# Springer Series in Operations Research

*Editor:*
Peter Glynn

# Springer Series in Operations Research

*Yao (Ed.):* Stochastic Modeling and Analysis of
Manufacturing Systems

David D. Yao
Editor

# Stochastic Modeling and Analysis of Manufacturing Systems

With 18 Illustrations

Springer-Verlag

New York Berlin Heidelberg London Paris
Tokyo Hong Kong Barcelona Budapest

David D. Yao
Department of Industrial Engineering
  and Operations Research
Columbia University
New York, NY 10027-6699
USA

*Series Editor*:
Peter Glynn
Department of Operations
  Research
Stanford University
Stanford, CA 94305
USA

Library of Congress Cataloging-in-Publication Data
Stochastic modeling and analysis of manufacturing systems / David D.
  Yao. (ed.).
    p.  cm. — (Springer series in operations research)
    Includes bibliographical references.
    ISBN 0-387-94319-6. — ISBN 3-540-94319-6
    1. Production management—Mathematical models.  2. Stochastic
analysis.  I. Yao, David D., 1950–  .  II. Series.
TS155.S787  1994
658.8′01′5118—dc20                                    94-19979

Printed on acid-free paper.

Production managed by Natalie Johnson; manufacturing supervised by Vincent Scelta
Photocomposed using the editor's LaTeX files.
Printed and bound by Edwards Brothers, Inc., Ann Arbor, MI.
Printed in the United States of America.

9 8 7 6 5 4 3 2 1

ISBN 0-387-94319-6 Springer-Verlag New York Berlin Heidelberg
ISBN 3-540-94319-6 Springer-Verlag Berlin Heidelberg New York

# Preface

This book is a collection of chapters, each focusing on a specific topic. The selection of topics attempts to reflect the development in recent years of those new probabilistic models and methodologies that have been either motivated by manufacturing systems research or demonstrated to have important potential in such research. Here, manufacturing systems research is broadly interpreted to include modeling and analysis, design, planning, scheduling and control. Each chapter is written by one or several experts, in a self-contained, expository style, and aimed at the graduate level.

The authors who wrote for the book were urged to make a special effort to be both informative and expository in their writing. From the outset, we agreed that no chapter should be a general survey (such as who did what when, etc.). Instead, I would like each chapter to be a detailed exposition on a well-selected subset of topics, with a carefully thought-out theme and focus, and self-contained in coverage (for instance, proofs of main results are included wherever necessary). I suggested to the authors that they should write with their graduate students in mind, and as if they were preparing a polished version of their lecture notes.

My main objective is that the book be a useful text or reference, at the graduate level, that can be effectively used both in classroom and for self-study. For instance, I have used some of the chapters for graduate courses at Columbia that teach modeling and analysis of manufacturing systems. Students who take the courses come mostly from Operations Research, Electrical Engineering, Mathematical Statistics, Industrial Engineering, Management Science, and occasionally from Applied Mathematics and Economics. It is exactly this type of readership that I would like the book to serve.

Alternatively, selected chapters of the book can be used to supplement the teaching and readings of other graduate courses in systems and control theory, stochastic processes, queueing theory, decision analysis, and advanced simulation. Used this way, the book offers not only detailed exposition to important methodologies (which might relate closely to the core of the courses in question), but also motivating applications of the methodologies.

The book can also be a useful reference for researchers in manufacturing systems who want to learn new tools and new methodologies, as well as for researchers in mathematical sciences who are interested in studying manufacturing problems and applications of stochastic modeling.

Roughly the book consists of two parts. The first four chapters are basically concerned with *models*, while the remaining four chapters address *design and control* methodologies.

In the first part, Chapter 1 studies Jackson networks, emphasizing the effectiveness of the models in capturing the fundamental qualitative and structural features of batch manufacturing, and in providing insight for the design and efficient operation of such systems. Chapters 2 and 3 present a modeling hierarchy that consists of three levels: micro, macro and the intermediate, *meso* models. In this hierarchy, queueing networks are micro models, fluid networks are macro models, while diffusion and strong approximations are meso models. Focusing on the macro and meso models, the two chapters detail the space-time scaling and related limit theorems in a unifying framework. In Chapter 4, the main model is the GSMP (generalized semi-Markov process). The treatment is to view the GSMP as a *scheme* driven by a sequence of clock times (event life times), with a focus on the *language* – the set of feasible strings (sequences) of events. Structural properties of the language lead to important implications in system performance. The theory is illustrated through analyzing in depth a production line operating under a *generalized kanban* mechanism, which controls at each stage the work-in-process and finished goods inventory, as well as overall buffer content.

In the second part, Chapter 5 presents the essentials of the recently developed theory of stochastic convexity and stochastic majorization, emphasizing their interplay and their role in understanding system behavior and supporting system design. Various aspects of the theory are illustrated through numerous applications that include a random yield model, a joint setup problem, a process involving trial runs, a network with constant WIP (work-in-process) and WIP-dependent production rates, and scheduling in tandem production lines and parallel assembly systems. Chapter 6 is a self-contained introduction to the fundamentals of derivative estimation via perturbation analysis and its applications in a variety of production networks, including kanban systems, systems with rework and scrap, with alternative sourcing, and with subassemblies. This chapter, along with Chapter 4, also introduces the reader to the newly developed *discrete-event systems* perspective in the modeling and analysis of manufacturing systems. The common theme of the last two chapters, Chapter 7 and Chapter 8, is dynamic scheduling. Chapter 7 presents an approach that is based on modeling the production facilities as Brownian networks. It addresses the objective of minimizing a weighted summation of the sojourn time and the sojourn-time inequity. This treatment unifies and generalizes previous works that focus on single-criterion objectives. Chapter 8 studies scheduling in re-entrant lines, which typically model the configuration of semiconductor manufacturing systems. The focus of the chapter is on developing simple but effective scheduling rules, and providing rigorous analytical justification to support the performance of such rules.

Each chapter was reviewed by one or several independent readers, whose critical reading and constructive comments and suggestions have enhanced the quality of the chapters. For their assistance, I thank the following readers: Rajeev Agrawal (Wisconsin-Madison), Hong Chen (British Columbia), Dinah Cheng (NYU), Jim Dai (Georgia Tech.), Michael Fu (Maryland), Paul Glasserman (Columbia), Shin-Gang Kou (Columbia), Xiao-Gao Liu (Waterloo), Rajendra Rajan (Wisconsin-Madison), Rhonda Righter (Santa Clara), Aliza Schachter (Columbia), Dequan Shaw (GTE Labs.), and Li Zhang (Columbia).

The initial organization of the book and much of my own writing took place during the 1991/92 academic year, when I was on sabbatical leave at Yale. I thank my hosts, Eric Dernardo and Offer Kella, for their hospitality. During the period, I was also a recipient of a Fellowship from the Guggenheim Foundation, and research grants from the National Science Foundation. I am grateful to these foundations for their support.

*New York City, March 1994*                                    *David D. Yao*

# Contents

# Contributors

JOHN A. BUZACOTT
Faculty of Administrative Studies, York Univeristy, North York, Ontario M3J 1P3, Canada

CHENG-SHANG CHANG
IBM Research Division, T.J. Watson Research Center, Yorktown Heights, NY 10598, USA

HONG CHEN
Faculty of Commerce, University of British Columbia, Vancouver, B.C. V6T 1Z2, Canada

PAUL GLASSERMAN
Graduate School of Business, Columbia University, New York, NY 10027, USA

P.R. KUMAR
Department of Electrical and Computer Engineering, University of Illinois, 1308 West Main Street, Urbana, IL 61801, USA

AVI MANDELBAUM
Faculty of Industrial Engineering and Management, Technion, Israel Institute of Technology, Haifa 32000, Israel

J. GEORGE SHANTHIKUMAR
Haas School of Business Administration, University of California, Berkeley, CA 94720, USA

LAWRENCE M. WEIN
Sloan School of Management, Massachussets Institute of Technology, Cambridge, MA 02139, USA

DAVID D. YAO
IEOR Department, Columbia University, New York, NY 10027-6699, USA

# 1
# Jackson Network Models of Manufacturing Systems

John A. Buzacott
J. George Shanthikumar
David D. Yao

ABSTRACT Focusing on discrete-part batch manufacturing systems, we illustrate the relevance and usefulness of Jackson network models. The emphasis is on demonstrating the effectiveness of the models in capturing the fundamental qualitative and structural features of batch manufacturing, so as to provide insight and support for the design and efficient operation of the systems. In particular, we study the relationship between the production rate and the work-in-process, the implications of resource sharing, and the different schemes in workload allocation and assignment. We also bring out the connections to other familiar subjects such as likelihood ratio ordering, majorization and arrangement orderings, and coupling techniques.

## 1.1 Introduction

Most manufacturing systems have a layout, or system configuration, that falls into one of two broad classes. Systems that manufacture products in large volume and low variety usually adopt a *product layout*: Each type of product is processed by a separate subsystem, in which parts go through a number of stages in sequence, known as *flow line*, because of the essentially linear configuration. (The term "flow" also suggests that the discrete nature of part movement within the system becomes less important, due to the high volume.) In this case, setting up separate lines for each product type is justified by the economy of scale through the large volume on the one hand and the homogeneity of processing requirements due to low variety on the other hand. In contrast, systems that process products with high variety and in small to medium sized batches typically follow a *process layout*. The primary example is a job shop, which consists of a set of functional departments, each performing a particular type of operation, e.g., lathing, drilling, milling, and so forth.

In recent years two variations of process layout have emerged: the *cellular layout*, which modifies each functional department of a job shop into a multi-functional cell, based on the principles of group technology; and the *flexible manufacturing system*, in which every cell is represented by one or more versatile, multi-functional machines. For our purpose here, we will not differentiate these variations from process layout; instead, below we will use the generic term, *workcenters*, to refer to both the functional departments and the multi-functional cells in a process layout.

In terms of modeling, there are at least two aspects in which systems with a process layout are significantly different from those with a product layout. First, the job (part) flows in process layout are much more complex than the simple, linear flow in product layout, since different types of jobs follow different routes in visiting the workcenters. Second, since in a process layout different types of jobs circulate in the system simulataneously, the processing requirements at each workcenter could vary widely; while in contrast, in a product layout the processing times at each stage are essentially homogeneous among the jobs.

For both types of layout, the main performance measures of interest, at both the workcenter level and the system level, are: the production rate (or throughput), the cycle time, and the level of work-in-process (WIP).

The focus of this chapter is on discrete-part, batch manufacturing systems that follow a process layout (including celluar layout and flexible manufacturing systems). Our task is to present formal models of the systems, and to analyze the models so as to enhance understanding of system behavior, and thereby provide useful insights and tools for system design.

To start with, the features that we look for in a formal model are as follows:

- The model should be versatile and rich enough to capture the essence of batch manufacturing systems. This includes not only the heterogeous routing and processing requirements mentioned earlier, but also the various operating characteristics of the systems. For instance, the production rate of each workcenter as well as the overall production rate of the system should in general be WIP-dependent, so as to reflect the throughput-inventory tradeoff that is essential to batch manufacturing.

- The model should have the capability not only to capture the essential qualitative behavior of the system, but also to make it precise, and to bring out explicitly the role played by different resources and control parameters. For instance, it is normally expected that with additional resource, e.g., more or faster machines and operators, the production rate of the system will increase. A more subtle issue is resource sharing and pooling. For instance, will aggregating two workcenters increase the production rate of the system? The power and relevance of the model are best reflected in its effectiveness in studying and resolving issues as such.

- The model should lead to easy and efficient computational means for evaluating major performance measures such as throughput, cycle time, WIP levels, and so forth. These performance evaluations are much needed in system design and in addressing "what-if" questions.

It turns out that a class of queueing networks, called *Jackson networks* (named after J.R. Jackson; see Section 10, Notes), is very well suited for our purpose. Much of our exposition here is to demonstrate that the model indeed has the desired features stated above.

Since we are concerned mainly with design issues, naturally, we focus on the long-run, or, *equilibrium (steady-state)* behavior of the model. Furthermore, we restrict ourselves to what's essentially a systems point of view. Specifically, our emphasis is almost entirely on the production rate of the *system* as a function of WIP levels and the production rate of the workcenters, as opposed to *job*-related performance measures, such as delay (although in some aggregated sense, delay relates to throughput and WIP level via Little's law). Therefore, we aggregate all types of jobs into a single class. In terms of the processing requirement at each workcenter, this is tantamount to taking the average of the processing times of different job types as the mean of a single exponential distribution. In terms of routing, the aggregation results in a Markovian transition mechanism among stations, with the transition probabilities interpreted as proportions of job flows. (Obviously, this aggregation will not be suitable to study, for instance, type-specific job delays, which often depend on much more detailed, type-dependent information such as routing and scheduling, as well as processing requirements.)

On the other hand, we retain the important feature of state-dependent service rates in the Jackson network, and focus prominently on the role they play as functions of the WIP, and the effect of their changes on the production rate — after all, these issues consititute the primary focus of the design and operation of the system. In other words, between the two basic aspects of the system — the qualitative, structural aspect and the quantitive, distributional aspect, we clearly put more emphasis on the former. It is exactly in this sense that we emphasize that the model is for insights, not numbers; at least, the value of the numbers should be judged relatively rather than absolutely.

The rest of the chapter is organized as follows. In Section 2 we introduce the three configurations of the Jackson network: the open, closed, and semi-open models, and derive the equilibrium distributions. We then continue in Section 3 to derive the throughput function and discuss its computation. The monotonicity of the throughput function is analyzed in detail in Section 4. The main approach there is through the notion of *equilibrium rate* and its linkage to the likelihood ratio ordering. In Section 5 we further exploit this connection, and use coupling techniques to establish concavity/convexity properties of the throughput function. The important special case of networks with multi-server nodes is the focus of Section 6, where we establish properties with respect to the number of servers and the service rates. Properties that correspond to resource sharing, in terms of aggregation of servers and nodes, are studied in Section 7. Connections to majorization and arrangement orderings, as motivated by the allocation or assignment of workload, are studied in Section 8. Concluding remarks and bibliographical notes are summarized in Sections 9 and 10.

## 1.2   Jackson Networks

Consider a network of $m$ nodes. Each node represents a workcenter, as motivated in the last section . Jobs travel among the workcenters following some routing matrix $[r_{ij}]$, where, for $i, j = 1, ..., m$, $r_{ij}$ is the probability that a job leaving node $i$ will go to node $j$. Implicit here is the assumption that job routing follows a Markovian mechanism. In applications, however, $r_{ij}$ can be interpreted as the *proportion* of jobs leaving node $i$ that next visit node $j$.

The processing times of jobs at all workcenters are assumed independent and identically distributed (iid), following an exponential distribution, with unit mean. The processing (or, service) rate, i.e, the rate work is depleted, at each node $i$ is a function of the number of jobs present at that node. Specifically, given there are $x_i$ jobs at node $i$, the processing rate is $\mu_i(x_i)$. Assume $\mu_i(0) = 0$ and $\mu_i(x) > 0$ for all $x > 0$.

Let $X_i(t)$ denote the number of jobs at node $i$ at time $t$, a random quantity. We are interested in studying the process $\{(X_i(t))_{i=1}^m; \ t \geq 0\}$, modeled as a continuous-time Markov chain. Since we are mainly concerned with equilibrium results, we will omit the argument $t$. Let $\mathbf{X} = (X_i)_{i=1}^m$. Let $\pi(\mathbf{x}) = \mathsf{P}[\mathbf{X} = \mathbf{x}]$ denote the equilibrium distribution. We will refer to $X_i$ as the state at node $i$, which represents the (steady-state) WIP level of workcenter $i$, and refer to $\mathbf{X}$ as the state of the system.

Note that the assumption of homogeneous job processing times among all workcenters is not as restrictive as it might appear, since any inhomogeneity of processing times among workcenters can be reflected in the service rates, which are indeed node- (as well as state-) dependent. On the other hand, it is convenient, in terms of modeling, to have state-dependent service rates at each node, since this captures the behavior of the production rate of each workcenter, which is often dependent on the level of WIP (work-in-process) there.

To summarize, the routing matrix and the service rates are the given data required for the network models to be discussed below. In applications, these data can be obtained from the material flow of the system (e.g., a "from-to" routing table in a jobshop) and the WIP dependent production rate of each workcenter, as well as the processing requirements of the jobs.

According to different specifications of the routing matrix, there are three different types of network models: *open*, *closed* and *semi-open*.

## 1.2.1   The Open Model

In an open network, jobs arrive from outside following a Poisson process with rate $\alpha > 0$. Each arrival is independently routed to node $j$ with probability $r_{0j} \geq 0$, and $\sum_{j=1}^{m} r_{0j} = 1$. Equivalently, this can be viewed as each node $j$ having an external Poisson stream of job arrivals with rate $\alpha r_{0j}$. Upon service completion at node $i$, a job may leave the network with probability $r_{i0}$ (or go to another node $j$ with probability $r_{ij}$ as specified earlier).

Hence, the Markov chain, $\{\mathbf{X}(t)\} = \{(X_i(t))_{i=1}^{m}\}$, is governed by the following transition rates:

$$
\begin{aligned}
q(\mathbf{x}, \mathbf{x} + \mathbf{e}_i) &= \alpha r_{0i} \\
q(\mathbf{x}, \mathbf{x} - \mathbf{e}_i) &= \mu_i(x_i) r_{i0} \\
q(\mathbf{x}, \mathbf{x} - \mathbf{e}_i + \mathbf{e}_j) &= \mu_i(x_i) r_{ij},
\end{aligned}
$$

where $\mathbf{e}_i$ and $\mathbf{e}_j$ denote the $i$ th and the $j$ th unit vector.

Assume that the augmented routing matrix, $[r_{ij}]_{i,j=0}^{m}$ (i.e., including the external source, indexed as node 0), is *irreducible*, i.e., every node can be reached, directly or indirectly, by every other node, including node 0. This implies, in particular, that every node will be visited by some jobs, i.e., no node is superfluous in the network. This also implies that without node 0 the routing matrix, $[r_{ij}]_{i,j=1}^{m}$, is *substochastic*, i.e., at least one of its row sums is strictly less than one, hence every job entering the network will eventually leave.

Let $\lambda_i$ be the overall arrival rate to node $i$, including both external arrivals and internal transitions. We have the following *traffic equations*:

$$
\lambda_i = \alpha r_{0i} + \sum_{j=1}^{m} \lambda_j r_{ji}, \quad i = 1, ..., m. \tag{1.1}
$$

The above assumption on the routing matrix guarantees that the solution to the traffic equations necessarily exists and is positive, i.e, $\lambda_i > 0$ for all $i$. It also gurantees the existence of an equilibrium (or, ergodic) distribution of the Markov chain $\mathbf{X}$.

Indeed the equilibrium distribution $\pi(\mathbf{x})$ is determined by the following system of *equilibrium* (or, *full*) *balance equations*, which equates the total "probablity flow" out of the state $\mathbf{x}$ with the total flow into the same state.

$$
\pi(\mathbf{x}) \sum_{i=1}^{m} [\alpha r_{0i} + \mu_i(x_i)]
$$

$$= \sum_{i=1}^{m} [\pi(\mathbf{x} - \mathbf{e}_i)\alpha r_{0i} + \pi(\mathbf{x} + \mathbf{e}_i)\mu_i(x_i + 1)r_{i0}]$$

$$+ \sum_{i=1}^{m} \sum_{j=1}^{m} \pi(\mathbf{x} + \mathbf{e}_i - \mathbf{e}_j)\mu_i(x_i + 1)r_{ij}, \qquad (1.2)$$

where $\mathbf{e}_i$ and $\mathbf{e}_j$ denote the $i$ th and the $j$ th unit vector.

Let $\{Y_1, ..., Y_m\}$ be a set of *independent* random variables with probability mass functions (pmf) as follows:

$$P[Y_i = n] = P[Y_i = 0] \cdot \frac{\lambda_i^n}{M_i(n)}, \qquad (1.3)$$

where

$$M_i(n) = \mu_i(1) \cdots \mu_i(n), \quad n = 1, 2, \ldots;$$

and we assume

$$\sum_{n=1}^{\infty} \frac{\lambda_i^n}{M_i(n)} < \infty, \qquad (1.4)$$

so that $P[Y_i = 0]$ is well defined. Note that $Y_i$ is the number of jobs in a birth-death queue in equilibrium, with arrival (birth) rate $\lambda_i$ and state-dependent service (death) rates $\mu_i(n)$.

**Theorem 1.2.1** Provided the condition in (1.4) is satified for all $i = 1, ..., m$, the equilibrium distribution of the open Jackson network has the following product form:

$$\pi(\mathbf{x}) = \prod_{i=1}^{m} P[Y_i = x_i],$$

where $Y_i$ follows the distribution in (1.3).

**Proof.** It suffices to verify that the equilibrium balance equations in (1.2) are satisfied. From the given product-form distribution of $\pi(\mathbf{x})$, we have

$$\pi(\mathbf{x}) = \pi(\mathbf{x} + \mathbf{e}_i)\mu_i(x_i + 1)/\lambda_i$$
$$= \pi(\mathbf{x} + \mathbf{e}_i - \mathbf{e}_j)\mu_i(x_i + 1)\lambda_j/[\lambda_i\mu_j(x_j)].$$

Substituting these into the right side of (1.2) and cancelling out $\pi(\mathbf{x})$ from both side, we have

$$\sum_{i=1}^{m} [\alpha r_{0i} + \mu_i(x_i)]$$

$$= \sum_{i=1}^{m} [\frac{\alpha r_{0i}}{\lambda_i}\mu_i(x_i) + \lambda_i r_{i0}] + \sum_{i=1}^{m} \sum_{j=1}^{m} \frac{\lambda_i}{\lambda_j} r_{ij}\mu_j(x_j). \qquad (1.5)$$

Making use of (1.1), we have

$$\sum_{i=1}^{m}\sum_{j=1}^{m}\frac{\lambda_i}{\lambda_j}r_{ij}\mu_j(x_j) = \sum_{j=1}^{m}[\sum_{i=1}^{m}\frac{\lambda_i}{\lambda_j}r_{ij}]\mu_j(x_j)$$

$$= \sum_{j=1}^{m}[1 - \frac{\alpha r_{0j}}{\lambda_j}]\mu_j(x_j).$$

Substituting the above into (1.5) simplifies the latter to

$$\sum_{i=1}^{m}\alpha r_{0i} = \sum_{i=1}^{m}\lambda_i r_{i0}.$$

To verify the above, from (1.1), summing over $i$, we have

$$\sum_{i=1}^{m}\alpha r_{0i} = \sum_{i=1}^{m}\lambda_i - \sum_{i=1}^{m}\sum_{j=1}^{m}\lambda_j r_{ji}$$

$$= \sum_{i=1}^{m}\lambda_i - \sum_{j=1}^{m}\lambda_j(1 - r_{j0})$$

$$= \sum_{i=1}^{m}\lambda_i r_{i0}.$$

□

**Remark 1.2.2** The condition in (1.4) is satisfied, if for each $i$ there exists a positive constant $\rho_i < 1$ such that

$$\lambda_i^n/[\mu_i(1)\cdots\mu_i(n)] < \rho_i^n$$

whenever $n \geq K_i$ for some $K_i$. Two special cases are of particular interest:

(i) Constant service rate: $\mu_i(x) = \mu_i > 0$ for all $x > 0$. Then, $\rho_i = \lambda_i/\mu_i < 1$ becomes the required condition. In this case, $Y_i$ follows a geometric distribution: $P[Y_i = n] = (1 - \rho_i)\rho_i^n$ for $n = 0, 1, 2, \dots$.

(ii) Multiple parallel servers: there are $c_i$ servers at node $i$, each with a constant rate $\mu_i$. That is, $\mu_i(x) = \min\{x, c_i\} \cdot \mu_i$. In this case, the required condition becomes $\rho_i = \lambda_i/(c_i\mu_i) < 1$.

Theorem 1.2.1 reveals that in equilibrium, the $m$ nodes in the network are independent, each following the distribution of a birth-death queue.

## 1.2.2   The Closed Model

Here the total number of jobs in the network is a constant $N$. There are no external arrivals, and no job ever leaves the network. We will refer to $N$ as the (total) job population of the network. The model can also be equivalently interpreted as follows: the network starts with a total of $N$ jobs, and as soon as a job completes all its processing requirement and leaves the network, a new job is immediately released into the network.

This mode of operation resembles the "base-stock" (or, one-for-one replenishment) inventory system. It is quite common in manufacturing systems. For instance, in many automated systems, each job has to be mounted on a *pallet* throughout its circulation within the system. Usually, the number of pallets is a given constant, say $N$. Whenever a job is completed and the pallet that carries it becomes vacant, another job is immediately mounted on to the palllet to enter the system. Even in systems that do not use pallets, it is quite often that there is a prespecified constant level of WIP to be maintained within the system. This WIP level then becomes the $N$ parameter. One advantage of this operating rule is that the (WIP-dependent) production rate of the system can be maintained at a desirable, constant level.

In the closed model, since no job enters or leaves the network, the routing matrix $[r_{ij}]_{i,j=1}^m$ is *stochastic* i.e., all the row sums are equal to one. Let $(v_i)_{i=1}^m$ be the positive solution to

$$v_i = \sum_{j=1}^m v_j r_{ji}, \quad i = 1, ..., m. \tag{1.6}$$

Since the routing matrix is stochastic, the solution to the above system is only unique up to a constant multiplier: there is one degree of freedom. To make the solution unique, we normally add another equation: set $\sum_{i=1}^m v_i = v$, for some positive constant, e.g., $v = 1$; or set $v_j = 1$ for some $j$. Either way, $v_i$ has the interpretation of the (relative) visit frequency (or, visit ratio) to node $i$.

The equilibrium balance equations are similar to those of the open network [cf. (1.2)], except here $\alpha = 0$ and $r_{0i} = r_{i0} = 0$ for all $i$. Hence, we have

$$\pi(\mathbf{x}) \sum_{i=1}^m \mu_i(x_i) = \sum_{i=1}^m \sum_{j=1}^m \pi(\mathbf{x} + \mathbf{e}_i - \mathbf{e}_j) \mu_i(x_i + 1) r_{ij}.$$

Below we denote $|\mathbf{x}| = x_1 + \cdots + x_m$, and similarly, $|\mathbf{X}| = X_1 + \cdots + X_m$ and $|\mathbf{Y}| = Y_1 + \cdots + Y_m$, for $\mathbf{X} = (X_i)_{i=1}^m$ and $\mathbf{Y} = (Y_i)_{i=1}^m$.

**Theorem 1.2.3** The closed Jackson network, with a total of $N$ jobs, has the following equilibrium distribution: for all $\mathbf{x}$ such that $|\mathbf{x}| = N$,

$$\pi(\mathbf{x}) = \prod_{i=1}^m P[Y_i = x_i]/P[|\mathbf{Y}| = N],$$

where $Y_i$ follows the distribution in (1.3), with $\lambda_i$ replaced by $v_i$ (solution to the traffic equations in (1.6)), and $x_i \leq N$ for all $i$.

**Proof.** Follow the proof of Theorem 1.2.1, verify (1.5) by letting the terms that involve $\alpha$ or $r_{i0}$ be equal to zero. The denominator in $\pi(\mathbf{x})$ comes from the normality condition, since

$$P[|\mathbf{Y}| = N] = \sum_{|\mathbf{X}|=N} \prod_{i=1}^{m} P[Y_i = x_i].$$

(Recall, the $Y_i$'s are independent by definition.) □

**Remark 1.2.4** Note that in contrast to the open model, in the closed model the $X_i$'s are *not* independent: they cannot be, since they are constrained by adding up to the constant $N$. But Theorem 1.2.3 reveals that this turns out to be the only twist. In other words, conditioning upon summing up to $N$, the $X_i$'s are independent. Another contrast is that in the closed model, the state space of $\mathbf{X}$ is finite; hence, no condition such as the one in (1.4) is needed for the equilibrium distribution.

### 1.2.3  The Semi-Open Model

This model imposes an overall buffer capacity on the open model. Specifically, the network is open, but it can only accommodate a maximum of $K$ jobs at any time. When the buffer limit $K$ is reached, external arrivals will be blocked and lost. Since the arrivals follow a Poisson process, due to the memoryless property of the interarrival times, this blocking mechanism is equivalent to stopping the arrival process as soon as the buffer limit is reached. (The arrival process will be resumed when a job next leaves the network, bringing the total number of jobs in the network down to $K - 1$.) So, in contrast to the closed model, the operation of a semi-open network resembles the "order-up-to" inventory systems.

It turns out that this model can be reduced to a closed network, with a constant of $K$ jobs. Add another node, node 0, to the network, and set $\mu_0(n) = \alpha$ for all $n \geq 1$, and $\mu_0(0) = 0$. Routing from and to node 0 follows the probabilties $r_{0j}$ and $r_{i0}$ as in the open network. The routing matrix of this closed network of $m + 1$ nodes is then $[r_{ij}]_{i,j=0}^{m}$. (Note: this is exactly the augmented routing matrix of the open network. However, node 0 here is part of the constructed *closed* network.) This way, node 0 effectively generates the arrival process of the original (semi-open) network. In particular, $x_0 = 0$ means that there are $K$ jobs in the other $m$ nodes (which consititute the original network), and hence $\mu_0(0) = 0$ correctly captures the blocking of external arrivals when the buffer is full.

Modify the traffic equation in (1.1) as follows: Divide both sides by $\alpha$, and let $v_0 = 1$, $v_i = \lambda_i/\alpha$ for $i = 1, ..., m$. Then, (1.1) becomes

$$v_i = \sum_{i=0}^{m} v_j r_{ji}, \quad i = 0, 1, ..., m,$$

which is the traffic equation of the closed model [cf. (1.6)] — for a network with $m + 1$ nodes.

**Theorem 1.2.5** The semi-open Jackson network, with an overall buffer capacity of $K$, has the following equilibrium distribution: for all $\mathbf{x}$ such that $|\mathbf{x}| \leq K$,

$$\pi(\mathbf{x}) = \prod_{i=1}^{m} P[Y_i = x_i]/P[|\mathbf{Y}| \leq K],$$

where $Y_i$ follows the distribution in (1.3), with $x_i \leq K$ for all $i = 1, ..., m$.

**Proof.** From the earlier analysis, we can apply Theorem 1.2.3 to a closed network with $m + 1$ nodes. Following the discussion above, we have $v_0 = 1$, $v_i = \lambda_i/\alpha$, and $x_0 = K - |\mathbf{x}|$. Hence,

$$
\begin{aligned}
\pi(\mathbf{x}) &= P[X_1 = x_1, \cdots, X_m = x_m] \\
&= P[X_0 = x_0, X_1 = x_1, \ldots, X_m = x_m] \\
&= \frac{1}{C} \cdot \frac{(1)^{x_0}(\frac{\lambda_1}{\alpha})^{x_1} \cdots (\frac{\lambda_m}{\alpha})^{x_m}}{\alpha^{x_0} M_1(x_1) \cdots M_m(x_m)} \\
&= \frac{\lambda_1^{x_1} \cdots \lambda_m^{x_m}}{C\alpha^K M_1(x_1) \cdots M_m(x_m)},
\end{aligned}
$$

where $C$ denotes the normalizing constant. Now, the last expression above can be written as $\prod_{i=1}^{m} P[Y_i = x_i]/C'$, with a new normalizing constant $C'$, which is simply determined as:

$$C' = \sum_{|\mathbf{x}| \leq K} \prod_{i=1}^{m} P[Y_i = x_i] = P[|\mathbf{Y}| \leq K];$$

hence, the desired expression. $\square$

**Remark 1.2.6** It is obvious, comparing Theorems 1.2.1 and 1.2.5, that letting $K \to \infty$ in the semi-open model yields the open model. On the other hand, letting $\alpha \to \infty$ in the semi-open model, while maintaining $0 < v_i = \lambda_i/\alpha < \infty$, recovers the closed model. To see this, note from the proof above that because of the $\alpha^{x_0}$ factor in the denominator, the pmf in Theorem 1.2.5 will vanish as $\alpha \to \infty$ unless $x_0 = 0$, or equivalently $|\mathbf{x}| \equiv K$ (instead of $|\mathbf{x}| \leq K$). But this reduces to exactly the pmf of the closed model. Intuitively, an infinitely large external arrival rate makes blocking happen all the time. It also makes external new jobs available all the time to be released into the network as soon as an internal job leaves the network.

## 1.3  The Throughput Function and Computation

A brief summary of the three models discussed in the last section is in order. The open model can be viewed as a special case of the semi-open model — one with infinite buffer capacity. The closed model can be viewed as a special case of the semi-open model — one with an infinite external arrival rate. On the other hand, a semi-open network can be reduced to a closed network by adding one more node. In this sense, the semi-open and the closed models have the same "modeling power". Since the equilibrium distribution of the closed model has a simpler form, below we focus on the closed model.

From the joint distribution $\pi(x)$ in Theorem 1.2.3, we can derive the marginal distribution for $X_i$. Let $\mathbf{Y}_{-i} = (Y_1, ..., Y_{i-1}, Y_{i+1}, Y_m)$ be the random vector that removes the component $Y_i$ from $\mathbf{Y}$. Let $|\mathbf{Y}_{-i}|$ denote the sum of the components of $\mathbf{Y}_{-i}$. We have, for $n = 0, 1, ..., N$,

$$P[X_i = n] = P[Y_i = n] \cdot \frac{P[|\mathbf{Y}_{-i}| = N - n]}{P[|\mathbf{Y}| = N]}. \qquad (1.7)$$

Based on this, the throughput (i.e., average output rate) from node $i$ is:

$$
\begin{aligned}
&E[\mu_i(X_i)] \\
&= \sum_{n=1}^{N} \mu_i(n) P[Y_i = n] \cdot \frac{P[|\mathbf{Y}_{-i}| = N - n]}{P[|\mathbf{Y}| = N]} \\
&= v_i \sum_{n=1}^{N} P[Y_i = n - 1] \cdot \frac{P[|\mathbf{Y}_{-i}| = N - n]}{P[|\mathbf{Y}| = N]} \\
&= v_i \left\{ \sum_{n=0}^{N-1} P[Y_i = n] \cdot \frac{P[|\mathbf{Y}_{-i}| = N - n - 1]}{P[|\mathbf{Y}| = N - 1]} \right\} \cdot \frac{P[|\mathbf{Y}| = N - 1]}{P[|\mathbf{Y}| = N]} \\
&= v_i \cdot \frac{P[|\mathbf{Y}| = N - 1]}{P[|\mathbf{Y}| = N]},
\end{aligned}
$$

where the second equality is due to

$$\mu_i(n) P[Y_i = n] = v_i P[Y_i = n - 1],$$

[cf. (1.3)], while the last equality results from recognizing [cf. (1.7)] that the sum in curly brackets is over the marginal distribution of node $i$ in a closed network with $N - 1$ jobs.

Therefore, the throughput of each node in a closed Jackson network is the visit frequency to that node times a node-independent quantity, which is a function of the total number of jobs in the network. The latter is often referred to as the throughput (function) of the closed Jackson network:

$$TH(N) = \frac{P[|\mathbf{Y}| = N - 1]}{P[|\mathbf{Y}| = N]}. \qquad (1.8)$$

The throughput of each node $i$ is then

$$TH_i(N) = \mathsf{E}[\mu_i(X_i)] = v_i \cdot TH(N). \tag{1.9}$$

Therefore, while the service rates at each node $i$, $\mu_i(n)$, describe the *intrinsic* (or potential) WIP-dependent production rate of the workcenter, the throughput function, $TH(N)$, is the *actual* production rate of the entire network when it is loaded to a WIP level of $N$.

We can derive similar WIP-dependent production rates for open and semi-open models. From Theorem 1.2.1, for the open network, we have

$$\frac{\mathsf{P}[|\mathbf{X}| = n-1]}{\mathsf{P}[|\mathbf{X}| = n]} = \frac{\sum_{|\mathbf{x}|=n-1} \prod_{i=1}^{m} \frac{\lambda_i^{x_i}}{M(x_i)}}{\sum_{|\mathbf{x}|=n} \prod_{i=1}^{m} \frac{\lambda_i^{x_i}}{M(x_i)}}.$$

Dividing both the numerator and the denominator by $\alpha^n$ and letting $v_i = \lambda_i/\alpha$, we have

$$\frac{\mathsf{P}[|\mathbf{X}| = n-1]}{\mathsf{P}[|\mathbf{X}| = n]} = \frac{\mathsf{P}[|\mathbf{Y}| = n-1]}{\alpha \mathsf{P}[|\mathbf{Y}| = n]} = \frac{TH(n)}{\alpha}.$$

The above relation between $\mathsf{P}[|\mathbf{X}| = n-1]$ and $\mathsf{P}[|\mathbf{X}| = n]$ indicates that the total number of jobs in the open network, $|\mathbf{X}|$, follows the same distribution as the number of jobs in a *single* birth-death queue with arrival rate $\alpha$ and state-dependent service rates $\mu(n) = TH(n)$. In other words, when the total number of jobs in the open network is $n$, its overall output rate is equal to the throughput function of a closed network with $n$ jobs. Hence, the WIP-dependent production rate of an open network is equal to the throughput of a closed network with the same, but *constant*, WIP level.

Similarly, based on Theorem 1.2.5, we can show that the total number of jobs in a semi-open Jackson network follows the same distribution as the number of jobs in a single birth-death queue with finite buffer capacity $(K)$; and that its WIP-dependent production rate is also equal to the throughput of a closed network with the same WIP level. The only twist is that the WIP level here is bounded by the overall buffer limit $K$.

**Proposition 1.3.1** (i) The production rate of a closed Jackson network with a constant WIP level of $N$ equals $TH(N)$ in (1.8).
(ii) In equilibrium, the total number of jobs in the open (resp. semi-open) Jackson network follows the same distribution as the number of jobs in a birth-death queue with the following specification: infinite (resp. finite buffer capacity), arrival rate $\alpha$ (same as the external arrival rate to the network), and state-dependent service rates that are equal to the throughput function, $TH(n)$, of the same network operating in a closed fashion with a constant WIP level of $n$. In other word, $TH(n)$, is the WIP-dependent production rate of the open and semi-open Jackson networks.

In the rest of this section, we briefly illustrate the computation of the throughput function and related performance measures.

## The Convolution Algorithm

It is evident from comparing (1.3) and (1.8) that the factors $P[Y_i = 0]$ will cancel out in computing the throughput function. For $1 \le j \le m$ and $n \le N$, let

$$g_i(n) = v_i^n / M_i(n), \ n \ge 1; \quad g_i(0) = 1;$$

$$G(j, n) = \sum_{n_1 + \cdots + n_j = n} \prod_{i=1}^{j} g_i(n_i).$$

Then,

$$TH(N) = \frac{G(m, N-1)}{G(m, N)}.$$

Hence, the computation can be carried out as follows:

- Boundaries: $G(1, n) = g_1(n)$ for all $n = 0, 1, ..., N$; and $G(i, 0) = 1$ for all $i = 1, ..., m$.

- For $j = 2, ..., m$, do:

  - for $n = 1, ..., N$, do:

$$G(j, n) = \sum_{\ell=0}^{n} G(j-1, \ell) g_j(n - \ell); \tag{1.10}$$

  - continue;

- continue.

The above algorithm also applies to the computation of the marginal distributions in (1.7). Write $G(n) = G(m, n)$; and denote $G_{-i}(n)$ as the $G$ value of a network with $n$ jobs and $m - 1$ nodes — node $i$ removed. Then, the marginal probability

$$P[X_i = n] = g_i(n) G_{-i}(N - n) / G(N). \tag{1.11}$$

For networks with single-server nodes and fixed service rate (per server), $\mu_i$ for node $i$, we have $g_i(n) = \rho_i g_i(n - 1)$, where $\rho_i = v_i / \mu_i$. In this case, the above algorithm simplifies significantly; in particular, (1.10) becomes:

$$
\begin{aligned}
G(j, n) &= \sum_{\ell=0}^{n-1} G(j-1, \ell) g_j(n-1-\ell) \rho_j + G(j-1, n) \\
&= \rho_j G(j, n-1) + G(j-1, n).
\end{aligned}
$$

## Mean Value Analysis

For simplicity, consider the special case of single-server nodes specified above. Let $L_i(N)$ and $W_i(N)$ denote the expected total number of jobs and expected delay (queueing plus service) at node $i$, with the argument $N$ denoting the job population of the network. In this case, $g_i(n) = \rho_i^n$. From (1.11), we have

$$
\begin{aligned}
L_i(N) &= \sum_{n=0}^{N} n P[X_i = n] \\
&= \sum_{n=1}^{N} n \rho_i^n G_{-i}(N-n)/G(N) \\
&= \sum_{n=0}^{N-1} (n+1)\rho_i^{n+1} G_{-i}(N-1-n)/G(N) \\
&= \rho_i [ \sum_{n=0}^{N-1} n\rho_i^n G_{-i}(N-1-n) \\
&\quad + \sum_{n=0}^{N-1} \rho_i^n G_{-i}(N-1-n) ]/G(N) \\
&= \rho_i [L_i(N-1)G(N-1) + G(N-1)]/G(N) \\
&= \rho_i \cdot TH(N) \cdot [L_i(N-1) + 1].
\end{aligned}
$$

On the other hand, from Little's Law, we have, for all $i$,

$$L_i(N) = TH_i(N) \cdot W_i(N) = v_i \cdot TH(N) \cdot W_i(N). \tag{1.12}$$

Hence, for all $i$,

$$W_i(N) = \frac{1}{\mu_i}[L_i(N-1) + 1]. \tag{1.13}$$

(Note the above indicates that on arrival at node $i$, the job observes an average congestion level that corresponds to a network with a total of $N-1$ jobs — intuitively, with the arriving job itself removed.)

Since $\sum_{i=1}^{m} L_i(N) = N$, summing over $i$ on both sides of (1.12), we have

$$TH(N) = N/[\sum_{i=1}^{m} v_i W_i(N)].$$

Substituting back into (1.12) yields, for all $i$,

$$L_i(N) = \frac{N v_i W_i(N)}{\sum_{j=1}^{m} v_j W_j(N)}. \tag{1.14}$$

Therefore, recursively making use of (1.13) and (1.14), with the boundaries $L_i(0) = 0$ for all $i$, we can compute the mean values $L_i(N)$, $W_i(N)$ and $TH_i(N)$ for all $i$ and for any desired value of $N$.

While the advantage of mean value analysis is that the main performance measures (means) are computed directly, it also leads to marginal distributions. For instance, to compute the marginal distribution in (1.11), we have

$$G(N) = [TH(1) \cdots TH(N)]^{-1};$$

and the $G_{-i}$ factor is similarly computed via the throughput of a network with node $i$ removed.

## 1.4   Monotonicity of the Throughput Function

Since the throughput function in (1.8) represents the (WIP-dependent) production rate in all three types of Jackson networks, it is usually the most important performance measure in the design of such networks. It is hence crucial that we understand some of its qualitative properties. For instance, whether it is monotone in the WIP level, and whether it is monotone in the service rates at the nodes. These translate into important system issues: whether increasing the WIP level (e.g. by adding more pallets) or whether speeding up the rates at the workcenters (e.g., by adding more operators or installing faster machines) will result in an increased overall production rate.

We address these monotonicity properties of the throughput function in this section. In the next section, we will go one step further to study the second-order properties, i.e., monotone properties of the *marginal* changes in the production rate.

### 1.4.1   Equilibrium Rate

In the last section we have seen repeatedly the role played by the *ratio* of certain pmf's. For instance, in (1.8), the throughput function is expressed as the ratio of two consecutive probabilities of the random variable $|\mathbf{X}|$; while following (1.3), we have a similar expression for the service rate at node $i$, in terms of the pmf of $Y_i$: $\mu_i(n)/\lambda_i = \mathsf{P}[Y_i = n - 1]/\mathsf{P}[Y_i = n]$. So, below we first formalize this ratio of probabilities.

Suppose $X$ is a non-negative, integer valued random variable. Let $p(n) = P(X = n) > 0$ for all $n \in \mathcal{N} = \{0, 1, ..., N\}$, where $N$ is a given integer. We allow $N$ to be infinite.

**Definition 1.4.1** The *equilibrium rate* of $X$ is a real valued, non-negative function, $r : \mathcal{N} \mapsto \Re_+ = [0, \infty)$, defined as

$$r(0) = 0, \qquad r(n) = p(n-1)/p(n), \quad n = 1, ..., N.$$

It follows that the equilibrium rate of $X$ and its probability mass function (pmf) uniquely define each other. In particular,

$$p(n) = p(0)/[r(1) \cdots r(n)], \qquad n = 1, ..., N;$$

and

$$p(0) = [1 + \sum_{n=1}^{N} 1/(r(1) \cdots r(n))]^{-1}.$$

(When $N$ is infinite, convergence of the summation is required.)

**Example 1.4.2** For a birth-death queue in equilibrium, with *unit* arrival rate and state-dependent service rate $\mu(n)$, we have

$$\mu(n) = \mathsf{P}[Y = n - 1]/\mathsf{P}[Y = n] = r_Y(n),$$

where $Y$ denotes the number of jobs in the system, and $r_Y(n)$, its equilibrium rate. That is, the equilibrium rate equals the service rate.

Next, notice that in all three network models of the last section, the routing probabilities only play a role indirectly through the solution to the traffic equations, $(\lambda_i)_i$ or $(v_i)_i$. Hence, we can assume, without loss of generality, that $\lambda_i = 1$ or $v_i = 1$, for all $i$, via replacing the service rates $\mu_i(n)$ by $\mu_i(n)/\lambda_i$ or by $\mu_i(n)/v_i$. (For simplicity, though, below we shall continue using $\mu_i(n)$ to denote the modified service rates.) This way, all the results, including the equilibrium distribution and the throughput function will remain unchanged. Note this modification is equivalent to assuming that all networks under discussion have a *serial* (or *tandem*) configuration. (In a closed network, this is more precisely a *cyclic* configuration.)

With this observation, following (1.3) and Theorem 1.2.3, we can express the service rate at each node $i$ as the equilibrium rate of $Y_i$: $\mu_i(n) = r_{Y_i}(n)$. Furthermore, following (1.8), we can express the throughput function as the equilibrium rate of $|\mathbf{Y}|$, the summation of the independent $Y_i$'s:

$$TH(n) = r_{|\mathbf{Y}|}(n). \qquad (1.15)$$

That is, the production rate of the network is nothing but some sort of "convolution" of the service rates of the nodes.

The above also suggests that the issues regarding monotonicity raised at the beginning of this section can be reduced to the *preservation* of monotonicity by equilibrium rates under convolution (of the random variables they represent).

## 1.4.2  $PF_2$ *Property*

The increasingness of the equilibrium rate, $r(n - 1) \le r(n)$ for all $n$, expressed in terms of the pmf, is: $p(n - 1)p(n + 1) \le p^2(n)$ for all $n$. In other words, the pmf is log-concave in $n$. This is known as the $PF_2$ property (Polya frequency of order two). We use $X \in PF_2$ to denote that the pmf of a random variable satisfies the $PF_2$ property.

**Definition 1.4.3** $X \in PF_2$ if any only if the equilibrium rate of $X$, $r_X(n)$, is increasing in $n$.

**Example 1.4.4** For the birth-death queue considered earlier with unit arrival rate and state-dependent service rate $\mu(n)$. The number of jobs in system $Y$ has the $PF_2$ property if and only if $\mu(n)$ is increasing in $n$.

It is known that the $PF_2$ property is preserved under convolution. That is, for a set of *independent* random variables $\{Y_1, ..., Y_m\}$, if $Y_i \in PF_2$ for all $i$, then $|\mathbf{Y}| \in PF_2$. (This will be proved later as part of the proof of a second-order property in Proposition 1.5.1, also see Proposition 1.5.4.) Hence, from (1.15), we immediately have

**Theorem 1.4.5** The throughput function $TH(N)$ is increasing in $N$, the total number of jobs in the network, if for every node $i$, the service rate, $\mu_i(n)$, is an increasing function.

In other words, the production rate of a Jackson network is increasing in the network WIP level if the service rate at every node is an increasing function of the node WIP level.

### 1.4.3  Likelihood Ratio Ordering

To address the other monotonicity issue raised earlier — whether speeding up the service at each node will translate into a high throughput, we first need to be more specific about what we mean by "speeding up the service". One way to make this precise is to use a *pointwise* ordering of the service rate function, i.e., increasing $\mu(n)$ to $\nu(n)$, for instance, such that $\nu(n) \geq \mu(n)$ for each $n$. Because of the equivalence between the service rate and the equilibrium rate, this translates to a pointwise ordering for the equilibrium rate as well. It turns out that this ordering relates to the *likelihood ratio ordering* in stochastic comparisons.

**Definition 1.4.6** $X$ and $Y$ are two discrete random variables. Suppose their pmf's have a common support set $\mathcal{N}$. Let $r_X$ and $r_Y$ denote their equilibrium rates. Then $X \geq_{\ell r} Y$ if and only if $P[X = n]P[Y = n - 1] \geq P[X = n - 1]P[Y = n]$ for all $n \in \mathcal{N}$, or equivalently, $r_X(n) \leq r_Y(n)$ for all $n \in \mathcal{N}$.

The more standard stochastic ordering, $X \geq_{st} Y$, is defined as $P[X \geq n] \geq P[Y \geq n]$ for all $n \in \mathcal{N}$, which is easily verified to be equivalent to $E\phi(X) \geq E\phi(Y)$ for all increasing function $\phi(\cdot)$.

**Lemma 1.4.7** $X \geq_{\ell r} Y \Rightarrow X \geq_{st} Y$.

**Proof.** Suppose $X, Y \in \mathcal{N} = \{0, 1, \ldots, N\}$. Denote

$$s(0) = 1, \quad s(n) = [r_X(1) \cdots r_X(n)]^{-1}, \quad n \geq 1;$$

$$S(n) = \sum_{k=0}^{n} s(k).$$

Denote $t(n)$ and $T(n)$ similarly, replacing $r_X$ with $r_Y$. Then, following Definition 1.4.6, $X \geq_{\ell r} Y$ implies $s(n)t(m) \geq s(m)t(n)$ for all $n \geq m$, which, in turn, implies

$$[s(n) + \cdots + s(N)][t(1) + \cdots + t(n-1)]$$
$$\geq [s(1) + \cdots + s(n-1)][t(n) + \cdots + t(N)].$$

Hence,

$$
\begin{aligned}
\mathsf{P}[X \geq n] &= \frac{s(n) + \cdots + s(N)}{S(N)} \\
&\geq \frac{t(n) + \cdots + t(N)}{T(N)} = \mathsf{P}[Y \geq n],
\end{aligned}
$$

for all $n \leq N$; i.e., $X \geq_{st} Y$. $\square$

**Example 1.4.8** In the birth-death queueing example considered earlier, increasing the service rate function $\mu(n)$, in the pointwise sense, will decrease the equilibrium number of jobs in system, in the sense of likelihood ratio ordering. Equivalently, for two random variables $X, Y \in \mathcal{N}$, the likelihood ratio ordering $X \geq_{\ell r} Y$ can be viewed as corresponding to two birth-death queues with the same arrival rate, and with state-dependent service rates $r_X(n)$ and $r_Y(n)$, and $r_Y(n) \geq r_X(n)$.

Now we know that the gist of the question we posed at the beginning of this subsection is whether the likelihood ratio ordering is preserved under convolution. The answer to this is in fact known. The precise statement is:

**Lemma 1.4.9** $Y_1 \geq_{\ell r} Y_2$, and $Z \in PF_2$ is independent of $Y_1$ and $Y_2$. Then $Y_1 + Z \geq_{\ell r} Y_2 + Z$.

In contrast, if the likelihood ratio ordering in the above lemma is changed to the stochastic ordering, then the $PF_2$ property is *not* needed. That is, $Y_1 \geq_{st} Y_2$ implies $Y_1 + Z \geq_{st} Y_2 + Z$, for any $Z$ that is independent of $Y_1$ and $Y_2$.

Below, we restate the above lemma in the context of a two-node closed ( cyclic) network, and supply a proof.

**Proposition 1.4.10** Let $Y_1$, $Y_2$ and $Z$ be the random variables in Lemma 1.4.9. Construct a two-node cyclic network with $N$ jobs. Let the service rates at the two nodes be the equilibrium rates of $Y_1$ (for node 1) and $Z$

(for node 2). Next, construct a second network, with the service rate at node 1 increased to the equilibrium rate of $Y_2$ (since $Y_1 \geq_{\ell r} Y_2$); other things stay unchanged. Then, the second network has a higher throughput.

**Proof.** For $i, j = 1, 2$, let $X_j^i$ denote the number of jobs at node $j$ in network $i$. Then, for $i = 1, 2$,

$$P[X_1^i = n] = \frac{P[Y_i = n]P[Z = N - n]}{P[Y_i + Z = N]},$$

and hence,

$$r_{X_1^i}(n) = r_{Y_i}(n)/r_Z(N + 1 - n).$$

Therefore, $Y_1 \geq_{\ell r} Y_2$ implies $X_1^1 \geq_{\ell r} X_1^2$, and hence $N - X_1^1 \leq_{\ell r} N - X_1^2$, i.e., $X_2^1 \leq_{\ell r} X_2^2$. This, in turn, implies $X_2^1 \leq_{st} X_2^2$, from Lemma 1.4.7. Therefore, $Er_Z(X_2^1) \leq Er_Z(X_2^2)$, since $r_Z(\cdot)$ is an increasing function ($Z \in PF_2$). But the two expectations are exactly the throughputs of the two networks. $\square$

From the above proof, we note that the $PF_2$ property is not needed for the likelihood ratio ordering of the number of jobs at the two nodes.

**Corollary 1.4.11** In the network of Proposition 1.4.10, increasing the service rate at node 1 decreases the number of jobs there $(X_1)$, and hence increases the number of jobs at node 2 $(X_2)$, both in the sense of likelihood ratio ordering. This holds regardless whether or not the service rate (at either node) is an increasing function.

**Remark 1.4.12** In fact, from the proof of Proposition 1.4.10, we can write, $X_1^i$ and $X_2^i$, for $i = 1, 2$, as conditional random variables:

$$X_1^i = [Y_i | Y_i + Z = N], \quad X_2^i = [Z | Y_i + Z = N].$$

Then the result in Corollary 1.4.11 takes the following form:

$$Y_1 \geq_{\ell r} Y_2 \quad \Rightarrow \quad [Y_1 | Y_1 + Z = N] \geq_{\ell r} [Y_2 | Y_2 + Z = N],$$

$$Y_1 \geq_{\ell r} Y_2 \quad \Rightarrow \quad [Z | Y_1 + Z = N] \leq_{\ell r} [Z | Y_2 + Z = N];$$

and no $PF_2$ property is required.

To summarize, we have

**Theorem 1.4.13** In a closed Jackson network, suppose the service rates at all nodes are increasing functions. Then, increasing the service rate functions, in a pointwise sense, at a subset (say, $B$) of nodes will increase the equilibrium number of jobs at each of the nodes *not* in $B$, in the sense of likelihood ratio ordering. Consequently, the throughput will be increased.

In other words, when the production rates at all workcenters are increasing functions, speeding up some workcenters will increase the overall production rate of the network. In a closed network, this will result in an increased WIP level at each of the other workcenters (where the production rates stay unchanged).

**Remark 1.4.14** Notice that the result above regarding the increased number of jobs applies to *each* of the nodes that is not in $B$. To see this, pick one particular node that is not in $B$, and aggregate all the other nodes, including those in $B$, into a single node. Since the service rates at all nodes are increasing functions, increase those functions (in a pointwise sense) that correspond to the nodes in $B$ will translate into an increased service rate function of the aggregated node. (This explains why the nodes in $B$ are required to have increasing service rate functions, which was not required in the two-node model in Proposition 1.4.10 and Corollary 1.4.11.) Now we can apply Corollary 1.4.11 to this aggregated two-node network.

### 1.4.4   Shifted Likelihood Ratio Ordering

From Theorem 1.4.13, we know that speeding up the service at one or several nodes will increase the overall production rate of the network, provided all nodes in the network have increasing service rate functions, i.e., the production rate of each node is increasing in the WIP level of the node. In applications, this need not always be the case. For instance, suppose the workcenter is a clean room, which is quite typical in semiconductor manufacturing. A higher WIP means longer delay, and delay beyond a certain level could degrade the quality of the waiting jobs (wafers) — due to contamination, for instance, creating additional complications to the production process, and thereby slowing it down. So the question we ask here is, when a network contains nodes where the service rates are not necessarily increasing functions of the WIP level, how do we speed up such nodes so as to increase the production rate of the whole network.

Based on the earlier analysis, we know an equivalent way to ask the same question is this: can the likelihood ratio ordering be strengthened, so that it is preserved under convolution *without* the $PF_2$ property. From Definition 1.4.6, we know strengthening the likelihood ratio ordering is tantamount to strengthening the pointwise dominance relation among equilibrium rates. This motivates the "shifted" dominance relation below:

**Definition 1.4.15** For two functions $f, g : \mathcal{N} \mapsto \Re_+$, denote $f \leq_\uparrow g$, if $f(m) \leq g(n)$ for all $m \leq n$, $m, n \in \mathcal{N}$.

The following properties are easily verified ($f \leq g$ denotes the usual pointwise ordering):

**Lemma 1.4.16** The shifted dominance $\leq_\uparrow$ satisfies the following properties:

(i) $f \leq_\uparrow g$ implies $f \leq g$;

(ii) If either $f$ or $g$ is an increasing function, then $f \leq_\uparrow g$ if and only if $f \leq g$;

(iii) $f \leq_\uparrow g$ if and only if there exists an increasing function $h$, such that $f \leq h \leq g$.

Based on the ordering $\leq_\uparrow$ among equilibrium rates, we can define a strengthened likelihood ratio ordering.

**Definition 1.4.17** Two random variables $X$ and $Y$, ordered under *shifted likelihood ratio ordering*, denoted $X \geq_\uparrow^{\ell r} Y$, if their equilibrium rates are ordered as $r_X \leq_\uparrow r_Y$.

Properties of the shifted likelihood ratio ordering follow immediately from combining Lemma 1.4.16 with Definition 1.4.17.

**Proposition 1.4.18** The shifted likelihood ratio ordering satisfies the following properties:

(i) $X \geq_\uparrow^{\ell r} Y$ implies $X \geq_{\ell r} Y$;

(ii) If either $X \in PF_2$ or $Y \in PF_2$, then $X \geq_\uparrow^{\ell r} Y$ if and only if $X \geq_{\ell r} Y$;

(iii) $X \geq_\uparrow^{\ell r} Y$ if and only if there exists a random variable $Z \in PF_2$, such that $X \geq_{\ell r} Z \geq_{\ell r} Y$.

Now we have the analog of Lemma 1.4.9 without requiring the $PF_2$ property.

**Lemma 1.4.19** If, for $i = 1, 2$, $Y_i$ and $Z_i$ are independent, then $Y_1 \geq_\uparrow^{\ell r} Y_2$, $Z_1 \geq_\uparrow^{\ell r} Z_2$ implies $Y_1 + Z_1 \geq_\uparrow^{\ell r} Y_2 + Z_2$.

Although the above can also be rephrased in the context of a two-node cyclic network, similar to Proposition 1.4.10, it cannot be proved by simply adapting the proof there. Nevertheless, there is another way to prove Proposition 1.4.10, which we illustrate below. This new approach extends readily to Lemma 1.4.19 as well.

For $i, j = 1, 2$, let $X_j^i(t)$ denote the number of jobs at node $j$ in network $i$ at time $t$. Note $X_1^i(t) + X_2^i(t) = N$ for $i = 1, 2$ and for all $t$. Let $D_j^i(t)$ denote the cumulative number of departures (i.e., service completions), up to time $t$, from node $j$ in network $i$. Recall in Proposition 1.4.10, node 1 of the two networks have service rates $r_{Y_1}(\cdot)$ and $r_{Y_2}(\cdot)$, respectively, and $r_{Y_1} \leq r_{Y_2}$; while node 2 in both networks has the same service rate $r_Z(\cdot)$, which is an increasing function. Below we establish a pathwise stochastic ordering among the state $(X)$ and the counting $(D)$ processes of the two networks. This result then implies the throughput result in Proposition 1.4.10.

**Proposition 1.4.20** Suppose the two networks in Proposition 1.4.10 start from the same initial state, i.e., $X_1^1(0) = X_1^2(0)$ [hence, $X_2^1(0) = X_2^2(0)$], and $D_j^1(0) = D_j^2(0) = 0$ for $j = 1, 2$. Then

$$\{X_1^1(t)\} \geq_{st} \{X_1^2(t)\}, \quad \{(D_1^1(t), D_2^1(t))\} \leq_{st} \{(D_1^2(t), D_2^2(t))\}.$$

**Proof.** We use uniformization to "couple" the two networks as well as to discretize time, and inductively construct the paths of the stochastic processes in question such that the desired order relations are maintained at all times.

For $j = 1, 2$, write $r_{Y_j}$ as $r_j$ for simplicity. Let

$$\eta := \max_k \{r_2(k)\} + r_Z(N) := \eta_1 + \eta_2$$

be the uniformization constant. Let $0 = \tau_0 < \tau_1 < \ldots$ be a sequence of Poisson event epochs with occurrence rate $\eta$. Let $\{U_k; k = 0, 1, 2, \ldots\}$ be a sequence of iid random variables uniformly distributed on the interval $[-\eta_2, \eta_1]$, and independent of the Poisson event epochs $\{\tau_k\}$. Below, using the two sequences $\{\tau_k\}$ and $\{U_k\}$, we generate the paths of the processes in the two networks.

Let $x_j^i(k)$ and $d_j^i(k)$ denote the sample values of $X_j^i(\tau_k)$ and $D_j^i(\tau_k)$ through the construction. Initially, set $x_1^i(0) = X_1^i(0)$ and $d_j^i(0) = 0$ for $i, j = 1, 2$. Inductively, suppose the construction has been carried out to $\tau_k$, and the following relations hold:

$$x_1^1(k) \geq x_1^2(k); \qquad d_j^1(k) \leq d_j^2(k), \quad j = 1, 2. \tag{1.16}$$

[The first inequality above implies $x_2^1(k) = N - x_1^1(k) \leq N - x_1^2(k) = x_2^2(k)$.] We specify the construction at $\tau_{k+1}$, and show the relations in (1.16) also hold at $\tau_{k+1}$. Note, for $t \in (\tau_k, \tau_{k+1})$, $x_j^i(t) = x_j^i(k)$, $d_j^i(t) = d_j^i(k)$, $i, j = 1, 2$. That is, in between two consecutive Poisson event epochs, there are no changes in either network, following the construction. At $\tau_{k+1}$, for $i = 1, 2$, set

$$x_1^i(k+1) = x_1^i(k) - 1_1^i + 1_2^i, \quad x_2^i(k+1) = N - x_1^i(k+1);$$

$$d_j^i(k+1) = d_j^i(k) + 1_j^i, \quad j = 1, 2;$$

where $1_j^i$ are indicator functions defined as:

$$1_1^i = 1\{U_k \in (0, r_i(x_1^i(k))]\}, \quad 1_2^i = 1\{U_k \in [-r_Z(x_2^i(k)), 0]\}.$$

(Hence, the two indicator functions correspond to whether or not there is a service completion at either node 1 or node 2 in the two networks.) This construction is valid, i.e., the constructed processes are indeed the correct probabilistic replicas of the orginal processes, since the service completions occur with the right rates: $r_i(x_1^i(k))$ for node 1 and $r_Z(x_2^i(k))$ for node 2 in network $i = 1, 2$.

We next show that the induction hypotheses in (1.16) also hold at $\tau_{k+1}$. If $x_1^1(k) > x_1^2(k)$, then, since regardless of what value $U_k$ takes, $x_1^1(k+1) \geq x_1^2(k+1)$ always holds. On the other hand, if $x_1^1(k) = x_1^2(k)$, then

$$r_1(x_1^1(k)) \leq r_2(x_1^2(k)),$$

implying $1_1^1 \leq 1_1^2$, and hence $x_1^1(k+1) \geq x_1^2(k+1)$. (Note: $1_2^1 = 1_2^2$ in this case.)

For the counting processes, $d_2^1(k+1) \leq d_2^2(k+1)$ obviously holds, since $r_Z(x_2^1(k)) \leq r_Z(x_2^2(k))$ follows from the increasingness of $r_Z(\cdot)$ and $x_2^1(k) \leq x_2^2(k)$. That $d_1^1(k+1) \leq d_1^2(k+1)$ holds is also obvious when $x_1^1(k) = x_1^2(k)$, since $r_1 \leq r_2$. On the other hand, when $x_1^1(k) > x_1^2(k)$, we have

$$d_1^2(k) - d_1^1(k) = [x_1^1(k) - x_1^2(k)] + [d_2^2(k) - d_2^1(k)] > 0,$$

making use of the induction hypothesis, $d_2^2(k) \geq d_2^1(k)$. Hence, in both cases, $d_1^1(k+1) \leq d_1^2(k+1)$ still holds. $\square$

Now we can adapt the above proof to prove a network analog of Lemma 1.4.19.

**Proposition 1.4.21** Consider the two cyclic networks in Proposition 1.4.10. Suppose the service rates at node 1 and node 2 are, respectively, equal to the equilibrium rates of $Y_i$ and $Z_i$, in network $i$, for $i = 1, 2$. When $Y_i$ and $Z_i$ satisfy the conditions in Lemma 1.4.19, the counting processes in the two networks satisfy

$$\{(D_1^1(t), D_2^1(t))\} \leq_{st} \{(D_1^2(t), D_2^2(t))\}.$$

**Proof.** Let $r_j^i$ denote the service rate at node $j$ in network $i$, for $i, j = 1, 2$. Then, $r_j^1 \leq_\uparrow r_j^2$ for $j = 1, 2$, following the conditions on $Y_i$ and $Z_i$ in Lemma 1.4.19. Also, following Lemma 1.4.16(iii), we can assume without loss of generality that either $r_j^1$ or $r_j^2$ is increasing, for $j = 1, 2$. Proceed by adapting the proof of Proposition 1.4.20 as follows:

(i) Let the uniformization constant be $\eta := \max_k\{r_1^2(k)\} + \max_k\{r_2^2(k)\}$.

(ii) Apply induction only to $d_j^i$'s, i.e., remove the part on $x_j^i$ in (1.16).

(iii) Replace $r_i$ by $r_1^i$, and $r_Z$ by $r_2^i$.

The two nodes are now symmetric, arguing for one node suffices. For instance, for node 1, the key is $x_1^1(k) \leq x_1^2(k) \Rightarrow r_1^1(x_1^1(k)) \leq r_1^2(x_1^2(k))$ (since $r_1^1 \leq_\uparrow r_1^2$); while $x_1^1(k) > x_1^2(k) \Rightarrow d_1^1(k) < d_1^2(k)$ (same as in the last part of the proof of Proposition 1.4.20). $\square$

Same as before, extension to the general closed network is immediate.

**Theorem 1.4.22** In a closed Jackson network, increasing the service rates at a subset of nodes, in the sense of the shifted ordering in Definition 1.4.15, will increase the throughput of the network, provided the service rates at all the other nodes are increasing functions.

Hence, in the context of the clean room example mentioned earlier, in order to increase the overall production rate of the network, the WIP-dependent production rate of the clean room must be increased according to the stronger shifted dominance ordering; the usual pointwise ordering is not good enough.

**Remark 1.4.23** Note the stronger result of stochastic ordering among departure processes in Proposition 1.4.21 does not apply to the general network in Theorem 1.4.22. It will, however, apply to any aggregated two-node model of the network.

## 1.5   Concavity and Convexity

In Theorem 1.4.5, we have established that the throughput function is an increasing function of the network WIP level, provided all nodes have increasing service rate functions. We also know that this result is equivalent to the preservation of the $PF_2$ property (or, the increasingness of the equilibrium rates) under convolution of the pmf's of independent random variables.

Here we study the concavity/convexity of the throughput function, with respect to the network WIP level. We will show that not only the increasingness of the equilibrium rates but also the increasing concavity and increasing convexity are preserved under convolution.

Below we start with a two-node cyclic network, and present a coupling proof of the increasing concavity of the departure processes, and hence the throughput, with respect to the job population. In contrast to the monotonicity proof, such as the one in Proposition 1.4.10, where the coupling is applied to two networks, here we need to construct *four* networks.

**Proposition 1.5.1** Consider four two-node cyclic networks, indexed by the superscript $i$, with job population $N^1 = N$, $N^2 = N^3 = N + 1$, and $N^4 = N + 2$, respectively. The service rates at the two nodes are $\mu_1(\cdot)$ and $\mu_2(\cdot)$, common for all four networks. Both $\mu_1$ and $\mu_2$ are increasing and concave functions. For $j = 1, 2$ and $i = 1, 2, 3, 4$, let $D_j^i(t)$ be the cumulative number of service completions up to time $t$, and $X_j^i(t)$, the number of jobs at time $t$, in network $i$ at node $j$. Assume initially, $X_1^i(0) = N^i$, $X_2^i(0) = 0$, and $D_j^i(0) = 0$ for all $i, j$. Then,

$$
\begin{aligned}
&\{(D_1^1(t) + D_1^4(t), D_2^1(t) + D_2^4(t))\} \\
\leq_{st} \ &\{(D_1^2(t) + D_1^3(t), D_2^2(t) + D_2^3(t))\};
\end{aligned} \tag{1.17}
$$

and

$$\{(D_1^1(t), D_2^1(t))\} \leq_{st} \{(D_1^i(t), D_2^i(t))\}, \quad i = 2, 3. \tag{1.18}$$

**Proof.** The uniformization procedure is similar to the proof of Proposition 1.4.20. Let the uniformization constant be $\eta := 2\mu_1(N + 2) + 2\mu_2(N + 2) := \eta_1 + \eta_2$. Let $\{\tau_k\}$ be the sequence of Poisson event epochs with rate $\eta$; let $\{U_k\}$ be an iid sequence of uniform random variables on $[-\eta_2, \eta_1]$, independent of $\{\tau_k\}$.

Again, let $x_j^i(k)$ and $d_j^i(k)$ denote the sample values of the state and the counting processes at $\tau_k$ generated by the construction. Initially, as specified in the theorem, for $i = 1, 2, 3, 4$, set $x_1^i(0) = N^i$, and $x_2^i(0) = 0$; set $d_j^i(0) = 0$ for $j = 1, 2$.

Inductively, suppose the construction has been carried out up to $\tau_k$. As induction hypotheses, suppose

$$d_j^1(k) + d_j^4(k) \leq d_j^2(k) + d_j^3(k), \quad j = 1, 2; \tag{1.19}$$

and, in addition,

$$x_j^1(k) \leq x_j^2(k) \leq x_j^4(k), \quad x_j^1(k) \leq x_j^3(k); \quad j = 1, 2. \tag{1.20}$$

Note that the relations in (1.20) will guarantee, via the construction below, the increasingness property in (1.18).

The construction at $\tau_{k+1}$ takes the same form as in the coupling proof of Proposition 1.4.20. For simplicity, write $x_j^i := x_j^i(k)$ and $d_j^i := d_j^i(k)$. For $i = 1, 2, 3, 4$, set:

$$x_1^i(k+1) = x_1^i - 1_1^i + 1_2^i, \quad x_2^i(k+1) = N^i - x_1^i(k+1);$$

$$d_j^i(k+1) = d_j^i + 1_j^i, \quad j = 1, 2.$$

Here, however, the indicator functions are specified differently:

$$1_1^i = 1\{U_k \in (0, \mu_1(x_1^i)]\}, \quad 1_2^i = 1\{U_k \in (-\mu_2(x_2^i), 0]\}; \quad i = 1, 2, 4;$$

and

$$\begin{aligned} 1_1^3 &= 1\{U_k \in (0, \mu_1(x_1^1)]\} \\ &\quad + 1\{U_k \in (\mu_1(x_1^2), \mu_1(x_1^2) + \mu_1(x_1^3) - \mu_1(x_1^1)]\}, \\ 1_2^3 &= 1\{U_k \in (-\mu_2(x_2^1), 0]\} \\ &\quad + 1\{U_k \in (-\mu_2(x_2^2), -\mu_2(x_2^2) - \mu_2(x_2^3) + \mu_2(x_2^1)]\}. \end{aligned}$$

That is, $1_j^i$ signifies a service completion at node $j$ in network $i$. Clearly, the above construction yields the correct service completion rates in all four networks. Note, for instance, in $1_1^3$, the two non-overlapping intervals add up to a total length of $\mu_1(x_1^3)$, the right service rate for node 1 in network 3. (In particular, based on the induction hypothesis and the increasingness of the service rates, we have $\mu_1(x_1^1) \leq \mu_1(x_1^2)$ and $\mu_1(x_1^3) \geq \mu_1(x_1^1)$.) The construction for network 3 might appear somewhat unusual; but it is crucial, as will become evident below.

That (1.20) holds at $\tau_{k+1}$ is obvious, following the construction. So we focus on (1.19). Due to symmetry, we only need to argue for $j = 1$. Consider two cases:

(i) Suppose $x_1^1 + x_1^4 \leq x_1^2 + x_1^3$. This, along with (1.20) and the increasing concavity of $\mu_1$, implies

$$\mu_1(x_1^2) + \mu_1(x_1^3) - \mu_1(x_1^1) \geq \mu_1(x_1^4).$$

Therefore, we have:

(ia) $\mathbf{1}_1^4 = 1 \Rightarrow$ either $\mathbf{1}_1^2 = 1$ or $\mathbf{1}_1^3 = 1$ (or both),

in addition to the more obvious implication,

(ib) $\mathbf{1}_1^1 = 1 \Rightarrow \mathbf{1}_1^2 = \mathbf{1}_1^3 = 1$.

In words, the construction guarantees, in this case, that a service completion (at node 1) in network 1 implies a service completion in both networks 2 and 3 [(ib)], while a service completion in network 4 implies a service completion in either network 2 or 3, or both [(ia)]. Hence, (1.19) also holds at $\tau_{k+1}$.

(ii) Suppose $x_1^1 + x_1^4 > x_1^2 + x_1^3$. Then, together with the induction hypothesis in (1.19) for $j = 2$, this implies

$$\begin{aligned} d_1^2 + d_1^3 &= d_2^2 + d_2^3 - (x_1^2 + x_1^3) + (2N + 2) \\ &> d_2^1 + d_2^4 - (x_1^1 + x_1^4) + (2N + 2) = d_1^1 + d_1^4. \quad (1.21) \end{aligned}$$

So, although we do not have (ia) in this case, we still have (ib), which is sufficient, due to the strict inequality in (1.21). In other words, the construction rules out the possibility of having service completions in both networks 1 and 4, without any service completion in either network 2 or network 3. The worst thing that can happen is there is a service completion in network 4 but no service completion in the other networks. But this poses no harm, due to the strict inequality in (1.21).

The induction is now completed, and hence the proof. □

It is not difficult to observe that the above proof applies equally well to the convex case, i.e., the service rates are increasing and convex functions. The only change is the conclusion: increasing convexity for the counting processes, and hence the throughput, with respect to the job population.

**Corollary 1.5.2** In the setting of Proposition 1.5.1, if the service rates at all nodes are increasing and convex functions, then the conclusion there changes to increasing convexity, i.e., the inequality in (1.17) is reversed, while (1.18) stays the same.

The linear case corresponds to an infinite-server node (i.e., the number of servers at each node is at least $N$), with each server having a constant service rate. Since linearity is both convex and concave, Proposition 1.5.1 and Corollary 1.5.2 both apply. That is, (1.17) should satisfy as an equality. This implies the throughput is also linear in the job population.

To summarize, the main result in this section can be stated as follows:

**Theorem 1.5.3** In a closed Jackson network, if the service rates at all nodes are increasing and concave (resp. increasing and convex) functions, then the throughput is increasing and concave (resp. increasing and convex) in the job population.

From the relation of the throughput function and the equilibrium rate of a convolution of independent random variables [refer to (1.15)], we know that the conclusion of Proposition 1.5.1 and more generally that of Theorem 1.5.3 can be interpretated as the preservation of concavity and convexity, in addition to monotonicity, of the equilibrium rates under convolution.

**Proposition 1.5.4** $\{Y_1, ..., Y_m\}$ is a set of independent random variables, each with an increasing and concave (increasing and convex) equilibrium rate. Then, the equilibrium rate of $Y_1 + \cdots + Y_m$ is also increasing and concave (increasing and convex).

## 1.6   Multiple Servers

An important special case of an increasing and concave service rate function is when a node has multiple, say $c$, parallel servers. Suppose each server has a constant service rate $\nu$, then $\mu(n) = \min\{n, c\}\nu$ is increasing and concave (in $n$) (since min is increasing and concave). Adapting the proof in the last section, Proposition 1.5.1 in particular, we can establish a concavity result with respect to the number of parallel servers.

**Proposition 1.6.1** Suppose the four networks in Proposition 1.5.1 all have the same job population $N$, and the same service rate at node 2, $\mu_2(\cdot)$, which is an increasing and concave function. They differ at node 1, which has $c^i$ parallel servers, each with a constant service rate $\nu > 0$, for network $i$, $i = 1, 2, 3, 4$. Suppose $c^1 = c$, $c^2 = c^3 = c + 1$, $c^4 = c + 2$. Then the conclusions in Proposition 1.5.1, in particular, (1.17, 1.18), still hold. Consequently, the throughput is increasing and concave in the number of servers $c$ (at node 1).

**Proof.** Follow essentially the proof of Proposition 1.5.1, with necessary modifications. Keep the induction hypothesis in (1.19), but change the one in (1.20) to the following:

$$x_1^1(k) \geq x_1^2(k) \geq x_1^4(k), \quad x_1^3(k) \geq x_1^4(k), \tag{1.22}$$

which then implies

$$x_2^1(k) \leq x_2^2(k) \leq x_2^4(k), \quad x_2^3(k) \leq x_2^4(k),$$

since all four networks have the same job population. Hence, the construction for node 2 stays the same as in the proof of Proposition 1.5.1, while the construction for node 1 needs to be modified.

Omit the argument $k$ from $x_j^i(k)$. The service rate at node 1 is now $\mu_1(x_1^i) = \min\{x_1^i, c^i\}\nu$, for $i = 1, 2, 3, 4$. Write these as $r^i := (x_1^i \wedge c^i)\nu$. Without loss of generality, set $\nu = 1$. First observe that we have

$$\text{either} \quad r^1 \leq r^2 \quad \text{or} \quad r^4 \leq r^3, \quad \text{or both.} \tag{1.23}$$

To see this, consider two cases: (a) $x_1^4 \geq c + 2$, and (b) $x_1^4 \leq c + 1$. In (a), we have $r^2 = c + 1 > c = r^1$, taking into account (1.22). In (b), we have $r^4 = x_1^4 \leq r^3$, since $x_1^4 \leq x_1^3$ and $r^3 = x_1^3 \wedge (c + 1)$.

Therefore, if both $r^1 \leq r^2$ and $r^4 \leq r^3$, follow the construction (for node 1) in Proposition 1.5.1, with

$$1_1^i = \mathbf{1}\{U_k \in (0, r^i]\}, \quad i = 1, 2, 3, 4. \tag{1.24}$$

If $r^1 \leq r^2$ but $r^4 > r^3$, there are two sub-cases: If $r^3 \geq r^1$, then follow $1_1^i$ above for $i = 1, 3, 4$, while for $i = 2$, set

$$1_1^2 = \mathbf{1}\{U_k \in (0, r^1]\} + \mathbf{1}\{U_k \in (r^3, r^2 + r^3 - r^1]\}.$$

Otherwise, i.e., if $r^3 < r^1$, then follow $1_1^i$ in (1.24) for $i = 1, 2, 3$ instead, while for $i = 4$, set

$$1_1^4 = \mathbf{1}\{U_k \in (0, r^3]\} + \mathbf{1}\{U_k \in (r^1, r^1 + r^4 - r^3]\}.$$

If $r^4 \leq r^3$ but $r^1 > r^2$, the construction is similar: replace $1_1^2$ and $1_1^4$ above by $1_1^3$ and $1_1^1$, respectively, according to whether $r^2 \geq r^4$ or $r^2 < r^4$.

Regardless, however, we still have, same as in the proof of Proposition 1.5.1,

$$x_1^1 + x_1^4 \leq x_1^2 + x_1^3 \quad \Rightarrow \quad r^1 + r^4 \leq r^2 + r^3. \tag{1.25}$$

The above follows trivially if either $x_1^4 \geq c + 2$ or $x_1^1 \leq c$. So suppose $x_1^4 \leq c + 1 \leq x_1^1$. Then, $r^1 + r^4 = c + x_1^4$, which, under the induction hypothesis in (1.22), is clearly dominated by

$$r^2 + r^3 = [x_1^2 \wedge (c + 1)] + [x_1^3 \wedge (c + 1)]$$

$$= (x_1^2 + x_1^3) \wedge [(x_1^2 \wedge x_1^3) + c + 1] \wedge (2c + 2).$$

Therefore, (1.25) ensures the validity of the argument for case (i) in the proof of Proposition 1.5.1, while (1.23) supports the argument in case (ii). □

Consider again the two-node cyclic network in Proposition 1.5.1. Suppose node one has $c$ parallel server, each with a service rate $r$; and the other node has an increasing and concave service rate function. Following essentially the proof there, we can show that the throughput function is increasing and concave in $r$ (for any given job population $N$). Let the four networks differ in the service rate (of each server) at node 1, which equals $r^1 = r$ for network 1, $r^2 = r^3 = r + \Delta$ for networks 2 and 3 (where $\Delta > 0$ is a real value), and $r^4 = r + 2\Delta$ for network 4. Keep the induction hypothesis in (1.19), while limit the one in (1.20) to $j = 2$ only (which then implies a relationship, with the inequalities reversed, for $j = 1$, since the four networks now have the same job population). The service rates at node 1 is $\mu_1^i(x_1^i) = (x_1^i \wedge c)r^i$ in network $i$. The rest of the construction and the proof simply follows the argument in the proof of Proposition 1.5.1.

To extend this to a more general closed Jackson network, suppose a node $i$ has $c_i$ servers, each with service rate $\mu_i$, and the visit frequency is $v_i$. Then, letting $r_i = \mu_i/v_i$ and aggregating the other nodes into a single node, we get back to the two-node network above, and reach the conclusion that the throughput is increasing and concave in $r_i$. Furthermore, the *reciprocal* of the throughput is decreasing and *convex* in $r_i$ (the reciprocal of a concave function is convex). Note that the reciprocal throughput, when multiplied by the total job population $N$, yields the average job delay (i.e., sojourn time in the network), via Little's law. Since following Proposition 1.6.1, the throughput function is concave in the number of servers at a multiple-server node, say $c_i$, the average job delay is decreasing and convex in $c_i$. To summarize, we have

**Theorem 1.6.2** In a closed Jackson network, suppose a node $i$ has $c_i$ servers, each with service rate $\mu_i$, and the visit frequency is $v_i$. Denote $r_i = \mu_i/v_i$. Suppose the service rates at the other nodes are increasing and concave functions. Then, for each $N$,

(i) the throughput function, $TH(N, c_i, r_i)$, is increasing and concave in $c_i$ and in $r_i$;

(ii) the reciprocal throughput, $TH^{-1}(N, c_i, r_i)$, and hence the average job delay, $N/TH(N, c_i, r_i)$, is decreasing and convex in $c_i$, and in $r_i$.

Write $\rho_i = v_i/\mu_i = 1/r_i$, and $\rho := (\rho_i)_{i=1}^m$. When all nodes have single servers, the above can be strengthened to a *joint* convexity with respect to $\rho$. To see this, first recall that the network can be equivalently viewed as having a cyclic configuration, with each node $i$ having a service rate $r_i = 1/\rho_i$. Let $T_i(n)$ be the time epoch of the $n$th service completion at node $i$. Let $\{U_i(n); i = 1, ..., m; n = 1, 2, ...\}$ be a sequence of iid uniform $[0,1]$ random variables. Then the exponential service time of job $n$ at node $i$ can be expressed as $\rho_i[-\log U_i(n)]$. Assume initially all $N$ jobs are in front of node 1. We have the following recursion:

$$T_i(n) = \rho_i[-\log U_i(n)] + \max\{T_{i-1}(n), T_i(n-1)\}, \qquad (1.26)$$

for all $n$ and all $i$, with the understanding that $T_i(n) \equiv 0$ if $n \leq 0$, and $T_0(n) = T_m(n-N)$ (i.e., both node index $i$ and job index $n$ are cyclic, with modulus $m$ and $N$, resepectively). Since max is increasing and convex, the above recursion preserves increasingness and convexity, with respect to $\rho = (\rho_i)_{i=1}^m$. Let $D_i(t)$ denote the cumulative number of service completions from node $i$ up to $t$. Then,

$$\lim_{n \to \infty} \frac{T_i(n)}{n} = \lim_{t \to \infty} \frac{T_i(D_i(t))}{D_i(t)} = \lim_{t \to \infty} \frac{t}{D_i(t)} = TH^{-1}(N, \rho).$$

(The existence of the limits above can be rigorously justified by the analysis in Chapter 4; see also Section 10, Notes.)

**Theorem 1.6.3** In a closed Jackson network where each node $i$ has a single server with fixed service rate $\mu_i$, and visit frequency $v_i$, the reciprocal throughput function, $TH^{-1}(N, \rho)$, and hence the average job delay, are increasing and convex in $\rho = (\rho_i)_{i=1}^m$, where $\rho_i = v_i/\mu_i$.

## 1.7   Resource Sharing

### 1.7.1   Aggregation of Servers

To motivate, we start with a simple example.

**Example 1.7.1** Consider a simple multi-server queue $M/M/c/N$. Suppose each server serves at a constant rate $1/c$ (hence the maximum output rate is 1). Now, reduce the number of servers to $c' < c$, with each server serving at a constant rate $1/c'$ (hence the maximum output rate is maintained at 1). To illustrate the effect of this change, consider the special case of $c' = 1$. In other words, we aggregate the processing capacity of multiple servers to form a single server with the same overall capacity. The obvious advantage is that the aggregated single server always works at full capacity whenever there is at least one job in the node, while in the orginal case, full capacity is only achieved when there are at least $c$ jobs.

Let $X$ and $X'$ denote the total number of jobs in system before and after the aggregation. Then clearly,

$$r_X(n) = \min\{n, c\}/c \leq \min\{n, c'\}/c' = r_{X'}(n), \quad n = 0, 1, \ldots, N;$$

hence, $X \geq_{\ell r} X'$. Furthermore, this implies $X \geq_{st} X'$, and hence $\mathsf{P}[X = N] \geq \mathsf{P}[X' = N]$. That is, the aggregation results in a higher throughput, since the blocking probability, $\mathsf{P}[X' = N]$, is lower. In summary, server aggregation in $M/M/c/N$ leads to a reduced total number of jobs in system, in the sense of likelihood ratio ordering, and an increased throughput.

Similar results also hold in a network setting. Although server aggregation is a special case of increasing the service rate function (in the pointwise sense), and hence belongs to the context of Theorem 1.4.13, more results can be established in this special case; in particular, there is a lower bound on the throughput, in addition to the upper bound.

**Proposition 1.7.2** Consider a two-node cyclic network with $N$ jobs: node 1 has $c$ parallel servers, each with a constant service rate $1/c$; node 2 has an increasing service rate function $\mu_2(\cdot)$. Index this network by superscript 0. Now, replace the $c$ servers at node 1 by $c'$ $(c' < c \leq N)$ servers, each with a constant service rate $1/c'$. Index this network by superscript 1. Further reduce the job population of network 1 to $N - (c - c')$, and index the network by superscript 2. Let $X_j^i$ be the number of jobs at node $j$ in network $i$; $j = 1, 2$; $i = 0, 1, 2$. Then,

$$X_1^0 \geq_{\ell r} X_1^1, \quad X_2^0 \leq_{\ell r} X_2^1; \quad X_j^0 \geq_{\ell r} X_j^2, \quad j = 1, 2.$$

Furthermore, let $TH^i$, $i = 0, 1, 2$, denote the throughput of the three networks. Then,

$$TH^2 \leq TH^0 \leq TH^1.$$

**Proof.** Without loss of generality, assume $c' = c - 1$. Let $Y_1$ and $Y_2$ denote two random variables with equilibrium rates

$$r_{Y_1}(n) = \min\{n, c\}/c, \quad \text{and} \quad r_{Y_2}(n) = \min\{n, c - 1\}/(c - 1),$$

respectively. Then, clearly,

$$r_{Y_2}(n - 1) \leq r_{Y_1}(n) \leq r_{Y_2}(n).$$

Let $Z$ denote a third random variable, independent of $Y_1$ and $Y_2$, with equilibrium rate $r_Z(n) = \mu_2(n)$. Then, similar to the proof of Proposition 1.4.10, we have

$$
\begin{aligned}
r_{X_1^0}(n) &= r_{Y_1}(n)/r_Z(N + 1 - n) \\
&\leq r_{Y_2}(n)/r_Z(N + 1 - n) = r_{X_1^1}(n)
\end{aligned}
$$

for all $n$. Hence, $X_1^0 \geq_{\ell r} X_1^1$, which also implies $X_2^0 \leq_{\ell r} X_2^1$. On the other hand,

$$r_{X_1^0}(n) \leq r_{Y_1}(n)/r_Z(N - n) = r_{X_1^2}(n),$$

since $r_Z$ is an increasing function; and

$$
\begin{aligned}
r_{X_2^0}(n) &= r_Z(n)/r_{Y_1}(N + 1 - n) \\
&\leq r_Z(n)/r_{Y_2}(N - n) = r_{X_2^2}(n).
\end{aligned}
$$

(When $n = N$, define $r_{X_j^2}(N) = \infty$, for $j = 1, 2$.) Therefore, $X_j^0 \geq_{\ell r} X_j^2$ for $j = 1, 2$.

The throughput relations now follow immediately, since the throughput for network $i$ is equal to $Er_Z(X_2^i)$ for $i = 0, 1, 2$, and $r_Z$ is an increasing function. $\square$

**Theorem 1.7.3** For any multi-server node in the $B$ part of the network considered in Theorem 1.4.13, reducing the number of servers while maintaining the maximal service capacity will lead to the same conclusions. Furthermore, if the the total number of jobs in the network is also reduced by the same number (as the number of reduced servers), then the throughput of the network will decrease.

The above theorem indicates that in increasing the overall production rate, the effect of server aggregation, in terms of reducing the number of servers while maintaining the capacity at the nodes, will be canceled out if the WIP level of the network is also reduced. Specifically, increasing the WIP level, by say $k$ jobs, will have more effect in increasing the overall production rate than reducing the number of servers, by $k$ servers, through aggregation.

### 1.7.2  Aggregation of Nodes

Consider again a closed, cyclic network with two nodes and $N$ jobs. There are $c_j \geq 1$ parallel servers at node $j$, each with a service rate $\mu_j$, $j = 1, 2$. Suppose we now formulate a second network by aggregating the two nodes into a single node, with $c := c_1 + c_2$ parallel servers. The total number of jobs is still $N$. Each job still requires two stages of service as before; specifically, the service times are exponentially distributed with mean $1/\mu_j$ at stage $j$, for $j = 1, 2$. But now the service of both stages of any job can be handled by any one of the $c$ servers.

Note in the second network, although there is only one node, there are still two stages of service for each of the $N$ jobs. In particular, each job goes through the two stages of service in sequence; and at any time each job is either in stage 1 (waiting or being processed for stage 1 service) or in stage 2. Indeed, we can think of the $N$ jobs as formulating two queues, one for each stage, while each of the $c$ servers can take jobs from both queues.

Use the superscript $i$ ($=1,2$) to index the two networks. Let $D_j^i(t)$ be the cumulative number of service completions up to time $t$ from stage $j$ in network $i$. We want to show

$$\{(D_1^1(t), D_2^1(t)\} \leq_{st} \{(D_1^2(t), D_2^2(t)\}. \tag{1.27}$$

Again, we use coupling. Let the uniformization constant be $\eta := c\mu := (c_1 + c_2)(\mu_1 \vee \mu_2)$. Let $\{\tau_k\}$ be the sequence of Poisson event epochs with rate $\eta$; let $\{U_k\}$ be a sequence of iid uniform random variables on $[-c\mu, c\mu]$, independent of $\{\tau_k\}$.

For $i, j = 1, 2$, let $d_j^i(k)$ denote the sample values of the counting processes at $\tau_k$ generated by the construction; let $x_j^i(k)$ denote the number of stage $j$ jobs in network $i$ at $\tau_k$. Initially, for $i = 1, 2$, set $x_1^i(0) = N$, and $x_2^i(0) = 0$; set $d_j^i(0) = 0$ for $j = 1, 2$.

As induction hypothesis, suppose

$$(d_1^1(k), d_2^1(k)) \leq (d_1^2(k), d_2^2(k)). \tag{1.28}$$

We want to show that the above also holds at $\tau_{k+1}$.

To specify the construction in network 2, we assume the following mode of operation: Among the $c$ servers, at any time there will be no more than $c_1$ servers working on stage 1 jobs unless the number of stage 2 jobs is less than $c_2$; and similarly, at any time there will be no more than $c_2$ servers working on stage 2 jobs unless the number of stage 1 jobs is less than $c_1$. In other words, among the $c$ servers there will always be $c_1$ (not necessarily always the same servers) giving priority to stage 1 jobs, and $c_2$ giving priority to stage 2 jobs. Hence, for instance, initially all $c$ servers start with stage 1 jobs (suppose $N > c$). As some of the servers complete their service, they may continue, on the same job, into stage 2. But once the number of servers working on stage 2 jobs reaches $c_2$, any server that completes a stage 1 job will have to switch to another stage 1 job.

Due to work conservation, the operation of network 2 assumed above will deplete work at the same rate as any other work conserving schemes (i.e., no server will be idle as long as there is job to be processed), and hence the same throughput (i.e., the same rate of depleting *jobs*) as well. Consider, for instance, the original mode of operation in network 2: every server works on the two stages of service of each job in sequence; after completing both stages consecutively at a server, a job will join the end of the queue and the server will pick up another job from the front of the queue. Let $D^2(t)$ be the number of jobs completed up to time $t$, under this mode of operation (in network 2). For $j = 1, 2$, let $S_j$ denote the generic exponential service time at stage $j$; let $S = S_1 + S_2$. Then, the long-run average rate of work depletion is

$$\lim_{t \to \infty} [S(1) + \cdots + S(D^2(t))]/t$$
$$= \lim_{t \to \infty} [S(1) + \cdots + S(D^2(t))]/D^2(t) \cdot \lim_{t \to \infty} D^2(t)/t$$
$$= (\frac{1}{\mu_1} + \frac{1}{\mu_2}) \cdot TH,$$

where $S(i)$ are iid replicas of $S$, and $TH$ denotes the throughput.

On the other hand, the long-run average rate of work depletion under the operation mode specified earlier can be similarly derived as follows:

$$\lim_{t \to \infty} [S_1(1) + \cdots + S_1(D_1^2(t)) + S_2(1) + \cdots + S_2(D_2^2(t))]/t$$

$$= \frac{1}{\mu_1} \lim_{t\to\infty} D_1^2(t)/t + \frac{1}{\mu_2} \lim_{t\to\infty} D_1^2(t)/t$$

$$= (\frac{1}{\mu_1} + \frac{1}{\mu_2}) \cdot TH',$$

where

$$TH' = \lim_{t\to\infty} D_1^2(t)/t = \lim_{t\to\infty} D_2^2(t)/t.$$

Since the two work-depletion rates are the same, we have $TH' = TH$.

Therefore, we specify the construction in network 2, assuming the mode of operation specified earlier, and verify the induction hypothesis (1.28) at $\tau_{k+1}$, and thereby establish the desired relation in (1.27).

Again, dropping the argument $k$ from $x_j^i(k)$ and $d_j^i(k)$, we set, for $i = 1, 2$,

$$x_1^i(k+1) = x_1^i - 1_1^i + 1_2^i, \quad x_2^i(k+1) = x_2^i - 1_2^i + 1_1^i;$$

and

$$d_j^i(k+1) = d_j^i + 1_j^i, \quad j = 1, 2;$$

where

$$
\begin{aligned}
1_1^1 &= 1\{U_k \in (-(x_1^1 \wedge c_1)\mu_1, 0]\}, \\
1_2^1 &= 1\{U_k \in (0, (x_2^1 \wedge c_2)\mu_2]\}; \\
1_1^2 &= 1\{U_k \in (-(x_1^2 \wedge [c_1 + (c_2 - x_2^2)^+])\mu_1, 0]\}, \\
1_2^2 &= 1\{U_k \in (0, (x_2^2 \wedge [c_2 + (c_1 - x_1^2)^+])\mu_2]\}.
\end{aligned}
$$

Note that in network 2, the number of jobs in the two stages of service is, respectively, $x_1^2 \wedge [c_1 + (c_2 - x_2^2)^+]$ and $x_2^2 \wedge [c_2 + (c_1 - x_1^2)^+]$.

Consider two cases: If $x_1^2 \geq x_1^1$, then $1_1^2 \geq 1_1^1$, and hence $d_1^2(k+1) \geq d_1^1(k+1)$. On the other hand, if $x_1^2 < x_1^1$, then

$$d_1^2 = d_2^2 + N - x_1^2 > d_2^2 + N - x_1^1 = d_1^1,$$

which also guarantees $d_1^2(k+1) \geq d_1^1(k+1)$, no matter what transition takes place at $\tau_{k+1}$. The proof of $d_2^2(k+1) \geq d_2^1(k+1)$ follows similarly.

It is easy to see that if we add a third common node into the two networks, the above proof can be slightly modified (adding $x_3^2(k) \geq x_3^1(k)$ to the induction hypothesis) to reach the same conclusion. (The third node needs to have an increasing service rate function.) This third node can represent the aggregation of the other parts of a more general network.

Finally, suppose for $j = 1, 2$, node $j$ has a visit frequency $v_j$ and $c_j$ servers, each with service rate $\mu_j$. We can equivalently view these two nodes as having the same, unit visit frequency, but with modified service rates $\mu_1/v_1$ and $\mu_2/v_2$. Aggregating the two nodes then yields one with $c_1 + c_2$ servers, and jobs with mean service times $v_1/\mu_1$ and $v_2/\mu_2$ for the two stages of service. The cyclic network result above then applies.

To summarize, we have

**Theorem 1.7.4** In a closed Jackson network with all nodes having increasing service rate functions, aggregating a set, say $B$, of multiple-server nodes into a single node will increase the overall network throughput. Furthermore, it will reduce the total number of jobs in $B$, in the sense of likelihood ratio ordering. When the network is open, the aggregation will reduce the total number of jobs in $B$, and hence in the network, in the sense of likelihood ratio ordering.

## 1.8  Arrangement and Majorization

Recall the visit ratios, $(v_i)_{i=1}^m$, are the solution to the equations in (1.6). The visit ratios can be interpreted as the proportion of the (total) workload assigned to the nodes. Suppose the service rate functions at the $m$ nodes, $\mu_i(\cdot)$, $i = 1, \ldots, m$ are given; we want to distribute the workload among the nodes. We start with a two-node network.

**Lemma 1.8.1** Consider a two-node closed Jackson network in equilibrium, with $N$ jobs. For $j = 1, 2$, let $\mu_j(\cdot)$ and $v_j$ be, respectively, the service rate function and the visit ratio at node $j$. Suppose $v_1 > v_2$. Let $X_1$ and $N - X_1$ be the number of jobs at node 1 and node 2, respectively. In addition, consider another two-node closed network (indexed by a superscript "$\prime$"), which differs from the first one only in visit ratios: $v_1' = v_1 - \Delta$ and $v_2' = v_2 + \Delta$, where $0 < \Delta \le v_1 - v_2$.

(i) Suppose $\mu_1(n) \ge \mu_2(n)$ for all $n$, and let $\Delta = v_1 - v_2$ (i.e., the second network is obtained through interchanging the visit ratios at the two nodes in the first network). Then,

$$\min(X_1, N - X_1) \ge_{st} \min(X_1', N - X_1').$$

(ii) Suppose $\mu_1(n) = \mu_2(n)$ for all $n$. Then,

$$\min(X_1, N - X_1) \le_{st} \min(X_1', N - X_1').$$

**Proof.** For (i), we want to show

$$P(X_1 \le n) + P(X_1 \ge N - n)$$
$$\le \ P(X_1' \le n) + P(X_1' \ge N - n) \qquad (1.29)$$

for all $n \le \lfloor \frac{N}{2} \rfloor$, where $\lfloor \frac{N}{2} \rfloor$ denotes the integer part of $N/2$. Write $\rho = v_1/v_2 \ge 1$, and for $j = 1, 2$, $M_j(0) = 1$, $M_j(n) = \mu_j(1) \cdots \mu_j(n)$ for $n \ge 1$. The above can be written explicitly as:

$$\frac{\sum_{k=0}^n \frac{\rho^k}{M_1(k)M_2(N-k)} + \frac{\rho^{N-k}}{M_1(N-k)M_2(k)}}{\sum_{k=0}^{\lfloor \frac{N}{2} \rfloor} \frac{\rho^k}{M_1(k)M_2(N-k)} + \frac{\rho^{N-k}}{M_1(N-k)M_2(k)}}$$

$$\leq \frac{\sum_{k=0}^{n} \frac{\rho^{N-k}}{M_1(k)M_2(N-k)} + \frac{\rho^k}{M_1(N-k)M_2(k)}}{\sum_{k=0}^{\lfloor \frac{N}{2} \rfloor} \frac{\rho^{N-k}}{M_1(k)M_2(N-k)} + \frac{\rho^k}{M_1(N-k)M_2(k)}}, \tag{1.30}$$

which can be directly verified, taking into account $\mu_1(n) \geq \mu_2(n)$.

To prove (ii), write $M(n) = M_1(n) = M_2(n)$, since $\mu_1(n) = \mu_2(n)$ for all $n$. We want to establish (1.29) with the inequality reversed. In place of (1.30), it suffices to show

$$\frac{\sum_{k=0}^{n} \frac{\rho^k + \rho^{N-k}}{M(k)M(N-k)}}{\sum_{k=0}^{\lfloor \frac{N}{2} \rfloor} \frac{\rho^k + \rho^{N-k}}{M(k)M(N-k)}}$$

is decreasing in $\rho$, since $\rho = v_1/v_2 \geq (v_1 - \Delta)/(v_2 + \Delta)$. Again, this can be directly verified. $\square$

**Theorem 1.8.2** Consider the two networks in Lemma 1.8.1. Suppose $v_1 \geq v_2$.

(i) If, in addition to the conditions in Lemma 1.8.1(i), $\mu_2(n)$ is concave in $n$ and $\mu_1(n) - \mu_2(n)$ is increasing in $n$, then $TH(N) \geq TH'(N)$ for any given $N$.

(ii) If, in addition to the conditions in Lemma 1.8.1(ii), $\mu_1(n) = \mu_2(n)$ is concave in $n$, then $TH(N) \leq TH'(N)$ for any given $N$.

**Proof.** To show (i), following (1.9), we have

$$TH(N) = E\mu_1(X_1)/v_1 = E\mu_2(N - X_1)/v_2,$$

and hence, assuming $v_1 + v_2 = 1$ without loss of generality,

$$\begin{aligned} TH(N) &= E[\mu_1(X_1) + \mu_2(N - X_1)] \\ &= E[\mu_1(X_1) - \mu_2(X_1) + \mu_2(X_1) + \mu_2(N - X_1)]. \end{aligned} \tag{1.31}$$

Replacing $X_1$ by $X_1'$ yields a similar expression for $TH'(N)$.

Now, a larger visit ratio is equivalent to a smaller service rate, hence, $v_1 \geq v_2$ implies $X_1 \geq_{\ell r} X_1'$, and hence $X_1 \geq_{st} X_1'$. Since $\mu_1(n) - \mu_2(n)$ is increasing in $n$ as assumed, we have

$$\mu_1(X_1) - \mu_2(X_1) \geq_{st} \mu_1(X_1') - \mu_2(X_1'). \tag{1.32}$$

On the other hand, since $\mu_2(n)$ is concave in $n$, and

$$\min(X_1, N - X_1) \geq_{st} \min(X_1', N - X_1')$$

(from Lemma 1.8.1(i)), we have,

$$\mu_2(X_1) + \mu_2(N - X_1) \geq_{st} \mu_2(X_1') + \mu_2(N - X_1'), \qquad (1.33)$$

following a simple coupling argument.

The desired result, $TH(N) \geq TH'(N)$ then follows from adding up (1.32) and (1.33), taking expectations on both sides, and comparing against (1.31).

To prove (ii), (1.32) becomes trivial (both sides are zero), and (1.33), with the inequality reversed, follows from Lemma 1.8.1(ii). $\square$

Note that the required conditions in Theorem 1.8.2 are easily satisfied by the case of multiple parallel servers. Let $c_1$ and $c_2$ be the number of servers at the two nodes. Suppose $c_1 \geq c_2$, and suppose all servers have the same service rate $\nu$, then, in addition to the increasing concavity of both $\mu_1(n)$ and $\mu_2(n)$, we also have

$$\mu_1(n) - \mu_2(n) = \nu[\min\{n, c_1\} - c_2]^+$$

increasing in $n$.

In Theorem 1.8.2(i) (as well as Lemma 1.8.1), the second network is obtained through interchanging the workload assignment of the first network (i.e., $v_2$ to node 1 and $v_1$ to node 2). Since $\mu_1(n) \geq \mu_2(n)$ for all $n$, the result simply states that the throughput is increased by assigning a higher workload to a faster node (or, in the multi-server case, a node with more servers, provided all servers have the same service rate). More formally, when $v_1 \geq v_2$, write

$$v = (v_1, v_2) \geq_A v' = (v_2, v_1),$$

where $\geq_A$ denotes the so-called *arrangement ordering*. In general, $x \geq_A y$, if two vectors, $x$ and $y$, are different permutations of the same set of components, and $x$ can be obtained from a sequence of pairwise interchange of the components of $y$, with each interchange resulting in a decreasing order of the two components. In other words, $x$ is a rearrangement of $y$'s components in the direction of decreasing order among the components. For instance, $(2, 1) \geq_A (1, 2)$, and $(3, 2, 1) \geq_A (3, 1, 2) \geq_A (1, 3, 2)$, etc.

The result in Theorem 1.8.2(i) says, if the two nodes in the closed network are numbered in decreasing order of their service rates, i.e., $\mu_1(n) \geq \mu_2(n)$ for all $n$, then, $v = (v_1, v_2) \geq_A v' = (v_2, v_1)$ implies $TH(v) \geq TH(v')$. In other words, the throughput function preserves the arrangement ordering. Functions that preserve arrangement orderings are called *arrangement increasing functions*.

On the other hand, the result in Theorem 1.8.2(ii) indicates another property of the throughput function. When $v_1 > v_2$ and $\Delta < v_1 - v_2$, we write

$$v = (v_1, v_2) \geq_m v' = (v_1 - \Delta, v_2 + \Delta),$$

where $\geq_m$ denotes the so-called *majorization* ordering, and the operation above that changes $v$ to $v'$ (i.e., moves $\Delta$ from the larger component $v_1$ to the smaller component $v_2$) is termed *transposition*. More generally, two vectors $x \geq_m y$ if $y$ can be obtained from $x$ through a sequence of transpositions. Intuitively, while the components of $x$ and the components of $y$ sum up to the same value, say $s$, $s$ is more evenly distributed among the components of $y$. A function that preserves (reverses) the majorization ordering is termed *Schur convex* (*Schur concave*). Since $v \geq_m v'$ implies $TH(v) \leq TH(v')$ in Theorem 1.8.2(ii), the throughput is a Schur concave function of the visit ratio $v$.

Note that both arrangement and majorization orderings are pairwise orderings; that is, $x \geq_A y$ if and only if there exist a sequence of vectors, $z^1, \ldots, z^k$, such that

$$x \geq_A z^1 \geq_A \cdots \geq_A z^k \geq_A y,$$

and the *neighboring* vectors above (e.g., $x$ and $z^1$) only differ in two components. In other words, $y$ can be obtained from $x$ through a sequence of *pairwise* interchanges of its components. The same holds for $x \geq_m y$. Hence, the results in Theorem 1.8.2 extend immediately to an $m$-node network as follows. Repeatedly apply the theorem, each time to one pair of nodes in the network (while hold the other nodes fixed): switch the visit ratios so that the faster node gets visted more often, or make the visit ratios more even through the transposition operation. Either results in a higher overall throughput from the two nodes (since the theorem holds for any $N$), and hence a higher throughput of the entire network (provided the service rates are increasing functions).

**Theorem 1.8.3** In a closed Jackson network with $m$ nodes and $N$ jobs, where the service rates at all nodes are increasing and concave functions,

(i) if the nodes are ordered such that $\mu_i(n) - \mu_{i+1}(n)$ is increasing in $n$, for all $i = 1, ..., m-1$, then the throughput is arrangement increasing in the visit ratios $(v_i)_{i=1}^m$;

(ii) if all nodes have the same service rate function, i.e., $\mu_i(n) = \mu(n)$ for all $i$ and all $n$, then the throughput is Schur concave in $(v_i)_{i=1}^m$.

In the special case of multiple parallel servers, we can allow the servers at different nodes to have different service rates, say $\nu_i$ for node $i$, by treating $\rho_i = v_i/\nu_i$ as $v_i$. The arrangement and majorization results then apply to $\rho_i$.

**Corollary 1.8.4** In the network of Theorem 1.8.3, suppose node $i$ has $c_i$ parallel servers, each with rate $\nu_i$. Let $\rho_i = v_i/\nu_i$ for all $i = 1, ..., m$.

(i) If the nodes are ordered such that $c_1 \geq \cdots \geq c_m$, then the throughput is arrangement increasing in $(\rho_i)_{i=1}^m$.

(ii) If all nodes have the same number of servers (i.e., $c_i = c$ for all $i$), then the throughput is Schur concave in $(\rho_i)_{i=1}^m$. In particular, given $\sum_{j=1}^m \rho_j = w$ — a constant, the balanced loading, i.e., $\rho_i = w/m$ for all $i$, yields the highest throughput.

## 1.9   Conclusions

We have demonstrated the many advantages in using Jackson networks to model and analyze the operation of manufacturing systems. The first advantage lies in the ease and flexibility in modeling:

- The WIP-dependent production rates of the workcenters and the overall system can be modeled, respectively, as the state-dependent service rate functions and the throughput function.

- The open, closed, and semi-open networks provide convenient models for different control mechanisms exercised on the system.

Second, the networks correctly describe the qualitative and structural behavior of manufacturing systems. That is, analysis of the networks leads to conclusions and phenomena that we normally observe or expect from batch-manufacturing operations. Some examples are as follows:

- The overall production rate of the system can be increased through increasing the production rate at each workcenter.

- The production rate of the system can also be increased, but at a decreasing marginal (i.e., concavity), via increasing the overall WIP level, provided the production rates at the workcenters are increasing and concave functions of the local WIP level. The same property holds true with respect to other resources, such as the number of severs (operators/machines), and their rates of service. (In practice, this increasing concavity is often a result of economies of scale.)

- Another way to increase the overall production rate is through resource sharing, for instance, aggregating servers at a node while maintaining the overall service capacity, or aggregating several nodes into a single node while maintaining the same number of servers and the processing requirements.

However, the models do more than merely predict expected system behavior: they make precise the characterization of both the qualitative system structure and the quantitative performance measures. The analysis of the models also brings out connections to likelihood ratio and stochastic orderings, the equilibrium rate, the $PF_2$ property, the majorization and arrangement orderings.

Yet another advantage of the networks lies in the simplicity and efficiency in data acquisition and computation:

- The only required data are the workload (visit ratios and average processing times) and the WIP-dependent production rates of each workcenter. The former is easily derived from the material flows. The latter can be either collected directly from real or simulated systems or computed indirectly from other distributional information of the production process at the workcenters.

- With the given data, the main performance measures are easily computed, via the convolution or mean value analysis algorithms.

These easily computable performance measures, along with the qualitative results, provide a powerful means in supporting the design and operation of the systems.

## 1.10    Notes

Jackson networks orginated from the studies of J.R. Jackson [10, 11]. Gordon and Newell [9] considered the case of closed networks. The convolution algorithm was proposed by Buzen in [7]. The mean value analysis belongs to Reiser and Lavenberg, see [17]. Sections 2 and 3 are mostly based on those early works. Most of the results there are also available in standard texts on queueing networks, e.g., Kelly [27], and Walrand [34]. The main feature of Jackson networks, namely, the product-form equilibrium distribution, in fact extends to networks that are much more general than what we focused upon here. For instance, jobs can be divided into several classes, the routing mechanism need not be Markovian, a variety of service disciplines can be allowed (e.g., processor sharing, last come first served). Indeed, product-form results are often associated with a class of networks that connect together the so-called *quasi-reversible* queues (Kelly [27]).

There is a rich body of literature that applies Jackson networks to the modeling and analysis of manufacturing systems under various configurations and operating schemes, e.g., flow lines, job shops and flexible manufacturing systems. The book of Buzacott and Shanthikumar [4] presents the detailed modeling of many such systems. Also see Buzacott and Shanthikumar [1, 3], Buzacott and Yao [5, 6], Gershwin [8], Suri, Sanders and Kamath [32], and Viswanadham and Narahari [33].

The likelihood ratio ordering and the stochastic ordering in Section 4 are standard stochastic order relations; refer to Ross [26] (Chapter 8) and Stoyan [29]. In particular, a result such as likelihood ratio ordering implying stochastic ordering (see Lemma 1.4.7) is easily proved for continuous random variables with densities (see [26] for instance). The proof for the discrete case is more difficult. (Our proof of Lemma 1.4.7 illustrates the effective use of the relation between the pmf and the equilibrium rate.)

The concept of equilibrium rate and its role in linking together the throughput function of a closed Jackson network and the likelihood ratio ordering were first developed in Shanthikumar and Yao [21, 22]. The motivation there was to address the issue: whether speeding up the servers at one or more nodes in a closed Jackson network will yield an increased throughput. With the notion of equilibrium rate, the issue can be equivalently viewed as the preservation of the likelihood ratio ordering under convolution, which, for $PF_2$ distributions, is a standard result; see, e.g., Keilson and Sumita [15]. The extension of this to *shifted* likelihood ratio ordering, without the $PF_2$ property, is due to Shanthikumar and Yao [21]. In both cases, the results have made it precise how to speed up servers in a closed network so as to increase the overall throughput.

It used to be a long-standing open problem that the throughput function of a closed Jackson network is concave in the job population. But proofs, based on rather tedious algebra, were only available for special cases, e.g., single-server nodes with constant service rates. With the machinery of equilibrium rate, Shanthikumar and Yao transformed this into comparisons of the service completion processes in two-node cyclic networks. The proof was then based on coupling arguments. The general result was first established in [24], upon which much of Section 5 is based.

That the $PF_2$ property is preserved under convolution is a classical result, see Karlin and Proschan [26]. As pointed out at the end of Section 5, the increasing concavity/convexity of the throughput function, via equilibrium rates, in fact has extended this classical result to the preservation of second-order properties (i.e., concavity and convexity), in addition to the first-order (monotonicity) property, $PF_2$.

The coupling arguments in the proof of Proposition 1.5.1, as well as in similar proofs of other results in Section 5 and Section 6, are based on the basic idea of constructing sample paths of stochastic processes under comparison on a common probability space, and demonstrating that they possess certain desired relations. Refer to Kamae, Krengel and O'Brien [12]. Note, however, that the concavity result in Proposition 1.5.1 requires the construction and comparison of *four* processes (as versus the usual three points that define concavity of a function: two end points and their convex combination). This type of concavity falls into the framework of a notion of *stochastic* convexity/concavity developed in Shaked and Shanthikumar [16, 17].

In contrast, the convexity through the recursion in (1.26) relates more directly to the usual functional (deterministic) convexity. It corresponds to a stronger notion of stochastic convexity developed in Shanthikumar and Yao [44]. This type of stochastic convexity will be studied further in Chapter 4, in particular through recursions that are similar to the one in (1.26).

The result regarding the aggregation of servers in Section 7.1 first appeared in [22] (where it was called "server reduction"). One application of the bounds in Proposition 1.7.2 is to bound the throughput of a closed network with multi-server nodes by the throughput of one with single-server nodes (see Shanthikumar and Yao [29]), since the computation of the latter is simpler by an order of magnitude, refer to the algorithms in Section 3. The result in Section 7.2 concerning aggregation of nodes is new.

On at least two occasions (in Sections 6 and 7) we expressed the throughput as the limit of the service-completion (counting) processes over time. The existence of the limit was implicitly assumed. This can be rigorously justified from the analysis in Chapter 4, based on the subadditive ergodic theory.

The majorization and arrangement results in Section 8 are motivated by the allocation or assignment of workload in manufacturing systems. Although it was known that balanced loading in a closed Jackson network with single-server nodes (constant service rate) maximizes the throughput, Yao [36] was the first to establish the Schur concavity of the throughput function and related the workload allocation and assignment problems to the majorization and arrangement orderings. Similar results in related or more general settings appeared in Shanthikumar and Stecke [23], Yao [37], and Yao and Kim [38]. The results presented in Section 8 follow Shanthikumar [21]. Applications of these results in the optimal allocation of servers in manufacturing system appeared in Shanthikumar and Yao [26, 23].

Marshall and Olkin [11] is a standard reference for majorization and related topics. More formal and extensive studies on stochastic majorization and arrangement, along with stochastic convexity, will be presented in Chapter 5.

Finally, we note that the Jackson network models also provide a sound basis for developing and analyzing approximation models, based on decomposition approaches, for more general networks; refer to Buzacott and Shanthikumar [4, 2], Buzacott and Yao [6], Shanthikumar and Buzacott [22], and Whitt [48].

*Acknowledgments:* John Buzacott is supported in part by NSERC via Operating and Strategic Grants on "Modeling and Implementation of Just-in-Time Cells" and "Robust Planning and Scheduling". George Shanthikumar is supported in part by NSF Grant DDM-91-13008 and by a Sloan Foundation Grant for the study on "Competitive Semiconductor Manufacturing". David Yao is supported in part by NSF Grants DDM-91-08540 and MSS-92-16490.

## 1.11   References

[1] Buzacott, J.A. and Shanthikumar, J.G. 1980. Models for Understanding Flexible Manufacturing Systems, *AIIE Transactions,* **14**, 339-350.

[2] Buzacott, J.A. and Shanthikumar, J.G. 1985. Approximate Queueing Models of Dynamic Job Shops, *Management Science,* **31**, 870-887.

[3] Buzacott, J.A. and Shanthikumar, J.G. 1992. Design of Manaufacturing Systems Using Queueing Models, *Queueing Systems: Theory and Applications,* **12**, 96-135.

[4] Buzacott, J.A. and Shanthikumar, J.G. 1993. *Stochastic Models of Manaufacturing Systems,* Prentice Hall, Englewood Cliffs, NJ.

[5] Buzacott, J.A. and Yao, D.D. 1986. Flexible Manufacturing Systems: A Review of Analytic Models, *Management Science,* **32**, 890-905.

[6] Buzacott, J.A. and Yao, D.D. 1986. On Queueing Network Models of Flexible Manufacturing Systems, *Queueing Systems: Theory and Applications,* **1**, 5-27.

[7] Buzen, J.B. 1973. Computational Algorithms for Closed Queueing Networks with Exponential Servers. *Comm. ACM,* **16**, 527-531.

[8] Gershwin, S.B. 1994. *Manufacturing Systems Engineering,* Prentice Hall, Englewood Cliffs, NJ.

[9] Gordon, W.J. and Newell, G. F. 1967. Closed Queueing Networks with Exponential Servers. *Operations Research,* **15**, 252-267.

[10] Jackson, J.R. 1957. Networks of Waiting Lines. *Operations Research,* **5**, 518-521.

[11] Jackson, J.R. 1963. Jobshop-Like Queueing Systems. *Management Science,* **10**, 131-142.

[12] Kamae, T. Krengel, U., and O'Brien, G.L. 1977. Stochastic Inequalities on Partially Ordered Spaces. *Annals of Probability,* **5**, 899-912.

[13] Karlin, S. and Proschan, F. 1960. Polya-Type Distributions of Convolutions. *Ann. Math. Stat.,* **31**, 721-736.

[14] Kelly, F.P. 1979. *Reversibility and Stochastic Networks.* Wiley, New York.

[15] Keilson, J. and Sumita, U. 1982. Uniform Stochastic Ordering and Related Inequalities. *Canadian Journal of Statistics,* **10**, 181-198.

[16] Marshall, A.W. and Olkin, I. 1979. *Inequalities: Theory of Majorization and Its Applications.* Academic Press, New York.

[17] Reiser, M. and Lavenberg, S.S. 1980. Mean Value Analysis of Closed Multichain Queueing Networks. *J. Assoc. Comp. Mach.*, **27**, 313-322.

[18] Ross, S.M. 1983. *Stochastic Processes.* Wiley, New York.

[19] Shaked, M. and Shanthikumar, J.G. 1988. Stochastic Convexity and Its Applications. *Advances in Applied Probability*, **20**, 427-446.

[20] Shaked, M. and Shanthikumar, J.G. 1990. Convexity of a Set of Stochastically Ordered Random Variables. *Advances in Applied Probability*, **22**, 160-167.

[21] Shanthikumar, J.G. 1987. Stochastic Majorization of Random Variables with Propotional Equilibrium Rates. *Advances in Applied Probability*, **19**, 854-872.

[22] Shanthikumar, J.G. and Buzacott, J.A. 1981. Open Queueing Network Models of Dynamic Job Shops. *Internatonal Journal of Production Research*, **19**, 1440-1452.

[23] Shanthikumar, J.G. and Stecke, K.E. 1986. Reducing the Work-in-Process Inventory in Certain Class of Flexible Manufacturing Systems. *European J. of Operational Res.*, **26**, 266-271.

[24] Shanthikumar, J.G. and Yao, D.D. 1986. The Preservation of Likelihood Ratio Ordering under Convolution. *Stochastic Processes and Their Applications*, **23**, 259-267.

[25] Shanthikumar, J.G. and Yao, D.D. 1986. The Effect of Increasing Service Rates in Closed Queueing Networks. *Journal of Applied Probability*, **23**, 474-483.

[26] Shanthikumar, J.G. and Yao, D.D. 1987. Optimal Server Allocation in a System of Multi-Server Stations. *Management Science*, **34**, 1173-1180.

[27] Shanthikumar, J.G. and Yao, D.D. 1988. On Server Allocation in Multiple-Center Manufacturing Systems. *Operations Research*, **36**, 333-342.

[28] Shanthikumar, J.G. and Yao, D.D. 1988. Second-Order Properties of the Throughput in a Closed Queueing Network. *Mathematics of Operations Research*, **13**, 524-534.

[29] Shanthikumar, J.G. and Yao, D.D. 1988. Throughput Bounds for Closed Queueing Networks with Queue-Dependent Service Rates. *Performance Evaluation*, **9**, 69-78.

[30] Shanthikumar, J.G. and Yao, D.D. 1991. Strong Stochastic Convexity: Closure Properties and Applications. *Journal of Applied Probability*, **28** (1991), 131-145.

[31] Stoyan, D. 1983. *Comparison Methods for Queues and Other Stochastic Models*. Wiley, New York.

[32] Suri, R., Sanders, J.L. and Kamath, M. 1993. Performance Evaluation of Production Networks. In: *Handbook in OR & MS*, Vol. 4, S.C. Graves et al (eds.), Elsevier Science.

[33] Viswanadham, N. and Narahari, Y. 1992. *Performance Modeling of Automated Manufacturing Systems*, Prentice Hall, Englewood Cliffs, NJ.

[34] Walrand, J. 1988. *An Introduction to Queueing Networks*. Prentice Hall, Englewood Cliffs, NJ.

[35] Whitt, W. 1983. The Queueing Network Analyzer, *Bell Syst. Tech. J.*, **62**, 2779-2815.

[36] Yao, D.D. 1984. Some Properties of the Throughput Function of Closed Networks of Queues. *Operations Research Letters*, **3**, 313-317.

[37] Yao, D.D. 1987. Majorization and Arrangement Orderings in Open Networks of Queues. *Annals of Operations Research*, **9**, 531-543.

[38] Yao, D.D. and Kim, S.C. 1987. Reducing the Congestion in a Class of Job Shops, *Management Science*, **34**, 1165-1172.

# 2
# Hierarchical Modeling of Stochastic Networks, Part I: Fluid Models

Hong Chen
Avi Mandelbaum

## 2.1 Introduction

Decision processes in complex operations are frequently hierarchical. It is natural, therefore, for models that support such decisions to be hierarchical as well, and here we explore such a hierarchy. Specifically, we are concerned with stochastic flow networks, typified by queueing networks, which will be analyzed within a framework that distinguishes three aggregation levels of *time* and *state-space*: a *microscopic* level that acknowledges individual particles (which is the level at which queueing network models are typically set up), a *macroscopic* level, in which the network is approximated by a deterministic fluid model, and an intermediate *mesoscopic* level, that quantifies the deviations between the micro and the macro in terms of stochastic diffusion approximations. It might be useful to start with an example, of a closed nonparametric Jackson queueing network, that attempts to concretize these levels.

*Micro, Macro and Meso Models of a Closed Network:* Consider $n$ identical customers that circulate among $K$ single-server service stations. Service stations are indexed by $k = 1, \ldots, K$, and the service times at each station $k$ are i.i.d. with unit mean, independently of the other stations. Suppose that the initial configuration of the $n$ customers is drawn from a uniform distribution over all possible configurations. Independently thereafter, a customer who is served at station $j$ joins immediately station $k$ with probability $p_{jk}$. The description thus far has been at the microscopic level. To illustrate the macroscopic and mesoscopic levels, let us assume for simplicity that the matrix $P = [p_{jk}]$ is irreducible doubly stochastic. We shall single out the $K$-dimensional stochastic process $Q^n = \{Q^n(t), t \geq 0\}$ whose $k$-th coordinate at time $t$, $Q_k^n(t)$, represents the number of customers present at station $k$ at time $t$.

A macroscopic description is in terms of a fluid network. It consists of $K$ buffers, which are connected by pipes to form a network within which fluid circulates. The transition of fluid between buffers is assumed to be instantaneous. There is a total of one unit of fluid, and the initial configuration of fluid in the buffers is uniformly distributed on the $K$-dimensional unit simplex. Deterministically thereafter, each buffer releases fluid at a constant unit rate, and a fraction $p_{jk}$ of the fluid released from buffer $j$ flows into the pipe leading directly to buffer $k$. Such dynamics turn out to maintain a constant fluid level at all the buffers at all times. This constant fluid configuration is the almost sure limit of $Q^n(nt)/n$ as $n \to \infty$. Generally, one arrives at the fluid approximation by increasing the number of particles $n$ to infinity, while simultaneously accelerating time and aggregating space both by a factor of $n$.

A mesoscopic description is in terms of a diffusion network, obtained via rescaling time by a factor of $n^2$ and space by a factor of $n$. In particular, when the $K$ servers are independent, and the i.i.d. service times have unit variance, as $n \to \infty$ the process $Q^n(n^2t)/n$ converges weakly to a Reflected/Regulated Brownian motion (RBM) supported on the $K$-dimensional unit simplex. This RBM is stationary with initial state that is uniformly distributed on the simplex. It evolves inside the simplex like some $K$-dimensional Brownian motion. Upon reaching the facet of the simplex where the $k$-th coordinate vanishes, $k = 1, \ldots, K$, the RBM is reflected instantaneously towards the interior of the simplex, with a direction of reflection that equals the $k$-th row of the matrix $I - P$.

Our review has two parts. The present Part I is devoted to flow (micro) networks and their fluid (macro) approximations. Part II introduces diffusion (meso) approximations for the important family of nonparametric open Jackson networks. The stark difference in scope between the two parts stems from the fact that our fluid models are technically straightforward to motivate, construct and analyze, while many of their diffusion counterparts are yet to be even rigorously formulated. One consequence is that intuition, rather than concrete examples, provides our main support to the claim that the importance of the fluid-view increases with the complexity of the system from which it originates.

Hierarchies of levels at which mathematical modelling is exercised have been, of course, fundamental across scientific disciplines. Here are some quotes on hierarchical modelling which we plainly cannot improve on. Following the quotes is a table that summarizes a *preliminary* possible attempt at a hierarchy, in the context of managerial decision making. The entries of the table provide mere examples, and are rather self-explanatory. Hence they will not be elaborated on here, except for saying that the strategic level is roughly matched with the macro models, the tactical with meso and the operational with micro.

*Quotes On Hierarchical Modelling:*

> "My thesis has been that one path to the construction of a nontrivial theory of complex systems is by way of a theory of

hierarchy. Empirically a large proportion of the complex systems we observe in nature exhibit hierarchic structure." (page 229 of Simon [1981])


"Classical limit theorems play a vital role in probability theory because they reveal the statistical regularity associated with a macroscopic view of uncertainty. Just as in statistical mechanics or macroeconomics, there is order associated with the macroscopic view which is not apparent from the microscopic view. . . . It is the general principle provided by the limit theorem which is the most important. The limit theorem acts like a physical law explaining common tendencies in a wide range of phenomena. This is why the classical limit theorems form the core of probability theory." (page 312 of Whitt [1974])

"An omnipresent observer could specify the exact state of a physical system at all times. A human observer must be content with a greatly reduced set of variables, and the problem of defining the system lies in how to specify this set, for a given system and a given observer. The observer's time and length scales are the most important elements in the problem. These scales depend on the observer's objective and knowledge. They must be compared with the variety of time and length scales occurring naturally in the system, due to either purely internal changes or to interaction between the system and its environment. Two observers may have the same scales, but different views of what is important. They would emphasize different variables, and with different objectives they could both be correct. Such subjective aspects are, of course, present in all idealized models of real physical systems and can never be completely removed." (The Introduction of Woods [1975])

"Production management encompasses a large number of decisions that affect several organizational echelons. Anthony's framework groups these decisions into three broad categories: strategic, tactical and operational. These three categories differ markedly in terms of the level of management participation, scope of decision, level of aggregation of the required information, time horizon and degree of uncertainties and risks. The framework suggests a hierarchical integrative approach to managerial decision support systems, which guarantees an appropriate coordination of the overall decision-making process, but, at the same time, recognizes the intrinsic characteristics of each decision level." (Hax and Candea [1984] on Anthony [1965])

Our hierarchy of models emerges via the classical limit theorems of probability, specifically the law of large numbers, refined by the law of the iterated logarithm and the central limit theorem (large deviations, unfortunately, fits only partially and is omitted for space constraints). The limit theorems, however, only reveal candidate levels of the hierarchy. The integration of these levels, both theoretically and in practice, has been left open, and we believe it to be a challenging important research area. (Integration could perhaps be first demonstrated via some "grand model", in which "decisions that are made at higher levels provide constraints for lower level decision making; in turn, detailed decisions provide the necessary feedback to evaluate the quality of aggregate decision making;" quoted from Hax and Candea [1984].)

*Acknowledgements, and a Final Quote:* The hierarchical framework discussed here is by no means new. Our thoughts have been influenced mainly by works of and conversations with D. Berman, D. Johnson, M. Harrison, M. Reiman, W. Whitt, R. Williams, and D.D. Yao. We gratefully acknowledge the editorial contribution of Liz Schwerer to our presentation. Finally, in the introduction to the much quoted Antony [1965], the author asserts and we conveniently agree that "I kept recalling the point that President James B. Conant demonstrated so vividly in *On Understanding Science*, namely, that development of a framework or a conceptual scheme often has led to progress, *even though the framework turns out to be wrong* ... the framework will have served a useful purpose if it prepares the way for a better one."

### 2.1.1  Macro, Meso and Microscopic Models for an i.i.d. Sequence

Our mathematical hierarchical framework will now be motivated through the very simple, yet fundamental, stochastic model $\xi = \{\xi_i, i = 1, 2, ...\}$, consisting of a sequence of nonnegative i.i.d. random variables in $\Re^K$. ($\Re^K$ denotes $K$-dimensional Euclidean space, endowed with the norm $\|x\| = \max_{1 \le k \le K} |x_k|$.) For concreteness, interpret $\xi_i$ as demand for some product during period $i$, $i = 1, 2 \ldots$. Then, the random variable

$$X(t) \equiv \sum_{i=1}^{\lfloor t \rfloor} \xi_i, \quad t \ge 0, \tag{2.1}$$

represents the cumulative demand over the time period $[0, t]$. We take the view that $X = \{X(t), t \ge 0\}$ is a *microscopic* model of demand, microscopic in the sense that it (or more precisely, its distribution) embodies all the information about demand that has been deemed worthy of analysis.

## Hierarchical Production Planning and Control

| Level | Decides | Every | On | Performance | Subject to | Processes | Methods |
|---|---|---|---|---|---|---|---|
| **Strategic** (planning) | Corporate | Year/Quarter (Long Range) | Market Products Processes | Market Share (Long-run Average) | Technology Market Size | Fluid Networks (Linear) | Linear & Integer Programming |
| **Tactical** (Planning + Control) | Plant Mgt. | Month (Medium Range) | Aggregate Plan Budget  Load/Input | Profit (Discounted) | Capacity  Timeliness & Priorities | Diffusion Networks (Locally Brownian) | Stochastic Control |
| **Operational** (Control) | Supervisor | Week/Day (Short Range) | Routing Sequencing | Cost | Bottlenecks | Queueing Networks (Point Processes) | Dynamic Programming |
| **Regulatory** (Control) | Shop Floor | hr/min/sec (Instantaneous) | Dispatching | Feasibility | Quality Breakdowns | Fluid Nets (Non-linear) & Diffusion Nets | Heuristics/NLP |

Suppose that the $\xi_i$'s share a common finite mean $\mu$, naturally interpreted as the average demand per unit of time. Then $X$ conforms to a functional strong law of large numbers (FSLLN), mathematically articulated as

$$FSLLN: \qquad \bar{X}^n(t) \equiv \frac{1}{n}X(nt) \xrightarrow{\text{a.s.}} \mu t \equiv \bar{X}(t), \qquad u.o.c.$$

The convergence $\xrightarrow{\text{a.s.}}$ is almost surely as $n \uparrow \infty$, and $u.o.c.$ stands for "uniformly on compact" subsets of $t \in [0, \infty)$. The term "functional" emphasizes our concern with convergence of functions, namely sample paths of stochastic processes, rather than mere convergence of random variables. The classical SLLN for partial sums is deduced formally from the FSLLN by letting $t = 1$ in the latter, but the two theorems are, in fact, mathematically equivalent.

The process $\bar{X}^n = \{\bar{X}^n(t), t \geq 0\}$ is obtained from $X$ by accelerating time and aggregating space, both by a factor of $n \uparrow \infty$. The FSLLN asserts that, with probability one and for large $n$, the sample paths of the random $\bar{X}^n$, viewed as real-valued functions over $[0, \infty)$, can be uniformly approximated by the deterministic process $\bar{X} = \{\bar{X}(t), t \geq 0\}$. Thus,

$$\frac{1}{n}X(n\cdot) = \bar{X}^n(\cdot) \approx \bar{X}(\cdot) = \frac{1}{n}\bar{X}(n\cdot),$$

from which $\bar{X}$ emerges as a *macroscopic* approximation for the demand $X$, that captures its long-run average trend. Alternatively, $\bar{X}$ can be taken at the outset as a macroscopic model of demand, which is crude yet sufficiently informative for some purposes.

Now let us add the assumption that the $\xi_i$'s share a finite variance $\sigma^2$. This suffices to guarantee that the following functional central limit theorem (FCLT) prevails

$$FCLT: \qquad \hat{X}^n(t) \equiv \sqrt{n}[\bar{X}^n(t) - \bar{X}(t)] \xrightarrow{\text{d}} \sigma B(t) \equiv \hat{X}(t).$$

The convergence $\xrightarrow{\text{d}}$, as $n \uparrow \infty$, stands for convergence in distribution, or weak convergence, $B$ is a one-dimensional standard Brownian motion, or a Wiener process, and "functional" again emphasizes that the convergence is that of stochastic processes rather than random variables.

The process $\hat{X}^n = \{\hat{X}^n(t), t \geq 0\}$ is obtained from $X$ via accelerating time by $n$ and aggregating space by $\sqrt{n}$. The FCLT asserts that the distribution of the deviation of $\bar{X}^n$ from $\bar{X}$, amplified by a factor of $\sqrt{n}$ with $n$ large, can be approximated by the distribution of a Brownian motion, scaled by $\sigma$. We can now write the following:

$$\frac{1}{n}X(n\cdot) = \bar{X}^n(\cdot) \overset{\text{d}}{\approx} \bar{X}(\cdot) + \frac{1}{\sqrt{n}}\hat{X}(\cdot)$$

$$\overset{\text{d}}{=} \bar{X}(\cdot) + \frac{1}{\sqrt{n}}[\frac{1}{\sqrt{n}}\hat{X}(n\cdot)] = \frac{1}{n}[\bar{X}(n\cdot) + \hat{X}(n\cdot)]. \qquad (2.2)$$

The first $\overset{d}{\approx}$ is based on the FCLT, and the next $\overset{d}{=}$ is a consequnce of a rescaling property of the Brownian motion, mathematically articulated in (6) below. The process $\tilde{X} = \{\tilde{X}(t), t \geq 0\}$, given by

$$\tilde{X}(t) = \bar{X}(t) + \hat{X}(t),  \tag{2.3}$$

emerges from (2.2) as a *mesoscopic* (intermediate between micro and macro) approximation for $X$. Its component $\hat{X} = \{\hat{X}(t), t \geq 0\}$ quantifies statistically significant deviations between the random microscopic model $X$ and its deterministic macroscopic approximation $\bar{X}$.

The above FCLT, usually referred to as Donsker's Theorem, is strictly more general than the classical CLT for partial sums. It implies the latter by letting $t = 1$, observing that $\sigma B(1)$ is normally distributed with mean 0 and variance $\sigma^2$, and applying the continuous mapping theorem (Glynn [1990], Proposition 2) to $x \rightarrow x(1)$.

The mesoscopic model $\tilde{X}$ in (2.3) refines the crude deterministic macroscopic model $\bar{X}$ by adding to it the stochastic element $\hat{X}$. There exist other classical refinements of the FSLLN, notably the functional law of the iterated logarithm (FLIL) and the functional large deviations principle (FLDP). The latter will only be commented on very briefly in the sequel, but we shall be using the following weak version of FLIL: for all $T > 0$,

$$FLIL: \qquad ||\bar{X}^n - \bar{X}||_T = \sup_{0 \leq t \leq T} |\bar{X}^n(t) - \bar{X}(t)| = O\left(\sqrt{T \log \log T}\right).$$

The limit theorems FSLLN, FCLT, FLIL, and part of FLDP, can all be deduced from a unifying mathematical framework, due to Kolmós, Major and Tusnády [1975,1976], which we now introduce. The cost of this unification is the existence of moments beyond the second, and this is rather negligible from a modelling point of view.

## 2.1.2 Strong Approximations - A Unifying Framework

Consider a sequence of random variables $\xi = \{\xi_i, i = 1, 2, ...\}$, with finite moments of order $r > 2$. Kolmós, Major and Tusnády [1975,1976] showed that such $\xi$ can be realized on some probability space, supporting a one-dimensional Wiener process $W = \{W(t), t \geq 0\}$, in a way that

$$FSAT: \qquad ||X - \tilde{X}||_T \equiv \sup_{0 \leq t \leq T} |X(t) - \tilde{X}(t)| \overset{a.s.}{=} \circ(T^{1/r}), \quad \text{as } T \uparrow \infty.$$

Here $X$ is defined in terms of $\xi$ via (2.1), $\tilde{X}$ is given by

$$\tilde{X}(t) = \mu t + \sigma W(t), \quad t \geq 0,  \tag{2.4}$$

(as in (2.3)), and FSAT stands for *Functional Strong Approximation Theorem*. The above realization is commonly referred to as the Strong Approximation of $X$ by $\tilde{X}$.

We now deduce from FSAT the classical FSLLN, FCLT and a version of FLIL. (This suffices for our purposes here, but actually more can be obtained; see the commentary at the end of the present subsection.) Starting with the FCLT, fix $T > 0$, observe that FSAT implies

$$\sup_{0 \le t \le T} |\hat{X}^n(t) - \frac{\sigma}{\sqrt{n}} W(nt)| \stackrel{\text{a.s.}}{=} \frac{o(1)}{n^{(r-2)/(2r)}}, \quad \text{as } n \uparrow \infty, \tag{2.5}$$

and use the scaling property of $W$,

$$\frac{1}{\sqrt{n}} W(n \cdot) \stackrel{\text{d}}{=} B(\cdot), \quad \forall n \ge 1, \tag{2.6}$$

combined with the "converging together theorem" (Glynn [1990], Proposition 7), to deduce the FCLT. As for the FSLLN, divide (2.5) by $\sqrt{n}$ to get

$$\sup_{0 \le t \le T} |\bar{X}^n(t) - \bar{X}(t) - \frac{\sigma}{n} W(nt)| \stackrel{\text{a.s.}}{=} o(1), \quad \text{as } n \uparrow \infty,$$

and apply the FSLLN for the Brownian motion, namely

$$\frac{1}{n} W(nt) \stackrel{\text{a.s.}}{\longrightarrow} 0, \quad u.o.c.,$$

as $n \uparrow \infty$, to conclude the FSLLN. Finally, FSAT and Strassen's FLIL for the Brownian motion, namely

$$\|W\|_T = \sup_{0 \le t \le T} |W(t)| \stackrel{\text{a.s.}}{=} O\left(\sqrt{T \log \log T}\right),$$

(e.g., Theorem 1.3.1* in Csörgö and Révész [1981]) yield

$$\|X - \bar{X}\|_T = \sup_{0 \le t \le T} |X(t) - \bar{X}(t)| \stackrel{\text{a.s.}}{=} O\left(\sqrt{T \log \log T}\right). \tag{2.7}$$

*Remarks:*   (1)   A more common formulation of FSAT actually requires the existence of a moment generating function for the $\xi_i$'s. This is in fact stronger than existence of all moments, and it appropriately yields a stronger approximation (formulated in Glynn [1990], Theorem 5 and some of its consequences). Even stronger approximations can be tailored to specific distributional assumptions (see, for example, Ethier and Kurtz [1986], Corollary 5.3 on page 359, which deals with Levy processes).

(2)   As already mentioned, the classical FSLLN, FCLT and FLIL do *not* follow from FSAT, as the latter assumes finite moments of order higher than two on its data $\xi$. (The FSLLN requires first moments, FCLT and FLIL require second.)

### 2.1.3  Summary

The processes $X$ in (2.1), $\bar{X}$ in FSLLN and $\tilde{X}$ in FSAT constitute a three-level hierarchy of models, respectively called microscopic (highly detailed), macroscopic (highly aggregated) and mesoscopic (intermediate). In the following sections we shall adapt these levels to some simple representative stochastic networks. Most of these simple models were conceived to motivate a corresponding hierarchical approach to nonparametric Jackson networks, and some of their generalizations. These, in turn, have and will provide cornerstone models for manufacturing, computer and communication systems.

As far as information requirements are concerned, microscopic models require distributional information, macroscopic require long-run average information, and mesoscopic models are based on second-order information. Thus, macro and meso models are to be preferred, at least at the outset of the modelling process, when detailed information is either not available or hard to get. Macro and meso models are also more tractable than their microscopic counterpart, and for some purposes their analysis is all that is required.

In modelling real systems, the choice of macroscopic, mesoscopic or microscopic representation ought to depend primarily on the required level of detail, which should be traded off against the availability of information and the tractability of the resulting model. Take a production system as an example. Macroscopic, mesoscopic and microscopic models seem to fit best long-term, medium-term, and short-term planning respectively, and to support decisions at the corporate and factory shop-floor levels.

In some cases, a combination of the macro, meso and microscopic models may be appropriate. Consider, for example, a production system where machine operations are subject to interruptions (due, for example, to unexpected breakdowns or scheduled preventive maintenance). If the interruption intervals are significantly longer than the processing interval, then it might be desirable to model the interruption mechanism microscopically and the processing times macroscopically. This will be elaborated further in Section 2.6.

## 2.2  A Flow Network in Discrete Time

In this section we first introduce a microscopic model for a flow network that evolves in discrete time. Then we approximate it by macroscopic and mesoscopic models, both of which are derived, together with rates of convergence, through strong approximations. A link between the flow network and the i.i.d. model from the Introduction is revealed by a transformation that maps the latter to the former. This transformation, called "oblique reflection" for reasons to be explained later, turns out to be Lipschitz continuous. Continuity justifies the approximations, and the Lipschitz property preserves the rates of convergence.

### 2.2.1  The Microscopic Model and Its Dynamics

Consider a network with $K$ nodes, also referred to as buffers or stations, and indexed by $k = 1, ..., K$. Commodities (alternatively fluids, depending on the context) flow in and out of the network and circulate among the buffers. The network is described by a nonnegative vector $Z(0)$ in $\Re^K$, a $K \times K$ substochastic matrix $P = (p_{jk})$, and two sequences of i.i.d. random vectors in $\Re^K$, $\{\alpha(i), i \geq 1\}$ and $\{\mu(i), i \geq 1\}$. Both sequences are defined on a common probability space, and we assume that they are independent to simplify the exposition.

The process of primary interest is the $K$-dimensional inventory level (or buffer content) process $Z = \{Z(i), i \geq 1\}$. The $k$th coordinate $Z_k(i)$ of $Z(i)$ is the content of buffer $k$ at the end of period $i$. The dynamics of the system are as follows. Initially, the inventory level at buffer $k$ is $Z_k(0)$, the $k$th coordinate of $Z(0)$. During period $i \geq 1$, the given amount $\alpha_k(i)$ flows into buffer $k$ from outside the network; an amount $\delta_k(i)$, to be determined below, flows out of buffer $k$, as long as it does not exceed the given outflow capacity constraint $\mu_k(i)$. A fraction $p_{kj}$ of the outflow from buffer $k$ is transferred to buffer $j$, and the remaining fraction, $1 - \sum_{j=1}^{K} p_{kj}$, flows out of the system. We assume that whatever arrives to the system leaves eventually, or mathematically, that the matrix $P$ has a spectral radius less than unity (equivalently, $[I - P]^{-1}$ exists and is nonnegative). The buffer contents at times $i = 1, 2, \ldots$, are thus given recursively by the balance equations

$$Z_k(i) = Z_k(i-1) + \alpha_k(i) + \sum_{j=1}^{K} \delta_j(i) p_{jk} - \delta_k(i), \quad k = 1, \ldots, K,$$

where the $\delta_k(i)$'s are still to be determined. We shall find it convenient, however, to analyze a reformulation of the balance equations in terms of the quantities

$$y_k(i) = \mu_k(i) - \delta_k(i);$$

these represent the *lost potential* outflow from buffer $k$ during period $i$, and hence must be nonnegative. We get

$$Z_k(i) = Z_k(i-1) + x_k(i) + y_k(i) - \sum_{j=1}^{K} y_j(i) p_{jk},$$

where

$$x_k(i) = \alpha_k(i) + \sum_{j=1}^{K} \mu_j(i) p_{jk} - \mu_j(i),$$

$k = 1, ..., K$, and $i = 1, 2, ...$ are given (as they depend on the data). In vector form, we are to determine $y = \{y(i), i = 1, 2, ...\}$ so that

$$Z(i) = Z(i-1) + x(i) + [I - P']y(i), \qquad (2.8)$$
$$y(i) \geq 0, \qquad (2.9)$$

where

$$x(i) = \alpha(i) + [P' - I]\mu(i).$$

An operation of our network is called *feasible* if its lost potential output $y$ satisfies (2.8)-(2.9), as well as $Z(i) \geq 0$, for all $i \geq 0$. In that case we also refer to $y$ itself as being feasible. The network's operation is *efficient* if its lost potential $y$ is least among all the feasible ones; in other words, if another $\tilde{y}$ satisfies (2.8) and (2.9) with its corresponding $\tilde{Z}(i) \geq 0$, then $\tilde{y}_k(i) \geq y_k(i)$ for all $k = 1, ..., K$, and $i = 1, 2, ....$. The existence of an efficient operation, equivalently a least feasible $y$, will now be related to a classical problem in mathematical programming, the linear complementarity problem.

**Proposition 2.2.1** Consider

$$\mathcal{F}(x) = \{y \geq 0 : x + [I - P']y \geq 0\}, \quad x \in \Re^K.$$

If $\mathcal{F}(x)$ is non-empty, then $\mathcal{F}(x)$ has a least element (which must be unique). Furthermore, this least element is the unique solution to

$$z = x + [I - P']y, \qquad (2.10)$$
$$z \geq 0, \qquad y \geq 0, \qquad (2.11)$$
$$z'y = 0. \qquad (2.12)$$

The equality (2.12) is equivalent to saying that $z_k = 0$ whenever $y_k > 0$ for all $k = 1, ..., K$. The problem of finding $y, z \in \Re^K$ that satisfy (2.10)-(2.12) is known as the Linear Complementarity Problem (LCP), with data $x$ and matrix $[I - P']$. We shall denote it by $LCP(x, P)$.

An efficient operation of our network is obtained by iteratively solving LCP's as follows: start with $Z(0)$ as data; given $Z(i-1)$, $i \geq 1$, solve $LCP(Z(i-1) + x(i), P)$ to obtain the least loss $y(i)$, and then compute $Z(i)$ through (2.8). This solution is characterized by: $y_k(i) > 0$ only when $Z_k(i) = 0$; in words, losses of outflow capacity arise only when buffers are empty. The above procedure yields the efficient operation, and we shall refer to it as solving $DCP(x, P)$, the Dynamic Complementarity Problem with data sequence $x$ and matrix $[I - P']$. (Readers might benefit from attempting to solve DCP in dimensions $K = 1, 2$. The case $K = 1$ can be solved explicitly; $K = 2$ has an illuminating geometric interpretation. Section 2.3 in Mandelbaum [1989] provides the details.)

### 2.2.2   Reformulation in Terms of Cumulants and Oblique Reflection

We now reformulate our microscopic network model in terms of cumulative processes, as in the Introduction. This is a necessary step towards identifying its proper macroscopic and mesoscopic versions, which evolve in continuous time. Define

$$a(t) = \sum_{i=1}^{\lfloor t \rfloor} \alpha(i), \tag{2.13}$$

$$m(t) = \sum_{i=1}^{\lfloor t \rfloor} \mu(i), \tag{2.14}$$

$$
\begin{aligned}
X(t) &= Z(0) + \sum_{i=1}^{\lfloor t \rfloor} x(i) \\
&= Z(0) + a(t) + [P' - I]m(t), \tag{2.15}
\end{aligned}
$$

$$Y(t) = \sum_{i=1}^{\lfloor t \rfloor} y(i). \tag{2.16}$$

The process $X = \{X(t), t \geq 0\}$, given in (2.15), will be referred to as the *netflow* process, because $a(t) + P'm(t)$ and $m(t)$ represent cumulative potential inflow and outflow respectively. Note that the netflow process is completely determined by the data, namely the initial vector $Z(0)$, the cumulative inflow process $a = \{a(t), t \geq 0\}$, and the cumulative potential outflow process $m = \{m(t), t \geq 0\}$. As demonstrated by Proposition 2.2.2 below, the netflow process is all that is required to determine the dynamics of our flow network.

With the above notations, the fluid level process can be rewritten as

$$Z(t) = X(t) + [I - P']Y(t), \qquad t \geq 0.$$

Observe that this last equality holds also at non-integer $t$'s, which is the reason for replacing $i$ with $t$ as an index. For now, however, we focus on integer times.) The observations on DCP yield

**Proposition 2.2.2** Given $X$ of the form in (2.15), there exists a unique pair $(Y, Z)$ such that

$$Z(t) = X(t) + [I - P']Y(t) \geq 0, \quad t = 0, 1, \ldots, \tag{2.17}$$
$$Y(t) \text{ is non-decreasing in } t \text{ with } Y(0) = 0, \tag{2.18}$$
$$Z_k(t)[Y_k(t) - Y_k(t-1)] = 0, \quad t = 1, 2, \ldots, k = 1, \ldots, K \tag{2.19}$$

Moreover, this unique $Y$ is the least element among the $Y$'s that satisfy (2.17) and (2.18).

**Proof.**    Existence and uniqueness follow by induction from Proposition 2.2.1. One is left with showing that $Y$ is least, which is carried out also by induction on $t$. Clearly, this is true for $t = 0$; we assume it for times up to $t - 1$ ($t \geq 1$), and prove it for times up to $t$.

Let $\tilde{Y}$ satisfy (2.17) and (2.18). Then it suffices to prove that $Y(t) \leq \tilde{Y}(t)$. By Proposition 2.2.1 and the DCP procedure (used to construct $Y$), we know that $y(t) = Y(t) - Y(t - 1)$ solves $LCP(X(t) + [I - P']Y(t - 1), P)$, hence it is the least element of $\mathcal{F}(X(t) + [I - P']Y(t-1))$. Let $\tilde{y}(t) = \tilde{Y}(t) - \tilde{Y}(t-1)$. By the induction hypothesis, $\tilde{Y}(t-1) - Y(t-1) + \tilde{y}(t) \geq \tilde{y}(t) \geq 0$, and

$$X(t) + [I - P']Y(t - 1) + [I - P'](\tilde{Y}(t - 1) - Y(t - 1) + \tilde{y}(t)) = \tilde{Z}(t) \geq 0,$$

implying that $\tilde{Y}(t - 1) - Y(t - 1) + \tilde{y}(t)$ is an element of $\mathcal{F}(X(t) + [I - P']Y(t - 1))$. Thus,

$$y(t) \leq \tilde{Y}(t - 1) - Y(t - 1) + \tilde{y}(t),$$

or equivalently, $Y(t) \leq \tilde{Y}(t)$.    □

The unique pair $(Y, Z)$ from Proposition 2.2.2, with $Y = \{Y(t), t = 0, 1, ...\}$ and $Z = \{Z(t), t = 0, 1, ...\}$, will be called the *state process* of the flow network. As a function of the data $X$, it will be denoted by $Y = \Psi(X)$ and $Z = \Phi(X)$. Proposition 2.2.2 asserts that the state of the flow network is a well-defined function of $X$. The next proposition shows that this function is in fact Lipschitz continuous in $X$. Continuity enables one to transform approximations for the primitive data $X$ into approximations for the state process $(Y, Z)$. The Lipschitz property enables control over the magnitude of error in such approximations. We thus derive strong approximations, which lead to macroscopic and mesoscopic versions of our microscopic flow network.

For a sequence $\xi = \{\xi^i, i = 1, 2, ...\}$ of elements in $\Re^K$, introduce

$$\|\xi\|_T = \sup_{1 \leq i \leq T} \|\xi^i\| = \sup_{1 \leq i \leq T} \max_{1 \leq k \leq K} |\xi^i_k| \qquad \text{for } T = 1, 2, \ldots, \infty.$$

**Proposition 2.2.3** There exists a constant $h > 0$ such that

$$\|\Psi(X^1) - \Psi(X^2)\|_T \leq h\|X^1 - X^2\|_T, \qquad (2.20)$$

$$\|\Phi(X^1) - \Phi(X^2)\|_T \leq h\|X^1 - X^2\|_T, \qquad (2.21)$$

for all $X^1$ and $X^2$ of form (2.15), and $T = 0, 1, 2, ...$ (including $T = \infty$).

**Proof.**    Inequality (2.21), with $h$ large enough, follows from (2.20) via (2.17). Thus we only need to prove (2.20), and we start with the two observations on $LCP$. First, with $K = 1$ and $P = 0$, the unique solution to (2.10)-(2.12) is determined by $y = (-x)^+$. This, after rewriting (2.10) as

$z = (x - P'y) + y$, provides the following fixed-point representation for a solution $y$ to $LCP(x, P)$:

$$y = [P'y - x]^+.$$

Now let $Y^1 = \Psi(X^1)$ and $Y^2 = \Psi(X^2)$. From the fixed-point representation, combined with Proposition 2.2.2, one gets

$$Y^i(t) = Y^i(t - 1) + [P'Y^i(t) - X^i(t) - Y^i(t - 1)]^+, \qquad (2.22)$$

$t = 1, 2, ...$; $i = 1, 2$. We may assume, without loss of generality, that

$$\eta = \max_{1 \leq k \leq K} \sum_{j=1}^{K} p_{kj} < 1. \qquad (2.23)$$

[Otherwise, our setup can be transformed as follows. Take $v$ to be an eigenvector that corresponds to the largest positive (Peron-Frobenius) eigenvalue of the matrix $P$. Denote this eigenvalue by $\eta$, and recall that $\eta < 1$ has been assumed. With $\Lambda = \text{diag}(v)$, the matrix $P^* = \Lambda^{-1}P\Lambda$ satisfies (2.23); the pair $(\Lambda Y, \Lambda Z)$ solves (2.17)-(2.19), with $X$ replaced by $\Lambda X$ and $P$ replaced by $P^*$.] By enumerating all possibilities, it is easy to see that

$$\|(x^1 + [y^1 - x^1]^+) - (x^2 + [y^2 - x^2]^+)\| \leq \max\{\|x^1 - x^2\|, \|y^1 - y^2\|\}$$

for any $x^i \in \Re^K$ and $y^i \in \Re^K$, $i = 1, 2$. Thus, taking $x^i = Y^i(t - 1)$ and $y^i = P'Y^i(t) - X^i(t)$ in the above, we can see that (2.22) implies

$$\|Y^1(t) - Y^2(t)\| \leq \max\left\{\|Y^1(t - 1) - Y^2(t - 1)\|, \frac{1}{1 - \eta}\|X^1(t) - X^2(t)\|\right\}$$

for $t = 1, 2, ....$ Iterating this last inequality, until reaching $\|Y^1(0) - Y^2(0)\| = 0$, yields (2.20) with $h = 1/(1 - \eta)$. Since $h$ is independent of $T$, (2.20) also holds for $T = \infty$. □

Let $\mathcal{D}^K$ denote the set of $K$-dimensional RCLL functions, namely the $\Re^K$-valued functions on $[0, \infty)$ which are right-continuous with left limits (the latter on $(0, \infty)$). Let also $\mathcal{D}_0^K = \{x \in \mathcal{D}^K : x(0) \geq 0\}$. For $x \in \mathcal{D}^K$, its uniform norm over $\mathcal{T} \subset [0, \infty)$ is defined as

$$\|x\|_{\mathcal{T}} = \sup_{t \in \mathcal{T}} \max_{1 \leq k \leq K} |x_k(t)|,$$

with $\|x\|_{[0,T]}$ abbreviated to $\|x\|_T$, $T > 0$. A continuous-time version of Propositions 2.2.2 and 2.2.3 is formulated as

**Theorem 2.2.4** For any $X \in \mathcal{D}_0^K$, there exists a unique pair $(Y, Z) \in \mathcal{D}_0^{2K}$ satisfying

$$Z(t) = X(t) + [I - P']Y(t) \geq 0, \tau \geq 0, \qquad (2.24)$$
$$dY(t) \geq 0, \qquad Y(0) = 0, \qquad (2.25)$$
$$Z_k(t)dY_k(t) = 0, \quad k = 1, \ldots, K; \qquad (2.26)$$

this unique $Y$ is the least element among those $Y$'s that satisfy (2.24) and (2.25). Furthermore, the mappings $Y = \Psi(X)$ and $Z = \Phi(X)$ are both Lipschitz continuous in $\mathcal{D}_0^K$, under the uniform norm over any compact interval.

Note our use of $\Psi$ and $\Phi$, which were previously defined for processes in discrete time only; this should cause no confusion, since a process in discrete time can be viewed as a step function in $\mathcal{D}^K$. Indeed, for a discrete-time process $X$, $\Psi(X)$ and $\Phi(X)$, as defined in Proposition 2.2.3, coincide with $\Psi(\tilde{X})$ and $\Phi(\tilde{X})$, as defined in Theorem 2.2.4 and evaluated at integer time epochs, with $\tilde{X}(t) = X(\lfloor t \rfloor)$. This observation is the starting point for proving Theorem 2.2.4 via Propositions 2.2.2 and 2.2.3.

*Proof of Theorem 2.2.4*    We only sketch the proof of existence. First step is to prove the claim that there exists a unique least element $Y$ that satisfies (2.24) and (2.25). To this end, we note from Proposition 2.2.2 and Proposition 2.2.3 that the theorem holds for the set of functions of the form (2.15) with $a(t)$ and $m(t)$ step functions. Since any step functions in $\mathcal{D}_0^K$ must be locally of bounded variation, the theorem is proved for the set of step functions by using the fact (from Chen and Mandelbaum (1991c)) that any $X \in \mathcal{D}_0^K$, locally of bounded variation, can be written in the form (2.15) and that if, in addition, $X$ is a step function, both $a(t)$ and $m(t)$ are still step functions. The proof of the claim is completed by noting that the set of step functions is dense in $\mathcal{D}_0^K$ under the uniform norm and using the Lipschitz continuity of the mappings. Finally, one proves that this least element must satisfy (2.26), and that any $Y$ satisfying (2.24)-(2.26) must coincide with this least element.    □

### 2.2.3  Mesoscopic Models and Strong Approximations

We start with strong approximations. As illustrated in the Introduction, they provide a unified framework within which we derive both macroscopic and mesoscopic models of the above elaborated microscopic model.

Assume that all the vectors $\alpha(i)$ and $\mu(i)$ have finite moments of some order $r > 2$. Let $\alpha$ and $\mu$ denote their means, and $\Gamma_\alpha$ and $\Gamma_\mu$ their covariance matrices, respectively. Then the given data satisfies the functional strong approximation theorem (FSAT)

$$||a - \alpha e - \Gamma_\alpha^{1/2} W_\alpha||_T \overset{\text{a.s.}}{=} o(T^{1/r}), \qquad (2.27)$$

$$||m - \mu e - \Gamma_\mu^{1/2} W_\mu||_T \overset{\text{a.s.}}{=} o(T^{1/r}). \qquad (2.28)$$

Here $e = \{e(t), t \geq 0\}$ is the identity element in $\mathcal{D}^K$, whose $k$th component $e_k(t) = t$; the cumulative inflow process $a = \{a(t), t \geq 0\}$ and cumulative outflow capacity process $m = \{m(t), t \geq 0\}$ are given by (2.13) and (2.14) respectively; finally, $W_\alpha$ and $W_\mu$ are two independent standard

$K$-dimensional Brownian motions. Applying (2.27)-(2.28) to the representation (2.15) yields the following FSAT for the cumulative netflow process $X = \{X(t), t \geq 0\}$:

$$||X - \tilde{X}||_T \overset{\text{a.s.}}{=} o(T^{1/r}), \tag{2.29}$$

where

$$\tilde{X}(t) = Z(0) + \bar{X}(t) + \hat{X}(t), \tag{2.30}$$
$$\bar{X}(t) = (\alpha + [P' - I]\mu)t, \tag{2.31}$$
$$\hat{X}(t) = \Gamma_\alpha^{1/2}W_\alpha(t) + [P' - I]\Gamma_\mu^{1/2}W_\mu(t), \tag{2.32}$$

for all $t \geq 0$. The strong approximation $\tilde{X}$ for the primitive data $X$ is a Brownian motion that consists of three components: an initial state $Z(0)$, a deterministic (drift) process $\bar{X}$ and a driftless Brownian motion $\hat{X}$. The deterministic part $\bar{X}$, also known as fluid approximation, captures the drift of the microscopic model $X$. The Brownian part $\hat{X}$, called diffusion approximation, captures statistically significant deviations between $X$ and its macroscopic approximation $\bar{X}$. The source of the terminolgy "fluid" and "diffusion" will become apparent later.

The process $\tilde{X}$ provides a second-order approximation to the microscopic netflow $X$, and we refer to it as a mesoscopic model of netflow. Given $\tilde{X}$, we construct a mesoscopic flow network model through (2.24)-(2.26). Specifically, the "inventory" level process $\tilde{Z}$ for this mesoscopic "network" is defined to be

$$\tilde{Z} = \Phi(\tilde{X}).$$

It qualifies as a mesoscopic approximation of the microscopic inventory $Z = \Phi(X)$ in view of

$$||Z - \tilde{Z}||_T \overset{\text{a.s.}}{=} o(T^{1/r}), \tag{2.33}$$

which is a consequence of (2.29) and the Lipschitz property of $\Phi$ (Theorem 2.2.4). Similarly, the process $\tilde{Y} = \Psi(\tilde{X})$, the cumulative lost potential "outflow" for the mesoscopic model, is a second-order strong approximation of its microscopic counterpart $Y = \Psi(X)$, that is

$$||Y - \tilde{Y}||_T \overset{\text{a.s.}}{=} o(T^{1/r}). \tag{2.34}$$

The mapping $\Phi$ is often called *oblique reflection*. The reason for this (somewhat inappropriate) terminology is the following (somewhat loose) geometric interpretation, which applies to any continuous sample path of $X$: $Z = \Phi(X) = X + [I - P']Y$ evolves like $X$ within the interior of the nonnegative orthant $\Re_+^K$; when $Z$ hits the boundary face $\{z_k = 0\}$, thus "threatening" to go negative, it is reflected instantaneously towards the interior of $\Re_+^K$; the direction of reflection is the $k$-th column of the matrix

$[I - P']$ (which, indeed, points to the interior because $diag[I - P'] > 0$); finally, reflection is accomplished by the least increase in $Y_k$ that maintains the nonnegativity of $Z$ intact. A geometric interpretation also applies to $X$ with discontinuities (in which case "reflection" is even less appropriate): when $X$ jumps out of $\mathfrak{R}_+^K$, $dY$ is the least push that brings the outlier point back to within nonnegativity.

To recapitulate, the buffer content $Z = \Phi(X)$ of the microscopic flow network has a strong approximation $\tilde{Z} = \Phi(\tilde{X})$. The sample paths of $\tilde{Z}$ are uniquely determined by the conditions:

$$\tilde{Z}(t) = \tilde{X}(t) + [I - P']\tilde{Y}(t) \geq 0, \tag{2.35}$$

$$d\tilde{Y}(t) \geq 0, \qquad \tilde{Y}(0) = 0, \tag{2.36}$$

$$\tilde{Z}(t)d\tilde{Y}(t) = 0, \tag{2.37}$$

where $\tilde{X}$ is a $K$-dimensional Brownian motion, starting at $\tilde{X}(0) = Z(0)$, with drift vector

$$\theta = \alpha + [P' - I]\mu, \tag{2.38}$$

and covariance matrix

$$\Gamma = \Gamma_\alpha + \Gamma_\mu^{1/2}[P - I][P' - I]\Gamma_\mu^{1/2}. \tag{2.39}$$

This state of affairs will be summarized by writing $\tilde{Z} = RBM_{Z(0)}(\theta, \Gamma)$, and calling $\tilde{Z}$, as customary, *reflected Brownian motion* with drift $\theta$ and covariance matrix $\Gamma$. The unique $\tilde{Y} = \Psi(\tilde{X})$, defined through (2.35)-(2.37), will be referred to as the *regulator* of the reflected Brownian motion $\tilde{Z}$.

### 2.2.4   Macroscopic Models: FSLLN's

We follow the treatment of the simple random sequence in subsection 2.1.2, where fluid approximations, or equivalently macroscopic models, emerged as FSLLN limits through rescaling of time and space. First, the FSLLN for the Brownian motion implies that

$$\frac{1}{n}\tilde{X}(nt) \to \bar{X}(t) = \theta t, \qquad u.o.c., \tag{2.40}$$

with $\theta$ as in (2.38). The process $\bar{X}$ constitutes a macroscopic netflow model, from which we construct the inventory level of the macroscopic fluid network through $\bar{Z} = \Phi(\bar{X})$. This last model is called a *linear fluid network* since $\bar{X}(t)$ is linear in $t$. The terminology "fluid network" stems from the fact that $\bar{Z}$ can be animated as the fluid level of a continuous-time flow network where fluid flows in and out of buffers at constant rates. (This will be demonstrated in Sections 2.3 and 2.4, where it will be also shown that the sample paths of $\bar{Z}$ are linear.)

The continuity of the oblique reflection mapping now gives

$$\frac{1}{n}\tilde{Z}(nt) = \Phi(\frac{1}{n}\tilde{X}(n\cdot))(t) \to \Phi(\bar{X})(t) = \bar{Z}(t), \qquad u.o.c. \qquad (2.41)$$

Combining (2.40)-(2.41) with the strong approximation (2.33), we get the following FSLLN for the microscopic inventory level process $Z$:

$$\bar{Z}^n(t) \equiv \frac{1}{n}Z(nt) \to \bar{Z}(t) = \Phi(\bar{X})(t), \qquad u.o.c. \qquad (2.42)$$

In fact, a stronger result than (2.42) follows from FLIL and the Lipschitz property of $\Phi$, namely

$$\sup_{0\leq t\leq T} |Z(t) - \bar{Z}(t)| \stackrel{a.s.}{=} O(\sqrt{T \log\log T}), \qquad \text{for all } T > 0.$$

### 2.2.5  Deviations Between Micro and Macro Models: FCLT

Within the framework of strong approximations, we are seeking FCLT's for the processes

$$\hat{Z}^n(t) \equiv \sqrt{n}\,[\bar{Z}^n(t) - \bar{Z}(t)], \quad \hat{Y}^n(t) \equiv \sqrt{n}\,[\bar{Y}^n(t) - \bar{Y}(t)].$$

Such limit theorems quantify deviations between the micro and macro models. They give rise to limits that are diffusion processes, hence they are referred to as "diffusion approximations."

In parallel to subsection 2.1.2, the strong approximation estimates (2.33) and (2.34) imply that for any fixed $T > 0$,

$$\sup_{0\leq t\leq T} |\hat{Z}^n(t) - \sqrt{n}\,[\tfrac{1}{n}\tilde{Z}(nt) - \bar{Z}(t)]| \stackrel{a.s.}{=} \frac{o(1)}{n^{(r-2)/(2r)}}. \qquad (2.43)$$

$$\sup_{0\leq t\leq T} |\hat{Y}^n(t) - \sqrt{n}\,[\tfrac{1}{n}\tilde{Y}(nt) - \bar{Y}(t)]| \stackrel{a.s.}{=} \frac{o(1)}{n^{(r-2)/(2r)}}, \qquad (2.44)$$

Weak convergence of $\hat{Y}^n$ and $\hat{Z}^n$ is, therefore, equivalent to the weak convergence of

$$\frac{1}{\sqrt{n}}\tilde{Z}(n\cdot) - \sqrt{n}\bar{Z} = \Phi(\frac{1}{\sqrt{n}}\tilde{X}(n\cdot)) - \sqrt{n}\,\bar{Z}, \quad t \geq 0$$

and

$$\frac{1}{\sqrt{n}}\tilde{Y}(n\cdot) - \sqrt{n}\,\bar{Y} = \Psi(\frac{1}{\sqrt{n}}\tilde{X}(n\cdot)) - \sqrt{n}\bar{Y}.$$

That, in turn, is immediate to verify only in the special case when $\theta = 0$. Indeed, then $\bar{X}$, $\bar{Y}$ and $\bar{Z}$ all vanish and, as in (2.6),

$$\frac{1}{\sqrt{n}}\tilde{X}(n\cdot) = \frac{1}{\sqrt{n}}Z(0) + \frac{1}{\sqrt{n}}\hat{X}(n\cdot) \stackrel{d}{=} \frac{1}{\sqrt{n}}Z(0) + \hat{X},$$

which converges weakly to $BM(0,\Gamma)$. One concludes that $\hat{Z}^n$ adheres to a FCLT from which its limit, as $n \uparrow \infty$, has emerged to be the $RBM_0\,(0,\Gamma)$.

The above argument fails when $\theta \neq 0$. A more elaborate approach is then called for, and we present it in Part II.

## 2.3   Flow Networks in Continuous Time

In the previous section we analyzed discrete-time models. Their macroscopic and mesoscopic approximations, however, evolve continuously in time. In fact, many systems that arise in practice are most conveniently modelled as continuous-time models. Furthermore, discrete-time models can be embedded at discrete epochs of continuous-time models, hence we are going to focus hereafter on the latter.

In the present section we introduce two continuous fluid networks, one whose evolution is time-inhomogeneous and the other where it is state-dependent. The examples in Section 2.6 partially demonstrate that these fluid networks provide a fairly rich class of models for manufacturing and communication operations, either as direct microscopic models or as derived macroscopic approximations.

### 2.3.1   Flow Networks with Time Inhomogeneous Dynamics

The network consists of $K$ buffers, each with an infinite storage capacity. The buffers are interconnected by frictionless pipes through which fluid flows in and out of the buffers. To model this flow, take as primitives a $K$-dimensional nonnegative vector $Z(0)$, a substochastic $K \times K$ matrix $P$, and two $K$-dimensional vector valued processes $\{\alpha(t), t \geq 0\}$ and $\{\mu(t), t \geq 0\}$, which are non-decreasing functions in $\mathcal{D}^K$, with $\alpha(0) = \mu(0) = 0$. For $k = 1, ..., K$, interpret the $k$th coordinate $Z_k(0)$ of $Z(0)$ as the initial fluid level in buffer $k$, $\alpha_k(t)$ as the cumulative exogenous inflow to buffer $k$ during the time interval $(0, t]$, and $\mu_k(t)$ as the cumulative *potential* outflow from buffer $k$ (namely the maximum outflow that can be realized during $(0, t]$ if buffer $k$ never empties). The $(j, k)$-th element $p_{jk}$ of $P$ represents the fraction of total outflow from buffer $j$ that flows directly to buffer $k$; $1 - \sum_{k=1}^{K} p_{jk}$ is the fraction that leaves the network, immediately upon flowing out of $j$. As in subsection 2.2.1, we assume that $P$ has a spectral radius less than unity.

When a buffer is empty, some of its potential outflow may be lost. Let $Y_k(t)$ denote the cumulative amount of potential outflow that is lost due to emptiness at buffer $k$ during $(0, t]$. Then the actual outflow from $k$ up to time $t$ is $\mu_k(t) - Y_k(t)$, and the fluid level in buffer $k$ at time $t$ equals

$$Z_k(t) = Z_k(0) + \alpha_k(t) + \sum_{j=1}^{K}[\mu_j(t) - Y_j(t)]p_{jk} - [\mu_k(t) - Y_k(t)].$$

In vector notation, the *fluid level* process $Z = \{Z(t), t \geq 0\}$ takes the form

$$Z(t) = X(t) + [I - P']Y(t), \qquad t \geq 0, \tag{2.45}$$

where the *netflow* process $X = \{X(t), t \geq 0\}$ is defined to be

$$X(t) = Z(0) + [\alpha(t) + P'\mu(t)] - \mu(t), \qquad t \geq 0. \tag{2.46}$$

A process $Y = \{Y(t), t \geq 0\}$ as in (2.45) is called a *feasible* loss if it satisfies

$$Z(t) \geq 0, \qquad t \geq 0, \tag{2.47}$$

$$Y \text{ is non-decreasing with } Y(0) = 0, \tag{2.48}$$

$$\mu - Y \text{ is non-decreasing.} \tag{2.49}$$

Clearly, for any $X$ of the form (2.46), $Y \equiv \mu$ is a feasible loss. (Let us side-remark that any $X$ whose sample paths are locally of bounded variation is of the form (2.46).) Based on Proposition 2.2.2, one can then establish the existence of a feasible loss $Y$ which is least among all feasible losses. This unique minimum loss is also characterized by (2.47)-(2.48), supplemented with the *complementarity* condition

$$Z(t) dY(t) = 0, \qquad t \geq 0.$$

(In fact, a more general result was already stated as Theorem 2.2.4 in subsection 2.2.2.)

A special case of the above model is the *linear fluid* model, where exogenous flows arrive at constant rates, and fluid is released from each buffer at a maximal constant rate if the buffer is not empty. Formally, $\alpha(t) = \alpha t$ and $\mu(t) = \mu t$ in a linear fluid model, which is unambiguously characterized by $Z(0)$ and the triplet $(\alpha, P, \mu)$: $\alpha$ is the vector of *exogenous inflow* rates, $\mu$ is the vector of *processing capacity* rates, , and $P$ is the *flow-transfer* matrix.

Linear fluid models are the subject of the next section. They arise, among other circumstances, as the FSLLN limits of nonlinear fluid models and some nonparametric Jackson (queueing) networks (yet to be introduced).

## 2.3.2 State-Dependent Dynamics

In many applications, inflow or outflow rates may depend on the state of the network (for example, the inventory level at the buffers). In this section, we generalize the time inhomogeneous fluid model to cover such dependencies.

As before, the network consists of $K$ infinite-capacity buffers, and $Z = \{Z(t), t \geq 0\}$ denotes the inventory level process. Then the vectors of inflow and outflow *rates* at time $t$ are given, respectively, by $\alpha[t, Z(t)]$ and $\mu[t, Z(t)]$, where $\alpha = \{\alpha[t, z] : t \geq 0, z \geq 0\}$, the inflow rate process, and $\mu = \{\mu[t, z] : t \geq 0, z \geq 0\}$, the potential outflow rate process, are given as primitives. Denoting by $y = \{y(t), t \geq 0\}$ the lost potential outflow rate process, we get the flow-balance relations

$$\frac{dZ_k(t)}{dt} = \alpha_k[t, Z(t)] + \sum_{j=1}^{K} [\mu_j[t, Z(t)] - y_j(t)] p_{jk}$$

$$- [\mu_k[t, Z(t)] - y_k(t)]; \tag{2.50}$$

in integrated vector form

$$Z(t) = Z(0) + \int_0^t \theta[s, Z(s)]\, ds + [I - P']Y(t), \qquad t \geq 0, \qquad (2.51)$$

where

$$\theta[t, z] = \alpha[t, z] + [P' - I]\mu[t, z]$$

and $Y(t) = \int_0^t y(t)dt$. In later applications it will turn out convenient, and sometimes even necessary, to not assume that $Y$ is absolutely continuous. We thus take (2.51) as our working representation, defined in terms of $Y$, the *cumulative* lost potential outflow process. We say that $Y$ is *feasible* if it gives rise to an inventory level process $Z$ that is nonnegative; it is *efficient* if it is the least feasible loss. These definitions are justified by

**Theorem 2.3.1** Let $\theta[t, z]$ be a vector-valued function from $\Re_+^{K+1}$ to $\Re^K$, which is Lipschitz in $z \in \Re_+^K$, u.o.c. in $t \in \Re_+$. We assume that $\theta[t, 0]$ is bounded for $t$ in any compact subset of $\Re_+$. Then given $X \in \mathcal{D}_0^K$, there exist a unique pair $Y \in \mathcal{D}_0^K$ and $Z \in \mathcal{D}_0^K$ that satisfy

$$Z(t) - \int_0^t \theta[s, Z(s))\, ds = X(t) + [I - P']Y(t), \qquad (2.52)$$

$$Z(t) \geq 0 \qquad \text{for} \quad t \geq 0, \qquad (2.53)$$

$$dY(t) \geq 0 \qquad \text{for} \quad t \geq 0, \qquad \text{and} \qquad Y(0) = 0, \qquad (2.54)$$

$$\int_0^\infty Z(t)dY(t) = 0. \qquad (2.55)$$

Denote by $\Psi_\theta(X)$ and $\Phi_\theta(X)$ these unique $Y$ and $Z$ respectively. Then the mappings $\Psi_\theta$ and $\Phi_\theta$ are Lipschitz continuous on $\mathcal{D}_0^K$. Moreover, $Y = \Psi_\theta(X)$ is the least element among those that satisfy (2.52)-(2.54).

*Remarks*     (1) Here and later, the statement that $\theta[t, z]$ is Lipschitz in $z \in \Re_+^K$, u.o.c. in $t \in \Re_+$, means that for any given finite interval $[0, T]$, there exists a constant $C_1(T) > 0$ such that

$$||\theta[t, z'] - \theta[t, z'']|| \leq C_1(T)||z' - z''||$$

for all $z', z'' \in \Re_+^K$ and $t \in [0, T]$. The Lipschitz condition and the boundedness of $\theta[t, 0]$ entails existence of constants $C_2(T)$, $T > 0$, such that

$$||\theta[t, z]||^2 \leq C_2(T)(1 + ||z||^2),$$

for all $z \in \Re_+^K$ and $t \in [0, T]$.

(2)     When $\theta \equiv 0$, we write $\Phi_\theta \equiv \Phi_0 \equiv \Phi$ and $\Psi_\theta \equiv \Psi_0 \equiv \Psi$. The theorem then recovers the (standard) oblique reflection mapping from Theorem 2.2.4.

(3) Theorem 2.3.1 can be generalized to $\theta$ that is a mapping on $\Re_+ \times \mathcal{D}_0^K$ to $\mathcal{D}^K$. This enables one to cover inflow and the outflow rates that depend on the whole history of the state process.

We conclude with two special cases. First, with inflow and potential outflow rates of the form $\alpha[t, z] \equiv \alpha^*[t, z]1[z \leq b]$ and $\mu[t, z] \equiv \mu^*[t, z]1[z \leq b]$, the state-dependent fluid network effectively has finite capacity buffers. Second, when the inflow potential outflow rates do not depend on state, our model reduces to the nonlinear fluid networks in subsection 2.3.1.

Various choices of $\alpha[t, z]$ and $\mu[t, z]$ lead to sample path representations of manufacturing and communication systems. See Section 2.6.1 for some examples.

## 2.4   Linear Fluid Network and Bottleneck Analysis

The present section is devoted to the linear fluid model $(\alpha, P, \mu)$, where $\alpha \geq 0$, $\mu > 0$ and $P$ has spectral radius less than unity. Recall that such a network is constructed from a linear netflow process

$$X(t) = Z(0) + \theta t \qquad \text{with} \qquad \theta = \alpha + [P' - I]\mu,$$

and its minimum (efficient) cumulative loss process $Y$ and the corresponding fluid (inventory) level process $Z$ are characterized by

$$Z(t) = X(t) + [I - P']Y(t) \geq 0, \qquad t \geq 0, \qquad (2.56)$$
$$dY(t) \geq 0, \qquad Y(0) = 0, \qquad (2.57)$$
$$Z(t)dY(t) = 0. \qquad (2.58)$$

The simplicity of $X$ renders a precise description of $Y$ and $Z$, specifically in terms of nonbottleneck, balanced bottleneck and strict bottleneck buffers. We show that the network reaches equilibrium in the sense that flow rates stabilize within a finite time. In equilibrium, the fluid level at nonbottlenecks remains zero, at balanced bottlenecks it remains constant and at strict bottlenecks it increases indefinitely at a constant rate.

### 2.4.1   Traffic Equations and Bottleneck Definitions

Consider a linear fluid model $(\alpha, P, \mu)$. The *effective* inflow rates to buffers, denoted by $\lambda_k$ for buffer $k$, is the sum of exogenous and endogenous inflow rates. The effective outflow rate from a buffer is the minimum between its effective inflow rate and its processing capacity. Formally,

$$\lambda_k = \alpha_k + \sum_{j=1}^{K}(\lambda_j \wedge \mu_j)p_{jk}, \qquad k = 1, \ldots, K,$$

or in vector form,

$$\lambda = \alpha + P'(\lambda \wedge \mu). \tag{2.59}$$

These equations are called either the *flow-balance* equations, or *traffic* equations. They define implicitly the effective inflow rate vector $\lambda$ through

**Theorem 2.4.1** Equations (2.59) have a unique nonnegative solution $\lambda$.

*Remark*    The traffic equations are equivalent to a linear complementarity problem, as in (2.10)-(2.12). More precisely, $y = [\mu - \lambda]^+$ and $z = [\lambda - \mu]^+$ solve $LCP(x, P)$ with data $x = \theta$. Observe that $x = \theta$, $y = [\mu - \lambda]^+$ and $z = [\lambda - \mu]^+$ represent, respectively, the netflow rate, the lost potential outflow rate, and the fluid inventory growth rate. The interpretation of equations (2.10)-(2.12) then becomes transparent.

*Proof of Theorem 2.4.1*    Define a mapping $F$ from $\Re_+^K$ to $\Re_+^K$ by $F(x) = \alpha + P'(x \wedge \mu)$. Since $P$ has a spectral radius less than unity, $P^n$ converges to 0 as $n \uparrow \infty$. Consequently, a high enough power $F$ can be shown to be a contraction mapping. By Banach's fixed-point theorem, $F$ has a unique fixed point in $\Re_+^K$, which is the vector of effective inflow rates.    $\square$

Introduce the *traffic intensity* of station $k$ to be

$$\rho_k = \frac{\lambda_k}{\mu_k}, \qquad k = 1, ..., K.$$

Buffer $k$ is called a *bottleneck* if $\rho_k \geq 1$, a *strict* bottleneck if $\rho_k > 1$, a *nonbottleneck* if $\rho_k < 1$, and a *balanced* bottleneck if $\rho_k = 1$.

Suppose that one knows the set of nonbottleneck buffers, say $a$, and hence the complement set of bottlenecks, say $b$. Then the effective inflow rates can be computed explicitly as follows. Partition $\lambda$, $\alpha$, $P$ and $\mu$ according to $a$ and $b$, namely,

$$\lambda = \begin{pmatrix} \lambda_a \\ \lambda_b \end{pmatrix}, \alpha = \begin{pmatrix} \alpha_a \\ \alpha_b \end{pmatrix}, P = \begin{pmatrix} P_a & P_{ab} \\ P_{ba} & P_b \end{pmatrix}, \mu = \begin{pmatrix} \mu_a \\ \mu_b \end{pmatrix},$$

and rewrite (2.59) in block form as

$$\lambda_a = \alpha_a + P'_{ba}\mu_b + P'_a\lambda_a, \tag{2.60}$$
$$\lambda_b = \alpha_b + P'_b\mu_b + P'_{ab}\lambda_a, \tag{2.61}$$

having used the inequalities $\lambda_a < \mu_a$ and $\lambda_b \geq \mu_b$. The matrix $(I - P_a)$ turns out to be invertible (see Proposition 2.4.2 below). Hence, we can solve for $\lambda_a$ in (2.60), and then obtain $\lambda_b$ from (2.61):

$$\lambda_a = [I - P'_a]^{-1}(\alpha_a + P'_{ba}\mu_b), \tag{2.62}$$
$$\lambda_b = \hat{\alpha}_b + \hat{P}'_b\mu_b, \tag{2.63}$$

where

$$\hat{\alpha}_b = \alpha_b + P'_{ab}[I - P'_a]^{-1}\alpha_a, \qquad (2.64)$$

$$\hat{P}_b = P_b + P_{ba}[I - P_a]^{-1}P_{ab}. \qquad (2.65)$$

The matrix $\hat{P}_b$ arises in the theory of Markov chains as the transition matrix of a partially observed Markov chain. Its elements represent equilibrium fractions of outflow from $b$ that end up back in $b$ either immediately or through $a$.

It is possible, in fact, to define

$$\hat{\alpha}_v = \alpha_v + P'_{uv}[I - P'_u]^{-1}\alpha_u, \qquad (2.66)$$

$$\hat{P}_v = P_v + P_{vu}[I - P_u]^{-1}P_{uv}, \qquad (2.67)$$

for any partition $(u, v)$ of the set of $K$ buffers. Then the transformation

$$(\alpha, P, \mu) \longrightarrow (\hat{\alpha}_v, \hat{P}_v, \mu_v), \qquad (2.68)$$

from the original network to its subnetwork of buffers in $v$, plays a key role in the analysis of linear fluid models (and also the FCLT's in Chapter II). A formal account of some of the network properties that (2.68) preserves is provided by

**Proposition 2.4.2** For any partition $(u, v)$, $[I - P'_u]^{-1}$ exists; therefore, the transformation (2.68) is well-defined. If the set $u$ includes no strict bottlenecks, the transformation (2.68) leaves the effective inflow rate and traffic intensity vectors intact. Formally, $\lambda_u \le \mu_u$ implies that $\lambda_v = \hat{\lambda}_v$ and $\rho_v = \hat{\rho}_v$, where $(\lambda_v, \rho_v)$ and $(\hat{\lambda}_v, \hat{\rho}_v)$ are the effective inflow rate and traffic intensity vectors of the networks $(\alpha, P, \mu)$ and $(\hat{\alpha}_v, \hat{P}_v, \mu_v)$ respectively.

We close the subsection with an additional classification of buffers, based on *potential* rather than effective inflow rates, and used in the proof of Theorem 2.4.4 below. The vector $\nu = \alpha + P'\mu$ constitutes potential inflow rates of the linear fluid network $(\alpha, P, \mu)$. Let $\theta = \nu - \mu$. Buffer $k$ is called *sub-critical* if $\theta_k < 0$, *critical* if $\theta_k = 0$, and *super-critical* if $\theta_k > 0$. Noting that the potential inflow rate is an upper bound for the effective rate, one can prove that

**Proposition 2.4.3** Sub-critical buffers are nonbottleneck buffers. The converse need not hold. However, if none of the buffers are sub-critical then they are all bottlenecks.

Example:   Consider a tandem-network with three stations. By this we mean the open network

$$\lambda^0 = \begin{pmatrix} \lambda_1^0 \\ 0 \\ 0 \end{pmatrix}, P = \begin{pmatrix} 0 & 1 & 0 \\ 0 & 0 & 1 \\ 0 & 0 & 0 \end{pmatrix}, \mu = \begin{pmatrix} \mu_1 \\ \mu_2 \\ \mu_3. \end{pmatrix}.$$

Then $\nu' = (\lambda_1^0, \mu_1, \mu_2)$, and $\theta' = (\lambda_1^0 - \mu_1, \mu_1 - \mu_2, \mu_2 - \mu_3)$. When $\lambda_1^0 = \mu_1 < \mu_3 < \mu_2$, we have $\rho' = (1, \mu_1/\mu_2, \mu_1/\mu_3)$, station 1 is critical, station 2 is sub-critical, and station 3 is super-critical. Only station 1 is a bottleneck station. Station 3 is a non-bottleneck station which is not sub-critical.

## 2.4.2  Bottleneck Analysis

The main result of the present subsection is Theorem 2.4.4, which reveals the existence of an *equilibrium time*. The proof of the theorem suggests an iterative algorithm that identifies nonbottlenecks, balanced bottlenecks and strict bottlenecks. We conclude the subsection with some simple examples for which the equilibrium time can be computed.

**Theorem 2.4.4**  Consider a linear fluid network $(\alpha, P, \mu)$ with initial state $Z(0)$. Denote by $a$ and $b$ respectively the sets of its nonbottleneck and bottleneck buffers. Then there exists a finite time $\tau$ such that

$$Z_a(t) = 0, \qquad \text{for } t \geq \tau, \tag{2.69}$$
$$Z_b(t) = Z_b(\tau) + (\lambda_b - \mu_b)(t - \tau), \qquad \text{for } t \geq \tau, \tag{2.70}$$
$$Y_a(t) = Y_a(\tau) + (\mu_a - \lambda_a)(t - \tau), \qquad \text{for } t \geq \tau, \tag{2.71}$$
$$Y_b(t) = 0, \qquad \text{for } t \geq 0, \tag{2.72}$$

where

$$Z_b(\tau) = Z_b(0) + P'_{ab}[I - P'_a]^{-1} Z_a(0) + (\lambda_b - \mu_b)\tau,$$

and $\lambda$ is the unique solution of (2.59) (the effective inflow rate vector of $(\alpha, P, \mu)$).

*Remarks*    (1)  Note that $\lambda_k = \mu_k$ for balanced bottlenecks and $\lambda_k > \mu_k$ for strict bottlenecks. Therefore, equality (2.70) formalizes the previous claim that, within a finite time, the fluid level at balanced buffers remains constant and at strict bottlenecks it increases at a constant rate.

(2)  When $Z_a(0) = 0$, the network actually starts at equilibrium ($\tau = 0$). Then (2.69)-(2.72) simplify to

$$Z(t) = Z(0) + (\lambda - \mu)^+ t,$$
$$Y(t) = (\mu - \lambda)^+ t,$$

for all $t \geq 0$.

We now outline the proof of Theorem 2.4.4. One starts with

**Lemma 2.4.5**  If $k$ is a sub-critical buffer, then $Z_k(t) = 0$ for all $t$ large enough.

One then proceeds with

**Lemma 2.4.6**  There exists a finite time $\tau$ such that (2.69) holds.

The proof of Lemma 2.4.6 consists of repeated applications of Lemma 2.4.5. First, if there are no sub-critical buffers, then all buffers must be bottlenecks (Proposition 2.4.3); in this case, $a = \emptyset$, and the lemma is proved with $\tau = 0$. Otherwise, applying Lemma 2.4.5 to the set of all sub-critical buffers, we know that after a finite time $\tilde{\tau}$, the inventory $Z_k$ vanishes for all sub-critical buffers $k$. After time $\tilde{\tau}$, we take the set of sub-critical buffers as exogenous to the system, and focus on the sub-network consisting of the remaining buffers. The parameters of this sub-network are given by the transformation (2.68) with $v$ being the set of non-subcritical buffers. By Proposition 2.4.2, this sub-network has the same set of bottleneck buffers as the original network. Now we apply the previous procedure to this sub-network; first, if this sub-network has no sub-critical buffers, then we conclude all buffers in this sub-network are bottlenecks, and the lemma is proved with $\tau = \tilde{\tau}$ (time $\tilde{\tau}$ can be thought of as time 0 in this sub-network); otherwise, we apply Lemma 2.4.5 to the set of sub-critical buffers of the sub-network, and so on. Note that each iteration of the above procedure eliminates at least one buffer. Therefore, within $K$ iterations at the most, the procedure terminates by either eliminating all buffers, or by having a sub-network which includes no sub-critical buffers. In particular, the network that we end up with must consist of exactly the bottleneck buffers of the original network, thus revealing $\tau < \infty$ for which (2.69) holds.

The proof will be completed once we show that (2.69) implies (2.70)-(2.72). This can be accomplished by writing (2.56) in blocks $a$ and $b$.

The proof of Lemma 2.4.6 suggests an algorithm that identifies the sets of bottleneck and nonbottleneck buffers in at most $K$ steps. (As noted above, this suffices for calculating $\lambda$ via (2.62)-(2.63).)

*An Algorithm for Identifying Bottlenecks and Nonbottlenecks:*

**Step 0** Set $a := \emptyset$ and $b := \{1, ..., K\}$;

**Step 1** Compute

$$\hat{\alpha}_b := \alpha_b + P'_{ab}[I - P'_a]^{-1}\alpha_a,$$
$$\hat{P}_b := P_b + P_{ba}[I - P_a]^{-1}P_{ab},$$
$$\hat{\theta}_b := \hat{\alpha}_b + [\hat{P}_b - I]\mu_b;$$

**Step 2** If $\hat{\theta}_b \geq 0$, return $a$ as the set of nonbottlenecks, $b$ as the set of bottlenecks, then STOP; otherwise, set $a := a \cup \{k : \hat{\theta}_k < 0\}$ and $b := a^c$, then GOTO Step 1.

We close this section with some examples in which the equilibrium time can be computed. Consider a tandem fluid network $(\alpha, P, \mu)$, by which we mean $\alpha = (\lambda, 0, .., 0)$, $\mu = (\mu_1, ..., \mu_K)$ and $P = (p_{jk})$ with $p_{k,k+1} = 1$ for $k = 1, ..., K - 1$ and all the other $p_{jk}$ vanish. Thus, the network consists of $K$ buffers in series, fluids enter through buffer 1 at a rate $\lambda$; after being processed at buffer $k$, the fluid moves on to buffer $k + 1$ ($k = 1, 2, ..., K - 1$); the fluid leaves the network having been processed at buffer $K$. The processing capacity of buffer $k$ is $\mu_k$. Denote the initial inventory level by $z = Z(0)$.

First consider the case where there are no bottlenecks: $\lambda < \min\{\mu_1, ..., \mu_K\}$. The equilibrium time $\tau$ is then the first time after which the fluid level at all buffers remains zero. It can be computed as follows:

$$\tau = \min_{1 \le k \le K} \tau_k, \tag{2.73}$$

where

$$\tau_k = \min\left\{ \frac{z_1 + \cdots + z_k}{\mu_k - \lambda} , \frac{z_k}{[\mu_k - \mu_{k-1}]^+} \right\}, \tag{2.74}$$

and $z_k/[\mu_k - \mu_{k-1}]^+$ is understood to be infinity for $k = 1$ or $[\mu_k - \mu_{k-1}]^+ = 0$. [For $x \in \Re$, $x^+ = \max\{x, 0\}$.] The quantity $\tau_k$ is, in fact, the equilibrium time of buffer $k$, that is the first time that its fluid level settles down at zero. This observation yields (2.73) as follows. First observe that if buffer $k - 1$ releases the fluid at rate $\mu_{k-1}$, then the equilibrium time for buffer $k$ would be $\tau_k' \equiv z_k/[\mu_k - \mu_{k-1}]^+$. However, if buffer $k - 1$ reaches equilibrium before time $\tau_k'$, then the equilibrium time for buffer $k$ is the same as the equilibrium time for a single-buffer system, with initial inventory level $z_1 + \cdots + z_k$, inflow rate $\lambda$ and processing capacity $\mu_k$; in this case, the equilibrium time is $(z_1 + \cdots + z_k)/(\mu_k - \lambda)$ (which is larger than $\tau_{k-1}$). Thus, we have reached formula (2.74).

The extension to a tandem network with bottlenecks is straightforward. Suppose that buffer $\ell$ is the first bottleneck buffer (i.e., $\lambda < \mu_k$ for $1 \le k < \ell$ and $\lambda \ge \mu_\ell$). Then clearly the equilibrium time for buffer $\ell$ is the same as that for buffer $\ell - 1$, whereas all the downstream buffers $\ell + 1, ..., K$ (if any) can be treated as a separate tandem network whose inflow rate at buffer $\ell + 1$ is $\mu_\ell$. This procedure determines the equilibrium time for all buffers in at most $K$ steps, and the equilibrium time for the network is again given by (2.73) with $\tau_k$ being the equilibrium time for buffer $k$.

At the cost of cumbersome notation, the above argument for tandem networks can be extended to cover any feedforward network, where buffers can be numbered so that the fluid flows directly only from a lower-numbered buffer to a higher-numbered one ($p_{jk} > 0$ only when $j < k$).

## 2.5    Functional Strong Law of Large Numbers

We show in this section that the linear fluid network arises as the FSLLN limit for both nonlinear fluid networks and nonparametric Jackson queueing networks. Thus, the linear fluid network model provides a macroscopic crude model for a fairly wide class of flow networks. We then consider some state-dependent queueing networks, and prove that their FSLLN limit is the state-dependent flow network introduced in subsection 2.3.2. (FSLLN's for a time inhomogeneous single queue are described in Section 2.6.3.)

### 2.5.1    FSLLN's for Nonlinear Fluid Networks

In applications, it turns out convenient to consider a sequence of nonlinear fluid networks, which we index by $n = 1, 2, ....$ Let each of these networks be as in Subsetion 3.1, and assume that they operate efficiently (least feasible loss $Y$). We append a superscript $n$ to all processes associated with the $n$th network. In particular, the initial inventory level, the exogenous inflow process and the potential outflow process for the $n$th network are $Z^n(0)$, $\alpha^n = \{\alpha^n(t), t \geq 0\}$, and $\mu^n = \{\mu^n(t), t \geq 0\}$, respectively. For ease of presentation, the flow transfer matrix $P$ does not vary with $n$.

We now state a FSLLN theorem for the fluid level and cumulative loss processes, based on FSLLN's for the given primitive data. To this end assume that, as $n \to \infty$,

$$\bar{Z}^n(0) \equiv \frac{1}{n} Z^n(0) \to \bar{Z}(0), \tag{2.75}$$

$$\bar{\alpha}^n(t) \equiv \frac{1}{n} \alpha^n(nt) \to \alpha t, \qquad u.o.c., \tag{2.76}$$

$$\bar{\mu}^n(t) \equiv \frac{1}{n} \mu^n(nt) \to \mu t, \qquad u.o.c., \tag{2.77}$$

where $\alpha$ and $\mu$ are both nonnegative vectors. (Only $\mu > 0$, however, is interesting).

**Theorem 2.5.1** Let $Z^n = \{Z^n(t), t \geq 0\}$ and $Y^n = \{Y^n(t), t \geq 0\}$ denote the fluid level and the cumulative loss process for the $n$th fluid network. Then under (2.75)-(2.77),

$$(\bar{Y}^n(t), \bar{Z}^n(t)) \equiv \left( \frac{1}{n} Y^n(nt), \frac{1}{n} Z^n(nt) \right) \longrightarrow (\bar{Y}(t), \bar{Z}(t)), \quad u.o.c. \tag{2.78}$$

as $n \to \infty$, where $\bar{Y}$ and $\bar{Z}$ are respectively the cumulative loss and fluid level processes for the linear fluid network $(\alpha, P, \mu)$. Formally, $\bar{Y} = \Psi(\bar{X})$ and $\bar{Z} = \Phi(\bar{X})$ with

$$\bar{X}(t) = \bar{Z}(0) + (\alpha + [P' - I]\mu)t, \quad t \geq 0. \tag{2.79}$$

Theorem 2.5.1 is a direct consequence of the continuity of the oblique reflection mapping (Theorem 2.2.4). Its proof resembles that of Theorem 2.5.2 in the next subsection, hence we leave out the details here.

### 2.5.2  FSLLN's for Nonparametric Jackson Queueing Networks

Let us start by describing the queueing model under consideration. Our queueing network consists of $K$ service stations, indexed by $k = 1, \cdots, K$. Each station $k$ constitutes a server, called server $k$, and a queue, called queue $k$. Server $k$ is dedicated to serving customers waiting in queue $k$. After being served, customers either leave the network or rejoin one of its queues in anticipation of additional service. The network's dynamics are described in terms of a random vector and three stochastic processes, all defined on a common probability space: a $K$-dimensional *initial queue length* vector $Z(0)$, a $K$-dimensional vector-valued *arrival* process $A = \{A(t), t \geq 0\}$, a $K$-dimensional vector-valued *service* process $S = \{S(t), t \geq 0\}$, and a $K \times K$-dimensional matrix-valued *routing sequence* $\xi = \{\xi(\ell), \ell = 1, 2, \cdots\}$. The $k$th component of $Z(0)$, $Z_k(0)$, is an integer-valued random variable which represents the number of customers initially present at station $k$. The $k$th component of $A$, $A_k = \{A_k(t), t \geq 0\}$, models exogenous arrivals to station $k$: the integer-valued random variable $A_k(t)$ describes the *number* of customers that arrive at station $k$ from the outside world (as opposed to "from other stations") during the time interval $(0, t]$. The $k$th component of $S$, $S_k = \{S_k(u), u \geq 0\}$, models departures from station $k$: the random variable $S_k(u)$ represents the number of service completions by server $k$ during its first $u$ units of busy-time. Finally, the $k$th column of $\xi$, $\xi^k = \{\xi^k(\ell), \ell = 1, 2, \cdots\}$, models the routing mechanism enforced at station $k$: its $j$th component $\xi_j^k(\ell)$ is the indicator of the event that the $\ell$th customer served at station $k$, upon completion of its service, is routed directly to queue $j$, $j = 1, \cdots, K$. (Formally, $\xi_j^k(\ell)$ equals 1 when the event that it indicates occurs and 0 when it does not.) For ease of notation, introduce

$$R(t) = \sum_{\ell=1}^{\lfloor t \rfloor} \xi(\ell),$$

and call $R = \{R(t), t \geq 0\}$ the *routing process*.

The processes of primary interest are the *queue length process* $Z = (Z_1, ..., Z_K)'$ with $Z_k = \{Z_k(t), t \geq 0\}$, and the *busy-time* process $B = (B_1, ..., B_K)'$ with $B_k = \{B_k(t), t \geq 0\}$; $Z_k(t)$ represents the number of customers in station $k$ at time $t \geq 0$ (served or waiting to be served), and $B_k(t)$ the amount of time that server $k$ has been busy during the time interval $[0, t]$, $k = 1, ..., K$. The dynamics of these processes are summarized by the *flow-balance* relation

$$Z_k(t) = Z_k(0) + A_k(t) + \sum_{j=1}^{K} R_k^j(S_j[B_j(t)]) - S_k[B_k(t)], \quad t \geq 0, \quad (2.80)$$

and the *work-conservation* constraints

$$B_k(t) = \int_0^t 1[Z_k(u) > 0]du, \quad t \geq 0. \quad (2.81)$$

It can be verified, through a constructive proof, that there exists a unique pair $Z$ and $B$ that satisfy (2.80) and (2.81). This pair constitutes our model of a non-parametric Jackson network. (There are other processes of interest, for example sojourn times of customers, but they will not be considered here.)

Now consider a sequence of queueing networks, as above, which is indexed by a superscript $n$. Their primitives are assumed to satisfy

$$\lim_{n \to \infty} \frac{1}{n} Z^n(0) = \bar{Z}(0), \quad (2.82)$$

$$\lim_{n \to \infty} \frac{1}{n} A^n(nt) = \alpha t, \quad u.o.c., \quad (2.83)$$

$$\lim_{n \to \infty} \frac{1}{n} S^n(nt) = \mu t, \quad u.o.c., \quad (2.84)$$

$$\lim_{n \to \infty} \frac{1}{n} R(nt) = P't, \quad u.o.c. \quad (2.85)$$

Here, the $K \times K$ matrix $P = [p_{jk}]$ is substochastic with spectral radius less than unity, the vector $\mu = (\mu_1, \cdots, \mu_K)'$ is positive, and the vectors $\bar{Z}(0) = (\bar{Z}_1(0), \cdots, \bar{Z}_K(0))'$ and $\alpha = (\alpha_1, \cdots, \alpha_K)$ are nonnegative. One interprets the scalar $p_{jk}$ as the long-run average fraction of customers that are routed from station $j$ directly to station $k$. The parameters $\mu_k$ and $\alpha_k$ represent, respectively, the long-run average service rate and the exogenous arrival rate at station $k = 1, \cdots, K$. The integer $Z_k^n(0)$ corresponds to the number of customers that are waiting to be served by server $k$ at time $t = 0$. Indeed, if a single network is considered (i.e., if the sequence of networks does not depend on $n$), then (2.82) holds trivially with $\bar{Z}(0) = 0$, while (2.83)-(2.85) reduce to the existence of long-run averages of arrival rates $\alpha$, service rates $\mu$ and fractions of jobs' routing $P$.

Given the existence of limits (2.82)-(2.85), the long-run behavior of the networks is summarized by the triplet $(\alpha, P, \mu)$. We first identify the non-bottlenecks and bottlenecks of the queueing network with those of the linear fluid network $(\alpha, P, \mu)$. Other network concepts, such as effective inflow rates and traffic intensities are identified similarly.

**Theorem 2.5.2** Assume that (2.82)-(2.85) hold, and let $(Z^n, B^n)$ be associated with the $n$th network through (2.80) and (2.81). Then the limit

$$(\bar{Z}^n, \bar{B}^n) \equiv \left( \frac{1}{n} Z^n(n\cdot), \frac{1}{n} B^n(n\cdot) \right) \longrightarrow (\bar{Z}, \bar{B}) \quad u.o.c. \tag{2.86}$$

holds, as $n \to \infty$, with

$$\bar{Z} = \bar{X} + [I - P']\bar{Y}, \tag{2.87}$$
$$\bar{B}_k(t) = t - \mu_k^{-1} \bar{Y}_k(t), \quad t \geq 0, \quad k = 1, \cdots, K, \tag{2.88}$$
$$\bar{X}(t) = \bar{Z}(0) + (\alpha + [P' - I]\mu)t, \tag{2.89}$$

and $\bar{Y} = \Psi(\bar{X})$. Moreover, there exists a finite time $\tau$ such that

$$\bar{Z}_a(t) = 0, \quad \text{for } t \geq \tau, \tag{2.90}$$
$$\bar{Z}_b(t) = \bar{Z}_b(\tau) + (\lambda_b - \mu_b)(t - \tau), \quad \text{for } t \geq \tau, \tag{2.91}$$
$$\bar{B}_a(t) = \bar{B}_a(\tau) + \rho_a(t - \tau), \quad \text{for } t \geq \tau, \tag{2.92}$$
$$\bar{B}_b(t) = t, \quad \text{for } t \geq 0, \tag{2.93}$$

where

$$\bar{Z}_b(\tau) = \bar{Z}_b(0) + P'_{ab}[I - P'_a]^{-1}\bar{Z}_a(0) + (\lambda_b - \mu_b)\tau,$$

and $a$, $b$, $\lambda$ and $\rho$ are the set of nonbottlenecks, the set of bottlenecks, the inflow capacity and the traffic intensity of $(\alpha, P, \mu)$ respectively.

**Proof.**    The relations (2.90)-(2.93) follow immediately from Theorem 2.4.4 and (2.87)-(2.89). Therefore, it suffices to prove (2.86)-(2.89). First rewrite (2.80) for the scaled $n$th network,

$$\bar{Z}^n(t) = \bar{X}^n(t) + [I - P']\bar{Y}^n(t), \tag{2.94}$$

where

$$\bar{X}^n(t) = \bar{Z}^n(0) + (\alpha + [P' - I]\mu) - [\bar{S}^n(\bar{B}^n(t)) - \text{diag}(\mu)\bar{B}^n(t)]$$
$$+ \sum_{j=1}^{K} [\bar{R}^{j,n}(\bar{S}^n_j(\bar{B}^n_j(t))) - \mu_j p^j \bar{B}^n_j(t)] + [\bar{A}^n_k(t) - \alpha t], \tag{2.95}$$
$$\bar{Y}^n_k(t) = \mu_k \int_0^t 1[\bar{Z}^n_k(u) = 0]du, \tag{2.96}$$

and $p^j$ is the $j$th column of $P'$. It is clear from (2.94) and (2.96) that $\bar{Z}^n$ and $\bar{Y}^n$ jointly satisfy (2.24)-(2.26), with $X$ replaced by $\bar{X}^n$ (obviously, $\bar{Z}^n \geq 0$); therefore,

$$\bar{Z}^n = \Phi(\bar{X}^n) \quad \text{and} \quad \bar{Y}^n = \Psi(\bar{X}^n). \tag{2.97}$$

Using $0 \le \bar{B}^n(t) \le t$ for all $t \ge 0$ and $n \ge 1$, (2.82)-(2.85) imply

$$\bar{X}^n \to \bar{X}, \quad u.o.c., \quad \text{as} \quad n \to \infty, \tag{2.98}$$

with $\bar{X}$ as given in (2.89). The continuity of mappings $\Psi$ and $\Phi$ (Theorem 2.2.4), together with (2.97) and (2.98), gives

$$(\bar{Y}^n, \bar{Z}^n) \to (\bar{Y}, \bar{Z}), \quad u.o.c., \quad \text{as} \quad n \to \infty,$$

with $\bar{Y} = \Psi(\bar{X})$, and $\bar{Z} = \Phi(\bar{X})$ as in (2.87). The proof is completed by observing that

$$\bar{B}_k^n(t) = t - \mu_k^{-1} \bar{Y}_k^n(t), \quad t \ge 0, \quad k = 1, \cdots, K.$$

$\square$

### 2.5.3  FSLLN's for State-Dependent Networks

We now extend Jackson's model by allowing state-dependent arrivals and services. Specifically, the exogenous *arrival* process $A$ and the *service* process $S$ are both taken to be general point processes with state-dependent intensity processes $\alpha = \{\alpha[t, Z(t-)], t \ge 0\}$ and $\mu = \{\mu[t, Z(t-)], t \ge 0\}$. Here, $\alpha = \{\alpha[t, z] : t \ge 0, z \in \Re_+^K\}$ and $\mu = \{\mu[t, z] : t \ge 0, z \in \Re_+^K\}$ are the arrival and service intensities respectively, both of which are given as primitives (and they are both allowed to be stochastic; for example, $\alpha[t, z] = \alpha[t, z, \omega]$? could hold on some probability space); $Z = \{Z(t), t \ge 0\}$ is the queue length process, whose formal description will be provided momentarily.

As in subsection 2.5.2, the exogenous arrival process $A$ indicates the cumulative number of jobs that arrive to each station. A jump of $S_k(\cdot)$ at time $t$ indicates a departure of a job from station $k$ at time $t$ if and only if at least one such job is present at station $k$ immediately prior to time $t$. Formally,

$$D_k(t) \equiv \int_0^t 1[Z_k(u-) > 0] \, dS_k(u), \tag{2.99}$$

represents the cumulative number of jobs that actually depart from station $k$ during $(0, t]$, and the vector process $D = \{D(t), t \ge 0\}$ is naturally called the *departure process*. The times between successive jumps of $S_k$ are interpreted as potential service times. Each server can be thought of as constantly working, while generating an actual departure precisely when a jump of $S_k$ occurs at a non-empty station. (Such a server is frequently called an "autonomous server".)

The routing matrix-valued process $R = \{R(t), t \ge 0\}$ is taken to be the same as in the previous subsection. We then postulate that a model is given whose queue length process $Z$ is characterized by (2.99), together with

$$Z_k(t) = Z_k(0) + A_k(t) + \sum_{j=1}^{K} R_k^j(D_j(t)) - D_k(t), \quad k = 1, ..., K. \quad (2.100)$$

Denoting by $\mathcal{F}_t = \sigma\{Z(s); 0 \le s \le t\}$ the $\sigma$-field generated by $Z = \{Z(t), t \ge 0\}$, we further postulate that $A_k$ and $S_k$ are point processes with $\mathcal{F}_t$-compensators

$$M_k(t) = \int_0^t \alpha_k[s, Z(s-)] \, ds \quad \text{and} \quad N_k(t) = \int_0^t \mu_k[s, Z(s-)] \, ds$$

respectively. Thus, $A_k$ and $S_k$ admit $\mathcal{F}_t$-intensities $\alpha_k = \{\alpha_k[t, Z(t-)], t \ge 0\}$ and $\mu_k = \{\mu_k[t, Z(t-)], t \ge 0\}$ respectively. Finally, we impose the following assumptions to facilitate the presentation: the primitives are such that, with probability one, no two of the above mentioned point processes jump at the same time; $\alpha[t, z]$ and $\mu[t, z]$ both satisfy the conditions in Theorem 2.3.1, that is they are bounded, and Lipschitz in $z \in \Re_+^K$, u.o.c. in $t \in \Re_+$.

Similarly to (2.94)-(2.96), the representation (2.99)-(2.100) can be rewritten, after an appropriate centering of its ingredients, as

$$Z(t) - \int_0^t \theta[s, Z(s)] \, ds = X(t) + [I - P']Y(t), \quad (2.101)$$

where

$$\theta[s, z] = \alpha[s, z] + [P' - I]\mu[s, z], \quad (2.102)$$

$$X_k(t) = Z_k(0) + [A_k(t) - M_k(t)] + \sum_{j=1}^{K} p_{jk}[S_j(t) - N_j(t)]$$

$$+ \sum_{j=1}^{K} \left[ R_k^j(D_j(t)) - p_{jk}D_j(t) \right] - [S_k(t) - N_k(t)] \quad (2.103)$$

$$Y_k(t) = S_k(t) - D_k(t) = \int_0^t 1[Z_k(u-) = 0] \, dS_k(u). \quad (2.104)$$

The representation (2.101)-(2.104) is close to being in a form that is suitable for an application of Theorem 3.1. One must only verify the complementarity condition (2.55), which we write in the form

$$\int_0^\infty 1[Z_k(u) > 0] dY_k(t) = \int_0^\infty 1[Z_k(u) > 0, Z_k(u-) = 0] \, dS_k(u) = 0.$$

The event $\{Z_k(u) > 0, Z_k(u-) = 0\}$ describes an arrival at time $u$ to an empty station $k$, and this arrival must correspond to a jump of either $A_k$

or some $S_j$, $j \neq k$. But such a jump cannot occur simultaneously with a jump of $S_k$, in view of our underlying assumptions. Hence complementarity prevails and yields $Y = \Psi_\theta(X)$ and $Z = \Phi_\theta(X)$. The state of the network has thus been represented as a Lipschitz function of the primitive data $X$ in (2.103).

Now consider a sequence of state-dependent queueing networks, as above, with corresponding processes indexed by a superscript $n$ for the $n$th network, $n = 1, 2, ....$ For example, $Z^n(0)$ indicates the initial queue length vector and $\alpha^n$ the arrival intensity process for the $n$th network. The arrival and service intensities for the $n$th network are assumed to take the form

$$\alpha^n[t, z] = \alpha[\frac{t}{n}, \frac{z}{n}] \quad \text{and} \quad \mu^n[t, z] = \mu[\frac{t}{n}, \frac{z}{n}];$$

that is, $\alpha^n$ and $\mu^n$ are scaled versions of some fixed intensity processes $\alpha$ and $\mu$. For a sample-path interpretation of this rescaling, fix $n$, focus on the arrival processes $A^n$, and consider first the special case $\alpha[t, z] \equiv \alpha[t]$. Then for the $n$th network, accelerating time and aggregating space units, both by a factor of $n$, gives rise to the rescaled point process $\bar{A}^n = \{\bar{A}^n(t) = A(nt)/n, t \geq 0\}$, whose compensator $\bar{M}^n$ is given by

$$\bar{M}^n(t) = \frac{1}{n} M(nt) \equiv \int_0^t \alpha[s] ds = M(t) \quad t \geq 0,$$

which is independent $n$. A strong-law effect emerges by increasing $n \uparrow \infty$, in the sense that $\bar{A}^n$ tends to evolve closer and closer around $M$, u.o.c. and a.s. Similar convergence takes place when generalizing to $\alpha[t, z]$, which depends both on time and space. The compensator of $\bar{A}^n$ then equals

$$\bar{M}^n(t) = \frac{1}{n} M(nt) = \int_0^t \alpha[s, \bar{Z}^n(s)] ds.$$

Here, as usual, $\bar{Z}^n(t) = Z(nt)/n$ which, we now show, converges to the fluid level of the model in Section 2.3.2.

Remark:    Instead of using the above rescaling, one can equivalently introduce $\alpha^n[t, z] = n\alpha[t, \frac{z}{n}]$, $\mu^n[t, z] = n\mu[t, \frac{z}{n}]$; then, instead of analyzing $Z^n(nt)/n$ (as we do here), one considers $Z^n(t)/t$ (which we do in Section 2.6.3, in order to remain consistent with its origin).

Express the rescaled queue length process as follows:

$$\bar{Z}^n(t) - \int_0^t \theta[s, \bar{Z}^n(s)] \, ds = \bar{X}^n(t) + [I - P']\bar{Y}^n(t), \qquad (2.105)$$

where $\theta$ is defined in (2.102), and the bar-rescaling plays its usual role. In particular,

$$\bar{Y}_k^n(t) \equiv \frac{1}{n} Y^n(nt) = \bar{S}_k^n(t) - \bar{D}_k^n(t) = \int_0^t 1[\bar{Z}_k^n(u-) = 0] \, d\bar{S}_k^n(u),$$

and

$$\bar{X}_k^n(t) = \bar{Z}_k^n(0) + [\bar{A}_k^n(t) - \bar{M}_k^n(t)] + \sum_{j=1}^{K} p_{jk}[\bar{D}_j^n(t) - \bar{N}_j^n(t)]$$

$$+ \sum_{j=1}^{K} \left[ R_k^{j,n}\left(\bar{D}_j^n(t)\right) - p_{jk}\bar{D}_j^n(t) \right] - [\bar{D}_j^n(t) - \bar{N}_j^n(t)]. \qquad (2.106)$$

Note that $\bar{Y}^n = \Psi_\theta(\bar{X}^n)$ and $\bar{Z}^n = \Phi_\theta(\bar{X}^n)$. Since $\Psi_\theta$ and $\Phi_\theta$ are Lipschitz continuous, u.o.c. convergence of $\bar{Y}^n$ and $\bar{Z}^n$ will follow from the convergence of $\bar{X}^n$. To get the latter, we add the assumptions:

$$\lim_{n \to \infty} \bar{Z}^n(0) \to \bar{Z}(0), \qquad (2.107)$$

$$\lim_{n \to \infty} \bar{R}^n(t) = P't, \qquad u.o.c. \qquad (2.108)$$

and

$$M_k(\infty) = \infty \quad \text{and} \quad N_k(\infty) = \infty, \qquad k = 1, ..., K, \qquad (2.109)$$

all assumed to hold almost surely. (A sufficient condition for (2.109) is the existence of two nonnegative processes $a = \{a(t), t \geq 0\}$ and $m = \{m(t), t \geq 0\}$ in $\mathcal{D}^K$ such that, with probability one, $\alpha_k[t, z] \geq a(t)$ and $\mu_k[t, z] \geq m(t)$ for all $t \geq 0$ and $z \geq 0$, and $\int_0^\infty a(t)dt = \int_0^\infty m(t)dt = \infty$.)

**Theorem 2.5.3** Under the above assumptions, the limit

$$(\bar{Z}^n, \bar{Y}^n) \to (\bar{Z}, \bar{Y}), \qquad u.o.c., \qquad (2.110)$$

holds, as $n \to \infty$, where

$$\bar{Z}(t) - \int_0^t \theta[s, \bar{Z}(s)]\, ds = \bar{Z}(0) + [I - P']\bar{Y}(t), \quad t \geq 0,$$

$\theta$ is defined in (2.102) and $\bar{Y} = \Psi_\theta(\bar{X})$ with $\bar{X}(t) \equiv \bar{Z}(0)$.

Remarks: The remarkable ease in which our state-dependent model is analyzed traces to the autonomous-server discipline, which differs from the situation in Theorem 2.5.2. Theorem 2.5.3 covers also stochastic intensities $\alpha$ and $\mu$, hence the limiting fluid network need not be deterministic.

**Proof.**    Lemma 2.5.4 below provides convergence of the ingredients of $\bar{X}^n$ that is neccessary for the proof. Somewhat more specifically, one starts by noting that for all $t \geq 0$ and $n \geq 1$,

$$0 \leq \bar{D}^n(t) \leq \bar{S}^n(t) = \bar{N}^n(t) + [\bar{S}^n(t) - \bar{N}^n(t)],$$

with the first term on the right-hand-side bounded and the second term converging to zero (Lemma 2.5.4). Combining (2.107) and (2.108) with Lemma 2.5.4 now gives

$$\lim_{n \to \infty} \bar{X}^n \to \bar{Z}(0). \quad u.o.c. \tag{2.111}$$

Finally, applying Theorem 2.3.1 to the processes $\bar{Y}^n = \Psi_\theta(\bar{X}^n)$ and $\bar{Z}^n = \Phi_\theta(\bar{X}^n)$ yields the convergence (2.110), with the limits $\bar{Y}$ and $\bar{Z}$ identified in the theorem. □

**Lemma 2.5.4** Suppose that the stochastic intensities $\alpha$ and $\mu$ are bounded and that $M^n(\infty) = \infty$ and $N^n(\infty) = \infty$ almost surely. Then as $n \to \infty$,

$$\bar{A}^n - \bar{M}^n \to 0, \quad u.o.c., \tag{2.112}$$
$$\bar{S}^n - \bar{N}^n \to 0, \quad u.o.c.. \tag{2.113}$$

**Proof.**    Under the condition that $M^n(\infty) = \infty$, we have

$$\frac{A_k^n(t) - M_k^n(t)}{M_k^n(t)} \to 0, \quad \text{as } t \to \infty, \tag{2.114}$$

as a consequence of Theorem 1 in Liptser [1980]. The convergence (2.114) implies that

$$\frac{\bar{A}_k^n(t)}{\bar{M}_k^n(t)} \to 1, \quad u.o.c. \text{ in } (0, \infty), \quad \text{as } n \to \infty.$$

Noting that

$$\bar{A}_k^n(t) - \bar{M}_k^n(t) = \bar{M}_k^n(t) \left[ \frac{\bar{A}_k^n(t)}{\bar{M}_k^n(t)} - 1 \right],$$

we conclude (2.112) once we notice that $0 \le M_k^n(t) \le ct$ for some constant $c > 0$ and that $\bar{A}_k^n$ is right continuous at $t = 0$ with $\bar{A}^n(0) = 0$. The proof for (2.113) is similar. □

# 2.6    Applications and Hints at Prospects of Fluid Models

## 2.6.1    *Stochastic Fluid Models for Manufacturing and Communication Systems*

In this subsection we restrict attention to the very special cases of one-dimensional time- and state-dependent models, as in subsections 2.3.1–2.3.2. Simple as they are, such models already provide a useful range of applications for manufacturing and communication systems and, thus, indicate the potential embodied in their multi-dimensional (and other) generalizations.

Consider a single buffer, with initial content $Z(0) \geq 0$, exogenous inflow rate $\alpha = \{\alpha(t), t \geq 0\}$ and potential outflow rate $\mu = \{\mu(t), t \geq 0\}$. The process of primary interest is the inventory level process $Z = \{Z(t), t \geq 0\}$; its dynamics are prescribed by

$$Z(t) = X(t) + Y(t) \geq 0, \tag{2.115}$$

where

$$X(t) = Z(0) + \int_0^t \alpha(s)\, ds - \int_0^t \mu(s)\, ds, \tag{2.116}$$

is the netflow process [cf. (2.46)], and $Y(t)$ indicates the cumulative lost potential outflow due to the emptiness of the buffer. Mathematically, the process $Y = \{Y(t), t \geq 0\}$ is the regulator of $X$, which entails that $Y$ and $Z$ uniquely satisfy (2.115), combined with

$$dY(t) \geq 0, \ t \geq 0, \qquad Y(0) = 0, \qquad \text{and} \tag{2.117}$$
$$Z(t)dY(t) = 0, \ t \geq 0. \tag{2.118}$$

In this one-dimensional case, $Y$ can be explicitly written as

$$Y(t) = \sup_{0 \leq s \leq t} [-X(s)]^+,$$

which, of course, determines an expression for $Z$. (This explicit expression arises naturally once one recalls that one seeks the least $Y$, which is nondecreasing with $Y(0) = 0$, such that $Y(t) \geq -X(t)$, for all $t \geq 0$.)

The process $Z$ can represent inventory of jobs (to be processed) in a manufacturing system or an inventory of entities (for example calls or cells, to be transmitted) in a communication system. For example, in a tandem manufacturing system, $\alpha(t)$ can represent the number of machines that are in operation at time $t$, $Z(t)$ the inventory level of a product that is produced, and $\mu(t)$ the number of downstream machines that consume the product at time $t$. We proceed with two more detailed examples.

*A Fluid Model for Systems with Random Interruptions*

In many manufacturing processes, job arrivals and processing times are essentially deterministic, but the environment is typically random. Random interruptions are caused, for example, by unexpected machine breakdowns, tool wear, and absence of operators. Typically, the duration of random interruptions (due, for example, to repair times of machines) and the time between two consecutive random interruptions are much larger than the interarrival times and the processing times of jobs. Therefore, in such a system, arrivals of jobs can be modelled by continuous flows of fluid at a constant rate. Departures of jobs can also be modelled by flows of fluid, but this must be modified to account for the random interruptions.

Specifically, in such a model, we can take $\alpha(t) \equiv \alpha$, and $\mu(t)$ to be an alternating renewal process with values alternating between 0 and $\mu$. Here, both $\alpha$ and $\mu$ are given constants; the reciprocal of the former represents the interarrival time between two jobs, and the reciprocal of the latter represents the processing time for a job. One can establish a tight pathwise bound between the inventory level process associated with this fluid model and the inventory process of jobs in a system with deterministic arrival and service times, if both models are subject to the same random interruptions.

Several generalizations come to mind. First, taking $\alpha(t)$ to be an alternating renewal process corresponds to supplies of raw materials (arrivals of jobs) that are also subject to random interruptions. The outflow process may alternate among more than two values, for example, high, low and zero, which represent high performance, low performance, and complete breakdown of the machine. All these models can be extended to a network setting.

### A Fluid Model for ATM Communication Systems

We consider a communication standard, known as the *Asynchronous Transfer Mode*, where information is sent in blocks of small fixed-size cells. Specifically, packets of data, which will also be referred to as *bursts of data*, are broken down into cells before being transmitted. The cells are small and of uniform size (53 bytes), and a burst contains a very large number of cells. The generation times between two consecutive cells from a burst are deterministic. For convenience, the time scale is chosen so that one unit of time is required to generate one cell from a burst. The interarrival times between two bursts, and the time to completely break down a burst into cells are usually very large (compared to the time required to generate a single cell). In addition, the transmission times for cells are small and deterministic. Therefore, both arrivals and transmissions of cells are best modelled by continuous fluid flows.

The performance measures of interest are delays of transmissions and buffer content of cells. These two quantities are related by Little's formula, hence it suffices to focus on the buffer content of cells, namely $Z = \{Z(t), t \geq 0\}$. We take as primitives, on a common probability space, a nonnegative random variable $Z(0)$, a nonnegative integer valued stochastic process $m = \{m(t), t \geq 0\}$, and a constant $c$. The random variable $Z(0)$ indicates the initial buffer content, and the constant $c$ is the transmission capacity, i.e., the maximum rate at which cells can be transmitted. The process $m$ evaluated at $t$, $m(t)$, indicates the number of bursts (packets of data) that are in the process of being broken into cells at time $t$. In other words, $m(t)$ is the rate at which cells are generated at time $t$.

The dynamics of the buffer content process $Z$ follows (2.115)-(2.118), with $\alpha(t) = m(t)$ and $\mu(t) = c$. In this case, the cumulative loss of transmission capacity has the explicit expression

$$Y(t) = \int_0^t [c - m(s)]1[m(s) < c]1[Z(s) = 0]\, ds.$$

With different choices of process $m$, several variations of burst arrival patterns can be accommodated. One variation is to consider a finite number of sources. Each source is an alternating renewal process; it generates cells at a unit rate when it is "on" and does not generate cells when it is "off". In this case, $m(t)$ represents the number of sources that are "on" at time $t$. A special case is when the durations of "on" and "off" periods are exponentially distributed. Then $m$ is a finite-state birth-death process.

Another variation of the model is as follows. Bursts (packets of data) arrive according to a renewal process. Each burst contains a random number of cells (independent of other bursts); call it the size of a burst. In this case, $m$ is equivalent to the queue length process of a $G/G/\infty$ queue, where interarrival times and service times for the queue are the interarrival times of bursts and sizes of bursts, respectively. When both interarrival times and sizes of bursts are exponential, the process $m$ becomes an infinite state birth-death process.

If the process $m$ is a general Markov chain, or even a generalized semi-Markov process, more general variations are obtained. One could also generalize the model itself in many directions, for example, to including transmission failures and to a network setting

### 2.6.2  Heterogeneous Fluid Networks: Bottleneck Analysis and Scheduling Control

As seen in previous sections, flows of fluids in a network can represent customers in a service facility, jobs on a manufacturing floor, or packets of data in a communication channel. In many such applications, variations of customers (jobs, packets of data) in terms of their service requirements can be very large. An appropriate model must then acknowledge a classification of customers into groups or types. Customers from different classes may have different arrival patterns and service requirements, while following different routes within the network. A simple model for such systems is an extension of the previous fluid network, where one allows *heterogeneous* fluids. The term "heterogeneous" is chosen because fluids in this network are classified into different types, and fluids of different types are distinguishable in terms of exogenous inflow rates, processing rates and flow-transfer fractions. Analogously, the previously studied models are sometimes called *homogeneous* fluid networks. For a concrete illustration, we now present and analyze a linear heterogeneous fluid model.

The network consists of a collection of $I$ buffers, each with an infinite storage capacity. The buffers are interconnected by pipes to form a network within which several types of fluids are circulating simultaneously. There are $K$ types of fluid, indexed by $k = 1, \ldots, K$. Fluid of type $k$, hereafter referred to as fluid $k$, resides exclusively in buffer $i = s(k)$, where $s(\cdot)$ is a given many-to-one map from types to buffers. From buffer $s(k)$, a fraction $p_{kj}$ of fluid $k$ turns into fluid $j$, thus being routed instantaneously into buffer $s(j)$; a fraction $1 - \sum_{j=1}^{K} p_{kj}$ of fluid $k$ leaves the network.

Fluid $k$ enters buffer $s(k)$ exogenously at a constant rate $\alpha_k$, and its potential outflow rate is $\mu_k$. Alternatively, $\alpha_k t$ is the cumulative exogenous inflow of fluid $k$ during the time interval $[0, t]$, and $\mu_k t$ represents the cumulative outflow of fluid $k$ during $[0, t]$ if buffer $s(k)$ had been dedicated exclusively to processing fluid $k$, and if there had been enough of it to start with. Without loss of generality, we assume the buffers' processing capacity to be one unit of fluid per unit of time: equivalently, a maximum $(t - s)$ units of fluid can be processed during the time interval $[s, t]$, for all $t \geq s \geq 0$.

Let $Z(0)$ denote initial fluid levels. Call $P = [p_{jk}]$ the *flow-transfer* matrix, $\alpha$ the *exogenous inflow rate* and $\mu$ the *potential outflow rate* vector. As before, we focus on *open* fluid networks, in which $P$ has spectral radius less than unity.

Given $Z(0), \alpha, \mu$, and $P$, the fluid level $Z_k(t)$ of type $k$ at time $t$ is determined by allocation process $T_k = \{T_k(t), t \geq 0\}$: $T_k(t)$ represents the cumulative amount of time allocated to processing fluid $k$ by buffer $s(k)$, during $[0, t]$. Let $C(i) = \{k : s(k) = i\}$ record the fluid types processed in buffer $i$. Then the total busy time of buffer $i$ during $[0, t]$ equals $B_i(t) = \sum_{k \in C(i)} T_k(t)$, its cumulative idle time is $U_i(t) = t - B_i(t)$, the fluid level of type $k$ at time $t$ (in buffer $s(k)$) is given by the flow-balance relations

$$Z_k(t) = Z_k(0) + \alpha_k t + \sum_{j=1}^{K} \mu_j T_j(t) p_{jk} - \mu_k T_k(t), \qquad (2.119)$$

and the total fluid level in buffer $i$ at time $t$ is $Z_i^*(t) = \sum_{k \in C(i)} Z_k(t)$.

We call an allocation $T$ *feasible* if it gives rise to $U = (U_i)$ and $Z = (Z_k)$ that satisfy for all $k = 1, \ldots, K$ and $i = 1, \ldots, I$,

$T_k$ is non-decreasing, starting with $T_k(0) = 0$,

$U_i$ is non-decreasing, and

$Z_k$ is nonnegative.

A feasible allocation is *work-conserving* if it also satisfies the complementarity condition

$$Z^*(t) dU(t) = 0, \qquad t \geq 0.$$

*Traffic Equations*

In this subsection we describe the evolution of the linear heterogeneous fluid model. In Sections 2.4 and 2.5, we saw that the classification of buffers into nonbottlenecks and bottlenecks through traffic equations led to a complete characterization of the first-order (long-run) behavior of linear homogeneous fluid networks, as well as of nonlinear homogeneous fluid networks and of nonparametric Jackson networks. Here we make a similar attempt for the linear heterogeneous fluid network, but the situation is far more complicated and much is left to be done.

As in Section 2.4, we start by analyzing *effective* inflow and outflow rates. The effective inflow rate of fluid $k$, denoted by $\lambda_k$, represents the inflow rate of fluid $k$, summed over both exogenous and endogenous inflows. The effective outflow rate $\delta_k$ represents the actual outflow rate of fluid $k$. ($\lambda_k$ and $\delta_k$ are "to" and "from" buffer $s(k)$.) Given the triplet $(\alpha, \mu, P)$, the vectors $\lambda = (\lambda_k)$ and $\delta = (\delta_k)$ adhere to the following *"traffic equations"*:

$$\lambda_k = \alpha_k + \sum_{j=1}^{K} \delta_j p_{jk}, \tag{2.120}$$

$$\sum_{k \in C(i)} \frac{\lambda_k}{\mu_k} = \rho_i, \tag{2.121}$$

$$\sum_{k \in C(i)} \frac{\delta_k}{\mu_k} = \rho_i \wedge 1, \tag{2.122}$$

$$0 \leq \delta \leq \lambda, \tag{2.123}$$

for $k = 1, ..., K$ and $i = 1, ..., I$. Here equality (2.120) is the flow-balance relation, and equality (2.122) is the workload balance relation. Equality (2.121) is the defining relation of $\rho_i$, which will be referred to as the *traffic intensity of buffer i*. In vector notation, the traffic equations take the form

$$\lambda = \alpha + P'\delta,$$
$$CM^{-1}\lambda = \rho,$$
$$CM^{-1}\delta = \rho \wedge e,$$
$$\lambda \geq \delta \geq 0,$$

where $M = \text{diag}(\mu)$, and $C = [c_{ik}]$ is the $I \times K$ matrix with

$$c_{ik} = \begin{cases} 1 & \text{if } k \in C(i), \\ 0 & \text{otherwise.} \end{cases}$$

**Theorem 2.6.1** For a triplet $(\alpha, \mu, P)$ that arises from an open network, the traffic equations (2.120)-(2.123) have at least one solution $(\lambda, \delta)$.

*Remark:*    (1) The converse seems also to be true, namely that every solution $(\lambda, \delta)$ to (2.120)-(2.123) constitutes effective arrival and departure rates that arise from some work-conserving allocation $T$.

(2) Any solution to the traffic equations also solves a linear complementarity problem (LCP, as in subsection 2.4.1). Indeed, with matrices $M$ and $C$ as introduced above. consider the transformation $y = M^{-1}\delta$, $z = M^{-1}(\lambda - \delta)$, $r = M^{-1}\alpha$, $R = M^{-1}P'M - I$. This transformation reduces (2.120)-(2.123) to the equivalent $LCP$-like problem: find $K$-dimensional vectors $y$ and $z$ that satisfy

$$z = r + Ry,$$
$$z \geq 0,$$
$$Cy \leq e,$$
$$(Cz)'(e - Cy) = 0.$$

(Simply note that $e - Cy = (e - \rho)^+$ and $Cz = (e - \rho)^-$.)

(3)   A simple example where the traffic equations have a multitude of solutions is a single station with two customer types ($I = 1$ and $K = 2$), in which $\alpha_1 = \alpha_2 = 1$, $\mu_1 = \mu_2 = 1$ and $P = 0$. Clearly, $(\lambda, \delta) = ((1,0), (1,0))$ and $(\lambda, \delta) = ((0,1), (0,1))$ provide two pairs of solutions; in the former, fluid 1 enjoys priority over fluid 2, which is reversed in the latter. In this example capacity is scarce (strictly less than the workload), and it can be allocated among several types of fluid. We now give a sufficient condition for the solution to be unique. (The formulation of a necessary and sufficient condition is cumbersome, and we do not include it here.)

**Theorem 2.6.2** The set of traffic equations (2.120)-(2.123) has a unique solution if

$$CM^{-1}[I - P']^{-1}\alpha \leq e, \tag{2.124}$$

in which case

$$\lambda = \delta = [I - P']^{-1}\alpha, \tag{2.125}$$

as well as

$$\beta = M^{-1}\lambda = M^{-1}[I - P']^{-1}\alpha, \tag{2.126}$$
$$\rho = C\beta = CM^{-1}[I - P']^{-1}\alpha \leq e. \tag{2.127}$$

Remark:   The $(j,k)$th element of the matrix $[I - P]^{-1}$ could be loosely interpreted as the average total number of switches into type $k$ by a fluid molecule that enters the network as type $j$. Thus, the $i$th element $w_i$ of the *potential workload* vector $w$, given by $w = CM^{-1}[I - P']^{-1}\alpha$, quantifies the potential long-run average workload arrives to the network per unit of time and which is potentially destined to buffer $i$, When

$$w = CM^{-1}[I - P']^{-1}\alpha \leq e, \tag{2.128}$$

the potential workload $w$ qualifies as *actual* workload, in the sense that $w = \rho$.

*Bottleneck Analysis and Stability*

In Section 2.4, we have proved that for a homogeneous linear fluid network, there exists a unique feasible work-conserving allocation. Furthermore, there exists a finite time after which the fluid level reaches and remains zero at a nonbottleneck buffer, remains constant at a balanced bottleneck buffer, and increases at a constant rate at a strict bottleneck buffer. However, none of the above properties hold in general for a heterogeneous linear fluid network, and a complete analysis seems challenging. In this subsection, we present some examples that demonstrates the subtlety of the heterogeneous model.

To start with, we provide a classification for some simple networks. First, the network is said to have no strict bottlenecks, when condition (2.124) is met. If, furthermore, the condition holds with strict inequality, the network is said to have no bottlenecks. A complete classification of buffers into nonbottlenecks and bottlenecks is much more complicated than that for a homogeneous network, because the traffic intensity is not uniquely defined in general (Remark (3) after Theorem 2.6.1).

First, we illustrate by an example that a feasible work-conserving allocation is not unique in general. Consider a linear fluid network with $I = 1$, $K = 2$, $\alpha = (1,1)'$, $\mu = (1,1)'$ and $P = 0$. Then both allocations $T(t) = (t, 0)'$ and $T(t) = (0, t)'$ are work-conserving; the former dedicates capacity to the processing of fluid 1, and the latter to 2.

In a homogeneous linear fluid network under any work-conserving allocation, nonbottleneck buffers empty within a finite amount of time, and remain empty thereafter (Theorem 2.4.4). Such a conclusion is false for heterogeneous linear fluid networks, as the following example demonstrates. Consider a network with $I = 2$, $K = 4$, $C(1) = \{1, 4\}$, $C(2) = \{2, 3\}$, and

$$\alpha = \begin{pmatrix} 1 \\ 0 \\ 1 \\ 0 \end{pmatrix}, \mu = \begin{pmatrix} 4 \\ 3/2 \\ 4 \\ 3/2 \end{pmatrix}, P = \begin{pmatrix} 0 & 1 & 0 & 0 \\ 0 & 0 & 0 & 0 \\ 0 & 0 & 0 & 1 \\ 0 & 0 & 0 & 0 \end{pmatrix}.$$

In this case, $\rho_1 = \rho_2 = 11/12 < 1$, hence both buffers are nonbottlenecks. Assuming an initial fluid level $Z(0) = (\gamma, 0, 0, 0)$, with $\gamma > 0$, we shall present, in the subsequent paragraph, a work-conserving allocation for which $Z(4\gamma) = (4\gamma, 0, 0, 0)$. Proceeding with this allocation, one gets $Z(4n\gamma) = (4n\gamma, 0, 0, 0)$ for all $n \geq 1$. Thus, not only does buffer 1 not become empty, but actually $\limsup_{t \to \infty} Z_1(t) = \infty$ (and, in fact, it will be seen that $\limsup_{t \to \infty} Z(t) = \infty$).

Starting at time $t = 0$, buffer 1 processes type 1 and buffer 2 processes type 2, both at full capacity, until time $t_1 = \gamma/3$. Then $Z(t_1) =$

$(0, 5\gamma/6, \gamma/3, 0)$, buffer 1 is forced to process at 11/12th of its capacity, since it is empty, and Buffer 2 processes at full capacity. This continues until time $t_2 = 2\gamma$, at which $Z(t_2) = (0, 0, 2\gamma, 0)$. The state of the network is now symmetric to its state at time $t = 0$ in that the buffers switch roles. We thus proceed, in a similar manner, to obtain $Z(4\gamma) = (4\gamma, 0, 0, 0)$, and so on.

In the above example there also exist allocation processes under which the inventory level process ultimately reaches and then remains at zero. One could refer to such allocations as stable. One could also relax the notion of stability and require merely non-explosion, that is boundedness, of the resulting fluid level process. In any case, stability of heterogeneous networks depends on the allocation employed. This is unlike homogeneous models where it depends only on the traffic intensities.

As a last example, we illustrate that even when all stations are non-bottlenecks, a limiting (and/or stationary) distribution for a multiclass queueing network need not exist. We consider the functional strong law-of-large-numbers limit of the above example, namely, the limit of $Z(nt)/n$ as $n \to \infty$. From (2.56) and the fact that $Y(nt)/n$ is uniformly (in $n$) Lipschitz continuous, it follows that $Z(nt)/n$, as well as its associated allocation process, converge at least along a subsequence. The limit $\bar{Z}$ is the inventory level of the fluid linear fluid model with the same parameters $(\alpha, \mu, P)$ as above. Noting that $Z(0) = (\gamma, 0, 0, 0)$ and $Z(4n\gamma) = (4n\gamma, 0, 0, 0)$, we must have $\bar{Z}(0) = (0, 0, 0, 0)$ and $\bar{Z}(4\gamma) = (4\gamma, 0, 0, 0)$. Thus, for the above fluid model where both buffers are nonbottlenecks and the initial fluid level is zero, we have shown that there exists a feasible allocation process such that its associated inventory level does not remain zero. The implication of this example is that for a nonparametric multi-class queueing network, the departure rate may not equal the arrival rate, even if the network has no bottlenecks and the network is operated under work-conserving service disciplines; in other words, the limit superior of the queue length process may be infinite.

Stability of a queueing network is commonly taken to mean ergodicity, in particular the existence of a unique limiting distribution for its queue length process which, preferably, is also a stationary distribution. In simple cases, such as nonparametric Jackson networks, there exists an obvious relation between stability of the stochastic network and its homogeneous fluid approximation, namely the network is stable if and only if its fluid approximation eventually empties. A natural and important direction of research is the analysis of such relations between nonparametric multi-class queueing network and their heterogeneous fluid approximations.

*Dynamic Scheduling Control*

Optimal control of multi-type queueing networks is a difficult problem for which few analytical results are available. Fluid approximations of such models provide an attractively simple alternative, whose optimal control is typically much more tractable, yet potentially significant. This point will now be demonstrated in terms of a single buffer linear fluid model.

Consider the heterogeneous fluid model with $I = 1$ and $P = 0$. Our objective is to find a feasible allocation that minimizes inventory cost. (The final result is strong enough to apply to very general objectives, discounted cost over (in)finite horizon or long-run average cost). To be concrete, let $c_k$ be the unit cost of the inventory of type $k$. The goal is to

$$\text{minimize} \quad c'Z(t) \tag{2.129}$$
$$\text{subject to} \quad Z(t) = Z(0) + \alpha t - MT(t) \geq 0,$$
$$T(t) \text{ is non-decreasing with } T(0) = 0,$$
$$U(t) = t - e'T(t) \text{ is non-decreasing.}$$

Here $Z$ and $T$ are $K$-dimensional, $U$ is a 1-dimensional process, and $M = diag(\mu)$. We have not assumed that $T$ is work-conserving, but it is intuitively clear that the optimal allocation must be.

Let $r = Mc$. Then (2.128) is equivalent to

$$\max_{T(t)} \quad r'T(t) \tag{2.130}$$
$$\text{s.t.} \quad T(t) \leq M^{-1}[Z(0) + \alpha t], \tag{2.131}$$
$$T(t) \text{ is non-decreasing with } T(0) = 0, \tag{2.132}$$
$$t - e'T(t) \text{ is non-decreasing.} \tag{2.133}$$

Assume, without loss of generality, that

$$r_1 = c_1\mu_1 \geq r_2 = c_2\mu_2 \geq \ldots \geq r_K = c_K\mu_K.$$

Momentarily ignore constraint (2.132) and replace (2.133) by $e'T(t) \leq t$. Then the optimization problem (2.130) reduces to a simple linear program, which we now solve. First consider $t$ in a neighborhood of zero, and assume that $Z_1(0) > 0$. Then the optimal solution to (2.130) is

$$T_1(t) = t \quad \text{and} \quad T_k(t) = 0, \; k = 2, \ldots, K, \tag{2.134}$$

for $t$ near zero. Actually, (2.134) is the optimal solution as long as $Z_1(t) \geq 0$, or equivalently until the first constraint in (2.131) becomes binding. ($Z$ under consideration corresponds to the allocation given by (2.134)). Suppose this happens at time $t = t_1$ and $Z_2(t_1) > 0$. The optimal allocation $T$ for $t \geq t_1$ in a neighborhood of $t_1$ is then

$$T_1(t) = T_1(t_1) + \beta_1(t - t_1),$$
$$T_2(t) = (1 - \beta_1)(t - t_1),$$

and

$$T_k(t) = 0, \quad k = 3, \ldots, K,$$

where $\beta_k = \lambda_k/\mu_k$ and $\lambda_k = \alpha_k$.

Proceeding inductively, we derive the optimal solution over $[0, \infty)$. This optimal solution turns out to satisfy (2.132) and (2.133). (In fact, $e'T(t) = t$ when $e'Z(t) > 0$.) In words, we have discovered that the optimal $T$ allocates the highest (possible) effort to the fluid $k$ with the largest index $c_k \mu_k$, subject to availability of this fluid, thus reaffirming the optimality of the classical $c\mu$ rule. The above analysis can be extended to general linear fluid networks. In particular, it can be shown that a single station model with non-zero $P$ recovers Klimov's priority rule for optimal scheduling of a multiclass queueing system.

### 2.6.3    Transient Analysis of the $M_t/M_t/1$ Queue

In this subsection we explore approximations to a time-inhomogeneous single-server queue. It is denoted by $M_t/M_t/1$ since both its inflow of customers and potential services are modeled by time-inhomogeneous Poisson processes. The results presented here serve as a transition to the next chapter, on strong approximations of queueing networks. They also demonstrate that the paradigms of fluid-macroscopic-strategic and diffusion-mesoscopic-tactical are yet far from being definite.

*Notation*

In Section 2.6.3 only, $D = D[0, \infty)$ denotes the space of all functions $x$ : $[0, \infty) \to R^1$ such that $x(0) = 0$, $x$ is right-continuous at 0, and $x$ is *either* right or left continuous at every $t > 0$. (Until now, functions in $D$ have been right-continuous). We endow $D$ with Skorohod's $M_1$-topology, which is described in Section 2.7. Readers, however, need not consult Section 2.7 for the text that follows. One should simply note that $M_1$-convergence is metricizable, say by a metric $d$, under which $D$ becomes a complete separable metric (Polish) space. Consequently, the standard framework for weak convergence on Polish spaces covers $(D, M_1)$. Consider a sequence $\{x^n | n = 1, 2, \ldots\}$ and a function $y$, all elements in $D$. For some real-valued sequence $f(n)$, the little-$o$ notation

$$x^n = f(n)y + o(f(n)),$$

stands for

$$\lim_{n \uparrow \infty} d(\frac{1}{f(n)} x^n, y) = 0,$$

or, in words, $\lim_{n \uparrow \infty} x^n/f(n) = y$ in $M_1$. The big-$O$ notation

$$x^n = f(n) y + O(f(n)),$$

means that

$$\sup_n \| \frac{1}{f(n)} x^n - y \| < \infty,$$

where

$$||x|| = \int_0^\infty e^{-t} \left[1 \wedge ||x||_t\right] dt.$$

Finally, when used with stochastic processes $X^n$ and $Y$, defined on a common probability space with sample paths in $D$, little-$o$ and big-$O$ indicate the above type of asymptotic behaviour for almost all sample paths.

*General Asymptotic Expansions*

Our model of an $M_t/M_t/1$ system is taken to be

$$Z(t) \equiv X(t) - \inf_{0 \le s \le t} X(s), \quad t \ge 0, \tag{2.135}$$

where

$$X(t) \equiv N^+ \left(\int_0^t \alpha(r)\, dr\right) - N^- \left(\int_0^t \mu(r)\, dr\right), \tag{2.136}$$

$N^+$ and $N^-$ are two independent Poisson processes with unit rate, and $\alpha$ and $\mu$ are nonnegative continuous functions. The resulting stochastic process $Z$ models the queue length of an $M_t/M_t/1$ system that starts, for simplicity, with $Z(0) = 0$. At time $t \ge 0$, the input rate is $\alpha(t)$ and, assuming a non-empty queue, the output rate is $\mu(t)$. One derives asymptotic expansions of $Z$ by uniformly accelerating its governing transition rates. Formally, for each $n = 1, 2, \ldots$, introduce a stochastic process $Z^n$ by

$$Z^n(t) \equiv X^n(t) - \inf_{0 \le s \le t} X^n(s), \quad t \ge 0,$$

in which

$$X^n(t) \equiv N^+ \left(n \int_0^t \alpha(r)\, dr\right) - N^- \left(n \int_0^t \mu(r)\, dr\right).$$

**Theorem 2.6.3 (FSLLN)** We have the following functional strong law of large numbers for $Z^n$:

$$\lim_{n \uparrow \infty} \frac{1}{n} Z^n(t, \omega) = Z^f(t) \quad \text{a.s..}$$

where

$$Z^f(t) \equiv \int_0^t [\alpha(r) - \mu(r)]\, dr - \inf_{0 \le s \le t} \int_0^s [\alpha(r) - \mu(r)]\, dr,$$

and the convergence is uniform on compact subsets of $t \ge 0$.

The FSLLN gives rise to the asymptotic expansion

$$Z^n(t, \omega) = nZ^f(t) + o(n) \quad \text{a.s.,}$$

from which the deterministic process $Z^f$ emerges as a first-order, *macroscopic*, fluid approximation for $Z$. Indeed,

$$Z^f(t) = X^f(t) - \inf_{0 \le s \le t} X^f(s), \quad t \ge 0,$$

where

$$X^f(t) = \int_0^t [\alpha(r) - \mu(r)] \, dr,$$

in view of which $Z^f$ can be animated as the fluid level in a buffer that is governed by the following dynamics (recall the models in Subsections 2.3.1 and 2.6.1): the buffer is empty at time $t = 0$; at time $t > 0$, the exogenous inflow rate is $\alpha(t)$, and the potential outflow rate is $\mu(t)$; finally, the actual outflow rate is strictly below its potential only when the buffer is empty, in which case it coincides with the inflow rate. In this framework, the quantity

$$Y^f(t) \equiv - \inf_{0 \le s \le t} X^f(s),$$

represents the *cumulative potential outflow* that is lost prior to time $t$.

Now introduce $\Phi_t$ to be the set of all times $s$ up to $t$ at which the fluid level is zero, but no potential outflow is lost during $[s, t]$. Thus

$$\Phi_t \equiv \left\{ 0 \le s \le t \mid Z^f(s) = 0 \text{ and } Y^f(s) = Y^f(t) \right\}.$$

Equivalently, $\Phi_t$ consists of the times $s \le t$ such that the fluid level at time $t$ equals precisely the netflow over the period $[s, t]$. Formally,

$$\Phi_t = \left\{ 0 \le s \le t \mid Z^f(t) = X^f(t) - X^f(s) \right\}.$$

**Theorem 2.6.4 (FCLT)** We have the following functional central limit theorem for $Z^n$:

$$\lim_{n \uparrow \infty} \sqrt{n} \left( \frac{1}{n} Z^n(t) - Z^f(t) \right) \overset{\text{d}}{=} Z^d(t)$$

where

$$Z^d(t) \equiv W \left( \int_0^t [\alpha(r) + \mu(r)] \, dr \right) - \inf_{s \in \Phi_t} W \left( \int_0^s [\alpha(r) + \mu(r)] \, dr \right),$$

$W = \{W(t), t \ge 0\}$ is standard Brownian motion, and the convergence is weak with respect to Skorohod's $M_1$-topology on $D[0, \infty)$.

(The currently available proof of FCLT assumes that $Z^d$ has a finite number of discontinuities over finite subintervals of $[0, \infty)$.) The FCLT refines the FSLLN in *distribution*. It gives rise to the asymptotic expansion

$$Z^n(t) \stackrel{\mathrm{d}}{=} nZ^f(t) + \sqrt{n}Z^d(t) + o\left(\sqrt{n}\right),$$

from which the stochastic process $Z^d$ emerges as a second-order, *mesoscopic*, diffusion approximation for the deviation of $Z$ from its fluid approximation $Z^f$. Our FSLLN and FCLT are both consequences of

**Theorem 2.6.5 (Strong Approximation)** The parametrized family $\{Z^n\}$ can be realized on a probability space $(\Omega, \mathcal{F}, P)$, supporting two independent standard Brownian motions $W^+$ and $W^-$ in a way that

$$Z^n(t, \omega) = \tilde{X}^n(t, \omega) - \inf_{0 \le s \le t} \tilde{X}^n(s, \omega) + O(\log n) \quad \text{a.s.}$$

where

$$\tilde{X}^n(t) = n\int_0^t [\alpha(r) - \mu(r)]\,dr + W^+\left(n\int_0^t \alpha(r)\,dr\right) - W^-\left(n\int_0^t \mu(r)\,dr\right).$$

*Local Asymptotic Expansions*

The above asymptotic analysis of the $M_t/M_t/1$ queue can be further localized and refined. Specifically, the fluid approximation determines six time-regions, to be described momentarily, within each of which the mesoscopic expansion takes a different form. Let $\rho(t) \equiv \alpha(t)/\mu(t)$, for $t > 0$, and define

$$\rho^*(t) \equiv \sup_{0 \le s \le t} \frac{\int_s^t \alpha(r)\,dr}{\int_s^t \mu(r)\,dr}, \quad t > 0,$$

with the convention $\rho^*(0) = \alpha(0)/\mu(0)$. The quantity $\rho^*$ is the $M_t/M_t/1$ *traffic intensity function* introduced by Massey [1981]. It turns out that the functions $\rho$ and $\rho^*$ summarize the information embodied in the fluid model which is relevant to accelerating the stochastic model. In particular, the traffic intensity function $\rho^*$ identifies three exhaustive main asymptotic regions for $M_t/M_t/1$, given by:

Underloaded:      $\rho^*(t) < 1$;

Overloaded:      $\rho^*(t) > 1$;

Critically Loaded:   $\rho^*(t) = 1$.

The last case is further refined into the following four subregions:

Onset of Critical Loading: $\rho^*(t) = 1$, and there exists a sequence $\ell_n \uparrow t$ such that $\rho^*(\ell_n) < 1$, for all $n$;

Middle of Critical Loading: $\rho^*(t) = 1$, $\rho^* \geq 1$ on some open interval containing $t$, and there exists a sequence $\ell_n \uparrow t$ such that $\rho^*(\ell_n) = 1$ for all $n$;

End of Critical Loading: $\rho^*(t) = 1$, $\rho^* \geq 1$ on some open interval where $t$ is its right endpoint, there exists a sequence $\ell_n \uparrow t$ such that $\rho^*(\ell_n) = 1$ for all $n$, and there exists a sequence $r_n \downarrow t$ such that $\rho^*(r_n) < 1$ for all $n$;

End of Overloading: $\rho^*(t) = 1$, and $\rho^* > 1$ on some open interval where $t$ is its right endpoint.

It is possible for the time evolution of an $M_t/M_t/1$ queue to alternate among all the above regimes. (In contrast, only one regime applies to the time homogeneous $M/M/1$, where $\alpha(t) \equiv \alpha$, $\mu(t) \equiv \mu$: it is underloaded when $\alpha < \mu$, overloaded when $\alpha > \mu$ and critically loaded when $\alpha = \mu$.) Furthermore, based on Theorems 2.6.4 and 2.6.5, an asymptotic expansion can be tailored to each regime, as illustrated by the following two examples.

**Theorem 2.6.6** As the point $t$ varies through the middle or end of critical loading,

$$Z^n(t) \overset{\text{d}}{=} \sqrt{n} Z^d(t) + o(\sqrt{n}),$$

where $t = \sup \Phi_t$.

The limit $Z^d$ is continuous during the middle of critical loading, for almost all sample paths; on the other hand, for $t$ at the end of critical loading it is still left continuous for almost every sample path, but it is not right continuous with a positive probability.

**Theorem 2.6.7** As the point $t$ varies over the overloaded region,

$$Z^n(t) \overset{\text{d}}{=} n \int_{t^*}^{t} [\alpha(r) - \mu(r)] dr + \sqrt{n} \left[ Z^f(t^*) + \hat{W}(t^*, t) \right] + o(\sqrt{n}),$$

where

$$\hat{W}(s,t) = W \left( \int_0^t [\alpha(r) + \mu(r)] \, dr \right) - W \left( \int_0^s [\alpha(r) + \mu(r)] \, dr \right), \ 0 \leq s \leq t,$$

and $t^* = \sup \Phi_t < t$.

Over each open interval of time where overloading prevails, $t^*$ is independent of $t$. So for continuous $\alpha$ and $\mu$, a local maximum for the leading term of the asymptotic expansion for $Z^n$ will arise when $\alpha(t) = \mu(t)$, immediately after a time when $\alpha$ exceeds $\mu$. This corresponds to the phenomenon of the peak congestion or queue length lagging behind the peak arrival rate.

*Strategic Fluid and Diffusion Approximations*

Consider a periodic $M_t/M_t/1$ queue, that is $\alpha$ and $\mu$ in (2.135) and (2.136) are periodic. Suppose that $\alpha$ has period-length $T$, denote by

$$\bar{\alpha} = \frac{1}{T} \int_0^T \alpha(s)\, ds$$

the average inflow per period, and define $\bar{\mu}$ similarly. We now accelerate the time evolution by a factor of $n = 1, 2, \ldots$, as in Section 2.5 and in contrast to uniform acceleration. Formally, this entails looking at $Z^{(n)}(t) = Z(nt)$, $t \geq 0$, constructed from $X^{(n)}(t) = X(nt)$. Letting $n \uparrow \infty$ yields the M/M/1-like asymptotic expansions

$$Z^{(n)}(t) = n(\bar{\alpha} - \bar{\mu})^+ t + o(n) \quad \text{a.s.}$$

(linear fluid approximation, as in Section 2.5.1) and

$$Z^{(n)}(t) \overset{\mathrm{d}}{=} \begin{cases} n(\bar{\alpha} - \bar{\mu})t + \sqrt{n}W((\bar{\alpha} + \bar{\mu})t) + o(\sqrt{n}) & \text{if } \bar{\alpha} > \bar{\mu}, \\ \sqrt{n}[W((\bar{\alpha} + \bar{\mu})t) - \inf_{0 \leq s \leq t} W((\bar{\alpha} + \bar{\mu})s)] + o(\sqrt{n}) & \text{if } \bar{\alpha} = \bar{\mu}. \end{cases}$$

In real-world terms, these latter asymptotic expansions can be thought of as being appropriate for strategic planning, at the corporate level of decision making, where long-range goals are formulated. The time-horizon is then typically measured in quarters or years, hence details must be suppressed. In contrast, the time-inhomogeneous expansions might be suitable for operational/regulatory control, at the shop-floor level of decision making. Over there details count, since they must be responded to within a time-horizon of weeks or days, perhaps even hours or seconds.

## 2.7   References and Comments

*General Commentary:*  Descriptions of most discrete event dynamic systems are carried out at microscopic levels. Needless to say, we were mainly motivated by queueing networks, for which there exists an impressive existing body of knowledge. Much of it can be traced back to the pioneering works of Jackson [1963], Gordon and Newell [1967], Baskett et al. [1975] and Kelly [1979] on product-form queueing networks.

There is a fastly developing research on the approximations of queueing networks, including mesoscopic diffusion approximations and macroscopic fluid approximations. Here we mention only the pioneering works on diffusion approximations by Kingman [1965], Igelhart and Whitt [1970], Reiman [1984] and Harrison [1988]. Diffusion approximations are consequences of the strong approximations introduced in the next chapter (Chen and Mandelbaum [1992b]), to which readers are referred for further historical account and references.

The earliest systematic body of work on fluid approximations of networks is that of Newell, as summarized in Newell [1982]. There are various applications of microscopic fluid models, to manufacturing systems by, for example, Mitra [1988], Gershwin [1989], Chen and Yao [1992] and Kella and Whitt [1992], to communication systems by, for examples, Kosten [1974] and Anick, Mitra and Sondhi [1982], and to dynamic scheduling by Chen and Yao [1993]. Additional references are Vandergraft [1983], Chen and Mandelbaum [1991a], and Chen [1993].

As demonstrated in the introductory section, and supplemented by Part II (the next chapter), the mathematical framework of strong approximations unifies the macro and meso approximations for microscopic models. Examples of strong approximations for queueing systems are Zhang, Hsu and Wang [1990], Zhang [1990], Horváth [1992], and Mandelbaum and Massey [1992].

### Section 1

The Example of the closed queueing network is taken from Chen and Mandelbaum [1991b]. The stronger form of the FSAT, mentioned in Remark (1), implies the upper-bound part of FLDP, but not the lower-bound. We shall not discuss FLDP here any further, except for mentioning that FLDP actually implies FLIL. Strassen [1964] provides a deeper insight than our stated FLIL. (It is formulated, for example, by Csörgö and Révész [1981], as Theorems 3.3.2 and 1.3.2.) For references of the FLDP with applications, see Shwartz and Weiss [1993].

Proof of the equivalence between FSLLN and SLLN can be found in Glynn and Whitt [1988], Theorem 4. Glynn [1990] provides a tutorial on weak convergence and its applications, with a focus on diffusion approximations for queueing networks.

### Section 2

The linear complementarity result Proposition 2.2.1 dates back to Cottle and Veinott [1972]. Chen and Mandelbaum [1991c] generalized it to $P$ which is a stochastic matrix. Also see Yang [1993].

The reflection mapping in Theorem 2.2.4 and the $RBM_x(\mu, \Gamma^2)$ were introduced by Harrison and Reiman [1981]. Chen and Mandelbaum [1991c] generalized it to $P$ stochastic.

### Section 3

The time inhomogeneous fluid model is taken from the Introduction to Chen and Mandelbaum [1991a]. Krichagina et al. [1988] is another example of a state-dependent fluid model. Theorem 2.3.1 is proved in Chen [1990].

*Section 4*

This section is primarily from Chen and Mandelbaum [1991a], to which readers are referred if in need of complete proofs.

*Section 5*

Section 2.5.2 is taken from Chen and Mandelbaum [1991a]. Brémaud (1981) is a good reference for point processes, where with a point process representation, he constructed a Jackson queueing network. In proving Lemma 2.5.4, we used Theorem 1 of Liptser [1980], which Liptser attributed to Lepingle [1976/1977].

*Section 6*

The model of a manufacturing system with random interruptions was studied by Chen and Yao [1991,1992], and also studied by Kella and Whitt [1992] with a different approach.

The communication model was studied by Anick, Mitra and Sondhi [1982] (also see Kosten [1984] for the finite state birth-death process, and then generalized to the finite state Markov chain case by Stern and Elwalid [1991]; see also Elwalid and Mitra [1991]). Earlier, Kosten [1974] considered a limit case of Anick, Mitra and Sondhi (1982). Pan, Okazaki and Kino (1991) considered the case where the transmission capacity $c = 1$ and the number of active bursts are equivalent to the queue length in an $M/M/\infty$ queue. Finally, Mitra [1988] is also within the category of the models in Section 2.6.1.

Section 2.6.2 is part of Chen and Mandelbuam [1992a]. The two-station counter-example is from Perkins and Kumar [1989], and the dynamic scheduling control model was extended by Chen and Yao [1993] to cover networks. In particular, the single-station model with feedback recovers Klimov's priority scheme (Klimov [1974,1978]). The fluid scheduling approach in Chen and Yao [1993] has been implemented and tested in Connors et al. [1994] and Atkins and Chen [1993]. Perkins and Kumar [1989] also provides an algorithm that identifies an allocation process which leads to a stable fluid level process. Complete proofs of the stability of nonparametric open and closed Jackson networks can be found in Meyn and Down [1993] and Kaspi and Mandelbaum [1989], following the pioneering work of Borovkov [1986] and ideas from Sigman [1989,1990]. Recently, there has been some importance progress in the fluid approximation and the stability for multiclass queueing networks. Chen [1993] established the sufficient condition for the fluid approximation of multiclass queueing networks. Rybko and Stolyar [1991], Dai [1993], and Chen [1993] proved that the stability of the fluid network implies the stability of the corresponding queueing network with renewal arrival and service times. Kumar and Meyn [1993] established the stability of a class of multiclass queueing networks with Poisson arrivals and exponential services.

Section 2.6.3 is extracted from Mandelbaum and Massey [1992]. For readers familiar with Skorohod's $J_1$-topology, the following information on his $M_1$-topology is included for ease of reference.

$M_1$-convergence:    Define the completed graph $\mathcal{G}(x)$ of $x \in D$ to consists of all pairs $(t, \gamma) \in [0, \infty) \times R^1$ such that $x(t-) \leq \gamma \leq x(t+)$, with the convention $x(0-) = 0$. A parametric representation of $\mathcal{G}(x)$ is a function $(\tau, g) : [0, \infty) \to \mathcal{G}(x)$ which is onto, continuous, whose first component $\tau$ is non-decreasing. A sequence $x_n$ is $M_1$-convergent to $x$ if there exist parametric representations $(\tau_n, g_n)$ of $x_n$ which converge, uniformly on compact subsets of $[0, \infty)$, to some parametric representation $(\tau, g)$ of $x$. Formally, for all $t > 0$, $\|\tau_n - \tau\|_t \vee \|g_n - g\|_t \to 0$, as $n \uparrow \infty$, where

$$\|x\|_t = \sup_{0 \leq s \leq t} |x(s)|,$$

for any $x \in D$. $M_1$-convergence was introduced by Skorohod [1956], and shown by Pomerade [1976] to induce on $D$ a topology under which it is a Polish space. This $M_1$-topology is weaker than the more prevalent $J_1$-topolgy, but the latter turns out too strong for our purposes (as will be explained momentarily). $M_1$-convergence is metrizable, for example (similarly to Whitt [1980]) by

$$d(x_1, x_2) = \int_0^\infty e^{-t} \left[ 1 \wedge d_t(x_1, x_2) \right] dt,$$

where $d_t(x_1, x_2) = \inf(\|\tau_1 - \tau_2\|_t + \|g_1 - g_2\|_t)$, the infimum taken over all possible parametrizations $(\tau_i, g_i)$ of $x_i$, $i = 1, 2$.

We can now motivate the need for $M_1$-convergence in Theorem 2.6.4 (FCLT). The process $\tilde{X}^n$ has continuous sample paths, and so does $Z^f$. Thus, up to a negligible $O(\log n)/\sqrt{n}$ term, the left hand side of FCLT is continuous. The limit $Z^d$, on the other hand, need *not* be continuous. Since continuous functions can not converge to a discontinuos function in the commonly used $J_1$-topology (the "largest jump" functional is $J_1$-continuous), one must resort to $M_1$.

*Acknowledgments:* Hong Chen is supported in part by NSF grant DDM-89-09972, by NSERC grant OG0089698, and by a UBC-HSS Research Grant.

## 2.8   References

[1] Anick, D., Mitra, D. and Sondhi, M.M., Stochastic theory of a data-handling system with multiple sources, *Bell Sys. Tech. J.* **61**, 1971-1894, 1982.

[2] Anthony, R.N., *Planning and Control Systems: A Framework for Analysis*, Harvard University Press, Cambridge, Massachusetts, 1965.

[3] Atkins, D. and Chen, H., Performance evaluation of scheduling control of queueing networks: fluid model heuristics, preprint, 1993.

[4] Baskett, F., Chandy, K.M., Muntz, R.R. and Palacois, F.G., Open, closed and mixed networks of queues with different classes of customers, *J. ACM* **22**, 248–260, 1975.

[5] Borovkov, A.A., Limit theorems for queueing networks I, *Theor. Prob. Appl.* **31**, 413–427, 1986.

[6] Brémaud, P., *Point Processes and Queues: Martingale Dynamics*, Springer-Verlag, New York, 1981.

[7] Chen, H., Generalized regulated mapping, fluid and diffusion limits, unpublished note, 1990.

[8] Chen, H., Fluid Approximations and Stability of Multiclass Queueing Networks I: Work-Conserving Disciplines, submitted, 1993.

[9] Chen, H. and Mandelbaum, A., Discrete flow networks: bottleneck analysis and fluid approximations, *Math. of OR* **16**, 408–446, 1991a.

[10] Chen, H. and Mandelbaum, A., Discrete flow networks: diffusion approximations and bottlenecks, *Ann. of Prob.* **19**, 1463–1519, 1991b.

[11] Chen, H. and Mandelbaum, A., Leontief systems, RBV's and RBM's, in the *Proceedings of the Imperial College Workshop on Applied Stochastic Processes*, M.H.A. Davis and R.J. Elliott (eds.), Gordon and Breach Science Publishers, 1991c.

[12] Chen, H. and Mandelbaum, A., Open heterogeneous fluid networks, with applications to multiclass queues, preprint, 1992a.

[13] Chen, H. and Mandelbaum, A., Hierarchical modelling of stochastic networks, Part II: strong approximations, in the same volume, 1992b.

[14] Chen, H. and Yao, D.D., Studies on systems with random disruptions via fluid models, *Proceedings of the 1991 American Control Conference*, Boston, MA, 1991.

[15] Chen, H. and Yao, D.D., A fluid model for systems with random disruptions, *Operations Research* **40**, S239–S247, 1992.

[16] Chen, H. and Yao, D.D., Dynamic scheduling of a multi-class fluid network, *Operations Research* **41**, 1104 - 1115, 1993.

[17] Connors, D., Feigin, G. and Yao, D.D., Scheduling semiconductor lines using a fluid network model, *IEEE Trans. Robotics and Automation* (forthcoming), 1994.

[18] Cottle, R.W. and Veinott, A.F., Polyhedral sets having a least element, *Math. Prog.* **3**, 238–249, 1972.

[19] Csörgö, M. and Révész, P., *Strong Approximations in Probability and Statistics*, Academic Press, 1981.

[20] Dai, J.G., On the Positive Harris Recurrence for Multiclass Queueing Networks: a Unified Approach via Fluid Limit Models, submitted, 1993.

[21] Elwalid, A. and Mitra, D., Analysis and design of rate-based congestion control of high speed networks, I: stochastic fluid models, access regulation, *Queueing Systems* **9**, 29–64, 1991.

[22] Ethier, S.N. and Kurtz, T.G., *Markov Processes*, Wiley, 1986.

[23] Gershwin, S.B., Hierarchical flow control: A framework for scheduling and planning discrete events in manufacturing systems, *Proceedings of IEEE* **77**, 195–209, 1989.

[24] Glynn, P.W., Diffusion approximations, in *Stochastic Models, Handbooks in OR & MS, Vol. 2*, eds. D.P. Heyman and M.J. Sobel, North Holland, 145–198, 1990.

[25] Glynn, P.W. and Whitt, W., Ordinary CLT and WLLN versions of $L = \lambda W$, *Math. O.R.* **13**, 674–692, 1988.

[26] Goodman, J.B. and Massey, W.A., The non-ergodic Jackson network, *J. of Appl. Prob.* **21**, 860–869, 1984.

[27] Gordon ,W.J. and Newell, G.F., Closed queueing systems with exponential servers, *Operations Research* **15**, 254–265, 1967.

[28] Harrison, J.M., Brownian models of queueing networks with heterogeneous customer populations, in W. Fleming and P.L. Lions (eds.), *Stochastic Differential Systems, Stochastic Control Theory and Applications*, IMA Volume **10**, Springer-Verlag, 147–186, 1988.

[29] Harrison, J.M. and Reiman, M.I., Reflected Brownian motion on an orthant, *The Annals of Prob.* **9**, 302–308, 1981.

[30] Hax, A.C. and Candea, D., *Production and Inventory Management*, Prentice-Hall, 1984.

[31] Horváth, L., Strong Approximations of Open Queue Networks, *Math. Oper. Res.* **17**, 487–508, 1992.

[32] Igelhart, D.L. and Whitt, W., Multiple channel queues in heavy traffic, I and II, *Adv. Appl. Prob.* **2**, 150–177 and 355–364, 1970.

[33] Jackson, J.R., Jobshop-like queueing systems, *Management Science* **10**, 131–142, 1963.

[34] Kaspi, H. and Mandelbaum, A., On the ergodicity of a closed queueing network, technical report, Technion—Israel Institute of Technology, 1989.

[35] Kella, O. and Whitt, W., A stochastic storage system in a random environment, *Operations Research* **40**, S257–S262, 1992.

[36] Kelly, F.P., *Reversibility and Stochastic Networks*, Wiley, 1979.

[37] Kingman, J.F.C., The heavy traffic approximation in the theory of queues, in W.L. Smith et al. (eds.), *Proc. Symp. on Congestion Theory*, Univ. of North Carolina Press, 137–159, 1965.

[38] Klimov, G.P., Time sharing service systems I, *Theor. Prob. Appl.* **19**, 532–551, 1974.

[39] Klimov, G.P., Time sharing service systems II, *Theor. Prob. Appl.* **23**, 314–421, 1978.

[40] Kolmós, Major and Tusnády, An approximation of partial sums of independent RV's, and the sample DF, I; II, *Z. Wahrsch. verw. Gebiete* **32**, 111–131, 1975; **34**, 33–58, 1976.

[41] Kosten, L., Stochastic theory of a multi-entry buffer (1), *Delft Progress Report* **1**, 10–18, 1974.

[42] Kosten, L., Stochastic theory of data handling systems with groups of multiple sources, in *Performance of Computer-Communication Systems*, eds. H. Rudin and W. Bux, Elsevier, Amsterdam, 321–331, 1984.

[43] Krichagina, E., Liptser, R.SH. and Pukhalskh, A.A., Diffusion approximation of systems with arrival depending on queue and arbitrary service distribution, *Theory Proba. Appl.* **33**, 114–124, 1988.

[44] Kumar, P.R. and Meyn, S.P., Stability of Queueing Networks and Scheduling Policies, tech. rep., C.S.L., University of Illinois, 1993.

[45] Lepingle, D., Sur le comportment asymptotique des martingales locales, *Lecture Notes in Mathematics* **649**, 148–161, 1976/1977.

[46] Liptser, R.SH., A strong law of large numbers for local martingales, *Stochastics* **3**, 217–228, 1980.

[47] Mandelbaum, A., The dynamic complementarity problem, tech. rep., Stanford University, 1989.

[48] Mandelbaum, A. and Massey, W., Strong approximations for time dependent queues, tech. rep., AT&T Bell Lab., Murray Hill, 1992.

[49] Massey, W., *Nonstationary Queueing Networks*, Ph.D. dissertation, Stanford University, 1981.

[50] Meyn, S.P. and Down, D., Stability of generalized Jackson networks, *Ann. Appl. Prob.*, 1993.

[51] Mitra, D., Stochastic theory of a fluid model of producers and consumers coupled by a buffer, *Adv. Appl. Prob.* **20**, 646–676, 1988.

[52] Newell, G.F., *Applications of Queueing Theory*, Chapman-Hall, 1982.

[53] Pan, H., Okazaki, H. and Kino, I., Analysis of a gradual input model for bursty traffic in ATM, *Proceedings of the 13th International Teletraffic Congress*, Copenhagen, 795–800, 1990.

[54] Perkins, J. and Kumar, P.R., Stable, distributed, real-time scheduling of flexible manufacturing/assembly/disassembly systems, *IEEE Transactions on Automatic Control* **34**, 139–148, 1989.

[55] Pomerade, J.-M.L., *A Unified Approach via Graphs to Skorohod's Topologies on the Function Space D*, Ph.D dissertation, Department of Statistics, Yale University, 1976.

[56] Reiman, M.I., Open queueing networks in heavy traffic, *Math. of O.R.* **9**, 441–458, 1984.

[57] Rybko, A.N. and Stolyar, A.L., On the Ergodicity of Stochastic Processes Describing Open Queueing Networks, *Problemy Peredachi Informatsii* **28**, 2–26, 1991.

[58] Schweitzer, P.J., Bottleneck Determination, Disney, R.L. and Otts, T.J. (eds.), *Applied Prob.- Computer Science, The Interface*, Vol. **I**, 471–485, Birkhauser, 1981.

[59] Sethi, S. and Zhang, Q., *Hierarchical Decision Making in Stochastic Manufacturing Systems* (forthcoming), 1993.

[60] Sethi, S., Zhang, Q. and Zhou, X., Hierarchical Controls in Stochastic Manufacturing Systems with Machines in Tandem, *Stochastics and Stochastics Reports* (forthcoming), 1993.

[61] Shwartz, A. and Alan, W., *Large Deviations for Performance Analysis: queues, communication and computing* (forthcoming), 1993.

[62] Sigman, K., Notes on the stability of closed queueing networks, *J. Appl. Prob.* **26**, 678–682, 1989.

[63] Sigman, K., The stability of open queueing networks, *Stochastic Processes and Their Applications* **35**, 11–25, 1990.

[64] Simon, H.A., *The Science of the Artificial*, 2nd Edition, MIT Press, 1981.

[65] Skorohod, A.V., Limit theorems for stochastic processes, *Theor. Probability Appl.* **1**, 261–290, 1956.

[66] Stern, T.E. and Elwalid, A.I., Analysis of separable Markov-modulated rate models for information-handling systems, *Adv. Appl. Prob.* **23**, 105–139, 1991.

[67] Strassen, V., An invariance principle for the law of the iterated logarithm, *Z. Wahrscheinlichkeitstheorie verw. Gebiete* **3**, 211-226, 1964.

[68] Verdergraft, J.M., A fluid flow model of networks of queues, *Management Science* **29**, 1198–1208, 1983.

[69] Whitt, W., Heavy traffic theorems for queues: a survey, in A.B. Clarke (ed.), *Mathematical Methods in Queueing Theory*, Springer Verlag, 1974.

[70] Whitt, W., Some useful functions for functional limit theorems, *Math. OR.* **5**, 67–85, 1980.

[71] Woods, L.C., *The Thermodynamics of Fluid Systems*, Oxford University Press, 1975.

[72] Yang, P., Least Control for a Class of Constrained Linear Stochastic Systems, *Math. Oper. Res.* **18**, 275–291, 1993.

[73] Zhang, H., Hsu, G. and Wang, R., Strong approximations for multiple channel queues in heavy traffic, *J. Appl. Prob.* **28**, 658–670, 1990.

[74] Zhang, H., Strong approximations for open networks in heavy traffic, preprint, 1990.

# 3
# Hierarchical Modeling of Stochastic Networks, Part II: Strong Approximations

Hong Chen
Avi Mandelbaum

## 3.1 Introduction

The goal in this part is to establish strong approximations for a family of open queueing networks. We cover, in particular, nonparametric Jackson networks. These are the classical open Jackson queueing networks, but without the parametric assumptions of exponential interarrival and service times (Section 2.5.2 of Part I). The basic results are Functional Strong Approximations (FSAT, Theorem 3.4.1) and a Functional Law of Iterated Logarithm (FLIL, Theorem 3.4.2). These readily imply fluid approximations, formalized by a Functional Strong Law of Large Numbers (FSLLN, Corollary 3.4.3), and diffusion approximations, formalized by a Functional Central Limit Theorem (FCLT, Corollary 3.4.4).

Our approach entails representing performance measures of interest, for example queue-length, as transformations of primitives, for example interarrival and service times. These transformations turn out to be Lipschitz continuous. Thus limit theorems and approximations of the primitives, specifically FSAT's, FSLLN's and FCLT's, carry over to the desired performance measures, and with the same order of error.

In the literature, the prevalent justifications for fluid and diffusion approximations have been FSLLN's and FCLT's. Strong approximations provide a framework which is conceptually different and, whenever applicable, it is in our opinion also superior: the framework is simple and direct - one first derives strong approximations, without any explicit rescaling; it unifies the classical FSLLN's, FLIL's and FCLT's - and these theorems, which are magnifying by-products of the approximations, reveal further insight; the framework also enables quantification of errors, in a way that is visibly monotone in the assumptions on the primitives - as moments of higher order are assumed finite, the better the approximation; finally, the mathematical toll for making strong approximations rigorous is more-than-minimal moment-conditions on the primitives - but as far as current applications are concerned, this toll seems negligible.

## 3.2   The Model

### 3.2.1   Primitives and Dynamics

Our queueing network consists of $K$ service stations, indexed by $k = 1, \cdots, K$. Each station $k$ constitutes a server, called server $k$, and a queue, called queue $k$. Server $k$ is dedicated to serving customers waiting in queue $k$. After being served, customers either leave the network or rejoin one of its queues in anticipation of additional service.

The network's dynamics are described in terms of the following vector primitives, the coordinates of which are all integer-valued: a $K$-dimensional nonnegative vector $Z(0)$, and a sequence of $K$-dimensional RCLL vector processes $F^k = \{F^k(t), t \geq 0\}$, $k = 0, 1, ..., K$. The $k$th coordinate of $Z(0)$, $Z_k(0)$, represents the number of jobs initially at station $k$. The $k$th coordinate of $F^0(t)$, $F_k^0(t)$, indicates the accumulated number of exogenous arrivals to station $k$ up to time $t$. For $j, k = 1, ..., K$, with $j \neq k$, the $j$th coordinate of $F^k(s)$, $F_j^k(s)$, models the number of service completions at station $k$, which switch directly to station $j$ during its first $s$ units of busy-time; the negative of the $k$th coordinate, $-F_k^k(s)$, $k = 1, ..., K$, stands for the total number of departures (service completions minus immediate feedbacks) from station $k$ during its first $s$ units of busy time.

The sample paths of the *flow* processes $F_j^0$, $F_j^k$, $j \neq k$, and $-F_k^k$ are assumed to be nondecreasing, all with $F^k(0) = 0$, $k = 0, \ldots, K$. Adding the assumption that $-F_k^k$ has only unit jumps suffices to guarantee existence of the *queue length* process $Z = \{Z(t), t \geq 0\}$ and the *busy time* process $B = \{B(t), t \geq 0\}$. They are implicitly defined as the unique solutions to the *flow-balance* relation

$$Z(t) = Z(0) + F^0(t) + \sum_{k=1}^{K} F^k[B_k(t)], \tag{3.1}$$

subject to the *work-conserving* constraints

$$B_k(t) = \int_0^t 1[Z_k(s) > 0]ds, \qquad k = 1, ..., K \tag{3.2}$$

(Note that $Z(t) \geq 0$ must hold at all $t \geq 0$.)

### 3.2.2   Underlying Assumptions and Parameters

The primitives $Z(0)$ and $F^k$, $k = 0, \ldots, K$, are defined on a common probability space and, strictly for convenience, they are taken to be mutually independent. For $k = 0, \ldots, K$, we assume that there exist $K$-dimensional nonnegative vectors $\alpha^k$, $K \times K$ covariance matrices $\Gamma^k$, $K$-dimensional mutually independent standard Wiener processes $W^k = \{W^k(t), t \geq 0\}$ such that

$$FSAT: \quad \sup_{0 \leq t \leq T} |F^k(t) - \alpha^k t - (\Gamma^k)^{1/2} W^k(t)| = o(T^{1/r}), \quad \text{as } T \uparrow \infty, (3.3)$$

for some scalar $r > 2$. It is further assumed that the $K \times K$ matrix $[\alpha^1, ..., \alpha^K]$ has the form

$$[\alpha^1, ..., \alpha^K] = [P' - I]\mathrm{diag}(\mu), \tag{3.4}$$

where $P$ is a $K \times K$ substochastic matrix with spectral radius less than unity, and $\mu$ is a positive $K$-dimensional vector.

One interprets $\alpha_k^0$, the $k$th coordinate of $\alpha^0$, as the long-run average rate of exogenous arrivals to station $k$; $\mu_k$, the $k$th coordinate of $\mu$, as the long-run average potential rate of service completions from station $k$; out of these completions, a long-run average fraction $p_{jk}$, the $(j, k)$th component of $P$, switch directly to station $k$. We refer to $\alpha^0$ and $\mu$ as the *arrival* and *service* rates, and to $P$ as the *transition* matrix.

For later use we record that Strassen's FLIL for the Brownian motion (prior to (1.7) in Part I), applied to $W^k$ in (3.3), yields

$$FLIL: \quad \sup_{0 \leq t \leq T} |F^k(t) - \alpha^k t| = O(\sqrt{T \log\log T}), \quad \text{as } T \uparrow \infty, \tag{3.5}$$

for $k = 0, ..., K$.

### 3.2.3 Nonparametric Jackson Networks

Our framework, in particular FSAT (3.3) and FLIL (3.5), covers nonparametric open Jackson queueing networks (Section 2.5.2 in Part I). Here the flows are constructed from lower-level primitives, which constitute the following mutually independent $K$-dimensional entities: an arrival process $A$, a service process $S$ and a routing sequence $\xi^k = \{\xi^k(\ell), \ell = 1, 2, \cdots\}$. The $k$th component of $A$, $A_k = \{A_k(t), t \geq 0\}$, is a renewal process that models exogenous arrivals to station $k$. The $k$th component of $S$, $S_k = \{S_k(u), u \geq 0\}$, is a renewal process that models service completions from station $k$: $S_k(u)$ represents the number of service completions by server $k$ during its first $u$ units of busy-time. Finally, $\xi^k = \{\xi^k(\ell), \ell = 1, 2, \cdots\}$ models the routing mechanism enforced at station $k$: its $j$th component $\xi_j^k(\ell)$ is the indicator of the event that the $\ell$th customer served at station $k$, upon completion of its service, is routed directly to queue $j$, $j = 1, \cdots, K$. (Formally, $\xi_j^k(\ell)$ equals 1 when the event that it indicates occurs and 0 when it does not.) To ease the notation introduce

$$R^k(n) = \sum_{\ell=1}^{n} [\xi^k(\ell) - e^k], \quad n = 0, 1, 2, \ldots, \tag{3.6}$$

for $k = 1, \ldots, K$, and denote its coordinates by $R_j^k(t)$, $j, k = 1, \ldots, K$, $e^k$ is the $K$-dimensional $k$th unit vector, $k = 1, \ldots, K$. The connection with the model in Section 3.2.1 is revealed through

$$F^0(t) = A(t), \tag{3.7}$$
$$F^k(t) = R^k[S_k(t)], \quad k = 1, \ldots, K, \tag{3.8}$$

at all $t \geq 0$.

Consider station $k$, $k = 1, \ldots, K$. We assume that the renewal processes $A_k$ and $S_k$ are constructed from i.i.d. intervals with finite moments of order $r$, for some $r > 2$. Then FSAT's can be proved, that establish a probability space, supporting independent standard Wiener processes $W^k$, $k = 0, \ldots, K$, for which (3.3) holds. The parameters $\alpha^k$ and $\Gamma^k$ emerge from elementary calculations that we now outline.

Let the mean service time at station $k$ be $1/\mu_k$, and denote its squared coefficient of variation by $c_k^S$; the corresponding parameters for the exogenous interarrival times are $1/\alpha_k^0$ and $c_k^A$. A FSAT for the renewal process $A_j$ then takes the form

$$\sup_{0 \leq t \leq T} |A_j(t) - \alpha_j^0 t - \alpha_j^0 c_j^A W_j^0(t)| = o(T^{1/r}), \quad \text{as } T \uparrow \infty,$$

and the independence of $A_j$, $j = 1, \ldots, K$, yields (3.3) for $k = 0$, with means $\alpha^0 = (a_k^0)$ and covariance matrix

$$\Gamma_{j\ell}^0 = \alpha_j^0 c_j^A \delta_{j\ell}, \quad j, \ell = 1, \ldots, K \tag{3.9}$$

Similar FSAT's apply to each $S_k$, with asymptotic mean $\mu_k$ and variance $\mu_k c_k^S$. They are combined with FSAT's for sums of i.i.d. vectors, as in (3.6), to FSAT's for compound renewal processes, as in (3.8). The asymptotic means and covariances are calculated as follows.

Let $r^k(\ell)$, $l = 1, 2, \ldots$, denote the summands of $R^k$ in (3.6). By Wald's identities,

$$E[F^k(t)] = E[S_k(t)] E[r^k(1)],$$
$$\text{Cov}[F^k(t)] = E[S_k(t)] \text{Cov}[r^k(1)] + \text{Var}[S_k(t)] E[r^k(1)]E[r^k(1)]'.$$

Based on the multinomial distribution of the $\xi^k(\ell)$'s,

$$E[r_j^k(1)] = p_{kj} - \delta_{kj},$$
$$\text{Cov}[r_j^k(1), r_\ell^k(1)] = \text{Cov}[\xi_j^k(1), \xi_\ell^k(1)] = p_{kj} (\delta_{j\ell} - p_{k\ell}).$$

Finally, the asymptotic covariance of $F^k$, $\Gamma^k = [\Gamma_{j\ell}^k]$, comes out to be

$$\Gamma_{j\ell}^k = \mu_k p_{kj} (\delta_{j\ell} - p_{k\ell}) + \mu_k c_k^S (p_{kj} - \delta_{kj}) (p_{k\ell} - \delta_{k\ell}), \quad j, \ell = 1, \ldots K, \tag{3.10}$$

for $k = 1, \ldots K$.

## 3.3  Preliminaries

We briefly recall some concepts and results (from Part I), which are used in the sequel.

### 3.3.1  Traffic Equations and Bottlenecks

The *effective* arrival rate vector $\lambda$ is the unique solution to the (nonlinear) traffic equations

$$\lambda = \alpha^0 + P'(\lambda \wedge \mu) \tag{3.11}$$

Its $k$th coordinate, $\lambda_k$, represents the long-run average arrival rate to station $k$ (see Section 2.4 of Part I). The quantity $\rho_k = \lambda_k/\mu_k$ is called the *traffic intensity* at station $j$. Station $k$ is a *nonbottleneck* if $\rho_k < 1$, *balanced bottleneck* if $\rho_k = 1$, and *strict bottleneck* if $\rho_k > 1$. Denote by $a = \{k : \rho_k < 1\}$, $b = \{k : \rho_k = 1\}$, and $c = \{k : \rho_k > 1\}$, the set of nonbottlenecks, ballanced bottlenecks and strict bottlenecks respectively.

### 3.3.2  The Oblique Reflection Mapping

Let $D^K$ be the set of $K$-dimensional RCLL (right-continuous and with left limits) functions, and let $D_0^K = \{x \in D^K : x(0) \geq 0\}$. Let $P$ be a $K \times K$ nonnegative matrix with spectral radius strictly less than unity. The oblique reflection mapping (Section 2.2 of Part I) is characterized in terms of

**Theorem 3.3.1** For any $X \in \mathcal{D}_0^K$ there exists a unique pair of $(Y, Z) \in \mathcal{D}_0^{2K}$ satisfying at all $t \geq 0$

$$Z(t) = X(t) + [I - P']Y(t) \geq 0, \tag{3.12}$$
$$dY(t) \geq 0, \qquad Y(0) = 0, \qquad \text{and} \tag{3.13}$$
$$\int_0^\infty Z_k(t)\, dY_k(t) = 0, \quad k = 1, \ldots, K \tag{3.14}$$

Introduce the mappings $Y = \Psi_P(X)$ and $Z = \Phi_P(X)$. Then $\Psi_P$ and $\Phi_P$ are both Lipschitz continuous on $\mathcal{D}_0^K$ (with respect to the uniform norm on compact subsets of $[0, \infty)$). Furthermore, $Y = \Psi_P(X)$ is the least among the $Y$'s that satisfy (3.12) and (3.13).

*Remarks:*

(1) $Y = \Psi_P(X)$ also has a fixed-point characterization. It uniquely satisfies

$$Y(t) = \sup_{0 \leq s \leq t} [P'Y(s) - X(s)]^+, \quad t \geq 0.$$

(See Harrison and Reiman (1981).)

(2)  When the dependence on $P$ is obvious, we write $\Psi$ and $\Phi$ instead of $\Psi_P$ and $\Phi_P$.

### 3.3.3  Reflected Brownian Motion on the Orthant

Let $X$ be a $K$-dimensional Brownian motion, starting at $x = X(0) \geq 0$, with drift vector $\theta$ and covariance matrix $\Gamma$. The process $Z = \{Z(t), t \geq 0\}$, whose sample paths are determined by $Z = \Phi_P(X)$, is known as a Reflected Brownian motion on the nonnegative $K$-dimensional orthant. It will be denoted by $Z = RBM_x(\theta, \Gamma)$. The process $Y = \{Y(t), t \geq 0\}$, with sample paths $Y = \Psi_P(X)$, is called the regulator of $RBM_x(\theta, \Gamma)$.

The process $RBM_x(\theta, \Gamma)$, $x \geq 0$, is a diffusion process (strong Markov process with continuous sample paths). The $k$th component $Y_k$ of its regulator $Y$ is its local time on the orthant's face $\{z \geq 0 : z'e^k = 0\}$.
*Remarks:*

(1)  We believe that RBM is Harris recurrent if and only if $[I - P']^{-1}\theta \leq 0$. It has been proved that RBM is positive recurrent if and only if the inequalities are all strict, in which case RBM enjoys a unique stationary/limiting distribution with a density.

(2)  Suppose that $[I - P']^{-1}\theta < 0$ and that $P_{kk} = 0$, $k = 1, ..., K$. Under the structural constraints

$$2\Gamma_{jk} = -(P_{kj}\Gamma_{kk} + P_{jk}\Gamma_{jj}) \qquad \text{for} \qquad j \neq k, \tag{3.15}$$

the stationary density has the product-form

$$f(z) = \prod_{k=1}^{K} \eta_k e^{-\eta_k z_k}, \qquad z = (z_1, ..., z_K) \geq 0, \tag{3.16}$$

where $\eta = (\eta_k)$ is given by

$$\eta = -diag(\Gamma)^{-1}[I - P']^{-1}\theta \tag{3.17}$$

Thus, at stationarity or in the limit, $Z$ with (3.15) has independent coordinates, the $k$th one being exponential with mean $1/\eta_k$. (The constraints (3.15) are necessary and sufficient for the product form (3.16).)

## 3.4   The Main Results

We start with FSAT in Section 3.4.1 and FLIL in Section 3.4.2. These imply fluid approximations in Section 3.4.3 and diffusion approximations Section 3.4.4.

### 3.4.1  Functional Strong Approximations

**Theorem 3.4.1** Suppose that the primitives satisfy the FSAT (3.3) with $r > 2$. Then

$$\sup_{0 \le t \le T} |Z(t) - \tilde{Z}(t)| = o(T^{1/r'}), \quad \text{as } T \uparrow \infty, \tag{3.18}$$

where $Z$ is the queue length process in (3.1)-(3.2), $\tilde{Z} = RBM_{Z(0)}(\theta, \Gamma)$ given by

$$\tilde{Z} = \tilde{X} + [I - P']\tilde{Y}, \tag{3.19}$$
$$\tilde{X}(t) = Z(0) + \theta t + \Gamma^{1/2} W(t), \quad t \ge 0, \tag{3.20}$$
$$\theta = \alpha^0 + [P' - I]\mu, \tag{3.21}$$
$$\Gamma = \Gamma^0 + \sum_{k=1}^{K} (\rho_k \wedge 1)\Gamma^k, \tag{3.22}$$
$$\tilde{Y} = \Phi_P(\tilde{X}), \tag{3.23}$$

and $W$ is a $K$-dimensional standard Wiener process. In (3.18) we can choose $r' = r$ if $r < 4$ and any $r' < 4$ when $r \ge 4$.

*Remarks:*

(1) For $r \ge 4$, the bound of the FSAT (3.18) can be improved as follows:

$$\sup_{0 \le t \le T} |Z(t) - \tilde{Z}(t)| = O((T \log\log T)^{1/4} (\log T)^{1/2}) \quad \text{as } T \uparrow \infty.$$

[This can be justified by taking $g(T) = 5(\log T)^{1/2}$ in (3.54) and (3.55), in the proof of the theorem.] A stronger result would be that (3.18) holds with $r' = r$, $r > 2$, (regardless of whether $r < 4$ or $r \ge 4$). We are not sure, however, whether such a result actually holds.

(2) Let $I(t) = et - B(t)$ represent cumulative idle time, where $e$ is a vector of ones. Then

$$\sup_{0 \le t \le T} |I(t) - \text{diag}(\mu)^{-1}\tilde{Y}(t)| = o(T^{1/r'}).$$

(3) The theorem is specialized in Section 3.5 to nonparametric Jackson networks, with $\Gamma$ expressed in terms of arrival and service rates, transition probabilities and various coefficients of variations.

(4) Consider a queueing network without bottlenecks, namely $b = c = \emptyset$. This is equivalent to $\rho < e$, in which case

$$\rho = \text{diag}(\mu)^{-1}[I - P']^{-1}\alpha^0.$$

Now $\rho < e$ if and only if $[I - P']^{-1}\theta < 0$, for $\theta$ in (3.21). Thus, $\tilde{Z}$ has a unique stationary/limit density. Under (3.15), this density has the product form (3.6) with

$$\eta_k = \frac{2\mu_k(1 - \rho_k)}{\Gamma_{kk}}, \qquad k = 1, ..., K.$$

(5) We believe that, in general, $\tilde{Z}_a$ is positive recurrent, $\tilde{Z}_b$ is null recurrent and $\tilde{Z}_c$ is transient.

### 3.4.2  Functional Laws of the Iterated Logarithm

**Theorem 3.4.2** Suppose that FLIL (3.5) is satisfied. Then, as $T \uparrow \infty$,

$$\sup_{0 \le t \le T} |Z(t) - \bar{Z}(t)| = O(\sqrt{T\log\log T}), \tag{3.24}$$

$$\sup_{0 \le t \le T} |B(t) - (\rho \wedge e)t| = O(\sqrt{T\log\log T}), \tag{3.25}$$

where $Z$ and $B$ are, respectively, the queue and busy time processes in (3.1) and (3.2),

$$\bar{Z} = \bar{X} + [I - P']\bar{Y}, \tag{3.26}$$

$$\bar{X}(t) = Z(0) + \theta t, \tag{3.27}$$

$$\bar{Y} = \Phi(\bar{X}), \tag{3.28}$$

and $\theta$ is as in (3.21).

*Remarks:*

(1) The deterministic processes $\bar{Z}_k$, $k = 1, \ldots, K$, represent buffer contents of the linear fluid network $(\alpha, P, \mu)$, with initial inventory level $Z(0)$, as introduced in Section 2.4 of Part I, and described in Theorem 2.4.4 there.

(2) The approximations (3.24)-(3.25) still prevail with $\bar{Z}$ being buffer contents of the same linear fluid network $(\alpha, P, \mu)$, but with $Z(0) = 0$. [cf. Lemma 2.4.5.] Then $\bar{Z}(t) = [\lambda - \mu]^+ t$, where $\lambda$ is the effective arrival rate (see Remark 2 that follows Theorem 2.4.4 in Part I).

### 3.4.3  FSLLN's and Fluid Approximations

Recall the "bar" notation

$$\bar{Z}^n(t) = \frac{1}{n}Z(nt) \qquad \text{and} \qquad \bar{B}^n(t) = \frac{1}{n}B(nt).$$

The following FSLLN is an immediate consequence of Theorem 3.4.2.

**Corollary 3.4.3 (FSLLN)** Under the assumptions of Theorem 3.4.2,

$$(\bar{Z}^n, \bar{B}^n) \to (\bar{Z}, \bar{B}), \quad \text{u.o.c.,} \quad \text{as } n \to \infty, \tag{3.29}$$

where

$$\bar{B}(t) = (\rho \wedge e)\, t, \quad \text{and}$$
$$\bar{Z}(t) = [\lambda - \mu]^+ t.$$

*Remark:*    This corollary is, in fact, a consequence of Theorem 2.5.2 from Part I, specialized to a sequence of networks that does not vary with $n$. Consequently, the characterization of the fluid model in Section 3.4.2 of Part I applies here as well.

## 3.4.4  FCLT's and Diffusion Approximations

Recall that $a$, $b$ and $c$ represent nonbottleneck, balanced and strict bottleneck stations, respectively. Introduce the "hat" notation

$$\hat{Z}^n(t) = \sqrt{n}\left[\tfrac{1}{n}Z(nt) - (\lambda - \mu)^+ nt\right],$$
$$\hat{B}^n(t) = \sqrt{n}\left[(\rho \wedge e)t - \tfrac{1}{n}B(nt)\right].$$

The following FCLT is a consequence of Theorem 3.4.1.

**Corollary 3.4.4 (FCLT)** Under the assumption of Theorem 3.4.1, we have

$$(\hat{Z}^n, \hat{B}^n) \xrightarrow{d} (\hat{Z}, \hat{B}), \quad \text{as } n \to \infty, \tag{3.30}$$

where

$$
\begin{align}
\hat{Z}_a &= 0, \tag{3.31}\\
\hat{Z}_b &= \hat{X}_b(t) + [I - \hat{P}_b']\hat{Y}_b(t), \tag{3.32}\\
\hat{X}_b &= \xi_b + P_{ab}'[I - P_a']\xi_a, \tag{3.33}\\
\hat{X}_b &= \xi(t) = \Gamma^{1/2}W(t), \tag{3.34}\\
\hat{Y}_b &= \Psi_{\hat{P}_b}(\hat{X}_b), \tag{3.35}\\
\hat{P}_b &= P_b + P_{ba}[I - P_a]^{-1}P_{ab}, \tag{3.36}\\
\hat{Z}_c &= \xi_c + P_{ac}'[I - P_a']^{-1}\xi_a - \hat{P}_{bc}'\hat{Y}_b, \tag{3.37}\\
\hat{P}_{bc} &= P_{bc} + P_{ba}[I - P_a]^{-1}P_{ac}, \tag{3.38}\\
\hat{B}_a &= \mathrm{diag}(\mu_a)^{-1}[I - P_a']^{-1}[\xi_a - P_{ba}'\hat{Y}_b], \tag{3.39}\\
\hat{B}_b &= -\mathrm{diag}(\mu_b)^{-1} \cdot \hat{Y}_b, \tag{3.40}\\
\hat{B}_c &= 0, \tag{3.41}
\end{align}
$$

$\Gamma$ is the covariance matrix in (3.22), and $W$ is a $K$-dimensional standard Wiener process as in (3.20)).

*Remarks:*

(1) The corollary demonstrates that the diffusion limit of queue length vanishes at the nonbottlenecks $a$. The diffusion approximation of the balanced subnetwork $b$ is a $|b|$-dimensional reflected Brownian motion. The diffusion limit for queue lengths at strict bottlenecks requires centering. This is because $Z_c$ builds up at a rate of $(\lambda_c - \mu_c)$, which is also the buildup rate of the corresponding fluid approximation [cf. Corollary 3.4.3]. After both centering and rescaling, $Z_c^n$ converges to the semimartingale $Z_c$ in (3.37): the martingale component of $Z_c$ is a Brownian motion, which is associated with $a$ and $c$; its bounded-variation component is nonincreasing and is associated with $b$ [see (3.35)].

(2) The corollary provides limits in light-traffic (no bottlenecks: $b = c = \emptyset$). For example, the centered and rescaled busy time processes $\hat{B}^n$ converges weakly to the driftless Brownian motion

$$\hat{B} = \text{diag}(\mu)^{-1}[I - P']^{-1}\xi,$$

with $\xi$ in (3.34).

(3) Proposition 2.4.2 in Part I guarantees the existence of the inverse $[I - P_a]^{-1}$.

## 3.5    Fitting Parametes

In Section 3.5.1 we provide two approximations to the nonparametric Jackson queueing network from Section 3.2.3: a first order approximation by a fluid network, which is supported by the FLIL Theorem 3.4.2, and a refined second order approximation by an RBM, which is based on the FSAT Theorem 3.4.1. These are specialized in Section 3.5.2 to the product-form and single-station cases.

### 3.5.1    *Nonparametric Jackson Networks*

At a first order, the queue length process $Z$ can be approximated by the buffer content process $\bar{Z}$ of the linear fluid model

$$\begin{aligned}
\bar{Z} &= \bar{X} + [I - P']\bar{Y}, \\
\bar{X}(t) &= Z(0) + [\alpha^0 + (P' - I)\mu]t, \\
\bar{Y} &= \Phi(\bar{X}).
\end{aligned}$$

The order of the approximation is given by

$$\sup_{0 \le t \le T} |Z(t) - \bar{Z}(t)| = O(\sqrt{T \log\log T}), \quad \text{as } T \uparrow \infty.$$

A refined second-order approximation is the RBM

$$\tilde{Z} = \tilde{X} + [I - P']\tilde{Y},$$
$$\tilde{X}(t) = Z(0) + [\alpha^0 + (P' - I)\mu]\,t + \Gamma^{1/2}\,W(t),$$
$$\tilde{Y} = \Phi(\tilde{X}),$$

where $W$ is a $K$-dimensional Wiener process. The covariance matrix $\Gamma = [\Gamma_{k\ell}]$ is calculated from (3.9), (3.10) and (3.22), and takes the form

$$\Gamma_{k\ell} = \alpha_k^0 c_k^A \delta_{k\ell} + \sum_{j=1}^{K} (\lambda_j \wedge \mu_j)\left[p_{jk}(\delta_{k\ell} - p_{j\ell}) + c_j^S(p_{jk} - \delta_{jk})(p_{j\ell} - \delta_{j\ell})\right].$$

Assuming finite moments of order $r > 2$, and an ambient probability space on which all our stochastic elements are defined, the error is quantified by the pathwise bounds

$$\sup_{0 \le t \le T} |Z(t) - \tilde{Z}(t)| = o(T^{1/r}), \quad \text{as } T \uparrow \infty.$$

### 3.5.2   Product Form and Single Station

Consider the case of no-bottlenecks ($\rho < e$). It is then plausible to approximate the steady-state of $Z$ by that of $\tilde{Z}$. In particular, when (3.15) approximately applies, and in view of Remark 4 below Theorem 3.4.1, the steady-state queue-lengths $Z_k(\infty)$, $k = 1, \ldots, K$, are approximately independent exponential, with means

$$E[Z_k(\infty)] \approx \frac{\Gamma_{kk}}{2\mu_k(1 - \rho_k)}.$$

The special case of a single station ($K = 1$) reduces to

$$E[Z(\infty)] \approx \frac{\rho}{(1 - \rho)} \left[\frac{(c^A + c^S)}{2} + \frac{p(1 - c^S)}{2}\right](1 - p),$$

where $p$ is the probability of feedback, and $\rho = \alpha^0/[\mu(1 - p)]$. Finally, $p = 0$ reduces to the classical approximation

$$E[Z(\infty)] \approx \frac{\rho}{(1 - \rho)} \frac{(c^A + c^S)}{2},$$

which originated in Kingman's pioneering work on the G/G/1 queue in heavy traffic.

## 3.6   Proof of the Main Results

We start with the proof of Theorem 3.4.2. We then use it to prove Theorem 3.4.1. Finally we prove Corollary 3.4.3 and Corollary 3.4.4.

Note that Theorem 3.4.1 actually implies Theorem 3.4.2, if the stronger assumption (3.5) is imposed.

*Proof of Theorem 3.4.2*

First rewrite (3.1) as

$$Z(t) = X(t) + [I - P']Y(t), \tag{3.42}$$

where

$$
\begin{aligned}
X(t) &= Z(0) + \theta t + [F^0(t) - \alpha^0 t] \\
&\quad + \sum_{j=1}^{k} [F^j(B_j(t)) - \alpha^j B_j(t)], \tag{3.43} \\
Y(t) &= \mathrm{diag}(\mu)[et - B(t)], \tag{3.44}
\end{aligned}
$$

and $\theta$ is as defined in (3.21). Applying the FLIL assumption (3.5) to (3.43) yields

$$\|\bar{X} - X\|_T = \sup_{0 \le t \le T} |X(t) - \bar{X}(t)| = O(\sqrt{T \log\log T}), \quad T \uparrow \infty, \tag{3.45}$$

where $\bar{X}$ is as defined in (3.27). Thus, (3.45) and the Lipschitz continuity of the reflection mapping (Theorem 3.3.1) lead to equality (3.24) in the theorem, and

$$\|Y - \bar{Y}\|_T = \sup_{0 \le t \le T} |Y(t) - \bar{Y}(t)| = O(\sqrt{T \log\log T}) \tag{3.46}$$

The proof of equality (3.25) in the theorem is now completed by combining (3.44) and (3.46), with equality (3.47) to be proved in the following lemma.

**Lemma 3.6.1** Let $\bar{Y} = \Psi(\bar{X})$ with $\bar{X}$ as in (3.27). Then there exists an $M > 0$ such that

$$\sup_{0 \le t < \infty} \|\bar{Y}(t) - (\mu - \lambda)^+ t\| \le M, \tag{3.47}$$

where $\lambda$ is the effective arrival rate that solves (3.4).

**Proof.**    Let $\bar{X}^*(t) = \theta t$. Then $\Psi(\bar{X}^*)(t) \equiv (\mu - \lambda)^+ t$ (see the Remark below Theorem 2.4.4 in Part I). By the Lipschitz property of the reflection mapping, there exists an $M' > 0$ such that

$$\|\Psi(\bar{X}) - \Psi(\bar{X}^*)\| \le M'\|\bar{X} - \bar{X}^*\| = M'\|Z(0)\| \equiv M.$$

*Proof of Theorem 3.4.1*

Proving the theorem for $r < 4$ establishes it for $r \ge 4$ since (2.23) for $r \ge 4$ implies it for all $r < 4$. We thus restrict attention to $r < 4$.

First force (3.1) into the form (3.12) via

$$Z(t) = X(t) + [I - P']Y(t),$$

where

$$
\begin{aligned}
X(t) &= Z(0) + \left[\alpha^0 + (P' - I)\mu\right]t + \left[F^0(t) - \alpha^0 t - (\Gamma^0)^{1/2}W^0(t)\right] \\
&\quad + \sum_{k=1}^{K}\left[F^j(B_k(t)) - \alpha^j B_k(t) - (\Gamma^j)^{1/2}W^k(B_k(t))\right] \\
&\quad + \sum_{k=1}^{K}(\Gamma^k)^{1/2}\left[W^k(B_k(t)) - W^k((\rho_k \wedge 1)t)\right] \\
&\quad + (\Gamma^0)^{1/2}W^0(t) + \sum_{k=1}^{K}(\Gamma^k)^{1/2}W^k((\rho_k \wedge 1)t), \quad (3.48) \\
Y(t) &= \operatorname{diag}(\mu)\left[et - B(t)\right]. \quad (3.49)
\end{aligned}
$$

Let

$$
\begin{aligned}
\widetilde{X}(t) &= Z(0) + \theta t + (\Gamma^0)^{1/2}W^0(t) \\
&\quad + \sum_{k=1}^{K}(\Gamma^k)^{1/2}W^k((\rho_k \wedge 1)t), \quad (3.50) \\
&\equiv Z(0) + \theta t + \Gamma^{1/2}W(t). \quad (3.51)
\end{aligned}
$$

with $\theta$ as in (3.21), and (3.51) being a defining relation for the standard Brownian motion $W$. Once we prove that

$$\sup_{0 \le t \le T} |X(t) - \widetilde{X}(t)| = o(T^{1/r}), \quad (3.52)$$

then we immediately deduce (3.18) from the Lipschitz continuity of the mapping $\Psi$. By the FSAT assumption (2.23), to prove (3.52) it suffices to show (note that $|B(t) - B(s)| \le |t - s|$) that

$$\sup_{0 \le t \le T} |W_k^j(B_j(t)) - W_k^j((\rho_j \wedge 1)t)| = o(T^{1/r}),$$

for all $j, k = 1, \ldots K$. This we do now by showing that, for any Wiener process $W$ on our ambient probability space,

$$\sup_{0 \le t \le T} |W(B_j(t)) - W((\rho_j \wedge 1)t)| = o(T^{1/r}) \quad (3.53)$$

for all $j = 1, 2, \ldots, K$. We start with a lemma, whose proof is postponed to the end of this subsection.

**Lemma 3.6.2** Let $W = \{W(t), t \geq 0\}$ be a Wiener process. Then for any $\delta > 0$ there exists a constant $C = C(\delta) > 0$ such that the inequality

$$P\left\{\sup_{0 \leq u,v \leq T;\ |u-v| \leq h} |W(u) - W(v)| \geq x\sqrt{h}\right\} \leq C(1 + \frac{T}{h})e^{-x^2/(2+\delta)}$$

holds for every $T > 0$ and $0 < h < T$.

Taking $h = h(T)$ and $X = g(T)$ in the above inequality and then applying the Borel-Cantelli Lemma yields,

**Lemma 3.6.3** Let $W = \{W(t), t \geq 0\}$ be is a Wiener process. Suppose that there exists a pair of functions $h$ and $g$ satisfying

$$\frac{g(T)\sqrt{h(T)}}{T^{1/r}} \to 0, \qquad \text{as } T \to \infty, \tag{3.54}$$

$$\sum_{T=1}^{\infty} \frac{T}{h(T)} e^{-[g(T)]^2/(2+\delta)} < \infty, \qquad \text{as } T \to \infty. \tag{3.55}$$

Then with probability one,

$$\sup_{0 \leq u,v \leq T;|u-v| \leq h(T)} |W(u) - W(v)| = o(T^{1/r}), \qquad \text{as } T \uparrow \infty. \tag{3.56}$$

When $2 < r < 4$,

$$h(T) = M\sqrt{T \log\log T} \qquad \text{and} \qquad g(T) = T^{\frac{1}{2}(\frac{1}{r}-\frac{1}{4})}$$

clearly satisfy (3.54) and (3.55). On the other hand, from equality (3.25) of Theorem 3.4.2, we know that there exists an $M > 0$ such that

$$\sup_{0 \leq t \leq T} |B_j(t) - (\rho_j \wedge 1)t| \leq M\sqrt{T \log\log T}.$$

Now applying Lemma 3.6.3 yields (3.53).

Finally, if we note that $W^j$, $j = 0, 1, ..., K$, are independent Wiener processes, then (3.50) implies that the covariance matrix $\Gamma$ is of form (3.22).

*Proof of Lemma 3.6.2*    Noting that

$$\{(u,v) : |u - v| \leq h, \quad 0 \leq u \leq T, \quad 0 \leq v \leq T\}$$

is a subset of

$$\{(u,v) : 0 \leq u \leq T, 0 \leq v - u \leq h\} \bigcup \{(u,v) : 0 \leq v \leq T, 0 \leq u - v \leq h\},$$

we can use Lemma 1.2.1 of Csörgö and Revesz [1981] with $T$ replaced by $T + h$ and $C$ replaced by $C/2$ to obtain the desired results.    □

*Proof of Corollary 3.4.3*

We take $\bar{Z}$ as defined in Corollary 3.4.3. First, it follows from (3.24) and (3.25) of Theorem 3.4.2 (also note Remark (1) below the theorem) that for any fixed $T > 0$,

$$\sup_{0 \le t \le T} \left| \frac{1}{n} Z(nt) - \frac{1}{n} \bar{Z}(nt) \right| = O\left( \sqrt{\frac{1}{n} \log \log n} \right), \qquad (3.57)$$

$$\sup_{0 \le t \le T} \left| \frac{1}{n} B(nt) - (\rho \wedge e) t \right| = O\left( \sqrt{\frac{1}{n} \log \log n} \right). \qquad (3.58)$$

These two equalities clearly imply the convergence of (3.29).

*Proof of Corollary 3.4.4*

For fixed $T > 0$, the strong approximation (3.18) implies that

$$\sup_{0 \le t \le T} \left| \frac{1}{\sqrt{n}} Z(nt) - \frac{1}{\sqrt{n}} \tilde{Z}(nt) \right| = \frac{o(1)}{n^{(r-2)/(2r)}}, \qquad \text{as } n \uparrow \infty.$$

Thus, the proof for Corollary 3.4.4 amounts to proving a central limit theorem for the reflected Brownian motion $\tilde{Z}$ as defined through (3.19)-(3.23), which will be stated as Proposition 3.6.4 below.

To simplify notations, we remove the tilde notation from the reflected Brownian motion; namely, the reflected Brownian motion will be represented by

$$Z = X + [I - P']Y, \qquad (3.59)$$
$$X(t) = Z(0) + \theta t + \Gamma W(t), \qquad (3.60)$$
$$\theta = \alpha + [P' - I]\mu, \qquad (3.61)$$
$$Y = \Phi(X). \qquad (3.62)$$

We define

$$B(t) = e t - \text{diag}(\mu^{-1}) Y(t), \qquad (3.63)$$

and "hat" notations:

$$\hat{Z}^n(t) = \frac{1}{\sqrt{n}} \left[ Z(nt) - (\lambda - \mu)^+ nt \right],$$

$$\hat{B}^n(t) = \frac{1}{\sqrt{n}} \left[ (\rho \wedge e) t - B(nt) \right], \qquad \text{and}$$

$$\hat{Y}^n(t) = \frac{1}{\sqrt{n}} Y(nt).$$

**Proposition 3.6.4** For the processes defined in (3.59)-(3.62), the convergence (3.30) prevails with the limiting processes defined by (3.31)-(3.40).

First we state and prove two lemmas.

**Lemma 3.6.5** Recall that $a$ is the set of nonbottleneck stations. Then we have

$$\hat{Z}_a^n \xrightarrow{d} 0, \quad \text{as } n \to \infty \tag{3.64}$$

**Proof.** The proof proceeds as follows. First, we prove the convergence (3.64) for the set of sub-critical stations (those for which $\theta_j < 0$; see Section 2.4 of the previous chapter). Then we consider a subnetwork which is obtained from the original network by removing all sub-critical stations, and then we prove the convergence (3.64) for those stations that are sub-critical stations in the subnetwork. We continue with this process unless we reach a subnetwork which does not have sub-critical stations, and then, by Propositions 2.4.2 and 2.4.3 in the previous chapter, we know that the lemma is proved. This process is very similar to that used in the proof of Theorem 2.4.4 in last chapter. So we will only provide the first step here, i.e., to prove the convergence of (3.64) for the set of sub-critical stations.

Consider a sub-critical station $j$, i.e., $\theta_j < 0$. Let $\epsilon_n = \max\{\bar{Z}_k^n(0); k = 1, ..., K\}$ and note that $\epsilon_n \to 0$. Then introduce for $t \geq 0$,

$$\nu_j^n(t) = \sup\{s \leq t : \bar{Z}_j^n(s) \leq \epsilon_n\}$$

(abbreviated as $\nu_j^n$ when convenient and well defined because the set over which the supremum is taken always contains $s = 0$: $\hat{Z}_j^n(0) \leq \epsilon_n$). Now $\hat{Z}_j^n$ is a continuous function. It follows from the definition of $\nu_j^n(t)$ that $\hat{Z}_j^n(\nu_j^n) = \epsilon_n$. Furthermore, if $\nu_j^n(t) < t$ then $\hat{Z}_j^n(s) > \epsilon_n \geq 0$ for $s \in [\nu_j^n(t), t]$. Using the complementarity condition (3.14), applied to the "hat" representation of (3.59), implies that $\hat{Y}_j^n(\nu_j^n(t)) = \hat{Y}_j^n(t)$, which also holds when $\nu_j^n(t) = t$. One utilizes all this in

$$
\begin{aligned}
-\epsilon_n \quad \leq \quad & \hat{Z}_j^n(t) - \hat{Z}_j^n(\nu_j^n) \\
= \quad & \hat{\xi}_j^n(t) - \hat{\xi}_j^n(\nu_j^n) + n\theta_j(t - \nu_j^n) - \sum_{k=1}^{J} p_{kj}\left[\hat{Y}_k^n(t) - \hat{Y}_k^n(\nu_j^n)\right] \\
\leq \quad & \hat{\xi}_j^n(t) - \hat{\xi}_j^n(\nu_j^n) + n\theta_j(t - \nu_j^n),
\end{aligned}
\tag{3.65}
$$

where

$$\hat{\xi}^n(t) = \Gamma \frac{1}{\sqrt{n}} W(nt) \tag{3.66}$$

Consequently, for $t \geq 0$,

$$0 \leq (-\theta_j)[t - \nu_j^n(t)] \leq \frac{\epsilon_n}{n} + \frac{1}{n}\hat{\xi}_j^n(t) - \frac{1}{n}\hat{\xi}_j^n(\nu_j^n) \tag{3.67}$$

The functional law of iterated logarithm for Brownian motion guarantees that both $\hat{\xi}_j^n(t)/n$ and $\hat{\xi}_j^n(\nu_j^n(t))/n$ converge uniformly to zero on any compact subset of $[0, \infty)$. Thus, one concludes from (3.67) and $\theta_j < 0$ that

$$\nu_j^n(t) \to t \quad u.o.c. \tag{3.68}$$

Clearly,

$$\hat{\xi}^n \xrightarrow{d} \hat{\xi}, \quad \text{as } n \to \infty. \tag{3.69}$$

Going back to (3.65), we have

$$0 \leq \hat{Z}_j^n(t) \leq \hat{\xi}_j^n(t) - \hat{\xi}_j^n\left(\nu_j^n\right) + \hat{Z}_j^n\left(\nu_j^n\right),$$

for all $t \geq 0$. Finally, $0 \leq \hat{Z}_j^n\left(\nu_j^n\right) \leq \epsilon_n$, combined with (3.68) and (3.69), establishes the convergence (3.64) for all sub-critical stations.    $\square$

**Lemma 3.6.6**  Recall that $c$ is the set of strict bottlenecks. Then we have

$$\hat{Y}_c^n \xrightarrow{d} \hat{\xi}, \quad \text{as } n \to \infty \tag{3.70}$$

**Proof.**    Let $\beta$ be the union of $b$ and $c$, i.e., $\beta$ is the set of all bottleneck stations. The lemma will be proved in two steps. First, we prove that there exists a sequence of processes $\tilde{Y}_\beta^n$, $n = 1, 2, ...$, in $\mathcal{C}^{|\beta|}$ that dominates $\hat{Y}_\beta^n$, $n = 1, 2, ...$, and converges weakly to a finite process. Second, we show the desired convergence (3.70).

To the end of proving the first step, we rewrite $\hat{Z}^n$ of (3.59) in $a$ and $\beta$ block form,

$$\hat{Z}_a^n(t) = \hat{Z}_a^n(0) + \theta_a \sqrt{n}t + \hat{\xi}_a^n(t)$$
$$- P_{\beta a}' \hat{Y}_\beta^n(t) + [I - P_a']\hat{Y}_a^n(t), \tag{3.71}$$

$$\hat{Z}_\beta^n(t) + (\lambda_\beta - \mu_\beta)\sqrt{n}t = \hat{Z}_\beta^n(0) + \theta_\beta \sqrt{n}t + \hat{\xi}_\beta^n(t)$$
$$- P_{a\beta}' \hat{Y}_a^n(t) + [I - P_\beta']\hat{Y}_\beta^n(t), \tag{3.72}$$

where $\hat{\xi}^n$ is defined in (3.66).

Since $\sigma(P) < 1$, the inverse of $(I - P_a')$ exists [Proposition 2.4.2 of the last chapter]. Solving for $\hat{Y}_a^n$ in (3.71) and substituting the outcome into (3.72) yields

$$\hat{Z}_\beta^n(t) + (\lambda_\beta - \mu_\beta)\sqrt{n}t = \chi_\beta^n(t) + (\lambda_\beta - \mu_\beta)\sqrt{n}t + [I - \hat{P}_\beta']\hat{Y}_\beta^n, \tag{3.73}$$

where

$$\chi_\beta^n(t) = [\hat{Z}_\beta^n(0) + P_{a\beta}'(I - P_a')^{-1}\hat{Z}_a^n(0)] - P_{a\beta}'(I - P_a')^{-1}\hat{Z}_a^n$$
$$+ [\hat{\xi}_\beta^n + P_{a\beta}'(I - P_a')^{-1}\hat{\xi}_a^n], \tag{3.74}$$
$$\hat{P}_\beta = P_\beta + P_{\beta a}(I - P_a)^{-1}P_{a\beta},$$

and we used the fact that

$$\theta_\beta + P'_{a\beta}(I - P'_a)^{-1}\theta_a = \lambda_\beta - \mu_\beta \qquad (3.75)$$

By the definition of $\beta$, we know that $\lambda_\beta - \mu_\beta \geq 0$. Therefore, by the least element characterization of mapping $\Psi$ (Theorem 3.3.1), we have

$$\hat{Y}^n_\beta = \Psi_{\hat{P}_\beta}\left(\chi^n_\beta + (\lambda_\beta - \mu_\beta)\sqrt{n}e\right) \leq \tilde{Y}^n_\beta \equiv \Psi_{\hat{P}_\beta}(\chi^n_\beta). \qquad (3.76)$$

By (3.69) and Lemma 3.6.5, we can see that $\chi^n_\beta$ converges weakly to a Brownian motion, and therefore, the continuous mapping theorem implies that $\tilde{Y}^n_\beta$ converges weakly to a finite limit (in fact, the regulator of a reflected Brownian motion). Now, we have completed the first step.

To complete the proof, we rewrite $\hat{Z}^n$ of (3.59) in blocks $a$, $b$ and $c$:

$$\hat{Z}^n_a(t) = \hat{Z}^n_a(0) + \theta_a\sqrt{n}t + \hat{\xi}^n_a(t)$$
$$- P'_{ba}\hat{Y}^n_b(t) - P'_{ca}\hat{Y}^n_c(t) + [I - P'_a]\hat{Y}^n_a(t), \quad (3.77)$$
$$\hat{Z}^n_b(t) = \hat{Z}^n_b(0) + \theta_b\sqrt{n}t + \hat{\xi}^n_b(t)$$
$$- P'_{ab}\hat{Y}^n_a(t) - P'_{cb}\hat{Y}^n_c(t) + [I - P'_b]\hat{Y}^n_b(t), \quad (3.78)$$
$$\hat{Z}^n_c(t) + (\lambda_c - \mu_c)\sqrt{n}t = \hat{Z}^n_c(0) + \theta_c\sqrt{n}t + \hat{\xi}^n_c(t)$$
$$- P'_{ac}\hat{Y}^n_a(t) - P'_{bc}\hat{Y}^n_b(t) + [I - P'_c]\hat{Y}^n_c(t) \quad (3.79)$$

Then we solve for $\hat{Y}^n_a$ in (3.77), and substitute the outcome into (3.79) to obtain

$$\hat{Z}^n_c(t) + (\lambda_c - \mu_c)\sqrt{n} = \hat{X}^n(t) - \hat{P}'_{bc}\hat{Y}^n_b + (\lambda_c - \mu_c)\sqrt{n}t$$
$$+ [I - \hat{P}'_c]\hat{Y}^n_c, \qquad (3.80)$$

where

$$\hat{X}^n_c(t) = [\hat{Z}^n_c(0) + P'_{ac}(I - P'_a)^{-1}\hat{Z}^n_a(0)] - P'_{ac}(I - P'_a)^{-1}\hat{Z}^n_a$$
$$+ [\hat{\xi}^n_c + P'_{ac}(I - P'_a)^{-1}\hat{\xi}^n_a],$$
$$\hat{P}_c = P_c + P_{ca}(I - P_a)^{-1}P_{ac},$$

$\hat{P}_{bc}$ is defined in (3.38), and we also used (3.75).

Applying Remark (1) that succeeds Theorem 3.3.1 to (3.80) and observing inequality (3.76) yields

$$0 \leq \hat{Y}^n_c(t) = \sup_{0 \leq s \leq t}\left[\hat{P}'_c\hat{Y}^n_c(s) - \hat{X}^n(s) + \hat{P}'_{bc}\hat{Y}^n_b(s) - (\lambda - \mu)\sqrt{n}s\right]^+$$
$$\leq \sup_{0 \leq s \leq t}\left[\hat{P}'_c\tilde{Y}^n_c(s) - \hat{X}^n_c(s) + \hat{P}'_{bc}\tilde{Y}^n_b(s) - (\lambda_c - \mu_c)\sqrt{n}s\right]^+.$$
$$(3.81)$$

Now note that all processes $\hat{X}_c^n$, $\tilde{Y}_b^n$ and $\tilde{Y}_c^n$ converge weakly to finite limits, and that $\lambda_c - \mu_c > 0$ (since $c$ is the set of strict bottlenecks). Then applying the functional limit theorem for the supremum (Theorem 6.1 of Whitt [1980]), we prove that the process defined by the right hand side of inequality (3.81) converges weakly to zero, therefore, the convergence (3.70). □

*Proof of Proposition 3.6.4*     First solving for $\hat{Y}_a^n$ in (3.77) and substituting the outcome into (3.78) yields

$$\hat{Z}_b^n(t) = \hat{X}_b^n(t) + [I - \hat{P}_b']\hat{Y}_b^n, \qquad (3.82)$$

where

$$\hat{X}_b^n(t) = [\hat{Z}_b^n(0) + P_{ab}'(I - P_a')^{-1}\hat{Z}_a^n(0)] - P_{ab}'(I - P_a')^{-1}\hat{Z}_a^n$$
$$+ [\hat{\xi}_b^n + P_{ab}'(I - P_a')^{-1}\hat{\xi}_a^n] - [P_{cb}' + P_{ab}'(I - P_a')P_{ca}']\hat{Y}_c^n, \qquad (3.83)$$

$\hat{P}_b$ is defined in (3.36), and we used (3.75).

It follows from (3.69) and Lemmas 3.6.5 and 3.6.6 that $\hat{X}_b^n$ in (3.82) converges weakly to the Brownian motion $\hat{X}_b$ in (3.33). The continuous mapping theorem then implies that

$$\left(\hat{Y}_b^n = \Psi_{\hat{P}_b}\left(\hat{X}_b^n\right), \hat{Z}_b^n = \Phi_{\hat{P}_b}\left(\hat{X}_b^n\right)\right)$$

converges weakly to the reflected Brownian motion $(\hat{Y}_b, \hat{Z}_b)$ defined through (3.32)-(3.36). Next, the weak convergences of (3.69), $\hat{Y}_a^n$, $\hat{Y}_b^n$, and $\hat{Z}_b^n$, applied to (3.80), imply the weak convergence of $\hat{Z}_c^n$ with the limit $\hat{Z}_c^n$ in (3.37). The convergence of $\hat{B}^n$ is by observing (3.76) and

$$\hat{B}^n(t) = -\text{diag}(\mu^{-1})[\hat{Y}^n(t) - (\mu - \lambda)^+ \sqrt{n}t].$$

Finally, we remark that all of the convergences actually hold jointly.

## 3.7 References, Possible Extensions and Future Research

*General Commentary:* We have introduced strong approximations as a unifying framework, at the cost of imposing assumptions that are mathematically too stringent. Indeed, all of our corollaries can be established, individually, under weaker conditions. However, as far as current applications are concerned, such stronger results seem to offer no benefit.

In this chapter we focus on homogeneous single-server open networks. Natural extensions include multi-server, and homogeneous closed and mixed networks, as well as heterogeneous (multi-class) networks of all kinds. Fluid and diffusion approximations for heterogeneous multi-server nonparametric Jackson networks under heavy traffic are given in Chen and Shanthikumar (1990). Combining their approach with ours easily establishes the strong approximation for the heterogeneous multi-server network, with no heavy traffic assumptions. Fluid and diffusion approximations for nonparametric closed Jackson networks are given in Chen and Mandelbaum [1991b]. As far as FLIL and FSAT for closed networks, FLIL for the queue length process (3.24) still holds, but our approach does not carry over to the FLIL for the busy time process (3.25). Establishing FSAT for closed network takes a different approach; see recent work by Zhang [1993]. This state of affairs is consistent with the fact that the mapping $\Phi$ for closed networks is Lipschitz (Dupuis and Ishii [1991]) but $\Psi$ need not be (a counter example appears in Berger and Whitt [1992]). Mixed networks are currently under study by Nguyen [1993]. Heterogeneous open networks present a significant challenge, as apparent from Harrison [1988], Harrison and Nguyen [1990;1992], Dai and Wang [1993] and Whitt [1994].

There is an alternative, deeper but less "user friendly", form of strong approximations, in terms of exponential bounds on the probability of deviations from a central trend. (See Csörgö and Révśz [1981] and Glynn [1990]). We have not presented this form here but, with some modification, it can also be handled by our approach.

Work on strong approximations for queueing networks has been rather scarce. We are aware only of Zhang, Hsu and Wang [1990], who analyze a single station with multiple-servers, Zhang [1990], that covers super-critical nonparametric Jackson networks, Horváth [1990], who treats two-station open network, and Glynn and Whitt [1991] that deal with queue in series.

Meyn and Down [1993] proves existence of a stationary distribution for non-parametric closed and open Jackson networks. As in Horváth [1990], one should be able to use strong approximations refinements to show that this stationary distribution, properly normalized, converges to the stationary distribution of a corresponding RBM. (This is actually Kingman's approach in his pioneering work on heavy traffic: he showed convergence to the exponential distribution, which is the stationary distribution of the one-dimensional RBM; the issue is easy to settle for closed networks, as done in Kaspi and Mandelbaum [1989], but it is still open for open networks.

Harrison and Williams [1987] established an integral equation, known as a basic adjoint relation (BAR), to characterize the stationary distribution of the approximating diffusion process for open queueing networks. Harrison, Williams and Chen [1990] extends the result to irreducible closed networks. BAR enables calculations of useful performance measures. On rare occasions, the integral equations can be solved to yield an explicit expression for the stationary distribution (typically of a product-form). Dai and Harrison [1991,1992] have developed computational methods for more general cases.

Diffusion approximations are used not only for performance evaluation, but also for optimal control of queueing networks. Specifically, a queueing control problem is approximated by a diffusion control problem that is easier to handle, and then optimal, or near optimal, solutions to the latter problem are interpreted in the original queueing context. This line of research started in Harrison [1988], and continued for example in Yang [1988], Wein [1990], Harrison and Wein [1990]. Kelly and Laws [1991] expresses the hope that ultimate justification of results that propose asymptotically optimal control will not depend on the Brownian nature of the approximation. It is plausible that the framework of strong approximations is what they are searching for. We also note that Krichagina, Lou, Sethi and Taksar [1991] proved the asymptotic optimality of the diffusion approximation for a failure-prone manufacturing system.

*Section 1*

There is a voluminous literature on queueing networks, most of which traces back to the seminal works of Jackson [1963], Gorden and Newell [1967], Whittle [1967;1968], BCMP [1975] and Kelly [1979].

Diffusion approximations for queueing systems have been a subject of research for almost 30 years. Readers are referred to Kingman [1965], Iglehart and Whitt [1970a,b], Reiman [1984], Johnson[1983], and Chen and Mandelbaum [1991b]. More references can be found in the papers cited above and in the survey papers by Whitt [1974], Lemoine [1978], Flores [1985] and Glynn [1990].

Consider a non-parametric queueing network whose traffic intensities are all strictly less than unity. The approximation of such a single queueing network commonly entails perturbing (rescaling) it to get an approximating *sequence* of networks, and then taking limits. Such an approximation is informative at stations with traffic intensities that are very close to unity (in heavy traffic); otherwise, the diffusion limit is zero. Our strong approximations, on the other hand, are always applicable: no rescaling is needed, and they give rise to both an approximating diffusion and an error bound. In particular, strong approximations are applicable at stations with traffic intensities significantly less than unity. This is consistent with success of the numerical method developed by Dai and Harrison [1992], which perform well in heavy traffic as well as moderate traffic.

*Section 2*

The model and the notation are adopted from Harrison and Williams [1987]. The FSAT for renewal processes is Part (ii) of Corollary 3.1, in Csörgő, Horváth and Steinebach [1987]. The FSAT for compound renewal processes is Theorem A in the Appendix to Horváth [1992]. Horváth uses FSAT's for summands of random vectors, which he attributes to Einmal

[1989]. (Note that Horváth [1992] considers the probability-bound form of the FSAT's.)

*Section 3*

Most of this section is a recapitulation of Sections 2.2 and 2.4 from Part I. Remark (2) in Section 3.3.3 follows from Harrison and Williams [1987].

*Section 4*

Note that the strong approximation (3.18) implies the functional law-of-iterated-logarithm. The latter result holds under a weaker condition than the former.

Strong approximations can also be developed for a sequence of networks. Then, Corollary 3.4.4 would recover the diffusion limits of Reiman [1984] and Chen and Mandelbaum [1991b].

*Section 5*

For more details on how to fit a network, and the detailed calculations of the covariance matrix, readers are referred to Harrison [1988] and Harrison and Williams [1987].

*Acknowledgments:* We would like to thank S.G. Kou for pointing out an error in the earlier proof of Theorem 3.4.1. Hong Chen is supported in part by NSF grant DDM-89-09972, by NSERC grant OG0089698, and by a UBC-HSS Research Grant.

## 3.8   References

[1] Baskett, F., Chandy, K.M., Muntz, R.R. and Palacois, F.G. (1975). "Open, closed and mixed networks of queues with different classes of customers", *J. Assoc. Comput. Mach.* **22** 248-260.

[2] Berger, A.W., and Whitt, W., (1992). "The Brownian approximation for rate-control throttles and the $G/G/1/C$ queue", *Discrete Event Dynamic Systems: Theory and Applications* **2** 7-60.

[3] Chen, H., and Mandelbaum, A. (1991a). "Discrete flow networks: bottleneck analysis and fluid approximations", *Math of OR* **16** 408-446.

[4] Chen, H., and Mandelbaum, A. (1991b). "Discrete flow networks: diffusion approximations and bottlenecks", *Ann. of Prob.* **19** 1463-1519.

[5] Chen, H., and Shanthikumar, G. (1990). "Fluid limits and diffusion approximations for networks of multi-server queues in heavy traffic", *Discrete Event Dynamic Systems: Theory and Applications* (forthcoming).

[6] Csörgö, M., Horváth L. and Steinebach, J. (1987). "Invariance principles for renewal processes", *Ann. Probab.* **15** 1441-1460.

[7] Csörgö, M., and Revesz, P. (1981). *Strong Approximations in Probability and Statistics*, Academic Press, New York, 1981.

[8] Dai, J.G., and Harrison, J.M. (1991). "Steady-state analysis of reflected Brownian motions: characterization, numerical methods and a queueing application", *Annals of Applied Probability* **1** 16-35.

[9] Dai, J.G., and Harrison, J.M. (1991). "Reflected Brownian motion in an orthant: numerical methods and a queueing application", *Annals of Applied Probability* **2** 65-86.

[10] Dai, J.G., and Wang, Y. (1993). "Nonexistence of Brownian models of certain multiclass queueing networks", *Queueing Systems* **13** 41-46.

[11] Dupuis, P., and Ishii, H. (1991). "On when the solution to the Skorohod problem is Lipschitz continuous with applications", *Stochastics.* **35** 31-62.

[12] Einmahl, U. (1989). "Extensions of results of Komlós, Major and Tusnády to the Multivariate Case", *J. Multivariate Anal.* **28** 20-68.

[13] Flores, C. (1985). "Diffusion approximations for computer communications networks", in B. Gopinath (ed.), *Computer Communications, Proc. Symp. Appl. Math.*, American Math. Society, 83-124.

[14] Glynn, P. W. (1990). "Diffusion approximations", in D.P. Heyman and M.J. Sobel (eds.), *Handbooks in Operations Research and Management Science, II: Stochastic Models*, North-Holland, Amsterdam.

[15] Gordon ,W. J., and Newell, G. F. (1967). "Closed queueing systems with exponential servers", *Operations Research* **15** 254-265.

[16] Harrison, J. M. (1985). *Brownian Motion and Stochastic Flow Systems*, Wiley.

[17] Harrison, J. M. (1988). "Brownian models of queueing networks with heterogeneous customer populations", in W. Fleming and P.L. Lions (eds.), *Stochastic Differential Systems, Stochastic Control Theory and Applications*, IMA Volume **10**, Springer-Verlag, 147-186.

[18] Harrison, J. M., and Nguyen, V. (1990). "The QNET method for two-moment analysis of open queueing networks", *Queueing Systems* **6** 1-32.

[19] Harrison, J. M., and Nguyen, V. (1992). "Brownian models of multiclass queueing networks: current status and open problems", to appear in *Queueing Systems*.

[20] Harrison, J.M. and Reiman, M.I., "Reflected Brownian motion on an orthant", *The Annals of Prob.* **9**, 302–308, 1981.

[21] Harrison, J. M., and Wein, L.M. (1990). "Scheduling networks of queues: heavy traffic analysis of a two-station closed network", *Operations Research* **38** 1052-1064.

[22] Harrison, J. M., and Williams, R. (1987). "Brownian models of open queueing networks with homogeneous customer populations", *Stochastics* **22** 77-115.

[23] Harrison, J. M., Williams, R., and Chen, H. (1990). "Brownian models of closed queueing networks", *Stochastics and Stochastic Reports* **29** 37-74.

[24] Horváth, L. (1992). "Strong approximations of open queueing networks", *Math. O.R.* **17** 487-508.

[25] Iglehart D. L., and Whitt, W. (1970a). "Multiple channel queues in heavy traffic, I", *Adv. Appl. Prob.* **2** 150-177.

[26] Iglehart D. L., and Whitt, W. (1970b). "Multiple channel queues in heavy traffic, II", *Adv. Appl. Prob.* **2** 355-364.

[27] Jackson, J. R. (1963). "Jobshop-like queueing systems", *Management Science* **10** 131-142.

[28] Johnson, D. P. (1983). *Diffusion approximations for optimal filtering of jump processes and for queueing networks*, Ph.D. Dissertation, University of Wisconsin.

[29] Kaspi, H. and Mandelbaum, A. (1989). "On the ergodicity of a closed queueing network", submitted for publication.

[30] Kelly, F. P. (1979). *Reversibility and Stochastic Networks*, Wiley.

[31] Kelly, F. P., and C.N. Laws. (1991). "Dynamic routing in open queueing networks", preprint.

[32] Kingman, J.F. C. (1965). "The heavy traffic approximation in the theory of queues", in W.L. Smith et al. (eds.), *Proc. Symp. on Congestion Theory*, Univ. of North Carolina Press, 137-159.

[33] Kleinrock, L. (1976). *Queueing Systems Vol. II: Computer Applications*, Wiley.

[34] Krichagina, E., Lou, S., Sethi, S. and Taksar, M. (1991). "Production control in a failure-prone manufacturing system: diffusion approximation and asymptotic optimality", submitted to *Ann. Appl. Prob.*

[35] Lemoine, A. J. (1978). "Network of queues - a survey of weak convergence results", *Management Science* **24** 1175-1193.

[36] Meyn, S.P. and D. Down. (1993). "Stability of generalized Jackson networks", *Ann. Appl. Prob.*.

[37] Nguyen, V. (1993). "Fluid and diffusion approximations of a two-station mixed queueing network", Working paper WP# 3519-93-MSA, Sloan School, MIT.

[38] Reiman, M. I. (1984). "Open queueing networks in heavy traffic", *Math. of O.R.* **9** 441-458.

[39] Wein, L. M. (1990). "Scheduling networks of queues: heavy traffic analysis of a two-station network with controllable inputs", *Operations Research* **38** 1065-1078.

[40] Whitt, W. (1974). "Heavy traffic theorems for queues: a survey", in A.B. Clarke (ed.), *Mathematical Methods in Queueing Theory*, Springer Verlag.

[41] Whitt, W. (1980). "Some useful functions for functional limit theorems", *Math. of O.R.* **5** 67-85.

[42] Whitt, W. (1994). "An interesting example of a multiclass open queueing network", *Management Science*.

[43] Whittle, P. (1967). "Nonlinear migration processes", *Bull. Inst. Internat. Statist.* **42** 642-647.

[44] Whittle, P. (1968). "Equilibrium distributions for an open migration process", *J. Appl. Prob.* **5** 567-571.

[45] Yang, P. (1988). *Pathwise solutions for a class of linear stochastic systems*, Ph.D. dissertation, Department of Operations Research, Stanford University.

[46] Zhang, H., G. Hsu, and R. Wang. (1990). "Strong approximations for multiple channel queues in heavy traffic" *J. Appl. Prob.* **28**, 658-670.

[47] Zhang, H. (1990). "Strong approximations for open networks in heavy traffic", preprint.

[48] Zhang, H. (1993). "Strong approximations for irreducible closed queueing networks", preprint.

# 4
# A GSMP Framework for the Analysis of Production Lines

Paul Glasserman
David D. Yao

ABSTRACT We present the basics of the *generalized semi-Markov process* (GSMP), focusing on its *scheme* and related structural properties. We illustrate the various applications of these properties through a detailed study on a serial production line under the so-called *generalized kanban control*: the production of each stage is controlled by three parameters that are upper limits on the work-in-process inventory, finished-job inventory, and the overall buffer capacity. In particular, we show that the system satisfies monotonicity, convexity/concavity, and line reversibility, all of which have useful implications in system design. Furthermore the service-completion epochs at all stages satisfy a subadditive ergodicity, which guarantees the existence of long-run average cycle times (or, equivalently, the existence of a well-defined production rate).

## 4.1 Introduction

A manufacturing process is a dynamical system: it can in principle be described by a state evolving in time according to a specific set of rules, possibly subject to random disturbances or fluctuations. The essential features of a discrete manufacturing system are a set of *resources* capable of providing service of some type, and *jobs* utilizing these resources. The state of such a system records the status of the resources, the content of buffers that supply the resources, and the location and status of jobs. The rules that determine the evolution of the state coordinate interactions between jobs and resources and among different jobs competing for the same resource.

The complete specification of system state and transition rules may be complex — possibly too complex to be carried out explicitly. But a distinctive feature is the source of this complexity: ordinarily, the rules governing individual mechanisms or interactions are quite simple; the complexity comes from the magnitude of cases that can arise. To put it another way, the components of the system — resources and jobs — follow simple patterns so long as they evolve asynchronously; coordinating these asynchronous components into a coherent system requires a large number of queueing, routing, and scheduling rules that combine to create large-scale complexity. Most of the time, the various system components evolve independently of each other. Interactions among system components occur at variable, discrete time instants generically referred to as *events*. So, this type of process may well be called a *discrete-event system*.

A well-established line of research in classical dynamical systems examines qualitative properties when complexity rules out analytical evaluation of quantitative performance. It is this approach that we pursue here in the setting of discrete-event systems. The centerpiece of the qualitative theory of dynamical systems is the analysis of trajectories. In the discrete-event setting, one description of a trajectory is the sequence of events and their corresponding epochs of occurrence. These objects pervade our analysis. The types of models we consider do not lend themselves to closed-form solutions; our objective is to show what types of conclusions can still be drawn, based on an analysis of trajectories.

Our approach examines the *structure* of a system to draw conclusions about its temporal behavior. We separate the purely logical aspects of a discrete-event system from its temporal and stochastic elements, and show that conditions on the logical structure have interesting qualitative implications for the temporal, stochastic evolution of the system. The framework of *generalized semi-Markov processes* (GSMP) provides a natural setting for this separation. The first part of this chapter develops general results in the GSMP; the second part then carries out a detailed analysis of the implications of these results for production lines under a "generalized kanban" control mechanism.

A principal logical feature of a discrete-event system is its collection of possible event trajectories, which we call its *language* of feasible strings of events. Various conditions on languages are detailed later in this chapter; we mention two that underlie all the results contained here. These are *non-interruption*, requiring that the occurrence of one event not deactivate any other events, and *permutability*, requiring that the set of active events reached through a string of events be independent of the order of events in the string. These conditions are equivalent to the language of feasible strings forming an *antimatroid*. This antimatroid property leads to (min,max,+) recursions for event epochs and associated monotonicity results. A further condition on the language leads to (max,+) recursions and corresponding convexity properties. Additional consequences are developed in later sections.

Basic properties of GSMPs are discussed in Section 2; structural conditions and their consequences are introduced in Section 3. These include conditions for montonicity, convexity and concavity in a single GSMP or a family of such processes. In Section 4, we describe the generalized kanban control mechanism and its analysis through the GSMP framework. Concavity and line-reversibility properties for this system are developed in

Sections 5 and 6. Sections 7 and 8 exploit the subadditivity of (max,+) recursions to establish the existence of long-run average cycle times and the rate of convergence to these limits.

## 4.2    GSMP and Its Scheme

### 4.2.1    The Scheme: GSMS

The core of a GSMP is its *scheme*, the generalized semi-Markov scheme (GSMS), denoted $\mathcal{G}$. The scheme is a five-tuple, $\mathcal{G} = \{\mathbf{S}, \mathbf{A}, \mathcal{E}, \phi, s_0\}$, where,

- **S** denotes the state space, the set of states, or physical configurations of a system;

- $\mathbf{A} := \{\alpha_1, ..., \alpha_m\}$ is a finite set of events;

- $\mathcal{E} : \mathbf{S} \mapsto 2^{\mathbf{A}}$ is a function that specifies the set of active events, the "event list" $\mathcal{E}(s)$, when the system is in state $s \in \mathbf{S}$;

- $\phi : \mathbf{S} \times \mathbf{A} \mapsto \mathbf{S}$ is a second function that specifies the transition mechanism of the system: given state $s$ and the occurrence of event $\alpha$, the system transits into state $\phi(s, \alpha)$;

- $s_0$ denotes the initial state.

A *string* is a finite sequence of events: $\sigma = \beta_1 \beta_2 ... \beta_n$, i.e., event $\beta_1$ occurs first, followed by $\beta_2$, and so forth, with $\beta_i \in \mathbf{A}$ for all $i = 1, ..., n$. An empty string, denoted $\epsilon$, is one that contains no event. Let $\sigma\alpha$, $\sigma_1\sigma_2$, etc. denote the concatenation of strings. Let $\mathbf{A}^*$ denote the set of all strings, including the empty string $\epsilon$.

The "input" to the scheme is a random sequence of "clock times", $\omega := \{\omega_\alpha(n); \alpha \in \mathbf{A}, n = 1, 2, ...\}$, where $\omega_\alpha(n)$ denotes the $n$th clock time of event $\alpha$. We shall refer to $\omega$ as the "clock sequence". We make no distributional or independence assumptions on $\omega$. For simplicity, we make no notational distinction between the random sequence $\omega$ and its sample realizations. This is appropriate, since for our purpose the clock times are independent of the dynamics of the system. Indeed, $\omega$ can be viewed as a sequence that is *a priori* sampled from its population.

For regularity, we make the following assumptions:

(i) No superfluous event: $\mathbf{A} = \cup_{s \in \mathbf{S}} \mathcal{E}(s)$, i.e., each event will be active in some state.

(ii) State reachability: every state in **S** is reachable from the initial state $s_0$; i.e., for every state $s \in \mathbf{S}$, there is a string of events $\sigma = \alpha_1 \ldots \alpha_n$ such that $\phi(\cdots \phi(s_0, \alpha_1), \ldots, \alpha_n) = s$.

(iii) Non-explosiveness of the clock times: $\sum_{n=1}^{\infty} \omega_\alpha(n) = \infty$, for all $\alpha \in \mathbf{A}$; that is, no event can occur an infinite number of times within a finite time interval.

Given the scheme $\mathcal{G}$ and the input clock sequence $\omega$, the GSMP evolves as follows. At time zero, the events on the event list $\mathcal{E}(s_0)$ are activated, with clock life times set at the sample values $\{\omega_\alpha(1), \alpha \in \mathcal{E}(s_0)\}$. The clocks then start to run down (at a deterministic, unit rate). The event, say $\alpha^*$, whose clock is the first to run out, triggers the next transition, into state $s_1 = \phi(s_0, \alpha^*)$. (In case of ties among clock samples, for concreteness let the sequence of triggering follow the order of the events as they are specified in $\mathbf{A} = \{\alpha_1, \ldots, \alpha_m\}$.) The event list is updated to $\mathcal{E}(s_1)$: the original events on $\mathcal{E}(s_0)$, including the triggering event $\alpha^*$, could be either de-activated and hence removed from the event list or kept on the new event list. The clock times are also updated accordingly: the new clocks — those associated with the new events on $\mathcal{E}(s_1)$, including $\alpha^*$ — are sampled from $\omega$; while the old clocks — those associated with the original events that are kept on $\mathcal{E}(s_1)$ — continue to run down. The above process is then repeated, from the new state $s_1$.

The "output" of the system is the sequence of event epochs

$$T := \{T_\alpha(n); \alpha \in \mathbf{A}, n = 1, 2, \ldots\},$$

where $T_\alpha(n)$ denote the $n$th occurrence epoch of event $\alpha$. A related sequence of interest is

$$D := \{D_\alpha(t); \alpha \in \mathbf{A}, n = 1, 2, \ldots\},$$

where $D_\alpha(t) := \sup\{n : T_\alpha(n) \leq t\}$ denotes the number of occurrences of event $\alpha$ up to time $t$. We refer to $T$ and $D$ as the "event-epoch sequence" and the "event-counting process", respectively.

The setup introduced above can be made much more general. For instance, the transition mapping $\phi$ could be replaced by a probabilistic mechanism. The clocks can run down with "speeds" that are state dependent. For ease of exposition, however, here we will focus on the less general scheme specified above.

### 4.2.2  Language and Score Space

The set $\mathbf{A}^*$ of all strings mentioned earlier is usually too general to be of any particular interest. It does not characterize the behavior of the system, since many strings in $\mathbf{A}^*$ are simply *infeasible*: those particular sequences of events just cannot happen as the system evolves. To characterize the behavior of the system, we need the notion a "language" generated by $\mathcal{G}$, denoted $\mathcal{L}(\mathcal{G})$, or simply $\mathcal{L}$, which is a subset of $\mathbf{A}^*$, consisting of only those "feasible" strings defined as follows.

The prefix of a string $\sigma = \beta_1 \ldots \beta_n$ is any initial portion of it, $\beta_1 \ldots \beta_k$ with $k \leq n$, including the empty string $\epsilon$.

The notion of a feasible string is defined recursively as follows:

- the empty string $\epsilon$ is feasible;
- if $\sigma$ is feasible, then $\sigma\alpha$ is feasible for all $\alpha \in \mathcal{E}(\phi(s_0, \sigma))$.

Therefore, a feasible string is one that starts from an event on the initial event list $\mathcal{E}(s_0)$, and each event that is subsequently appended to it is picked from the current event list. Any prefix of a feasible string is feasible.

The language, $\mathcal{L}(\mathcal{G})$ is then simply defined as the set of all feasible strings. Under this definition, the language is prefix closed, i.e., if $\sigma \in \mathcal{L}$ then $\sigma' \in \mathcal{L}$ for any $\sigma'$ that is a prefix of $\sigma$. Extend the domain of $\phi$ to $\mathbf{S} \times \mathcal{L}$ in the natural way: $\phi(s, \sigma\alpha) = \phi(\phi(s, \sigma), \alpha)$.

When $\mathcal{L} = \mathbf{A}^*$, i.e., all strings are feasible, the scheme $\mathcal{G}$ is simply a "shuffle" of all the $m$ events in $\mathbf{A}$, in the sense that any permutation, repetition, and concatenation of the $m$ events is feasible. This corresponds to a system in which all the $m$ events run autonomously without any constraint or coordination; the event list in any state is always $\mathbf{A}$ itself.

Closely related to the language is the "score space". Define an $|\mathbf{A}|$-dimensional vector $[\sigma]$, with its $\alpha$-component, $[\sigma]_\alpha$, denoting the number of $\alpha$ events in the string $\sigma$. We shall refer to $[\sigma]$ as the "score" of $\sigma$. A score is feasible if it can be realized by a feasible string. The score space is then the set of all feasible scores:

$$\mathcal{N} := \{x \in Z_+^{|\mathbf{A}|} : x = [\sigma], \exists \sigma \in \mathcal{L}\}.$$

($Z_+$ denotes the set of non-negative integers.)

**Example 4.2.1** Consider a single-server queueing system that allows a maximum of $K$ jobs in it. Once a job arrives and brings the total number of jobs in the system (including the arriving job itself) to $K$, the arrival process is immediately stopped. The arrival process will be resumed at the next service completion, when the number of waiting jobs drops below $K$. The service discipline is first-come-first-served.

Let the state be the total number of jobs in the system, including the one in service. The state space is then $\mathbf{S} = \{0, 1, ..., K\}$. Let the initial state be zero, i.e., the system starts empty. There are two events, arrivals and service completions, denoted $\alpha$ and $\beta$, respectively. Hence, $\mathbf{A} = \{\alpha, \beta\}$. The event list can be specified as follows:

$$\mathcal{E}(0) = \{\alpha\}; \quad \mathcal{E}(k) = \{\alpha, \beta\}, \ k = 1, ..., K - 1; \quad \mathcal{E}(K) = \{\beta\}.$$

The transition function takes the following form:

$$\phi(k, \alpha) = k + 1, \quad \phi(k, \beta) = k - 1.$$

The language $\mathcal{L}$ consists of all feasible strings $\sigma$, characterized by the following relations in terms of scores:

$$0 \leq [\sigma']_\alpha - [\sigma']_\beta \leq K,$$

for any prefix $\sigma'$ of $\sigma$.

The input to the scheme is the sequence of interarrival times and service times. The output consists of the sequence of arrival and service completion epochs, as well as the related counting processes.

**Example 4.2.2** In the above example, suppose $K = \infty$, so that the arrival event is always active. In addition, suppose the server always serves, even when there is no job in the system (in which case the service completion produces no output from the system). This is known as an "autonomous server". Alternatively, the server can also be viewed as a "gating" mechanism: from time to time — whenever the service clock runs out — the "gate" opens, and one job from the queue, if any, is allowed to leave. Here, we have a shuffle scheme, and $\mathcal{L} = \mathbf{A}^*$; i.e., any string of $\alpha$'s and $\beta$'s is feasible.

# 4.3   Structural Properties of the Scheme

Unless otherwise stated, the initial state is understood to be $s_0$, and we will write $\phi(\sigma) := \phi(s_0, \sigma)$ and $\mathcal{E}(\sigma) := \mathcal{E}(\phi(s_0, \sigma))$. Throughout, $\vee$ and $\wedge$ denote the *max* and the *min* operators among vectors (in the componentwise sense). Any partial order between vectors is also in the componentwise sense.

## 4.3.1   Some Useful Properties

We start with presenting some useful properties of the scheme $\mathcal{G}$. Not all GSMS's possess those properties (see the examples below); those that do, however, are endowed with some very appealing structure, as we shall illustrate later in the section.

**Definition 4.3.1** The scheme $\mathcal{G}$ is said to satisfy

(i) *non-interruption,* if $s \in \mathbf{S}$, $\alpha, \beta \in \mathcal{E}(s)$, $\alpha \neq \beta \Rightarrow \beta \in \mathcal{E}(\phi(s, \alpha))$;

(ii) *permutability,* if $\sigma_1, \sigma_2 \in \mathcal{L}$, $[\sigma_1] = [\sigma_2] \Rightarrow \mathcal{E}(\sigma_1) = \mathcal{E}(\sigma_2)$;

(iii) *strong permutability,* if $\sigma_1, \sigma_2 \in \mathcal{L}$, $[\sigma_1] = [\sigma_2] \Rightarrow \phi(\sigma_1) = \phi(\sigma_2)$;

(iv) *min-closure,* if $\sigma_1, \sigma_2 \in \mathcal{L} \Rightarrow [\sigma] = [\sigma_1] \wedge [\sigma_2]$, for some $\sigma \in \mathcal{L}$.

Non-interruption states that the occurrence of one event never de-activates another: if both $\alpha$ and $\beta$ are active in state $s$ and $\alpha$ occurs, $\beta$ must remain active in the new state $\phi(s, \alpha)$. Hence, non-interruption guarantees that each event, once activated, always occurs at the scheduled time. Permutability states that two strings that have the same score will lead to two states that have the same event list. That is, the actual *sequence* of event occurrences is not important (and in this sense "permutable"); what matters is only the *number* of event occurrences (i.e., scores). Strong permutability strengthens this property by requiring that the two strings with the same score lead to the same state. Min-closure requires the score space to be closed under min: the minimum of any two feasible scores is also a feasible score.

We illustrate the above properties through some simple queueing examples. In all the examples below, non-interruption is automatically satisfied. In particular, this is guaranteed by a non-preemptive service discipline.

**Example 4.3.2** Consider a single-server queue that allows a maximum of one job in it (i.e., no extra waiting room). Suppose the arrival process is uncontrollable, in the sense that it is always an active event, regardless of the system state. When the server is occupied, the arrivals are blocked and lost. There are two events here: job arrival and service completion, denoted $\alpha$ and $\beta$, respectively. This model violates permutability. For instance, starting from an empty system, the string $\alpha\beta\alpha$ leads to an event list $\{\alpha, \beta\}$, while another string with the same score, $\alpha\alpha\beta$ leads to an event list $\{\alpha\}$ (the string results in an empty system, the second arrival being blocked).

On the other hand, suppose the arrival process is controllable: whenever an arrival occurs and the server is occupied, the arrival event is removed from the event list; it will only be re-activated when the service is completed and the system becomes empty again. In this case, *strong permutability* is satisfied: The state is a 0-1 binary variable, corresponding to system empty or not. Any feasible string has a score that satisfies $[\sigma]_\alpha - [\sigma]_\beta = 0$ or 1. Hence, any two feasible strings that have the same score will lead to the same state.

**Example 4.3.3** Consider a single-server queue with infinite waiting room. There are two job classes, indexed by the subscripts 1 and 2. Let $\alpha_i$ and $\beta_i$ denote the arrival and service completion event of class $i$, $i = 1, 2$. The service discipline is first come first served, regardless of class. This model also violates permutability: Start with an empty system, $\alpha_1\alpha_2$ leads to the event list $\{\alpha_1, \alpha_2, \beta_1\}$, while $\alpha_2\alpha_1$ leads to the event list $\{\alpha_1, \alpha_2, \beta_2\}$.

Suppose the service process is class-independent, hence $\beta_1 = \beta_2 = \beta$. Then, permutability is satisfied: whether $\beta$ is on the event list or not depends only on whether the score $[\sigma]_{\alpha_1} + [\sigma]_{\alpha_2} - [\sigma]_\beta$ is positive or zero ($\alpha_1$ and $\alpha_2$ are always on the event list). However, it is also clear that strong permutability is not satisfied, when the state is defined as the number of jobs of either class in the system. On the other hand, if the state is defined as the total number of jobs of both classes in the system, then strong permutability is satisfied.

When $\beta_1 = \beta_2 = \beta$, min-closure is not satisfied either. For instance, $[\sigma^1] = (j, n - j, n)$ ($j$ class 1 arrivals, $n - j$ class 2 arrivals, and $n$ service completions), and $[\sigma^2] = (k, n - k, n)$ are two feasible scores, and suppose

$j < k$. Then, $[\sigma^1] \wedge [\sigma^2] = (j, n - k, n)$ is not a feasible score, since $n - k + j < n$, i.e.,the total number of arrivals is less than the number of service completions. On the other hand, if in addition, $\alpha_1 = \alpha_2 = \alpha$ (i.e., the model becomes a single class queue), then the score becomes a 2-vector, and it is easy to verify that min-closure is satisfied.

### 4.3.2  Condition (M)

We now introduce condition **(M)** (for "monotonicity"), originally developed to characterize monotonicity in a GSMP with respect to clock times. It has three equivalent forms, one of which is simply non-interruption plus permutability, see Definition 4.3.1 (i,ii). Below, we will show that condition **(M)** is equivalent to the language generated by the scheme having an antimatroid structure. It is also equivalent to the event epochs of the GSMP having a (min,max, +) representation.

**Definition 4.3.4** The scheme $\mathcal{G}$ is said to satisfy

(i) Condition **(M)**: if $\sigma_1, \sigma_2 \in \mathcal{L}$, $[\sigma_1] \le [\sigma_2] \Rightarrow \mathcal{E}(\sigma_1) \backslash A_{12} \subseteq \mathcal{E}(\sigma_2)$, where $A_{12} := \{\alpha \in \mathbf{A} : [\sigma_1]_\alpha < [\sigma_2]_\alpha\}$;

(ii) Condition **(M1)**: if it satisfies non-interruption and permutability;

(iii) Condition **(M2)**: if $\sigma_1, \sigma_2 \in \mathcal{L}$, $[\sigma_1] \ne [\sigma_2] \Rightarrow \exists \sigma$ such that $\sigma_1 \sigma \in \mathcal{L}$ and $[\sigma_1 \sigma] = [\sigma_1] \vee [\sigma_2]$.

Condition **(M)** says that if a string has more events, it should lead to a state with a richer event list, except that a provision is made for events that occur more times on the longer string. This ensures that more event occurrences will enable more events to happen in the future. Hence, it can be succinctly described as "more $\Rightarrow$ more". It is a statement that tries to capture directly the monotone structure of the scheme. Condition **(M1)** is simply a combination of the two properties, non-interruption and permutability, explained earlier. In most applications, **(M1)** is perhaps the most convenient form. For instance, in queueing systems, non-interruption is typically satisfied whenever the service discipline is non-preemptive; the verification of **(M1)** then reduces to verifying permutability only, as we have already illustrated in Examples 4.3.2 and 4.3.3. Condition **(M2)** says that the score space is *max-closed*, hence a semi-lattice. That is, given any two feasible strings and their scores, the (componentwise) maximum of the two scores is also a feasible score. Furthermore, this maximum is achieved by simply appending to one of the two strings the extra events from the other string.

To prove the equivalence of the conditions, we need the following lemma.

**Lemma 4.3.5** Under **(M1)**, we have

$$\sigma_1, \sigma_2 \in \mathcal{L}, \ [\sigma_1] < [\sigma_2] \Rightarrow \exists \sigma \text{ such that } \sigma_1 \sigma \in \mathcal{L} \text{ and } [\sigma_1 \sigma] = [\sigma_2].$$

**Proof.** Use induction on the length of $\sigma_2$, denoted $|\sigma_2|$. The case of $|\sigma_2| = 1$ is obvious. As induction hypothesis, suppose the statement in the lemma holds when $|\sigma_2| \leq n - 1$. Consider $|\sigma_2| = n$. Let $\sigma$ be a string that consists of those extra events in $\sigma_2$ (i.e., *beyond* what is in $\sigma_1$), in the same order as they occur in $\sigma_2$. This way, clearly $[\sigma_1\sigma] = [\sigma_2]$. The only remaining task is to show that $\sigma_1\sigma$ is indeed a feasible string, i.e., every time an extra event in $\sigma_2$ is appended to $\sigma_1$, feasibility is maintained. Suppose at one point $\sigma_1$ has been extended to $\sigma_1\sigma'$, and the next event to be appended to $\sigma_1\sigma'$ is $\alpha$. We want to show $\sigma_1\sigma'\alpha \in \mathcal{L}$. Write $\sigma_2 = \eta\alpha\delta$. We have

$$[\eta]_\alpha = [\sigma_1\sigma']_\alpha, \quad [\eta] \leq [\sigma_1\sigma'].$$

If $\delta$ is an empty string, i.e., $\alpha$ is the last event in $\sigma_2$, then $[\eta] = [\sigma_1\sigma']$, and $\eta\alpha \in \mathcal{L}$ leads to $\sigma_1\sigma'\alpha \in \mathcal{L}$ due to permutability. Next, suppose $\delta \neq \epsilon$. Since $|\sigma_1\sigma'| \leq n - 1$, applying the induction hypothesis to $\eta$ and $\sigma_1\sigma'$, we can extend $\eta$ to $\eta\eta' \in \mathcal{L}$ with $[\eta\eta'] = [\sigma_1\sigma']$. Since $[\eta]_\alpha = [\sigma_1\sigma']_\alpha$, $\eta'$ contains no $\alpha$. Since both $\eta\alpha \in \mathcal{L}$ and $\eta\eta' \in \mathcal{L}$, applying non-interruption leads to $\eta\eta'\alpha \in \mathcal{L}$. But then permutability implies $\sigma_1\sigma'\alpha \in \mathcal{L}$. $\square$

**Theorem 4.3.6** The conditions **(M)**, **(M1)** and **(M2)** are equivalent.

**Proof. (M1)** $\Rightarrow$ **(M)**. To start with, assume that $\sigma_2$ has exactly one more $\alpha$ event than $\sigma_1$. Suppose $\beta \in \mathcal{E}(\sigma_1)$. We want to show $\beta \in \mathcal{E}(\sigma_2)$. Applying Lemma 4.3.5, we have $\sigma_1\alpha \in \mathcal{L}$, i.e., $\alpha \in \mathcal{E}(\sigma_1)$, since $\alpha$ is the extra event that is in $\sigma_2$ but not in $\sigma_1$. Since $\beta \in \mathcal{E}(\sigma_1)$, non-interruption implies $\beta \in \mathcal{E}(\sigma_1\alpha)$. Since $[\sigma_1\alpha] = [\sigma_2]$, permutability implies $\beta \in \mathcal{E}(\sigma_2)$. If $\sigma_2$ has more than one extra event, apply the above argument repeatedly.

**(M)** $\Rightarrow$ **(M2)**. Follow the proof of Lemma 4.3.5, construct $\sigma$ in a similar fashion. The only difference is here we do not have $[\sigma_2] \geq [\sigma_1]$, but $\sigma$ still takes all the events that are present in $\sigma_2$ but not in $\sigma_1$. To argue that $\alpha$ can be appended to $\sigma_1\sigma'$, let $\eta$ denote the prefix of $\sigma_2$ immediately preceding $\alpha$, then $[\eta] \leq [\sigma_1\sigma']$. Hence $\eta\alpha \in \mathcal{L}$ implies $\sigma_1\sigma'\alpha \in \mathcal{L}$, due to **(M)**.

**(M2)** $\Rightarrow$ **(M1)**. For non-interruption, suppose $s$ is the state reached by a string $\sigma$. Since $\alpha, \beta \in \mathcal{E}(s)$, both $\sigma\alpha$ and $\sigma\beta$ are feasible strings. Hence, **(M2)** guarantees the feasibility of $\sigma\alpha\beta$, i.e., $\beta \in \mathcal{E}(\phi(s, \alpha))$. For permutability, suppose two feasible strings $\sigma_1$ and $\sigma_2$ have the same score: $[\sigma_1] = [\sigma_2]$, and suppose $\beta \in \mathcal{E}(\sigma_2)$, i.e., $\sigma_2\beta \in \mathcal{L}$. Then, $[\sigma_1\beta] = [\sigma_1] \vee [\sigma_2\beta]$; hence **(M2)** implies $\sigma_1\beta \in \mathcal{L}$, i.e., $\beta \in \mathcal{E}(\sigma_1)$. The other way round, i.e., $\beta \in \mathcal{E}(\sigma_1) \Rightarrow \beta \in \mathcal{E}(\sigma_2)$, follows from symmetry. $\square$

## The Antimatroid Connection

Under **(M)**, the scheme, or more specifically, the language it generates, has a special structure, namely, an *antimatroid with repetition*. Below, we first briefly review the concepts of *matroid*, *antimatroid*, and *greedoid*. Refer to Dietrich [12] for more details.

Let $S$ be a finite set, and $\mathcal{F}$, a family of subsets (of $S$). Let $A, B$ be subsets of $S$, and $|A|, |B|$ denote their cardinality. $(S, \mathcal{F})$ is a *matroid*, if $\mathcal{F}$ satisfies the following properties:

(i) $\emptyset \in \mathcal{F}$;

(ii) *(subclusive)* $A \in \mathcal{F} \Rightarrow B \in \mathcal{F}, \forall B \subseteq A$;

(iii) *(exchange)* $A, B \in \mathcal{F}, |A| > |B| \Rightarrow B \cup e \in \mathcal{F}$, for some $e \in A \backslash B$.

Now, *antimatroid* is the same $(S, \mathcal{F})$ that satisfies (i), but weakens (ii) while strengthens (iii) as follows:

(iia) *(accessible)* $A \in \mathcal{F} \Rightarrow B \in \mathcal{F}$, for some $B \subset A$;

(iiia) *(strong exchange)* $A, B \in \mathcal{F}, A \nsubseteq B \Rightarrow B \cup e \in \mathcal{F}, \exists e \in A \backslash B$.

[Note that (iia) weakens (ii) by weakening its conclusion, while (iiia) strengthens (iii) by relaxing its condition.]

The simplest example of a matroid is based on linear independence of vectors. (In fact matroid was originally introduced by Whitney [47] as an abstraction of linear independence.) Suppose $S$ is a set of vectors and $\mathcal{F}$ consists of all subsets of linearly independent vectors. If $B \in \mathcal{F}$, then any of its subsets is also linearly independent, hence subclusiveness. Given $A, B \in \mathcal{F}$, if $A$ has a larger cardinality, then $B$ can be expanded by taking vectors from $A$ while still maintaining linear independence. This is the exchange property. However, this might not be possible, if $A$ is merely not a subset of $B$. For instance, suppose $A$ and $B$ are two different pairs of linearly independent vectors on a 2-dimensional plane, neither can be expanded to span the 3-dimensional space by adding a vector from the other.

The simplest example of an antimatroid is perhaps the so-called "shelling of a tree". Let $S$ be the set of edges of a tree, and $\mathcal{F}$, the family of subsets of edges such that the complement of each subset remains a tree. Then for any two such subsets $A$ and $B$, as long as $A$ is not a subset of $B$, $B$ can always be expanded by taking some edges from $A$, i.e., the strong exchange property is satisfied. To see this, consider two cases: (i) $B \subset A$, and (ii) $B \not\subset A$ (in addition to $A \not\subset B$). Case (i) is trivial: $B$ can be expanded to $A$. In case (ii) there must exist a "leaf" in $A$ that is not in $B$ and can hence be added to $B$ without disqualifying it from belonging to $\mathcal{F}$. On the other hand, if $A \in \mathcal{F}$, then clearly not all subsets of $A$ belong to $\mathcal{F}$, although the edge(s) in $A$ closest to the remaining tree can be removed without endangering its membership in $\mathcal{F}$. Hence, accessibility is satisfied, but not subclusiveness.

*Greedoid* (Korte and Lovász [30]) unifies matroid and antimatroid by taking both weaker properties (iia) (accessible) and (iii) (exchange). Hence both matroid and antimatroid are special cases of greedoid. Greedoid provides the essential characterization of the structure of many combinatorial optimization problems that are solvable by greedy algorithms.

Now, in the setting of GSMS, we are concerned with the antimatroid structure of the language $\mathcal{L}$. Here, the finite set $S$ is the event set $\mathbf{A}$, and $\mathcal{L}$ plays the same role as $\mathcal{F}$. However, $\mathcal{L}$ differs from $\mathcal{F}$ on two accounts: (i) each of its member is a string, i.e., an *ordered* sequence of events; and (ii) the events can repeatedly occur. Björner [4] proposed the concept of *antimatroid with repetition* to study a structure such as $(\mathbf{A}, \mathcal{L})$. Specifically, a language $\mathcal{L}$ is such an antimatroid if it (a) contains the empty string, (b) is prefix closed (corresponding to accessibility), and (c) satisfies a "strong exchange property" that is equivalent to two properties, "locally free" and "permutable" (Shor, Björner and Lovász [45]), which correspond, respectively, to non-interruption and permutability that constitute our condition (M1). Note that according to our definition of the language, namely, the set of feasible strings, (a) and (b) are automatically satisfied. Hence, in view of Theorem 4.3.6, we have

**Theorem 4.3.7** The scheme $\mathcal{G}$ satisfies condition (M) if and only if the language it generates, $\mathcal{L}$, is an antimatroid.

**Definition 4.3.8** The scheme $\mathcal{G}$ is said to satisfy Condition (C) if it is non-interruptive and strongly permutable.

The following are some rather obvious consequences of condition (C).

**Corollary 4.3.9** (i) Condition (C) implies (M) and its equivalent forms, (M1) and (M2). (ii) Under (C), for any $\sigma_1, \sigma_2 \in \mathcal{L}$, if $[\sigma_1] = [\sigma_2]$, then $\sigma_2$ can be obtained from $\sigma_1$ by a sequence of pairwise interchanges of consecutive events, with each interchange resulting in a feasible string. (In fact, this holds under (M).)

As we shall demonstrate later, in many applications (queueing systems in particular), with an appropriate state definition, it is almost trivial to verify (C) — which then implies (M) — while it could be quite tedious to verify (M) directly.

## 4.3.3  Condition (CX)

When the language $\mathcal{L}$ is an antimatroid, the strong exchange property guarantees that the score space is max-closed, that is, given any two feasible scores, their componentwise max is also a feasible score, i.e., there exists a string in the language whose score equals this max. In other words, the score space is a semi-lattice. However, in general, the antimatroid structure does not lead to a score space that is *min-closed*. That is, given $\sigma_1, \sigma_2 \in \mathcal{L}$, there need not exist a $\sigma \in \mathcal{L}$ such that $[\sigma] = [\sigma_1] \wedge [\sigma_2]$. In other words, even when **(M)** is satisfied, min-closure could still fail. We have shown such a case in Example 4.3.3.

Nevertheless, when **(M)** holds, we can meaningfully talk about a longest string (i.e., the one with the largest score), $\sigma \in \mathcal{L}$, that satisfies

$$[\sigma] \leq [\sigma_1] \wedge [\sigma_2]. \tag{4.1}$$

For instance, in Example 4.3.3, such a string $\sigma$ corresponds to the score $(j, n-k, n-k+j)$. Note that $\sigma$ must exist: the empty string always satisfies (4.1), and $\sigma$ must be unique: for any two feasible strings satisfying (4.1), taking max results in another feasible string satisfying the same inequality but with a larger score, due to the max-closure property of $\mathcal{L}$. Hence the question is: when would (4.1) become an *equality* ? It turns out that for this to happen we need the following condition, which has three equivalent forms.

**Definition 4.3.10** The scheme $\mathcal{G}$ is said to satisfy

(i) Condition **(CX)**: if
$$\sigma_1, \sigma_2, \sigma_3 \in \mathcal{L}, \ [\sigma_3] \geq [\sigma_1] \wedge [\sigma_2] \Rightarrow [\mathcal{E}(\sigma_1) \cap \mathcal{E}(\sigma_2)] \backslash A^\wedge \subseteq \mathcal{E}(\sigma_3),$$
where $A^\wedge := \{\alpha \in \mathbf{A} : [\sigma_3]_\alpha > [\sigma_1]_\alpha \wedge [\sigma_2]_\alpha\}$.

(ii) Condition **(CX1)**: if it satisfies non-interruption and
$$\sigma_1, \sigma_2, \sigma_3 \in \mathcal{L}, \ [\sigma_3] = [\sigma_1] \wedge [\sigma_2] \Rightarrow \mathcal{E}(\sigma_1) \cap \mathcal{E}(\sigma_2) \subseteq \mathcal{E}(\sigma_3).$$

(iii) Condition **(CX2)**: if it satisfies **(M)** and min-closure.

Here, **(CX)** stands for "convexity". The condition was originally developed to characterize the convexity of the event epochs with respect to the clock times. It is a strengthening of **(M)**. Under **(CX)**, the language $\mathcal{L}$ is not only an antimatroid, it also satisfies the min-closure property, and the score space $\mathcal{N}$ becomes a lattice.

**Theorem 4.3.11** The conditions **(CX)**, **(CX1)** and **(CX2)** are equivalent, and each is equivalent to $\mathcal{L}$ being an antimatroid that is min-closed, and implies that $\mathcal{N}$ is a lattice.

**Proof. (CX)** $\Rightarrow$ **(CX1)**. First observe that **(CX)** implies **(M)** [let $\sigma_1 = \sigma_2$ in **(CX)**] and hence non-interruption. That **(CX)** implies the other condition in **(CX1)** is obvious.

**(CX1)** $\Rightarrow$ **(CX2)**. The second condition in **(CX1)** obviously implies permutability, hence **(CX1)** $\Rightarrow$ **(M)**. To show that **(CX1)** also implies min-closure, we want to argue that (4.1) is satisfied as an equality. Based on Lemma 4.3.5, for $j = 1, 2$, we can extend $\sigma$ to $\sigma\sigma_j' \in \mathcal{L}$ with $[\sigma\sigma_j'] = [\sigma_j]$. It then suffices to argue that $\sigma_1'$ and $\sigma_2'$ have no common events. Use contradiction. Suppose $\alpha$ is the first common event in $\sigma_1'$ and $\sigma_2'$. Apply **(CX1)** to $\sigma$ and the two strings $\sigma\sigma_j''$, for $j = 1, 2$, where $\sigma_j''$ is the prefix of $\sigma_j'$, immediately preceding $\alpha$. (Note that $\sigma_1''$ and $\sigma_2''$ have no common events.) This leads to $\alpha \in \mathcal{E}(\sigma)$, and hence $\sigma\alpha \in \mathcal{L}$, contradicting the maximality of $\sigma$.

**(CX2)** $\Rightarrow$ **(CX)**. Let $\beta \in [\mathcal{E}(\sigma_1) \cap \mathcal{E}(\sigma_2)]\backslash A^\wedge$. We want to show $\beta \in \mathcal{E}(\sigma_3)$. Consider a string $\sigma_3' \in \mathcal{L}$, with $[\sigma_3'] = [\sigma_1] \wedge [\sigma_2]$, whose existence is guaranteed by min-closure, which also justifies the existence of another string $\sigma \in \mathcal{L}$ with $[\sigma] = [\sigma_1\beta] \wedge [\sigma_2\beta]$. Now, **(M)** ensures that $\sigma_3'$ can be extended to have the same score as $\sigma$. But this implies $\beta \in \mathcal{E}(\sigma_3')$, since $\beta$ is the only extra event that $\sigma$ has (beyond what $\sigma_3'$ has). Since $[\sigma_3] \geq [\sigma_3']$, and both strings have the same number of $\beta$ occurrences, **(M)** implies $\beta \in \mathcal{E}(\sigma_3)$ as well.

The last two statements in the theorem follow directly from Theorem 4.3.7 and Definition 4.3.10 (iii). $\square$

### 4.3.4 Minimal Elements

When the scheme satisfies condition **(M)**, the event list is determined by the score, instead of the string that achieves the score. So, given a feasible string $\sigma$ with score $[\sigma] = x \in \mathcal{N}$, we can meaningfully write $\mathcal{E}(x)$, instead of $\mathcal{E}(\sigma)$. For each $\alpha \in \mathbf{A}$ and each $n = 1, 2, ...$, define

$$\mathcal{N}_{\alpha,n} := \{x \in \mathcal{N} : x_\alpha = n - 1, \alpha \in \mathcal{E}(x)\}. \tag{4.2}$$

That is, $\mathcal{N}_{\alpha,n}$ is the set of feasible scores that can lead to the $n$th activation of $\alpha$. Let $x^k(\alpha, n)$, $k = 1, 2, ...$, denote the *minimal elements* of $\mathcal{N}_{\alpha,n}$, i.e., for each $k$,

$$x \in \mathcal{N}_{\alpha,n}, \quad x \leq x^k(\alpha, n) \quad \Rightarrow \quad x = x^k(\alpha, n). \tag{4.3}$$

In other words, a minimal element $x^k(\alpha, n)$ is the smallest score (in the componentwise sense) that enables the $n$th activation of event $\alpha$. Note that the number of such minimal elements is necessarily finite, since the event set $\mathbf{A}$ is finite.

**Theorem 4.3.12** If the scheme $\mathcal{G}$ satisfies condition **(M)**, then the event epochs $T$ admit the following (min,max, +) representation for any clock sequence $\omega$:

$$T_\alpha(n) = \omega_\alpha(n) + \min_k \max_{\beta \in \mathbf{A}} \{T_\beta(x_\beta^k(\alpha, n))\}, \tag{4.4}$$

where $x^k(\alpha, n)$ is a minimal element of $\mathcal{N}_{\alpha,n}$, and the min is taken over all such minimal elements. If $\mathcal{G}$ satisfies condition **(CX)**, then $T$ admits the following (max, +) representation for any clock sequence $\omega$:

$$T_\alpha(n) = \omega_\alpha(n) + \max_{\beta \in \mathbf{A}} \{T_\beta(x_\beta(\alpha, n))\}. \tag{4.5}$$

**Proof.** Denote the min-max part in (4.4) as $S_\alpha(n)$, which we argue is the time at which the $\alpha$ event is activated for the $n$th time; (4.4) then follows from non-interruption. Under condition **(M)**, the time epoch $S_\alpha(n)$ is reached as soon as one of the minimal elements $x^k(\alpha, n)$ is reached, hence the min part. For any given $k$, the minimal element $x^k(\alpha, n)$ is reached if and only if each event $\beta$ has occured $x_\beta^k(\alpha, n)$ times, hence the max part.

The (max, +) representation in (4.5) follows from the min-closure property implied by **(CX)**, since in this case the minimal element is unique. $\square$

**Example 4.3.13** Continue the single-server queue model of Example 4.3.3 with two classes of arrivals (but homogeneous in service requirement). The minimal elements of $\mathcal{N}_{\beta,n}$ are $(j, n - j, n - 1)$, for $j = 0, 1, ..., n$. That is, there have been a total of $n$ arrivals (from both classes) and $n - 1$ service completions (so that the $n$th service can be initiated). Consequently, the time epoch of the $n$th service completion has the following expression.

$$T_\beta(n) = \omega_\beta(n) + \min_{0 \le j \le n} \max\{T_{\alpha_1}(j), T_{\alpha_2}(n - j), T_\beta(n - 1)\}.$$

This (min,max, +) expression, as well as the multiplicity of the minimal elements, further explain why the model satisfies condition **(M)**, but not **(CX)**.

On the other hand, if there is only one class of arrivals, denoted $\alpha$, then the above event-epoch recursion reduces to

$$T_\beta(n) = \omega_\beta(n) + \max\{T_\alpha(n), T_\beta(n - 1)\}.$$

That is, the minimal element is unique, and **(CX)** is satisfied.

Under **(CX)**, there is an alternative expression for the event epochs, equivalent to (4.5). Denote the $n$th occurrence of the event $\alpha$ by the pair $(\alpha, n)$. Making use of the minimal element, we can define a precedence relation $\to$ on such pairs: $(\beta, j) \to (\alpha, n)$ if $x_\beta(\alpha, n) = j$. That is, the $j$th occurrence of $\beta$ precedes the $n$th occurrence of $\alpha$ if $\beta$ must occur at least $j$ times in order to activate $\alpha$ the $n$th time. In other words, the $\beta$ component of the minimal element $x_\beta(\alpha, n) = j$. Define a *path* $\pi$ as a finite sequence of such pairs ordered under $\to$, for instance,

$$\pi : (\alpha_1, n_1) \to \cdots \to (\alpha_\ell, n_\ell).$$

Let $\Pi(\alpha, n)$ denote the set of paths, each starting with $(\beta, 1)$, for some $\beta \in \mathcal{E}(s_0)$, and ending with $(\alpha, n)$. That is, each path in $\Pi(\alpha, n)$ corresponds to an "event trajectory" that leads from the initial state to the state reached at $(\alpha, n)$. Note that $\Pi(\alpha, n)$ is necessarily a finite set. Then, starting from (4.5) and arguing inductively, we have

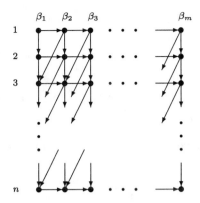

FIGURE 1. Longest-path interpretation of event epochs. Arcs represent precedence constraints. Node $(\beta_i, j)$ represents the $j$-th occurrence of event $\beta_i$ and has associated with it the duration $\omega_{\beta_i}(j)$. The event epoch $T_{\beta_m}(n)$ is the length of the longest path from the upper-left corner to the lower-right corner.

**Corollary 4.3.14** Under **(CX)**, an alternative expression for the event epochs in (4.5) is

$$T_\alpha(n) = \max_{\pi \in \Pi(\alpha, n)} \sum_{(\beta, j) \in \pi} \omega_\beta(j),$$

with the maximum over an empty set taken to be $+\infty$.

The above also suggests a graph interpretation. Let the pairs $(\beta, j)$ defined above be nodes in a graph. A directed edge between two nodes represents the precedence relation between the two corresponding pairs. Associated with each node $(\beta, j)$ is a "cost": the event life time $\omega_\beta(j)$. Then, $T_\alpha(n)$ is simply the maximum cost (or, longest path) traveling from a (dummy) source node [i.e., one that precedes $(\beta, 1)$, $\forall \beta \in \mathcal{E}(s_0)$] to the destination node $(\alpha, n)$. See Figure 1 (where the dummy node is omitted, since there is only a single event $\beta_1 \in \mathcal{E}(s_0)$).

### 4.3.5 Monotonicity and Convexity

We now discuss the implications of the representations of $T$ in Theorem 4.3.12, in terms of monotonicity and convexity. There are two stochastic order relations involved. (Let $X$ and $Y$ be two random vectors.) The *stochastic ordering*: $X \leq^{st} Y$ if and only if $\mathsf{E}f(X) \leq \mathsf{E}f(Y)$ for all increasing functions $f$; and the *convex ordering*: $X \leq^{icx} Y$ if and only if $\mathsf{E}f(X) \leq \mathsf{E}f(Y)$ for all increasing and convex functions $f$. (Here and below, $E$ denotes expectation, "increasing" means "non-decreasing".) For random sequences, these orderings hold if they are satisfied by all finite dimensional sub-sequences (random vectors). See, e.g., Ross [26] (Chapter 8); also, Stoyan [29], Kamae et al [25].

**Theorem 4.3.15** (i) Under **(M)**, $T$ is increasing in $\omega$. Under **(CX)**, $T$ is increasing and convex in $\omega$.

(ii) Under **(M)**, $\omega^1 \leq^{st} \omega^2 \Rightarrow T(\omega^1) \leq^{st} T(\omega^2)$. Under **(CX)**, we have, in addition, $\omega^1 \leq^{icx} \omega^2 \Rightarrow T(\omega^1) \leq^{icx} T(\omega^2)$.

**Proof.** The results under **(M)** follow immediately from (4.4), noticing that both min and max (as well as +) are increasing operators, and the minimal elements $x^k(\alpha, n)$ are independent of $\omega$. The results under **(CX)** follow from (4.5), since max and + are increasing and convex operators. □

**Example 4.3.16** Consider the two examples in Example 4.3.13. When there are two classes of arrivals, we only have monotonicity for the event epochs (with respect to the clock times). In the case of a single arrival class, however, the event epochs are not only increasing but also convex in the clock times. In addition, the convex ordering ($\leq^{icx}$) between clock times also translates into the same ordering between event-epoch sequences.

Now, suppose the $n$th clock time of $\alpha$ takes the form: $f_{\alpha,n}(\omega_\alpha(n), \theta_\alpha(n))$, where $\theta_\alpha(n)$ is a (deterministic) parameter, and $f_{\alpha,n}(\cdot, y)$ is an increasing and convex function with respect to $y$. Then, under **(CX)**, for any increasing and convex function $g$, $\mathbb{E}g[T(\omega, \theta)]$ is increasing and convex with respect to $\theta := \{\theta_\alpha(n); \alpha \in \mathbf{A}, n = 1, 2, ...\}$. In other words, when the clock times satisfy the notion of *strong stochastic convexity* of Shanthikumar and Yao [44], the same property carries over to the event-epoch sequence, under **(CX)**.

Also note that since the counting process $D$ relates directly to the event-epoch sequence $T$ through $D_\alpha(t) = \sup\{n : T_\alpha(n) \leq t\}$ for all $\alpha$ and all $t$, any monotonicity result of $T$ translates directly into a monotonicity result of $D$. Such translations, however, are not possible in general for convexity results.

### 4.3.6   Characteristic Function

**Definition 4.3.17** Define the function $\chi : \mathcal{L} \mapsto \mathbf{Z}_+^{|\mathbf{A}|}$ componentwise by

$$\chi_\alpha(\sigma) = [\sigma]_\alpha + \mathbf{1}[\alpha \in \mathcal{E}(\sigma)],$$

and refer to it as the *characteristic function* (of the scheme).

The characteristic function captures the one-step behavior of the evolution of feasible strings: $\chi_\alpha(\sigma) > [\sigma]_\alpha$ if and only if $\sigma$ can be followed by $\alpha$. Moreover, $\chi$ determines $\mathcal{L}$, since $\sigma = \beta_1 \ldots \beta_n \in \mathcal{L}$ if and only if $[\beta_1 \ldots \beta_{i-1}]_{\beta_i} < \chi_{\beta_i}(\beta_1 \ldots \beta_{i-1})$ for all $i = 1, ..., n$.

When the scheme satisfies **(M)**, as pointed out in Section 3.4, we can write $\mathcal{E}(\sigma)$ as $\mathcal{E}(x)$, where $x = [\sigma]$. The characteristic function then becomes a function on the score space:

$$\chi_\alpha(x) = x_\alpha + \mathbf{1}[\alpha \in \mathcal{E}(x)]. \tag{4.6}$$

Below, we show that the characteristic function also provides a characterization of the conditions (M) and (CX). Call $\chi$ (as a function on $\mathcal{L}$) *increasing* if for any two feasible strings $\sigma_1, \sigma_2 \in \mathcal{L}$, $[\sigma_1] \le [\sigma_2] \Rightarrow \chi(\sigma_1) \le \chi(\sigma_2)$. When (M) is satisfied, $\chi$ is increasing if $x^1 \le x^2 \in \mathcal{N} \Rightarrow \chi(x^1) \le \chi(x^2)$. Call $\chi$ *supermodular*, if

$$\chi(\sigma_1) + \chi(\sigma_2) \le \chi(\sigma_3) + \chi(\sigma_4), \tag{4.7}$$

whenever

$$[\sigma_3] = [\sigma_1] \wedge [\sigma_2], \quad [\sigma_4] = [\sigma_1] \vee [\sigma_2], \tag{4.8}$$

and all four strings are feasible. Under (M), the above simplifies to

$$\chi(x) + \chi(y) \le \chi(x \wedge y) + \chi(x \vee y), \tag{4.9}$$

whenever $x, y$ and $x \wedge y$ are all feasible scores (the feasibility of $x \vee y$ is guaranteed under (M)).

**Theorem 4.3.18** (i) $\mathcal{G}$ satisfies (M) if and only if $\chi$ is increasing;
(ii) $\mathcal{G}$ satisfies (CX) if and only if $\chi$ is increasing and supermodular.

**Proof.** Consider (i) first. If $\mathcal{G}$ satisfies (M), then following Theorem 4.3.6(i), suppose $[\sigma_1]_\alpha = [\sigma_2]_\alpha$; hence $\alpha \in \mathcal{E}(\alpha_1)\backslash A_{12} \Rightarrow \alpha \in \mathcal{E}(\sigma_2)$, implying $\chi_\alpha(\sigma_1) \le \chi_\alpha(\sigma_2)$, following Definition 4.3.17. [If $\alpha \in A_{12}$, then $[\sigma_1]_\alpha < [\sigma_2]_\alpha$, and $\chi_\alpha(\sigma_1) \le \chi_\alpha(\sigma_2)$ is automatically satisfied.] Conversely, if $[\sigma_1]_\alpha = [\sigma_2]_\alpha$, then from $\chi_\alpha(\sigma_1) \le \chi_\alpha(\sigma_2)$, we have $\alpha \in \mathcal{E}(\sigma_1)\backslash A_{12} \Rightarrow \alpha \in \mathcal{E}(\sigma_2)$.

Next we prove (ii). Suppose (CX) holds. Then, (M) holds, and (4.6) and (4.9) apply. The supermodularity in (4.9) reduces to,

$$\mathbf{1}[\alpha \in \mathcal{E}(x \wedge y)] + \mathbf{1}[\alpha \in \mathcal{E}(x \vee y)] \ge \mathbf{1}[\alpha \in \mathcal{E}(x)] + \mathbf{1}[\alpha \in \mathcal{E}(y)]. \tag{4.10}$$

Hence, it suffices to show

$$\alpha \in \mathcal{E}(x) \cup \mathcal{E}(y) \quad \Rightarrow \quad \alpha \in \mathcal{E}(x \wedge y) \cup \mathcal{E}(x \vee y), \tag{4.11}$$

$$\alpha \in \mathcal{E}(x) \cap \mathcal{E}(y) \quad \Rightarrow \quad \alpha \in \mathcal{E}(x \wedge y) \cap \mathcal{E}(x \vee y), \tag{4.12}$$

whenever $x, y \in \mathcal{N}$ [which guarantees both $x \wedge y \in \mathcal{N}$ and $x \vee y \in \mathcal{N}$, since $\mathcal{N}$ is a lattice under (CX)].

First suppose $\alpha \in \mathcal{E}(x)$, so $x + e_\alpha \in \mathcal{N}$, where $e_\alpha$ denotes the unit vector in the $\alpha$th direction. Then, when $x_\alpha \ge y_\alpha$, max-closure implies

$$(x + e_\alpha) \vee y = (x \vee y) + e_\alpha \in \mathcal{N};$$

that is, $\alpha \in \mathcal{E}(x \vee y)$. On the other hand, when $x_\alpha < y_\alpha$, min-closure implies

$$(x + e_\alpha) \wedge y = (x \wedge y) + e_\alpha \in \mathcal{N};$$

that is, $\alpha \in \mathcal{E}(x \wedge y)$. Reversing the roles of $x$ and $y$ completes the verification of (4.11).

To verify (4.12), suppose $\alpha \in \mathcal{E}(x) \cap \mathcal{E}(y)$. Then, **(M)** implies $\alpha \in \mathcal{E}(x \vee y)$, while **(CX)** [specifically, **(CX1)**] implies $\alpha \in \mathcal{E}(x \wedge y)$.

To prove the converse, $\chi$ increasing implies **(M)**, as has been shown earlier in (i), and hence it implies non-interruption. On the other hand, supermodularity leads to [cf. (4.7)]:

$$\mathbf{1}[\alpha \in \mathcal{E}(\sigma_1)] + \mathbf{1}[\alpha \in \mathcal{E}(\sigma_2)] \le \mathbf{1}[\alpha \in \mathcal{E}(\sigma_3)] + \mathbf{1}[\alpha \in \mathcal{E}(\sigma_4)], \qquad (4.13)$$

for any four feasible strings that satisfy (4.8). But this implies

$$\alpha \in \mathcal{E}(\sigma_1) \cap \mathcal{E}(\sigma_2) \quad \Rightarrow \quad \alpha \in \mathcal{E}(\sigma_3),$$

which is the other condition in **(CX1)** [Definition 4.3.10(ii)]. $\square$

**Example 4.3.19** Consider a single-server queue model with infinite waiting room. Let $\alpha$ and $\beta$ denote the arrival and service completion events. Suppose the system starts empty. From earlier discussions [cf. Examples 4.3.3 and 4.3.13], we know this model satisfies **(CX)**. So we want to verify the supermodularity of its characteristic function. Let $x = (x_\alpha, x_\beta)$ and $y = (y_\alpha, y_\beta)$ be two feasible scores, i.e., $x_\alpha \ge x_\beta$ and $y_\alpha \ge y_\beta$. Here, the supermodularity in (4.9) reduces to

$$\mathbf{1}[x_\alpha \wedge y_\alpha > x_\beta \wedge y_\beta] + \mathbf{1}[x_\alpha \vee y_\alpha > x_\beta \vee y_\beta] \ge \mathbf{1}[x_\alpha > x_\beta] + \mathbf{1}[y_\alpha > y_\beta].$$

Clearly, if both $x_\alpha > x_\beta$ and $y_\alpha > y_\beta$, then all four indicator functions above take value 1, and the inequality is satisfied as an equality. Suppose $x_\alpha > x_\beta$ but $y_\alpha = y_\beta$. The right side above is then equal to 1; while at least one of the indicator functions on the left side will take value 1, according to either $y_\alpha > x_\beta$ or $y_a \le x_\beta$. Hence the inequality is satisfied. The other case, $x_\alpha = x_\beta$, $y_\alpha > y_\beta$ is similar.

## 4.3.7  Subschemes

Below we use the superscripts $S$ and $B$ to index quantities that relate to two schemes, one is "smaller" and the other "bigger".

**Definition 4.3.20** One scheme $\mathcal{G}^S$ is a subscheme of another $\mathcal{G}^B$, denoted $\mathcal{G}^S \subseteq \mathcal{G}^B$, if

- $\mathbf{S}^S \subseteq \mathbf{S}^B$, $s_0^S = s_0^B$;

- $\mathbf{A}^S \subseteq \mathbf{A}^B$;

- $\mathcal{E}^S(s) \subseteq \mathcal{E}^B(s)$, for all $s \in \mathbf{S}^S$;

- $\phi^S(s, \alpha) = \phi^B(s, \alpha)$, for all $s \in \mathbf{S}^S$ and all $\alpha \in \mathcal{E}^S(s)$.

**Theorem 4.3.21** Suppose $\mathcal{G}^S$ and $\mathcal{G}^B$ generate languages $\mathcal{L}^S$ and $\mathcal{L}^B$, respectively.
(i) $\mathcal{G}^S \subseteq \mathcal{G}^B \Rightarrow \mathcal{L}^S \subseteq \mathcal{L}^B$;
(ii) Suppose $\mathcal{L}^S$ is non-interruptive and $\mathcal{L}^B$ an antimatroid. Then $\mathcal{L}^S \subseteq \mathcal{L}^B$
$\Rightarrow T^S \geq T^B$.

**Proof.** For (i), the feasibility of a string $\sigma = \alpha_1 \ldots \alpha_n \in \mathcal{L}^S$ implies

$$\alpha_{i+1} \in \mathcal{E}^S(\phi^S(s_0, \alpha_1, \ldots, \alpha_i)) \subseteq \mathcal{E}^B(\phi^B(s_0, \alpha_1, \ldots, \alpha_i)),$$

for all $i = 0, 1, \ldots, n - 1$ (when $n = 0$, $\sigma = \alpha_0 = \epsilon$). Hence, $\sigma \in \mathcal{L}^B$.

To prove (ii), the idea is to construct a modified clock sequence $w' \geq w$, such that when $\mathcal{G}^B$ is driven by $w'$, it "mimics" the evolution of $\mathcal{G}^S$. That is, $T^B(w') = T^S(w)$. In other words, we *prolong* the clock times for $\mathcal{G}^B$, so that it evolves in the same manner as $\mathcal{G}^S$ (driven by the original clock sequence $w$). Condition **(M)**, which is equivalent to $\mathcal{L}^B$ being an antimatroid, then leads to $T^B(w') \geq T^B(w)$, and hence the desired conclusion.

Construct the clock sequence $w'$ as follows. Initially, set $w'_\alpha(1) = w_\alpha(1)$ if $\alpha \in \mathcal{E}^S(s_0) \subseteq \mathcal{E}^B(s_0)$. (The $\subseteq$ relation is due to $\alpha \in \mathcal{L}^S \Rightarrow \alpha \in \mathcal{L}^B$.) Set $w'_\alpha(1) = T^S_\alpha(1)$ if $\alpha \in \mathcal{E}^B(s_0) - \mathcal{E}^S(s_0)$. Note, given $w$, $T^S$ is completely specified. Furthermore, if $\alpha \in \mathbf{A}^B - \mathbf{A}^S$, $T^S_\alpha(n)$ is understood to be $\infty$ for any $n$. Then clearly, $w'_\alpha(1) \geq w_\alpha(1)$ for all $\alpha \in \mathbf{A}^B$, and the first events generated by $\mathcal{G}^S$ and $\mathcal{G}^B$ are exactly the same type, and they occur at the same time.

Inductively, suppose the construction has been carried to the $n$th event epoch $\tau_n$, and $\sigma_n$ is the resulting string. Then, set

$$w'_\alpha([\sigma_n]_\alpha + 1) = w_\alpha([\sigma_n]_\alpha + 1)$$

for $\alpha \in \mathcal{E}^S(\sigma_n)$, while for $\alpha \in \mathcal{E}^B(\sigma_n) - \mathcal{E}^S(\sigma_n)$, set

$$w'_\alpha([\sigma_n]_\alpha + 1) = T^S_\alpha([\sigma_n]_\alpha + 1) - \tau_n.$$

This way, an event that is active in $\mathcal{G}^B$ but not active in $\mathcal{G}^S$ is assigned a (longer) clock time that only runs out when the same event next occurs in $\mathcal{G}^S$. Moreover, the evolution of $\mathcal{G}^B$ (driven by $w'$) is exactly the same as $\mathcal{G}^S$ (driven by $w$). Also notice that since $\mathcal{G}^B$ satisfies non-interruption, the same condition is required for $\mathcal{G}^S$ to make the above construction work. $\square$

**Example 4.3.22** Consider the single-server queue model in (4.2.1). Recall, the buffer limit is $K$, and the arrival process is stopped as soon as the buffer limit is reached. Now compare this with another similar queue with buffer limit $K + 1$, and index the two systems by superscripts $S$ and $B$, respectively.

Suppose at a time epoch $\tau$, an arrival, say the $n$th, brings the state to $K$. [This implies the $n - K + 1$ st service is currently underway; the service will complete at $T_\beta^S(n - K + 1)$.] The arrival event is then removed from the event list of $\mathcal{G}^S$, but it remains active on the event list of $\mathcal{G}^B$. Prolong the next interarrival time of $\mathcal{G}^B$ to

$$
\begin{aligned}
\omega_\alpha'(n + 1) &= T_\alpha^S(n + 1) - \tau \\
&= T_\beta^S(n - K + 1) + \omega_\alpha(n + 1) - \tau \\
&\geq \omega_\alpha(n + 1).
\end{aligned}
$$

[Note, the arrival process in $\mathcal{G}^S$ resumes at $T_\beta^S(n - K + 1)$.] This way, the next $(n + 1$ st) arrival will occur at the same time in both systems. ($K$ is in fact the only state in which prolonging the clock time is needed.)

In this case, both schemes satisfy (M). It is intuitively clear that prolonging the arrival times as above slows down the service completion (as well as the arrivals). Hence, enlarging the scheme, i.e., increasing the buffer limit, accelerates the occurrence of both arrivals and service completions.

## 4.3.8   Synchronized Schemes

We continue the discussion on comparing different schemes. Consider now a *family* of schemes, $\{\mathcal{G}^b, b \in \mathcal{B}\}$, parameterized by $b$. Without loss of generality, suppose the schemes in the family share a common event set **A**. Let $\mathcal{G}^*$ be the shuffle scheme of the events in **A** [cf. Section 2], and $\mathcal{L}^*$, the corresponding language. Given an input $\omega$, the event-epoch sequence generated by the shuffle scheme is simply the superposition of the sequences $\{T_\alpha(n)\}$, of all the events $\alpha \in \mathbf{A}$, where $T_\alpha(n) = \sum_{i=1}^n \omega_\alpha(i)$. Denote this superimposed sequence by $\{\tau_k^*\}$. The counting process $D^*$ changes values only at the $\tau_k^*$'s. Let $\alpha_k^*$ denote the triggering event at $\tau_k^*$. Hence, we focus on the sequence of values $\{D^*(\tau_k^*)\}$, denoted simply $\{D^*(k)\}$.

Rather than drive each scheme $\mathcal{G}^b$ separately, we synchronize them to the shuffle scheme, taking the event epochs of each $\mathcal{G}^b$ to be a subsequence of $\mathcal{G}^*$. For each scheme $\mathcal{G}^b$, the actual event epochs are "thinned" from this sequence through its event list $\mathcal{E}^b$. In other words, the events of each scheme $\mathcal{G}^b$ can only occur at the event epochs $\{\tau_k^*\}$ of the shuffle scheme. Specifically, $\alpha_k^*$ counts as an event occurrence (at $\tau_k^*$) for the scheme $\mathcal{G}^b$, if $\alpha_k^* \in \mathcal{E}^b$. In this sense, all the schemes in the family are "synchronized". On the other hand, at $\tau_k^*$, if $\alpha_k^* \notin \mathcal{E}^b$, then there will be no event occurring in $\mathcal{G}^b$. In this sense, $\{\tau_k^*\}$ is merely a "potential" event epoch for $\mathcal{G}^b$. Let $\{D^b(k)\}$ be the sequence of values of the counting process $D^b$ at $\{\tau_k^*\}$. Given the shuffle scheme is driven by $\omega$, and given the synchronization mechanism, $D^b(k)$ is the score achieved by $\mathcal{G}^b$ at $\tau_k^*$.

Now suppose (M) holds. The event list of $\mathcal{G}^b$ over the time interval $[\tau_k^*, \tau_{k+1}^*)$ can be expressed as $\mathcal{E}^b(D^b(k))$. Then we have the following simple recursion for each scheme $\mathcal{G}^b$:

$$
D_\alpha^b(k + 1) = D_\alpha^b(k) + \mathbf{1}[\alpha_{k+1}^* = \alpha] \cdot \mathbf{1}[\alpha \in \mathcal{E}^b(D^b(k))]. \tag{4.14}
$$

Let $\chi(b, \cdot)$ denote the characteristic function of $\mathcal{G}^b$. Then

$$\chi_\alpha(b, D^b(k)) = D^b_\alpha(k) + \mathbf{1}[\alpha \in \mathcal{E}^b(D^b(k))].$$

Hence, the recursion in (4.14) can also be written as

$$D^b_\alpha(k+1) = \{D^b_\alpha(k) + \mathbf{1}[\alpha^*_{k+1} = \alpha]\} \wedge \chi_\alpha(b, D^b(k)). \qquad (4.15)$$

We say that $D^b_\alpha(k)$ is concave in $b$ if

$$D^{b^1}_\alpha(k) + D^{b^3}_\alpha(k) \le 2D^{b^2}_\alpha(k),$$

for all $b^1$, $b^2$ and $b^3$ that satisfy $b^1 + b^3 = 2b^2$. Similarly, concavity of $\chi_\alpha(b, x)$ is defined by

$$\chi_\alpha(b^1, x^1) + \chi_\alpha(b^3, x^3) \le 2\chi_\alpha(b^2, x^2),$$

for all $b^1$, $b^2$ and $b^3$ that satisfy $b^1 + b^3 = 2b^2$, and all $x^1$, $x^2$ and $x^3$ that satisfy $x^1 + x^3 = 2x^2$.

**Theorem 4.3.23** If for all $\alpha \in A$, $\chi_\alpha(b, x)$ is increasing (resp. increasing and concave) in $(b, x)$, then $D^b_\alpha(k)$ is increasing (resp. increasing and concave) in $b$ for all $\alpha$ and for any given $k$.

**Proof.** Since $\chi$ is increasing (in particular, with respect to the score) **(M)** is satisfied, hence (4.15) applies. The desired conclusions then follow from the preservation of increasing concavity by the recursion in (4.15), in particular, since $\wedge$ (min) is an increasing and concave operator. $\square$

**Example 4.3.24** Continue with Example 4.3.22. We want to show concavity with respect to the buffer limit $K$. Here, we have to switch to the counting process (rather than the event epochs), and the schemes (parameterized by $K$) have to be synchronized. Note here synchronization makes the queue an autonomous-server model [cf. Example 4.2.2]. That is, service completion occurs at all event epochs of the shuffle scheme. But if at that point there is no job in the system then the service completion results in no *departure*.

Consider $b^1 = K - 1$, $b^2 = K$ and $b^3 = K + 1$. To verify the concavity of the characteristic function amounts to verifying the following (consider first the service completion event $\beta$):

$$\mathbf{1}[\beta \in \mathcal{E}(x^1)] + \mathbf{1}[\beta \in \mathcal{E}(x^3)] \le 2 \cdot \mathbf{1}[\beta \in \mathcal{E}(x^2)], \qquad (4.16)$$

for all feasible scores $x^j$ ($j = 1, 2, 3$) such that $x^1 + x^3 = 2x^2$. Recall, here a score $x = (x_\alpha, x_\beta)$ is feasible if and only if $0 \le x_\alpha - x_\beta \le K$, and $\beta \in \mathcal{E}(x)$ if and only if $x_\alpha > x_\beta$.

The only case that needs verification is when the indicator function on the right side of (4.16) vanishes. But this only happens when $x^2_\alpha = x^2_\beta$. Hence,

$$x^1_\alpha - x^1_\beta + x^3_\alpha - x^3_\beta = 2(x^2_\alpha - x^2_\beta) = 0,$$

which implies $x_\alpha^1 = x_\beta^1$ and $x_\alpha^3 = x_\beta^3$. Hence, both indicator functions on the left side of (4.16) must also vanish.

Replace $\beta$ by the arrival event $\alpha$ in (4.16). For any feasible score $x$, $\alpha \in \mathcal{E}(x)$ if and only if $x_\alpha - x_\beta < b$. Hence, the right side of (4.16) only vanishes when $x_\alpha^2 = x_\beta^2 + K$, which implies

$$x_\alpha^1 - x_\beta^1 + x_\alpha^3 - x_\beta^3 = x_\alpha^2 - x_\beta^2 = 2K,$$

and hence $x_\alpha^1 - x_\beta^1 = K - 1$ and $x_\alpha^3 - x_\beta^3 = K + 1$. That is, both indicator functions on the left side of (4.16) must also vanish.

Therefore, we conclude the counting process is increasing and concave in the buffer limit $K$.

## 4.4    The $(a, b, k)$ Tandem Queue

We now apply the general framework of the previous sections to the specific setting of a production line with control of intermediate inventories. We begin by describing the system in detail and noting some immediate consequences of the earlier general results. Further applications of the GSMP framework are developed in subsequent sections.

### 4.4.1    Production Lines Under Kanban Control

Consider a tandem-queue model with $m$ stages, each stage having a single server. Stage 1 draws jobs from an infinite source. Each job goes through the $m$ stages in sequence and leaves the system immediately upon completing service at the last stage, stage $m$. The service discipline at each stage is first-come-first-served.

There are three parameters associated with each stage $i$:

- $a_i$: an upper limit on the number of raw jobs at stage $i$, i.e., jobs in queue and in service at $i$;

- $b_i$: an upper limit on the number of finished jobs at stage $i$, i.e., completed jobs blocked from entry to the next stage, stage $i + 1$;

- $k_i$: an upper limit on the total number of jobs at stage $i$, i.e., including both raw jobs and finished jobs.

Let $(a, b, k) = (a_i, b_i, k_i)_{i=1}^m$. These parameters specify a blocking mechanism that works as follows: Server $i$ processes jobs so long as it has raw jobs available. Jobs completed at stage $i$ move to stage $i + 1$ unless either of the limits $a_{i+1}$ or $k_{i+1}$ has been reached, in which case the completed jobs remain in stage $i$. Server $i$ can continue to process jobs until the limit $b_i$ is reached, at which point the server becomes *blocked*. As room becomes available at stage $i + 1$ (so that neither $k_{i+1}$ nor $a_{i+1}$ is tight anymore) completed jobs from stage $i$ move to stage $i + 1$, the $b_i$ limit becomes non-binding, and server $i$ is permitted to resume processing.

One interpretation of the three control parameters is this: at each stage $i$, $a_i$ controls the number of raw jobs, $b_i$ controls the finished goods inventory, and $k_i$ represents the physical buffer capacity of the stage. To avoid trivial cases, it is natural to impose the following conditions on the parameters for each stage $i$:

$$1 \le a_i \le k_i, \quad 0 \le b_i \le k_i, \quad a_i + b_i \ge k_i; \tag{4.17}$$

otherwise, some of the limits will never be reached or a server will never be able to serve (e.g., if $a_i = 0$). Since, as stated earlier, stage 1 draws jobs from an infinite source and stage $m$ supplies completed jobs to an infinite demand, the parameters $a_1$ and $b_m$ are effectively superfluous. Furthermore, the buffer limit $k_m$ will never be reached unless $a_m = k_m$. Hence, to be specific, we set

$$a_1 = k_1, \quad a_m = b_m = k_m. \tag{4.18}$$

We will refer to the above blocking mechanism as "general blocking", since it includes other blocking mechanisms as special cases. To see this, recall in classical tandem-queue models jobs completed at any stage can always be released into the downstream stage as long as the buffer there is not full. In other words, the limit on the number of raw jobs at each stage is just the buffer capacity, i.e., $a_i = k_i$ for all stage $i$. The blocking of the server also involves checking whether the downstream buffer is full. There are two different mechanisms:

(i) The checking of the downstream buffer is conducted immediately before the server *initiates* a service. If the downstream buffer is full, the service cannot initiate. This mechanism corresponds to $b_i = 0$. That is, when stage $i$ server is blocked, there will be no finished job held in stage $i$. This is the so-called *communication blocking* in the literature. Another name is *block-and-hold* 0. It corresponds to the situation that messages can only be transmitted whenever a channel is available.

(ii) The checking of the downstream buffer takes place immediately after the server *completes* a service. If the downstream buffer is full, the completed job is held in the current stage, and the server is blocked. This corresponds to $b_i = 1$. That is, whenever stage $i$ server is blocked, there is exactly one finished job in the stage. This mechanism is known in the literature as *manufacturing blocking*, or *block-and-hold* 1.

More recently, there have been studies on tandem queues operating under the so-called *kanban* blocking. It works as follows. For each stage $i$, there is a total of $k_i$ cards ("kanbans"). A card is attached to a job as soon as it enters stage $i$. The card stays with the job throughout its sojourn in the stage. The card is only detached from the job when it moves on to the downstream stage. (Hence, while jobs move from one stage to the next, cards always stay in their home stage.) In order for a job to move from stage $i$ to the downstream stage $i + 1$, there must be a card available at stage $i + 1$ (i.e., a card that is not attached to any job in stage $i + 1$). The server in stage $i$ can serve as long as there are raw jobs to be served. It will only be blocked if the number of completed but blocked jobs in stage $i$ reaches $k_i$. At that point all cards are attached to finished jobs in stage $i$, and no raw job can be admitted into the stage. Clearly, this mechanism corresponds to $a_i = b_i = k_i$.

In view of the kanban blocking described above, the $(a, b, k)$ model can be viewed as a *generalized kanban blocking* mechanism. At each stage $i$, in addition to the $k_i$ kanbans, there are two other types of cards: $a_i$ "conveyance cards" and $b_i$ "production cards". The kanbans function in exactly the same manner as before. The conveyance cards and the production cards are attached to, respectively, the raw jobs and the finished jobs. (Hence, each job has two cards attached to it: a kanban plus either a conveyance card or a production card.) The function of the conveyance cards at stage $i$ is to authorize job movement into the stage: For any job to enter stage $i$, there must be one conveyance card, in addition to one kanban, available at stage $i$. Both cards are then attached to the entering job. The production cards at stage $i$, on the other hand, authorize production: For server $i$ to process any job, a free production card (i.e., one that is not attached to any finished job in stage $i$) must be available. When the raw job completes its service, the production card is attached to it, while the conveyance card is detached from it. (When $b_i = 0$, there is no production card at stage $i$. Instead, production is authorized by a free conveyance card at stage $i + 1$, and each job moves into stage $i + 1$ immediately upon service completion at stage $i$.) Clearly, this way in each stage $i$, the total number of raw jobs is limited to $a_i$, the total number of finished jobs is limited to $b_i$, while the sum of both is limited to $k_i$.

### 4.4.2   Properties with Respect to Service Times

Denote service completion at stage $i$ by event $\alpha_i$. The event set is then $\bar{\alpha} = \{\alpha_i, i = 1, \ldots, m\}$. Denote a typical state by $s = (s_i)_{i=1}^{m-1}$, where $s_i$ is the total number of jobs that have completed service by server $i$ but not yet by server $i + 1$. This includes the finished jobs in stage $i$ and the raw jobs in stage $i + 1$. Then, $s_i + \cdots + s_{j-1}$ is the total number of jobs that have been completed by server $i$ but not yet by server $j$. Clearly, this quantity is dominated by $u_{ij}$ defined as follows:

$$u_{ij} = b_i + \sum_{\ell=i+1}^{j-1} k_\ell + a_j, \qquad i = 1, \ldots m-1, \quad j = i+1, \ldots m. \quad (4.19)$$

In other words, there is a maximum of $u_{ij}$ buffer positions to accommodate those jobs that have been completed by server $i$ but not yet by server $j$. The $u_{ij}$ values are also useful in characterizing the blocking mechanism:

**Lemma 4.4.1** Server $i$ ($i = 1, \ldots, m$) is blocked if and only if for some $j \geq i+1$, the upper limit $u_{ij}$ is reached.

**Proof.** Server $i$ is blocked if and only if $b_i$ is reached. But this can happen if and only if either $a_{i+1}$ or $k_{i+1}$ is reached; otherwise, a job would move from stage $i$ to stage $i+1$. If $a_{i+1}$ is reached, then $u_{i,i+1}$ meets the condition of the lemma. If $k_{i+1}$ is reached but $a_{i+1}$ is not, then $k_{i+1} > a_{i+1}$; hence there must be finished but blocked jobs at stage $i+1$. In other words, either $a_{i+2}$ or $k_{i+2}$ is reached. Repeating this argument, we eventually reach a $j$ for which the limit $a_j$ is reached since, at the last stage, $a_m = k_m$. $\square$

Hence, the state space is

$$\mathbf{S} = \{ s \in Z_+^{m-1} : \sum_{\ell=i}^{j-1} s_\ell \leq u_{ij},$$

$$i = 1, \ldots, m-1; j = i+1, \ldots, m \}. \quad (4.20)$$

Henceforth, fix the initial state $s^0 = \mathbf{0}$; i.e., the system starts empty.

The state transition function takes the following form:

$$\phi(s, \alpha_1) = s + e_1, \quad \phi(s, \alpha_m) = s - e_{m-1},$$

$$\phi(s, \alpha_i) = s - e_{i-1} + e_i, \quad i = 2, \ldots, m-1,$$

where $e_i$ denotes the $i$-th unit vector. In words, a service completion at stage $i$ transforms a raw job into a finished job, reducing $s_{i-1}$ by one unit while increasing $s_i$ by one unit (except at the first and the last stages).

For event $\alpha_i$ to be active, server $i$ must not be blocked and there must be jobs available to be processed. Hence, based on Lemma 4.4.1, we have the following event list specification:

$$\mathcal{E}(s) = \{ \alpha_i \in \bar{\alpha} : s_{i-1} > 0, \sum_{\ell=i}^{j-1} s_\ell < u_{ij},$$

$$i = 1, \ldots, m-1; j = i+1, \ldots, m \}. \quad (4.21)$$

For $i = 1$ and $i = m$, respectively, the first and the second constraints are vacuously satisfied: the first stage always has jobs available; the last stage is never blocked.

Consider any feasible string $\sigma$ and let $x = [\sigma]$ be its score. If $s$ is the state reached from $s^0 = \mathbf{0}$ via $\sigma$, then

$$s_i = x_i - x_{i+1}, \qquad i = 1, \ldots, m - 1. \tag{4.22}$$

For after all, $s_i$, the total number of jobs completed by server $i$ but not yet by server $i + 1$, is simply the difference in the number of service completions between the two servers. This relation leads immediately to strong permutability: any two strings that have the same scores lead to the same state. (Non-interruption is automatically satisfied by the first-come-first-served discipline at all stages.)

From the state-score relation in (4.22), the specification of the score space follows immediately from that of the state space, since a score is feasible if and only if its corresponding state is feasible:

$$\begin{aligned} \mathcal{N} &= \{x \in Z_+^m : 0 \le x_i - x_j \le u_{ij}; \\ &\quad i = 1, \ldots, m - 1; \; j = i + 1, \ldots, m\}. \end{aligned} \tag{4.23}$$

Given permutability, the event list can be expressed as a function of the scores. Hence (4.21) takes the following form:

$$\mathcal{E}(x) = \{\alpha_i \in \bar{\alpha} : x_i < x_{i-1} \bigwedge_{j \ge i+1} (x_j + u_{ij})\}. \tag{4.24}$$

It is easy to verify that $\mathcal{N}$ in (4.23) is min-closed: if $x, y \in \mathcal{N}$, then

$$x_{i-1} \wedge y_{i-1} \ge x_i \wedge y_i,$$

and

$$x_i \wedge y_i \le (x_j + u_{ij}) \wedge (y_j + u_{ij}) = (x_j \wedge y_j) + u_{ij}, \quad j \ge i+1;$$

that is, $x \wedge y \in \mathcal{N}$.

Summarizing the above discussions, we have

**Proposition 4.4.2** The GSMS of the $(a, b, k)$ tandem-queue model satisfies non-interruption, strong permutability, and min-closure. In other words, conditions **(C)** and **(CX)** are satisfied.

From the score space specification in (4.23), it is clear that the minimal element of $\mathcal{N}_{\alpha_i, n}$ can be specified as follows (in terms of its components);

$$x_1 = \cdots = x_{i-1} = n; \quad x_i = n-1; \quad x_j = n-u_{ij}, \quad j = i+1, \ldots m. \tag{4.25}$$

That is, stage $i$ can only initiate its $n$-th service if all the upstream stages ($\le i - 1$) have completed at least $n$ jobs and server $i$ has completed $n - 1$ jobs and is not blocked. Thus, by Lemma 4.4.1, each downstream stage $j$ ($\ge i + 1$) must have completed at least $n - u_{ij}$ jobs.

To lighten notation, replace the index $\alpha_i$ with $i$. Let $\omega = \{\omega_i(n); i = 1, \ldots, m; n = 1, 2, \ldots\}$ be the input clock sequence to the GSMS, with $\omega_i(n)$ the service time of the $n$-th job at stage $i$. Denote by $T_i(n)$ the epoch of the $n$-th service completion at stage $i$. From (4.25), we have the following recursion:

$$T_i(n) = \omega_i(n) \quad + \quad \max\{T_j(n), j = 1, \ldots, i - 1; T_i(n - 1);$$
$$T_j(n - u_{ij}), j = i + 1, \ldots, m\}.$$

[By convention $T_j(\ell) = 0$ for all $\ell \leq 0$ and all $j$.] However, since $T_1(n) \leq T_2(n) \leq \cdots \leq T_{i-1}(n)$, the first $i - 2$ terms under max above are superfluous. We may write instead

$$T_i(n) \quad = \quad \omega_i(n) + \max\{T_{i-1}(n), T_i(n - 1),$$
$$T_j(n - u_{ij}), j = i + 1 \ldots, m\}. \tag{4.26}$$

Hence, based on the recursion in (4.26), we have

**Proposition 4.4.3** In the $(a, b, k)$ model, $T$ is increasing and convex in $\omega$. Each component of $T$ is Lipschitz continuous in every finite set of components of $\omega$.

In the stochastic setting, the above translates into stochastic monotonicity and strong stochastic convexity of $T$, with respect to the clock times. Furthermore, $T$ preserves the $\leq_{\mathrm{icx}}$ order of the clock times.

So far we have assumed that any completed job at the last stage $m$ leaves the system immediately. This is tantamount to assuming there is an infinite demand process to absorb the completed jobs from the last stage. Here we modify the model to account for a finite demand process. Index the arrival event as the $m + 1$ st event; hence $\omega_{m+1}(n)$ denotes the interarrival times. Assume at time zero there is an arrival, the 0 th. There are two basic ways to operate the system: *make-to-stock* and *make-to-order*.

Under make-to-stock, the dynamics of the system are essentially the same as before, except for some boundary conditions. Specifically, now completed jobs at stage $m$ have to be held in stage $m$ if there is no demand waiting "at the door". Therefore, the parameter $b_m$ is no longer superfluous; in particular we do not assume $b_m = k_m$ [cf. (4.18)]. Furthermore, there is one more component for the minimal element in (4.25), namely, $x_{m+1} = n - u_{i,m+1}$, where,

$$u_{i,m+1} = b_i + \sum_{j=i+1}^{m} k_j, \tag{4.27}$$

in particular, $u_{m,m+1} = b_m$. Accordingly, the event-epoch recursion in (4.26) is modified to

$$T_i(n) = \omega_i(n) \quad + \quad \max\{T_{i-1}(n), T_i(n - 1),$$
$$T_j(n - u_{ij}), j = i + 1 \ldots, m, m + 1\}. \tag{4.28}$$

Note $T_{m+1}(n) = \sum_{k=1}^{n} \omega_{m+1}(k)$ is simply the $n$th arrival epoch.

Under make-to-order, production at the first stage is activated by the arrival of an order (demand), and then propagated to all the downstream stages. Hence, whenever a job is completed at the last stage, there is always a waiting order to carry it away. Therefore, effectively $b_m = 0$. In order for all $k_m$ buffer positions to be utilized, assume $a_m = k_m$.

Conceptually, the make-to-order operation can be equivalently viewed as orders arriving at the first stage, getting processed at all the intermediate stages, and leaving the system after service completion at the last stage. This is in fact the standard way to view a tandem queue, except here the operation of each stage follows the $(a, b, k)$ mechanism.

Hence the dynamics of make-to-order also follow the recursion in (4.28), with $b_m = 0$, and in particular $u_{m,m+1} = 0$. All the other parameters are the same. Note that since $\{u_{ij}\}$ determines the state space and the event list, the scheme under make-to-order is a subscheme of the scheme under make-to-stock; in particular $u_{m,m+1} = b_m > 0$ under make-to-stock, while $u_{m,m+1} = 0$ under make-to-order. (Note, in order to make this comparison, we need to assume $a_m = k_m$ under make-to-stock as well.)

Summarizing the above discussions, we have

**Proposition 4.4.4** (i) The results in Proposition 4.4.2 also hold when the demand process is finite and the system is operated under either make-to-stock or make-to-order.
(ii) The scheme under make-to-order is a subscheme of the scheme under make-to-stock. Consequently, with the same input clock sequence (interarrival and service times), service completions at all stages happen faster under make-to-stock.

## 4.5    Properties with Respect to $(a, b, k)$

From the earlier model description, we know the parameters $(a, b, k)$ essentially control the operation of the system. Here we consider the effect of varying these parameters on system performance, mainly the event-epoch sequence $T$ and the counting process $D$. We start with monotonicity results with respect to $(a, b, k)$. For second-order results, we only have the concavity of $D$, under synchronization.

### 4.5.1    Monotonicity with Respect to $(a, b, k)$

We first consider letting all parameters $(a, b, k)$ increase, then letting some increase while others decrease to keep total capacity fixed. For ease of discussion, we focus on the infinite demand process. Modifications under make-to-order and make-to-stock can be carried out much the same as the analysis at the end of the last section.

**Proposition 4.5.1** Consider two systems with control parameters $(a, b, k)$ and $(a', b', k')$. Let $\mathcal{G}$ and $\mathcal{G}'$ denote the corresponding schemes; let $T, T'$ and $D, D'$ be the corresponding event-epoch sequence and counting process. If $(a, b, k) \le (a', b', k')$ (componentwise) then $\mathcal{G} \subseteq \mathcal{G}'$. Consequently, $T \ge T'$ and $D \le D'$.

**Proof.** Let $\mathcal{G} = (\mathbf{S}, \bar{\alpha}, \mathcal{E}, \phi)$ and $\mathcal{G}' = (\mathbf{S}', \bar{\alpha}', \mathcal{E}', \phi')$ be the schemes for the two systems. From Proposition 4.4.2, we know both schemes are non-interruptive and permutable. Since $(a, b, k) \le (a', b', k')$ implies $u_{ij} \le u'_{ij}$ for all $i = 1, \ldots, m-1$ and $j = i+1, \ldots, m$, we have $\mathbf{S} \subseteq \mathbf{S}'$ and $\mathcal{E}(s) \subseteq \mathcal{E}'(s)$ for all $s \in \mathbf{S}$. Clearly, $\bar{\alpha} = \bar{\alpha}'$; by definition, while $\phi$ and $\phi'$ agree on $\mathbf{S} \times \bar{\alpha}$. Thus, we indeed have $\mathcal{G} \subseteq \mathcal{G}'$. The implications on the event-epoch sequence and the event-counting process then follow from Theorem 4.3.21. $\square$

From the proof above it becomes evident that the result depends on $(a, b, k)$ only through $u_{ij}$'s. Since it is possible for the $u_{ij}$'s to increase while some of the $(a, b, k)$ parameters decrease, we next obtain the subscheme relation letting some parameters increase while letting others decrease.

It is useful to display $\{u_{ij}, i = 1, \ldots, m-1, j = 2, \ldots, m\}$ in a matrix form:

$$
u = \begin{pmatrix} b_1 + a_2 & b_1 + k_2 + a_3 & \cdots & b_1 + k_2 + k_3 + \cdots + k_{m-1} + a_m \\ 0 & b_2 + a_3 & \cdots & b_2 + k_3 + \cdots + k_{m-1} + a_m \\ \vdots & \vdots & \ddots & \vdots \\ 0 & 0 & \cdots & b_{m-1} + a_m \end{pmatrix}.
$$

(4.29)

We can now observe the various changes in $(a, b, k)$ that will increase $u$ (in the componentwise sense). Notice that $b_i$ only appears in the $i$-th row of the matrix. Hence, decreasing $b_i$ by any positive amount and adding the same amount to $a_{i+1}$ and to $k_{i+1}$ increases $u$. Similarly, decreasing $a_j$ by any positive amount and adding the same amount to $b_{j-1}$ and to $k_{j-1}$ also increases $u$. Thus, we have

**Proposition 4.5.2** The event-epoch sequence $T$ decreases and the counting process $D$ increases under the following changes:
(i) reducing $b_i$ and adding the reduced amount to $a_{i+1}$ and to $k_{i+1}$;
(ii) reducing $a_j$ and adding the reduced amount to $b_{j-1}$ and to $k_{j-1}$.

In another direction, suppose the total number of buffer positions (or, kanbans), $k_1 + \cdots + k_m$, is a given constant. Then from the $u$ matrix it is obvious that both $k_1$ and $k_m$ should be made as small as possible (recall that we always take $k_m = a_m$). Thus, we should set $k_1 = b_1$ and $k_m = 1$:

**Corollary 4.5.3** Given a fixed, total number of buffer positions, $T$ is decreased and $D$ increased by making the first and last buffers as small as possible, i.e., by setting $k_1 = b_1$ and $k_m = 1$.

When $k_1$ and $k_m$ are reduced, the reduced amount can be added to the other buffers to increase $u$. The reduction in $k_m$ must be added to $k_{m-1}$ as well as to $b_{m-1}$; the reduction in $k_1$ can be added to any other buffer.

**Remark 4.5.4** We can rewrite the $u$ matrix in (4.29) by eliminating the $a_i$ parameters, i.e., letting $a_i = k_i$:

$$
u = \begin{pmatrix}
b_1' + k_2' & b_1' + k_2' + k_3' & \cdots & b_1' + k_2' + k_3' + \cdots + k_{m-1}' + k_m' \\
0 & b_2' + k_3' & \cdots & b_2' + k_3' + \cdots + k_{m-1}' + k_m' \\
\vdots & \vdots & \ddots & \vdots \\
0 & 0 & \cdots & b_{m-1}' + k_m'
\end{pmatrix}.
$$
(4.30)

Equating the entries in the matrix to their counterparts in (4.29), we have

$$
\begin{aligned}
b_i' &= a_i + b_i - k_i, \quad i = 1, ..., m-1; \\
a_i' &= k_i' = k_{i-1} - a_{i-1} + a_i, \quad i = 2, ..., m.
\end{aligned}
$$
(4.31)

Similarly, we can also eliminate the $b_i$ parameters by letting $b_i = k_i$:

$$
\begin{aligned}
a_i' &= a_i + b_i - k_i, \quad i = 2, ..., m; \\
b_i' &= k_i' = k_{i+1} - b_{i+1} + b_i, \quad i = 1, ..., m-1.
\end{aligned}
$$
(4.32)

Since the dynamics of the $(a, b, k)$ system, in terms of the service completion processes at the stages, are determined entirely by the $u$ matrix, we now know that the counting processes will remain the same if the model is reduced to a two-parameter $(a', k')$ or $(b', k')$ model as specified above.

### 4.5.2   Concavity with Respect to $(a, b, k)$

We now supplement the monotonicity results in the last subsection with concavity properties of the counting process $D$ with respect to $(a, b, k)$. For this, we need to focus on *synchronized schemes*. Recall this mechanism generates *potential* event epochs autonomously. A potential epoch is accepted as a genuine epoch if the corresponding event is in the event list. (This mechanism is reminiscent of uniformization. Indeed, when all event lifetimes are exponential, synchronization is equivalent to uniformization.)

Now, potential service completions at stage $i$ occur at times

$$
T_i^*(n) = \omega_i(1) + \cdots + \omega_i(n), \ n = 1, 2, \ldots .
$$

Let $\alpha_1^*, \alpha_2^*, \ldots$ be the sequence of stages at which potential service completions occur. (In case of ties, suppose for concreteness that upstream stages complete first.)

Fix some $c \equiv (a, b, k)$; objects superscripted by $c$ correspond to this parameter set. Let $D_i^c(k)$ be the number of accepted stage-$i$ service completions (under $c$) among the first $k$ potential events, with $D_i^c(0) \equiv 0$ for all $i = 1, \ldots, m$. Then

$$D_i^c(k+1) = D_i^c(k) + [\mathbf{1}\{\alpha_{k+1}^* = \alpha_i\} \wedge \mathbf{1}\{\alpha_i \in \mathcal{E}^c(D^c(k))\}]; \qquad (4.33)$$

i.e., the number of genuine stage-$i$ service completions is increased at the $(k+1)$-st potential event if and only if $\alpha_i$ is in the event list *and* $\alpha_{k+1}^* = \alpha_i$. Recall that under permutability we may express the event list unambiguously as a function of the number of events $D^c(k) = (D_i^c(k))_{i=1}^m$ that have occurred thus far. This completely specifies the evolution of the system. Here service completions are synchronized across schemes, in that they occur at time instants specified independently of $(a, b, k)$.

From the event list specification in (4.21), the characteristic functions can be expressed as

$$\chi_i(c, x) = x_i + \mathbf{1}\{x_i < x_{i-1} \bigwedge_{j \geq i+1} (x_j + u_{ij})\}. \qquad (4.34)$$

The recursion for $D^c$ can be rewritten as

$$D_i^c(k+1) = \{D_i^c(k) + \mathbf{1}[\alpha_{k+1}^* = \alpha_i] \wedge \chi_i(c, D^c(k))\}. \qquad (4.35)$$

To show that $D^c$ is concave in $c$, it suffices to check the concavity of $\chi_i$ in $(c, x)$ for all $\alpha_i$. Below we show a stronger result instead, that $\chi_i$ is concave in $(u, x)$, where $u$ is the $u$-matrix corresponding to $c$. This is stronger because $c^1 + c^2 = 2c^3$ implies $u^1 + u^2 = 2u^3$.

For $r = 1, 2, 3$ write the indicator function in $\chi_i(c^r, x^r)$ as $\mathbf{1}_i^r$. Suppose $\mathbf{1}_i^1 = 1$. Then,

$$x_i^1 < x_{i-1}^1 \bigwedge_{j \geq i+1} (x_j^1 + u_{ij}^1).$$

In addition, feasibility requires

$$x_i^2 \leq x_{i-1}^2 \bigwedge_{j \geq i+1} (x_j^2 + u_{ij}^2).$$

Hence,

$$
\begin{aligned}
2x_i^3 &= x_i^1 + x_i^2 \\
&< [x_{i-1}^1 \bigwedge_{j \geq i+1} (x_j^1 + u_{ij}^1)] + [x_{i-1}^2 \bigwedge_{j \geq i+1} (x_j^2 + u_{ij}^2)] \\
&\leq (x_{i-1}^1 + x_{i-1}^2) \bigwedge_{j \geq i+1} (x_j^1 + x_j^2 + u_{ij}^1 + u_{ij}^2) \\
&= 2x_{i-1}^3 \bigwedge_{j \geq i+1} (2x_j^3 + 2u_{ij}^3).
\end{aligned}
$$

That is,

$$x_i^3 < x_{i-1}^3 \bigwedge_{j \geq i+1} (x_j^3 + u_{ij}^3),$$

and hence, $1_i^3 = 1$. By symmetry, $1_i^2 = 1$ also implies $1_i^3 = 1$. Hence, $1_i^1 + 1_i^2 \leq 2 \cdot 1_i^3$, which is the desired concavity. To summarize, we have

**Proposition 4.5.5** In the $(a, b, k)$ tandem model, under synchronization the counting process $D^c$ is concave in $u$ and hence concave in $c = (a, b, k)$.

## 4.6    Line Reversal

Line reversal is essentially a symmetry property with respect to $(a, b, k)$. In the general case, symmetry holds only for the departure epochs of each job from the entire system (i.e., from the last stage). In a special case, which requires $a_i + b_i = k_i$ for all $i$, the symmetry holds for the completion epoch of each job at every stage. We discuss these two cases in two subsections.

(A word of caution, for readers familiar with the notion of *time reversibility* and its applications in queueing networks (e.g., Kelly [27]), it is an entirely different concept from the *line* reversibility discussed here.)

### 4.6.1    Reversibility of Departure Epochs

Refer to the system described so far as the *original system*, where jobs move through the stages in the sequence $1, 2, \ldots, m$. In the *reversed system*, jobs move instead through the sequence $m, m - 1, \ldots, 1$. Both the original and the reversed systems process the same set of $n$ jobs, following the same job sequence: the first job, which starts at stage $m$ in the reversed system, is the first job that starts at stage 1 in the original system, and so forth. Call this *line reversal*. If the job sequence in the reversed system is also reversed (job $n$ first, job 1 last), call the transformation *line-and-job reversal*. Note that reversing the sequence of jobs means replacing a clock sequence (service times at stage $i$, say) $(\omega_i(1), \ldots, \omega_i(n))$ by the sequence $(\omega_i(n), \ldots, \omega_i(1))$.

Below, we use a "tilde" to index quantities that relate to the reversed system. Let $u^R$ denote a "rotation" operation of the $u$ matrix [cf. (4.29)] along the northeast-southwest diagonal. That is,

$$u_{ij}^R = u_{m+1-j, m+1-i},$$

for all $i = 1, \ldots, m - 1$ and $j = 2, \ldots, m$. The key condition for line reversal is

$$u^R = \tilde{u}. \tag{4.36}$$

In other words, the rotation of the $u$ matrix of the original system should represent the corresponding matrix of the reversed system.

Note (4.36) is indeed a very reasonable condition. For instance, it is automatically satisfied if the control parameters $a_i$ and $b_i$ at each stage $i$ in the reversed system switch roles: $b_i$ controls the work-in-process, while $a_i$ controls the finished goods inventory. (The role of $k_i$ remains unchanged.)

That is,

$$\tilde{a}_i = b_{m+1-i}, \quad \tilde{b}_i = a_{m+1-i}, \quad \tilde{k}_i = k_{m+1-i}, \quad i = 1, \ldots, m. \qquad (4.37)$$

Then, (4.36) is obviously satisfied.

Another common case that satisfies (4.36) is the so-called *flow-line* model: $m$ single servers are connected by $m - 1$ intermediate buffers, indexed as $i = 2, \ldots, m$. (Server 1 takes in jobs from an infinite source, and server $m$ supplies an infinite demand.) Each buffer $i$ has $k_i - 1$ "positions" to accommodate a maximum of $k_i - 1$ jobs; in addition, each server also corresponds to another buffer position. The line operates under either communication or manufacturing blocking. When the line is reversed, server $m$ becomes the first server, feeding jobs into buffer $m$, followed by server $m - 1$, which in turn feeds jobs into buffer $m - 1$, and so forth; the last stage is server 1, taking in jobs from buffer 2. Obviously, the original system can be modeled as an $(a, b, k)$ system with $b_i = 0$ or 1 (communication or manufacturing blocking), and $a_i = k_i$, for $i = 1, \ldots, m - 1$. For the reversed system, we have $\tilde{b}_i = 0$ or 1, $\tilde{k}_i = k_{m+2-i}$, and $\tilde{a}_i = \tilde{k}_i$. It is easy to verify that (4.36) is satisfied.

We now show that under line-and-job reversal, for any job $n$, the departure epoch from the system (i.e., leaving the last stage) remains the same. Under line reversal only, the same holds in a weaker (distributional) sense, and only under independence assumptions on the service times. The precise result is:

**Proposition 4.6.1** Suppose (4.36) holds.
(i) Under line-and-job reversal, $\tilde{T}_m(n) = T_m(n)$, for all $n = 1, 2, \ldots$.
(ii) If the service times are independent at different stages and iid at each stage, then under line-reversal, $\tilde{T}_m(n) \stackrel{d}{=} T_m(n)$, for all $n = 1, 2, \ldots$, where $\stackrel{d}{=}$ denotes equality in distribution.

**Proof.** The result is an application of the "longest path" representation of the event epochs under **(CX)**; refer to Corollary 4.3.14. Let $(i, \ell)$ denote the $\ell$-th occurrence of event $i$. Write $(j, p) \rightarrow (i, \ell)$ if $x_j(i, \ell) = p$, where $x(i, \ell)$ is the minimal element of $\mathcal{N}_{i,\ell}$. In other words, in order for $(i, \ell)$ to happen, $(j, p)$ must already have happened. From the earlier discussion that led to (4.25) and (4.26), we see that $(j, p) \rightarrow (i, \ell)$ if and only if

$$(j, p) \in \{(1, \ell), \ldots, (i - 1, \ell), (i, \ell - 1); (j, \ell - u_{ij}), j \geq i + 1, \ell \geq u_{ij}\}.$$

When the system starts empty, the only active event is $\alpha_1$. Thus, every path to $(m, n)$ has the form

$$\pi : \quad (1, 1) \rightarrow \cdots \rightarrow (j, p) \rightarrow (i, \ell) \rightarrow \cdots \rightarrow (m, n).$$

Let $\Pi(m, n)$ denote the set of all such paths. The event epoch $T_m(n)$ can be expressed as

$$T_m(n) = \max_{\pi \in \Pi(m,n)} \Big\{ \sum_{(i,\ell) \in \pi} \omega_i(\ell) \Big\}. \qquad (4.38)$$

When (4.36) holds, it is easy to verify that $(j,p) \to (i,\ell)$ in the original system if and only if $(m+1-i, n+1-\ell) \to (m+1-j, n+1-p)$ in the reversed system. Therefore, the path $\pi$ in the original system becomes the following path in the reversed system:

$$\tilde{\pi}: \quad (m,n) \to \cdots \to (m+1-i, n+1-\ell) \to (m+1-j, n+1-p) \to \cdots \to (1,1).$$

So each path in the original system corresponds to a path in the reversed system and vice versa. Hence, $\Pi(m,n) = \tilde{\Pi}(m,n)$. Also, due to line-and-job reversal, the processing times in the original and the reversed systems satisfy $\tilde{\omega}_i(\ell) = \omega_{m+1-i}(n+1-\ell)$. Hence, for any $\pi \in \Pi(m,n)$,

$$
\begin{aligned}
\sum_{(i,\ell)\in\tilde{\pi}} \tilde{\omega}_i(\ell) &= \sum_{(m+1-i,n+1-\ell)\in\pi} \omega_{m+1-i}(n+1-\ell) \\
&\equiv \sum_{(i,\ell)\in\pi} \omega_i(\ell).
\end{aligned}
\tag{4.39}
$$

Via (4.38), $\tilde{T}_m(n) = T_m(n)$ follows.

Next, drop job reversal and impose the independence conditions of (ii). This makes $\tilde{\omega}_i(\ell) = \omega_{m+1-i}(\ell)$, and $\omega_j(p) \stackrel{d}{=} \omega_j(p')$ for all $j,p$ and $p'$. Replace (4.39) with

$$
\begin{aligned}
\sum_{(i,\ell)\in\tilde{\pi}} \tilde{\omega}_i(\ell) &= \sum_{(m+1-i,n+1-\ell)\in\pi} \omega_{m+1-i}(\ell) \\
&\stackrel{d}{=} \sum_{(m+1-i,n+1-\ell)\in\pi} \omega_{m+1-i}(n+1-\ell) \\
&\equiv \sum_{(i,\ell)\in\pi} \omega_i(\ell)
\end{aligned}
$$

to get $\tilde{T}_m(n) \stackrel{d}{=} T_m(n)$. $\square$

The above line-reversal result, together with the concavity in Proposition 4.5.5, can be used to characterize optimal buffer allocation in certain settings. Consider the problem of optimizing over possible $u$ matrices. Call the set of such matrices under consideration the parameter space. Call an element of the parameter space optimal if it maximizes the expected cumulative number of job completions (at the last stage) up to time $t$, $E[D_m(t)]$, for every $t \geq 0$. We have

**Proposition 4.6.2** Consider the $(a,b,k)$ tandem model with iid exponential service times at each stage, independent across stages. Suppose that for every allocation $u$ in the parameter space, $u^R$ and $(u+u^R)/2$ are also in the parameter space. Then, if there is an optimal allocation, there is a symmetric optimal allocation; that is, one for which $u = u^R$. More generally, given any allocation $u$, there is a symmetric allocation that achieves at least the same $E[D_m(t)]$.

**Proof.** The assumptions of iid exponential service times at each stage and independence across stages meet the required conditions in both Proposition 4.6.1 (ii) and Proposition 4.5.5. Suppose the parameter selection $u$. Consider the reversed system, with parameter $\tilde{u} = u^R$. Then via line reversibility of Proposition 4.6.1(ii), the two systems give rise to the same $T_m(n)$ (equal in distribution), and hence the same $\mathsf{E}[D_m(t)]$. Take the mean of the two vectors, $(u + u^R)/2$, which also belongs to the parameter space as assumed. This allocation is symmetric; furthermore, it cannot do worse than $\mathsf{E}[D_m(t)]$, following the concavity established in Proposition 4.5.5. $\square$

### 4.6.2  Full Reversibility

Under a stronger condition on the $(a, b, k)$ parameters, namely, $a_i + b_i = k_i$ for all $i$, the type of reversibility established in Proposition 4.6.1 can be strengthened to imply the (deterministic) equality of the entire event epoch sequences for the original and the reversed systems, under *line reversal* only, i.e., $\tilde{\omega}_\ell(\ell) = \omega(m + 1 - i, \ell)$ for any $\ell$. We want to show that when (4.36) is satisfied, $\tilde{T}(i, n) = T(m + 1 - i, n)$ for all $n$ and all $i$.

To this end, we need to start the two systems in different, but corresponding, states. Typically, if the original system starts empty, then its only initially active event is service completion at the first stage. This corresponds to service completion at the last stage in the reversed system. So, we will have the reversed system start in a state in which its first $m - 1$ stages are all blocked so that only the final stage can serve a job. The following result includes the proper correspondence between states in the original and reversed system:

**Proposition 4.6.3** Suppose the parameters of the original system satisfy $a_i + b_i = k_i$, $i = 1, \ldots, m$, and the parameters of the reversed system satisfy $\tilde{u} = u^R$. Suppose the reversed system starts in state $\tilde{s}$, with $\tilde{s}_i = \tilde{u}_{i,i+1} - s_{m-i}$, $i = 1, \ldots, m - 1$, where $s$ is the initial state of the original system. Then $\tilde{T}(i, n) = T(m + 1 - i, n)$ for all $n = 1, 2, \ldots$, for all $i = 1, \ldots, m$.

**Proof.** The condition $a_i + b_i = k_i$ for all $i$ is easily seen to be equivalent to the following additivity condition on the $u_{ij}$ parameters: $u_{i\ell} = u_{ij} + u_{j\ell}$ whenever $i < j < \ell$. It follows that in this case server $i$ is blocked if and only if the upper limit $u_{i,i+1}$ is reached, via Lemma 4.4.1. As a consequence, (4.26) simplifies to

$$T(i, n) = \omega(i, n) + \max\{T(i - 1, n), T(i, n - 1), T(i + 1, n - u_{i,i+1})\},$$

when the (original) system starts empty. When it starts in state $s$, the above recursion becomes:

$$\begin{aligned} T(i, n) &= \omega(i, n) + \max\{T(i - 1, n - s_{i-1}), \\ &\quad T(i, n - 1), T(i + 1, n + s_i - u_{i,i+1})\}. \end{aligned} \qquad (4.40)$$

Similarly, when the reversed system starts in state $\tilde{s}$, we have

$$
\begin{aligned}
\tilde{T}(i,n) &= \tilde{\omega}(i,n) + \max\{\tilde{T}(i-1, n - \tilde{s}_{i-1}), \tilde{T}(i, n-1), \\
&\quad \tilde{T}(i+1, n + \tilde{s}_i - \tilde{u}_{i,i+1})\} \\
&= \tilde{\omega}(i,n) + \max\{\tilde{T}(i-1, n - \tilde{u}_{i-1,i} + s_{m+1-i}), \\
&\quad \tilde{T}(i, n-1), \tilde{T}(i+1, n - s_{m-i})\},
\end{aligned}
$$

where the second equation makes use of the relation between the states: $\tilde{s}_i = \tilde{u}_{i,i+1} - s_{m-i}$. Now, letting $i$ be $m + 1 - i$ above, while noticing the relations:

$$
\tilde{\omega}_{m+1-i}(n) = \omega_i(n) \quad \text{and} \quad \tilde{u}_{m-i,m+1-i} = u_{i,i+1},
$$

we have

$$
\begin{aligned}
\tilde{T}(m+1-i, n) &= \tilde{\omega}(m+1-i, n) \\
&\quad + \max\{\tilde{T}(m-i, n + s_i - u_{i,i+1}), \\
&\quad \tilde{T}(m+1-i, n-1), \tilde{T}(m+2-i, n - s_{i-1})\}.
\end{aligned}
$$

But this coincides with (4.40) as $i$ ranges from 1 to $m$, hence the desired conclusion. $\square$

**Remark 4.6.4** (i) There is another way to interpret the result in Proposition 4.6.3. Let $\mathcal{G}$ and $\tilde{\mathcal{G}}$ denote the schemes of the orignal and the reversed systems. We can obtain $\tilde{\mathcal{G}}$ from $\mathcal{G}$ by relabeling each state $s$ (in $\mathcal{G}$) as $\tilde{s}$ (in $\tilde{\mathcal{G}}$) following the relation specified in Proposition 4.6.3, while holding all the event lists fixed. Then, $\mathcal{E}(s) = \tilde{\mathcal{E}}(\tilde{s})$, and $\phi(s, \alpha) = \tilde{\phi}(\tilde{s}, \alpha)$ for all $\alpha \in \bar{\alpha}$. This way, the only difference between the two schemes is that they start from different initial states. Otherwise they are subschemes of each other. Hence they should have exactly the same event-epoch sequence.
(ii) Unfortunately, the requirement $a_i + b_i = k_i$ in Proposition 4.6.3 has limited scope. In fact, any $(a, b, k)$ model satisfying this condition can be reduced to a system with communication blocking having parameters $b_i' = 0$, $k_i' = b_{i-1} + a_i = a_i'$. It does not seem possible to establish this strong type of reversibility without the condition $a_i + b_i = k_i$.

## 4.7 Subadditivity and Ergodicity

Recall $T_m(n)$ is the time to complete $n$ jobs from all $m$ stages in the system. This is the so-called *makespan* of $n$ jobs. The average, $T_m(n)/n$ is the *cycle time* (of each job) through the system. In this and the next sections, we are interested in studying the existence of the limit, $\lim_{n\to\infty} T_m(n)/n$, and more generally, the cycle time limit at each stage $i$: $\lim_{n\to\infty} T_i(n)/n$, for all $i = 1, ..., m$. The reciprocal of the cycle time limit is often referred to as the throughput, or production rate.

It turns out that the key to the existence of such limit is the (max,+) recursion of the event epochs, a direct consequence of condition **(CX)**. This recursion makes it possible to apply, with appropriate adaptation, the powerful subadditive ergodic theory of Kingman [28, 29]. In this section, we lay down the general theoretical framework, and in the next section discuss the convergence and the rate of convergence.

### 4.7.1 Event-Epoch Vectorization

Our starting point is the event-epoch recursion in (4.26). Note that on the right side, only $T_{i-1}$ has an argument $n$; all the other event epochs have arguments that are less than $n$. But letting $u_{jj} = 1$, and starting from

$$T_1(n) = \omega_1(n) + \bigvee_{j=1}^{m} T_j(n - u_{1j})$$

(again, using $\vee$ to denote max), we can rewrite the recursion in (4.26) as follows:

$$T_i(n) = \bigvee_{k=1}^{i} [\bigvee_{j=k}^{m} T_j(n - u_{kj}) + \sum_{\ell=k}^{i} \omega_\ell(n)]. \tag{4.41}$$

Next, we want to turn the above into a recursion for matrix product in (max,+) algebra. For real numbers $a, b$ define $a \oplus b = \max(a, b)$ and $a \otimes b = a + b$. Extend $\Re$ to include $-\infty$ with $a \oplus -\infty = a$ for all $a$. Clearly, $a \otimes 0 = a$ and $a \otimes (-\infty) = -\infty$ for all $a$. That is, 0 and $-\infty$ play the role of 1 and 0 in (ordinary) $(+,\times)$ algebra. If $v$ is a (row) vector over $\Re \cup \{-\infty\}$ and $A$ is a matrix, define $v \otimes A$ by replacing $+, \times$ in ordinary vector-matrix multiplication with $\oplus, \otimes$; more specifically,

$$(v \otimes A)_i = \bigoplus_j (v_j \otimes A_{ji})$$
$$= \max_j (v_j + A_{ji}).$$

Extend this to matrix multiplication in the usual way.

To vectorize the recursion in (4.41), we have to first decide upon the vector of event epochs, upon which the matrix product, under (max,+), will be built. Here, as well as in the sections to follow, we allow some of the stages to have infinite buffers. In other words, we allow the entries in the $u$ matrix to equal $\infty$. Let $d = \max_{i \leq j}\{u_{ij} < \infty\}$. Note that $d$ is well defined. In particular, if all stages have infinite buffers, then $d = u_{ii} \equiv 1$. On the other hand, if $u_{ij} < \infty$ for all $i \leq j$, then $d = u_{1,m}$ [note $u_{1,m}$ is the largest entry in the $u$ matrix; see (4.29)]. Now, define

$$\hat{T}(n) = (\hat{T}_i(n))_{i=1}^{m} \quad \text{where} \quad \hat{T}_i(n) = (T_i(n - v))_{v=0}^{d}, \tag{4.42}$$

with $T_i(n) \equiv 0$ for any $n \leq 0$. That is, for each $n$, $\hat{T}(n)$, is a vector of $m$ sub-vectors, and each sub-vector, $\hat{T}_i(n)$ is a $(d+1)$-vector.

We can now write the recursion in (4.41) as a generalized matrix product:

$$\hat{T}(n) = \hat{T}(n-1) \otimes A(n). \tag{4.43}$$

Here $A(n)$ is a matrix of $m \times m$ blocks, with each block being a $(d+1) \times (d+1)$ matrix. All the blocks in the diagonal have the following form:

$$\begin{pmatrix} * & 0 & -\infty & \cdots & -\infty \\ * & -\infty & 0 & \cdots & -\infty \\ \vdots & \vdots & \ddots & \ddots & \vdots \\ * & -\infty & \cdots & -\infty & 0 \\ * & -\infty & -\infty & \cdots & -\infty \end{pmatrix} ; \tag{4.44}$$

and all the non-diagonal blocks have a similar form, with the zero entries replaced by $-\infty$. Here the asterisks denote entries that are either the sum of clock times, $\sum_\ell w_\ell(n)$ in (4.41), or $-\infty$.

To see this, consider the $i$th column of blocks in $A(n)$, which post-multiplies $\hat{T}(n-1)$ to yield the sub-vector $\hat{T}_i(n) = (T_i(n), T_i(n-1), ..., T_i(n-d))$ of $\hat{T}(n)$. Note that except for the first component $T_i(n)$, all the other components also appear in $\hat{T}(n-1)$. [Specifically, the $i$th sub-vector of $\hat{T}(n-1)$ is $\hat{T}_i(n-1) = (T_i(n-1), ..., T_i(n-d), T_i(n-1-d))$.] Hence, with the exception of the first column, all the other columns in this block must be identity vectors, under (max,+). On the other hand, the first column, which transforms $\hat{T}(n-1)$ into $T_i(n)$, should add to the relevant components of $\hat{T}(n-1)$ the corresponding $\sum_\ell w_\alpha(n)$ terms, following (4.41), and $-\infty$ to the other components.

To summarize, we have

**Lemma 4.7.1** The event-epoch recursion of the $(a, b, k)$ model satisfies the generalized matrix product relation in (4.43), where each matrix in the sequence $\{A(n), n \geq 0\}$ has only three types of entries: $0$, $-\infty$, or sums of service times, with the structure following (4.44). Furthermore, it satisfies the following property: if $w'$ denotes the shifted sequence defined by $w'_\alpha(n) = w_\alpha(n+1)$, then $A(n+1, w) = A(n, w')$

The last statement above clearly follows from the structure of the $A$ matrices as discussed above.

## 4.7.2   The Subadditive Ergodic Theorem

For background, we include in this section a statement of Kingman's subadditive ergodic theorem, followed by its application to the generalized products of random matrices. We start with an elementary result. A sequence $\{a_1, a_2, ...\}$ of real numbers is called *subadditive* if

$$a_{m+n} \leq a_m + a_n, \quad m, n = 1, 2, ....$$

If $\{a_n, n \geq 1\}$ is subadditive, then $\{a_n/n, n \geq 1\}$ has a limit as $n \to \infty$, possibly equal to $-\infty$. (Cohen [8] cites this result as an exercise in Pólya and Szegö [36].) To see this, note that given $m$, any $n$ can be written as $n = k_n m + \ell$, where $\ell < m$ and $k_n$ is a multiplier that depends on $n$. The subadditivity of $\{a_n\}$ implies

$$a_n \leq k_n a_m + a_\ell.$$

Dividing both sides by $n$ and noticing that $k_n/n \to 1/m$ and $a_\ell/n \to 0$, we have

$$\limsup_n \frac{a_n}{n} \leq \frac{a_m}{m}.$$

Since $m$ is arbitrary, we have

$$\limsup_n \frac{a_n}{n} \leq \liminf_n \frac{a_n}{n}.$$

Therefore, the limit $\lim_n a_n/n$ exists and is equal to $\liminf_n a_n/n$.

Kingman's [29] result is formulated in terms of *subadditive processes*. These are processes $X = \{X_{mn} : m = 0, 1, \ldots; n = m + 1, m + 2, \ldots\}$ satisfying the following conditions:

**(S1)** If $i < j < k$, then $X_{ik} \leq X_{ij} + X_{jk}$, a.s.

**(S2)** The joint distributions of the process $\{X_{m+1,n+1}, n > m\}$ are the same as those of $\{X_{mn}, n > m\}$.

**(S3)** The expectation $g_n = \mathsf{E}[X_{0n}]$ exists and satisfies $g_n \geq -cn$ for some finite constant $c$ and all $n = 1, 2, \ldots$.

A consequence of (S1), (S3) and the elementary result given above is that $\gamma = \lim_{n \to \infty} g_n/n$ exists and is finite. We can now state Kingman's subadditive ergodic theorem: If $X$ is a subadditive process, then the finite limit

$$\zeta = \lim_{n \to \infty} X_{0n}/n$$

exists almost surely, and $\mathsf{E}[\zeta] = \gamma$

Condition (S2), on the shift $\{X_{mn}\} \mapsto \{X_{m+1,n+1}\}$, is a stationarity condition. If all events defined in terms of $X$ that are invariant under this shift have probability zero or one, then $X$ is *ergodic*. In this case, as discussed by Kingman [29, p.885], the limiting random variable $\zeta$ is almost surely constant and equal to $\gamma$. It is this version of the result that we will use. Notice that the limit provided by Kingman's theorem holds in expectation, as well as almost surely: $\lim_{n \to \infty} n^{-1} \mathsf{E}[X_{0n}] = \mathsf{E}[\zeta]$.

Cohen [8] gives an excellent account of connections between subadditive ergodic theory and products of random matrices, and considers, among other settings, the case of (max, +) matrix multiplication. For purposes of reference and comparison, we paraphrase his Theorem 4:

**Theorem 4.7.2** (Cohen [8])    Let $\{A(n), n = 1, 2, \ldots\}$ be a stationary and ergodic sequence of random $d \times d$ real matrices and let

$$P(m, n) = A(m+1) \otimes \cdots \otimes A(n), \quad m+1 \leq n. \tag{4.45}$$

If $\mathsf{E}|A_{ij}(n)| < \infty$ for all $1 \leq i, j \leq d$, then the finite limit

$$\lim_{n \to \infty} n^{-1} P(1, n)_{ij} = \gamma$$

exists almost surely, is a constant, and is independent of $i$ and $j$.

**Remark 4.7.3** The main step in Cohen's proof is showing that $X_{mn} = -P(m, n)_{11}$ is a subadditive process. The remarkable fact that the limiting matrix is constant is a consequence of the requirement that $A_{ij}(n) > -\infty$. This condition in (max, +) algebra is analogous to the assumption of strictly positive matrix entries in ordinary matrix multiplication.

Cohen also gives an intuitive explanation of this result which is helpful in what comes next. Think of the indices $i = 1, \ldots, d$ as points, and $A(n)_{ij}$ as the "distance" from $i$ to $j$ at time $n$. With this interpretation, $(A(1) \otimes \cdots \otimes A(n))_{ij}$ is the length of the longest $n$-stage path from $i$ to $j$. (This is a consequence of (max, +) matrix multiplication.) Requiring $A(n)_{ij} > -\infty$ ensures that any point can be reached from any other at every stage. The limit $\gamma$ is the average length per stage of the longest path from $i$ to $j$. For large $n$, the longest path from $i$ to $j$ consists of an initial segment from $i$ to a maximum average length cycle among the $d$ points, followed by a large number of such cycles, and then a path from the cycle to $j$. As $n$ increases, the initial and final segments become negligible, so the length of the longest path becomes independent of $i$ and $j$.

If the matrices in the recursion (4.43) satisfied the hypotheses of Cohen's theorem, we would immediately be able to conclude that

$$\lim_{n \to \infty} n^{-1} \tilde{T}(n) = \lim_{n \to \infty} n^{-1} \mathbf{0} \otimes (A(1) \otimes \cdots \otimes A(n)) = [\gamma],$$

where $\mathbf{0}(\equiv \hat{T}(0))$ is the zero vector and $[\gamma]$ is a vector with all entries equal to $\gamma$. Unfortunately, even if the matrices $A(n)$ in (4.43) are stationary and ergodic, we have seen that they typically include entries equal to $-\infty$. So, we need a generalization of Cohen's result for the types of matrices arising in our setting.

### 4.7.3    More General Matrices

To start with, we need some properties of ordinary (non-random) matrices in (max, +) algebra. All of these are straightforward analogs of results for non-negative matrices under standard matrix multiplication (as in Chapter 2 of Pullman [37]) with $-\infty$ playing the role usually played by 0. So, we omit most of the proofs. We write $A^{\otimes n}$ for the $n$-fold $\otimes$-product of $A$ with itself. We will use $d$ to denote the generic dimension of any matrix under discussion; it does not necessarily relate to the $d$ value in §7.1.

**Definition 4.7.4** The $d \times d$ matrix $A$ is *reducible* if $d \geq 2$ and if there exists a permutation of the rows and columns of $A$ under which it has the block form

$$\begin{pmatrix} B & C \\ -\infty & D \end{pmatrix}, \tag{4.46}$$

where $B$ and $D$ are square matrices. Otherwise, $A$ is *irreducible*. In particular, every $1 \times 1$ matrix is irreducible.

**Lemma 4.7.5** The $d \times d$ matrix $A$, $d \geq 2$, is irreducible if and only if for all $i$ and $j$ there exists an $n$ such that $A_{ij}^{\otimes n} > -\infty$.

**Definition 4.7.6** The $d \times d$ matrix $A$, $d \geq 2$ is *periodic* if its rows and columns can be permuted to give it the block form

$$\begin{pmatrix} -\infty & B^1 & -\infty & \cdots & -\infty \\ -\infty & -\infty & B^2 & \cdots & -\infty \\ \vdots & \vdots & \ddots & \ddots & \vdots \\ -\infty & -\infty & \cdots & -\infty & B^{k-1} \\ B^k & -\infty & \cdots & -\infty & -\infty \end{pmatrix}.$$

Otherwise, $A$ is called *aperiodic*. Every $1 \times 1$ matrix is aperiodic.

**Lemma 4.7.7** If $A$ is irreducible and aperiodic, and $A$ is not the $1 \times 1$ matrix $(-\infty)$, then for some $n$, $A_{ij}^{\otimes n} > -\infty$ for all $i, j$.

**Lemma 4.7.8** Through a permutation of its rows and columns, any matrix $A$ can be put in the block form

$$\begin{pmatrix} A^1 & & & * \\ & A^2 & & \\ & & \ddots & \\ -\infty & & & A^K \end{pmatrix}, \tag{4.47}$$

where $A^1, \ldots, A^K$ are irreducible, the entries below the block diagonal are $-\infty$, and the entries above the block diagonal are arbitrary.

**Proof.** Let $A$ be $d \times d$ and proceed by induction on $d$. The result holds for $d = 1$. If $d \geq 2$ and $A$ is irreducible, there is nothing to prove. Otherwise, $A$ can be put into the form (4.46). Now apply the induction hypothesis to $B$ and $D$ in (4.46). Through repeated such reduction, $A$ attains the form (4.47). □

It is not hard to see that in multiplying matrices with $(\max, +)$ algebra, the location of $-\infty$'s in the product depends only on the location of $-\infty$'s in the matrices multiplied. (The same is true of 0's when we multiply non-negative matrices in standard algebra.) We use this observation frequently.

We now impose some stochastic conditions:

**(A1)** The matrix sequence $\{A(n), n \geq 0\}$ is stationary and ergodic.

**(A2)** For each $i, j$, the entry $A_{ij}(1)$ is integrable on the event that it exceeds $-\infty$; i.e., $\mathsf{E}[|A_{ij}(1)|; A_{ij}(1) > -\infty] < \infty$.

**(A3)** For each $i, j$ the probability that $A_{ij}(1) = -\infty$ is zero or one.

Condition (A3) ensures that the location of $-\infty$'s is the same among all $\{A(n), n \geq 0\}$; results for powers of a single matrix, concerning the location of $-\infty$'s, therefore extend to products of the $\{A(n), n \geq 0\}$. Given (A3), condition (A2) simply states that each entry not identically equal to $-\infty$ is integrable.

We can now prove a preliminary generalization of Theorem 4.7.2. Let $P(m, n)$ be as in (4.45).

**Lemma 4.7.9** Assume (A1)-(A3). Suppose the matrix $A(1)$ is irreducible and aperiodic. Then

$$\lim_{n \to \infty} n^{-1} P(1, n)_{ij} = \gamma$$

exists almost surely and is independent of $i$ and $j$. The limit is finite unless $A(1)$ is the $1 \times 1$ matrix $(-\infty)$.

**Proof.** In the $1 \times 1$ case, the claim reduces to the strong law of large numbers for ergodic, stationary sequences. Suppose then that the matrices are $d \times d$, $d \geq 2$. From conditions (A1) and (A3), Lemma 4.7.7 and our observation about the location of $-\infty$'s, it follows that, for some $n_*$, $(A(1) \otimes \cdots \otimes A(n_*))_{ij} > -\infty$ for all $i, j$. Moreover, if a matrix $B$ has all entries greater than $-\infty$, then $B \otimes D$ has all entries greater than $-\infty$ unless $D$ has some column identically equal to $-\infty$. Since $A(n_* + 1)$ is irreducible, it cannot have a column identically equal to $-\infty$. So, for all $k \geq 0$, $P(1, n_* + k)_{ij} > -\infty$. Indeed, under (A2), all such entries are integrable: this follows from the fact that max is subadditive; i.e., $\max(a, b) \leq |a| + |b|$ for all real numbers $a, b$.

The rest of the proof is that of Cohen's [8] Theorem 4 and Kingman's [29] Theorem 5, but for one modification which we will point out. Let $X_{mn} = -P(m, n)_{11}$. Then, again by the subadditivity of max,

$$X_{\ell n} \leq X_{\ell m} + X_{mn},$$

for all $\ell < m < n$. This is hypothesis (S1) of the subadditive ergodic theorem. Under (A1), we have stationarity and even ergodicity of $\{X_{mn}\}$, as required by (S2). With $n_*$ as above, $g_n = \mathsf{E}[X_{0n}] = -\mathsf{E}[P(1, n)_{11}]$ exists and is finite for all $n \geq n_*$. This is slightly weaker than the first part of

(S3), but the subadditive ergodic theorem applies with this modification because only finitely many terms are affected. For the second part of (S3), observe that for $n \geq n_*$ we have

$$-g_n = \mathsf{E}[P(1, n)_{11}] \leq \mathsf{E}[\sum_{k=1}^{n} \max_{i,j} A(k)_{ij}] = n\mathsf{E}[\max_{i,j} A(1)_{ij}].$$

Since $A(1)$ has some entry greater than $-\infty$ (by irreducibility), (A2) implies that the expectation on the far right is finite and

$$g_n/n \geq -\mathsf{E}[\max_{i,j} A(1)_{ij}] > -\infty.$$

With (S1)-(S3) verified, the lemma is proved for $i = j = 1$.

To extend the result to arbitrary $i$ and $j$, observe (much as in Cohen's proof), that for $n > 2n_*$,

$$P(1, n)_{ij} \geq P(1, n_*)_{i1} + P(n_*, n - n_* - 1)_{11} + P(n - n_* - 1, n)_{1j}$$
$$P(1, n)_{11} \geq P(1, n_*)_{1i} + P(n_*, n - n_* - 1)_{ij} + P(n - n_* - 1, n)_{j1}.$$

These inequalities become obvious when the matrix entries are given the longest-path interpretation. Now divide through by $n$ and take liminf in the first inequality and limsup in the second. In both cases, the first term on the right vanishes as $n \to \infty$ by the integrability of $P(1, n_*)$. A Borel-Cantelli argument using integrability of $P(n - n_* - 1, n)$, $n \geq n_* + 1$, shows that in both cases the last term also vanishes; pages 76-77 of Cohen [8] and page 892 of Kingman [29] detail analogous cases. Thus, the limit for all $i, j$ exists and equals the limit for $i = j = 1$. $\square$

Lemma 4.7.9 allows matrix entries equal to $-\infty$, but it is not yet adequate for the types of matrices arising in (4.43); the irreducibility condition is too strong. To obtain a sufficiently general result, we need to look more closely at the matrix decomposition (4.47).

This decomposition of a $d \times d$ matrix $A$ partitions the indices $\{1, \ldots, d\}$ into $K$ classes corresponding to the $K$ irreducible submatrices on the block diagonal. Denote these classes by $S_1, \ldots, S_K$. For fixed $A$, let us say that there is a path from $i$ to $j$ if for some $n$, $A_{ij}^{\otimes n} > -\infty$. Thus, for $d \geq 2$ an irreducible matrix is one in which there is a path between every pair of indices. The condition $A_{ij}^{\otimes n} > -\infty$ corresponds to the existence of a sequence $k_1, \ldots, k_{n+1}$ with $k_1 = i$, $k_{n+1} = j$, and $A_{k_r k_{r+1}} > -\infty$ for $r = 1, \ldots, n$. Let us say that there is a path from $i$ to $j$ through $S_\ell$ if, for some $k \in S_\ell$, $A_{ik}^{\otimes n_1} > -\infty$ and $A_{kj}^{\otimes n_2} > -\infty$, for some $n_1, n_2$. We now have

**Lemma 4.7.10** Suppose that in the decomposition (4.47) of $A$ the submatrices $A^1, \ldots, A^K$ are aperiodic (as well as irreducible). Then $A$ has the following property: there exists an $n_*$ such that

$$A_{ij}^{\otimes n_*} > -\infty \quad \Rightarrow \quad A_{ij}^{\otimes n} > -\infty \text{ for all } n \geq n_*;$$
$$A_{ij}^{\otimes n_*} = -\infty \quad \Rightarrow \quad A_{ij}^{\otimes n} = -\infty \text{ for all } n \geq n_*.$$

**Proof.** The block structure of the matrix is preserved by powers. The elements below the block diagonal remain identically equal to $-\infty$. If some submatrix $A^\ell$ on the block diagonal is the $1 \times 1$ matrix $(-\infty)$, it remains so for all powers of $A$, by upper-triangularity. The elements of all other submatrices on the block diagonal are greater than $-\infty$ after a finite number $n_1$ of products of $A$ with itself, because these matrices are irreducible and aperiodic (Lemma 4.7.7). So, it only remains to consider entries above the block diagonal.

Suppose, then, that $i < j$ and $i \in S_{\ell_1}$, $j \in S_{\ell_2}$, $\ell_1 \neq \ell_2$. If there is a path from $i$ to $j$, then, by the upper-triangularity of $A$, it passes through classes $S_{\ell_1}, S_{m_1}, \ldots, S_{m_r}, S_{\ell_2}$ in increasing order, $\ell_1 < m_1 < \cdots < m_r < \ell_2$. In other words, there is a path $k_1, \ldots, k_{n+1}$ such that the index of the class containing $k_s$ does not exceed the index of the class containing $k_{s+1}$, $s = 1, \ldots, n$. Now let $n_* = dn_1 + 1$, with $n_1$ as above and $d \times d$ the dimension of the matrix. Suppose there is a path from $i$ to $j$ of length $n_*$; i.e., $A_{ij}^{\otimes n} > -\infty$. Any such path must make at least $n_1$ consecutive visits to at least one class $S_\ell$. Let $i'$ be the first index in $S_\ell$ along this path and let $j'$ be the last. By the definition of $n_1$ and the irreducibility and aperiodicity of $A^\ell$, there exist $n$-step paths from $i'$ to $j'$ for all $n \geq n_1$. Hence, if there exists a path from $i$ to $j$ of $n_*$ steps, there exists one of $n$ steps for all $n$ greater than $n_*$.

Now suppose $A_{ij}^{\otimes n_*} = -\infty$. We claim that the same is true for all $n \geq n_*$. By way of contradiction, suppose there is a path of $n_2$ steps, $n_2 > n_*$, from $i$ to $j$, and suppose $n_2$ is the smallest such number. As before, the path must include strictly more than $n_1$ consecutive indices in some class $S_\ell$, beginning with some $i'$ and ending with some $j'$. However, there exists a path from $i'$ to $j'$ in no more than $n_1$ steps; hence, the path from $i$ to $j$ could be shortened, contradicting the minimality of $n_2$. $\square$

## 4.8    Cycle Time Limits

### 4.8.1    Existence of the Limits

In order to apply Lemmas 4.7.9 and 4.7.10, to start with, we want to make sure that the $A(n)$ matrix in (4.43) can indeed be transformed into the form in (4.47), with the diagonal blocks being irreducible and aperiodic matrices. From §7.1, we know that these diagonal blocks have the form in (4.44). Now, noticing that $T_i(k) \geq T_i(k-1) + \omega_i(k)$ for any $i$ and any $k$, we can modify each of these matrices as follows without affecting the recursion in (4.43):

$$\begin{pmatrix} \omega_i(n) & 0 & -\infty & \cdots & -\infty \\ \omega_i(n) & \omega_i(n-1) & 0 & \cdots & -\infty \\ \vdots & \vdots & \ddots & \ddots & \vdots \\ \omega_i(n) & -\infty & \cdots & \omega_i(n-d+1) & 0 \\ \omega_i(n) & -\infty & -\infty & \cdots & \omega_i(n-d) \end{pmatrix}. \quad (4.48)$$

This way, all the diagonal blocks become irreducible and aperiodic.

Next, assume there are $K - 1$ ($K \geq 1$) stages that have infinite buffer limit, at stages $i_1, \ldots, i_{K-1}$, and $i_1 < \ldots < i_{K-1}$. To be specific, if stage $i_\ell$ has an infinite $k_{i_\ell}$ value, assume $a_{i_\ell} = k_{i_\ell} = \infty$ and $b_{i_\ell} < \infty$. Other possibilites are similarly treated.

This way, the $A(n)$ matrix is partitioned into $K$ irreducible classes, $S_\ell$, $\ell = 1, \ldots, K$. Each class $S_\ell$ corresponds to a segment of the production line that includes the stages $i_\ell, i_\ell + 1, \ldots, i_{\ell+1} - 1$. Say a class $S_j$ can *reach* another class $S_\ell$, if there is a path from any member of $S_j$ to any member of $S_\ell$. (Here, "path" follows the definition in §7.3 preceding Lemma 4.7.10.) Then clearly, any class with a smaller index can reach any class with a larger index, but the converse does not hold. This is simply because a service completion at an upstream segment of the line is indeed a precedent constraint for a service completion in a downstream segment; but with the infinite buffer(s) decoupling the downstream segment from the upstream segment, the former can no longer block the latter, and hence there is no precedence constraint from the former on to the latter.

To summarize, we have

**Lemma 4.8.1** For the $(a, b, k)$ tandem model, suppose $K - 1$ ($1 \leq K \leq m$) stages have infinite buffer limits as specified above. Then the matrix $A(n)$, for any given $n \geq 1$, in the event-epoch recursion (4.43) decomposes into $K$ classes, $S_\ell$, $\ell = 1, \ldots, K$; and for any $\ell > j$, $S_\ell$ is reachable from $S_j$, but not vice versa. Consequently, the matrix has the upper-triangular form in (4.47), with all the blocks below the diagonal being $[-\infty]$ (a matrix with all entries equal to $-\infty$), all the blocks above the diagonal *not* equal to $[-\infty]$, and all the diagonal blocks irreducible and aperiodic.

**Proposition 4.8.2** For the $(a, b, k)$ model as specified in Lemma 4.8.1, suppose the service times are integrable, stationary and ergodic, then the limit (of cycle times)

$$\gamma_\ell = \lim_{n \to \infty} n^{-1} T_{i_\ell}(n) < \infty$$

exists almost surely for each stage $i_\ell \in S_\ell$ (i.e., the $\ell$th segment of the production line), and is independent of the initial state.

**Proof.** From (4.43) we have that

$$n^{-1}\hat{T}(n) = n^{-1}\mathbf{0} \otimes A(1) \otimes \cdots \otimes A(n).$$

For $n \leq d$, some entries of $A(n)$ may include $\omega_\alpha(k)$'s with $k \leq 0$, so we do not have stationarity. However, the sequence $\{A(d+n), n = 1, 2, \ldots\}$ is stationary and ergodic, and all entries of every $A(n)$, $n = 1, 2, \ldots$ are either integrable or equal to $-\infty$. By the specification in Lemma 4.8.1, (A3) holds. Pick $n_*$ following Lemma 4.7.10, and without loss of generality, let it be greater than $d$. We first show

$$\lim_{n \to \infty} n^{-1} A(n_* + 1) \otimes \cdots \otimes A(n_* + n) = \Gamma,$$

with $\Gamma$ being a matrix that admits the same decomposition as $A(n)$; specifically,

$$\Gamma_{ij} = [-\infty], \ j > \ell; \quad \Gamma_{jj} = [\gamma_j]; \quad \Gamma_{j\ell} = [\gamma_\ell], \ j < \ell;$$

where $\Gamma_{j\ell}$ denotes the $(j, \ell)$ th block in $\Gamma$, $[x]$ denotes a matrix with all elements equal to $x$. (Note $\gamma_\ell$ is the constant corresponding to the diagonal block $A^\ell(n)$, via Lemma 4.7.9.)

The assumptions on the service times imply (A1)-(A3). For $j > \ell$, i.e., those blocks that are below the (block) diagonal, the result is automatic. For the diagonal blocks, the result follows from Lemma 4.7.9. (In particular, take into account Lemma 4.8.1, about the irreducibility and aperiodicity of the diagonal blocks.) So, we only need to consider blocks above the block diagonal.

Pick $j < \ell$, and consider an element, $\Gamma_{i_j, i_\ell}$, at the $(i_j i_\ell)$ th position of $\Gamma$, with $i_j \in S_j$ and $i_\ell \in S_\ell$. We know $\Gamma_{i_j, i_\ell}$ is the limiting average of the longest path between $i_j$ and $i_\ell$. Following the argument of Cohen [8] (see Remark 4.7.3), this longest path is formed by an initial path from $i_j$ to the maximum (average length) cycle, followed by an infinite number of such cycles, and then a path from this cycle to $i_\ell$. Now in our context, a cycle corresponds to exactly the cycle time of a segment of the production line (which corresponds to a class). For the segments between $j$ and $\ell$, the longest cycle time (limiting average) is $\gamma_\ell$ (since the event epochs are increasing in the stage indices). As $n$ increases, the initial and the final portions of the path become negligible, hence $\Gamma_{i_j, i_\ell} = \gamma_\ell$.

Next, let

$$B = \lim_{n \to \infty} n^{-1} A(1) \otimes \cdots \otimes A(n_*)$$

be a matrix of 0's and $-\infty$'s. Note that the location of its $-\infty$'s corresponds to that in $\Gamma$, by Lemma 4.7.10, and pre-multiplying it by $\mathbf{0}$ yields column maxima. It is then obvious that

$$\mathbf{0} \otimes B \otimes \Gamma = \mathbf{0} \otimes \Gamma = (\gamma_\ell)_{\ell=1}^K.$$

It now follows that

$$
\begin{aligned}
\lim n^{-1}\hat{T}(n) &= \mathbf{0} \otimes \left(\lim n^{-1}A(1) \otimes \cdots \otimes A(n_*)\right) \\
&\quad \otimes \left(\lim n^{-1}A(n_* + 1) \otimes \cdots \otimes A(n_* + n)\right) \\
&= \mathbf{0} \otimes B \otimes \Gamma = \mathbf{0} \otimes \Gamma = (\gamma_\ell)_{\ell=1}^K.
\end{aligned}
$$

Finally, we establish independence of the initial state. Write $T^{(s)}$ for event times starting from state $s$ and write $T^{(s)}(\cdot, \omega)$ to stress the dependence on the clock sequence $\omega$. For any score $y$, let $\omega_y$ be the shifted clock sequence defined by $\omega_{y,\alpha}(n) = \omega_\alpha(n + y_\alpha)$, $\alpha \in \bar{\alpha}$, $n = 1, 2, \ldots$.

Now let $s$ and $s'$ be any states. By irreducibility, there is a string $\sigma$ such that $s' = \phi(s, \sigma)$. Let $y$ be its score. For any $n = 1, 2, \ldots$ and any $\alpha \in \bar{\alpha}$,

$$
T_\alpha^{(s')}(n, \omega) \leq \max_\beta \{T_\beta^{(s')}(y_\beta, \omega)\} + T_\alpha^{(s)}(n - y_\alpha, \omega_y).
$$

If we now divide by $n$ and let $n \to \infty$, then the max term vanishes because it is integrable. Moreover, the limit through the shifted clocks $\omega_y$ is the same as through $\omega$, by stationarity. Consequently, $\gamma_\alpha^{(s')} \leq \gamma_\alpha^{(s)}$. Reversing the roles of $s$ and $s'$ proves equality. $\square$

**Remark 4.8.3** If $u_{ij} < \infty$ for all $i, j$, which is the case when the buffer limit is finite at all stages, then the $A(n)$ matrix has a single irreducible class. Hence, following Proposition 4.8.2, the production line has a unique cycle time limit, and hence a unique production rate, at all stages. Another extreme case is when the buffer limit is infinite at all stages (implying $u_{ij} = \infty$ for all $i, j$). Then, there will be $m$ cycle time limits (not necessarily all distinct), one for each stage. In general, we allow a combination of finite and infinite buffers; and the result points out precisely the decoupling role played by infinite buffers.

## 4.8.2   Rate of Convergence

The subadditive ergodic theorem guarantees the existence of a limit for a (normalized) subadditive process, but says nothing about the rate of convergence. All ergodic theorems may be viewed as generalizations of the strong law of large numbers; convergence rates and error bounds for strong laws are provided by central limit theorems. In this section, we develop bounds to complement the convergence of the cycle times $\{n^{-1}T_\alpha(n), n \geq 0\}$. (Here and below, we use $\alpha$ to denote a generic service completion event at any stage.) These bounds are formally similar to Gaussian approximations but are not based on central limit theorems (which are not generally available for subadditive sequences). Instead, they follow from a martingale inequality. The main additional assumptions we need are that the clock times are i.i.d. and bounded. Our use of this method follows the application in Rhee and Talagrand [39] to bin-packing and traveling-salesman problems.

Our first step bounds the difference $T_\alpha(n) - \mathsf{E}[T_\alpha(n)]$ for any $\alpha$ and $n$. Write $\omega(\ell)$ for the vector of service times $(\omega_\alpha(\ell), \alpha \in \bar\alpha = \{\alpha_1 \ldots, \alpha_m\})$. Define

$$\mathcal{F}_k = \sigma\text{-algebra generated by } \{\omega(\ell), \ell = 1, \ldots, k\},$$

and let $\mathcal{F}_0$ be the trivial $\sigma$-algebra. Clearly, $\{\mathcal{F}_n, n \geq 0\}$ is an increasing family. For fixed $\alpha$ and $n$, define

$$\Delta_k = \mathsf{E}[T_\alpha(n)|\mathcal{F}_k] - \mathsf{E}[T_\alpha(n)|\mathcal{F}_{k-1}], \quad i = 1, \ldots, n. \tag{4.49}$$

We always have $\mathsf{E}[T_\alpha(n)|\mathcal{F}_0] = \mathsf{E}[T_\alpha(n)]$, and $\mathsf{E}[T_\alpha(n)|\mathcal{F}_n] = T_\alpha(n)$ if $T_\alpha(n)$ is $\mathcal{F}_n$-measurable. Hence, by telescoping the sum we get

$$\sum_{k=1}^n \Delta_k = T_\alpha(n) - \mathsf{E}[T_\alpha(n)]. \tag{4.50}$$

This expresses the total error $T_\alpha(n) - \mathsf{E}[T_\alpha(n)]$ as the sum of individual errors $\Delta_k$.

For this decomposition to be useful, the $\Delta_k$'s must have some structure. The relevant property is this:

**Definition 4.8.4** Random variables $\{Y_n, n \geq 1\}$ form a *martingale difference sequence* (MDS) with respect to an increasing family $\{\mathcal{F}_n, n \geq 0\}$ of $\sigma$-algebras if each $Y_n$ is $\mathcal{F}_n$-measurable and $\mathsf{E}[Y_n|\mathcal{F}_{n-1}] = 0$.

By its very definition, each $\Delta_k$ in (4.49) is $\mathcal{F}_k$-measurable. Moreover,

$$\mathsf{E}[\Delta_k|\mathcal{F}_{k-1}] = \mathsf{E}[\mathsf{E}[\Delta_k|\mathcal{F}_k]|\mathcal{F}_{k-1}] - \mathsf{E}[\Delta_k|\mathcal{F}_{k-1}] = 0,$$

so $\{\Delta_k, k = 1, \ldots, n\}$ is an MDS. The MDS representation becomes useful through the following result:

**Lemma 4.8.5** Let $\{\Delta_k, k = 1, \ldots, n\}$ be an MDS. Then for each $t \geq 0$,

$$\mathsf{P}[|\sum_{k=1}^n \Delta_k| > t] \leq 2\exp\left(-t^2/(2\sum_{k=1}^n \|\Delta_k\|_\infty^2)\right), \tag{4.51}$$

where $\|\Delta_k\|_\infty$ is the essential supremum of $\Delta_k$.

This result is stated in Rhee and Talagrand [39], where a reference to a proof also appears. With this lemma we have a way to bound $T_\alpha(n) - \mathsf{E}[T_\alpha(n)]$ using (4.50) if we can bound the $\Delta_k$'s.

We impose the following assumptions:

**(B1)** The vectors $\{\omega(n), n \geq 1\}$ are i.i.d. and integrable.

**(B2)** There exists a constant $c$ such that $\mathsf{P}[\omega_\alpha(1) \leq c] = 1$ for all $\alpha \in \bar\alpha$.

Condition (B1) strengthens our earlier assumption of stationarity and ergodicity of the service times, but still allows dependence among the components of $\omega(n)$ for each $n$. Condition (B2) requires that the service times be bounded. We now have

**Lemma 4.8.6** If (B1) and (B2) hold, then for any $t \geq 0$,

$$P[|T_\alpha(n) - E[T_\alpha(n)]| > t] \leq 2\exp(-t^2/(2nm^2c^2)),$$

where $c$ is the constant in (B2), and $m = |\bar{\alpha}|$.

**Proof.** For $i = 1, \ldots, n$, denote by $T_\alpha^k(n)$ the time of the $n$-th occurrence of $\alpha$ when $\omega(i)$ is replaced by the zero vector; i.e., when each $\omega_\beta(i)$, $\beta \in \bar{\alpha}$, is set to zero. We know that event epochs are increasing functions of clock times; so, $T_\alpha^k(n) \leq T_\alpha(n)$. It also follows from (4.26) that $T_\alpha(n) \leq T_\alpha^k(n) + \sum_{\beta \in \bar{\alpha}} \omega_\beta(k)$. To put it another way, replacing $\omega_\beta(i)$ with zero reduces the time of the $n$-th occurrence of $\alpha$ by at most $\omega_\beta(k)$. Taking conditional expectations across these inequalities we get

$$E[T_\alpha^k(n)|\mathcal{F}_k] \leq E[T_\alpha(n)|\mathcal{F}_k] \leq E[T_\alpha^k(n)|\mathcal{F}_k] + mc,$$

$$E[T_\alpha^k(n)|\mathcal{F}_{k-1}] \leq E[T_\alpha(n)|\mathcal{F}_{k-1}] \leq E[T_\alpha^k(n)|\mathcal{F}_{k-1}] + mc.$$

However, under (B1), $T_\alpha^k(n)$ is independent of $\omega_i$, so

$$E[T_\alpha^k(n)|\mathcal{F}_k] = E[T_\alpha^k(n)|\mathcal{F}_{k-1}].$$

Combining the inequalities therefore yields

$$|E[T_\alpha(n)|\mathcal{F}_k] - E[T_\alpha(n)|\mathcal{F}_{k-1}]| \leq mc;$$

i.e., $\|\Delta_k\|_\infty \leq mc$. The result now follows from (4.51). $\square$

The main result of this subsection is the following:

**Proposition 4.8.7** Suppose in addition to the conditions of Proposition 4.8.2 that (B1)-(B3) hold. Then for all $\epsilon > 0$ there exists an $n_0 < \infty$ such that for all $n \geq n_0$,

$$P[|n^{-1}T_\alpha(n) - \gamma_\alpha| > \epsilon] \leq 2\exp(-n\epsilon^2/(2m^2c^2)). \qquad (4.52)$$

**Proof.** For all $n$,

$$P[|n^{-1}T_\alpha(n) - \gamma_\alpha| > \epsilon]$$
$$\leq \quad P[|n^{-1}T_\alpha(n) - n^{-1}E[T_\alpha(n)]| + |n^{-1}E[T_\alpha(n)] - \gamma_\alpha| > \epsilon].$$

Moreover, as noted at the end of §7.2, the subadditive ergodic theorem implies convergence in expectation, so $n^{-1}E[T_\alpha(n)] \to \gamma_\alpha$. In particular, for any $\delta > 0$ and all sufficiently large $n$, $|n^{-1}E[T_\alpha(n)] - \gamma_\alpha| < \delta\epsilon$. Consequently,

$$P[|n^{-1}T_\alpha(n) - \gamma_\alpha| > \epsilon]$$
$$\leq \quad P[|n^{-1}T_\alpha(n) - n^{-1}E[T_\alpha(n)]| > \epsilon(1 - \delta)].$$

By the previous result, the probability on the right is less than or equal to

$$2\exp\left(\frac{-n\epsilon^2(1-\delta)^2}{2m^2c^2}\right).$$

Since this upper bound is valid for all $\delta > 0$, it remains valid for $\delta = 0$, which is what we needed to show. $\square$

The bound in (4.52) is useful in estimating $\gamma_\alpha$ through simulation. It can be used to construct a confidence interval for $\gamma_\alpha$ that is valid for all sufficiently large $n$, not just asymptotically. Moreover, using (4.52) obviates the sometimes difficult task of estimating an asymptotic variance: the (known) constant $m^2c^2$ replaces the variance. Of course, when $\{\sqrt{n}(n^{-1}T_\alpha(n) - \gamma_\alpha), n \geq 0\}$ satisfies a central limit theorem, we would expect $m^2c^2$ to be an upper bound on its variance constant. Confidence interval halfwidths provided by (4.52) are $O(n^{-1/2})$ just as with a central limit theorem.

The utility of (4.52) is diminished if $m$ or $c$ is large. In specific models, we can typically improve these constants. If, for example, we can show that some events $\beta_1, \ldots, \beta_k$ are never in the path that attains the maximum in the event-epoch recursion, then $m$ may be reduced to $m - k$ and $c$ need only bound clock times for events other than $\beta_1, \ldots, \beta_k$.

## 4.9  Notes

**Section 1.** Refer to the articles in Ho [24] for an introduction to the various facets of research in discrete-event systems and related applications.

**Section 2.** This treatment of the GSMP as a GSMS driven by clock sequence follows Glasserman and Yao [16, 17, 18]. Discussions of other features, such as *speeds* and *probabilistic routing*, can be found in [17].

The earliest work on GSMP focuses on insensitivity of stationary distributions with respect to distributions of clock times; see, for instance, Matthes [31], Schassberger [42] and Whitt [48]. A more recent article, Glynn [23], discusses modeling of discrete-event systems using GSMPs with special attention to regenerative properties.

The role of a GSMS as generator of a language is reminiscent of the *supervisory control* framework of Ramadge and Wonham [40]. The event list function $\mathcal{E}$ plays the role of a supervisor, in that it enables and disables events.

**Sections 3.1 and 3.2.** Condition (**C**) was introduced in Glasserman [13, 14] as a condition for continuity of path functionals in the context of perturbation analysis derivative estimation. The original version of (**C**) is this: If $\alpha, \beta \in \mathcal{E}(s)$, then $\phi(s, \alpha\beta) = \phi(s, \beta\alpha)$, i.e., both sides are defined and equal.

Condition (M) was originally developed in [17] as a condition for monotonicity in GSMPs. In [18], (M) was shown to be equivalent to non-interruption plus permutability, which is (M1) in Definition 4.3.4. In addition, (C) was shown to be stronger than (M) in that it strengthens permutability to strong permutability. This is the form adopted here.

In [18], the connection between (M) and antimatroid was also established. This connection was motivated by the antimatroid with repetition of Björner [4], and Shor, Björner and Lovász [45]. The key structural property of antimatroid with repetition is the strong exchange property, (M2) in Definition 4.3.4, which is equivalent to (M).

**Section 3.3.** Condition (CX) was introduced as a condition for convexity in [18]. From this perspective, it is a natural extension of (M). It can alternatively be viewed as the result of adding min-closure to the antimatroid property.

**Sections 3.4 and 3.5.** Under (M) and (CX), the score space becomes a semi-lattice and a lattice, respectively. The notion of minimal elements was first developed in [18] as a basis for event-epoch recursions. It also captures the notion of event *activation* under (M): $\alpha$ can be activated for the $n$th time if and only if one of the minimal elements of $\mathcal{N}_{\alpha,n}$ is reached. Thus, under (M), event activation is determined by scores, rather than strings. This greatly simplifies the dynamics of a GSMP and yields the (min,max,+) recursion in (4.4). Strengthening (M) to (CX) further simplifies the recursion to (max,+). Monotonicity and convexity, which were the original motivation of [17, 18], now follow as simple consequences of these recursions.

The Lipschitz continuity of min, max and + plays a key role in the convergence of perturbation analysis derivative estimates; see Glasserman [13, 14, 14]. Their monotonicity guarantees variance reduction using common random numbers; see Glasserman and Yao [16, 19].

**Section 3.6.** The characteristic function is a useful tool in establishing consequences of (M) or (CX). Indeed Theorem 4.3.18 points out alternative ways to specify (M) and (CX) through the characteristic function. In Section 3.7, it also plays a key role in relating families of schemes.

The characteristic function is also a useful device in modeling optimal control problems for GSMPs. This application is developed in Glasserman and Yao [21].

**Section 3.7.** The idea of comparing different schemes and characterizing subscheme relations first appeared in [17, 18]. Specifically, a subscheme relation always implies a sub-language relation. And in order to compare the event completion sequences, in addition to the sub-language relationship, the smaller language has to be non-interruptive and the larger language has to satisfy (M), i.e., both non-interruption and permutability.

**Section 3.8.** Synchronization becomes uniformization in a Markov setting; for background on uniformization see, e.g., Ross [26]. Without Markovian assumptions, synchronization models a different type of system than the standard construction. For instance, it corresponds to gated or autonomous service in Example 4.2.2.

**Sections 4, 5 and 6.** The $(a, b, k)$ tandem model was originally developed in Cheng [6], and Cheng and Yao [8]. For earlier work on kanban models, see Mitra and Mitrani [33, 34] and the references there.

The fact that the $(a, b, k)$ model can be reduced to a two-parameter $(b, k)$ model (see Remark 4.5.4) was first observed by Rajan and Agrawal [38] (where a third, independent parameter is used to model a so-called "server starvation" mechanism). On the other hand, in practice, there are "two-card" kanban systems, conveyance card plus kanban, which are equivalent to a two-parameter $(a, k)$ model (i.e., $b_i = k_i$ for all $i$); see [8]. From Remark 4.5.4, we now know that at least in terms of analyzing the service completion processes, the $(a, b, k)$ model itself, as well as all its variations, can all be reduced to a two-parameter model, either $(a, k)$ or $(b, k)$.

The concavity results in §5.2 have generalized similar results previously established for communication or manufacturing blocking assuming exponential service times and using uniformization; see, for instance, Anantharam and Tsoucas [2], Meester and Shanthikumar [32], and Shanthikumar and Yao [43]. Assuming a synchronized model from the outset, these types of results go through for the $(a, b, k)$ model without the exponential assumption.

The line reversal results given here generalize similar results for classical tandem queues, e.g., Yamazaki and Sakasegawa [49], and Muth [35]. Previous work on this topic typically uses either an associated activity network (e.g., [35]) or a "duality" between jobs and "holes" (e.g., [49]). Proposition 4.6.1 makes a direct connection between reversibility and the representation for event epochs.

The full reversibility result was shown in Ammar and Gershwin [1] for a tandem queue with exponential servers under communication blocking. In [1], the key idea is to relabel the state of the Markov chain for the original system, while preserving the transition rates, and thereby obtain the transition diagram of the Markov chain for the reversed system. Our Proposition 4.6.3 shows that while communication blocking is essential for this type of strong reversibility, exponential service time distributions are not. The same result (i.e., in the same generality as Proposition 4.6.3) also appeared in Buzacott and Shanthikumar [5] (p. 219), where the argument was based on the job-hole duality.

The symmetry of line reversal, when combined with the concavity properties of §5, has useful implications in buffer allocation, as illustrated in Proposition 4.6.2.

Results in these three sections are taken from Glasserman and Yao [20], where we also consider systems with other configurations operating under the $(a, b, k)$ control mechanism. These include cyclic and fork-join networks, which are useful models for production systems that operate at constant WIP, and systems that involve parallel service and assembly. Related studies that address similar issues but use different approaches or consider different blocking schemes include Dallery, Liu and Towsley [11], and Rajan and Agrawal [38], among others.

**Sections 7 and 8.** For background material on stationarity, ergodicity and martingales see, e.g., Karlin and Taylor [26]. Applications of (max,+) and related algebras appear to have been first put forward by Cunninghame-Green; see [10] and references there. Cohen *et al* [9] contains many interesting applications of random matrices.

As discussed in Baccelli [3] and Cohen [8], the constants $\gamma_\ell$ appearing in Lemma 4.7.9 and Proposition 4.8.2 are analogs of *Lyapunov exponents* in ordinary products of random matrices. In [3] and [8], a corresponding connection is made with *Oseledec's multiplicative ergodic theorem* (for which see [9, Section I.A] and references there). Oseledec's theorem (and its analog in [3]) is concerned with the action of random matrix products on individual vectors. It includes a partial characterization of certain random subspaces for the limiting product associated with the Lyapunov exponents. In our (more specialized) setting, we give, instead, a complete characterization of the limiting matrix $\Gamma$ itself (Proposition 4.8.2). Results in these two sections are specialized from the general setting of Glasserman and Yao [22].

*Acknowledgments:* Paul Glasserman and David Yao are both supported in part by NSF grant MSS-92-16490; David Yao is also supported in part by NSF grant DDM-91-08540.

## 4.10   References

[1] Ammar, M.A. and Gershwin, S.B. 1989. Equivalence Relations in Queueing Models of Fork/Join Networks with Blocking, *Performance Evaluation,* **10**, 233-245.

[2] Anantharam, V., and Tsoucas, P. 1990. Stochastic Concavity of Throughput in Series of Queues with Finite Buffers, *Advances in Applied Probability,* **22**, 761-763.

[3] Baccelli, F. 1992. Ergodic Theory of Stochastic Petri Networks, *Ann. Prob.* **20**, 375-396.

[4] Björner, A. 1985. On Matroids, Groups, and Exchange Languages, in *Matroid Theory and its Applications,* Coll. Math. Soc. J. Bolyai **40**. North-Holland, Amsterdam, 25-60.

[5] Buzacott, J.A. and Shanthikumar, J.G. 1992. *Stochastic Models of Manufacturing Systems,* Prentice-Hall, Englewood Cliffs, NJ.

[6] Cheng, D.W. 1990. *Tandem Queues with General Blocking: Stochastic Comparisons and Structural Properties,* Ph.D. thesis, Graduate School of Business, Columbia University, New York.

[7] Cheng, D.W., and Yao, D.D. 1993. Tandem Queues with General Blocking: A Unified Model and Stochastic Comparisons, *Discrete Event Dynamic Systems: Theory and Applications,* **2**, 207-234.

[8] Cohen, J.E. 1988. Subadditivity, Generalized Products of Random Matrices and Operations Research, *SIAM Review,* **30**, 69-86.

[9] Cohen, J.E., Newman, C.M., and Kesten, H., eds. 1986. *Random Matrices and Their Applications,* Contemporary Mathematics, vol. 50, American Mathematical Society, Providence.

[10] Cunninghame-Green, R. 1979. *Minimax Algebra,* Lecture Notes in Economics and Mathematical Systems 166, Springer-Verlag, New York.

[11] Dallery, Y., Liu, Z. and Towsley, D. Properties of Fork/Join Queueing Networks with Blocking under Various Operating Mechanisms, submitted for publication.

[12] Dietrich, B.L. 1989. Matroids and Antimatroids—A Survey, *Discrete Math.* **78**, 223-237.

[13] Glasserman, P. 1988. *Equivalence Methods in the Perturbation Analysis of Queueing Networks,* Ph.D. Thesis, Division of Applied Sciences, Harvard University, MA.

[14] Glasserman, P. 1991. Structural Conditions for Perturbation Analysis Derivative Estimation: Finite-Time Performance Indices, *Oper. Res.* **39**, 724-738.

[15] Glasserman, P. 1991. *Gradient Estimation via Perturbation Analysis,* Kluwer Academic Publishers, Norwell, Massachusetts.

[16] Glasserman, P., and Yao, D.D. 1991. Algebraic Structure of Some Stochastic Discrete-Event Systems, with Applications, *Discrete Event Dynamic Systems, Theory and Appications,* **1**, 7-35.

[17] Glasserman, P., and Yao, D.D. 1992. Monotonicity in Generalized Semi-Markov Processes, *Math. Oper. Res.* **17**, 1-21.

[18] Glasserman, P., and Yao, D.D. 1992. Generalized Semi-Markov Processes: Antimatroid Structure and Second-Order Properties, *Math. Oper. Res.* **17**, 444-469.

[19] Glasserman, P., and Yao, D.D. 1992. Some Guidelines and Guarantees for Common Random Numbers, *Mgmt. Sci.* **38**, 884-908.

[20] Glasserman, P., and Yao, D.D. Structured Buffer-Allocation Problems, *Discrete Event Dynamic Systems, Theory and Appications,* to appear.

[21] Glasserman, P., and Yao, D.D. Monotone Optimal Control of Permutable GSMPs, *Math. Oper. Res.,* to appear.

[22] Glasserman, P., and Yao, D.D. Subadditivity and Stability of a Class of Discrete-Event Systems, submitted for publication.

[23] Glynn, P.W. 1989. A GSMP Formalism for Discrete Event Systems. *Proceedings of IEEE* **77**, 14-23.

[24] Ho, Y.C., (ed.) 1989. Special Issue on Discrete Event Dynamical Systems, *Proceedings of the IEEE* (January issue).

[25] Kamae, T., Krengel, U., and O'Brien, G.L. 1977. Stochastic Inequalities on Partially Ordered Spaces, *Ann. Prob.* **5**, 899-912.

[26] Karlin, S. and Taylor, H.M. 1975. *A First Course in Stochastic Processes,* (2nd ed), Academic Press.

[27] Kelly, F.P. 1979. *Reversibility and Stochastic Networks,* Wiley, New York.

[28] Kingman, J.F.C. 1968. The Ergodic Theory of Subadditive Stochastic Processes. *J. Roy. Statist. Soc.,* Ser. B. **30**, 499-510.

[29] Kingman, J.F.C. 1973. Subadditive Ergodic Theory. *Ann. Probability* **1**, 883-909.

[30] Korte, B., and Lováz, L. 1983. Structural Properties of Greedoids, *Combinatorica* **3**, 359-374.

[31] Matthes, K. Zur Theorie der Bedienungsprozess, *Trans. 3rd Prague Conf. Inform. Theory, Statist. Dec. Funct., Random Processes,* Prague, 513-528, Prague.

[32] Meester, L.E., and Shanthikumar, J.G. 1990. Concavity of the Throughput and Optimal Buffer Space Allocation for Tandem Queueing Systems with Finite Buffer Storage Space, *Advances in Applied Probability,* **22**, 764-767.

[33] Mitra, D. and Mitrani, I. 1990. Analysis of a Kanban Discipline for Cell Coordination in Production Lines, I, *Management Science,* **36**, 1548-1566.

[34] Mitra, D. and Mitrani, I. 1991. Analysis of a Kanban Discipline for Cell Coordination in Production Lines, II: Stochastic Demands, *Operations Research*, **39**, 807-823.

[35] Muth, E. 1979. The Reversibility Property of Production Lines, *Management Science*, **25**, 152-158.

[36] Pólya, G., and Szegö, G. 1976. *Problems and Theorems in Analysis, Vol.1*, Second Edition, Springer-Verlag, New York.

[37] Pullman, N.J. 1976. *Matrix Theory and its Applications: Selected Topics*. Marcel Dekker, New York.

[38] Rajan, R. and Agrawal, R. Structural Properties of the Throughput in Cyclic Networks with General Blocking and Starvation, *Queueing Systems, Theory and Applications*, submitted.

[39] Rhee, W., and Talagrand, M. 1987. Martingale Inequalities and NP-Complete Problems, *Math. Oper. Res.* **12**, 177-181.

[40] Ramadge, P.J., and Wonham, W.M. 1987. Supervisory Control of a Class of Discrete-Event Processes, *SIAM J. Control and Optimization* **25**, 206-230.

[41] Ross, S.M. 1983. *Stochastic Processes*. Wiley, New York.

[42] Schassberger, R. 1976. On the Equilibrium Distribution of a Class of Finite-State Generalized Semi-Markov Processes, *Math. Oper. Res.* **1**, 395-406.

[43] Shanthikumar, J.G. and Yao, D.D. 1989. Monotonicity and Concavity Properties in Cyclic Queueing Networks with Finite Buffers, in *Queueing Networks with Blocking*, H. Perros and T. Altiok, eds., Elsevier Science, 325-344.

[44] Shanthikumar, J.G., and Yao, D.D. 1991. Strong Stochastic Convexity: Closure Properties and Applications, *J. Appl. Probab.* **28**, 131-145.

[45] Shor, P.W., Björner, A., and Lovász, L. Chip-Firing Games on Graphs, *European J. Combinatorics* **12**, 283-291.

[46] Stoyan, D. 1983. *Comparion Methods for Queues and Other Stochastic Models*, D.J. Daley (Ed.), Wiley, New York.

[47] Whitney, H. 1935. On the Abstract Properties of Linear Dependence, *Amer. J. Math.* **57**, 507-533.

[48] Whitt, W. 1980. Continuity of Generalized Semi-Markov Processes, *Math. Oper. Res.* **5**, 494-501.

[49] Yamazaki, G., and Sakasegawa, H. 1975. Properties of Duality in Tandem Queueing Systems. *Ann. Inst. Stat. Math.* **27**, 201-212.

# 5
# Stochastic Convexity and Stochastic Majorization

Cheng-Shang Chang
J. George Shanthikumar
David D. Yao

ABSTRACT Convexity and submodularity are useful second-order properties in optimization. Majorization and the related arrangement ordering
are key properties that support pairwise-interchange arguments. Together
these properties play an important role in resource allocation, production
planning, and scheduling. Here we present the essentials of the recently
developed theory of stochastic convexity and stochastic majorization, emphasizing their interplay. We illustrate the many applications of the theory
through examples in production systems, including a random yield model, a
joint setup problem, a manufacturing process with trial runs, a production
network with constant work-in-process (WIP) and WIP-dependent production rate, and scheduling in tandem production lines and parallel assembly
systems.

## 5.1 Introduction

Consider a production process that involves two stages. The first stage
consists of $m$ subassemblies, each producing one type of component. A set
of components, one or several units from each type, are then assembled
at the second stage. For instance, the subassemblies produce electronic
components — various types of transistors, resistors, capacitors, etc., which
are assembled at a second stage into circuit boards. Suppose the component
yield of each type $i$ is random: given a production lot of $n_i$ units, the yield
— number of good units — is a random variable $Y_i(n_i, p_i)$, where $p_i$ denotes
the yield ratio, a deterministic parameter that measures the quality of the
subassembly. Without loss of generality, suppose a single unit from each
type is needed for the assembly, then the number of assembled products,
i.e., the assembly yield, is

$$Y(n, p) = \min\{Y_i(n_i, p_i), i = 1, ..., m\},$$

where $n = (n_i)_{i=1}^m$ and $p = (p_i)_{i=1}^m$.

In studying the optimal design of the above process, we would like to know properties of the yield, at both the component and assembly levels, with respect to the parameters $(n, p)$. For instance, is $Y_i$ increasing in $n_i$ and $p_i$ in some sense? (Naturally, one would expect the yield to be higher when the lot size is larger and the quality is better — in terms of a higher yield ratio.) What about second-order properties of the yield with respect to the parameters, such as concavity or convexity, submodularity or super-modularity? We know these are all useful properties in optimization. For instance, concavity implies decreasing marginals in yield, and supermodularity in $(n_i, p_i)$ implies that lot size and yield ratio enhance each other in increasing the number of assembled units.

Obviously, in order to address these issues we need to know more about the random variable $Y_i$ as a function of the parameters $(n_i, p_i)$. In other words, we need to be more specific about the "yield model". Consider the simplest case,

$$Y_i(n_i, p_i) = \sum_{j=1}^{n_i} Y_i^j(p_i),$$

where $Y_i^j(p_i)$, $j = 1, ..., n_i$, are iid Bernoulli random variables with success probability $p_i$. In other words, this is an additive yield model: each unit $j$ in the lot is independently good or bad modeled as a Bernoulli variate. This way, $Y_i(n_i, p_i)$ is a binomial variate with parameters $(n_i, p_i)$. When $n_i$ is large, $Y_i$ can also be viewed as a normal variate with mean $n_i p_i$ and variance $n_i p_i (1 - p_i)$. So it appears as if the parametric behavior of the yield can be studied through its distribution function.

However, the distribution function of the yield may not be easily accessible. For instance, even if the $Y_i$'s are independent, and all follow binomial or normal distributions (with different parameters), it is still difficult to derive the distribution function of $Y = \min_i \{Y_i\}$. Therefore, what is needed is a theory that does not rely on explicit distribution functions.

In another direction, one can ask questions such as whether a subassembly with a higher yield ratio should be given a larger lot size, and if all the yield ratios are the same then shouldn't the lot sizes be divided as evenly as possible among the subassemblies? These allude to properties of the yield with respect to the parameters under *arrangement* and *majorization* orderings.

Arrangement and majorization orderings often arise in pairwise interchange arguments. In addition to the assembly example above, consider the following simple scheduling problem: Two jobs are to be processed in sequence on a single processor. Their processing times are $x$ and $y$ time units, respectively ($x$ and $y$ are real values). Process $x$ first and then $y$, and the total delay ("flow time") of the jobs is $x + (x + y) = 2x + y$. Interchange the processing sequence, i.e., process $y$ first and then $x$, and the flow time is $y + (x + y) = x + 2y$. Suppose $x > y$, then $2x + y > x + 2y$. That is, the second sequence is better in terms of a smaller flow time. This is essentially the argument for optimality of the so-called SPT (shortest processing time) rule in deterministic scheduling. (When there are more than two jobs, re-peatedly apply the above argument to each pair, each interchange of the processing sequence — shorter job first — results in a decrease of the flow time.) The natural question to ask here is whether the result still holds in the stochastic setting, i.e., when the processing times are random variables.

In the deterministic setting, there is a rich theory of convexity and its applications in optimization (e.g., Rockafellar [14]), and an equally rich theory of rearrangement and majorization inequalities (e.g., Hardy, Little-wood and Polya [9], Marshall and Olkin [11]). In contrast, studies of the stochastic counterpart of these theories have been largely a recent endeavor.

The purpose of this chapter is to introduce the reader to those recent developments in the stochastic convexity and stochastic majorization. To facilitate the exposition, we will focus on a selected set of special cases, and motivate them through concrete examples in production and scheduling such as the ones introduced above.

In Section 2, we start with reviewing the definitions of several commonly used stochastic order relations: likelihood ratio ordering, hazard rate or-dering, stochastic ordering, and convex ordering. In particular, we focus on the functional representation of likelihood ratio and hazard rate order-ings. (Functional representations for stochastic and convex orderings are standard and well known.) We demonstrate that the class of functions that preserve the arrangement ordering, i.e., *arrangement increasing function*, form a defining class for the likelihood ratio ordering. The weaker, hazard rate ordering can then be characterized by a subclass of the arrangement increasing functions. These functional characterizations will play a crucial role in the later sections.

We next move on to the discussion of second-order stochastic properties in Section 3. We start with stochastic convexity. In addition to a natural, functional definition, we also present two sample-path based defintions: one is stronger, which mimics the three-point definition of deterministic convexity (the third point being the convex combination of any two given points); the other is weaker, requiring a four-point construction. Several examples are presented to illustrate in detail the techniques involved in the four-point construction. We then introduce the definitions for stochastic supermodularity and submodularity, and illustrate them through several examples. These, when combined with stochastic convexity, are particu-larly useful in applications. For instance, the component yield, $Y_i(n_i, p_i)$, introduced earlier is stochastically linear (i.e., both convex and concave) in $n_i$ and in $p_i$ in the weaker (four-point) sense, and stochastically su-permodular in $(n_i, p_i)$, and these properties hold independent of the yield distribution. These properties are also useful in characterizing the spatial and temporal behavior of Markov processes.

Section 4 serves as a transition into stochastic majorization. Motivated by the characterization of likelihood ratio ordering via arrangement increasing functions (Section 2), we now know that random variables that are ordered in likelihood ratio naturally induce arrangement and majorization orderings as well. This is indeed the case in a class of production networks modeled as closed queueing networks. Majorization and arrangement orderings in this context greatly facilitate the solutions to several resource allocation problems.

Motivated by the relation between the (stochastic) likelihood ratio ordering and the (deterministic) arrangement and majorization orderings, in Section 5 we systematically develop the stochastic counterpart of deterministic rearrangement and majorization inequalities such as the well known Hardy-Littlewood-Polya inequality, and the more general Day's inequality (see, [9, 6]; also, [11]). We consider two different settings. The first one is non-parametric, where the random variables involved are ordered under certain stochastic order relation, which determines the defining class of functions that characterizes the stochastic majorization. (Typically, a stronger stochastic order corresponds to a larger class of functions.) The second setting is parametric, i.e., the random variables involved are from parametric families (such as those involved in the yield model). There, in addition to characterizaing the defining class of functions, we also require the family of random variables involved to satisfy stochastic convexity (or stochastic supermodularity). It is through this close interplay between stochastic convexity and stochastic majorization that we are able to solve a variety of problems that involve pairwise-interchange arguments. We illustrate this through several scheduling examples.

## 5.2   Stochastic Order Relations: Functional Characterizations

Throughout this section, let $X$ and $Y$ be two random variables; let $F(\cdot)$ and $G(\cdot)$ denote their distribution functions, $f(\cdot)$ and $g(\cdot)$ their densities, and let $\bar{F} = 1 - F$ and $\bar{G} = 1 - G$. Throughout, the existence of any expectations is implicitly assumed; $\overset{\text{d}}{=}$ denotes equal in distribution; "increasing" and "decreasing" are used in the non-strict sense.

First recall the following definitions of some commonly used stochastic order relations.

**Definition 5.2.1**   (i)  *Likelihood ratio ordering:* $X \geq_{\ell r} Y$, if their likelihood ratios are ordered: $f(y)/f(x) \leq g(y)/g(x)$ for all $x \geq y$.

(ii)  *Hazard rate ordering:* $X \geq_{hr} Y$, if their hazard rates are ordered: $f(x)/\bar{F}(x) \leq g(x)/\bar{G}(x)$ for all $x$.

(iii)  *Stochastic ordering:* $X \geq_{st} Y$, if $\bar{F}(x) \geq \bar{G}(x)$ for all $x$.

(iv)  *Increasing convex ordering:* $X \geq_{icx} Y$, if $\int_a^\infty \bar{F}(x)dx \geq \int_a^\infty \bar{G}(x)dx$ for all $a$.

For discrete random variables, likelihood ratio and hazard rate orderings are similarly defined: replace the density functions in Definition 5.2.1(i,ii) by probability mass functions (pmf's). The following results are easily verified from Definition 5.2.1.

**Theorem 5.2.2**    (i) $X \geq_{\ell r} Y \Rightarrow X \geq_{hr} Y \Rightarrow X \geq_{st} Y \Rightarrow X \geq_{icx} Y$.

(ii) $X \geq_{st} Y$ if and only if $\mathsf{E}\phi(X) \geq \mathsf{E}\phi(Y)$ for any function $\phi(x)$ that is increasing in $x$.

(iii) $X \geq_{icx} Y$ if and only if $\mathsf{E}\phi(X) \geq \mathsf{E}\phi(Y)$ for any function $\phi(x)$ that is increasing and convex in $x$.

Following Theorem 5.2.2(iii) above, we can also define the *increasing concave ordering*: $X \geq_{icv} Y$ if and only if $\mathsf{E}\phi(X) \geq \mathsf{E}\phi(Y)$ for any function $\phi(x)$ that is increasing and concave in $x$. Since $\phi(x)$ is increasing and convex if and only if $-\phi(-x)$ is increasing and concave in $x$, we have $X \geq_{icx} Y$ if and only if $-X \leq_{icv} -Y$.

From Theorem 5.2.2(i,ii), the class of increasing (resp. increasing and convex) functions can be viewed as the defining class for stochastic (resp. increasing convex) ordering. In this sense, Theorem 5.2.2(ii, iii) provides functional characterizations for stochastic and convex orderings. It does not seem possible, however, to come up with similar univariate functions as defining classes for likelihood ratio and hazard rate orderings. Hence, we resort to *bivariate* functions. We start with the likelihood ratio ordering. Below, we denote $\Delta\phi(x,y) = \phi(x,y) - \phi(y,x)$.

**Theorem 5.2.3** Define a class of bivariate functions as follows:

$$\mathbf{C}_{\ell r} = \{\phi(x,y) : \Delta\phi(x,y) \geq 0, \forall x \geq y\}.$$

Then, for two independent random variables $X$ and $Y$, $X \geq_{\ell r} Y$ if and only if $\mathsf{E}\phi(X,Y) \geq \mathsf{E}\phi(Y,X)$, for all $\phi \in \mathbf{C}_{\ell r}$.

**Proof.** For the "if" part, given $u > v$, let $\phi(x,y) = \mathbf{1}[u \leq x \leq u+du, v \leq y \leq v+dv]$, where $du > 0$, $dv > 0$ and $dv < u-v$, then $\phi \in \mathbf{C}_{\ell r}$. Hence, $\mathsf{E}\phi(X,Y) \geq \mathsf{E}\phi(Y,X)$, or $f(u)g(v) \geq f(v)g(u)$, i.e., $X \geq_{\ell r} Y$.

For the "only if" part, taking into account $\Delta\phi(x,y) = -\Delta\phi(y,x)$, we have

$$\mathsf{E}\Delta\phi(X,Y) = \int_y \int_x \Delta\phi(x,y)f(x)g(y)dxdy$$

$$= \int_y \int_{x \geq y} \Delta\phi(x,y)[f(x)g(y) - f(y)g(x)]dxdy \geq 0,$$

since $\phi \in \mathbf{C}_{\ell r} \Rightarrow \Delta\phi \geq 0$, and $X \geq_{\ell r} Y \Rightarrow f(x)g(y) \geq f(y)g(x)$ for all $x \geq y$. $\square$

Note that since likelihood ratio ordering (as well as all the other orderings in Definition 5.2.1) is a relation concerning the *marginal* distributions of

$X$ and $Y$, i.e., there is no reference to any *joint* distributional relation of $(X, Y)$, it is only natural to assume independence among the two random variables $X$ and $Y$. Hence Theorem 5.2.3 can be rephrased as follows:

**Corollary 5.2.4** $X \geq_{\ell r} Y$ if and only if there exist two independent random variables $\hat{X}$ and $\hat{Y}$, such that $\hat{X} \overset{d}{=} X$, $\hat{Y} \overset{d}{=} Y$, and $E\phi(\hat{X}, \hat{Y}) \geq E\phi(\hat{Y}, \hat{X})$ for all $\phi \in \mathbf{C}_{\ell r}$.

Similarly, we have the following defining class for the hazard rate ordering.

**Theorem 5.2.5** Define $\mathbf{C}_{hr} = \{\phi(x, y) : \text{both } \phi(x, y) \text{ and } \Delta\phi(x, y) \text{ are increasing in } x, \forall x \geq y\}$.
Then, $X \geq_{hr} Y$ if and only there exist two independent random variables $\hat{X}$ and $\hat{Y}$, such that $\hat{X} \overset{d}{=} X$, $\hat{Y} \overset{d}{=} Y$, and $E\phi(\hat{X}, \hat{Y}) \geq E\phi(\hat{Y}, \hat{X})$ for all $\phi \in \mathbf{C}_{hr}$.

**Proof.** First note that we have the following equivalent conditions to $X \geq_{hr} Y$ in Definition 5.2.1(ii):

$$\bar{F}(y)/\bar{F}(x) \leq \bar{G}(y)/\bar{G}(x), \quad \forall x \geq y, \tag{5.1}$$

and

$$f(y)/\bar{F}(x) \leq g(y)/\bar{G}(x), \quad \forall x \geq y. \tag{5.2}$$

For instance, Definition 5.2.1(ii) $\Rightarrow$ (5.1) follows from the following identities:

$$\bar{F}(x) = \exp\{-\int_{-\infty}^{x} \frac{f(t)}{\bar{F}(t)}\}dt, \quad \bar{G}(x) = \exp\{-\int_{-\infty}^{x} \frac{g(t)}{\bar{G}(t)}\}dt,$$

since

$$\frac{\bar{F}(y)}{\bar{F}(x)} = \exp\{\int_{y}^{x} \frac{f(t)}{\bar{F}(t)}dt\} \leq \exp\{\int_{y}^{x} \frac{g(t)}{\bar{G}(t)}dt\} = \frac{\bar{G}(y)}{\bar{G}(x)}.$$

Conversely, (5.1) implies, for $\delta > 0$,

$$\frac{\bar{F}(x-\delta) - \bar{F}(x)}{\delta\bar{F}(x)} \leq \frac{\bar{G}(x-\delta) - \bar{G}(x)}{\delta\bar{G}(x)}.$$

Letting $\delta \to 0$ gives Definition 5.2.1(ii). Next, Definition 5.2.1(ii) and (5.1) together imply (5.2):

$$\frac{f(y)}{\bar{F}(x)} = \frac{f(y)}{\bar{F}(y)} \cdot \frac{\bar{F}(y)}{\bar{F}(x)} \leq \frac{g(y)}{\bar{G}(y)} \cdot \frac{\bar{G}(y)}{\bar{G}(x)} = \frac{g(y)}{\bar{G}(x)}.$$

Finally, that (5.2) implies Definition 5.2.1(ii) is trivial: let $y = x$.

Now, to prove the "if" part, let $\phi(x, y) = \mathbf{1}[x \geq u, y \geq v]$, where $u \geq v$ are given. Then clearly, $\phi \in \mathbf{C}_{hr}$, in particular, $\Delta\phi(x, y) = \mathbf{1}[x \geq u, u > y \geq v]$ is increasing in $x$. Hence, $E\Delta\phi(\hat{X}, \hat{Y}) \geq 0$ recovers (5.1).

For the "only if" part, assuming differentiability of $\phi$ for simplicity, we have, similar to the proof of Theorem 5.2.3,

$$E\Delta\phi(\hat{X}, \hat{Y})$$

$$= \int_y \int_{x \geq y} \Delta\phi(x, y)[f(x)g(y) - f(y)g(x)]dxdy$$

$$= \int_y \int_{x \geq y} [\frac{\partial}{\partial x}\Delta\phi(x, y)][\bar{F}(x)g(y) - f(y)\bar{G}(x)]dxdy \geq 0,$$

where the second equality follows from integration by parts, and the inequality is due to (5.2), as well as $\Delta\phi(x, y)$ increasing in $x$ for $x \geq y$. $\square$

Clearly, $\mathbf{C}_{hr} \subset \mathbf{C}_{\ell r}$. It is also easy to verify that the class $\mathbf{C}_{\ell r}$ is closed under composition with increasing functions. That is, $\phi \in \mathbf{C}_{\ell r} \Rightarrow h(\phi(x, y)) \in \mathbf{C}_{\ell r}$ for any $h(z)$ that is increasing in $z$. Similarly, the class $\mathbf{C}_{hr}$ is closed under composition with increasing and convex functions: $\phi \in \mathbf{C}_{hr} \Rightarrow h(\phi(x, y)) \in \mathbf{C}_{hr}$ for any $h(z)$ that is increasing and convex in $z$. In particular, denoting $h'$ as the derivative, we have

$$\frac{\partial}{\partial x}[h(\phi(x, y)) - h(\phi(y, x))]$$

$$= h'(\phi(x, y))\frac{\partial}{\partial x}\phi(x, y) - h'(\phi(y, x))\frac{\partial}{\partial x}\phi(y, x)$$

$$\geq h'(\phi(y, x))\frac{\partial}{\partial x}[\phi(x, y) - \phi(y, x)] \geq 0,$$

where the first inequality follows from the convexity of $h(\cdot)$, the increasingness of $\phi(x, y)$ in $x$ for $x \geq y$ [so that $\frac{\partial}{\partial x}\phi(x, y) \geq 0$], and $\phi(x, y) \geq \phi(y, x)$, which is implied by $\Delta\phi(x, y)$ increasing in $x$ for $x \geq y$. [Note, from the proof of (2.4), it is clear that the increasingness of $\phi(x, y)$ in $x$ for $x \geq y$ is *not* needed there. It is only needed to make the class $\mathbf{C}_{hr}$ closed under composition with functions that are increasing and convex.] To summarize, taking into account Theorem 5.2.2, we have

**Corollary 5.2.6** For two independent random variables, $X$ and $Y$,

(i) $X \geq_{\ell r} Y \Leftrightarrow \phi(X, Y) \geq_{st} \phi(Y, X)$, $\forall\phi \in \mathbf{C}_{\ell r}$;

(ii) $X \geq_{hr} Y \Leftrightarrow \phi(X, Y) \geq_{icx} \phi(Y, X)$, $\forall\phi \in \mathbf{C}_{hr}$.

**Example 5.2.7** Consider a single machine stochastic scheduling problem, where $n$ jobs are to be scheduled with the objective of minimizing the flow time (i.e., sum of the time until completion for each job) in some stochastic sense. Let $\pi$ denote a schedule such that job $i$ is scheduled at the $\pi(i)$ th position, $i = 1, 2, ..., n$. (That is, $\pi$ denotes a permutation of $\{1, 2, ..., n\}$.)

Let $X_i$ be the processing time of job $i$. The flow time under schedule $\pi$, denoted as $T_\pi$, can be derived as follows:

$$T_\pi = \sum_{i=1}^{n} [n + 1 - \pi(i)] X_i. \tag{5.3}$$

Consider two jobs $a$ and $b$, and suppose $\pi(a) > \pi(b)$. Compare the schedule $\pi$ with another schedule $\pi'$ which interchanges the processing order of $a$ and $b$: $\pi'(a) = \pi(b)$, $\pi'(b) = \pi(a)$, and $\pi'(i) = \pi(i), \forall i \neq a, b$. Denote $A = \sum_{i \neq a, b} [n + 1 - \pi(i)] X_i$. Then, we have

$$T_\pi = A + [n + 1 - \pi(a)] X_a + [n + 1 - \pi(b)] X_b, \tag{5.4}$$
$$T_{\pi'} = A + [n + 1 - \pi(a)] X_b + [n + 1 - \pi(b)] X_a. \tag{5.5}$$

Let $\phi(x, y) = [n + 1 - \pi(b)] x + [n + 1 - \pi(a)] y$. Since $\pi(a) > \pi(b)$, it is easy to verify that $\phi \in \mathbf{C}_{hr} \subset \mathbf{C}_{\ell r}$.

**Proposition 5.2.8** For independent processing times, if $X_n \geq_{\ell r} \ldots \geq_{\ell r} X_1$ (resp., if $X_n \geq_{hr} \ldots \geq_{hr} X_1$), then $\pi = (1, ..., n)$ minimizes the flow time in the sense of stochastic (resp., convex) ordering.

Note that in comparing the two flow times in (5.4) above, if the processing times are deterministic, then all that's needed is the following simple fact

$$a \geq b, \ x \geq y \quad \Rightarrow \quad ax + by \geq ay + bx, \tag{5.6}$$

where all variables are real. In the stochastic setting, however, the situation is much more complicated: different order relations among the stochastic processing times lead to different orderings in the flow times, as demonstrated in Proposition 5.2.8.

The inequality in (5.6) belongs to the class of "rearrangement inequalities", which play a key role in supporting pairwise interchange arguments that often arise in scheduling and other settings. Also, the class of functions $\mathbf{C}_{\ell r}$ preserves a certain "arrangement" ordering, for instance, if $\phi(x, y) = ax + by$ with $a \geq b$, then $\phi(x, y)$ is larger than $\phi(y, x)$ when $x \geq y$. Therefore, the results in Proposition 5.2.8 can be viewed as stochastic versions of (5.6). In Section 4 and Section 5, we will pursue these ideas in a more formal and general way so as to derive stochastic versions of more general rearrangement inequalites to support more complicated applications.

## 5.3   Second-Order Stochastic Properties

### 5.3.1   Stochastic Convexity

Consider a family of random variables parameterized by a real or integer valued scalar $\theta$, $\{X(\theta)\}$. Following (2.1 iii), $\{X(\theta)\}$ is stochastically increasing in $\theta$, if $X(\theta_1) \leq_{st} X(\theta_2)$ for any $\theta_1 \leq \theta_2$. This is what we mean by *stochastic monotonicity*. An equivalent definition for stochastic monotonicity is:

**Definition 5.3.1** $\{X(\theta)\}$ is stochastically increasing in $\theta$, if for any given $\theta_1 \leq \theta_2$, there exist on a common probability space $(\Omega, \mathcal{F}, P)$ two random variables $\hat{X}_1$ and $\hat{X}_2$ that are equal in distribution to $X(\theta_1)$ and $X(\theta_2)$ respectively, and $\hat{X}_1(\omega) \leq \hat{X}_2(\omega)$ for all $\omega \in \Omega$.

**Lemma 5.3.2** Suppose $F(x, \theta)$ denotes the distribution function of $X(\theta)$. Let $F^{-1}(u, \theta) = \inf\{x : F(x, \theta) > u\}$, where $u \in [0, 1]$, denote the inverse distribution function. Then Definition 5.3.1 is also equivalent to $F^{-1}(u, \theta)$ increasing in $\theta$, for any given $u \in [0, 1]$. (The common probability space in this case is the one in which the uniform variate $U \in [0, 1]$ is defined. In particular, note that $F^{-1}(U, \theta_i) \stackrel{d}{=} X(\theta_i)$ for $i = 1, 2$.)

From the above, it is easy to verify

**Lemma 5.3.3** $X(\theta)$ is stochastically increasing in $\theta$, if and only if for any real-valued function $\phi(x)$ that is increasing in $x$, $\mathsf{E}\phi[X(\theta)]$ (as a *deterministic* function of $\theta$) is increasing in $\theta$. [Note this is consistent with the equivalence relation in Theorem 5.2.2(ii).]

Therefore, we have three equivalent definitions for stochastic monotonicity. We shall refer to the two definitions in Definition 5.3.1 and Lemma 5.3.2 as "sample-path" definitions, as versus the "functional" definition in Lemma 5.3.3. Roughly speaking, the sample-path definitions are easier to use in proofs (i.e., to establish stochastic monotonicity) while the functional version is more convenient in applications (for instance, when $\phi$ is part of an objective function that is to be optimized).

Now consider the stochastic *convexity* of $\{X(\theta)\}$. Parallel to the above discussion, we have the following definitions, which, however, are *not* equivalent, as we shall explain shortly below.

**Definition 5.3.4** (SICX-sp). $\{X(\theta)\}$ is stochastically increasing and convex in the sample-path sense, denoted $\{X(\theta)\} \in$ SICX-sp, if for any four parameter values $\theta_i$, $i = 1, 2, 3, 4$, that satisfy $\theta_1 + \theta_4 = \theta_2 + \theta_3$ and $\theta_4 \geq \max\{\theta_2, \theta_3\}$, there exist on a common probability space $(\Omega, \mathcal{F}, P)$ four random variables $\hat{X}_i$, $i = 1, 2, 3, 4$, such that $\hat{X}_i \stackrel{d}{=} X(\theta_i)$, for all four $i$, and

$$\hat{X}_4(\omega) \geq \max\{\hat{X}_2(\omega), \hat{X}_3(\omega)\}, \quad \hat{X}_1(\omega) + \hat{X}_4(\omega) \geq \hat{X}_2(\omega) + \hat{X}_3(\omega),$$

for all $\omega \in \Omega$.

**Definition 5.3.5** (SSICX). $\{X(\theta)\}$ is said to satisfy *strong* stochastic increasing convexity, denoted $\{X(\theta)\} \in$ SSICX, if $X(\theta)$ can be expressed as $X(\theta) \stackrel{d}{=} \phi(\xi, \theta)$ where $\phi$ is an increasing and convex function with respect to $\theta$, and $\xi$ is a random variable whose distribution function is independent of $\theta$. In particular, $X(\theta) \in$ SSICX if $F^{-1}(u, \theta)$ is increasing and convex in $\theta$ (for any given $u \in [0, 1]$).

**Definition 5.3.6** (SICX). $\{X(\theta)\}$ is stochastically increasing and convex in $\theta$, denoted $\{X(\theta)\} \in$ SICX, if $\mathsf{E}\phi[X(\theta)]$ is increasing and convex in $\theta$ for any function $\phi(x)$ that is increasing and convex in $x$.

Definitions for stochastic *concavity* are similar. Also, stochastic *linearity* is defined to be the condition when both stochastic convexity and concavity are satisfied. We shall use CV and L (in place of CX) to denote concavity and linearity, respectively. Stochastically *decreasing* and convex (concave) can be similarly defined by replacing the condition for increasingness in the above definitions by an appropriate condition for decreasingness. For instance, to define stochastic decreasing convexity in the *sp* sense, replace the inequality $\hat{X}_4 \geq \max\{\hat{X}_2, \hat{X}_3\}$ in Definition 5.3.4 by $\hat{X}_1 \geq \max\{\hat{X}_2, \hat{X}_3\}$.

**Remark 5.3.7** (i) The following implications, SSICX $\Rightarrow$ SICX-sp $\Rightarrow$ SICX, are easily verified from the definitions above.
(ii) The strong version of stochastic convexity in Definition 5.3.5 can also be stated as follows: for any parameter values $\theta$ and $\eta$, and any constant $\alpha \in [0,1]$, there exist on a common probability space $(\Omega, \mathcal{F}, P)$ three random variables, $\hat{X}_1 \overset{\mathrm{d}}{=} X(\theta)$, $\hat{X}_2 \overset{\mathrm{d}}{=} X(\eta)$, and $\hat{X}_3 \overset{\mathrm{d}}{=} X(\alpha\theta + (1 - \alpha)\eta)$ such that

$$\hat{X}_3(\omega) \leq \alpha\hat{X}_1(\omega) + (1 - \alpha)\hat{X}_2(\omega)$$

for all $\omega \in \Omega$. In this sense, the sample values of $X(\omega, \theta)$ behave like a convex function with respect to $\theta$. This version mimics the convexity definition of a deterministic function. In contrast, Definition 5.3.4 relaxes the regular convexity definition to a four-point version, and hence a weaker stochastic convexity. (Note that here "four-point" refers to four instances of the random variables, not necessarily four parameters. In many applications, as we shall demonstrate below, to verify Definition 5.3.4, it suffices to have three (distinct) parameters; for instance, set $\theta_2 = \theta_3$, but use these to generate two instances of the random variable $X(\theta)$, $\theta = \theta_2 = \theta_3$.)
(iii) The strong version in Definition 5.3.5 is satisfied by many families of random variables. For instance, if $X(\theta)$ is an exponential random variable with mean $\theta$, then $X(\theta) = \theta\xi$ where $\xi$ follows the exponential distribution with unit mean. Hence, $\{X(\theta)\} \in$ SSIL. The reader will verify that this property in fact extends to the exponential families (i.e., summations and mixtures of exponentials). Similarly, if $X(\theta)$ is a normal variate with mean $\mu$ and standard variation $\theta$, then $X(\theta) = \theta Z + \mu$, where $Z$ denotes the standard normal variate. Hence, for fixed $\mu$, $\{X(\theta)\}$ is also stochastically linear in $\theta$.
(iv) When the distribution function $F(x, \theta)$ is differentiable, it is also easy to verify SSICX, following Definition 5.3.5, via checking the first and second

derivatives of $X$ with respect to $\theta$. To this end, write $X$ as $X(\xi, \theta)$, and for each sample value of $\xi$, view $X$ as a deterministic function of $\theta$. Omitting reference to $\xi$, and taking derivatives from $F(X(\theta), \theta) = U$, we have

$$F_x X_\theta + F_\theta = 0, \quad F_x X_{\theta\theta} + F_{xx} X_\theta^2 + 2F_{x\theta} X_\theta + F_{\theta\theta} = 0,$$

where $F_x, F_\theta, X_\theta$, etc. denote partial derivatives with respect to $x$ or $\theta$. From the above, solve for $X_\theta$ and $X_{\theta\theta}$. Then $\{X(\theta)\} \in$ SSICX if both derivatives are non-negative.

Below, we illustrate that certain useful families of random variables do *not* satisfy SSICX, although they do satisfy the weaker SICX-sp property.

**Example 5.3.8** Let $\{X(p)\}$ denote a family of Bernoulli random variables: $X(p) = \mathbf{1}[U \leq p]$, where $\mathbf{1}$ denotes the indicator function, $p \in (0, 1)$ is the parameter, and $U \in [0, 1]$ is the uniform variate. Since $\mathsf{E}\phi[X(p)] = \phi(1)p$ is a linear function of $p$, for *any* function $\phi$, convex or concave, $\{X(p)\}$ satisfies stochastic linearity in the sense of Definition 5.3.6. However, it is clear that $\{X(p)\}$ does not satisfy SSICX (or SSICV) in the sense of Definition 5.3.5, since the indicator function is neither convex nor concave.

The non-obvious fact here is that $\{X(p)\}$ satisfies SIL-sp in the sense of Definition 5.3.4. To show this, consider four parameter values: $p_1 \leq p_2 = p_3 \leq p_4$ and $p_1 + p_4 = p_2 + p_3$. Let

$$\hat{X}_i = \mathbf{1}[U \leq p_i], \quad i = 1, 2, 4;$$

and

$$\hat{X}_3 = \mathbf{1}[U \leq p_1] + \mathbf{1}[p_2 \leq U \leq p_4].$$

Then clearly $\hat{X}_i \overset{d}{=} X(p_i)$ for all four $i$. In particular $\hat{X}_3 \overset{d}{=} \mathbf{1}[U \leq p_3]$, since $p_4 - p_2 + p_1 = p_3$. Also, $\hat{X}_4 \geq \max\{\hat{X}_2, \hat{X}_3\}$, and

$$\begin{aligned} \hat{X}_1 + \hat{X}_4 &= \mathbf{1}[U \leq p_1] + \mathbf{1}[U \leq p_2] + \mathbf{1}[p_2 \leq U \leq p_4] \\ &= \hat{X}_2 + \hat{X}_3. \end{aligned}$$

Hence, $\{X(p)\}$ does satisfy SIL-sp.

**Example 5.3.9** Now suppose $X(p)$ follows a geometric distribution with parameter $p$. $\mathsf{E}X(p) = 1/p$ is decreasing and convex in $p$. Hence, $\{X(p)\}$ is stochastically decreasing and convex in the weak sense of Definition 5.3.6. We can further show that $\{X(p)\}$ in fact satisfies the stronger *sp* notion of stochastically decreasing and convex (cf. Definition 5.3.4). To this end, consider the four $p_i$ values in Example 5.3.8. Use a common sequence of iid uniform variates $\{U_n \in [0, 1]; n = 1, 2, ...\}$ to generate the four replicas:

$$\hat{X}_i = \inf\{n : U_n \in [0, p_i]\}, \quad i = 1, 2, 4;$$

$$\hat{X}_3 = \inf\{n : U_n \in [0, p_1] \cup [p_2, p_4]\}.$$

Then, it is easy to see that $\hat{X}_1 \geq \hat{X}_i$ for $i \neq 1$, and $\hat{X}_4$ equals either $\hat{X}_2$ or $\hat{X}_3$, or both, hence $\hat{X}_1 + \hat{X}_4 \geq \hat{X}_2 + \hat{X}_3$.

**Example 5.3.10** Let $X(n) = \sum_{i=1}^{n} Y_i$, where $Y_i$ are iid non-negative random variables. We show $\{X(n)\}$ satisfies SIL-sp. To this end, pick four parameter values: $n, n+1, n+1$, and $n+2$. Use a sequence of independent uniform variates, $U_1, ..., U_n, U_{n+1}, U_{n+2}$ to generate, from the common distribution of $Y_i$, the sample values $\hat{Y}_1, ..., \hat{Y}_n, \hat{Y}_{n+1}, \hat{Y}_{n+2}$, respectively. Let

$$\hat{X}_1 = \sum_{i=1}^{n} \hat{Y}_i, \quad \hat{X}_2 = \sum_{i=1}^{n+1} \hat{Y}_i, \quad \hat{X}_4 = \sum_{i=1}^{n+2} \hat{Y}_i,$$

and

$$\hat{X}_3 = \sum_{i=1}^{n} \hat{Y}_i + \hat{Y}_{n+2}.$$

The conditions involved in Definition 5.3.4 are obviously satisfied by this construction. In particulr, $\hat{X}_3 \stackrel{d}{=} X(n+1)$, since the $\hat{Y}_i$'s are iid; and $\hat{X}_1 + \hat{X}_4 = \hat{X}_2 + \hat{X}_3$. It is also clear that $X(n)$ is *not* convex or concave in $n$, in the sense of Definition 5.3.5.

**Example 5.3.11** Continue with the above example. Suppose $Y_i$ are independent, but not identically distributed. Specifically, suppose $Y_i \leq_{st} Y_{i+1}$ for all $i$. Then, $\{X(n)\} \in$ SICX-sp. To show this, modify the construction of $\hat{X}_3$ in Example 5.3.10: replace $\hat{Y}_{n+2}$ by $\hat{Y}'_{n+1}$, which is sampled from the distribution of $Y_{n+1}$, but using the uniform variate $U_{n+2}$ that generates $\hat{Y}_{n+2}$. Since $Y_{n+1} \leq_{st} Y_{n+2}$, we have $\hat{Y}'_{n+1} \leq \hat{Y}_{n+2}$. Hence, $\hat{X}_1 + \hat{X}_4 \geq \hat{X}_2 + \hat{X}_3$. Similarly, if $Y_i \geq_{st} Y_{i+1}$ for all $i$, then $\{X(n)\} \in$ SICV-sp.

Combining the two examples in Example 5.3.8 and Example 5.3.10, we have a useful model for manufacturing processes with random yield introduced in Section 1. Let $Y_i(p)$ be a set of iid Bernoulli random variables parameterized by $p$. Suppose $p$ is the yield ratio. Then $Y_i$ represents whether the unit $i$ is good ($Y_i = 1$) or bad ($Y_i = 0$). Let $n$ be the lot size; then $X(n)$ gives the number of good units (i.e., "yield") that come out of this lot. Write $X$ in the examples as $X(n, p)$. We can also define the stochastic supermodularity of $X$ with respect to $(n, p)$, mimicking the SICX-sp definition in Definition 5.3.4. We do this in the next subsection.

### 5.3.2    Stochastic Supermodularity and Submodularity

**Definition 5.3.12** A family of random variables, $\{X(s, t)\}$, where $s$ and $t$ are real or integer valued scalars, is stochastically increasing and supermodular (resp. increasing and submodular) in $(s, t)$ if for any given $s_1 \leq s_2$, $t_1 \leq t_2$, there exist on a common probability space $(\Omega, \mathcal{F}, P)$ four random variables $\hat{X}_i$, $i = 1, 2, 3, 4$, that are equal in distribution to $X(s_1, t_1), X(s_1, t_2), X(s_2, t_1)$, and $X(s_2, t_2)$, respectively, and for all $\omega \in \Omega$,

$$\hat{X}_4(\omega) \geq \max\{\hat{X}_2(\omega), \hat{X}_3(\omega)\};$$

$$\hat{X}_1(\omega) + \hat{X}_4(\omega) \geq \text{(resp. } \leq)\hat{X}_2(\omega) + \hat{X}_3(\omega).$$

The property of stochastically *decreasing* and supermodular is similarly defined: replace $\hat{X}_4$ in the first inequality above by $\hat{X}_1$.

**Remark 5.3.13** (i) Recall, in the deterministic setting, a bivariate function $\phi(x, y)$ is supermodular (resp. submodular), if for any $x_1 \leq x_2$, $y_1 \leq y_2$,

$$\phi(x_1, y_1) + \phi(x_2, y_2) \geq \text{(resp. } \leq)\phi(x_1, y_2) + \phi(x_2, y_1).$$

Hence, the stochastic version above simply states that the sample realization of $X$ (i.e., for any given $\omega$) behaves as a (deterministic) supermodular or submodular function. In particular, Definition 5.3.12 implies that $EX(s, t)$ is increasing and supermodular or submodular in $(s, t)$. Also notice that supermodularity (or submodularity) is always a four-point definition (in contrast to convexity or concavity). Hence, there are no analogous versions to Definitions 5.3.4 and 5.3.5 in the convexity/concavity setting.

(ii) Two useful properties of a deterministic supermodular or submodular function are worth noting. When $\phi$ is twice differentiable, supermodularity (resp. submodularity) is equivalent to the cross partial derivative $\phi_{xy} \geq 0$ (resp. $\leq 0$). (Hence, supermodularity and submodularity are quite different properties from convexity and concavity.) To maximize a supermodular function $\phi(x, y)$, suppose $y_1 < y_2$, and let $x_1^*$ be the $x$ that maximizes $\phi(x, y_1)$ given $y_1$. That is, $\phi(x_1^*, y_1) \geq \phi(x, y_1)$ for all $x$. Similarly, let $x_2^*$ be the $x$ that maximizes $\phi(x, y_2)$ given $y_2$. We then have the "isotone" property: $x_1^* \leq x_2^*$. In other words, any $x_2 < x_1^*$ cannot be a candidate to maximize $\phi(x, y_2)$. This is simply because the supermodularity implies

$$\phi(x_2, y_2) - \phi(x_1^*, y_2) \leq \phi(x_2, y_1) - \phi(x_1^*, y_1).$$

But the RHS above is $\leq 0$, since $x_1^*$ maximizes $\phi(x, y_1)$. Hence, $\phi(x_2, y_2) \leq \phi(x_1^*, y_2)$, for any $x_2 < x_1^*$. This isotone property has useful applications in maximizing a supermodular function. A similar isotone property exists in minimizing a submodular function. (Maximizing submodular functions or minimizing supermodular functions lead to "antitone" properties. For more details in a general lattice setting, refer to Topkis [30].)

**Example 5.3.14** Continue with the random yield model described earlier. Following Definition 5.3.12, it is easy to verify that $X(n, p) = \sum_{i=1}^{n} Y_i(p)$, where $Y_i(p)$ are iid Bernoulli random variables with parameter $p$, is stochastically supermodular in $(n, p)$. In fact, the Bernoulli distribution here is not important; supermodularity holds as long as for each $i$, $Y_i(p)$ is stochastically increasing in $p$. This supermodularity, as well as the SIL-sp property in $n$ and in $p$ established earlier, will become useful when we study below an assembly operation with random component yield.

We can now combine stochastic supermodularity with stochastic convexity into a new property: *directional convexity*.

**Definition 5.3.15** A (deterministic) bivariate function $\phi(x,y)$ is termed "directionally convex " (resp. directionally concave) if it satisfies the following property:

$$\phi(z^1) + \phi(z^4) \geq \text{(resp. } \leq) \; \phi(z^2) + \phi(z^3),$$

for any $z^i = (x_i, y_i)$, $i = 1, 2, 3, 4$, such that

$$x_1 \leq x_2, x_3 \leq x_4, \quad y_1 \leq y_2, y_3 \leq y_4,$$

and

$$x_1 + x_4 = x_2 + x_3, \quad y_1 + y_4 = y_2 + y_3.$$

**Lemma 5.3.16** The bivariate function $\phi(x,y)$ is directionally convex (resp. directionally concave) in $(x,y)$ if and only if $\phi(x,y)$ is convex (resp. concave) in $x$ and in $y$ (individually), and supermodular (resp. submodular) in $(x,y)$.

**Proof.** We prove the equivalence between directional convexity and (individual) convexity plus supermodularity, the other case being completely analogous. Note the four points $(z^i)$ in Definition 5.3.15 have the following relation: $z^1$ and $z^4$ are at the southwest and northeast corners of a rectangle, while $z^2$ and $z^3$ lie within the rectangle. Hence directional convexity implies supermodularity by simply letting $z^2$ and $z^3$ coincide with the other two corner points, and convexity in each variable follows by reducing (collapsing) the rectangle to one of its sides, parallel to either the horizontal or the vertical axis.

For the converse, let $(x_i, y_i)$, $i = 1, 2, 3, 4$, be the four points in Definition 5.3.12. Then,

$$
\begin{aligned}
& \phi(x_4, y_4) - \phi(x_3, y_3) \\
= \; & \phi(x_4, y_4) - \phi(x_4, y_3) + \phi(x_4, y_3) - \phi(x_3, y_3) \\
\geq \; & \phi(x_4, y_2) - \phi(x_4, y_1) + \phi(x_4, y_1) - \phi(x_3, y_1) \\
\geq \; & \phi(x_2, y_2) - \phi(x_2, y_1) + \phi(x_2, y_1) - \phi(x_2, y_1) \\
= \; & \phi(x_2, y_2) - \phi(x_2, y_1),
\end{aligned}
$$

where the first inequality makes use of the convexity in $y$ and the supermodularity, while the second inequality makes use of the convexity in $x$ as well as supermodularity. $\square$

Based on Lemma 5.3.16, combining Defintion 5.3.12 with the earlier definitions of stochastic convexity, we have:

**Theorem 5.3.17** If the family of random variables $\{X(s,t)\}$ is stochastically increasing and supermodular (resp. increasing and submodular) in $(s,t)$, and in addition, increasing and convex (resp. increasing and concave) in $s$ and in $t$, following any one of Definitions 5.3.4, 5.3.5 and 5.3.6, then $\mathsf{E}X(s,t)$ is increasing and directionally convex (resp. increasing and directionally concave) in $(s,t)$.

Based on Definition 5.3.15, we can define stochastic versions of directional convexity. There can be several versions, corresponding to the different versions of stochastic convexity. Below we list one.

**Definition 5.3.18** A family of random variables, $\{X(s,t)\}$, where $s$ and $t$ are real or integer valued scalars, is stochastically increasing and directionally convex in $(s,t)$, in the $sp$ (sample-path) sense, if for any four given points $z^i = (s_i, t_i)$, $i = 1, 2, 3, 4$, specified in Defintion 5.3.15, there exist on a common probability space $(\Omega, \mathcal{F}, P)$ four random variables $\hat{X}_i$ that are equal in distribution to $X(z^i)$, $i = 1, 2, 3, 4$, respectively, and for all $\omega \in \Omega$,

$$\hat{X}_4(\omega) \geq \max\{\hat{X}_2(\omega), \hat{X}_3(\omega)\};$$

$$\hat{X}_1(\omega) + \hat{X}_4(\omega) \geq (\text{resp. } \leq)\hat{X}_2(\omega) + \hat{X}_3(\omega).$$

**Remark 5.3.19** Obviously, if $\{X(s,t)\}$ is stochastically increasing and directionally convex in $(s,t)$, following Defintion 5.3.18, then it is stochastically increasing and convex in $s$ and in $t$ (in the $sp$ sense), and stochastically increasing and supermodular in $(s,t)$. The converse need not hold in general. However, following Theorem 5.3.17, the converse does hold for *expectation*; and this often has useful applications, as we shall demonstrate in Section 3.4 below.

## 5.3.3   Markov Chain Applications

Let $\{X_n(s)\}$ be a discrete-time homogeneous Markov chain with state space on the non-negative integers, and initial state $s$, i.e., $X_0 = s$. Let $Y(x)$ denote the generic random variable that has the same distribution as the position taken by the Markov chain in one transition starting from $x$; that is, $Y(x)$ equals in distribution to $X_{n+1}$ given $X_n = x$. Not surprisingly, the spatial and temporal behavior of this homogeneous Markov chain is completely characterized by $Y(x)$. For instance, clearly, if $Y(x) \geq x$, then $X_n$ is stochastically increasing in $n$. Furthermore, if $\{Y(x) - x\}$ is stochastically increasing in $x$ (note this implies $Y(x) \geq x$), then, for any $s_1 \leq s_2$ (using "hat" to denote sample values),

$$X_0(s_1) + X_1(s_2) \stackrel{d}{=} s_1 + \hat{Y}(s_2) \geq s_2 + \hat{Y}(s_1) \stackrel{d}{=} X_0(s_2) + X_1(s_1).$$

Inductively, we can then show that $X_n(s)$ is supermodular in $(n,s)$. Under the same conditions, we also have

$$\hat{X}_2 - \hat{X}_1 = \hat{Y}'(\hat{Y}(s)) - \hat{Y}(s) \geq \hat{Y}'(s) - s = \hat{X}'_1 - \hat{X}_0,$$

where $\hat{Y}$ and $\hat{Y}'$ denote the sample values of the $Y$'s that correspond to the two transitions, $\hat{X}_1 \stackrel{d}{=} \hat{X}'_1 \stackrel{d}{=} X_1$, and the inequality is due to the increasingness of $\{Y(x) - x\}$, taking into account $\hat{Y}(s) \geq s$. Hence inductively, $\{X_n(s)\}$ satisfies SICX-sp in $n$ (for any given $s$). Finally, $\{Y(x)\}$ satisfying

SICX-sp implies $\{X_1(s)\} \in$ SICX-sp. Hence, for any four initial states, $s_i$, $i = 1, 2, 3, 4$, satifying

$$s_4 \geq \max\{s_2, s_3\}, \quad s_1 + s_4 = s_2 + s_3,$$

we can generate, on a common probability space, $\hat{X}^i$, $i = 1, 2, 3, 4$, such that $\hat{X}^i \overset{d}{=} X_1(s_i)$, and

$$\hat{X}^4 \geq \max\{\hat{X}^2, \hat{X}^3\}, \quad \hat{X}^1 + \hat{X}^4 \geq \hat{X}^2 + \hat{X}^3.$$

Making use of the SICX-sp property of $Y(x)$ again, we can generate, on a common probability space, $\hat{Y}^i$, $i = 1, 2, 3, 4$, such that $\hat{Y}^i \overset{d}{=} Y(\hat{X}^i)$, and

$$\hat{Y}^4 \geq \max\{\hat{Y}^2, \hat{Y}^3\}, \quad \hat{Y}^1 + \hat{Y}^4 \geq \hat{Y}^2 + \hat{Y}^3.$$

But $\hat{Y}^i \overset{d}{=} X_2(s_i)$; hence, $\{X_2(s)\} \in$ SICX-sp. This way, we can show that $\{X_n(s)\} \in$ SICX-sp in $s$ for any given $n$. To summarize, we have

**Theorem 5.3.20** If $\{Y(x)-x\}$ is stochastically increasing in $x$, and $\{Y(x)\}$ satisfies SICX-sp, then the Markov chain $\{X_n(s)\}$ satisfies SICX-sp in $n$ and in $s$, and is stochastically increasing and supermodular in $(n, s)$. In particular, $\mathsf{E}X_n(s)$ is directionally increasing and convex in $(n, s)$.

As an application of Theorem 5.3.20, consider a continuous-time pure death process that starts at the initial state $X_0 = s$. Later in Section 3.4, we will use this as a basic model for a production process.

**Theorem 5.3.21** $\{X_t(s)\}$ is a pure death process with initial state $X_0 = s$ and death rate $\mu(x)$ given $X_t = x$. If $\mu(x)$ is increasing and concave in $x$, with $\mu(0) = 0$ and $\mu(x) > 0$ for all $x > 0$, then $\{X_t(s)\}$ satisfies SICX-sp in $s$ and in $-t$, and is stochastically increasing and supermodular in $(s, -t)$. In particular, $\mathsf{E}X_t(s)$ is directionally increasing and convex in $(s, -t)$ [or, equivalently, increasing and convex in $s$, decreasing and convex in $t$, and submodular in $(s, t)$.]

**Proof.** We use uniformization to generate the sample path of the pure death process. Let $\eta = \mu(s)$ be the uniformization constant. [Note $\eta \geq \mu(x)$ for all $x \leq s$, due to the increasingness of $\mu(x)$.] Let $0 = \tau_0 < \tau_1 < \ldots < \tau_n < \ldots$ be a sequence of event epochs associated with the Poisson process with rate $\eta$. Below, we construct a discrete-time Markov chain, $\{X_n(s)\}$, with initial state $s$, and use it to generate the path of the death process $X_t$ by setting, for $n = 0, 1, 2, \ldots$,

$$\hat{X}_{\tau_n} = X_n, \quad \hat{X}_t = X_n, \quad t \in [\tau_n, \tau_n + 1).$$

In order for the path generated to follow the same probability law as the original death process, the $Y(x)$ that associates with $\{X_n(s)\}$ is specified as follows:

$$Y(x) = x - \mathbf{1}[\eta U \leq \mu(x)]. \tag{5.7}$$

We want to show it satisfies conditions similar to those listed in Theorem 5.3.20; specifically, (i) $\{x - Y(x)\}$ is stochastically increasing in $x$, and (ii) $\{Y(x)\}$ satisfies SICX-sp.

Since (i) follows immediately from (5.7), we show (ii). Pick $x_i$, $i = 1, 2, 3, 4$, such that

$$x_1 \leq x_2, x_3 \leq x_4; \quad x_1 + x_4 = x_2 + x_3.$$

Let

$$
\begin{aligned}
\hat{Y}_i &= x_i - \mathbf{1}[\eta U \leq \mu(x_i)], \quad i = 1, 2, 4; \\
\hat{Y}_3 &= x_3 - \mathbf{1}[\eta U \leq \mu(x_1)] \\
&\quad - \mathbf{1}[\mu(x_2) \leq \eta U \leq \mu(x_2) + \mu(x_3) - \mu(x_1)].
\end{aligned}
$$

Then clearly $\hat{Y}_i \stackrel{\mathrm{d}}{=} Y(x_i)$ for $i = 1, 2, 3, 4$, and $\hat{Y}_1, \hat{Y}_2, \hat{Y}_3 \leq \hat{Y}_4$. Furthermore, $\hat{Y}_1 + \hat{Y}_4 \geq \hat{Y}_2 + \hat{Y}_3$ is then equivalent to

$$
\begin{aligned}
&\mathbf{1}[\eta U \leq \mu(x_4)] \\
\leq\ &\mathbf{1}[\eta U \leq \mu(x_2)] + \mathbf{1}[\mu(x_2) \leq \eta U \leq \mu(x_2) + \mu(x_3) - \mu(x_1)] \\
=\ &\mathbf{1}[\eta U \leq \mu(x_2) + \mu(x_3) - \mu(x_1)],
\end{aligned}
$$

which follows immediately from the concavity of $\mu(x)$, i.e., $\mu(x_1) + \mu(x_4) \leq \mu(x_2) + \mu(x_3)$. $\square$

**Corollary 5.3.22** When $\{X_t(s)\}$ is the death process in Theorem 5.3.21, $\{s - X_t(s)\}$ is a birth process that satisfies SICV-sp in $s$ and in $t$, and stochastically supermodular in $(s, t)$.

**Proof.** The birth process in question, denoted $Z(t)$, starts at 0, increases over time, and eventually reaches $s$ and stays at $s$. The corresponding one-step transition [cf. (5.7)] is characterized by

$$Y(z) = z + \mathbf{1}[\eta U \leq \mu(s - z)].$$

Similar to the proof of Theorem 5.3.21, we can show that $\{Y(z) - z\}$ is stochastically decreasing in $z$ and $\{Y(z)\}$ satisfies SICV-sp. The desired properties then follow, much similar to the way the conclusions in Theorem 5.3.20 are reached. $\square$

### 5.3.4  A Joint Setup Problem

Here we study the problem of jointly setting up a set of production facilities. We model the state (work in process) at each facility as a pure death process with state-dependent death rate (production rate), and apply the results derived in Section 3.3.

**Example 5.3.23** Consider a set of production facilities indexed by $i = 1, 2, ..., m$. From time to time (e.g., a shift) a joint setup is performed for all $m$ facilities: a number of jobs are prepared (pre-processed) and released into each facility for processing. The state of facility $i$ at time $t$ is defined as the number of jobs that have not been finished — work in process, or *WIP*; denote this state as $X_t^i(x_i)$, where $x_i = X_0^i$ is the initial state, i.e., the number of jobs immediately after the setup. Suppose for all $i$, $\{X_t^i\}$ is modeled as a pure death process with death rate $\mu^i(x)$ when the state is in $x$. Suppose for all $i$, $\mu^i(0) = 0$, $x > 0 \Rightarrow \mu^i(x) > 0$, and that $\mu^i(x)$ is increasing and concave in $x$. This last assumption appears appropriate for most production facilities, where the production rate increases as the WIP level increases, but gradually flattens out as the system capacity approaches saturation.

Suppose that the facilities are jointly set up at time zero and are then run for a given length of $t$ units of time. The decision at time zero is to determine the number of jobs that are initially allocated to each facility, $x = (x_i)_{i=1}^m$. For each facility $i$, there is a profit earned from the total number of completed jobs by time $t$, $g_i(x_i - X_t^i(x_i))$, a penalty cost for the number of unfinished jobs (if any) at time $t$, $h_i(X_t^i(x_i))$, and a cost for the setup, $c_i(x_i)$; here $g_i, h_i$ and $c_i$ are all real-valued functions. Let

$$\phi_i(x_i) = \mathsf{E}g_i(x_i - X_t^i(x_i)) - \mathsf{E}h_i(X_t^i(x_i)) - c_i(x_i), \quad i = 1, ..., m.$$

Then $\phi_i(x_i)$ is the expected net profit (over the $t$ time units) from facility $i$, given its initial allocation $x_i$. We want to solve the following optimization problem:

$$\max_{x \leq N, |x| \leq R} \phi(x) = \sum_{i=1}^m \phi_i(x_i), \tag{5.8}$$

where $N = (N_i)_{i=1}^m$; $N_i$ is a given upper limit (integer) on $x_i$, reflecting the capacity at facility $i$; and $R$ the (given) maximal total number of jobs to be allocated.

**Proposition 5.3.24** If for all $i = 1, ..., m$, $g_i(x_i)$ is increasing and concave, while $h_i(x_i)$ and $c_i(x_i)$ are increasing and convex, then the objective function in (3.9a), $\phi(x)$, is (jointly) concave in $x$.

**Proof.** From Theorem 5.3.21 and Corollary 5.3.22, $\{X_t^i(x_i)\}$ is stochastically increasing and convex in $x_i$, and $\{x_i - X_t^i(x_i)\}$ stochastically increasing and concave in $x_i$, both in the *sp* sense. Under the given conditions, it is then easy to see that $\phi_i(x_i)$ is concave in $x_i$. Joint concavity then follows from the separable form of $\phi(x)$. $\square$

**Remark 5.3.25** Proposition 5.3.24 implies that the optimal solution to (5.8) can be generated using a greedy type of marginal allocation algorithm (Fox [7]). The algorithm runs as follows. Start from $x^0 = \mathbf{0}$. Suppose $x^k$ is the allocation at the $k$'th iteration of the algorithm. Set $x^{k+1} = x^k + e_j$, where $e_j$ is the $j$ th unit vector, and

$$j = \arg\max_i\{\Delta_i^k = \phi_i(x_i^k + 1) - \phi_i(x_i^k)|x_i^k < N_i, \Delta_i^k > 0\}.$$

Once $x_i^k = N_i$ or $\Delta_i^k \le 0$, eliminate facility $i$ from further allocation. The algorithm stops when all facilities are eliminated or all $R$ jobs are allocated, whichever occurs first.

**Example 5.3.26** Continue with Example 5.3.23. Suppose the time length $t$ is also a decision variable (for instance, $t$ is the time between successive setups). For simplicity, assume that $t$ is also discrete (e.g., number of minutes or hours), and $t \le T$, where $T$ is a given integer. Write the expected net profit functions as $\phi_i(x_i, t)$. The optimization problem is then

$$\max_{(x,t)\le(N,T),|x|\le R} \phi(x,t) = \sum_{i=1}^m \phi_i(x_i, t). \qquad (5.9)$$

**Proposition 5.3.27** Under the conditions of Proposition 5.3.24, if in addition we assume a linear profit function $g_i$ for facility $i$, then $\phi_i(x_i, t)$ is concave in $t$ (as well as concave in $x_i$), and supermodular in $(x_i, t)$ for all $i$.

**Proof.** From Theorem 5.3.21, in the stochastic $sp$ sense, $\{X_t^i(x_i)\}$ is increasing and convex in $x_i$ decreasing and convex in $t$, and submodular in $(x_i, t)$. Since $h_i(\cdot)$ is increasing and convex, it is easy to verify that $Eh_i(X_t^i(x_i))$ is convex in $x_i$ and in $t$, and submodular in $(x_i, t)$. Similarly, from Corollary 5.3.22, in the stochastic $sp$ sense, $\{x_i - X_t^i(x_i)\}$ is increasing and concave in $x_i$ and in $t$, and supermodular in $(x_i, t)$. It is easy to verify that $Eg_i(x_i - X_t^i(x_i))$ is concave in $x_i$ and in $t$, and supermodular in $(x_i, t)$, taking into account that $g_i$ is a linear function. The stated properties of $\phi_i$ then follow. $\square$

**Remark 5.3.28** To find the optimal solution to (5.9), for each $t \le T$, use the marginal allocation to obtain the optimal $x^*(t)$. The final optimal solution is then obtained by comparing these $x^*(t)$, $t \le T$. The supermodularity in Proposition 5.3.27 implies the isotone property [cf. Remark 5.3.13(ii)]: $x^*(t)$ is increasing in $t$. Hence, the marginal allocation for $t + 1$ can start from $x^*(t)$ (instead of $\mathbf{0}$ as in Remark 5.3.25).

### 5.3.5   Production with Trial Runs

**Example 5.3.29** We study a manufacturing process that involves trial runs. A job to be processed consists of $J$ units. To process the job, a setup is required. Although the entirety of the job can be set up and processed in a single batch, it is not desirable to do so, since the setup is prone to failure, resulting in loss of units. (So, if all $J$ units are set up in a single batch, they would all be lost if the setup fails.) On the other hand, if a setup is good, then the next setup is guaranteed to be good as well, hence the remaining units can be set up and processed in a single batch. (The remaining process is routine and reliable.) Therefore, the common practice is to conduct trial runs of the setup using small batches until a successful setup is performed. This models, for instance, the photolithographic process in semiconductor wafer fabrication. There, the manual allignment of the mask, which exposes the photoresist on the wafer to form the designed circuitry, is known to be such a failure-prone setup.

The time required for each setup is usually deterministic and independent of the number of units involved (batch size). Hence, without loss of generality, assume each setup takes one unit of time. The time for processing the batch that follows the $j$ th setup is random and dependent on the batch size; denote this as $S(x_j)$, given the batch size is $x_j$, $1 \le x_j \le J$. To capture the economies of scale, $S(x_j)$ is assumed to be SICV-sp in $x_j$. That is, it increases with the batch size, but with decreasing marginals. For instance, suppose $S(x_j) = \xi_1 + \cdots + \xi_{x_j}$, where $\xi_i$'s are independent random variables that are stochastically decreasing in $i$ [cf. Example (5.3.11)].

Let $\mathbf{x} = (x_j)_{j=1}^k$ be a $k$-vector of positive integers, where $k \le J - 1$ and $|\mathbf{x}| = \sum_{j=1}^k x_j \le J - 1$. We are interested in studying a control policy that prescribes up to a maximum number of $k$ trials, with the $j$ th trial involving a batch of $x_j$ units, $j \le k$. If all $k$ trials fail, the remaining $J - |\mathbf{x}|$ units are set up and processed as a single batch. Refer to this as the $k(\mathbf{x})$ policy.

Let $p_j > 0$ be the probability of success for the $j$ th setup, let $q_j = 1 - p_j$, $j = 1, ..., J$. Let $\beta_0 = 1$ and $\beta_j = q_1 ... q_j$, $j = 1, ..., J$. Let $G(\mathbf{x})$ and $B(\mathbf{x})$ denote the number of good and bad units, $G(\mathbf{x}) = J - B(\mathbf{x})$; let $T(\mathbf{x})$ denote the time required to complete the whole job (all $J$ units). We have

$$
\begin{aligned}
B(\mathbf{x}) &= x_1 + \cdots + x_j \quad \text{w.p.} \quad \beta_j p_{j+1}, \quad j = 0, 1, ..., k; \\
B(\mathbf{x}) &= J \quad \text{w.p.} \quad \beta_{k+1};
\end{aligned} \tag{5.10}
$$

where "w.p." stands for "with probability", and $B$ is defined to be 0 when $j = 0$; and

$$
\begin{aligned}
T(\mathbf{x}) &= j + \sum_{i=1}^j S(x_i) + S(J - x_1 - \cdots - x_j) \\
&\quad \text{w.p.} \quad \beta_{j-1} p_j, \quad j = 1, ..., k; \\
T(\mathbf{x}) &= k + 1 + \sum_{i=1}^k S(x_i) + S(J - x_1 - \cdots - x_k) \tag{5.11} \\
&\quad \text{w.p.} \quad \beta_k. \tag{5.12}
\end{aligned}
$$

Below, we show that given $k$, the maximum number of trial runs, the optimal policy is to set $x_i = 1$ for all $i$, i.e., to have single-unit batches for the trial runs. This will be denoted as the $k(\underline{1})$ policy.

**Proposition 5.3.30** Given $k$, the $k(\underline{1})$-setup policy

(i) stochastically maximizes the number of good units $(G)$; and

(ii) minimizes the expected completion time $(ET)$, provided the expected processing time $ES(x)$ is concave in $x$.

**Proof.** (i) We show that $B(\mathbf{x})$ $[= J - G(\mathbf{x})]$ is stochastically minimized by letting $\mathbf{x} = \underline{1}$. Specifically, we generate on a common probability space the sample values of $B(\underline{1})$ and $B(\mathbf{x})$ (for any given $\mathbf{x}$) such that the former is dominated by the latter. To this end, divide the interval $[0,1]$ into a set of $k + 2$ segments with length $\beta_j p_{j+1}$ for the $j$ th segment, $j = 0, 1, ..., k$, and $\beta_{k+1}$ for the last segment [cf. (5.10)]. Generate a uniform variate $U \in [0,1]$. If $U$ falls into the $j$ th segment, $j \leq k + 1$, then $\hat{B}(\underline{1}) = j$ while $\hat{B}(\mathbf{x}) = x_1 + ... + x_j \geq j$. If $U$ falls into the last segment, then $\hat{B}(\underline{1}) = \hat{B}(\mathbf{x}) = J$. In any case we have $\hat{B}(\underline{1}) \leq \hat{B}(\mathbf{x})$, and hence the desired result.

(ii) Obivious: $ES(x)$ concave implies

$$\sum_{i=1}^{k} ES(1) + ES(J - k) \leq \sum_{i=1}^{k} ES(x_i) + ES(J - x_1 - \cdots - x_k),$$

for any $\mathbf{x} = (s_i)_{i=1}^{k}$. $\square$

Next, we study properties of the $k(\underline{1})$ policy with respect to $k$.

**Proposition 5.3.31** Under the $k(\underline{1})$-setup policy, the number of good units, $G(k)$, is stochastically increasing and concave in $k$, provided $p_j \geq q_j p_{j+1}$ for all $j = 1, ..., J - 1$.

**Proof.** Equivalently, we show that the number of bad units, denoted as $B(k)$, is stochastically decreasing and convex in $k$. Following Definition 5.3.4, we want to construct on a common probability space one replica each for $\hat{B}(k - 1)$ and $\hat{B}(k + 1)$, and two replicas for $\hat{B}(k)$ [denoting the second one as $\hat{B}'(k)$], such that

$$\hat{B}(k - 1) + \hat{B}(k + 1) \geq \hat{B}(k) + \hat{B}'(k) \tag{5.13}$$

is satisfied.

We use a common uniform variate $U \in [0,1]$ to generate all four replicas. For $\hat{B}(k - 1)$, the interval $[0,1]$ is divided into a sequence of segments of length $\beta_j p_{j+1}$ for the $j$ th segment, $j = 0, 1, ..., k - 1$, and $\beta_k$ for the last segment [cf. (5.10)]. Suppose $U$ falls into the $j$th segment, then $\hat{B}(k-1) = j$ if $j \leq k - 1$, and $\hat{B}(k - 1) = J$ if $j = k$ (the last segment). For $\hat{B}(k)$, $\hat{B}'(k)$ and $\hat{B}(k+1)$, follow the same construction, except in the last segment (i.e., the one with length $\beta_k$). For $\hat{B}(k)$, this segment is further divided into two sub-segments: the first one has a length $\beta_k p_{k+1}$, and the second one, $\beta_{k+1}$; and $\hat{B}(k) = k$ if $U$ falls into the first one, while $\hat{B}(k) = J$ if $U$ falls into the second one. For $\hat{B}'(k)$, interchange the two sub-segments. That is, the first one has a length $\beta_{k+1}$ and corresponds to $\hat{B}'(k) = J$, while the second one has a length $\beta_k p_{k+1}$ and corresponds to $\hat{B}'(k) = k$. To construct $\hat{B}(k+1)$, the last segment is divided into three sub-segments: the first one of length $\beta_{k+1} p_{k+2}$; the second one, $\beta_{k+2}$; and the third one, $\beta_k p_{k+1}$; and $\hat{B}(K+1)$ is set at $k+1$, $J$, and $k$, respectively, when $U$ falls into one of the three sub-segments.

Note that the given condition, $p_{k+1} \geq q_{k+1} p_{k+2}$, implies

$$\beta_k p_{k+1} \geq \beta_{k+1} p_{k+2},$$

i.e., the first sub-segment of $\hat{B}(k)$ is larger than that of $\hat{B}(k+1)$. This condition is crucial: it enables the above construction to rule out the possibility that both $\hat{B}(k-1)$ and $\hat{B}(k+1)$ take value $J$, while only one of $\hat{B}(k)$ and $\hat{B}'(k)$ equals $J$. Hence, the construction ensures that (5.13) is always satisfied.

The stochastic decreasing property of $B(k)$ is easy: just compare the replicas of $B(k-1)$ and $B(k)$ as constructed above. $\square$

**Proposition 5.3.32** Under the $k(\underline{1})$-setup policy, the completion time of the job, $T(k)$ is stochastically increasing and concave in $k$, provided the service times $S(x)$ are stochastically increasing and concave in $x$.

**Proof.** Follow the construction in the above proof. The situation here is, however, much more straightforward: all the segments just follow their natural order, no switching is needed [for instance, $\hat{T}(k)$ and $\hat{T}'(k)$ follow exactly the same construction). $\square$

With a suitable objective function, the concavity properties with respect to $k$ are useful in identifying the optimal number of trial runs to conduct, say $k^*$. It can then be shown that the overall optimal policy is the $k^*(\underline{1})$ policy.

## 5.4    Arrangement and Likelihood Ratio Orderings

The purpose of this section is two-fold: (a) to introduce the *arrangement* and *majorization* orderings, and the classes of functions that preserve these orderings, namely, *arrangement increasing* functions and *Schur convex* functions; and (b) to relate these deterministic orderings to the likelihood ratio ordering of random variables. Specifically, arrangement increasing functions constitute a defining class for the likelihood ratio ordering (as well as for the arrangement ordering). The primary application example in this section is the closed Jackson network (see Chapter 1).

## 5.4.1  The Connection

**Definition 5.4.1** Let $x = (x_i)_{i=1}^n$ and $y = (y_i)_{i=1}^n$ be two $n$-vectors of real-valued components. The arrangement ordering, denoted $x \geq_A y$, is defined as follows: $x$ can be obtained from $y$ through successive pairwise interchanges of its components, with each interchange resulting in a decreasing order of the two interchanged components. A function $\phi : \Re^n \mapsto \Re$ that preserves the arrangement ordering is termed an "arrangement increasing function"; that is, $\phi$ is arrangement increasing if $\phi(x) \geq \phi(y)$ for any $x \geq_A y$.

For instance, $(4, 5, 3, 1) \geq_A (4, 3, 5, 1) \geq_A (4, 1, 5, 3)$. Note $x \geq_A y$ implies that $x$ is necessarily a permutation of the components of $y$.

The arrangement ordering is easy to motivate. The inequality in (5.6) is such an ordering, and so is the scheduling model in Example 5.2.7, as well as other similar pairwise interchange arguments. Furthermore, in Section 2, the defining class of functions for the likelihood ratio ordering, $\mathbf{C}_{\ell r}$ [cf. Theorem 5.2.3], clearly belongs to the class of arrangement increasing functions. Indeed, based on Definition 5.4.1, we can extend Theorem 5.2.3 to the multivariate case as follows.

**Theorem 5.4.2** Let $X = (X_i)_{i=1}^n$ be a random vector of independent components. Let $\pi$ and $\sigma$ denote two permutations of the $n$ integers $\{1, 2, ..., n\}$. Let $X^\pi$ ($X^\sigma$) denote a random vector obtained through rearranging the components of $X$ according to the permutation $\pi$ ($\sigma$). Define $\pi \geq_A \sigma$ following the same definition as for vectors. Then, $X_n \geq_{\ell r} \cdots \geq_{\ell r} X_1$ if and only if $\mathsf{E}\phi(X^\pi) \geq \mathsf{E}\phi(X^\sigma)$ for all $\pi \geq_A \sigma$ and all arrangement increasing functions $\phi$.

The above in fact also suggests a likelihood ratio ordering among random variables that are not necessarily independent.

**Definition 5.4.3** Let $X$ be the random vector in Theorem 5.4.2, but the components are not necessarily independent. Let $\pi$ and $\sigma$ be the permutations in Theorem 5.4.2. Define a likelihood ratio ordering among the components of $X$, denoted $X_n \geq_{\ell r:j} \cdots \geq_{\ell r:j} X_1$, if $\mathsf{E}\phi(X^\pi) \geq \mathsf{E}\phi(X^\sigma)$ for all $\pi \geq_A \sigma$ and all arrangement increasing functions $\phi$.

Similar to the proof of Theorem 5.2.3, we can establish the following

**Theorem 5.4.4** The components of $X$ are ordered $X_n \geq_{\ell r:j} \cdots \geq_{\ell r:j} X_1$, if and only if the joint density function (or pmf) of $X$ is an arrangement increasing function.

Obviously, when the components are independent, the joint ordering $\geq_{\ell r:j}$ reduces to the regular ordering $\geq_{\ell r}$, since the joint density function factorizes under independence, recovering the original definition for $\geq_{\ell r}$. However, in the general case, $\geq_{\ell r:j}$ and $\geq_{\ell r}$ do not imply each other, as we shall demonstrate through an example below. (Note that in the dependent case, the ordering $\geq_{\ell r}$ is still well defined, although it is concerned with the marginal distributions only. In contrast, $\geq_{\ell r:j}$ is concerned with the joint distribution.)

Similar joint orderings can also be defined for the other stochastic order relations discussed in Section 2. The defining functional classes obviously have to be subsets of the arrangement increasing functions.

Closely related to the arrangement ordering is majorization, and the class of Schur convex functions that preserve majorization.

**Definition 5.4.5** Two $n$-vectors, $x$ and $y$, are ordered under majorization, denoted as $x \leq_m y$, if

$$\sum_{j=1}^{i} x_{[j]} \leq \sum_{j=1}^{i} y_{[j]}, \quad i = 1, ..., n-1;$$

$$\sum_{j=1}^{n} x_{[j]} = \sum_{j=1}^{n} y_{[j]};$$

where $x_{[j]}$ and $y_{[j]}$ denote the $j$ th largest components of $x$ and $y$, respectively. Replacing the last equality above by $\leq$ results in "weak majorization", denoted $x \leq_{wm} y$. A function $\phi$ is termed Schur convex if for any $x$ and $y$, $x \leq_m y \Rightarrow \phi(x) \leq \phi(y)$. In addition, $x \leq_{wm} y$ if and only if $\phi(x) \leq \phi(y)$ for any $\phi$ that is increasing and Schur convex. Finally, a function $\phi$ is Schur concave if $-\phi$ is Schur convex.

**Remark 5.4.6** (i) From the definition of majorization, we have $x \leq_m x^\pi$ as well as $x \geq_m x^\pi$ for any permutation $\pi$. Hence, if a Schur convex/concave function $\phi$ has a symmetric domain (i.e., $x$ belongs to the domain if and only if $x^\pi$ belongs to the domain), then $\phi$ is necessarily symmetric, i.e., $\phi(x) = \phi(x^\pi)$ for any permutation $\pi$. Below, we will assume this is indeed the case throughout.

(ii) Suppose a pair of components of $x$ is ordered: $x_i > x_j$. Then obviously, $x \geq_m x - \epsilon e^i + \epsilon e^j$, where $e^i$ and $e^j$ denote the $i$ th and the $j$ th unit vectors, and $0 < \epsilon < x_i - x_j$. In other words, $x$ can be made smaller, in the sense of majorization, by shifting a small, positive amount ($\epsilon$) from one of its larger component ($x_i$) to a smaller component ($x_j$) ($\epsilon$ should be small enough so that after the shift the larger component is still larger). Call such an operation on the vector $x$ "transposition". Then clearly, $x \leq_m y$ if and only if $x$ can be reached from $y$ through a sequence of such transpositions, each resulting in a vector that is majorized by the vector from the previous transposition.

(iii) There are two implications from the above. One is that to establish the Schur convexity of a function $f$, we only need to establish the dominance relation between the function values at $x$ and its transposition. In other words, Schur convexity is essentially a property with respect to each *pair* of components. The other implication is that for a differentiable function $f$, Schur convexity is equivalent to

$$x_i > x_j \quad \Rightarrow \quad f_i(x) \geq f_j(x),$$

for any $i \neq j$ and any $x$, where $f_i$ and $f_j$ denote the partial derivatives with respect to $x_i$ and $x_j$.

## 5.4.2  Queueing Network Applications

Applications of majorization and arrangement orderings in queueing networks appeared earlier in Chapter 1 (Section 1.8 in particular). Here we present more such applications, and in particular bring out the connection to the joint likelihood ratio ordering $\geq_{\ell r:j}$.

Consider a closed Jackson network in equilibrium, with $m$ nodes and $N$ jobs. (Refer to Section 1.2 for details. Here we use the same notation.) Let $X_i$ be the number of jobs in node $i$, and $X = (X_i)_{i=1}^m$. Let $\mu_i(n_i)$ be the (state-dependent) service rate at node $i$, when $X_i = n_i$. Suppose for all $i$, $\mu_i(0) = 0$ and $\mu_i(n_i) > 0$ for all $n_i > 0$. Let $r_{ij}$ denote the routing probability from node $i$ to node $j$. The routing matrix $[r_{ij}]$ is stochastic (i.e., each row sums to unity).

Let $v_i$ be the solution to

$$v_i = \sum_{j=1}^m v_j r_{ij}, \quad i = 1, ..., m. \tag{5.14}$$

Note that since the routing matrix $[r_{ij}]$ is stochastic, the solution to the above linear equation system is only unique to a constant multiplier. We can add a normalization condition, $\sum_{i=1}^m v_i = 1$, to (5.14) to make the solution unique. This way, $v_i$ can be interpreted as the "visit ratio" to node $i$, or the relative frequency that node $i$ is visited by the jobs. Formally, $v = (v_i)_{i=1}^m$ can also be viewed as the invariant probability vector of the Markov chain that governs job routing among the nodes.

Let $Y = (Y_i)_{i=1}^m$ be a vector of *independent* random variables, where each $Y_i$ has equilibrium rate $r_{Y_i}(n_i) = \mu_i(n_i)/v_i$, Then, the throughput function of the network, $TH(N)$, can be expressed as the equilibrium rate of the sum of random variables $Y_1 + \cdots + Y_m$ (refer to Section 1.4.1)

$$TH(N) = r_{Y_1 + \cdots + Y_m}(N). \tag{5.15}$$

From the results in Section 1.4.2 and 1.4.3, we have

$$Y_i \geq_{\ell r} Y_j \quad \Leftrightarrow \quad \mu_i(n)/v_i \leq \mu_j(n)/v_j \quad \forall n, \tag{5.16}$$

and

$$Y_i \in PF_2 \quad \Leftrightarrow \quad r_{Y_i}(k) \text{ increasing in } k. \tag{5.17}$$

**Lemma 5.4.7** $Y_1 \geq_{\ell r} \ldots \geq_{\ell r} Y_m \Rightarrow X_1 \geq_{\ell r:j} \ldots \geq_{\ell r:j} X_m.$

**Proof.** Make use of the product-form distribution (see Theorem 1.2.3). Pick any pair of indices $i < j$. Fixing $X_k$ for $k \neq i, j$, while interchanging the values of $X_i$ and $X_j$ in the pmf, we have, for any non-negative integers $x \geq y$,

$$P[..., X_i = x, ..., X_j = y, ...]/P[..., X_i = y, ..., X_j = x, ...]$$

$$= P[Y_i = x]P[Y_j = y]/P[Y_i = y]P[Y_j = x] \geq 1,$$

since $Y_i \geq_{\ell r} Y_j$. That is, the joint pmf of $X$ is an arrangement increasing function. The desired conclusion then follows from Theorem 5.4.4. $\square$

**Remark 5.4.8** Earlier, we mentioned that the orderings $\geq_{\ell r:j}$ and $\geq_{\ell r}$ do not imply each other in general. Lemma 5.4.7 now provides such an example; specifically, the result there does not hold for the ordering $\geq_{\ell r}$. To see this, from the marginal distribution of $X_i$ in (1.1.8) we can derive its equilibrium rate:

$$r_{X_i}(n_i) = r_{Y_i}(n_i)/r_{\Sigma_{(i)}}(N + 1 - n_i), \tag{5.18}$$

where, $\Sigma_{(i)}$ denotes the sum $Y_1 + \cdots + Y_m$ minus $Y_i$. (That is, $\Sigma_{(i)} = |\mathbf{Y}_{-i}|$, using the notation in Section 1.3.) A similar expression can be derived for the equilibrium rate of $X_j$. Hence, in order to have $r_{X_i}(k) \leq r_{X_j}(k)$ for all $k$, we need not only $Y_i \geq_{\ell r} Y_j$, but also $\Sigma_{(i)} \leq_{\ell r} \Sigma_{(j)}$. That is,

$$\Sigma_{(ij)} + Y_j \leq_{\ell r} \Sigma_{(ij)} + Y_i,$$

where $\Sigma_{(ij)}$ denotes the sum $Y_1 + \cdots + Y_m$ without $Y_i$ and $Y_j$. Now, from Sections 1.4.2 and 1.4.3 (in particular Lemma 1.4.9), we know that in general to preserve the likelihood-ratio ordering under convolution, the (independent) random variables involved have to satisfy the $PF_2$ property. Hence, in order for the above to be implied by $Y_i \geq_{\ell r} Y_j$, we need the $PF_2$ property of $\Sigma_{(ij)}$. Therefore, for Lemma 5.4.7 to hold for the ordering $\geq_{\ell r}$, the additional requirement that $Y_i \in PF_2$ for all $i$ is needed. For the application below, however, the result holds without the $PF_2$ property, thanks to the joint ordering $\geq_{\ell r:j}$.

**Example 5.4.9** Consider the following allocation problem in the closed Jackson network. There are $m$ sites for allocating $m$ workcenters (nodes). The service rates, $\{\mu_i(n)\}$, and the visit ratios, $\{v_i\}$, are known, reflecting the capacity and processing requirements at the workcenters. Therefore, the work-in-process (WIP) level of each workcenter is independent of its location. However, the sites have different cost structures for accommodating the WIP. (For instance, storage space has to be built for jobs in transition.) Suppose $\pi = (\pi(i))_{i=1}^m$ denotes an allocation with workcenter $\pi(i)$ located at site $i$. For $x = (x_i)_{i=1}^m$, let $h(x)$ be the holding cost of having $x_i$ jobs at site $i$, $i = 1, ..., m$. Let $X^\pi$ denote the equilibrium state of the network under allocation $\pi$. The problem is to minimize the expected holding cost:

$$\min_\pi \mathsf{E}h(X^\pi). \tag{5.19}$$

**Proposition 5.4.10** Suppose there exists a permutation $\pi^*$, such that for all $n = 1, ..., N$,

$$\mu_{\pi^*(1)}(n)/v_{\pi^*(1)} \leq \cdots \leq \mu_{\pi^*(m)}(n)/v_{\pi^*(m)}, \tag{5.20}$$

then $\pi^*$ is the optimal solution to (5.19) for any arrangement increasing function $h$.

**Proof.** Under condition (5.20), we have $Y_{\pi^*(m)} \geq_{\ell r} \cdots \geq_{\ell r} Y_{\pi^*(1)}$. Hence, $X_{\pi^*(m)} \geq_{\ell r:j} \cdots \geq_{\ell r:j} X_{\pi^*(1)}$ follows from Lemma 5.4.7. The optimality of $\pi^*$ then follows from Definition 5.4.3, since the cost function $h$ is arrangement increasing. $\square$

## 5.5 Stochastic Rearrangement and Majorization

### 5.5.1 The Deterministic Theory

In Section 2, we have seen in Example 5.2.7 the key role played by the pairwise interchange argument through a stochastic version of a simple rearrangement inequality (5.6). An immediate extension of (5.6) is the well known HLP inequality. Let $x$ and $y$ be two $n$-vectors of real-valued components; let $x^\pi$ and $y^\sigma$ denote the rearrangement of the components of $x$ and $y$ according to the permutations $\pi$ and $\sigma$, respectively. In particular, let the superscripts $\uparrow$ and $\downarrow$ denote rearrangements of components according to, respectively, increasing and decreasing orders. Then, the HLP inequality can be expressed as a relation among the inner products:

$$x^\uparrow \cdot y^\downarrow \leq x^\pi \cdot y^\sigma \leq x^\uparrow \cdot y^\uparrow,$$

for any permutations $\pi$ and $\sigma$.

A generalization of the HLP inequality is Day's inequality (Day [6]; also see Marshall and Olkin [11], Chapter 6).

**Lemma 5.5.1** (Day [6])     Denote

$$f \circ \phi(x, y) = f(\phi(x_1, y_1), ..., \phi(x_n, y_n)).$$

Then,

$$f \circ \phi(x^\uparrow, y^\downarrow) \leq f \circ \phi(x^\pi, y^\sigma) \leq f \circ \phi(x^\uparrow, y^\uparrow),$$

for any permutations $\pi$ and $\sigma$, any monotone (i.e., either increasing or decreasing) and supermodular function $\phi$ and any increasing Schur convex function $f$.

Since the increasing Schur convex functions form the defining class for weak majorization, Day's inequality can be equivalently expressed as

$$\phi(x^\uparrow, y^\downarrow) \leq_{wm} \phi(x^\pi, y^\sigma) \leq_{wm} \phi(x^\uparrow, y^\uparrow). \tag{5.21}$$

To prove Day's inequality, we only need to show, for $x_1 \leq x_2$ and $y_1 \leq y_2$,

$$f(\phi(x_1, y_1), \phi(x_2, y_2)) \geq f(\phi(x_1, y_2), \phi(x_2, y_1)). \tag{5.22}$$

Suppose $\phi$ is increasing. Denote the four arguments of $f$ above as $z_1, z_4, z_2$ and $z_3$, respectively. Then,

$$z_1 \leq z_2, z_3 \leq z_4, \quad z_1 + z_4 \geq z_2 + z_3,$$

since $\phi$ is increasing and supermodular. In other words,

$$(z_1, z_4) \geq_{wm} (z_2, z_3).$$

Hence (5.22) follows, since $f$ is increasing and Schur convex. If $\phi$ is decreasing, interchange $z_1$ and $z_4$, the remaining arguments still apply.

It is interesting to compare the above with the result in Theorem 1.8.2 (ii) of Chapter 1. There,

$$v = (v_1, v_2) \geq_m v' = (v_1', v_2')$$

led to

$$\min(X_1, N - X_1) \geq_{st} \min(X_1', N - X_1')$$

(see the proof of Theorem 1.8.2); that is, $X(v) \leq_m X(v')$ in the sense that $\mathsf{E}f(X(v)) \leq \mathsf{E}f(X(v'))$ for any Schur convex function $f$. This suggests that Schur convex functions be used as a defining class for stochastic majorization as well. However, this notion of stochastic majorization often turns out to be too strong in many applications, where any interesting results might only hold if $f$ belongs to a *subclass* of Schur convex functions. Another limitation is that the type of result in Theorem 1.8.2 was obtained primarily through algebraic manipulation (see the proof of Lemma 1.8.1), which reveals very little about the functional relationship of $X$ with respect to $v$.

### 5.5.2    The Stochastic Counterpart

Below, we shall attempt to directly "translate" Day's inequality in Lemma 5.5.1 into a stochastic version. In doing so, we find that for Schur convex functions to be the defining class, the required stochastic order relation among the random variables involved has to be the strongest, the likelihood ratio ordering. For weaker orderings, the defining class has to be restricted to a subclass of Schur convex functions. This subclass of functions have a "directional" property, analogous to (but different from) the directional convexity in Definition 5.3.15; see Lemma 5.5.4 below. The main theorem in this subsection is Theorem 5.5.2.

**Theorem 5.5.2** Let $X$ and $Y$ be two independent random $n$-vectors, each with independent components. Suppose the components of $X$ $(Y)$ are ordered in the sense of $\geq_a$ $(\geq_b)$ to be specified below. Suppose $\phi(\cdot, \cdot)$ is a monotone and supermodular function. Then, for any permutations $\pi$ and $\sigma$ of $\{1, 2, ..., n\}$, we have

$$\mathsf{E} f \circ \phi(X^\uparrow, Y^\downarrow) \leq \mathsf{E} f \circ \phi(X^\pi, Y^\sigma) \leq \mathsf{E} f \circ \phi(X^\uparrow, Y^\uparrow),$$

for any function $f$ that is

(i) increasing and Schur convex, if $(a, b) = (\ell r, \ell r)$;

(ii) symmetric, submodular, increasing and convex in each variable, if $(a, b) = (st, st)$;

(iii) expressible as $f = g \circ h$ with $h$ satisfying the properties in (ii) and $g: \Re \mapsto \Re$, an increasing and convex function, if $(a, b) = (\ell r, hr)$ or $(hr, \ell r)$, and $\phi$ increasing.

Moreover, when $\phi$ is submodular, the above results also hold with the increasingness of $f$, as well as the increasingness of $\phi$ in (iii), replaced by decreasingness.

**Remark 5.5.3** (i) A symmetric, convex function is Schur convex. To see this, without loss of generality, consider a bivariate function $f(x_1, x_2)$ that is symmetric and convex. Suppose $x_1 > x_2$, we want to show

$$f(x_1, x_2) \geq f(x_1 - \epsilon, x_2 + \epsilon) \tag{5.23}$$

for any $0 < \epsilon < x_1 - x_2$. The convexity of $f$ implies, for any $0 < \theta < 1$,

$$\theta f(x_1, x_2) + (1 - \theta) f(x_2, x_1) \geq f[\theta x_1 + (1 - \theta) x_2, \theta x_2 + (1 - \theta) x_1].$$

Now, the symmetry of $f$ implies the LHS above equals $f(x_1, x_2)$. Hence, pick $\theta$ such that $\epsilon = (1 - \theta)(x_1 - x_2)$. A Schur convex function, however, is not necessarily convex. In fact, it is not even necessarily convex in each variable.

(ii) A symmetric function that is convex in each variable is not necessarily Schur convex either. (As an example, consider $f(a, b) = a^2 + 3ab + b^2$. It is symmetric, convex in $a$ and in $b$. However, $f_a - f_b = -(a - b)$, making it Schur concave.) With the addition of submodularity, however, the function does become Schur convex. See Remark 5.5.5, following Lemma 5.5.4 below. Therefore, the class of functions in Theorem 5.5.2(ii) is indeed a subset of the Schur convex class.

(iii) While (joint) convexity implies convexity in each variable, the converse is not true in general. A special case that does make the converse true is when the function $f$ is *separable*, i.e., $f(x) = \sum_i g_i(x_i)$. When $g_i$ is convex in $x_i$, for all $i$, $f$ is (jointly) convex in $x$. (The symmetry of $f$ would further require that the $g_i$ functions are the same for all $i$.) When $f$ is separable, it is easily verified (Remark 5.3.13) that $f$ is both submodular and supermodular (hence *modular*), provided the $g_i$'s are either increasing for all $i$ or decreasing for all $i$.

(iv) The two classes of functions in Theorem 5.5.2 (ii) and (iii) are simply different classes: while the class in (iii) is preserved under composition with increasing and convex functions, the class in (ii) is not (submodularity would fail). However, $\max_i(x_i)$, is a function that belongs to both classes, since for any increasing function $g(z)$,

$$g(\max_i(x_i)) = \max_i(g(x_i)).$$

In particular, when $g$ is increasing and convex, $g(\max_i(x_i))$ belongs to both classes (max is increasing and convex).

(v) In the same spirit as expressing Day's rearrangement inequality as a majorization relation in (5.21), we can also formally express Theorem 5.5.2 as a *stochastic* majorization relation as follows:

$$\phi(X^\uparrow, Y^\downarrow) \leq_{wm} \phi(X^\pi, Y^\sigma) \leq_{wm} \phi(X^\uparrow, Y^\uparrow).$$

However here the ordering $\leq_{wm}$ among random vectors has different meanings that depend on the order relations among the components of the random vectors. For instance, in the setting of Theorem 5.5.2(ii), $\leq_{wm}$ means an order that is preserved by functions that are symmetric, submodular, increasing and convex in each variable. In this sense, the stochastic version of Day's rearrangement inequality requires restricting the Schur convex class of functions to the subclass specified in Theorem 5.5.2(ii), when the components of the random vectors are ordered in stochastic ordering. In contrast, this restriction is not needed when the components are ordered in the likelihood ratio ordering, such as in the setting of Theorem 5.5.2(i): Schur convex functions still form the defining class.

We now prove the three parts of Theorem 5.5.2 separately. Part (i) turns out to be the easiest. Since all the random variables involved are independent, no generality is lost in assuming that $X$ and $Y$ in Theorem 5.5.2 are 2-vectors. This is tantamount to applying a pairwise interchange argument, fixing all the other components in the original $X$ and $Y$ vectors.

**Proof.** [Theorem 5.5.2(i)]. For $x_1 \geq x_2$ and $y_1 \geq y_2$, we have

$$f(\phi(x_1, y_1), \phi(x_2, y_2)) \geq f(\phi(x_1, y_2), \phi(x_2, y_1)),$$

following the given conditions on $f$ and $\phi$ and Day's inequality in (5.22). Now, fixing $x_1$ and $x_2$, we can write the above as $g(y_1, y_2) \geq g(y_2, y_1)$ for $y_1 \geq y_2$, taking into account the symmetry of $f$ (implied by its Schur convexity). Hence, $g \in \mathbf{C}_{\ell r}$, and

$$\mathsf{E}f(\phi(x_1, Y_1), \phi(x_2, Y_2)) \geq \mathsf{E}f(\phi(x_1, Y_2), \phi(x_2, Y_1)),$$

since $Y_1 \geq_{\ell r} Y_2$. Next, repeat the argument by writing the above as $h(x_1, x_2) \geq h(x_2, x_1)$ for $x_1 \geq x_2$. $\square$

To prove Theorem 5.5.2(ii), we need two lemmas. The first one reveals more about the properties of the class of functions specified there. These properties relate closely to the directional convexity in Section 3.

**Lemma 5.5.4** $f$ is submodular, and convex in each variable, if and only if

$$f(z^1) + f(z^4) \geq f(z^2) + f(z^3) \tag{5.24}$$

for any four vectors $z^i = (x_i, y_i)$, $i = 1, 2, 3, 4$, satisfying:

$$x_1 \geq \max\{x_2, x_3\}, \quad y_4 \geq \max\{y_2, y_3\};$$

$$x_1 + x_4 = x_2 + x_3, \quad y_1 + y_4 = y_2 + y_3.$$

If, in addition, $f$ is increasing (resp. decreasing), the results also hold, with the last two equalities above replaced by $\geq$ (resp. $\leq$).

The proof of the lemma is completely analogous to the proof of Lemma 5.3.16, via the remark below, and hence omitted.

**Remark 5.5.5** Notice the close resemblance of the above lemma to the notion of directional convexity in Definition 5.3.15. In fact, following Lemma 5.3.16, directional convexity is equivalent to *supermodularity*, instead of submodularity, plus convexity in each variable. Hence, in contrast to directional convexity, the four points (vectors), $z^i$ ($i$=1,2,3,4), here have the following relation: $z^1$ and $z^4$ are, respectively the southeast and the northwest corners of the rectangle they form (on the $x$-$y$ plane), $z^2$ and $z^3$ are then two points which fall inside (or at most at the boundary) of the rectangle. That is, while directional convexity is a property along the northeast-southwest diagonal, the property in Lemma 5.5.4 above is along the northwest-southeast diagonal.

(ii) When the function $f$ in Lemma 5.5.4 is also symmetric, then it is Schur convex. To see this, let $x_1 > x_2$ and $0 < \epsilon < x_1 - x_2$ as in Remark 5.5.3, and set

$$z^1 = (x_1, x_2), \quad z^4 = (x_2, x_1);$$

$$z^2 = (x_1 - \epsilon, x_2 + \epsilon), \quad z^3 = (x_2 + \epsilon, x_1 - \epsilon).$$

Then (5.24) reduces to the desired inequality in (5.23).

**Lemma 5.5.6** Suppose $f$ is increasing (resp. decreasing), submodular and convex in each variable, and $\phi$ is monotone and supermodular (resp. submodular). Given $y_1 \geq y_2$, then

$$f(\phi(x_1, y_1), \phi(x_2, y_2)) - f(\phi(x_1, y_2), \phi(x_2, y_1))$$

is increasing in $x_1$.

**Proof.** Suppose $\phi$ is increasing. Let $a > 0$ be any given constant. Define the four points in Lemma 5.5.4 as follows:

$$z^1 = (\phi(x_1 + a, y_1), \phi(x_2, y_2)), \quad z^4 = (\phi(x_1, y_2), \phi(x_2, y_1));$$

$$z^2 = (\phi(x_1 + a, y_2), \phi(x_2, y_1)), \quad z^3 = (\phi(x_1, y_1), \phi(x_2, y_2)).$$

Then clearly $z^i$ satisfy the requirements in Lemma 5.5.4. In particular,

$$\phi(x_1 + a, y_1) + \phi(x_1, y_2) \geq \phi(x_1 + a, y_2) + \phi(x_1, y_1)$$

follows from the supermodularity of $\phi$. When $f$ is increasing, submodular and convex in each variable, we have $f(z^1) - f(z^2) \geq f(z^3) - f(z^4)$, following Lemma 5.5.4, hence the desired increasingness in $x_1$.

When $\phi$ is decreasing, interchange the definition of $z^1$ and $z^4$. The case $f$ is decreasing is similarly proved. $\square$

We are now ready to prove Theorem 5.5.2(ii).

**Proof.** [Theorem 5.5.2(ii)]. Consider $f$ increasing; the decreasing case is similarly proved. We first show, under the given conditions, that

$$\mathsf{E}f(\phi(x_1, Y_1), \phi(x_2, Y_2)) - \mathsf{E}f(\phi(x_1, Y_2), \phi(x_2, Y_1)) \qquad (5.25)$$

is increasing in $x_1$. Since $Y_1 \geq_{st} Y_2$, there exists a pair of random variables, $\hat{Y}_1 \geq \hat{Y}_2$, and $\hat{Y}_i \stackrel{d}{=} Y_i$ for $i=1,2$. Generate *independently* another pair, $\hat{Y}_1' \geq \hat{Y}_2'$, that are also equal in distribution to $Y_1$ and $Y_2$, respectively. Then, for any given $a > 0$, it is easy to verify that

$$f(\phi(x_1 + a, \hat{Y}_1), \phi(x_2, \hat{Y}_2')) - f(\phi(x_1 + a, \hat{Y}_2), \phi(x_2, \hat{Y}_1'))$$

$$\geq f(\phi(x_1, \hat{Y}_1), \phi(x_2, \hat{Y}_2')) - f(\phi(x_1, \hat{Y}_2), \phi(x_2, \hat{Y}_1')),$$

since the four points (the arguments of $f$) above correspond to the four $z^i$ in Lemma 5.5.4. Also note that involved in each $z^i$ is a pair of *independent* replicas of $Y_1$ and $Y_2$ (which is a requirement, since $Y_1$ and $Y_2$ are independent as assumed). Taking expectations on both sides, we obtain the desired increasingness in $x_1$. Since $f$ is symmetric, (5.25) can be written as $g(x_1, x_2) - g(x_2, x_1)$, which is increasing in $x_1$.

Next, since $X_1 \geq_{st} X_2$, in the same way as before, generate a pair of replicas of $X_1$ and $X_2$: $\hat{X}_1 \geq \hat{X}_2$, and generate *independently* another replica of $X_2$: $\hat{X}_2'$. Then, the increasing property (in $x_1$) just obtained yields

$$g(\hat{X}_1, \hat{X}_2') - g(\hat{X}_2', \hat{X}_1) \geq g(\hat{X}_2, \hat{X}_2') - g(\hat{X}_2', \hat{X}_2).$$

Taking expectations on both sides, the RHS vanishes, giving the desired conclusion. $\square$

**Proof.** [Theorem 5.5.2(iii)]. Suppose $(a, b) = (\ell r, hr)$. Fix $x_1 \geq x_2$, and write $f$ as

$$f(y_1, y_2) = g \circ h(\phi(x_1, y_1), \phi(x_2, y_2)),$$

where $g$ is an increasing and convex function and $h$ satisfies all the properties in (5.3 ii). Write the $h$ part above as $h(y_1, y_2)$. Then it is clear that $h \in \mathbf{C}_{hr}$, since it is increasing in $y_1$, and $h(y_1, y_2) - h(y_2, y_1)$ is also increasing in $y_1$, following Lemma 5.5.4. It then follows that $g \circ h \in \mathbf{C}_{hr}$, since the class $\mathbf{C}_{hr}$ is closed under composition with increasing and convex functions. Therefore, $Y_1 \geq_{hr} Y_2$ leads to

$$\mathsf{E}g \circ h(\phi(x_1, Y_1), \phi(x_2, Y_2)) \geq \mathsf{E}g \circ h(\phi(x_1, Y_2), \phi(x_2, Y_1)).$$

Now, write the LHS above as $\tilde{f}(x_1, x_2)$, so the RHS is $\tilde{f}(x_2, x_1)$, taking into account the symmetry of $h$. Hence, $\tilde{f} \in \mathbf{C}_{\ell r}$. Since $X_1 \geq_{\ell r} X_2$, we have

$$\mathsf{E}g \circ h(\phi(X_1, Y_1), \phi(X_2, Y_2)) \geq \mathsf{E}g \circ h(\phi(X_1, Y_2), \phi(X_2, Y_1)),$$

which is the desired conclusion. $\square$

We now illustrate the application of Theorem 5.5.2 through a scheduling example.

**Example 5.5.7** Consider the problem of scheduling $n$ jobs in a tandem queue of $m$ servers, with infinite intermediate buffers. All jobs are present at time zero. For any job $i$, the processing requirements at all servers are equal, denoted $P_i$. Let $D_i$ denote the due time for job $i$. Suppose the processing times and due times are independent among the $n$ jobs. Let $C_i$, $L_i$ and $T_i$ denote, respectively, the completion time, lateness and tardiness of job $i$. Then, $L_i = C_i - D_i$, and $T_i = \max\{L_i, 0\}$. Denote by $C$, $L$ and $D$ the corresponding vectors. Of particular interest are the *departure* epochs of the jobs. These are the components of the vector $C$ arranged in increasing order: $C^{\uparrow} = (C_{(i)})_{i=1}^{n}$, where $C_{(i)}$ denotes the $i$th smallest component of $C$. Suppose the schedule of the $n$ jobs follows the permutation $\pi$. Then, it is not difficult to derive the following expression (see Pinedo and Weber [12]): for $j = 1, ..., n$,

$$C_{(j)}^{\pi} = \sum_{i=1}^{j} P_{\pi(i)} + (m - 1) \max\{P_{\pi(1)}, ..., P_{\pi(j)}\}.$$

In particular, $C_{(n)}^{\pi}$ is the time to complete all $n$ jobs, the "makespan".

**Proposition 5.5.8** Suppose $P_1 \leq_a P_2 \leq_a \cdots \leq_a P_n$. Let $s$ and $\ell$ denote, respectively, the schedules $(1,2,...,n)$ (shortest processing time first) and $(n,...,2,1)$ (longest processing time first). Then, for any permutation schedule $\pi$,

$$\mathsf{E}f(C^{\uparrow s}) \leq \mathsf{E}f(C^{\uparrow \pi}) \leq \mathsf{E}f(C^{\uparrow \ell}),$$

(i) for any increasing function $f$, if $a = \ell r$;

(ii) for any increasing and supermodular function $f$, if $a = hr$.

**Proof.** To prove (i), we only need to show that for any two permutations $\pi$ and $\sigma$, $\pi \leq_A \sigma$ implies $f(C^{\uparrow\pi}) \leq f(C^{\uparrow\sigma})$, when $f$ is an increasing function. This is directly verified.

To prove (ii), denote $x_i = P_{\pi(i)}$ and write the completion times as $C^{\pi}_{(i)} = g_i(x_1, ..., x_i)$. Note that $g_i$ is symmetric in its arguments. We want to show, given $x_i \geq x_{i+1}$, the difference between the schedule $\pi$ and another schedule $\sigma$ that interchanges the processing sequence of $\pi(i)$ and $\pi(i+1)$, expressed as

$$f(\ldots, g_i(x_1, \ldots, x_{i-1}, x_i), g_{i+1}(x_1, \ldots, x_{i-1}, x_i, x_{i+1}), \ldots)$$
$$- \quad f(\ldots, g_i(x_1, \ldots, x_{i-1}, x_{i+1}), g_{i+1}(x_1, \ldots, x_{i-1}, x_{i+1}, x_i), \ldots),$$

is increasing in $x_i$, i.e., $f \in \mathbf{C}_{hr}$. Since $f$ is supermodular and $g$ is increasing and symmetric, for $a > 0$, the above difference is dominated by

$$f(\ldots, g_i(x_1, \ldots, x_{i-1}, x_i), g_{i+1}(x_1, \ldots, x_{i-1}, x_i + a, x_{i+1}), \ldots)$$
$$- \quad f(\ldots, g_i(x_1, \ldots, x_{i-1}, x_{i+1}), g_{i+1}(x_1, \ldots, x_{i-1}, x_{i+1}, x_i + a), \ldots),$$

which, in turn, is dominated by

$$f(\ldots, g_i(x_1, \ldots, x_{i-1}, x_i + a), g_{i+1}(x_1, \ldots, x_{i-1}, x_i + a, x_{i+1}), \ldots)$$
$$- \quad f(\ldots, g_i(x_1, \ldots, x_{i-1}, x_{i+1}), g_{i+1}(x_1, \ldots, x_{i-1}, x_{i+1}, x_i + a), \ldots),$$

since both $f$ and $g$ are increasing functions. Hence, we have established the desired increasing property (in $x_i$) of the difference. $\square$

**Proposition 5.5.9** If, in addition to the given conditions in Proposition 5.5.8, $D_1 \leq_b D_2 \leq_b \ldots \leq_b D_n$, then

$$\mathsf{E}f(L^s) \leq \mathsf{E}f(L^{\pi}) \leq \mathsf{E}f(L^{\ell}), \quad \mathsf{E}f(T^s) \leq \mathsf{E}f(T^{\pi}) \leq \mathsf{E}f(T^{\ell}),$$

(i) for any function $f$ that belongs to one of the three classes in Theorem 5.5.2(i,ii,iii), if $(a, b) = (\ell r, \ell r)$, $(\ell r, st)$, $(\ell r, hr)$, respectively;

(ii) for any function $f$ that belongs to one of the three classes in Theorem 5.5.2(i,ii,iii) with the additional property of supermodularity, if $(a, b) = (hr, \ell r)$, $(hr, st)$, $(hr, hr)$, respectively.

**Proof.** We show the results for the sequence $s$, results for the sequence $\ell$ are similarly proved. Consider lateness. Note, following the sequence $s$, $C^s_{(j)} = C^s_j$ for all $j$. For (i), since $f$ is increasing, applying Proposition 5.5.8(i), we have

$$\begin{aligned} \mathsf{E}f(L^s) &= \mathsf{E}f(C^s_{(1)} - D_1, \ldots, C^s_{(n)} - D_n) \\ &\leq \mathsf{E}f(C_{(1)} - D_1, \ldots, C_{(n)} - D_n). \end{aligned} \tag{5.26}$$

Now, since $C_{(1)} \leq \ldots \leq C_{(n)}$ (a.s.), applying Theorem 5.5.2 and viewing $\phi = C + (-D)$, we have

$$\mathsf{E}f(C_{(1)} - D_1, \ldots, C_{(n)} - D_n)$$
$$\leq \quad \mathsf{E}f(C_1 - D_1, \ldots, C_n - D_n) = \mathsf{E}f(L^\pi).$$

For (ii), the proof is the same. Note, however, to claim (5.26), based on Proposition 5.5.8(ii), it is further required that $f$ be supermodular, in addition to the properties in Theorem 5.5.2.

Finally, for tardiness, since $T_j = \max\{L_j, 0\}$ is an increasing and convex function of $L_j$, it will not change the properties (increasingness and supermodularity) of the $\phi$ function above. Hence, the same proof applies to tardiness. $\square$

The additional requirement of supermodularity in Proposition 5.5.9(ii) above virtually restricts the function $f$ to the separable class: When $f(x) = \sum_{i=1}^{n} g(x_i)$, with $g$ increasing and convex in its argument, it is a function that satisfies all the required properties in Proposition 5.5.9(ii). Specifically, it is symmetric and increasing; since it is separable and convex in each variable, it is also (jointly) convex, as well as both submodular and supermodular [cf. Remark 5.5.3(ii)].

### 5.5.3   Connections to Stochastic Convexity and Stochastic Supermodularity

We now turn to considering parameterized families of random variables. That is, we replace the components of the random vectors $X$ and $Y$ in Section 5.2 by parameterized random variables. Then, as we shall demonstrate below, properties (of the parameterized families of random variables) such as stochastic convexity and stochastic supermodularity developed in Section 3.1 and Section 3.2 become crucial in characterizing stochastic majorization. The main results here are Theorems 5.5.10 and 5.5.12. The class of functions in Theorem 5.5.2(ii) remains the defining class here.

**Theorem 5.5.10** $\{X(\theta)\}$ is a parameterized family of independent random variables. Suppose $\theta = (s_i, t_j)$ where $s_i$ and $t_j$ are real or integer valued scalars. Suppose $\{X(s_i, t_j)\}$ is stochastically monotone (i.e., either increasing or decreasing in the two parameters) in the sense of Definition 5.3.1, and stochastically supermodular in the sense of Definition 5.3.12. Consider two sets of parameter values: $s = (s_i)_{i=1}^{n}$ and $t = (t_j)_{j=1}^{n}$. Let $\pi$ and $\sigma$ be two permutations of $\{1, \ldots, n\}$. Let $X(s^\pi, t^\sigma)$ denote the random vector $(X(s_{\pi(i)}, t_{\sigma(i)}))_{i=1}^{n}$. Let $f : \Re^n \mapsto \Re$ be a function that is symmetric, increasing, submodular, and convex in each variable, i.e., $f$ belongs to the class of Theorem 5.5.2(ii). Then,

$$\mathsf{E}f(X(s^\uparrow, t^\downarrow)) \leq \mathsf{E}f(X(s^\pi, t^\sigma)) \leq \mathsf{E}f(X(s^\uparrow, t^\uparrow)).$$

If the increasingness of $f$ is changed to decreasingness, the above also holds if $\{X(s_i, t_j)\}$ is stochastically monotone and submodular.

**Proof.** As before, we only need to consider the two-dimensional case. Suppose $s = (s_1, s_2)$, $t = (t_1, t_2)$, and $s_1 \geq s_2$, $t_1 \geq t_2$. Consider first the case in which both $f$ and $X$ are increasing. Since $X$ is stochastically increasing and supermodular, following Definition 5.3.12, we can generate the replicas

$$\hat{X}_1 \stackrel{d}{=} X(s_1, t_1), \quad \hat{X}_2 \stackrel{d}{=} X(s_1, t_2),$$

$$\hat{X}_3 \stackrel{d}{=} X(s_2, t_1), \quad \hat{X}_4 \stackrel{d}{=} X(s_2, t_2);$$

such that

$$\hat{X}_1 \geq \max\{\hat{X}_2, \hat{X}_3\}, \quad \hat{X}_1 + \hat{X}_4 \geq \hat{X}_2 + \hat{X}_3. \tag{5.27}$$

In addition, independently of the four $\hat{X}$, generate four $\hat{Y}$:

$$\hat{Y}_4 \stackrel{d}{=} X(s_1, t_1), \quad \hat{Y}_3 \stackrel{d}{=} X(s_1, t_2),$$

$$\hat{Y}_2 \stackrel{d}{=} X(s_2, t_1), \quad \hat{Y}_1 \stackrel{d}{=} X(s_2, t_2);$$

such that

$$\hat{Y}_4 \geq \max\{\hat{Y}_2, \hat{Y}_3\}, \quad \hat{Y}_1 + \hat{Y}_4 \geq \hat{Y}_2 + \hat{Y}_3. \tag{5.28}$$

Let $z^i = (\hat{X}_i, \hat{Y}_i)$ for $i = 1, 2, 3, 4$. Then,

$$f(z^1) + f(z^4) \geq f(z^2) + f(z^3)$$

follows directly from (5.24). Taking expectations on both sides, and taking into account the symmetry of $f$, we have

$$\mathsf{E}f(X(s_1, t_1), X(s_2, t_2)) \geq \mathsf{E}f(X(s_1, t_2), X(s_2, t_1)), \tag{5.29}$$

the desired rearrangement result.

When $X$ is decreasing, interchange $\hat{X}_1$ and $\hat{X}_4$, and $\hat{Y}_1$ and $\hat{Y}_4$ in the above construction. When $f$ is decreasing and $X$ submodular, reverse the second inequality in (5.27) and (5.28). The rest still applies. □

The result in Theorem 5.5.10 can also be expressed as a stochastic majorization relation:

$$X(s^\uparrow, t^\downarrow) \leq_{wm} X(s^\pi, t^\sigma) \leq_{wm} X(s^\uparrow, t^\uparrow).$$

Notice the analogy between the above and its deterministic counterpart in (5.21). Here, $X$ plays exactly the same role as $\phi$.

**Example 5.5.11** Consider an assembly operation over a set of components of $m$ different types. Suppose one unit from each type is required to assemble the final product. Suppose the production of each component follows the yield model in Example 5.3.14. Let $n = (n_j)_{j=1}^m$ be the vector of lot sizes (of the components), and $p = (p_j)_{j=1}^m$, the vector of yield ratios. The number of final products assembled is then $\min\{X(n_j, p_j); j = 1, \ldots, m\}$, where $X(n_j, p_j) = \sum_{i=1}^{n_j} Y_i(p_j)$, and $Y_i$ are a set of iid Bernoulli random variables with parameter $p_j$. Since $X$ is stochastically increasing and supermodular, Theorem 5.5.10 applies:

$$\mathsf{E}\min\{X(n^\uparrow, p^\downarrow)\} \geq \mathsf{E}\min\{X(n^\pi, p^\sigma)\} \geq \mathsf{E}\min\{X(n^\uparrow, p^\uparrow)\}. \qquad (5.30)$$

That is, the best arrangement is to assign large lot sizes to low yielding components.

To derive (5.30) from Theorem 5.5.10, use the fact that $\min_i\{x_i\} = -\max_i\{-x_i\}$. Also, all the properties of min are preserved through composition with increasing and concave functions. Hence the inequalities in (5.30) also hold when the expectation is taken over an increasing concave (say, profit) function of the number of assembled products.

Note here all that is required is the supermodularity of $X$ in the lot size and the yield ratio. It is easy to verify that it suffices to have each component increasing in its yield ratio.

Next, following the spirit of Theorem 5.5.10, we develop a notion of stochastic majorization based on the SICX-sp property [cf. Definition 5.3.5].

**Theorem 5.5.12** Let $\{X(\eta)\}$ be a family of independent random variables, parameterized by a real or integer scalar $\eta$. Then, $(\theta_i^1)_{i=1}^n \leq_{wm} (\theta_i^2)_{i=1}^n$ implies

$$\mathsf{E}f(X(\theta_1^1), \ldots, X(\theta_n^1)) \leq \mathsf{E}f(X(\theta_1^2), \ldots, X(\theta_n^2))$$

for all functions $f$ that are increasing, symmetric, submodular, and convex in each variable [i.e., $f$ belongs to the class of (5.3 ii)], provided $\{X(\eta)\} \in$ SICX-sp.

**Proof.** Follow the proof of Theorem 5.5.10, making use of the SICX-sp property in place of the supermodularity. Without loss of generality, suppose

$$\theta_1^2 \geq \theta_1^1 \geq \theta_2^1 \geq \theta_2^2, \quad \theta_1^1 + \theta_2^1 \leq \theta_1^2 + \theta_2^2.$$

Hence, pick four parameter values:

$$\eta_1 = \theta_1^2, \quad \eta_2 = \theta_1^1, \quad \eta_3 = \theta_2^1, \quad \eta_4 = \theta_2^2,$$

and let $\hat{X}_i \overset{\mathrm{d}}{=} X(\eta_i)$, for $i = 1, 2, 3, 4$. Independent of the $\hat{X}_i$, generate four more replicas, $\hat{Y}_i$, in reverse order, i.e., $\hat{Y}_1 \overset{\mathrm{d}}{=} X(\theta_4)$, and so forth. The rest of the proof of Theorem 5.5.10 then follows through. In particular, (5.27) and (5.28) hold, due to the SICX-sp property; and (5.29) takes the form

$$\mathsf{E}f(X(\theta_1^2), X(\theta_2^2)) \geq \mathsf{E}f(X(\theta_1^1), X(\theta_2^1)),$$

which is the desired conclusion. $\square$

The above result can be expressed as the stochastic majorization of two parameterized random vectors,

$$(X(\theta_1^1), ..., X(\theta_n^1)) \leq_{wm} (X(\theta_1^2), ..., X(\theta_n^2)),$$

given the parameter vectors are ordered under weak majorization. Here, the stochastic majorization is in the same sense as in Theorem 5.5.10, namely, a relation that is preserved by functions that symmetric, increasing, submodular, and convex in each variable.

**Example 5.5.13** Continue with the assembly model in Example 5.5.11. Suppose all components have the same lot size, $n$. Since the yield of type $i$, $\{X(n, p_i)\} \in$ SIL-sp in $p_i$ (cf. Example 5.3.8), the total number of assembled products, $\min\{X(n, p_i), i = 1, ..., m\}$, fits into the setting of Theorem 5.5.12. Furthermore, thanks to the min function, the required properties in Theorem 5.5.12 will be preserved by composition with increasing and concave functions. Hence, the number of assembled products will be increased, in the sense of the increasing concave ordering, when the vector of yield ratio, $(p_i)_{i=1}^m$ is decreased in the sense of weak majorization. In other words, as might be expected, with equal lot size it helps when the yield ratio is more uniform among the components.

**Example 5.5.14** Consider a system of $m$ parallel servers, with resequencing of completed jobs — a useful model for assembly systems. Jobs arrive at the system following a Poisson process with rate $\lambda$. Each arrival is independently assigned to a server $i$ with probability $p_i$, $\sum_{i=1}^m p_i = 1$. For each $i$, the service times, $\{S_n^i; n = 1, 2, ...\}$, are iid among the jobs. Once assigned to a server, the job is not allowed to switch servers. Each server serves its own queue following the FCFS discipline. After service completion, the jobs wait in a resequencing area to be released according to their arrival sequence (i.e., a job won't be released until all the jobs that originally arrived before it have been released).

Let $W$ denote the stationary sojourn time in system of each job (including the time spent in the resequencing area). We can write $W$ explicitly as a function of $\theta = (p_i)_{i=1}^m$:

$$W(\theta) = \max\{X_1(p_1), ..., X_m(p_m)\}, \tag{5.31}$$

where $X_i(p_i)$ is the stationary workload in an M/G/1 queue with arrival rate $\lambda p_i$ and service times $\{S_n^i; n = 1, 2, ...\}$. Without loss of generality, assume $\lambda = 1$, and to ensure stationarity, assume $\mathsf{E}(S_n^i) < 1/p_i$ for all $i$.

Now, from standard queueing theory it is known that the stationary workload of an M/G/1 queue with arrival rate $p$ can be expressed as (omitting the script $i$)

$$X(p) \stackrel{\mathrm{d}}{=} \sum_{k=1}^{N(p)} R_k,$$

where $R_k$ is a set of iid random variables following the residual service time distribution [specifically, the density function $f_R(x) = P(S_n > x)/\mathsf{E}(S_n)$]; $N(p)$ follows a geometric distribution with parameter $1 - p$. From Example 5.3.9, we know $\{N(p)\} \in$ SICX-sp, and hence $\{X(p)\} \in$ SICX-sp as well.

When all the $m$ servers are identical, i.e., all the service times are iid, (5.31) can be written as

$$W(\theta) = \max\{X(p_1), \dots, X(p_m)\}.$$

Hence, Theorem 5.5.12 applies. That is, for any two job assignment schemes, indexed by the superscripts 1 and 2, if $\theta^1 \leq_m \theta^2$, then $W(\theta^1) \leq_{icx} W(\theta^2)$. (Note, for any increasing and convex function $g$, $g \circ \max$ still has all the required properties in Theorem 5.5.12, and hence the convex ordering.)

## 5.6   Notes

Introductory materials on likelihood ratio, hazard rate, stochastic and convex orderings can be found in Ross [26] (Chapter 8). Stoyan [29] is a more detailed reference on stochastic comparisons, including many queueing applications. Most of the materials in this section, in particular the functional characterization of likelihood ratio and hazard rate orderings, are from Shanthikumar and Yao [26]. Theorem 5.2.3 was partially known before, see Brown and Solomon [1] and Proposition 8.4.2 (p. 268) of [26].

The *sp* notion of stochastic convexity (Definition 5.3.4) was developed in Shaked and Shanthikumar [16, 17, 18], along with other notions of stochastic convexity. For instance, the *st* version, SICX-st, is defined as follows: $\{X(\theta)\}$ is stochastically increasing and convex in the *st* sense if $\mathsf{E}f[X(\theta)]$ is increasing and convex in $\theta$ for any increasing function $f$. (The convexity of $f$ is *not* required here.) It can be shown that SICX-st is equivalent to the distribution function of $X(\theta)$, $F(x, \theta)$, being decreasing and concave in $\theta$ (or $\bar{F} = 1 - F$ increasing and convex). It can also be shown that SICX-st $\Rightarrow$ SICX-sp. But SICX-st and SSICX (which also implies SICX-sp) do not imply each other. For instance, the family of degenerate random variables, $\{X(\theta) \equiv \theta\}$ satisfies SSICX but not SICX-st. On the other hand, $F(x, \theta)$ decreasing and concave in $\theta$ need not satisfy the conditions, in Remark 5.3.7, for SSICX.

The notion of strong stochastic convexity (Definition 5.3.5) is due to Shanthikumar and Yao [27]. The characterization of the spatial and temporal behavior of Markov chains and its applications in Section 3.3 are from Shanthikumar and Yao [25, 28]. The application to manufacturing processes with trial runs in Section 3.4 is from Gallego, Yao and Moon [8].

The notion of directional convexity and its properties in Definition 5.3.15 and Lemma 5.3.16 were developed in [18], including the stochastic version (see Definition 5.3.18). Although in this chapter we did not elaborate on *stochastic* directional convexity, it appears to be particularly useful in characterizing the spatial-temporal behavior of stochastic processes, for instance in strengthening the results in Section 3.3. Refer to [18] and Chang et al [3, 4] for a variety of applications along this line.

Marshall and Olkin [11] is a standard reference for majorization and arrangement orderings, as well as the related functional classes, such as Schur convex and arrangement increasing functions. The results in Theorems 5.4.2 and 5.4.4, as well as the queueing network results in Example 5.4.9 and Proposition 5.4.10, are from [27]. The notion of equilibrium rate plays an important role in queueing networks (See Chapter 1 for a more detailed discussion.) It was first introduced in Shanthikumar and Yao [21, 22], and applied in a variety of settings, including Shanthikumar [20] and Shanthikumar and Yao [24].

Theorem 5.5.2, its proof, and the scheduling applications in Example 5.5.7 and Propositions 5.5.8 and 5.5.9, first appeared in Chang and Yao [5], which includes many more examples that apply Theorem 5.5.2 to stochastic scheduling. (Also see Righter [13].) The class of functions (in Theorem 5.5.2(ii)) that are symmetric, submodular, and convex in each variable first appeared in Chang [2], where it was denoted $\mathbf{C}_5$, and was shown to be a subclass of Schur convex functions (cf. Lemma 5.5.4 and Remark 5.5.5). In [2] the main motivation is to develop a new notion of stochastic majorization that is weaker (and hence more broadly applicable) than the earlier, standard notion (see [11]), of which the defining class is Schur convex functions.

In the parametric case, Theorems 5.5.12 and 5.5.10 are results of combining stochastic majorization with stochastic convexity and stochastic supermodularity. Note that Theorem 5.5.12 is just one way to generate stochastic majorization, in the parametric case, via stochastic convexity. Specifically, it is based on the *sp* notion of stochastic convexity (Definition 5.3.4). It is possible to develop different versions of stochastic majorization, based on other notions of stochastic convexity. These different versions of stochastic majorization and their applications in reliability and resource allocation have recently appeared in Liyanage and Shanthikumar [10] and in Shaked and Shanthikumar [19]. For instance, one such version in [10] is based on the *st* notion of stochastic convexity, which, as we mentioned above, is stronger than the *sp* notion. The defining class for the resulting stochastic majorization is composed of functions that are symmetric, increasing, and submodular, but not necessarily convex in each variable. In other words, it *includes* $\mathbf{C}_5$ as a subclass. (However, it does not appear to have a subset relationship with the class of Schur convex functions.) One advantage of this class is that it is preserved under composition with functions that are increasing and convex. Hence the corresponding stochastic majorization can be expressed in terms of the increasing convex ordering. [In this regard, it is similar to the functional class in Theorem 5.5.2(iii).] Based on the *st* notion of stochastic convexity, in [10] an example similar to Example

5.5.14 is shown to satisfy the corresponding stronger version of stochastic majorization.

*Acknowledgments:* George Shanthikumar is supported in part by NSF grant DDM-91-13008 and by a Sloan Foundation Grant for the study on "Competitive Semiconductor Manufacturing". David Yao is supported in part by NSF grants DDM-91-08540 and MSS-92-16490.

## 5.7    References

[1] Brown, M. and Solomon, H. 1973. Optimal Issuing Policies under Stochastic Field Lives. *Journal of Applied Probability,* **10**, 761-768.

[2] Chang, C.S. 1990. A New Ordering for Stochastic Majorization: Theory and Applications. *Advances in Applied Probability,* **24**, 604-634.

[3] Chang, C.S., Chao, X.L. and Pinedo, M. 1991. Monotonicity Results for Queues with Doubly Stochastic Poisson Arrivals: Ross's Conjecture. *Advances in Applied Probability,* **23**, 210-228.

[4] Chang, C.S., Chao, X.L., Pinedo, M. and Shanthikumar, J.G. 1991. Stochastic Convexity for Multidimensional Process and Its Applications. *IEEE Transactions on Automatic Control,* **36**, 1347-1355.

[5] Chang, C.S. and Yao, D.D. 1990. Rearrangement, Majorization, and Stochastic Scheduling. *Mathematics of Operations Research,* **18**, 658-684.

[6] Day, P.W. 1972. Rearrangement Inequalities. *Canadian Journal of Mathematics,* **24**, 930-943.

[7] Fox, B. 1966. Discrete Optimization via Marginal Analysis. *Management Science,* **13**, 210-216.

[8] Gallego, G., Yao, D.D. and Moon, I. 1993. Optimal Control of a Manufacturing Process with Trial Runs. *Management Science,* **39**, 1499-1505.

[9] Hardy, G.H., Littlewood, J.E. and Polya, G. 1952. *Inequalities.* Cambridge U. Press, London.

[10] Liyanage, L. and Shanthikumar, J.G. 1992. Allocation through Stochastic Schur Convexity and Stochastic Arrangement Increasingness. In: *Stochastic Inequalities,* M. Shaked and Y.L. Tong (eds.), IMS Lecture Notes/Monographs Series, **22**, 253-273.

[11] Marshall, A.W. and Olkin, I. 1979. *Inequalities: Theory of Majorization and Its Applications.* Academic Press, New York.

[12] Pinedo, M. and Weber, R.R. 1984. Inequalities and Bounds in Stochastic Shop Scheduling. *SIAM Journal of Applied Mathematics,* **44**, 869-879.

[13] Righter, R. 1992. Scheduling. In: *Stochastic Orders,* M. Shaked and J.G. Shanthikumar (eds.), to appear.

[14] Rockafellar, R.T. 1970. *Convex Analysis.* Princeton U. Press, Princeton, N.J.

[15] Ross, S.M. 1983. *Stochastic Processes.* Wiley, New York.

[16] Shaked, M. and Shanthikumar, J.G. 1988. Stochastic Convexity and Its Applications. *Advances in Applied Probability,* **20**, 427-446.

[17] Shaked, M. and Shanthikumar, J.G. 1990. Convexity of a Set of Stochastically Ordered Random Variables. *Advances in Applied Probability,* **22**, 160-167.

[18] Shaked, M. and Shanthikumar, J.G. 1990. Parametric Stochastic Convexity and Concavity of Stochastic Processes. *Ann. Inst. Statist. Math.,* **42**, 509-531.

[19] Shaked, M. and Shanthikumar, J.G. 1992. Optimal Allocation of Resources to Nodes of Parallel and Series Systems. *Advances in Applied Probability,* **24**, 894-914.

[20] Shanthikumar, J.G. 1987. Stochastic Majorization of Random Variables with Propotional Equilibrium Rates. *Advances in Applied Probability,* **19**, 854-872.

[21] Shanthikumar, J.G. and Yao, D.D. 1986. The Preservation of Likelihood Ratio Ordering under Convolution. *Stochastic Processes and Their Applications,* **23**, 259-267.

[22] Shanthikumar, J.G. and Yao, D.D. 1986. The Effect of Increasing Service Rates in Closed Queueing Networks. *Journal of Applied Probability,* **23**, 474-483.

[23] Shanthikumar, J.G. and Yao, D.D. 1988. On Server Allocation in Multiple-Center Manufacturing Systems. *Operations Research,* **36**, 333-342.

[24] Shanthikumar, J.G. and Yao, D.D. 1988. Second-Order Properties of the Throughput in a Closed Queueing Network. *Mathematics of Operations Research,* **13**, 524-534.

[25] Shanthikumar, J.G. and Yao, D.D. 1989. Second Order Stochastic Properties in Queueing Systems. *Proceedings of IEEE,* **77**(1), 162-170.

[26] Shanthikumar, J.G. and Yao, D.D. 1991. Bivariate Characterization of Some Stochastic Order Relations. *Advances in Applied Probability*, **23**, 642-659.

[27] Shanthikumar, J.G. and Yao, D.D. 1991. Strong Stochastic Convexity: Closure Properties and Applications. *Journal of Applied Probability*, **28** (1991), 131-145.

[28] Shanthikumar, J.G. and Yao, D.D. 1992. Spatiotemporal Convexity of Stochastic Processes and Applications. *Probability in the Engineering and Information Sciences*, **6**, 1-16.

[29] Stoyan, D. 1983. *Comparison Methods for Queues and Other Stochastic Models*. Wiley, New York.

[30] Topkis, D.M. 1978. Minimizing a Submodular Function on a Lattice. *Operations Research*, **26**, 305-321.

# 6
# Perturbation Analysis of Production Networks

## Paul Glasserman

ABSTRACT This chapter treats the problem of evaluating the sensitivity of performance measures to changes in system parameters for a class of stochastic models. The technique presented, called perturbation analysis, evaluates sensitivities from sample paths, based either on a simulation or on real data.

The chapter begins with an overview, based on a single-machine model. It proceeds to address underlying theoretical issues and then examines a variety of examples of production networks. It concludes with a discussion of issues arising in the estimation of steady-state sensitivities.

## 6.1 Introduction

Purified widget gas is separated from naturally occurring widget dioxide in a relatively simple industrial process. The widget dioxide is fed into a tank, from which it is drawn into a reactor; purified gas flows out of the reactor into a second tank for intermediate storage. A knob on the operator's control panel controls the flow from the first tank into the reactor. The gas levels in both the input and output tanks affect the rate of purification. So, the process is described by a differential equation

$$\dot{x}(t,\theta) = f(x(t,\theta), y(t,\theta)), \qquad (6.1)$$

where $x$ is the level of widget gas in the second tank, $y$ is the level of widget dioxide in the first tank, and $\theta$ is the setting of the operator's knob.

Fundamental to controlling this process is understanding what happens when the operator turns the knob. To investigate this, we examine the sensitivity of $x(t,\theta)$ to $\theta$: we differentiate, obtaining a second differential equation

$$\partial_\theta \dot{x}(t,\theta) = \partial_x f \cdot \partial_\theta x(t,\theta) + \partial_y f \cdot \partial_\theta y(t,\theta). \qquad (6.2)$$

The level of widget gas at time $t$ is

$$x(t,\theta) = x(0,\theta) + \int_0^t \dot{x}(s,\theta)\, ds;$$

its sensitivity to $\theta$ is given by

$$\partial_\theta x(t,\theta) = \partial_\theta x(0,\theta) + \int_0^t \partial_\theta \dot{x}(s,\theta)\, ds.$$

In the solid state, individual widgets are stamped out of widget blanks. Blanks are loaded through a chute onto an input pallet, from which they pass one at a time through the stamping machine. A knob on the machine controls its operation. Let $u_n$ be the time between the arrival to the pallet of the $(n-1)$-st and $n$-th blanks and let $s_n(\theta)$ be the time to stamp the $n$-th blank when the knob is set to $\theta$. Then the interval $w_n$ from the time the $n$-th blank arrives at the pallet to the time it passes under the stamp satisfies a recursion

$$w_n(\theta) = \phi(w_{n-1}(\theta), u_{n-1}, s_{n-1}(\theta)),$$

meaning that the $n$-th such interval is completely determined by the $(n-1)$-st and by the preceding interarrival and stamping times.

Fundamental to controlling this system is understanding what happens when an operator turns the knob on the machine. To investigate this, we once again compute derivatives:

$$\partial_\theta w_n(\theta) = \partial_w \phi \cdot \partial_\theta w_{n-1}(\theta) + \partial_s \phi \cdot \partial_\theta s_{n-1}(\theta). \tag{6.3}$$

Generally, the operation of the machine is somewhat variable, and so is the loading of blanks. We model this variability by replacing the deterministic quantities $w_n$, $u_n$, $s_n$ with random variables $W_n$, $U_n$, $S_n$. In this case, (6.3) becomes a recursion for derivatives of random variables.

*Perturbation analysis*, as the term is used here, is the study of how parameters of a stochastic system influence performance of the system. In more specific terms, it is a method for computing and validating expressions like (6.3) when applied to random variables. Two important features distinguish perturbation analysis from the more classical study of (6.2). One is the central role played by variability, modeled as randomness. The other, even more important, is the discrete nature of processes like that described around (6.3); indeed, these now go by the name of *discrete-event systems*. It is clear that $\{W_n(\theta), n \geq 0\}$ evolves in discrete time and $\{x(t,\theta), t \geq 0\}$ in continuous time, but the distinction goes deeper than that. The *dynamics* of the stamping process are fundamentally discrete. The system is driven by the occurrence of *events*—the arrival of blanks and the initiation and completion of stamping of each blank—at discrete time instants. In contrast, the gas-purification system is inherently continuous.

From a mathematical viewpoint, these considerations translate to a rather different analysis for (6.3) than would be available for (6.2). The introduction of randomness calls for a statistical interpretation and analysis of the derivatives $\{W_n'(\theta), n \geq 0\}$. The presence of discrete dynamics means that

the smoothness conditions one could usually expect $f$ in (6.1) to satisfy—
say, continuous differentiability—are entirely unreasonable for $\phi$. At best,
we can expect $\phi$ to be piecewise smooth, and this complicates the analysis
of derivatives. This chapter develops the necessary theory to accomodate
these features and illustrates the theory with a variety of examples.

We keep this introduction short because Section 2 of this chapter gives
a more detailed overview of perturbation analysis as applied to a simple
model with a single machine. Section 3 gives background on derivatives of
random functions and investigates differentiation of seemingly nondifferen-
tiable dynamics. Using this apparatus, Section 4 re-examines the single-
machine model. Section 5 details the application of perturbation analysis
to a variety of production networks, including a serial line, systems with
finite buffers, a line with kanban control, and systems with defects, among
others. Section 6 extends the analysis for finite horizons to steady state.
We make some concluding remarks in Section 7.

Perturbation analysis originates in Ho, Eyler, and Chien [20], the parametric case studied here in Ho and Cao [21] and Suri and Zazanis [33]. The
book by Ho and Cao [22] gives a comprehensive treatment and casts perturbation analysis in the more general setting of the analysis of discrete event
systems. The book by Glasserman [14] stresses theoretical underpinnings
of the subject. The presentation here is significantly different from that in
[14] (or [22]), the most notable contrast being the prominence given here
to explicit recursions. Except for the exposition, not much of what is here
is new. To limit interruptions of the general discussion, we have collected
references in notes at the end of the chapter.

A comment on terminology: For brevity, we use the term "perturbation
analysis" to refer specifically to what is usually called "*infinitesimal* perturbation analysis." References to other perturbation analysis techniques
are provided in the notes.

# 6.2   Overview Through the Single-Machine Model

In order that technical issues not obscure fundamental intuitive ideas,
in this section we give an informal introduction to perturbation analysis through a simple model. We postpone mathematical detail and precise
statements of results to later sections.

Our illustrative example is a model of a single facility. At the level we consider, it makes no difference whether the facility is a machine forming one
part of a larger production network or an entire factory. For convenience,
we call it a machine. The machine is operated in response to requests for
its output. The requests may be generated by a production plan, by other
machines that use the output, or by customer demands, for example. If,
when a request is received, the machine is idle, processing begins imme-

diately; otherwise, the request is queued with any other pending requests. Each request constitutes a *job*. Jobs are processed in the order they arrive.

## The Waiting Times

A critical measure of the performance of this system is the time taken to complete a job. The processing time itself is generally known, at least approximately; in any case, it is unavoidable. Thus, it makes sense to examine the waiting time—the time between the arrival of a request and the initiation of processing for that request.

Let $\{U_n, n \geq 0\}$ be the times between arrivals: the $(n+1)$-st request arrives $U_n$ time units after the $n$-th. A 0-th job arrives at time zero. For $n \geq 0$, let $S_n$ be the work required to complete the $n$-th job. Our machine performs work at a rate of $1/\theta$ work units per time unit, so a work requirement of $s$ is completed in $\theta s$ time units. For now, the $S_n$'s and $U_n$'s are just sequences of (nonnegative) numbers; in particular, we have not made any statistical assumptions about them. If we let $\{W_n, n \geq 0\}$ be the sequence of waiting times, then $W_0 = 0$ and subsequent waiting times follow the Lindley recursion

$$W_{n+1} = \max(0, W_n + \theta S_n - U_n). \tag{6.4}$$

We now ask, How do the waiting times change with $\theta$? Clearly, decreasing $\theta$ (and thereby speeding up the machine) should decrease the waiting times. Can this effect be quantified? How sensitive are the $W_n$'s to changes in $\theta$?

To stress the dependence on the parameter $\theta$, let us write the waiting times as $W(\theta) = \{W_n(\theta), n \geq 0\}$ when the machine runs at rate $1/\theta$. To quantify sensitivity, we compute derivatives. Let us first rewrite (6.4) as

$$W_{n+1}(\theta) = \begin{cases} W_n(\theta) + \theta S_n - U_n, & \text{if } W_n(\theta) + \theta S_n - U_n > 0; \\ 0, & \text{otherwise.} \end{cases} \tag{6.5}$$

Let $W'_n(\theta)$ denote the derivative with respect to $\theta$ of the $n$-th waiting time with $S = \{S_n, n \geq 0\}$ and $U = \{U_n, n \geq 0\}$ held fixed. Since the 0-th job never waits, $W'_0(\theta) = 0$ for all $\theta$. Now consider the two cases in (6.5). So long as $W_n(\theta) + \theta S_n - U_n \neq 0$, a sufficiently small change in $\theta$ does not change which of the two cases applies. For all sufficiently small $h$, we have

$$W_{n+1}(\theta+h) = \begin{cases} W_n(\theta+h) + (\theta+h)S_n - U_n, & \text{if } W_n(\theta) + \theta S_n - U_n > 0; \\ 0, & \text{otherwise;} \end{cases}$$

see Figure 1. Thus, we find that the waiting-time derivatives satisfy

$$W'_{n+1}(\theta) = \begin{cases} W'_n(\theta) + S_n, & \text{if } W_n(\theta) + \theta S_n - U_n > 0; \\ 0, & \text{otherwise.} \end{cases} \tag{6.6}$$

We have ignored the case $W_n(\theta) + \theta S_n - U_n = 0$; special cases like this one arise in all our examples and applications. Part of the purpose of Section 3

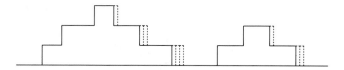

FIGURE 1. How the evolution of the number of waiting jobs changes under a small increase in $\theta$. Each job takes longer to process, delaying the service initiation of subsequent jobs. Under a sufficiently small change in $\theta$, the order of arrivals and departures is unchanged.

is to justify ignoring them and to legitimize the seemingly cavalier passage from (6.5) to (6.6).

What do these derivatives tell us? If we faced the same sequence of service and interarrival times with a different $\theta$, then $W_n'(\theta)$ predicts the change in $W_n$ under a small parameter change. Instead of individual waiting times, we might examine averaged waiting times

$$\overline{W}_n(\theta) = (W_1(\theta) + \cdots + W_n(\theta))/n, \quad n > 0,$$

and their derivatives

$$\overline{W}_n'(\theta) = (W_1'(\theta) + \cdots + W_n'(\theta))/n, \quad n > 0.$$

This should better reflect overall sensitivity to $\theta$ than would any individual waiting-time derivative. Even so, we are unlikely to face again exactly the same service and interarrival times. The derivatives we compute are only useful if they reflect sensitivity to $\theta$ of *expected* performance.

At this point, we need to impose some statistical assumptions. To make these as simple as possible, suppose $S$ and $U$ are independent sequences of i.i.d. (independent and identically distributed) nonnegative random variables. So long as $E[S_0]$ is finite, every $W_n(\theta)$, $n \geq 0$ has finite expectation for all $\theta$. Measure the performance of our process by $E[\overline{W}_n(\theta)]$ for some (typically large) $n$. The sensitivity of performance is then given by the derivative $E[\overline{W}_n(\theta)]'$. Averaging i.i.d. copies of $\overline{W}_n'(\theta)$ (generated by i.i.d. copies of $S$ and $U$) we obtain, in the limit, $E[\overline{W}_n'(\theta)]$, by the strong law of large numbers. Thus, we have a systematic way of computing $E[\overline{W}_n'(\theta)]$; but what we would really like to know is $E[\overline{W}_n(\theta)]'$. We must investigate whether or not

$$E[\overline{W}_n'(\theta)] = E[\overline{W}_n(\theta)]'. \tag{6.7}$$

Each $W_i(\theta)$ is a sum of terms $\theta S_j - U_j$ with $j$ ranging over a subset of $\{0, \ldots, i\}$. In fact, if we let

$$l_i(\theta) = \max\{0 \leq j \leq i : W_j(\theta) = 0\},$$

then unraveling (6.4) yields

$$W_i(\theta) = \sum_{j=l_i(\theta)}^{i-1} \theta S_j - U_j,$$

with empty sums equal to zero by convention. From this we get, for any $h > -\theta$, the bound

$$|W_i(\theta + h) - W_i(\theta)| \le h \sum_{j=0}^{i-1} S_j$$

and therefore also

$$|\overline{W}_n(\theta + h) - \overline{W}_n(\theta)| \le h \sum_{j=0}^{n-1} S_j.$$

(Indeed, the realizations of $W_n(\cdot)$ and $\overline{W}_n(\cdot)$ are of the type to be illustrated in Figure 3.) If $S_0$ has finite expectation, then the right side is an integrable bound on the left side. Dividing by $h$, letting $h \to 0$ and invoking the dominated convergence theorem (see Section 3.1) we obtain

$$\begin{aligned} \mathsf{E}[\overline{W}'_n(\theta)] &= \mathsf{E}[\lim_{h \to 0} h^{-1}\{\overline{W}_n(\theta + h) - \overline{W}_n(\theta)\}] \\ &= \lim_{h \to 0} h^{-1}\mathsf{E}[\overline{W}_n(\theta + h) - \overline{W}_n(\theta)] \\ &= \mathsf{E}[\overline{W}_n(\theta)]'. \end{aligned}$$

This validates $\overline{W}'_n(\theta)$ as an estimate of $\mathsf{E}[\overline{W}_n(\theta)]'$. In later sections, we allow a more general dependence on the parameter: the service times and interarrival times themselves will be fairly arbitrary functions of $\theta$. This will make verification of (6.7) a bit more involved without altering the essence of the argument above.

In Section 6, we address the issue of *steady-state* derivative estimation. If $\theta\mathsf{E}[S_0] < \mathsf{E}[U_0]$, then the distribution of $W_n(\theta)$ has a limit as $n \to \infty$. If $w(\theta)$ is the mean of this limiting distribution—i.e., the steady-state mean waiting time—then

$$\lim_{n \to \infty} n^{-1} \sum_{i=1}^{n} W'_i(\theta) = w'(\theta). \tag{6.8}$$

The proof of (6.8) is not difficult but requires some background results, so we postpone it.

### The Length of the Queue

When arrivals to our machine are orders placed by customers, the waiting times examined above measure the responsiveness of the machine; the average wait is one measure of the level of service provided to customers. Suppose, however, that the machine is just one stage in a larger production process. Arrivals now represent parts processed at upstream stages, requiring processing at our machine before moving on to downstream stages. In this setting, we are also interested in the *work-in-process inventory* at our machine; that is, the number of parts waiting in the queue.

For all $t \geq 0$, let $A_t(\theta)$ and $D_t(\theta)$ be, respectively, the number of arrivals and the number of departures in the interval $[0, t]$. Suppose the first interarrival time begins at zero, but drop the convention that there is a 0-th arrival at time zero. Then we have

$$A_t(\theta) = \sup\{n \geq 0 : U_0 + \cdots + U_{n-1} \leq t\},$$

and

$$D_t(\theta) = \sup\{n \geq 0 : U_0 + \cdots + U_{n-1} + W_n(\theta) + \theta S_n \leq t\}.$$

The number of arrivals does not depend on $\theta$; it would if the $U_n$'s did, so we still use the argument $\theta$. Let $Q_t(\theta)$ denote the number of parts waiting or in service at time $t$, $t \geq 0$; then, in general,

$$Q_t(\theta) = Q_0(\theta) + A_t(\theta) - D_t(\theta) \tag{6.9}$$

for all $t \geq 0$. In our setting, $Q_0(\theta) = 0$ for all $\theta$. Equation (6.9) plays a role somewhat analogous to that of the Lindley recursion (6.4) for the waiting times. However, differentiating both sides of (6.9) yields only $0 = 0$ because each of the terms is integer-valued. A different approach is needed if we are to study the sensitivity to $\theta$ of the queue-length process.

The key is to look at the instants when the queue length changes. For $n \geq 1$, define

$$T_{a,n}(\theta) = U_0 + \cdots + U_{n-1}$$

and

$$T_{d,n}(\theta) = T_{a,n}(\theta) + W_n(\theta) + \theta S_n;$$

$T_{a,n}(\theta)$ is the the epoch of the $n$-th arrival and $T_{d,n}(\theta)$ that of the $n$-th departure. Repeatedly substituting for $W_n(\theta)$, or else directly from the dynamics of the system, we could write also

$$T_{d,n}(\theta) = \theta S_n + \max\{T_{a,n}(\theta), T_{d,n-1}(\theta)\}.$$

The second term on the right is the instant the $n$-th part enters service: when it arrives or when the previous part departs, whichever comes later.

Taking derivatives, we get $T'_{a,n}(\theta) = 0$ for all $n$ (the arrival times do not depend on $\theta$), and, much as in (6.6),

$$T'_{d,n}(\theta) = \begin{cases} S_n, & \text{if } T_{a,n}(\theta) \geq T_{d,n-1}(\theta); \\ S_n + T'_{d,n-1}(\theta), & \text{otherwise.} \end{cases}$$

Again, the case $T_{a,n}(\theta) = T_{d,n-1}(\theta)$ requires some care.

We use the derivatives of the arrival and departure epochs to evaluate the derivative of the time-averaged queue length

$$\overline{Q}_t(\theta) = t^{-1} \int_0^t Q_s(\theta)\,ds.$$

From (6.9) we confirm that the queue changes size only at arrivals or departures. Let $\{\tau_n, n \geq 1\}$ be the epochs of state transitions of the queue-length process, due either to arrivals or departures. Then, with

$$N_t(\theta) = A_t(\theta) + D_t(\theta),$$

we have for $n = 1, 2, \ldots$,

$$\tau_n(\theta) = \inf\{t \geq 0 : N_t(\theta) \geq n\}.$$

Fix $\tau_0(\theta) = 0$ for all $\theta$. During intervals $[\tau_i, \tau_{i+1})$, the queue length remains constant; thus,

$$\overline{Q}_t(\theta) = t^{-1}\left(\sum_{i=0}^{N_t(\theta)-1} Q_{\tau_i(\theta)}(\theta)[\tau_{i+1}(\theta) - \tau_i(\theta)] + Q_t(\theta)[t - \tau_{N_t(\theta)}]\right).$$
(6.10)

We now take derivatives. Each summand in (6.10) is a product of two factors. When we differentiate, each summand therefore generates two terms. However, in each case the first factor is a queue length. Each $Q_{\tau_i}$ and $Q_t$ is integer-valued, so its derivative is zero and only the second term remains. Thus,

$$\overline{Q}'_t(\theta) = t^{-1}\left(\sum_{i=0}^{N_t(\theta)-1} Q_{\tau_i(\theta)}(\theta)[\tau'_{i+1}(\theta) - \tau'_i(\theta)] + Q_t(\theta)[-\tau'_{N_t(\theta)}(\theta)]\right).$$
(6.11)

This is the limiting case of the perturbations illustrated in Figure 1.

How do we compute the derivatives $\tau'_i(\theta)$ needed for this expressions? If $\tau_i(\theta) = T_{d,j}(\theta)$ (the $i$-th transition occurs at the $j$-th departure) then $\tau'_i(\theta) = T'_{d,j}(\theta)$. If $\tau_i(\theta) = T_{a,j}(\theta)$ (the $i$-th transition occurs at the $j$-th arrival) then $\tau'_i(\theta) = T'_{a,j}(\theta)$, and we have already seen how $T'_{d,j}(\theta)$ and $T'_{a,j}(\theta)$ are computed. Here, too, some care is needed when arrivals and departures occur simultaneously, since then $\tau'_i(\theta)$ is not determined and may not be defined.

It remains to connect the derivative $\overline{Q}'_t(\theta)$ and the sensitivity of the *expected* average queue length $\mathsf{E}[\overline{Q}_t(\theta)]$. For this, we bound $|\overline{Q}_t(\theta + h) - \overline{Q}_t(\theta)|$. The service time of the $n$-th part increases by $hS_n$; but an increase beyond $ht/\theta$ does not affect the increment in $\overline{Q}_t$ because a service time greater than $t$ will not be completed in $[0, t]$. Each service-time increment

$\Delta$ delays subsequent parts by at most $\Delta$ and keeps the queue one unit higher for an interval of length at most $A_t\Delta$. Any such increment therefore contributes at most $t^{-1}(A_t \cdot \Delta)$ to the change in $\overline{Q}_t$. In total, there are $A_t$ such increments in $[0, t]$, so

$$|\overline{Q}_t(\theta + h) - \overline{Q}_t(\theta)| \leq t^{-1}(A_t \cdot ht/\theta) \cdot A_t = A_t^2 h/\theta.$$

It now follows from the dominated convergence theorem that $\mathsf{E}[\overline{Q}_t'(\theta)] = \mathsf{E}[\overline{Q}_t(\theta)]'$, provided that $\mathsf{E}[A_t^2] < \infty$. When interarrival times are i.i.d., a sufficient condition for this is that the interarrival times not be identically zero.

## The Workload

The queue length measures the work-in-process inventory in number of parts. If we consider instead the time needed to process all waiting parts, we obtain the workload. Measure work in fixed time units independent of $\theta$. In this case, the total work brought to the machine in $[0, t]$ is

$$\theta \sum_{i=1}^{A_t(\theta)} S_i.$$

So long as there is work in the system, the workload decreases at unit rate, jumping up by $\theta S_n$ at the epoch of the $n$-th arrival. Let $V_t(\theta)$, $t \geq 0$ be the work in the system at time $t$. The $n$-th waiting time $W_n(\theta)$ equals $V_t(\theta)$ at $t = T_{a,n}^-(\theta)$, and when either $V_t(\theta)$ or $Q_t(\theta)$ is zero, so is the other.

Varying $\theta$ changes the evolution of $\{V_t(\theta), t \geq 0\}$ at the arrival epochs: increasing $\theta$ to $\theta + h$ increases the $n$-th jump from $\theta S_n$ to $(\theta + h)S_n$. The difference $V_t(\theta + h) - V_t(\theta)$ remains constant between jumps, so long as $V_t(\theta) > 0$. Thus, if we let $\theta \cdot B_t(\theta)$ be the total work brought by time $t$ during a busy period that contains $t$, we have

$$V_t(\theta + h) - V_t(\theta) = \begin{cases} hB_t(\theta), & \text{if } V_t(\theta) > 0; \\ 0, & \text{if } V_t(\theta + h) = V_t(\theta) = 0. \end{cases}$$

The case $V_t(\theta + h) > 0 = V_t(\theta)$ is negligible as $h \to 0$. Dividing by $h$ and passing to the limit we obtain $V_t'(\theta) = B_t(\theta)$. See Figure 2.

With

$$\overline{V}_t(\theta) = t^{-1} \int_0^t V_s(\theta)\, ds$$

and $\overline{B}_t(\theta)$ similarly defined, we have $\overline{V}_t'(\theta) = \overline{B}_t(\theta)$. The difference $|\overline{V}_t(\theta + h) - \overline{V}_t(\theta)|$ is maximized if all work brought in during $[0, t]$ actually arrives at time zero. In this case, $V_0(\theta + h) = (\theta + h)V_0(\theta)/\theta$ and the difference between the two workload processes does not increase with time. Thus,

$$|\overline{V}_t(\theta + h) - \overline{V}_t(\theta)| \leq h \cdot \sum_{i=1}^{A_t(\theta)} S_i.$$

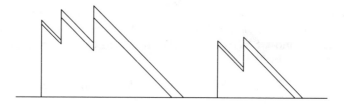

FIGURE 2. The workload processes $V_t(\theta)$ and $V_t(\theta + h)$ corresponding to the queue-length processes in Figure 1.

If $\mathsf{E}[A_t(\theta)] < \infty$ and $\mathsf{E}[S_1] < \infty$ then the right side is integrable (by Wald's identity) and the dominated convergence theorem gives $\mathsf{E}[\overline{V}'_t(\theta)] = \mathsf{E}[\overline{V}_t(\theta)]'$.

## Summary

Our examination of the waiting times and the queue length in this simple example suggests the following categories of processes and techniques:

(i) Discrete time, continuous state space: For each fixed time $n$, examine the change in state under a parameter perturbation. Compute the derivative at each $n$.

(ii) Continuous time, discrete state space: For each state, examine the change in the time of entry to and exit from that state under a parameter perturbation. Compute the derivative of a time average of the process.

The waiting-time process is an example of (i), the queue-length process an example of (ii). In both cases, we found recursive formulas for derivatives that can be computed from observational data. Bounding the increment of a performance measure led to verification that the expectation of the derivative is the derivative of the expectation.

The workload process is intermediate to (i) and (ii): it evolves in continuous time on a continuous state space, but between (random) jumps its evolution is completely deterministic. Once the sensitivity of the waiting times and the queue length have been analyzed, it is relatively straightforward to extend the analysis to the workload, so we will not consider it further. Our main objective in subsequent sections is to extend the foregoing example to more general systems and more general parameter dependence. Carrying this out requires first a more careful look at differentiation and allied concepts.

## 6.3   Differentiation

This section covers three related topics. We first consider, in a fairly abstract way, derivatives of random functions and their connection to derivatives of expectations. We then examine differentiability of *inputs* to production systems, primarily processing times and interarrival times. Finally, we look at how differentiability in inputs carries over to differentiability of outputs.

### 6.3.1   Classes of Random Functions

Differentiability is a local phenomenon, and we could discuss derivatives at a point $\theta$ purely in terms of conditions near $\theta$. However, rather than attach "in a neighborhood of $\theta$" to every condition, we enforce hypotheses throughout a fixed interval $[a, b]$. Our results then hold at all points in this interval.

All our random variables and stochastic processes are defined on a probability space $(\Omega, \mathcal{F}, P)$. An $\mathbf{R}^d$-valued random function on $[a, b]$ is a (measurable) mapping from $\Omega \times [a, b]$ to $\mathbf{R}^d$. Denote by $\mathcal{M}$ the set of all such mappings. If $X \in \mathcal{M}$, we write $X(\theta)$ for its value at $\theta$, omitting the argument $\omega$. The functions on $[a, b]$ obtained by fixing a value of $\omega$ are the *sample functions* of $X$. As usual, we say that an event holds almost surely (a.s.) if it holds with probability one. A property holds almost everywhere (a.e.) on $[a, b]$ if it holds everywhere on $[a, b]$ except possibly for a set of Lebesgue measure zero.

For any $\theta \in [a, b]$ we have the class

$$\mathcal{D}_\theta = \{X \in \mathcal{M} : X \text{ is differentiable at } \theta, \text{ a.s.}\};$$

i.e., $X \in \mathcal{D}_\theta$ if

$$\lim_{h \to 0} h^{-1}[X(\theta + h) - X(\theta)]$$

exists with probability one. In this case, we write $X'(\theta)$ for the limiting random variable. At the endpoints of $[a, b]$, take one-sided limits. Little more can be said about random functions in $\mathcal{D}_\theta$ than that they possess its defining property. Generally, we work with

$$\mathcal{D}_{[a,b]} = \bigcap_{\theta \in [a,b]} \mathcal{D}_\theta = \{X \in \mathcal{M} : \forall \theta \in [a, b], X \text{ is differentiable at } \theta, \text{ a.s.}\}.$$

(This class should not be confused with the space, usually denoted $D[a, b]$, of functions on $[a, b]$ that are right-continuous and have left-limits.) Membership in $\mathcal{D}_{[a,b]}$ is a prerequisite for the application of perturbation analysis. However, $X$ belonging to $\mathcal{D}_{[a,b]}$ implies almost nothing about the derivatives $\{X'(\theta), \theta \in [a, b]\}$. In particular, $X \in \mathcal{D}_{[a,b]}$ does *not* imply that the sample functions of $X$ are, with probability one, differentiable functions on $[a, b]$.

As an example, suppose $X$ is a standard Poisson process with $\theta$ playing the role usually played by a time parameter. Then the probability that $X$ fails to be differentiable at $\theta$ equals the probability that $X$ has a jump at $\theta$, which is zero. Thus, $X \in \mathcal{D}_{[a,b]}$ for all $0 < a < b$. However, since the sample functions of $X$ are piecewise constant, $X'(\theta) = 0$, a.s., at all $\theta$. In contrast, $\mathsf{E}[X(\theta)]$ is strictly increasing in $\theta$. Thus, $X'(\theta)$ and its expectation tell us nothing about $\mathsf{E}[X(\theta)]'$.

The problem in this example is a failure of *uniform integrability*. A family $\{Y_n, n \geq 0\}$ of real-valued random variables is uniformly integrable if

$$\lim_{c \to \infty} \sup_{n \geq 0} \mathsf{E}[Y_n \mathbf{1}\{|Y_n| > c\}] = 0.$$

Here, $\mathbf{1}\{\cdot\}$ is the indicator function for the event in braces. If $\{Y_n, n \geq 0\}$ converges to a limit random variable $Y$ (almost surely, or merely in probability) then uniform integrability implies that $\mathsf{E}[Y] = \lim \mathsf{E}[Y_n]$. In fact, uniform integrability is a necessary condition for this interchange of limit and expectation. In the Poisson example, the family $Y_h = h^{-1}[X(\theta + h) - X(\theta)]$, $0 < h \leq b - \theta$, is not uniformly integrable: if $h \leq 1/c$,

$$\begin{aligned}\mathsf{E}[Y_h \mathbf{1}\{|Y_h| > c\}] &\geq P(X \text{ jumps in } [\theta, \theta + h]) \cdot c \\ &\geq (1 - e^{-h})c.\end{aligned}$$

The supremum over $h$ of the left side is, then, at least $(1 - \exp[-1/c])c$, and does not vanish as $c$ increases.

A sufficient condition for a family $\{Y_n, n \geq 0\}$ to be uniformly integrable is that there exist a random variable $K$ with $|Y_n| \leq K$, a.s., for all $n$, and $\mathsf{E}[K] < \infty$. This is the dominated convergence theorem. Applying it to difference quotients suggests the condition

$$|h^{-1}[X(\theta + h) - X(\theta)]| \leq K,$$

or, for $\mathbf{R}^d$-valued random functions,

$$\|X(\theta + h) - X(\theta)\| \leq Kh,$$

where $\|\cdot\|$ is the Euclidean norm. In general, a (deterministic) function $f : S \to \mathbf{R}^m$, $S \subseteq \mathbf{R}^n$, satisfies a *Lipschitz condition* with *modulus* $k_f$ if

$$\|f(x_2) - f(x_1)\| \leq k_f \|x_2 - x_1\|$$

for all $x_1, x_2 \in S$. Such an $f$ is called *Lipschitz*. Let us therefore define

$$\text{Lip} = \{X \in \mathcal{M} : X \text{ is almost-surely Lipschitz}\}.$$

For uniform integrability we need the subclasses

$$\text{Lip}^p = \{X \in \text{Lip} : \text{a modulus of } X \text{ has finite } p\text{-th moment}\}.$$

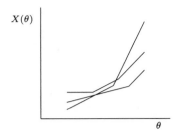

FIGURE 3. Sample functions of an almost-surely piecewise-linear element of $\mathrm{Lip}_D$. No $\theta$ is a point of nondifferentiability with positive probability; $X'(\theta)$ exists, a.s., for all $\theta$. But along a fixed sample function there may be points where the derivative fails to exist. Averaging over all possible paths yields a smooth curve.

Thus, a random function $X$ is in $\mathrm{Lip}^p$ if $\|X(\theta_2) - X(\theta_1)\| \le K_X |\theta_2 - \theta_1|$ for all $\theta_1, \theta_2 \in [a, b]$, for some $K_X$ with $\mathsf{E}[K_X^p] < \infty$. The most important cases for us are $p = 1$ and $p = 2$. Let $\mathrm{Lip}_D = \mathrm{Lip} \cap \mathcal{D}_{[a,b]}$ and $\mathrm{Lip}^p_D = \mathrm{Lip}^p \cap \mathcal{D}_{[a,b]}$; see Figure 3 for an example. The random functions suitable for perturbation analysis are those in $\mathrm{Lip}^1_D$:

**Lemma 6.3.1** If $X \in \mathrm{Lip}^1_D$ and each $X(\theta)$ is integrable, then the derivatives $\{\mathsf{E}[X(\theta)]', \theta \in [a, b]\}$ exist and $\mathsf{E}[X'(\theta)] = \mathsf{E}[X(\theta)]'$ for all $\theta \in [a, b]$.

**Proof.** Existence of all $X'(\theta)$'s is the definition of $\mathcal{D}_{[a,b]}$. If $\theta, \theta + h \in [a, b]$, then

$$\|X(\theta + h) - X(\theta)\| \le K_X h.$$

hence, for each component function $X_i$, $i = 1, \ldots, d$,

$$h^{-1}|X_i(\theta + h) - X_i(\theta)| \le K_X.$$

The dominated convergence theorem now implies that

$$\lim_{h \to 0} h^{-1}(\mathsf{E}[X_i(\theta + h)] - \mathsf{E}[X_i(\theta)])$$

exists and equals

$$\mathsf{E}[\lim_{h \to 0} h^{-1}(X_i(\theta + h) - X_i(\theta))] = \mathsf{E}[X_i'(\theta)].$$

Since this holds for each component function, we have the vector equality $\mathsf{E}[X'(\theta)] = \mathsf{E}[X(\theta)]'$. $\square$

An important additional consequence of the Lipschitz property is *absolute continuity*. A function $f : [a, b] \to \mathbf{R}$ is absolutely continuous if for every $\epsilon > 0$ there is a $\delta > 0$ such that

$$\sum_{i=1}^n |f(y_i) - f(x_i)| < \epsilon$$

for every collection $\{(x_i, y_i), i = 1, \ldots, n\}$ of disjoint subintervals of $[a, b]$ with

$$\sum_{i=1}^{n} |y_i - x_i| < \delta.$$

A function into $\mathbf{R}^d$ is absolutely continuous if each of its component functions is. The importance of this property is that an absolutely continuous function is differentiable almost everywhere *and equals the integral of its derivative.* Lipschitz functions are absolutely continuous: choose $\delta$ equal to $\epsilon$ divided by the modulus. For purposes of reference we record

**Lemma 6.3.2** If $X \in$ Lip then, almost surely, $X'(\theta)$ exists at almost every $\theta \in [a, b]$. Moreover,

$$X(\theta_2) = X(\theta_1) + \int_{\theta_1}^{\theta_2} X'(\theta) \, d\theta, \quad \text{a.s.,} \tag{6.12}$$

for any $\theta_1, \theta_2 \in [a, b]$.

A representation of the form (6.12), but with $X'$ replaced by an arbitrary function, by itself implies differentiability at almost every $\theta$. However, an $X$ in Lip that is not in $\mathcal{D}_{[a,b]}$ may, with positive probability, fail to be differentiable at the particular $\theta$ of interest. For this reason, in perturbation analysis we work with $\text{Lip}_D^1$ rather than $\text{Lip}^1$.

A few additional properties of Lipschitz functions will be useful in later sections; we state them here without proof.

**Lemma 6.3.3** The following properties hold:

(a) A composition of Lipschitz functions is Lipschitz.

(b) The functions min, max, and + (from $\mathbf{R}^2$ to $\mathbf{R}$) are Lipschitz with unit modulus.

(c) A convex function on a compact set is Lipschitz.

(d) A continuously differentiable function on a compact set is Lipschitz.

(e) A modulus of a Lipschitz function is an upper bound on the norm of its gradient.

Combining parts (a) and (b), we see that the random functions $W_n(\cdot)$, $T_{a,n}(\cdot)$, and $T_{d,n}(\cdot)$ of Section 2 are almost-surely Lipschitz. This is always the case when we have a composition of min, max, and addition.

## 6.3.2   Differentiability of Inputs

Often, as part of a model we have an i.i.d. sequence of inputs. In Section 2, the service requirements $\{S_n, n \geq 0\}$ and the interarrival times $\{U_n, n \geq 0\}$ were i.i.d. sequences. There, the parameter $\theta$ was the reciprocal of the processing rate, making $\theta S_n$, $n \geq 0$, the actual service times. We would like, now, to consider more general parameters and more general sequences $\{S_n(\theta), n \geq 0\}$ and $\{U_n(\theta), n \geq 0\}$ of random variables depending on a parameter.

In modeling a system, the starting point is often a set of probability distributions for random inputs, rather than the random variables themselves. Thus, when we refer to an input depending on a parameter, this is initially specified through a collection $\{F_\theta, \theta \in [a, b]\}$ of distribution functions. The field of random variate generation develops algorithms for sampling from some $F_\theta$ — i.e., for generating variates with specified distributions for use in simulation. In perturbation analysis, we examine the effect of small changes in $\theta$. So, we would like our samples from $\{F_\theta, \theta \in [a, b]\}$ to change smoothly with $\theta$. This leads us to

**Definition 6.3.4** A *differentiable representation* of a family $\{F_\theta, \theta \in [a, b]\}$ of distributions on $\mathbf{R}$ is a real-valued random function $X$ on $[a, b]$ for which

(i)  $P(X(\theta) \leq x) = F_\theta(x)$ for all $x \in \mathbf{R}$, and

(ii)  $X'(\theta)$ exists, a.s., for all $\theta \in [a, b]$.

Thus, a differentiable representation is an element of $\mathcal{D}_{[a,b]}$ with marginal distributions $\{F_\theta, \theta \in [a, b]\}$. Our purpose in this section is to construct differentiable representations and to compute their derivatives. These derivatives will then allow us to compute derivatives of system-level performance measures.

We begin with two important special cases, scale and location parameters. The distributions $\{F_\theta, \theta \in [a, b]\}$, $a > 0$, are a *scale family* if, for all $\theta$ and $x$, $F_\theta(x) = F(x/\theta)$ for some distribution $F$ not depending on $\theta$. In this setting, we obtain a differentiable representation by setting $X(\theta) = \theta Y$ where $Y$ has distribution $F$. Since, for any $x \in \mathbf{R}$,

$$
\begin{aligned}
P(X(\theta) \leq x) &= P(\theta Y \leq x) \\
&= P(Y \leq x/\theta) \\
&= F(x/\theta) = F_\theta(x),
\end{aligned}
$$

this $X$ has the specified marginal distributions. It is clearly differentiable, with $X'(\theta) = Y = X(\theta)/\theta$. Thus, $Y$ plays no explicit role but is merely a vehicle in establishing that $X'(\theta) = X(\theta)/\theta$ for a scale parameter.

Quite analogously, the distributions $\{F_\theta, \theta \in [a, b]\}$ are a *location family* if, for all $\theta$ and $x$, $F_\theta(x) = F(x - \theta)$ for some $F$ not depending on $\theta$. Here, we may set $X(\theta) = Y + \theta$, $Y$ having distribution $F$. It is easy to check that this $X$ is a representation of $\{F_\theta, \theta \in [a, b]\}$. It is differentiable with $X'(\theta)$ identically one.

Examples of scale parameters are the mean of the exponential distribution and the standard deviation of the normal distribution. One of the two parameters usually used to identify a gamma density is a scale parameter. The mean of a uniform distribution with fixed spread, the mean of the normal distribution, and any atom of a discrete distribution are examples of location parameters.

Though the scale and location cases arise frequently in practice, they are by no means exhaustive. A somewhat more general method follows from the fact that, if $U$ is uniformly distributed on the unit interval, then

$$X(\theta) = F_\theta^{-1}(U)$$

has distribution $F_\theta$, where

$$F_\theta^{-1}(u) = \sup\{x : F_\theta(x) \le u\}.$$

This is the *inversion* method of generating random variates. If, for every $\theta \in [a, b]$, $F^{-1}(u)$ is differentiable at $\theta$ for almost every $u \in [0, 1]$, then this construction yields a differentiable representation.

As an example, consider the exponential distribution $F_\theta(x) = 1 - e^{-x/\theta}$ with mean $\theta$. Setting $F_\theta(x) = u$ and solving for $x$ yields $x = -\theta \ln(1-u)$. If $U$ is uniformly distributed on the unit interval, then $X(\theta) = -\theta \ln(1 - U)$ is exponentially distributed with mean $\theta$. This differentiable representation also follows from the fact that $\theta$ is a scale parameter.

Under additional conditions, inversion leads to an important simplification, as the following result shows:

**Proposition 6.3.5** Suppose that for every $\theta \in (a, b)$, $F_\theta(\cdot)$ has a density that is strictly positive on an open interval $I_\theta$. Suppose also that, as a function of two variables, $F.(\cdot)$ is continuously differentiable on $\{(\theta, x) : \theta \in (a, b), x \in I_\theta\}$. Let $X(\theta, u) = F_\theta^{-1}(u)$. Then for any $\theta \in (a, b)$

$$\frac{\partial X}{\partial \theta} = -\frac{\partial_\theta F_\theta(X)}{\partial_x F_\theta(X)}, \tag{6.13}$$

almost surely.

**Proof.** Write $X(\theta, u)$ for $F_\theta^{-1}(u)$. The assumption of continuous differentiability implies that the equation $F_\theta(X(\theta, u)) = u$ uniquely determines $X$ for any $\theta$ and any $0 < u < 1$. Thus, for $\theta + h \in (a, b)$,

$$F_{\theta+h}(X(\theta + h, u)) = u = F_\theta(X(\theta, u)). \tag{6.14}$$

The mean value theorem asserts the existence of a point $(x^*, \theta^*)$ on the line segment joining $(X(\theta, u), \theta)$ and $(X(\theta + h, u), \theta + h)$, for which

$$
\begin{aligned}
F_{\theta+h}(X(\theta + h, u)) = {} & F_\theta(X(\theta, u)) + \partial_\theta F_{\theta^*}(x^*)h \\
& + \partial_x F_{\theta^*}(x^*)[X(\theta + h, u) - X(\theta, u)].
\end{aligned}
$$

Subtracting the far left and far right sides of (6.14) from this equation and rearranging terms gives

$$X(\theta + h, u) - X(\theta, u) = -\partial_\theta F_{\theta^*}(x^*)h/\partial_x F_{\theta^*}(x^*).$$

Now divide both sides by $h$. As $h \to 0$, $(x^*, \theta^*)$ approaches $(X(\theta, u), \theta)$. Thus, (6.13) follows from the continuity of the partial derivatives of $F$. □

One important consequence of this result is that it provides a representation of the general form

$$X'(\theta) = \psi(X(\theta), \theta). \tag{6.15}$$

Once such a relation is established, how $X(\theta)$ is generated is unimportant. In particular, it is not necessary that $X(\theta)$ be generated by inversion in order that we use (6.13). Often, specialized methods faster than inversion are available. Indeed, in (6.13) or more generally (6.15), it is not necessary that $X(\theta)$ be generated at all—it may simply be an observed value which is then substituted into the corresponding formula.

Another feature of (6.13) is that it sometimes applies when inversion does not. A good example is the hyperexponential distribution

$$F_\theta(x) = 1 - \theta e^{-\mu_1 x} - (1 - \theta)e^{-\mu_2 x}.$$

Here, $\theta$ is constrained to the unit interval and functions as a mixing probability between exponential distributions with means $\mu_1^{-1}$ and $\mu_2^{-1}$. This distribution cannot be inverted in closed form (though hyperexponential samples are easily generated). However, since

$$\partial_\theta F_\theta(x) = -\theta e^{-\mu_1 x} + \theta e^{-\mu_2 x}$$

and

$$\partial_x F_\theta(x) = \theta \mu_1 e^{-\mu_1 x} + (1 - \theta)\mu_2 e^{-\mu_2 x},$$

Proposition 6.3.5 permits us to set

$$X'(\theta) = \frac{\theta e^{-\mu_1 X(\theta)} - \theta e^{-\mu_2 X(\theta)}}{\theta \mu_1 e^{-\mu_1 X(\theta)} + (1 - \theta)\mu_2 e^{-\mu_2 X(\theta)}},$$

as though $X(\theta)$ had been generated by inversion.

For both scale and location families, we obtain differentiable representations that are almost-surely linear in $\theta$, hence Lipschitz. When (6.13) applies, it is reasonable to expect inputs to be almost-surely continuously differentiable.

## 6.3.3  Differentiability of Recursions

Having investigated the differentiability of inputs—random variables representing service times and interarrival times—we can now investigate when differentiability carries over to outputs—system performance measures. We saw in Section 2 that outputs often satisfy recursions driven by inputs; so, we consider the general question of differentiability of random variables $\{X_n(\theta), n \geq 0\}$ satisfying a recursion of the form

$$X_{n+1}(\theta) = \phi(X_n(\theta), U_n(\theta)) \tag{6.16}$$

with input $\{U_n, n \geq 0\}$. We let each $U_n(\theta)$ be an $l$-dimensional random vector; $\phi$ maps $\mathbf{R} \times \mathbf{R}^l$ into $\mathbf{R}$.

As noted in Lemma 6.3.3, the Lipschitz property is preserved under composition. It follows that every $X_n$ is almost-surely Lipschitz if $X_0$ and $\{U_n, n \geq 0\}$ are, and if $\phi$ is Lipschitz. Integrability of moduli is also preserved:

**Lemma 6.3.6** Suppose (6.16) holds for some Lipschitz $\phi$. Then if $X_0$ and $\{U_i, 0 \leq i \leq n-1\}$ are in Lip, so is $X_n$. If $X_0$ and $\{U_i, 0 \leq i \leq n-1\}$ are in Lip$^1$, so is $X_n$.

**Proof.** Let $\phi$ have modulus $k_\phi$, $X_0$ modulus $K_{X_0}$ and $U_i$ modulus $K_i$, $i = 0, \ldots, n-1$. For any $\theta_1, \theta_2$,

$$
\begin{aligned}
&|X_n(\theta_2) - X_n(\theta_1)| \\
&= |\phi(X_{n-1}(\theta_2), U_{n-1}(\theta_2)) - \phi(X_{n-1}(\theta_1), U_{n-1}(\theta_1))| \\
&\leq k_\phi(|X_{n-1}(\theta_2) - X_{n-1}(\theta_1)| + \|U_{n-1}(\theta_2) - U_{n-1}(\theta_1)\|) \\
&\leq k_\phi(|X_{n-1}(\theta_2) - X_{n-1}(\theta_1)| + K_{n-1}|\theta_2 - \theta_1|).
\end{aligned}
$$

Iterating this inequality gives

$$|X_n(\theta_2) - X_n(\theta_1)| \leq (k_\phi^n K_{X_0} + \sum_{j=0}^{n-1} k_\phi^{n-j} K_j)|\theta_2 - \theta_1|. \tag{6.17}$$

This shows that $X_n$ is Lipschitz. It has an integrable modulus if $\mathsf{E}[K_{X_0}]$ and $\mathsf{E}[K_i]$, $i = 0, \ldots, n-1$, are finite. $\square$

The recursions in Section 2 were compositions of max and addition. In some systems, we find recursions using also min. All such recursions are Lipschitz, so the condition on $\phi$ in Lemma 6.3.6 is appropriate.

As a consequence of Lemma 6.3.1, we said that the random functions suitable for perturbation analysis are those in Lip$_D^1$, so we would like to supplement Lemma 6.3.6 with conditions for almost-sure differentiability at every $\theta \in (a, b)$. Suppose $X_0$ and $U_n$, $n \geq 0$, are differentiable, a.s., at every $\theta$. If $\phi$ were continuously differentiable, then we could conclude immediately that each $X_n$ is in $\mathcal{D}_{[a,b]}$, because the composition of a continuously differentiable function and a function differentiable at a given point is differentiable at that point. However, since min and max are not continuously differentiable, imposing this type of condition does not lead to a useful theory.

We need, instead, a chain rule for compositions of Lipschitz functions with isolated points of non-differentiability. Let us first examine a deterministic setting. Suppose $f$ and $g$ are differentiable real-valued functions on $\mathbf{R}$, and let $h(x) = \max(f(x), g(x))$. Then $h$ is differentiable on $\{x : f(x) \neq g(x)\}$ with

$$h'(x) = \begin{cases} f'(x) & \text{if } f(x) > g(x) \\ g'(x) & \text{if } g(x) > f(x). \end{cases}$$

This follows from the fact that, for all $x$ at which $f(x) \neq g(x)$ and all sufficiently small $|\delta|$,

$$h(x + \delta) - h(x) = \begin{cases} f(x + \delta) - f(x) & \text{if } f(x) > g(x) \\ g(x + \delta) - g(x) & \text{if } g(x) > f(x). \end{cases}$$

The analogous statement is true for $\min(f, g)$.

On the set $\{x : f(x) = g(x)\}$, $h$ may or may not be differentiable, and this prevents us from asserting differentiability of the composition $\max(f(\cdot), g(\cdot))$. Here, however, the stochastic setting offers a simplification: if $X$ and $Y$ are almost-surely differentiable at $\theta$, and if $P(X(\theta) = Y(\theta)) = 0$, then we may indeed assert that $Z(\theta) \stackrel{\triangle}{=} \max(X(\theta), Y(\theta))$ is almost-surely differentiable with

$$Z'(\theta) = \begin{cases} X'(\theta) & \text{if } X(\theta) > Y(\theta) \\ Y'(\theta) & \text{if } Y(\theta) > X(\theta). \end{cases}$$

On the null event $\{X(\theta) = Y(\theta)\}$, we may define $Z'(\theta)$ as we please.

To formalize and generalize these observations, let

$$G_\phi = \{(x, u) \in \mathbf{R} \times \mathbf{R}^l : \nabla \phi \text{ is continuous in a neighborhood of } (x, u)\}.$$

Here, $\nabla \phi$ is the vector of partial derivatives of $\phi$. From $G_\phi$ define

$$G_\theta = \{x \in \mathbf{R} : P((x, U_0(\theta)) \in G_\phi) = 1\}.$$

We now have

**Lemma 6.3.7** Let $\{U_n, n \geq 0\}$ be an i.i.d. sequence driving the recursion (6.16). Suppose

$$x \in G_{\theta_0} \Rightarrow P(\phi(x, U_0(\theta_0)) \in G_{\theta_0}) = 1 \qquad (6.18)$$

for some $\theta_0$. Suppose further that $X_0$ and $U_0$ are almost-surely differentiable at $\theta_0$, and that $X_0(\theta_0) \in G_{\theta_0}$, a.s. Then every $X_n$, $n \geq 1$ is also almost-surely differentiable at $\theta_0$.

**Proof.** We use induction. Take as induction hypothesis that $X_n$ is differentiable at $\theta_0$, a.s., and that $X_n(\theta_0) \in G_{\theta_0}$. This hypothesis is satisfied with $n = 0$. By the definition of $G_{\theta_0}$, $(X_n(\theta_0), U_n(\theta_0))$ is in $G_\phi$ with probability one. It follows that the composition $X_{n+1}(\cdot) = \phi(X_n(\cdot), U_n(\cdot))$ is differentiable at $\theta_0$, a.s. By (6.18), $X_{n+1}(\theta_0) \in G_{\theta_0}$, a.s. $\square$

As an example, consider the Lindley mapping $\phi : \mathbf{R} \times \mathbf{R}^2$ given by $\phi(x, (u_1, u_2)) = \max(0, x + u_1 - u_2)$. For this $\phi$,

$$G_\phi = \{(x, (u_1, u_2)) : x + u_1 - u_2 \neq 0\}.$$

Let $\{U_{1,n}, n \geq 0\}$ and $\{U_{2,n}, n \geq 0\}$ be independent sequences of, respectively, i.i.d. service and interarrival times. Then

$$G_\theta = \{x : P(U_{1,0}(\theta) - U_{2,0}(\theta) = x) = 0\}.$$

Thus, if $U_{1,0}(\theta) - U_{2,0}(\theta)$ has a density, this set is all of $\mathbf{R}$. In this case, Lemma 6.3.7 applied to

$$W_{n+1}(\theta) = \max\{0, W_n(\theta) + U_{1,n}(\theta) - U_{2,n}(\theta)\}$$

allows us to write

$$W'_{n+1}(\theta) = \begin{cases} W'_n(\theta) + U'_{1,n}(\theta) - U'_{2,n}(\theta), & \text{if } W_n(\theta) + U_{1,n}(\theta) > U_{2,n}(\theta); \\ 0, & \text{otherwise.} \end{cases}$$

The case $W_n(\theta) + U_{1,n}(\theta) = U_{2,n}(\theta)$ occurs with probability zero. A similar analysis applies to the recursion for $T_{d,n}(\theta)$ given in Section 2.

We can summarize this example and many others by saying that differentiability is preserved (i.e., the complement of $G_\phi$ is never visited) if two or more events never occur at the same instant. The case $W_n(\theta) + U_{1,n}(\theta) = U_{2,n}(\theta)$ corresponds to the simultaneous occurrence of an arrival and a service completion that ends a busy period. So long as this occurs with probability zero, the waiting times are differentiable. Also, when events occur one at a time, each transition time $\tau_i$, $i = 1, 2, \ldots$, corresponds to just one event. In the notation of Section 2, we have $\tau_i = T_{a,j}$ or $\tau_i = T_{d,n}$, but not both. The differentiation rule that sets $\tau'_i = T'_{a,j}$ or $\tau'_i = T'_{d,n}$, accordingly, is thus legitimate.

## 6.4   Analysis of the Single-Machine Model

We now apply the tools developed in the previous section to perturbation analysis of the example outlined in Section 2. Analyzing this model in detail simplifies the analysis of subsequent, more complex systems.

Let $S = \{S_n, n \geq 0\}$ and $U = \{U_n, n \geq 0\}$ be independent sequences of i.i.d. random functions from $[a, b]$ into $[0, \infty)$. Each $S_n(\theta)$ is the $n$-th service time at parameter value $\theta$, each $U_n(\theta)$ is the $n$-th interarrival time at that parameter value. Let $\{W_n(\theta), n \geq 0\}$ be the corresponding sequence of waiting times, with $W_0 \equiv 0$, a.s. As in Section 2, let $\overline{W}_n(\theta)$ be the sample mean of the first $n$ waiting times.

**Theorem 6.4.1** Suppose $S_0 \in \text{Lip}_D^1$ and $U_0 \in \text{Lip}_D^1$ and $P(S_0(\theta) - U_0(\theta) = x) = 0$ for all $x \in \mathbf{R}$, for all $\theta \in [a, b]$. Then for all $n = 1, 2, \ldots, \overline{W}_n \in \text{Lip}_D^1$. In particular, $\mathsf{E}[\overline{W}'_n(\theta)] = \mathsf{E}[\overline{W}_n(\theta)]'$ for all $\theta \in [a, b]$.

**Proof.** We need only combine earlier observations. From Lemma 6.3.6, we know that $\overline{W}_n$ is in $\text{Lip}^1$. Lemma 6.3.7 gives differentiability, as illustrated at the end of Section 3.3. The last statement is Lemma 6.3.1. $\square$

We next examine the queue-length process, under the standing assumption that $Q_0$ does not depend on $\theta$. For added generality, we consider

$$\overline{Q}_{f,t}(\theta) = t^{-1} \int_0^t f(Q_s(\theta))\, ds,$$

with $f$ mapping $\mathbf{N} = \{0, 1, 2, \ldots\}$ into $\mathbf{R}$. For example, if $f(x) = \mathbf{1}\{x > k\}$, then $\overline{Q}_{f,t}$ is the proportion of time the work-in-process exceeds $k$ units. For any such $f$, define

$$\delta_f = \sup\{|f(x) - f(y)| : x, y \geq 0,\ |x - y| = 1\}. \tag{6.19}$$

If $\{\tau_n, n \geq 0\}$ are the transition times of $\{Q_t, t \geq 0\}$, then

$$|f(Q_{\tau_i}) - f(Q_{\tau_{i+1}})| \leq \delta_f,$$

for all $i$. When $f$ is the identity, $\delta_f = 1$ because the queue-length process only increases or decreases in unit jumps. A requirement that $\delta_f$ be finite is a type of discrete Lipschitz condition on $f$.

Since $\{Q_t(\theta), t \geq 0\}$ is piecewise constant,

$$\overline{Q}_{f,t}(\theta) = t^{-1} \left( \sum_{i=0}^{N_t(\theta)-1} f(Q_{\tau_i(\theta)}(\theta))[\tau_{i+1}(\theta) - \tau_i(\theta)] + f(Q_t(\theta))[t - \tau_{N_t(\theta)}(\theta)] \right), \tag{6.20}$$

where $N_t$ is the number of events in $[0, t]$. If events occur one at a time and no event occurs just at time $t$, then

$$\overline{Q}'_{f,t}(\theta) = t^{-1} \left( \sum_{i=0}^{N_t(\theta)-1} f(Q_{\tau_i(\theta)}(\theta))[\tau'_{i+1}(\theta) - \tau'_i(\theta)] + f(Q_t(\theta))[-\tau'_{N_t(\theta)}(\theta)] \right), \tag{6.21}$$

as argued at (6.11). This can also be written as

$$\overline{Q}'_{f,t}(\theta) = t^{-1} \left( \sum_{i=1}^{N_t(\theta)} \tau'_i(\theta)[f(Q_{\tau_{i-1}(\theta)}(\theta)) - f(Q_{\tau_i(\theta)}(\theta))] \right). \tag{6.22}$$

We can now establish

**Theorem 6.4.2** Suppose that

(i) $S_0, U_0 \in \text{Lip}_D^2$;

(ii) for all $\theta \in [a, b]$, $U_0(\theta)$ has a density;

(iii) $P(\inf_{a \leq \theta \leq b} U_0(\theta) = 0) < 1$ and $P(\inf_{a \leq \theta \leq b} S_0(\theta) = 0) < 1$;

(iv) $\delta_f < \infty$.

Then $\overline{Q}_{f,t} \in \text{Lip}_D^1$ and consequently $\mathsf{E}[\overline{Q}'_{f,t}(\theta)] = \mathsf{E}[\overline{Q}_{f,t}(\theta)]'$ for all $\theta \in [a, b]$.

**Proof.** Our first task is to find a modulus for the transition times $\{\tau_n, n \geq 0\}$. Let $K_{S_i}, K_{U_i}, i = 0, 1, 2, \ldots$, be moduli for the corresponding service and interarrival times. If we vary $\theta$, the resulting change in the $n$-th transition time cannot exceed the change in the first $n$ service and interarrival times:

$$|\tau_n(\theta_2) - \tau_n(\theta_1)| \leq \sum_{i=1}^{n} |U_i(\theta_2) - U_i(\theta_1)| + |S_i(\theta_2) - S_i(\theta_1)|$$

$$\leq \sum_{i=1}^{n} (K_{U_i} + K_{S_i})|\theta_2 - \theta_1|.$$

Let $N_t^* = \sup_\theta N_t(\theta)$. Then for $n \leq N_t^*$,

$$|\tau_n(\theta_2) - \tau_n(\theta_1)| \leq \sum_{i=1}^{N_t^*} (K_{U_i} + K_{S_i})|\theta_2 - \theta_1|.$$

Let $K^*$ be the modulus implied by this inequality; i.e., $K^*$ is the right side divided by $|\theta_2 - \theta_1|$.

To bound moments of $K^*$, observe that

$$N_t^* \leq \sup_\theta \sup\{n : \sum_{i=1}^{n} U_i(\theta) \leq t\} + \sup_\theta \sup\{n : \sum_{i=1}^{n} S_i(\theta) \leq t\}$$

$$\leq \sup\{n : \sum_{i=1}^{n} \inf_\theta U_i(\theta) \leq t\} + \sup\{n : \sum_{i=1}^{n} \inf_\theta S_i(\theta) \leq t\}.$$

The sequences $\{\inf_\theta U_n(\theta), n \geq 1\}$ and $\{\inf_\theta S_n(\theta), n \geq 0\}$ are i.i.d. Hence, their partial sums define renewal processes, and we have bounded $N_t^*$ by the superposition of two renewal processes. The number of renewals in an interval $[0, t]$ has moments of all orders provided only that the inter-renewal times are not identically zero. Consequently, under hypothesis (iii), $N_t^*$ has finite moments. Since, by hypothesis (i), $\mathsf{E}[K_{U_i}^2 + K_{S_i}^2] < \infty$ for all $i = 1, 2, \ldots$, we also conclude that $K^*$ has finite second moment.

We can now examine $\overline{Q}_{f,t}$ itself. Under hypotheses (i) and (ii), $\overline{Q}_{f,t}$ is differentiable with probability one at each $\theta \in [a, b]$. As a function of $\theta$, $\overline{Q}_{f,t}$ is almost-surely piecewise differentiable, with possible points of non-differentiability occurring at those $\theta$'s where two events in $[0, t]$ occur at the same time or some event occurs just at time $t$. In the former case, some $\tau_i$ may fail to be differentiable, in the latter case, $N_t$ has a discontinuity. We verify that even at these points $\overline{Q}_{f,t}$ is continuous.

Because $Q_s(\theta) = Q_0 + A_s(\theta) - D_s(\theta)$, a potential discontinuity in $Q_s(\cdot)$, or more generally $f(Q_s(\cdot))$, occurs only when two events — arrivals or departures — occur at time $s$. The simultaneous occurrence of two or more events at some time before $s$ does not alter $Q_s$, because the queue length depends on the number of arrivals and departures but not their order. From (6.20) and the continuity of the $\tau_i$'s, we see that a potential discontinuity in $\overline{Q}_{f,t}$ occurs only at a discontinuity of some $Q_{\tau_i}$ or of $N_t$. However, as just argued, a discontinuity in $Q_{\tau_i}$ occurs only if $\tau_i = \tau_{i+1}$; similarly, a discontinuity in $N_t$ occurs only if $\tau_{N_t} = t$. In either case, we see from (6.20) that the discontinuity in $Q_{\tau_i}$ or $Q_t$ is weighted by a quantity $[\tau_{i+1} - \tau_i]$ or $[\tau_{N_t} - t]$ equal to zero. We conclude, therefore, that $\overline{Q}_{f,t}$ is continuous even at its points of non-differentiability. In short, $\overline{Q}_{f,t}(\cdot)$ is almost-surely continuous and piecewise differentiable.

These two properties and a generalized mean-value theorem yield

$$|\overline{Q}_{f,t}(\theta_2) - \overline{Q}_{f,t}(\theta_1)| \leq (\sup_\theta |\overline{Q}'_{f,t}(\theta)|) \cdot |\theta_2 - \theta_1|,$$

for all $\theta_1, \theta_2$. The supremum is taken over the all-but-countably-many $\theta$'s at which the derivative exists. This supremum is a Lipschitz modulus for $\overline{Q}_{f,t}$. Our proof will be complete if we can show that it is integrable. From (6.21), and the definitions of $N_t^*$, $K^*$ and $\delta_f$, we have

$$\sup_\theta |\overline{Q}'_{f,t}(\theta)| \leq \sup_\theta \sum_{i=1}^{N_t^*} |\tau_i'(\theta)| \cdot |f(Q_{\tau_{i-1}}(\theta)) - f(Q_{\tau_i}(\theta))|$$
$$\leq N_t^* K^* \delta_f.$$

Since $\delta_f$ is finite and $N_t^*$ and $K^*$ are square-integrable, the Cauchy-Schwarz inequality makes this bound integrable. $\square$

We have examined this model in complete detail because it contains the essential ingredients of the corresponding analysis of more complex systems. In subsequent examples, we will not repeat all the steps that lead to unbiasedness. So, pointing out the key features that make the proof work is worthwhile. They are these:

- The event times are almost-surely Lipschitz in $\theta$ because they satisfy recursions that are compositions of Lipschitz operations.

- As a consequence, $\overline{Q}_{f,t}$ is differentiable, except possibly where the order of events changes.

- Because the queue length at any time depends only on the number of events of each type and not their order, a change in the order of events introduces no discontinuity in $\overline{Q}_{f,t}$.

- In this case, the supremum of $|\overline{Q}'_{f,t}|$ is a Lipschitz modulus for $\overline{Q}_{f,t}$.

Thus, in subsequent examples, our main tasks will be to verify that the event times satisfy Lipschitz recursions, and that the *state* of the system (typically, a vector) depends only on the number of events of each type, not their order.

# 6.5    Production Networks

We now extend the analysis for a single machine to certain networks of machines. We begin with the simplest network—a serial production line—then incorporate finite buffers, a kanban control scheme and rework of defects. Further generalizing the serial system, we obtain networks with alternative sourcing and with subassemblies.

## 6.5.1    The Production Line

Consider a facility consisting of $m$ machines in series. Production is initiated by the arrival of customer demands. Each job is processed at the first machine and then moves on to the second, continuing through the line until processing is completed at the $m$-th machine, at which point the job leaves the facility. Between machines, jobs are held in buffers, which, for now, we take to have unlimited capacity.

Let $\{U_n, n \geq 0\}$ be the times between arrivals of customer demands, and for $i = 1, \ldots, m$ let $\{S_{i,n}, n \geq 0\}$ be the processing times of consecutive jobs at machine $i$. If a 0-th demand arrives at time zero, then the $n$-th demand arrives at

$$T_{0,n} = U_0 + \ldots + U_{n-1}.$$

Denote by $T_{i,n}$ the time of the $n$-th completion of processing at machine $i$. Processing of the $n$-th job at machine $i$ begins when that job is completed at machine $i - 1$ and when the $(n - 1)$-st job is completed at machine $i$. Whichever of these events occurs later triggers the initiation of service. Thus, for $i = 1, \ldots, m$ and $n \geq 0$, we have

$$T_{i,n} = S_{i,n} + \max\{T_{i-1,n}, T_{i,n-1}\}.$$

This puts us in the setting of event times obeying Lipschitz recursions. If the service and interarrival times are functions of $\theta$, we obtain $T'_{0,n}(\theta) = U'_0(\theta) + \cdots + U'_{n-1}(\theta)$ and

$$T'_{i,n}(\theta) = S'_{i,n}(\theta) + \begin{cases} T'_{i-1,n}(\theta), & T_{i-1,n}(\theta) \geq T_{i,n-1}(\theta); \\ T'_{i,n-1}(\theta), & T_{i-1,n}(\theta) < T_{i,n-1}(\theta). \end{cases}$$

In the first case, the $n$-th job finds the $i$-th machine idle, in the second case, busy. The ambiguous case $T_{i-1,n} = T_{i,n-1}$ can be resolved either way.

Let $W_{i,n}$ be the time from the arrival of the $n$-th customer demand to initiation of processing of the $n$-th job at machine $i$. In other words, $W_{i,n} = T_{i,n} - S_{i,n} - T_{0,n}$. With $i = m$, $W_{m,n} + S_{m,n}$ is the *makespan* for the $n$-th job: the total time from its initiation to its completion. It follows from the expressions above for the $T_{i,n}$'s that

$$W_{i,n} = \max\{W_{i-1,n} + S_{i-1,n}, W_{i,n-1} + S_{i,n-1} - U_{n-1}\},$$

with the convention that a variable is zero if it is indexed with a machine index less than one or a customer index less than zero. This gives

$$W'_{i,n}(\theta) = \begin{cases} W'_{i-1,n}(\theta) + S'_{i-1,n}(\theta), & T_{i-1,n}(\theta) \geq T_{i,n-1}(\theta); \\ W'_{i,n-1}(\theta) + S'_{i,n-1}(\theta) - U'_{n-1}(\theta), & T_{i-1,n}(\theta) < T_{i,n-1}(\theta). \end{cases}$$

For each $n$, $W_n$ is the vector $(W_{1,n}, \ldots, W_{m,n})$, $\overline{W}_n$ is the sample mean of $W_1, \ldots, W_n$, and $\overline{W}'_n$ is that of $W'_1, \ldots, W'_n$.

As in previous sections, $\{\tau_n, n \geq 0\}$ are the times of events of any type— i.e., the superposition of the event times $\{T_{i,n}, i = 0, \ldots, m, n \geq 0\}$, with $\tau_0 = 0$. The corresponding counting process is

$$N_t = \sup\{n \geq 0 : \tau_n \leq t\}.$$

Suppose that inputs—the interarrival and processing times—are independent sequences of i.i.d. functions of the parameter $\theta$. Arguing just as in Theorem 6.4.1, we obtain

**Theorem 6.5.1** Suppose that

(i) $U_0, S_{1,0}, \ldots, S_{m,0} \in \mathrm{Lip}_D^1$;

(ii) $P(\text{there exists } i \text{ such that } \tau_i(\theta) = \tau_{i+1}(\theta) \leq t) = 0$ for all $\theta \in [a,b]$.

Then the $\mathbf{R}_+^m$-valued random functions $\overline{W}_n$, $n \geq 0$ are in $\mathrm{Lip}_D^1$. Consequently, $\mathsf{E}[\overline{W}'_n(\theta)] = \mathsf{E}[\overline{W}_n(\theta)]'$ (componentwise) for all $n$ and all $\theta \in [a,b]$.

From the delays $W_{i,n}$ it is a simple matter to obtain waiting times at individual nodes. Between the instant the $n$-th job completes service at machine $i$ and the instant that job initiates service at machine $i + 1$, an interval of length $W_{i+1,n}(\theta) - W_{i,n}(\theta) - S_{i,n}(\theta)$ elapses. The derivative of the waiting time at machine $i$ is thus $W'_{i+1,n}(\theta) - W'_{i,n}(\theta) - S'_{i,n}(\theta)$. Under the conditions of Theorem 6.5.1, this has expectation $\mathsf{E}[W_{i+1,n}(\theta)]' - \mathsf{E}[W_{i,n}(\theta)]' - \mathsf{E}[S_{i,n}(\theta)]'$, which is the derivative of the expected waiting time at node $i$ for job $n$.

Consider, next, the process $Q_t = (Q_{1,t}, \ldots, Q_{m,t})$, $t \geq 0$, where $Q_{i,t}$ is the number of jobs that, by time $t$, have completed service at machine $i - 1$

but not machine $i$. In other words, for $i > 1$, $Q_{i,t}$ is the number of jobs in the buffer separating machines $i - 1$ and $i$, plus any job currently being processed at machine $i$. For $i = 1$, $Q_{1,t}$ is the number of jobs waiting or in service at the first machine. Take $Q_{i,0}$ to be identically zero for all $i$. For any $f : \mathbf{N}^m \to \mathbf{R}$, where $\mathbf{N} = \{0, 1, 2, \ldots\}$, let $\overline{Q}_{f,t}$ be the time average of $f(Q_s)$ over the interval $[0, t]$. Define

$$\delta_f = \sup\{|f(x) - f(y)| : x, y \in \mathbf{N}^m, \sum_{i=1}^{m} |x_i - y_i| \le 2\}.$$

We now have

**Theorem 6.5.2** Suppose that

(i) $U_0, S_{1,0}, \ldots, S_{m,0} \in \text{Lip}_D^2$;

(ii) $P(\text{there exists } i \text{ such that } \tau_i(\theta) = \tau_{i+1}(\theta) \le t) = 0$ and $P(\tau_{N_t(\theta)}(\theta) = t) = 0$ for all $\theta \in [a, b]$;

(iii) $P(\inf_{a \le \theta \le b} U_0(\theta) = 0) < 1$ and $P(\inf_{a \le \theta \le b} S_0(\theta) = 0) < 1$;

(iv) $\delta_f < \infty$.

Then $\overline{Q}_{f,t} \in \text{Lip}_D^1$ and consequently $\mathsf{E}[\overline{Q}'_{f,t}(\theta)] = \mathsf{E}[\overline{Q}_{f,t}(\theta)]'$ for all $\theta \in [a, b]$.

Rather than detail the proof of this result, we examine the key steps as outlined after Theorem 6.4.2. The proof given there shows that the $\tau_i$'s are almost-surely Lipschitz with a square-integrable modulus depending on the horizon $t$ but not the index $i$. Consider, now, a typical state $(n_1, \ldots, n_m) \in \mathbf{N}^m$. If $n_j \ge 1$, $1 \le j \le m - 1$, then a service completion at machine $j$ changes the state to $(n_1, \ldots, n_m) - e_j + e_{j+1}$, where $e_k$, $k = 1, \ldots, m$ are the standard unit vectors in $\mathbf{R}^m$. The arrival of a customer demand makes the state $(n_1, \ldots, n_m) + e_1$, and if $n_m \ge 1$ then a service completion at the $m$-th machine makes the state $(n_1, \ldots, n_m) - e_m$. Since, in every case, the state transition corresponds to adding and subtracting vectors, changing the order of events does not change the state reached. Observe, also, that if state $y$ is reached from state $x$ through the occurrence of just one event, then $|f(x) - f(y)| \le \delta_f$. The proof given at Theorem 6.4.2 therefore applies here as well.

### 6.5.2   Finite Buffers

Let us now modify the previous example to account for limited buffer space between machines. Suppose there is room for $k_i$ jobs between machines $i-1$ and $i$, for $i = 2, \ldots, m$, including any job in service at machine $i$. We put no limit on the number of jobs that can wait to enter the system, so $k_1 = \infty$.

When processing of a job at machine $i$ is completed, $i = 1, \ldots, m - 1$, the job is transported to the next buffer, unless that buffer is full. If the buffer between machines $i$ and $i+1$ is full, the job remains at machine $i$, impeding processing of the next job. In this case, we say that machine $i$ is *blocked*. So long as machine $i$ is blocked, its buffer (the storage space between machines $i - 1$ and $i$) will continue to fill, until it too reaches capacity, at which time machine $i - 1$ may become blocked. In this way, blocking propagates upstream. A job completed at the last machine immediately leaves the system, so machine $m$ is never blocked.

We use the notation of Section 5.1. Clearly, the expression $T_{0,n} = U_0 + \cdots + U_{n-1}$ for the time of the $n$-th arrival remains valid. For the service-completion times $T_{i,n}$, $i = 1, \ldots, m$, we must look more closely at when service at a machine is initiated; that is, we must re-evaluate $T_{i,n} - S_{i,n}$.

Processing of the $n$-th job at machine $i$ obviously cannot initiate before that job completes service at machine $i - 1$, so

$$T_{i,n} - S_{i,n} \geq T_{i-1,n}.$$

Also, the $n$-th job must wait until the $(n-1)$-st job has completed service, so

$$T_{i,n} - S_{i,n} \geq T_{i,n-1}.$$

However, even if the $n$-th job has arrived and the $(n-1)$-st job has completed service, the next service cannot be initiated if the $(i + 1)$-st buffer is full. For in this case, upon completion of its $(n - 1)$-st job, machine $i$ would become blocked. This is the case if less than $n - 1 - k_{i+1}$ jobs have completed service at machine $i + 1$, so

$$T_{i,n} - S_{i,n} \geq T_{i+1,n-1-k_{i+1}}.$$

But completion of $n - 1 - k_{i+1}$ jobs at machine $i + 1$ is not enough to ensure space at the $(i+1)$-st buffer: machine $i+1$ may itself be blocked by machine $i + 2$, machine $i + 2$ by machine $i + 3$, and so on. Thus,

$$T_{i,n} - S_{i,n} \geq T_{j,n-1-k_{i+1}-\cdots-k_j}, \quad j = i + 1, \ldots, m.$$

When all of these conditions have been met, the $n$-th processing time at machine $i$ begins; so, with

$$k_{ij} = 1 + k_{i+1} + \cdots + k_j,$$

we have

$$T_{i,n} = S_{i,n} + \max\{T_{i-1,n}, T_{i,n-1}, T_{j,n-k_{ij}}, j = 1, \ldots, m\}. \tag{6.23}$$

Given this representation, we can easily extend earlier results. Let $W_{i,n}$ be, once again, the time between the arrival of the $n$-th job and its service initiation at machine $i$. To streamline the recursion for these delays, define

$$U_j^k = U_j + U_{j+1} + \cdots + U_k,$$

with the usual convention that empty sums are zero. From (6.23) we obtain

$$W_{i,n} = \max\{W_{i-1,n} + S_{i-1,n}, W_{i,n-1} + S_{i,n-1} - U_{n-1},$$
$$W_{j,n-k_{ij}} + S_{j,n-k_{ij}} - U_{n-k_{ij}}^{n-1}\}.$$

Though this recursion is more complex than those we encountered previously, it preserves the Lipschitz property central to perturbation analysis. Recursions for $T'_{i,n}$ and $W'_{i,n}$ follow by differentiating each case separately, just as before. Theorem 6.5.1 holds here without modification.

As in Section 5.1, let $Q_{i,t}$ be the number of jobs completed by machine $i - 1$ not yet completed by machine $i$, $i = 2, \ldots, m$. At $i = 1$, replace "jobs completed by machine $i - 1$" with "jobs that have arrived." Let $Q_t = (Q_{1,t}, \ldots, Q_{m,t})$. This is not quite the usual vector of queue lengths. If at time $t$ machine $i$ is blocked, then the last job completed at machine $i$ is recorded in $Q_{i+1,t}$, though physically that job remains at machine $i$. The vector $Q_t$ tells us all we need to know about the disposition of jobs and machines. For example, in state $(n_1, \ldots, n_m)$, machine $i$ is blocked if and only if

$$n_{i+1} + \cdots + n_j = 1 + k_{i+1} + \cdots + k_j,$$

for some $j = i + 1, \ldots, m$. Since, as before, state transitions correspond to adding and subtracting unit vectors, changing the order of events does not change the state reached. For the same reason, the definition of $\delta_f$ given in Section 5.1 remains appropriate here. We summarize the foregoing observations in

**Theorem 6.5.3** Theorems 6.5.1 and 6.5.2 remain valid for the serial network with finite buffers.

Several variants of the model above admit a similar analysis. For example, we might consider a protocol in which processing at machine $i$ does not begin until there is room in the $(i + 1)$-st buffer. This blocks the $i$-th machine one service time earlier than would be the case with the previous mechanism. Accordingly, the recursions for $T_{i,n}$ and $W_{i,n}$ are modified by decreasing each index $k_{ij} = 1 + k_{i+1} + \cdots + k_j + 1$ to $k_{i+1} + \cdots + k_j$.

Another variant models make-to-stock production instead of demand-triggered production. Recall that in the specification above we required that the first buffer—the one for arriving jobs—have unlimited capacity. Otherwise, demands received when the first buffer is full would be lost, and it would not be possible to write (Lipschitz) recursions for the event times or waiting times. If, however, the production line supplies an essentially infinite demand, then a new job is initiated whenever the first machine becomes available. In this setting, it is natural to set $k_1 = 0$; no buffer is needed before the first machine, because a new job is started at that machine whenever the previous job moves to the second machine. Equation (6.23) remains valid. The external arrival times $T_{0,n}$ are replaced with the new service-initiation times $T_{1,n} - S_{1,n}$.

### 6.5.3  Implementation

At this point, it seems appropriate to make a small digression into questions of implementation. We have given expressions for derivatives of waiting times and queue-length functionals in terms of derivatives of service times and interarrival times; Section 3.2 discussed computation of derivatives of inputs. It remains to comment on how these are combined to compute derivatives of performance measures.

Once we have the derivatives of the event times $\{T_{i,n}\}$ and $\{\tau_n\}$, it is a simple matter to combine them to obtain the derivatives of the performance measures. So, we only consider computation of the event time derivatives. For this, there is a remarkably simple procedure.

With machine $i$ associate a variable $\Delta_i$, $i = 1, \ldots, m$, and with the arrival stream associate $\Delta_0$. Initially, all the $\Delta_i$'s are set to zero. Each event— arrival or service completion—corresponds to just one of these variables, so we may refer unambiguously to a type-$i$ event, $i = 0, \ldots, m$. In order that we may treat service completions and arrivals together, write $S_{0,n}$ for $U_n$. Now consider the following scheme:

> if the $n$-th event is the $k$-th occurrence of a type-$i$ event
> > then $\Delta_i \leftarrow \Delta_i + S'_{i,k}(\theta)$
> > if, in addition, this initiates a new type-$j$ event
> > > then $\Delta_j \leftarrow \Delta_i$.

If this procedure is followed at each transition, then just after the $k$-th occurrence of a type-$i$ event, $\Delta_i$ contains the value $T'_{i,k}(\theta)$. If this is the $n$-th event (of any type) to occur, then this is also $\tau'_n(\theta)$.

It is a relatively straightforward matter to verify that these rules correctly implement the derivative recursions obtained by differentiating (6.23). Indeed, this algorithm applies to derivatives of all such recursions. Rather than show this in detail, we interpret the two parts of the algorithm. The first step merely reflects the fact that since $S_{i,k}$ is always a term in $T_{i,k}$, $S'_{i,k}$ is always a term in $T'_{i,k}$. The second step corresponds to a type-$i$ event attaining the max (or, if applicable, the min) in a recursion for $T_{j,.}$. In the serial line with infinite buffers there are two ways this could happen:

1. If $j = i + 1$ and the $k$-th job finds machine $i + 1$ idle, then $T_{i+1,k} = S_{i+1,k} + T_{i,k}$ and $T'_{i+1,k} = S'_{i+1,k} + T'_{i,k}$. In this case, the contents of $\Delta_i$ are passed to $\Delta_{i+1}$.

2. If $j = i$, then $T_{i,k+1} = S_{i,k+1} + T_{i,k}$ and $T'_{i,k+1} = S'_{i,k+1} + T'_{i,k}$. In this case, $\Delta_i$ is just passed to itself.

With infinite buffers, these are the only pairs of $(i, j)$ for which the occurrence of a type-$i$ event can initiate a type-$j$ event. With finite buffers, more cases arise. If a service completion at machine $i$ unblocks machine $i - 1$, this may initiate a new service time at machine $i - 1$. In this case, $\Delta_i$

would be passed to $\Delta_{i-1}$ in the second step of the algorithm above. Since a service completion at $i$ potentially unblocks all machines $j = 1, \ldots, i-1$, it is possible in the second step to pass $\Delta_i$ to $\Delta_j$ for any $j = 1, \ldots, i-1$.

### 6.5.4   A Kanban System

Finite buffers reflect, in part, the fact that space between machines is always limited. However, they also serve as a means of controlling work-in-process inventory: in the model of Section 5.2, the number of jobs waiting for service that are actually in the system (i.e., jobs that have at least initiated processing at the first machine) cannot exceed the buffer capacity of machines 2 through $m$.

Kanbans similarly control intermediate inventories in a production line. A kanban is just a card. Machine $i$ has a number $k_i$ of cards, $i = 1, \ldots, m$, and an *input* and an *output* buffer. When a job moves to the input buffer of machine $i$, one of the $k_i$ kanbans are attached to it; if no kanbans are available at machine $i$, the job must remain in the output buffer of machine $i-1$. An initial (infinite) buffer, not controlled by kanbans, holds arriving jobs when no kanbans are available at the first machine. When a job leaves machine $i$, it relinquishes its kanban, making it possible for a job to move from the output buffer of machine $i-1$ to the input buffer of machine $i$. So long as there are jobs in its input buffer, machine $i$ may continue to work, moving completed jobs to its output buffer. Thus, at any time, the total number of jobs at machine $i$ — in its input buffer, its output buffer, or in service — cannot exceed $k_i$. The main difference between the kanban mechanism and the finite-buffer model of Section 5.2, is that with kanbans machine $i$ may continue to work even when the input buffer at machine $i+1$ is full.

Arguing as in Section 5.2, we find that the event times admit the representation (see also Chapter 4)

$$T_{i,n} = S_{i,n} + \max\{T_{i-1,n}, T_{i,n-1}, T_{j,n-k_{ij}}, j = 1, \ldots, m\}, \qquad (6.24)$$

where now

$$k_{ij} = k_i + k_{i+1} + \cdots + k_j.$$

In this redefinition, the initial term, formerly equal to 1, has been replaced with $k_i$. This reflects the fact that in (6.23) a machine can only process one more job when the downstream buffer is full, but with kanban control it can complete as many jobs as it has kanbans.

Using, again, the notation

$$U_j^k = U_j + U_{j+1} + \cdots + U_k,$$

from (6.24) we obtain

$$W_{i,n} = \max\{W_{i-1,n} + S_{i-1,n}, W_{i,n-1} + S_{i,n-1} - U_{n-1},$$
$$W_{j,n-k_{ij}} + S_{j,n-k_{ij}} - U_{n-k_{ij}}^{n-1}\}.$$

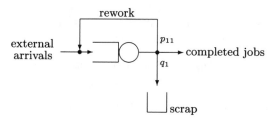

FIGURE 4. Routing probabilities at a single machine with rework and scrap

The state representation used in Sections 5.1 and 5.2 remains valid: $Q_{i,t}$ is the number of jobs that have completed service at machine $i - 1$ but not machine $i$. From this information, we could reconstruct the number in the output buffer of machine $i - 1$ and the number in the input buffer of machine $i$. Not distinguishing these provides a simpler encoding of the state space and the transitions. In particular, it is still the case that at each transition no more than two components of the state vector change, and no component changes by more than one unit. As a result, we have

**Theorem 6.5.4** Theorems 6.5.1 and 6.5.2 remain valid for the serial network with kanban control.

As in Section 5.2, this model can be modified to reflect a system in which new jobs are initiated whenever the first machine becomes available, regardless of external demands.

### 6.5.5    Systems with Rework and Scrap

In the examples discussed thus far, we have made the simplifying assumption that all parts and processes are defect-free. To incorporate defects, we could associate with each machine $i$, $i = 2, \ldots, m$, the following parameters:

- probabilities $p_{ij}$, $j = 1, \ldots, i$, where $p_{ij}$ is the fraction of jobs leaving machine $i$ that must be reworked at machines $j, j + 1, \ldots, i$;

- a probability $q_i$ giving the fraction of jobs leaving machine $i$ that must be scrapped.

Of course, we require that for every $i$,

$$0 \leq q_i + p_{i1} + \cdots + p_{ii} < 1.$$

The complementary probability $1 - q_i - p_{i1} - \cdots - p_{ii}$ gives the fraction of jobs leaving machine $i$ that are free of defects.

If all machines have infinite buffers, it is possible—at least in principle— to write certain analogs of our previous recursions for the event times. To illustrate, let us consider the case of a single machine; see Figure 4. The arrival times of external demands are $T_{0,n}$, $n \geq 1$, and the times of service completions (whether or not defective) are $T_{1,n}$, $n \geq 1$. In addition, let

$$
\begin{aligned}
T_{c,n} &= \text{time of completion of } n\text{-th non-defective item;} \\
T_{s,n} &= \text{time of completion of } n\text{-th scrapped item;} \\
T_{r,n} &= \text{time of completion of } n\text{-th item for rework;} \\
T_{a,n} &= \text{time of } n\text{-th arrival, whether from external demand or rework.}
\end{aligned}
$$

The job completed at $T_{c,n}$ leaves the system; the one completed at $T_{s,n}$ is scrapped. But the job completed at $T_{r,n}$ is routed back into the buffer where it waits to be processed again by the machine. The arriving job at $T_{a,n}$ could be an external demand, or it could be a job fed back for rework

Suppose, for purposes of illustration, that $q_1 = p_{11} = 1/3$; in other words, a completed job is equally likely to be scrapped, reworked, or shipped. Imagine, next, that the fate of each job is determined in advance, rather than when its service is completed. Though physically contrived, this model is mathematically equivalent to the original one. With this modification, the sequence of routes followed by jobs leaving the machine—to scrap, to rework, or out of the system—is fixed. For any such sequence, the event times can be expressed recursively.

To illustrate further, consider an outcome in which the first job is completed successfully, the second is reworked and the third is scrapped, and in which the same cyclic pattern repeats. In this case, we have

$$
T_{c,n} = T_{1,3n-2}, \quad T_{r,n} = T_{1,3n-1}, \quad T_{s,n} = T_{1,3n}.
$$

Also, much as in the standard single-machine model,

$$
T_{1,n} = S_n + \max\{T_{a,n}, T_{1,n-1}\}.
$$

It remains to consider the arrival times. The $n$-th job arrives the first time $j$ external jobs have arrived and $n - j$ reworked jobs have arrived, as $j$ ranges from 0 to $n$. Thus,

$$
T_{a,n} = \min_{0 \leq j \leq n} \max\{T_{0,j}, T_{r,n-j}\};
$$

as usual,

$$
T_{0,j} = U_0 + \cdots + U_{j-1},
$$

where the $U_i$'s are external interarrival times.

The possibility of expressing the event times using only min, max, and $+$ shows that they are Lipschitz in the service and interarrival times. Analogous expressions could be derived (in principle) for any other outcome of the routing decisions. It follows that if the service and interarrival times are Lipschitz in a parameter $\theta$, then so are the event times, *provided the routing probabilities do not change with $\theta$*. It is central to the foregoing argument that we be able to fix the routing outcomes before we vary $\theta$.

As in previous models, if the event times are Lipschitz, so too are the waiting times. Let us next investigate the extent to which the routing alternatives above can be incorporated into our previous models, examining in particular the continuous-time vector queue length process. Recall that following the proof of Theorem 6.4.2 we noted an important property: changing the order of events did not change the state reached. In a serial system with infinite buffers, this remains true with scrap and rework for every outcome of the routing decisions. It matters not whether a job to be reworked completes service before or after an external arrival; in either order, the same state is reached. So, in this case, essentially the same proof used before applies. Suppose, however, that some machines have finite buffers. In this setting, if machine $i$ completes a job and feeds it back to machine $j$ for rework, it is possible for machine $j$ to block machine $i$ if its buffer is full. If there is room for just one more job at machine $j$, and if a job is about to complete at machine $j - 1$, then the order in which jobs at $i$ and $j - 1$ complete service determines which machine is blocked and which successfully passes on its job. Thus, in this case, the order of events cannot be ignored. As a result, $\overline{Q}_t$ is not, in general, continuous in the service and interarrival times. Of course, if machine $j$ had an infinite buffer, this problem would not arise. To summarize, we have

**Theorem 6.5.5** Theorems 6.5.1 and 6.5.2 continue to hold in the serial line with infinite buffers and scrap and rework probabilities. In fact, they hold whenever $p_{2j} + \cdots + p_{mj} > 0$ implies that machine $j$ has an infinite buffer, $j = 2, \ldots, m$; that is, whenever every machine to which work may be fed back has an infinite buffer.

The recursions used above, conditional on the routing outcomes, were for illustration only; it is by no means necessary to write out such recursions in each case. Indeed, the algorithm of Section 5.3 is applicable even with routing probabilities. If, for example, a job from machine $i$ is sent back to machine $j$ for rework, and if that job finds machine $j$ idle, then the second step in the algorithm sets $\Delta_j \leftarrow \Delta_i$. Other cases work the same way.

## 6.5.6   A System with Alternative Sourcing

A natural extension of the serial networks considered so far allows tree-like topologies. We have in mind a system in which certain intermediate parts can be produced by any of a set of subsystems. These subsystems feed a common machine which processes jobs as they arrive from the various sources on a first come, first served basis. Thus, the network forms a tree, in which subsystems merge into smaller systems which may merge again, until the last stage in which there is just one machine.

The simplest example consists of three machines, machines 1 and 2 feeding machine 3; see Figure 5. Jobs arrive separately at machines 1 and 2

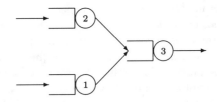

FIGURE 5. Machines 1 and 2 supply machine 3.

according to interarrival times $\{U_{1,n}, n \geq 0\}$ and $\{U_{2,n}, n \geq 0\}$, respectively. Denote the corresponding arrival times by $T_{0_i,n}$, $i = 1, 2$; i.e.,

$$T_{0_i,n} = U_{i,0} + \cdots + U_{i,n-1}.$$

When a job completes service at either of the first two machines, it moves immediately to machine 3. The service completion times at machine $i$, $i = 1, 2$, are given by

$$T_{i,n} = S_{i,n} + \max\{T_{0_i,n}, T_{i,n-1}\}.$$

The $n$-th job arrives at machine 3 the first time $j$ jobs have arrived from machine 1 and $n - j$ have arrived from machine 2, as $j$ ranges from 0 to $n$. Thus,

$$T_{3,n} = S_{3,n} + \min_{0 \leq j \leq n} \max\{T_{1,j}, T_{2,n-j}, T_{3,n-1}\}.$$

Given this Lipschitz representation of the event times, the rest of the analysis is the same as before.

**Theorem 6.5.6** Theorems 6.5.1 and 6.5.2 continue to hold in a tree-like network with infinite buffers.

In fact, the result remains valid if the restriction to infinite buffers is relaxed to require only that every machine fed by more than one other machine has an infinite buffer. The reasoning is the same as in the case of rework: the order of events matters if one machine potentially blocks two or more other machines.

### 6.5.7   A System with Subassemblies

The structure of this system is similar to the previous one, but the dynamics are different. Before, various subsystems were alternative sources of the same input to downstream machines. In the example, machine 3 processes jobs from machine 1 *or* machine 2 as they arrive. Now, the subsystems produce subassemblies which must be further assembled by downstream machines. In the three-machine example, this means that machine 3 must take one job from machine 1 *and* one job from machine 2 and combine them into a finished product.

Rather than restrict ourselves to the three-machine example, we consider a general setting. There are $m$ machines, machine $i$ having a set of *predecessor* machines $\pi(i) \subseteq \{1, \ldots, i - 1\}$. The predecessor machines produce components or subassemblies required by machine $i$; and machine $i$ cannot begin processing until at least one component from each predecessor machine is available. Each machine supplies exactly one other machine: no $j$ is in more than one $\pi(i)$. In intermediate stages of production, jobs move from one machine to the next immediately upon completion of service. All machines have infinite buffers.

Customer demands arrive to the system in a single stream. Each arrival triggers the initiation of the first subassemblies. To model this, set $\pi(i) = \{0\}$ if machine $i$ is not supplied by any other machines. The fictitious machine 0 represents the source of external demands. With this convention, we have

$$T_{i,n} = S_{i,n} + \max\{\max_{j \in \pi(i)} T_{j,n}, T_{i,n-1}\}, \quad i = 1, \ldots, m,$$

and, as usual,

$$T_{0,n} = U_0 + \cdots + U_{n-1}.$$

If $W_{i,n}$ is the time from the arrival of the $n$-th demand to the $n$-th service initiation at machine $i$, then

$$W_{i,n} = \max\{\max_{j \in \pi(i)} W_{j,n} + S_{j,n}, W_{i,n-1} + S_{i,n-1} - U_{n-1}\}.$$

From this Lindley-like recursion, the Lipschitz property follows.

In continuous time, let $Q_{i,t}$ be a $|\pi(i)|$-dimensional subvector recording how many jobs from each of machine $i$'s predecessors are at machine $i$. All told, $Q_t$ has $d = |\pi(1)| + \cdots + |\pi(m)|$ components. Not more than $m + \max|\pi(i)|$ of them change at any transition. Thus, for $f : \mathbf{N}^d \to \mathbf{R}$, we define

$$\delta_f = \sup\{|f(x) - f(y)| : x, y \in \mathbf{N}^d, \sum_{i=1}^{d} |x_i - y_i| \le m + \max|\pi(i)|\}.$$

With this modification, we have

**Theorem 6.5.7** Theorems 6.5.1 and 6.5.2 continue to hold in systems with subassemblies.

In the model above, subjobs are *joined*. To model operations with more complex precedence constraints, we could allow jobs to *fork* into subjobs to be processed independently and then rejoined. This leads to the class of *acyclic fork-join queues,* for which the results above also hold.

# 6.6 Steady-State Derivative Estimation

Thus far, we have only discussed derivatives over finite horizons. In that setting, the fundamental statistical issue for perturbation analysis estimates is unbiasedness: when there is no bias, the law of large numbers guarantees convergence to the correct value as independent replicates are averaged. In steady-state derivative estimation, we examine, instead the question of convergence as the time horizon grows. For a discrete-time process $\{W_n(\theta), n \geq 0\}$, we ask if, given that

$$\lim_{n \to \infty} n^{-1} \sum_{i=1}^{n} W_i(\theta) = w(\theta), \quad \text{a.s.}, \tag{6.25}$$

for some deterministic $w(\theta)$, is it also true that

$$\lim_{n \to \infty} n^{-1} \sum_{i=1}^{n} W_i'(\theta) = w'(\theta), \quad \text{a.s.} \tag{6.26}$$

In continuous time, we ask when

$$\lim_{t \to \infty} t^{-1} \int_0^t f(Q_s(\theta))\, ds = m_f(\theta), \quad \text{a.s.}, \tag{6.27}$$

extends to

$$\lim_{t \to \infty} \overline{Q}_{f,t}'(\theta) = m_f'(\theta), \quad \text{a.s.} \tag{6.28}$$

Less is known about these questions than about finite-horizon derivative estimates. Indeed, even the validity of (6.25) and (6.27) is a non-trivial issue; analysis of (6.26) and (6.28) is at least as difficult. No truly general theory exists, but various important cases have been studied, and we touch on some of these. We first examine waiting-time-like processes (in discrete time), then queue-length-like processes (in continuous time). For systems satisfying Little's law, either would suffice; but the two cases are of independent interest.

## 6.6.1 Discrete Time

A useful starting point is a *vector* recursion of the general form

$$W_{n+1}(\theta) = \phi(W_n(\theta), U_n(\theta)), \tag{6.29}$$

$\phi$ mapping $\mathbf{R}_+^d \times \mathbf{R}^l \to \mathbf{R}_+^d$. Think of $W_n$ as a vector of waiting times and of $U_n$ as a vector of inputs. The inputs are i.i.d. All the examples of Section 5 fit this framework.

We discussed, in Section 3.3, what conditions on $\phi$ and the inputs make the $W_n$'s Lipschitz and almost-surely differentiable. To streamline the discussion, here we generally just assume that all $W_n$'s are in $\mathcal{D}_{[a,b]}$ and ask when the limit of $\overline{W}_n'(\theta)$ is the derivative of the limit of $\overline{W}_n(\theta)$.

A simple but powerful approach to this problem, based on convexity conditions, has been developed by J.Q. Hu. Recall that a function $f : \mathbf{R}^n \to \mathbf{R}$ is convex if, for all $0 < \alpha < 1$,

$$f(\alpha x + (1 - \alpha)y) \leq \alpha f(x) + (1 - \alpha)f(y),$$

for all $x, y \in \mathbf{R}^d$. The relevance of this property comes from the following fact: if the functions $\{f_n, n \geq 1\}$ are convex and differentiable on an open convex set $S$, and if they converge pointwise to a function $f$, also differentiable, then the derivatives (gradients) of the $f_n$'s converge to that of $f$. (In fact, since convex functions are always differentiable off a countable set, the hypotheses in this result can be weakened.) Briefly put, for convex functions derivatives and limits can be interchanged.

What makes this attractive theoretical property useful in practice is the fact that max and + are increasing and convex. Compositions of increasing convex functions are convex. Hence, whenever $\phi$ in (6.29) is a composition of max and +, convexity in the inputs is passed to the outputs. Combining these observations, we obtain

**Theorem 6.6.1** Suppose that

(i) $W_0(\cdot)$ and $U_0(\cdot)$ are almost-surely convex;

(ii) $\phi$ is increasing and convex;

(iii) for all $\theta \in (a, b)$, $W_n'(\theta)$, $n \geq 0$, exist, a.s.;

(iv) for all $\theta \in (a, b)$, $\overline{W}_n'(\theta)$ has an almost-sure limit as $n \to \infty$; and,

(v) equation (6.25) holds with $w$ differentiable.

Then $\overline{W}_n'(\theta) \to w'(\theta)$, a.s., as $n \to \infty$.

As already noted, condition (ii) is satisfied by (max,+)-recursions. Condition (i) is part of the formulation of a model; it holds for scale and location parameters since then the inputs are almost-surely linear. Condition (iii) is the topic of Section 3.3 so we do not comment further. The most difficult conditions to verify are the remaining ones, (iv) and (v). Both of these are facilitated by the presence of *regenerative* structure:

**Definition 6.6.2** A process $\{X_t\}$, with either $t \in \mathbf{N}$ or $t \in \mathbf{R}_+$, is *regenerative* if there exists an increasing sequence $\{\sigma_n, n \geq 1\}$ of stopping times for $X$ making the cycles $\{X_t, \sigma_i \leq t < \sigma_{i+1}\}$, $i = 1, 2, \ldots$, independent and identically distributed.

Recall that $\sigma$ is a stopping time for $X$ if the occurrence or non-occurrence of the event $\{\sigma \leq t\}$ is completely determined by $\{X_s, 0 \leq s \leq t\}$. A regenerative process is called *non-delayed* if $X_0$ has the same distribution as $X_{\sigma_1}$. For simplicity, we consider only this case; accordingly, we define

$\sigma_0 = 0$, a.s. If $\mathsf{E}[\sigma_1] < \infty$, the process is positive recurrent. If an **R**-valued process $X$ is positive recurrent regenerative and non-negative, then

$$n^{-1} \sum_{i=1}^{n} X_i$$

converges, a.s., in the case of discrete time, and

$$t^{-1} \int_0^t X_s \, ds$$

converges, a.s., in the case of continuous time. Moreover, the limits are deterministic. (If the sign of $X$ changes, these results remain true under an integrability condition.) Thus, except for the differentiability of $w$, conditions (iv) and (v) are met when $\{W_n(\theta), n \geq 0\}$ and $\{W_n'(\theta), n \geq 0\}$ are positive recurrent regenerative. To illustrate, we prove

**Proposition 6.6.3** Let $\{W_n, n \geq 0\}$ be the waiting times in the single-machine model. Suppose that

(i)  $S_0$ and $-T_0$ are almost-surely increasing and convex;

(ii)  for all $\theta \in (a, b)$, $\mathsf{E}[S_0(\theta)] < \mathsf{E}[T_0(\theta)]$;

(iii)  for all $\theta \in (a, b)$, $W_n'(\theta)$, $n \geq 0$, exists, a.s.

Then for each $\theta \in (a, b)$, $\overline{W}_n(\theta)$ converges almost-surely to a deterministic limit $w(\theta)$ that is differentiable off a countable subset of $(a, b)$. Wherever $w'(\theta)$ exists, $\overline{W}_n'(\theta)$ converges to it, a.s.

**Proof.** The modified one-step Lindley mapping $(w, s, -t) \mapsto (w+s+(-t))^+$ is increasing and convex; so, under condition (i), the waiting times are almost-surely increasing and convex. With (iii), we have $W_n'(\theta) \geq 0$. Under condition (ii), each $\{W_n(\theta), n \geq 0\}$ is a positive recurrent regenerative process: the sequence regenerates every time $W_n(\theta)$ visits zero. The same is true of $\{W_n'(\theta), n \geq 0\}$ since $W_n'(\theta) = 0$ whenever $W_n(\theta) = 0$; see (6.6). Thus, $\{W_n(\theta), n \geq 0\}$ and $\{W_n'(\theta), n \geq 0\}$ converge with probability one to deterministic limits. Moreover, since convexity is preserved under pointwise limits, the steady-state mean waiting time $w$ is convex in $\theta$. $\square$

Similar arguments can be made for any of the convex recursions of Section 5. However, convexity clearly cannot handle all interesing cases: it restricts the form of the input, and it precludes, for example, recursions with min. To illustrate what can be done without convexity, we present one more result for discrete-time processes. Call $\phi$ *non-expansive* if

$$\|\phi(x) - \phi(y)\| \leq \|x - y\|;$$

i.e., if it is Lipschitz with unit modulus. If $\phi$ is a function of two arguments, call it non-expansive in its second argument it is Lipschitz with unit modulus for all values of its first argument. For such $\phi$ we have

**Theorem 6.6.4** Suppose that

  (i) $\phi(w, u)$ is non-expansive in $u$;

  (ii) $W_0$ and $U_0$ are in $\text{Lip}_D^1$;

  (iii) for all $\theta \in (a, b)$, $\{(W_n(\theta), W_n'(\theta_0)), n \geq 0\}$ is regenerative with respect to stopping times $\{\sigma_k(\theta), k \geq 1\}$ for which $W_{\sigma_k(\theta)}'(\theta) = 0$, $k = 1, 2, \ldots$;

  (iv) $\sup_{\theta \in (a,b)} \mathsf{E}[\sigma_1(\theta)] < \infty$.

Then $\lim \overline{W}_n(\theta)$ exists, a.s., at every $\theta$, and at almost every $\theta \in (a, b)$ this limit is differentiable with derivative equal to $\lim \overline{W}_n'(\theta)$.

**Proof.** In the non-expansive case, (6.17) and the fact that $W_{\sigma_k}' = 0$ give

$$\|W_n'(\theta)\| \leq \sum_{i=\sigma_{k_{n}-1}}^{\sigma_{k_n}-1} K_{U_i},$$

where $\sigma_{k_{n}-1} \leq n < \sigma_{k_n}$ and $K_{U_i}$ is a modulus for $U_i$. Taking expectations and using the regenerative property, we get

$$\mathsf{E}[\|W_n'(\theta)\|] \leq \mathsf{E}[\sigma_1(\theta)]\mathsf{E}[K_{U_1}].$$

Under conditions (ii) and (iv), this is bounded uniformly in $\theta$.
  As in Lemma 6.3.2, (ii) gives

$$W_n(\theta_2) = W_n(\theta_1) + \int_{\theta_1}^{\theta_2} W_n'(\theta) \, d\theta, \quad \text{a.s.},$$

for all $\theta_1, \theta_2$. The same is true for $\overline{W}_n$ and $\overline{W}_n'$. By Lemma 6.3.6, each $W_n$ is in $\text{Lip}^1$, and so is each $\overline{W}_n$. Thus, we may apply Fubini's theorem to obtain

$$\mathsf{E}[\overline{W}_n(\theta_2)] = \mathsf{E}[\overline{W}_n(\theta_1)] + \int_{\theta_1}^{\theta_2} \mathsf{E}[\overline{W}_n'(\theta)] \, d\theta.$$

From regenerative-process theory, we know that $\lim_{n \to \infty} \mathsf{E}[\overline{W}_n(\theta)]$ equals $\lim_{n \to \infty} \overline{W}_n(\theta)$, and the same applies to $\overline{W}_n'(\theta)$. Letting $n$ increase, we thus obtain

$$
\begin{aligned}
w(\theta_2) &= w(\theta_1) + \lim_{n \to \infty} \int_{\theta_1}^{\theta_2} \mathsf{E}[\overline{W}_n'(\theta)] \, d\theta \\
&= w(\theta_1) + \int_{\theta_1}^{\theta_2} \lim_{n \to \infty} \mathsf{E}[\overline{W}_n'(\theta)] \, d\theta \\
&= w(\theta_1) + \int_{\theta_1}^{\theta_2} \lim_{n \to \infty} \overline{W}_n'(\theta) \, d\theta.
\end{aligned}
$$

The interchange of limit and integral is justified by the uniform bounded-ness established above. Since $\theta_1, \theta_2$ are arbitrary, this representation shows that $w'(\theta)$ exists at almost every $\theta$, and where it exists it is given by the limit inside the integral. $\square$

### 6.6.2   Continuous Time

A thorough investigation of the convergence of derivatives in continuous time requires the introduction of more background and more notation than seems appropriate here. We choose, instead, merely to draw attention to the key issues and to show one way of resolving them. We comment on the practical implications of these issues and give guidelines for predicting the infinite-horizon behavior of perturbation analysis estimates.

In examining the validity of (6.28), it turns out to be somewhat more convenient to take the limit through the subsequence $\{\tau_n, n \geq 0\}$ of transition times. Thus, we consider

$$\overline{Q}_{\tau_n, f} = \tau_n^{-1} \sum_{i=0}^{n-1} f(Q_{\tau_i})[\tau_{i+1} - \tau_i].$$

In fact, it is enough to consider

$$n^{-1} \sum_{i=0}^{n-1} f(Q_{\tau_i})[\tau_{i+1} - \tau_i], \quad n \geq 1, \tag{6.30}$$

because $\overline{Q}_{\tau_n, f}$ is the ratio of two such terms: take $f \equiv 1$ for the denom-inator. If we have convergent derivative estimates for the numerator and the denominator, we can combine them to obtain a convergent derivative estimate for the ratio.

Incorporating $\theta$ and differentiating (6.30) gives

$$n^{-1} \sum_{i=0}^{n-1} f(Q_{\tau_i(\theta)}(\theta))[\tau'_{i+1}(\theta) - \tau'_i(\theta)], \quad n \geq 1. \tag{6.31}$$

In a stable system—one for which (6.27) is valid—we can expect

$$n^{-1} \sum_{i=0}^{n-1} f(Q_{\tau_i(\theta)}(\theta))$$

to converge. So, convergence of (6.31) depends critically on the stability of the sequence

$$[\tau'_{n+1}(\theta) - \tau'_n(\theta)], \quad n \geq 0.$$

Three cases emerge, each with a distinct interpretation:

(i) $[\tau'_{n+1}(\theta) - \tau'_n(\theta)]$ has a limiting distribution and so does $\tau'_n(\theta)$;

(ii) $[\tau'_{n+1}(\theta) - \tau'_n(\theta)]$ has a limiting distribution but $\tau'_n(\theta)$ does not;

(iii) $[\tau'_{n+1}(\theta) - \tau'_n(\theta)]$ fails to have a limiting distribution.

Let us comment on these cases and when they can be expected to arise (under reasonable additional conditions). Case (i) is common among open systems—i.e., systems with external arrivals and departures—in which the service times but not the interarrival times depend on $\theta$. In this case, service-time derivatives generated during a system-level busy period cease to affect the system whenever it empties. If the system empties infinitely often, the derivatives of the event times remain stochastically bounded, and so do the derivatives of the inter-event times.

Case (ii) arises in closed networks—networks with a fixed job population—and in open networks with a single arrival stream, in which the interarrival times do depend on $\theta$. In the former, service-time derivatives potentially affect the timing of events indefinitely, because jobs affected by those derivatives never leave the system. In the latter, the derivative of any interarrival time propagates to all subsequent arrival times. There is a subsequence of $\{\tau'_n(\theta), n \geq 0\}$, corresponding to the arrival epochs, taking the values

$$T'_{0,i}(\theta) = U'_0(\theta) + \cdots + U'_{i-1}(\theta).$$

The limit of $n^{-1}T'_{0,n}(\theta)$ is $\mathsf{E}[U'_0(\theta)]$. The limit of $n^{-1}\tau'_n(\theta)$ depends on what fraction of transitions are arrivals, but in any case $\tau'_n(\theta)$ diverges. Nevertheless, since all events are equally affected, derivatives for all event types grow together, and the inter-event time derivatives remain stable.

The canonical instance of Case (iii) is an open system with multiple arrival streams in which one or more of the streams depends on the parameter. For simplicity, suppose there are two streams and only interarrival times of the first depend on $\theta$. Suppose they are increasing in this parameter. Then through the subsequence of events corresponding to first-stream arrivals, $\tau'_n(\theta)$ increases to infinity. At arrivals from the second stream, $\tau'_n(\theta)$ is always zero. Suppose now that, infinitely often, arrivals from either or both of the two streams are consecutive events, and consider the sequence $[\tau'_n(\theta) - \tau'_{n-1}(\theta)]$. When an arrival from the first streams follows an arrival from the second, this is a large positive number; when the order is reversed, it is a large negative number. As $n$ increases, this difference takes increasingly large positive and negative values and fails to have a limiting distribution. If only the service times depended on $\theta$, the presence of multiple arrival streams is generally not a problem.

In practice, then, it is essential to be able to rule out case (iii). A precise formulation of the cases and conditions that imply them can be given by supplementing $\{Q_t(\theta), t \geq 0\}$ with residual service and interarrival times, thereby making it a general state-space Markov process. Rather than carry this out, we give an informal description that, nevertheless, captures essential features of the precise theory.

To avoid case (iii), we can require that $\{Q_t(\theta), t \geq 0\}$ possess a special regenerative structure. We require that there be a state $x$ such that

$$Q_{\sigma_i^-(\theta)}(\theta) = x, \text{ a.s.}, \tag{6.32}$$

for all $\theta$, with either of the following additional properties:

$$\text{in state } x \text{ there is just one active event;} \tag{6.33}$$

or

$$\text{no events active in state } x \text{ are affected by } \theta. \tag{6.34}$$

We need to explain the terms used in these conditions. A service-completion event is *active* whenever the corresponding machine is not idle; an external arrival event is active in all states. What it means for the timing of an event to depend on $\theta$ also requires some explanation. An arrival event is affected by $\theta$ if its interarrival times depend on the parameter; a service-completetion at, say, machine $i$ is affected by $\theta$ if the service times at $i$ depend on $\theta$, or if machine $i$ is fed by an arrival stream depending on $\theta$, or if jobs can move from machine $j$ to machine $i$ (possibly through intermediate machines), for some machine $j$ depending on $\theta$ or fed by arrivals depending on $\theta$. Thus both (6.33) and (6.34) rule out the possibility of more than one arrival stream unless no arrival times depend on $\theta$.

Though informally stated, conditions (6.33) and (6.34) can be made precise without changing their meaning. With this understanding, we state a result. We need one additional piece of notation: define (discrete-time regeneration points) $M_n$, $n \geq 0$ by $\sigma_n = \tau_{M_n}$.

**Theorem 6.6.5** Suppose that

(i) for all $t > 0$, $\overline{Q}_{f,t} \in \text{Lip}_D^1$;

(ii) for all $\theta$, (6.32) and either (6.33) or (6.34) hold;

(iii) the following quantities are bounded independently of $\theta$:

$$\mathsf{E}[\sum_{n=0}^{M_1-1} f(Q_{\tau_i(\theta)}(\theta))^2], \quad \mathsf{E}[\sigma_1^4(\theta)], \quad \text{and } \mathsf{E}[M_1^3(\theta)].$$

Then (6.27) holds for every $\theta \in (a, b)$, and at almost every $\theta$,

$$\lim_{t \to \infty} \overline{Q}'_{f,t}(\theta) = m'_f(\theta), \text{ a.s.}$$

## 6.7   Concluding Remarks

The following theme emerges from our coverage of perturbation analysis of production networks: meaningful derivatives are easily computed when the timing of events is pathwise sufficiently smooth. The appropriate level of smoothness is a Lipschitz condition. A stronger property would rule out most systems of interest, while a weaker one might fail to ensure the statistical validity of the derivatives computed. The Lipschitz property is easily verified when explicit recursions are available, and the availability of recursions is intimately connected to the behavior of a system when events change order. Additional stability conditions permit passage to steady state.

We should, perhaps, touch on what has not been covered here. A variety of specialized variants of perturbation analysis have been developed to compute derivatives in cases where the smoothness needed for ordinary perturbation analysis fails to hold. These are discussed in Ho and Cao [22] and, to a lesser extent, in Glasserman [14]. No one method works in all settings. Most systems with multiple job types fall outside the scope of at least the simplest perturbation analysis techniques. Finding an efficient method for general multi-class networks remains an important open problem.

An alternative approach to derivative estimation starts from likelihood ratios. Put simply, whereas perturbation analysis differentiates random variables, the likelihood-ratio method differentiates distributions. For more on this idea, see Glynn [18], Reiman and Weiss [25], and Rubinstein [29].

Whether obtained through likelihood ratios or through perturbation analysis, derivative estimates compute sensitivities only with respect to continuous parameters. In practice, it is at least as important to understand sensitivies with respect to discrete parameters: buffer sizes, kanban allocations, etc. There is a need for efficient methods of exploring alternative designs that differ in values of discrete parameters.

## 6.8   Notes

**Section 1.** The similarities and differences between traditional continuous systems and modern discrete-event systems have been put forth by Y.C. Ho in several settings. For a broad discussion, see Chapters 1 and 2 of Ho and Cao [22]. Extensive references and some coverage of other derivative estimation techniques appear there as well.

**Section 2.** The study of waiting-time derivatives in the single-server queue originates in Suri and Zazanis [33], Zazanis [35], and Zazanis and Suri [36]. Zazanis has also investigated derivatives of the workload process. General expressions for derivatives of queue-length like processes are given in Suri [32] and in Glasserman [13] where (6.11) appears.

**Section 3.1.** The importance of the class $\mathrm{Lip}_D^1$ for perturbation analysis is pointed out in Glasserman [12], though the characterization there uses a mean value theorem and an integrability condition on the supremum of the derivative norm, rather than the Lipschtiz property *per se*. For more on uniform integrability, dominated convergence and their role in perturbation analysis, see Chapter 1 of Glasserman [14]. For background on absolute continuity and differentiation of integrals, see, e.g., Chapter 5 of Royden [28], and for uniform integrability and its consequences see Chung [9]. Derivatives of Lipschitz functions are treated in Clarke [10] and in Chapter 4 of Rockafellar [27].

We could make the results of this section a bit more general by considering one-sided derivatives. For the models we consider, the almost-sure existence of one-sided derivatives is nearly automatic, though membership in $\mathcal{D}_{[a,b]}$ is not quite. The drawback to this alternative is that when we validate the interchange of expectation and one-sided limit, we only obtain a one-sided derivative of the *expected* performance. If expected performance is known to be differentiable, this drawback disappears.

**Section 3.2.** Derivatives of scale and location families and of the inversion representation come from Suri [31] and Suri and Zazanis [33]. For a general discussion, see the Appendix of Suri [32]. Related issues are studied in Glynn [17], from which the proof of Proposition 6.3.5 is taken.

**Section 3.3.** The point of view and some of the details behind Lemmas 6.3.6 and 6.3.7 are from Glasserman [15]. Derivatives of compositions involving max are considered (in a deterministic setting) in Rockafellar [27], for example.

As noted in this section, differentiability typically fails at points where two events occur simultaneously. However, even at such points, right- and left-derivatives typically exists, a.s., and simply correspond to taking the simultaneous events in one order or another.

**Section 4.** Results much like Theorem 6.4.1 appear in Glasserman [12, 15] and Zazanis [35]. Multi-server queues, not considered here, can be handled similarly; see, e.g., Fu and Hu [11]. Theorem 6.4.2 is similar to results in Glasserman [13] (which see for the generalized mean value theorem mentioned in the proof); the case of unbounded $f$ (requiring $\delta_f < \infty$) appears here for the first time. As noted in this section, a crucial role is played by the condition that the state depend on the *number* of events of each type but not their *order*. This condition is introduced in Glasserman [13]. Its application in perturbation analysis is further developed in Glasserman [14]. There is an intimate connection between this structure and (min,max,+)-recursions for event times; Chapter 4 of this volume.

**Section 5.1.** The validity of perturbation analysis for queues in series follows from more general results in Chapter 4 of Glasserman [14]. There, all *generalized Jackson networks* are considered, but from a rather different point of view; in particular, no use is made there of explicit recursions. This makes the extension to routing probabilities easier, but makes the analysis of systems with deterministic routing less transparent.

**Section 5.2.** That finite buffers cause perturbations to propagate upstream is an important early observation; see Ho et al. [20] and Cao and Ho [5]. The recursions used here appear in Shanthikumar and Yao [30]. They are differentiated in Hu [24]. Our formulation is based on the general blocking model of Cheng [7] and Cheng and Yao [8].

**Section 5.3.** This general algorithm extracts the essential features of those in Ho and Cao [21] and Suri [32], and also appears in Glasserman [13].

**Section 5.4.** This kanban system is a special case of the general blocking model of Cheng [7] and Cheng and Yao [8], and our formulation follows theirs. Cheng and Yao [8] provide additional references and background on kanbans. Cheng [7] applies perturbation analysis to the general model.

**Section 5.5.** The routing considered here is a special case of that allowed in Chapter 4 of Glasserman [14]. For routing probabilities that depend on $\theta$, Reiman and Weiss [25] discuss derivative estimates based on likelihood ratios. The importance of the requirement that no buffer block more than one machine is noted and discussed in Cao and Ho [5]. This turns out to be a consequence of general conditions in Glasserman [13], as discussed in [14].

**Section 5.6.** These results follow from results for generalized Jackson networks given in Glasserman [14] without the simplicity that comes from explicit recursions.

**Section 5.7.** The recursions used here are from the treatment of fork-join queues in Baccelli, Massey, and Towsley [2].

**Section 6.1.** The elegant and remarkably powerful use of convexity to establish convergence of derivatives is due to Hu [23, 24]. Results like Theorem 6.6.1 are given there. This method meshes nicely with the prominence of max in our examples. For the Lindley equation, Chen and Yao [6] use related but slightly weaker conditions.

For background on regenerative processes, see, e.g., Asmussen [1] and Ross [26]. Theorem 6.6.4 is from Glasserman [15]. Regeneration is certainly not a necessary condition for convergence of perturbation analysis; recent work using instead stationary and ergodic assumptions includes Wardi and Hu [34].

**Section 6.2.** This section is an informal treatment of Glasserman, Hu, and Strickland [16], which may be consulted for a proof of Theorem 6.6.5. The model used there is a generalized semi-Markov process. In that setting, it is easy to give precise meaning to conditions (6.33) and (6.34). Other work on convergence of perturbation analysis derivative estimates includes Cao [3, 4] and Heidelberger et al. [19].

*Acknowledgments:* This work is supported by the National Science Foundation under grant MSS-9216490.

## 6.9  References

[1] ASMUSSEN, S., *Applied Probability and Queues,* Wiley, New York, 1987.

[2] BACCELLI, F., MASSEY, W.A., AND TOWSLEY, D., Acyclic Fork-Join Queueing Networks, *J.ACM* **36**, 615-642 , 1989.

[3] CAO, X.R., Realization Probability in Closed Jackson Queueing Networks and its Application, *Adv. Appl. Prob.* **19**, 708-738, 1987.

[4] CAO, X.R., A Sample Performance Function of Closed Jackson Queueing Networks, *Operations Research* **36**, 128-136, 1988.

[5] CAO, X.R., AND HO, Y.C., Estimating Sojourn Time Sensitivity in Queueing Networks Using Perturbation Analysis, *JOTA* **53**, 353-375, 1987.

[6] CHEN, H., AND YAO, D.D., Derivatives of the Expected Delay in the GI/G/1 Queue, *J. Appl. Prob.* **28**, 899-907, 1990.

[7] CHENG, D.W. *Tandem Queues with General Blocking,* Ph.D. thesis, Columbia University 1990.

[8] CHENG, D.W., AND YAO, D.D., Tandem Queues with General Blocking: A Unified Model and Stochastic Comparisons, 1991. To appear in *DEDSTA.*

[9] CHUNG, K.L., *A Course in Probability Theory,* Academic Press, Orlando, Florida, 1974.

[10] CLARKE, F.H., *Optimization and Nonsmooth Analysis,* Wiley-Interscience, New York, 1983.

[11] FU, M.C., AND HU, J.Q., Consistency of Infinitesimal Perturbation Analysis for the GI/G/m queue, *European J. Oper. Res.* **54**, 121-139, 1991.

[12] GLASSERMAN, P., Performance Continuity and Differentiability in Monte Carlo Optimization, *Proc. Winter Sim. Conf.,* The Society for Computer Simulation, San Diego, California, 518-524, 1988.

[13] GLASSERMAN, P., Structural Conditions for Perturbation Analysis Derivative Estimation: Finite-Time Performance Indices, *Oper. Res.* **39**, 724-738, 1991.

[14] GLASSERMAN, P., *Gradient Estimation via Perturbation Analysis,* Kluwer Academic Publishers, Norwell, Massachusetts, 1991.

[15] GLASSERMAN, P., Regenerative Derivatives of Regenerative Sequences, *Adv. Appl. Prob.* **25**, 116-139, 1993.

[16] GLASSERMAN, P., HU, J.Q., AND STRICKLAND, S.G., Strongly Consistent Steady-State Derivative Estimates, *Prob. Eng. Inf. Sci.* **5**, 391-413, 1991.

[17] GLYNN, P.W., Construction of Process Differentiable Representations for Parametric Families of Distributions, Technical Report, University of Wisconsin Mathematics Research Center, Madison, Wisconsin, 1986.

[18] GLYNN, P.W., Likelihood Ratio Gradient Estimation: An Overview, *Proc. Winter Sim. Conf.*, The Society for Computer Simulation, San Diego, California, 366-374, 1987.

[19] HEIDELBERGER, P., CAO, X.R., ZAZANIS, M., AND SURI, R., Convergence Properties of Infinitesimal Perturbation Analysis Estimates, *Mgmt. Sci.* **34**, 1281-1302, 1988.

[20] HO, Y.C., EYLER, M.A., AND CHIEN, T.T., A Gradient Technique for General Buffer Storage Design in a Serial Production Line, *Internatl. J. Prod. Res.* **17**, 557-580, 1979.

[21] HO, Y.C., AND CAO, X.R., Optimization and Perturbation Analysis of Queueing Networks, *JOTA* **40**, 559-582, 1983.

[22] HO, Y.C., AND CAO, X.R., *Perturbation Analysis of Discrete Event Dynamic Systems,* Kluwer Academic Publishers, Norwell, Massachusetts, 1991.

[23] HU, J.Q., Stong Consistency of Infinitesimal Perturbation Analysis for the G/G/1 Queue, Technical Report, Harvard University Division of Applied Sciences, Cambridge, Massachusetts, 1990.

[24] HU, J.Q., Convexity of Sample Path Performances and Strong Consistency of Infinitesimal Perturbation Analysis, *IEEE Trans. Aut. Ctrl.* **37**, 258-262, 1992.

[25] REIMAN, M.I. AND WEISS, A., Sensitivity analysis for simulations via likelihood ratios, *Oper. Res.* **37**, 830-844, 1989.

[26] ROSS, S.M., *Stochastic Processes,* John Wiley and Sons, New York, 1983.

[27] ROCKAFELLAR, R.T., *The Theory of Subgradients and its Applications to Problems of Optimization. Convex and Nonconvex Functions.* Research and Education in Mathematics, No. 1, Heldermann Verlag, Berlin, 1981.

[28] ROYDEN, H.L., *Real Analysis,* Second Edition, Macmillan, New York, 1968.

[29] RUBINSTEIN, R., Sensitivity Analysis and Performance Extrapolation for Computer Simulation Models, *Oper. Res.* **37**, 72-81, 1989.

[30] SHANTHIKUMAR, J.G., AND YAO, D.D. Second-Order Stochastic Properties of Queueing Systems, *Proc. IEEE* **77**, 162-170, 1989.

[31] SURI, R., Implementation of Sensitivity Calculations on a Monte-Carlo Experiment, *JOTA* **40**, 625-630, 1983.

[32] SURI, R., Infinitesimal Perturbation Analysis for General Discrete Event Systems, *J.ACM* **34**, 686-717, 1987.

[33] SURI, R., AND ZAZANIS, M., Perturbation Analysis Gives Strongly Consistent Estimates for the M/G/1 Queue, *Mgmt. Sci.* **34**, 39-64, 1988.

[34] WARDI, Y., AND HU, J.Q., Strong Consistency of Infinitesimal Perturbation Analysis for Tandem Queueing Networks, *DEDSTA* **1**, 37-60, 1991.

[35] ZAZANIS, M., Weak Convergence of Sample Path Derivatives for the Waiting Time in a Single-Server Queue, *Proc. 25th Allerton Conf.,* 297-304, 1987.

[36] ZAZANIS, M., AND SURI, R., Perturbation Analysis of the GI/G/1 Queue, Working Paper, Northwestern University, 1986.

# 7
# Scheduling Networks of Queues: Heavy Traffic Analysis of a Bi-Criteria Problem

Lawrence M. Wein

ABSTRACT We consider bi-criteria scheduling problems for three queueing systems (a single queue, a two-station closed network, and a two-station network with controllable inputs) populated by various customer types. The objective is to minimize the long run expected average value of a linear combination of the customer sojourn time and the *sojourn time inequity*. The inequity at time $t$ is the sum of squares of the pairwise differences of the total number of customers in the system at time $t$ of each type divided by their respective arrival rates. Brownian approximations to these three scheduling problems are solved, and the solutions are interpreted in order to obtain scheduling policies. Simulation results show that the second objective criteria tends to equalize the mean sojourn times of the various customer types, and may lead to a reduction in sojourn time variance. The simulation results also show that in the network settings, in contrast to the single queue case, there are priority sequencing policies that significantly reduce the variance of sojourn times relative to the first-come first-served policy.

## 7.1 Introduction

Random events, such as machine breakdowns, variable yield and cancelled orders, occur in all factories. In order to develop scheduling policies that respond to these events, the job-shop needs to be viewed from a dynamic and stochastic perspective, as opposed to a static, deterministic one. A *multiclass network of queues*, or queueing network, is the prototypical mathematical model of a job-shop when viewed from a dynamic and stochastic viewpoint. Each node of the queueing network corresponds to a workstation of machines, and each customer in the network corresponds to a particular job that requires processing. Typically, as much as 90–95% of a job's time in the shop is spent waiting (in a queue) to be processed. The traditional job-shop scheduling decision is to decide, at each machine in the shop, which of the waiting jobs to work on next.

Although a large literature is devoted to the analysis of predictive performance of queueing networks, very little progress has been made in the optimal scheduling of a multiclass queueing network, which is considered a mathematically intractable problem. Consequently, computer simulation is still the primary tool of analysis, and the best hope for further progress on these scheduling problems appears to be in the analysis of cruder, more tractable models. One such model is the Brownian network model developed by Harrison [12], which approximates a queueing network with dynamic scheduling capability under balanced heavy loading conditions. These heavy loading conditions result in the model focusing only on the *bottleneck*, or most heavily loaded, machines in the factory. Fortunately, this is where most of the congestion and queueing occurs, and where scheduling can have its biggest impact. Several multiclass queueing network scheduling problems with important manufacturing applications have been analyzed using this model. The procedure employed in these studies is to (1) formulate a queueing network scheduling problem, (2) formulate the approximating Brownian control problem (using Harrison's Brownian network model), (3) reformulate the Brownian control problem in terms of workloads, (4) solve the workload formulation, and (5) interpret the solution of the workload formulation in terms of the queueing system in order to obtain an effective scheduling policy for the original queueing network scheduling problem.

In this chapter, this five step procedure will be used to analyze a bicriteria scheduling problem for three multiclass queueing systems. In order to describe and motivate these problems, several definitions are required. The three primary *system* performance measures (as opposed to due-date performance measures, which are not considered here) in a job-shop are the *sojourn time*, which is the length of time a job spends on the shop floor, the *work-in-process (WIP) inventory*, which is the number of jobs on the shop floor, and the *throughput*, which is the number of jobs completed per unit of time. In stable queueing systems, the long run expected average values of these three quantities are related by Little's formula (Little [32]), which states that the mean WIP inventory equals the product of the mean throughput and the mean sojourn time. In general, it is desirable to keep the sojourn time and WIP inventory as small as possible (in order to achieve the benefits of Just-In-Time manufacturing, for example; see Schonberger [37]), and to keep the throughput as large as possible.

Although the objective in scheduling most multiclass queueing systems is to minimize the mean sojourn time of customers, it is also desirable in many practical situations to keep the variance of the sojourn times as small as possible. For example, in many manufacturing systems, all arriving jobs are quoted the same due-date lead time (due-date minus arrival date), and so a smaller sojourn time variance will lead to better due-date performance. In some service systems, the desire to treat all customers as equitably as possible dictates that a small sojourn time variance is required. In many production facilities, low variability in sojourn times leads to easy coordination with its downstream customers and upstream suppliers. The two criteria we are interested in are the mean and variance of the sojourn time, although the latter quantity will only be addressed indirectly, as explained below.

For single server, single class queueing systems, the first-come first-served (FCFS) policy minimizes sojourn time variance over the class of work-conserving scheduling policies (see Kingman [24]). Furthermore, Groenevelt [9] has shown that FCFS is effective in reducing sojourn time variance in single server, multiclass queues. It is also well known that the shortest expected processing time (SEPT) rule (see Klimov [27], for example) minimizes the mean sojourn time in many single server, multiclass queueing systems. The SEPT rule, however, can lead to a very large sojourn time variance; when the load on the system is very heavy, customers with the largest expected processing times may sit in the queue for a long period of time, while customers with the shortest expected processing time will usually move through the system relatively quickly. Thus, a fundamental tradeoff exists in single server, multiclass queues between system *efficiency* (minimizing mean sojourn time) and system *equitability* (minimizing sojourn time variance). As a result, some authors (see Jackson [16], [17], [18], Kleinrock [25], and Shanthikumar [38], for example) have suggested and analyzed alternative scheduling policies that attempt to address this tradeoff in an effective manner.

However, very little is known about this tradeoff in a network setting. Indeed, just obtaining sojourn time variances in single class queueing networks under the FCFS policy is an arduous task (see Chapter 4 of Walrand [41] and references therein). The bi-criteria scheduling problems analyzed here will attempt to address this tradeoff. Before describing the various criteria, the basic queueing network underlying all three queueing systems will be defined. Using the terminology of Kelly [23], we assume the queueing network is visited by various *types* of customers, each with its own arbitrary deterministic route through the system. In a manufacturing setting, a customer type represents a particular product that is produced by the facility. A different customer *class* will be defined for each combination of type and stage of completion, and each customer class is served at a particular single server station in the network, and has its own general service time distribution.

The first of the three queueing systems is a single server queue, where each customer type has its own independent renewal input process and has one stage on its route. The second system is a two-station *closed* network, where the total population in the network is held constant, and when a customer departs the network, the type of the new customer is chosen exogenously (in a Markovian or deterministic fashion) according to a specified product mix. In both of these systems, the scheduling decision is to dynamically decide which customer class to serve next at each station; we will refer to these decisions as *sequencing* decisions. The third system is a two-station network with controllable inputs, where the scheduler also decides when to release the next customer into the network. We assume that a specified expected average throughput rate must be maintained, and an infinite number of customers are lined up outside the network waiting to gain entrance. The type of each entering customer is again exogenously specified according to a particular product mix.

Since analyzing the variance of sojourn times is so difficult in a multiclass queueing network, and since the five step procedure is most easily used when the objective is in terms of the vector queue length process, we propose a surrogate measure for the bi-criteria scheduling problems. In order to motivate our measure, notice that although all customers in a single server, single class FCFS queue have the same steady-state mean sojourn time, a customer's actual sojourn time depends on two random variables, its actual processing time and the workload in the queue at the time of its arrival. However, in a FCFS network populated by various types of customers, different customer types will have different steady state mean sojourn times; customer types with longer routes (or larger mean processing times) will experience longer steady state mean sojourn times than customer types with shorter routes (or smaller mean processing times). Furthermore, a significant portion of the overall sojourn time variance may be due to the difference in sojourn times across types, rather than within types.

In this chapter, we will focus on reducing the variability of sojourn times *across* types by minimizing the long run expected average *sojourn time inequity*, where the inequity at time $t$ is the sum of squares of pairwise differences of the total number of customers in the system of each type at time $t$ divided by their respective arrival rates. If one could maintain the sojourn time inequity process at zero for all times $t$, then (by Little's formula) each customer type will have the same mean sojourn time in steady state.

The sojourn time inequity is a cruder measure than the sojourn time variance; for example, the inequity in a single class queue is always zero, regardless of the queueing discipline in use. However, the inequity process does allow us to capture the first-order effects of equalizing the sojourn times across types. In many cases, a reduction in the sojourn time inequity may lead to a reduction in the actual sojourn time variance. However, if the reduction in inequity results in a large increase in the mean sojourn time, an increase in actual sojourn time variance may occur. In such cases, solving the bi-criteria scheduling problem for various values of the weighting factor $c$ (defined in the next paragraph) may lead to a reduction in sojourn time variance.

The first of the two criteria in each of the three minimization problems is to minimize the long run expected average sojourn time inequity. In the single station queue and the network with controllable inputs, the second criterion is the long run expected average number of customers in the system, which is proportional to the long run expected average sojourn time in both systems by Little's formula. In the closed network, the second criterion is the long run expected average idleness rate at an arbitrarily chosen server, which is inversely proportional to the mean throughput rate of the network. Hence, minimizing the mean idleness rate of a server will minimize the mean sojourn time of customers. In all three problems, a weight $c$ will be put on the second criterion, and the objective is to minimize the weighted average of the two criteria. When $c = 0$, the objective is to minimize the sojourn time inequity, and when $c \to \infty$, the objective is to minimize the mean sojourn time.

In the limiting $c \to \infty$ case, the three scheduling problems described above have been analyzed in [12] (single queue), Harrison and Wein [14] (closed network), and Wein [42], [43] (network with controllable inputs) by solving and interpreting a reformulation of the approximating Brownian control problem. In this chapter, we generalize these analyses to include the bi-criteria objective for any value of $c$. For the single queue, we find in Section 7.2 that FCFS is effective in minimizing the sojourn time inequity, which is not surprising in light of Groenevelt's [9] results. The closed network and network with controllable inputs are analyzed in Sections 7.3 and 7.4, respectively, and a simulation experiment involving a two-station network is undertaken in Section 7.5 that demonstrates the effectiveness of the procedure. In Section 7.6, we provide a brief survey of research on heavy traffic analysis of queueing network scheduling problems.

In the simulation experiment, significant reductions in sojourn time inequity are achieved under the proposed policies, and these reductions are accompanied by corresponding reductions in sojourn time variance. However, the nature of the tradeoff between mean sojourn time and sojourn time variance is problem specific; as the parameter in the objective function is reduced from $c \to \infty$ to $c = 0$, it is possible to achieve a small reduction in sojourn time variance coupled with a large increase in mean sojourn time, or a large reduction in sojourn time variance combined with a small increase in mean sojourn time (see Tables III and IV, respectively). We show how the Brownian analysis can predict the nature of this tradeoff for any given example, and simulate our test example under two sets of data in order to illustrate these two extreme cases.

Although FCFS is effective at minimizing sojourn time variance in the single server case, we find that it is easily outperformed on this dimension in the network case. Moreover, in both simulated examples, a sequencing policy is found that simultaneously reduced the mean sojourn time and the sojourn time variance with respect to FCFS.

This section concludes with the probabilistic formalisms that will be adopted in this chapter. When we say that $X$ is a $K$-dimensional $(\mu, \Sigma)$ Brownian motion (readers are referred to Karatzas and Shreve [22] for a definition), it is assumed there is a given $(\Omega, \mathbf{F}, \mathbf{F_t}, X, P_x)$, where $(\Omega, \mathbf{F})$ is a measurable space, $X = X(\omega)$ is a measurable mapping of $\Omega$ into $\mathbf{C}(\mathbf{R^K})$, which is the space of continuous functions on $\mathbf{R^K}$, $\mathbf{F_t} = \sigma(X(s), s \leq t)$ is the filtration generated by $X$, and $P_x$ is a family of probability measures on $\Omega$ such that the process $\{X(t), t \geq 0\}$ is a Brownian motion with drift $\mu$, covariance matrix $\Sigma$, and initial state $x$ under $P_x$. Let $E_x$ be the expectation operator associated with $P_x$. If $Y = \{Y(t), t \geq 0\}$ is a process that is $\mathbf{F_t}$-measurable for all $t \geq 0$, then we say that the process $Y$ is *non-anticipating* with respect to the Brownian motion $X$. More generally, we will say that one process $Y$ is non-anticipating with respect to another process $X$ when $Y$ is adapted to the coarsest filtration with respect to which $X$ is adapted.

## 7.2    A Single Server Queue

### 7.2.1    The Scheduling Problem

Consider a single server queue visited by $K$ customer types who arrive according to independent renewal processes $\{A_k(t), t \geq 0\}$, and who exit the system after receiving service. Thus, a one-to-one correspondence exists between class and type. The interarrival times of type $k$ have mean $\lambda_k^{-1}$ and variance $a_k^2$. Each customer type has a general service time distribution with mean $m_k$ and variance $s_k^2$, and following queueing theory convention, we will refer to $\mu_k = m_k^{-1}$ as type $k$'s service rate. The service times for type $k$ are equivalently characterized by the renewal process $\{S_k(t), t \geq 0\}$, which is the number of type $k$ service completions up to time $t$ if the server were continuously serving type $k$ jobs in the interval $[0, t]$. No set-up costs or times are incurred when switching service from one job type to another.

The state of the system is described by the $K$-dimensional process $Q = (Q_k)$, where $Q_k(t)$ is the number of type $k$ customers in the system at time $t$. The decisions in our scheduling problem take the form of cumulative control processes. In particular, let the *allocation process* $\{T_k(t), t \geq 0\}$ be the cumulative amount of time that the server devotes to serving type $k$ jobs in $[0, t]$. Then the vector $T = (T_k)$ represents the scheduling policy. If we assume that $Q(0) = 0$, then it follows that for $k = 1, \ldots, K$ and $t \geq 0$,

$$Q_k(t) = A_k(t) - S_k(T_k(t)). \tag{7.1}$$

Furthermore, if we define the *cumulative idleness process* $\{I(t), t \geq 0\}$ to be the cumulative amount of time the server is idle in $[0, t]$, then

$$I(t) = t - \sum_{k=1}^{K} T_k(t) \text{ for } t \geq 0. \tag{7.2}$$

As in [12], a scheduling policy $T$ must satisfy

$$Q(t) \geq 0 \text{ for } t \geq 0, \tag{7.3}$$

$$T \text{ is nondecreasing and continuous with } T(0) = 0, \qquad (7.4)$$
$$T \text{ is nonanticipating with respect to } Q, \qquad (7.5)$$
$$I \text{ is nondecreasing with } I(0) = 0, \qquad (7.6)$$

where constraint (7.5) implies that the scheduler cannot observe future arrival times or service times.

Recall from the introduction that the sojourn time inequity at time $t$ was defined as the sum of squares of pairwise differences of the number of customer of each type in the system at time $t$ divided by their respective arrival rates. Thus our objective function can be written as

$$\limsup_{T \to \infty} \frac{1}{T} E\Big[ \int_0^T \Big( c \sum_{k=1}^K Q_k(t) + \frac{1}{2} \sum_{j=1}^K \sum_{k=1}^K \Big( \frac{Q_j(t)}{\lambda_j} - \frac{Q_k(t)}{\lambda_k} \Big)^2 \Big) dt \Big]. \quad (7.7)$$

The first term in (7.7) is proportional to the mean steady-state sojourn time by Little's formula, and the second term is the long run expected average sojourn time inequity. Ideally, the process $Q$ would be chosen so that the sojourn time inequity process is zero for all times $t$, in which case each customer type will have the same long run average mean sojourn time. Although this state of affairs cannot always be achieved, the second term in the objective should still aid in equating the sojourn times across customer types. The scheduling problem is to choose a policy $T$ to minimize (7.7) subject to constraints (7.1)–(7.6).

## 7.2.2   The Limiting Control Problem

In this subsection, we follow the approach taken in Sections 3 through 5 of [12] to develop a Brownian approximation to the control problem (7.1)–(7.7). Only the basics of the approximation are provided, and readers are referred to [12] for a more detailed presentation and justification. The first step in the approximation is to define a collection of *centered processes*. Let $\rho_k = \lambda_k/\mu_k$ be the proportion of time that must be devoted to serving type $k$ jobs in order to satisfy the average customer demand. The *traffic intensity* of the system, defined by $\rho = \sum_{k=1}^K \rho_k$, is the average server utilization required to satisfy average demand. Define $\alpha_k = \rho_k/\rho$ to be the proportion of the server's busy time that would be devoted to serving type $k$ jobs if the server met average demand exactly. For $k = 1, \ldots, K$ and $t \geq 0$, define the centered processes

$$V_k(t) = \alpha_k t - T_k(t) \qquad \text{and} \qquad (7.8)$$
$$\eta_k(t) = S_k(t) - \mu_k t. \qquad (7.9)$$

Finally, define the $K$-dimensional process $\chi_k$ by

$$\chi_k(t) = (\lambda_k - \mu_k \alpha_k)t - \eta_k(T_k(t)) + A_k(t) - \lambda_k t$$
$$\text{for } k = 1, \ldots, K \text{ and } t \geq 0. \quad (7.10)$$

Then it follows from (7.1) and (7.2), respectively, that

$$Q_k(t) = \chi_k(t) + \mu_k V_k(t) \text{ for } k = 1, \ldots, K \text{ and } t \geq 0, \text{ and} \quad (7.11)$$

$$I(t) = \sum_{k=1}^{K} V_k(t) \text{ for } t \geq 0. \quad (7.12)$$

The key to the approximation is to replace the allocation process $T_k(t)$ in (7.10) by $\alpha_k t$; readers are referred to Section 5 of [12] for an informal defense of this substitution, and to Section 11 of that paper for an alternative substitution. The final step in the Brownian approximation is to *rescale* the basic processes under heavy traffic conditions, which assume the existence of a large integer $n$ that equals $(1 - \rho)^{-2}$. A representative example is to choose $n = 100$ if the traffic intensity $\rho = 0.9$. Using the system parameter $n$, we define the scaled processes

$$Z_k(t) = \frac{Q_k(nt)}{\sqrt{n}} \quad \text{for } k = 1, \ldots, K \text{ and } t \geq 0, \quad (7.13)$$

$$Y_k(t) = \frac{V_k(nt)}{\sqrt{n}} \quad \text{for } k = 1, \ldots, K \text{ and } t \geq 0, \text{ and} \quad (7.14)$$

$$U(t) = \frac{I(nt)}{\sqrt{n}} \quad \text{for } k = 1, \ldots, K \text{ and } t \geq 0, \quad (7.15)$$

and the Brownian approximation is essentially obtained by letting the parameter $n \to \infty$. The processes $Z$, $Y$ and $I$ now represent limiting scaled processes, but will be referred to simply as the queue length, allocation and idleness processes, respectively.

The process $\chi$ in (7.10) also needs to be rescaled. Define $\chi_k^n$ by

$$\chi_k^n(t) = \frac{\chi_k(nt)}{\sqrt{n}} \text{ for } k = 1, \ldots, K \text{ and } t \geq 0. \quad (7.16)$$

Then a straightforward application of the functional central limit theorem for renewal processes, the random time change theorem (see Section 17 of Billingsley 1968 [2]) and the continuous mapping theorem ([2], Theorem 5.1) implies that

$$\chi_k^n \Rightarrow X_k \text{ for } k = 1, \ldots, K, \quad (7.17)$$

where $\Rightarrow$ denotes weak convergence, and $X_1, \ldots, X_k$ are independent Brownian motion processes with drift $\sqrt{n}(\lambda_k - \mu_k \alpha_k)$ and variance $\lambda_k^3 a_k^2 + \alpha_k \mu_k^3 s_k^2$. Although the heavy traffic parameter $n$ appears in the drift term, we will see later that the proposed scheduling policy is independent of $n$.

We are now in a position to state the *limiting control problem*, which is to choose a $K$-dimensional RCLL (right continuous with left limits) process $Y$ to

$$\min \limsup_{T \to \infty} \frac{1}{T} E\left[ \int_0^T \left( c \sum_{k=1}^{K} Z_k(t) + \frac{1}{2} \sum_{j=1}^{K} \sum_{k=1}^{K} \left( \frac{Z_j(t)}{\lambda_j} - \frac{Z_k(t)}{\lambda_k} \right)^2 \right) dt \right]$$

$$(7.18)$$

subject to $Z_k(t) = X_k(t) + \mu_k Y_k(t)$ for $k = 1, \ldots, K$ and $t \geq 0$,  (7.19)

$$U(t) = \sum_{k=1}^{K} Y_k(t) \text{ for } t \geq 0, \tag{7.20}$$

$Z(t) \geq 0$ for $t \geq 0$,  (7.21)

$U$ is nondecreasing with $U(0) = 0$, and  (7.22)

$Y(0) = 0$ and $Y$ is nonanticipating with respect to $X$. (7.23)

### 7.2.3  The Workload Formulation

The state of the system in the Brownian control problem (7.18)–(7.23) is the $K$-dimensional queue length process $Z$ defined in (7.19). The next step in our procedure is to find an *equivalent* reformulation of the problem where the state of the system is described by the the one-dimensional *workload* process

$$W(t) = \sum_{k=1}^{K} m_k Z_k(t) \text{ for } t \geq 0, \tag{7.24}$$

which represents the amount of work present in the system at time $t$. Define $B(t) = \sum_{k=1}^{K} m_k X_k(t)$, so that $B$ is a one-dimensional Brownian motion process with drift $\sqrt{n}(\rho - 1)$ and variance $\sum_{k=1}^{K} \lambda_k^3 a_k^2 m_k^2 + \sum_{k=1}^{K} \alpha_k \mu_k s_k^2$. The workload formulation of the limiting control problem is to choose RCLL processes $Z$ and $U$ ($K$-dimensional and one-dimensional, respectively) to

$$\min \limsup_{T \to \infty} \frac{1}{T} E\left[ \int_0^T \left( c \sum_{k=1}^{K} Z_k(t) + \frac{1}{2} \sum_{j=1}^{K} \sum_{k=1}^{K} \left( \frac{Z_j(t)}{\lambda_j} - \frac{Z_k(t)}{\lambda_k} \right)^2 \right) dt \right]$$

(7.25)

subject to $\sum_{k=1}^{K} m_k Z_k(t) = B(t) + (t)$ for all $t \geq 0$,  (7.26)

$Z(t) \geq 0$ for $t \geq 0$,  (7.27)

$U$ is nondecreasing with $U(0) = 0$, and  (7.28)

$Z$ and $U$ are nonanticipating with respect to $X$.  (7.29)

A policy $Y$ is said to be *feasible* for the limiting control problem if it satisfies (7.19)–(7.23) and a policy $(Z, U)$ is feasible for the workload formulation if it satisfies (7.26)–(7.29). The following proposition, which was derived for open queueing networks in Section 6 of [12], allows us to analyze the workload formulation of the limiting control problem in lieu of studying problem (7.18)–(7.23) directly.

**Proposition 7.2.1** Every feasible policy $Y$ for the limiting control problem yields a corresponding feasible policy $(Z, U)$ for the workload formulation, and every feasible policy $(Z, U)$ yields a corresponding feasible policy $Y$.

**Proof.** Let $Y$ be any feasible policy for the limiting control problem, thus yielding an associated pair of processes $(Z, U)$ from equations (7.19)–(7.20). Premultiplying (7.19) by $m_k$ and summing over $k$ gives equation (7.26). Since constraints (7.21)–(7.23) are satisfied, the policy $(Z, U)$ is feasible.

Reversing the argument, suppose that $(Z, U)$ is a feasible policy for the workload formulation. Then constraints (7.21)–(7.22) are satisfied and, using equation (7.19), one can define a corresponding control process $Y$ satisfying (7.23) by

$$Y_k(t) = m_k^{-1}[Z_k(t) - X_k(t)] \text{ for } k = 1, \ldots, K \text{ and } t \geq 0. \tag{7.30}$$

The associated queue length and cumulative idleness processes in (7.19) and (7.20) are precisely the processes $Z$ and $U$, respectively, that we started with. Hence, $Y$ is a feasible policy. $\square$

Not only is the workload formulation easier to solve than the limiting control problem, but its solution is also easier to interpret in terms of the original queueing system. As will be seen in the next subsection, the solution $(Z, U)$ to the workload formulation will not only be nonanticipating with respect $X$, but will also be nonanticipating with respect to $B$. Furthermore, the form of the scheduling policy is independent of the parameters of the various Brownian motion processes.

### 7.2.4   Solution to the Workload Formulation

The workload formulation (7.25)–(7.29) will be solved in two steps. In the first step, the optimal control process $Z$ is derived in terms of the control process $U$. The second step consists of deriving the optimal control process $U$. Let us begin with the limiting $c \to \infty$ case that was solved by [12], where the objective is to minimize the mean sojourn time. Suppose we are given a process $U$ that satisfies constraints (7.28)–(7.29). Consider the following linear program that is imbedded in the workload formulation at time $t$:

$$\min_{Z(t)} \sum_{k=1}^{K} Z_k(t) \tag{7.31}$$

$$\text{subject to } \sum_{k=1}^{K} m_k Z_k(t) = W(t), \tag{7.32}$$

$$Z(t) \geq 0, \tag{7.33}$$

where the righthand side value $W(t)$ is nonnegative and observable at time $t$ and, by (7.24)–(7.26) equals $B(t) + U(t)$.

Without loss of generality, let $m_j = \max_{1 \leq k \leq K} m_k$. Then for all non-negative values of the workload process $W(t)$, the solution to the linear program is $Z_j(t) = W(t)/m_j$ and $Z_k(t) = 0$ for $k \neq j$. If we denote the dual variable by $\pi(t)$, then the dual linear program of (7.31)–(7.33) is:

$$\max_{\pi(t)} \ W(t)\pi(t) \tag{7.34}$$

$$\text{subject to } m_k \pi(t) \leq 1 \text{ for } k = 1, \ldots, K. \tag{7.35}$$

The dual variable $\pi(t)$ is interpreted as the increase in the value of the primal objective function (7.31) per increase in the value of the righthand side value $W(t)$. For any nonnegative value of $W(t)$, the solution to the dual problem (7.17)–(7.20) is $\pi(t) = 1/m_j$ which is nonnegative. Thus it follows (see Yang [51] for details) that the workload formulation (7.25)–(7.29) can be solved by finding the process $U$ that minimizes the process $W$, and then solving the linear program (7.31)–(7.33) at each point in time.

It is well known (see Harrison [11]) that the process defined by

$$U(t) = -\inf_{0 \leq s \leq t} B(s) \tag{7.36}$$

minimizes the value of $U(t)$ for all times $t$ with probability one subject to constraints (7.26)–(7.29). Thus, the minimum righthand side value in (7.32) is

$$W^*(t) = B(t) - \inf_{0 \leq s \leq t} B(s), \tag{7.37}$$

which is nonnegative. Hence, the solution to the workload formulation is $(Z^*, U^*)$, where $Z_j^*(t) = W^*(t)/m_j$ and $Z_k^*(t) = 0$ for $k \neq j$. Notice that this solution is optimal in a much stronger sense than expressed in (7.25); the value of $\sum_{k=1}^{K} Z_k(t)$ is minimized for all times $t$ with probability one. Such a solution will be referred to as a *pathwise* solution to the workload formulation.

When $0 < c < \infty$, the following quadratic program must be solved at each point in time:

$$\min_{Z_k(t)} \ c \sum_{k=1}^{K} Z_k(t) + \frac{1}{2} \sum_{j=1}^{K} \sum_{k=1}^{K} \left( \frac{Z_j(t)}{\lambda_j} - \frac{Z_k(t)}{\lambda_k} \right)^2 \tag{7.38}$$

$$\text{subject to } \sum_{k=1}^{K} m_k Z_k(t) = W(t), \tag{7.39}$$

$$Z(t) \geq 0. \tag{7.40}$$

The dual to this quadratic program (see Dorn [5]) is

$$\max_{Z(t),\pi(t)} \ -\frac{1}{2} \sum_{j=1}^{K} \sum_{k=1}^{K} \left( \frac{Z_j(t)}{\lambda_j} - \frac{Z_k(t)}{\lambda_k} \right)^2 + W(t)\pi(t) \tag{7.41}$$

subject to    $-\dfrac{2(K-1)Z_k}{\lambda_k^2} + \dfrac{2}{\lambda_k}\sum_{j\neq k}\dfrac{Z_j}{\lambda_j} + m_k\pi(t) \le c$ for $k = 1,\dots,K$.

$$(7.42)$$

Since the objective function in (7.41) is convex, no duality gap exists and readers may verify that $\pi^*(t)$ is nonnegative for all nonnegative values of $W(t)$. Thus, the solution $Z^*$ to the quadratic program (7.38)–(7.40) coupled with $U^*$ in (7.36) yields a pathwise solution to the workload formulation.

For the $c = 0$ case, the solution to (7.38)–(7.40) is

$$Z_k^*(t) = \frac{\lambda_k W(t)}{\rho}\text{ for } k = 1,\dots,K\text{ and } t \ge 0, \qquad (7.43)$$

since it is feasible and achieves an objective function value of zero, regardless of the value of the workload process $W(t)$. Although any process $U$ satisfying (7.28)–(7.29) will lead to a pathwise solution when paired with $Z^*$, a natural candidate is to choose $U^*$ in (7.36), since it also minimizes the workload process.

### 7.2.5   Interpreting the Solution to the Workload Formulation

In this subsection, the solution $(Z^*, U^*)$ to the workload formulation will be interpreted in terms of the original queueing system in order to develop an effective scheduling policy. It is well-known that the optimal process $\{U^*(t), t \ge 0\}$ in (7.36) increases only when $W(t) = 0$. Recalling the definitions of the processes $U$ and $W$, we see that the server incurs idleness only when no customers are in the system. Thus, the natural interpretation of (7.36) is to allow the server to work whenever work is available.

According to (7.24), the scheduler can choose any nonnegative values of $Z_k(t), k = 1,\dots,K$, that are consistent with the present workload process $W(t)$. Hence, in the Brownian limit, the queue lengths of various types can be instantaneously exchanged for one another, as long as the work content in these queues remain unchanged. As explained in [12], these exchanges can be interpreted as reallocation of server time among the various types, and they appear to occur instantaneously because we are observing the system in scaled time.

In the $c \to \infty$ case, where minimization of the mean sojourn time is the objective, only one of the $K$ components of $Z$ is ever positive, namely, type $j$, where $\mu_j = max_{1\le k\le K}\mu_k$. This is interpreted to mean that customers of type $j$ are only served when there are no other customers present in the system. Under heavy traffic conditions, it does not matter in what order the other $K-1$ customer types are served, as long as the server is kept busy when there is work for them to do. This is because the $K-1$ customer types will not see the queueing system in a heavy traffic situation, and consequently their scaled queue lengths will be negligible compared to the bottom two priority types. This phenomenon of the normalized queue length processes of high priority customers vanishing in the heavy traffic limit has been observed in previous work. Whitt [49], Harrison [10], and Reiman [36] have obtained heavy traffic limit theorems in a single-station system, and Johnson [19] and Peterson [35] have obtained similar results in a network setting.

Since the $K - 1$ customer types each have zero scaled queue length in the limiting Brownian model, there is some ambiguity that remains in specifying a sequencing rule that emerges from the solution of the Brownian control problem. However, the quantity $\mu_k$ is a natural index to use to prioritize the various customer types. In particular, we propose to award higher priority to customer types with larger values of the index $\mu_k$. As noted in [12], this policy is equivalent to the well-known shortest expected processing time rule (see [27], for example), which minimizes the mean sojourn time in many single server multiclass queueing systems.

In the $c = 0$ case, where we are attempting to minimize the sojourn time inequity, the queue lengths of the various types are in direct proportion to their respective arrival rates. [19] and [35] have shown that this same proportionality also holds under the FCFS policy in the heavy traffic limit. Thus, our analysis suggests that the FCFS policy is effective in reducing sojourn time variance in single server, multiclass queues. It is encouraging to note that our analysis concurs with a related result using exact methods (see [9]).

When $0 < c < \infty$, we propose the following procedure to obtain an effective sequencing policy. First, find the solution $(Z_k^*(t), \pi^*)$ to the dual quadratic program (7.41)–(7.42). This solution $Z^*$ will yield a unique value of the unscaled workload vector in steady state by the conservation law in [25], and then the unique parameters for Kleinrock's delay dependent discipline (see [25], Kleinrock [26]) can be derived that will achieve this workload vector. In particular, the synthesis algorithm of Wood and Sargeant [50] offers a simple iterative algorithm (where a quadratic equation is solved at each step) to derive the necessary parameters (see also Federgruen and Groenevelt [6] for a generalization of this algorithm).

## 7.3  A Closed Network

The five steps in the procedure for analyzing queueing network scheduling problems were illustrated in detail for a particular problem in Subsections 7.2.1 through 7.2.5, respectively. To avoid redundancy and an excessive amount of notation, we will go directly to the workload formulation of the limiting control problem for the scheduling problems addressed in this section and the next section. The derivations of the limiting control problem and the equivalent workload formulation for these networks are very similar to the corresponding derivations for the single server system in Subsections

7.2.2 and 7.2.3, respectively. However, these derivations are considerably more involved due to the increased complexity of the underlying queueing system.

## 7.3.1   The Workload Formulation

For the networks in this section and the next section, we will index single server stations by $i = 1, 2$, customer classes by $k = 1, \ldots, K$, and customer types by $j = 1, \ldots, J$. Since a different customer class is defined for each combination of customer type and stage of completion, we have $K \geq J$. Let $\tau(j)$ be the set of classes that are on the route of type $j$. The total population size of the closed network considered in this section is always maintained at $N$, and this is achieved by releasing a new customer into the network whenever one exits. The new customer will be of class $k$ with probability $q_k$, independent of all previous history, where $\sum_{k=1}^{K} q_k = 1$; alternatively, entering customers can be chosen according to the mix $q_k$ in a deterministic fashion, and the only change in the analysis is the covariance matrix of the underlying Brownian motion. Of course, $q_k > 0$ only for those classes that correspond to the first stage of some customer type's route. We will also let $\bar{q}_j = \sum_{k \in \tau(j)} q_k$, so that entering customers are of type $j$ with probability $\bar{q}_j$.

Recall that each customer type has its own arbitrary deterministic route through the network. In the workload formulation of the Brownian control problem, the routing information is captured in the quantity $M_{ik}$, which is the expected remaining processing time at station $i$ for a class $k$ customer until that customer exits the network. The $2 \times K$ matrix $M = (M_{ik})$ will be referred to as the workload profile matrix. For $i = 1, 2$, define $v_i = \sum_{k=1}^{K} M_{ik} q_k$, so that $v_i$ is the expected total time over the long run that server $i$ devotes to each newly arriving customer. Define the relative traffic intensity $\rho_i$ for station $i$ to be $v_i / \max\{v_1, v_2\}$ for $i = 1, 2$. Then the balanced heavy loading conditions for the closed network assume the existence of a sufficiently large integer $N$ such that the total population size is $N$ and $N|\rho_1 - \rho_2|$ is of moderate size; a representative example is $N = 10$ and $\rho_1 = \rho_2 = 1$.

As in the previous section, the queue length process and server idleness process need to be rescaled, this time by the population parameter $N$. Let $Z_k(t) = Q_k(N^2 t)/N$ for $k = 1, \ldots, K$ and $t \geq 0$, and $U_i(t) = I_i(N^2 t)/N$ for $i = 1, 2$ and $t \geq 0$. Let $\{\hat{B}(t), t \geq 0\}$ be a one-dimensional Brownian motion process with drift $\mu$ and variance $\sigma^2$ (their specific values are not required here), and define the workload imbalance profile vector $\hat{M} = (\hat{M}_K)$ by

$$\hat{M}_k = \rho_2 M_{1k} - \rho_1 M_{2k} \text{ for } k = 1, \ldots, K. \tag{7.44}$$

By Propositions 2 and 7 in Harrison and Wein [15], the workload formulation can be expressed as choosing RCLL processes $(U, Z)$ that are nonanticipating with respect to $\hat{B}$ such that

$$\sum_{k=1}^{K} \hat{M}_k Z_k(t) = \hat{B}(t) + \rho_2 U_1(t) - \rho_1 U_2(t) \text{ for all } t \geq 0, \qquad (7.45)$$

$$\sum_{k=1}^{K} Z_k(t) = 1 \text{ for all } t \geq 0, \qquad (7.46)$$

$$Z_k(t) \geq 0 \text{ for } k = 1, \ldots, K \text{ and for all } t \geq 0, \text{ and} \qquad (7.47)$$

$$U_1 \text{ and } U_2 \text{ are nondecreasing with } U_1(0) = U_2(0) = 0. \qquad (7.48)$$

If the number of customers exiting the network per unit of time is $\lambda$ over the long run and $Z_k(\infty)$ denotes the scaled vector queue length process in steady-state, then by Little's formula, the mean steady-state sojourn time of type $j$ customers is $E[\sum_{k \in \tau(j)} Z_k(\infty)]/\bar{q}_j \lambda$. Even though the throughput rate of the network is unknown, we can express our bi-criteria objective as

$$\min \limsup_{T \to \infty} \frac{1}{T} E \left[ cU_1(T) + \left( \frac{\sum_{k \in \tau(i)} Z_k(t)}{\bar{q}_i} - \frac{\sum_{k \in \tau(j)} Z_k(t)}{\bar{q}_j} \right)^2 dt \right]. \qquad (7.49)$$

## 7.3.2   The $c \to \infty$ Case

We begin by analyzing the limiting case where the objective is to maximize the throughput rate of the network. This case was analyzed in [15]. Define the one-dimensional workload imbalance process $\hat{W}$ by

$$\hat{W}(t) = \sum_{k=1}^{K} \hat{M}_k Z_k(t) \text{ for } t \geq 0. \qquad (7.50)$$

It is clear from equations (7.46), (7.47) and (7.50) that the workload imbalance process must reside within the *workload imbalance interval* $[a^*, b^*]$, where $a^* = \min_{1 \leq k \leq K} \hat{M}_k$, $b^* = \max_{1 \leq k \leq K} \hat{M}_k$, $a^* \leq 0 \leq b^*$, and $a^* < b^*$.
By equations (7.45) and (7.50), it follows that

$$\hat{W}(t) = \hat{B}(t) + \rho_2 U_1(t) - \rho_1 U_2(t) \text{ for } t \geq 0. \qquad (7.51)$$

Thus, the workload imbalance formulation can be analyzed in a two-step procedure. The first problem is to find an optimal control $(U_1^*, U_2^*)$ (that is nonanticipating with respect to $\hat{B}$) to minimize $\limsup_{T \to \infty} T^{-1} E[U_1(T)]$ subject to constraints (7.48) and (7.51) and subject to the workload imbalance process $\hat{W}$ residing in the interval $[a^*, b^*]$. The solution $U^*$ to the first problem will lead to an optimal workload imbalance process $\hat{W}^*$ via equation (7.51) with $U^*$ replacing $U$, and the second problem is to choose an optimal process $Z^*$ that is nonanticipating with respect to $\hat{B}$ and satisfies equations (7.46), (7.47) and (7.50), with $\hat{W}^*$ replacing $\hat{W}$ in (7.50). We will now discuss the two problems in turn.

It is well known that the optimal solution $U^*$ to the first problem is

$$U_1^*(t) \quad = \quad \frac{1}{\rho_2} \sup_{0 \le s \le t} [a^* - \hat{B}(s) + \rho_1 U_2^*(s)]^+, \text{ and} \qquad (7.52)$$

$$U_2^*(t) \quad = \quad \frac{1}{\rho_1} \sup_{0 \le s \le t} [\hat{B}(s) + \rho_2 U_1^*(s) - b^*]^+, \qquad (7.53)$$

so that $\hat{B}(t) + \rho_2 U_1^*(t) - \rho_1 U_2^*(t), t \ge 0$, is a one-dimensional reflected (or regulated) Brownian motion (abbreviated by RBM; see [11] for a complete treatment) on the interval $[a^*, b^*]$. Since our objective function is to exert the control $U$ as little as possible subject to keeping $\hat{W}$ in $[a^*, b^*]$, it is not surprising that the control $U$ is exerted only when the process $\hat{W}$ reaches the two endpoints of the closed interval.

If we define

$$\hat{W}^*(t) = \hat{B}(t) + \rho_2 U_1^*(t) - \rho_1 U_2^*(t) \qquad (7.54)$$

and assume (without loss of generality) that the classes $k = 1, \ldots, K$ are ordered so that $\max_{1 \le k \le K} \hat{M}_k = \hat{M}_1$ and $\min_{1 \le k \le K} \hat{M}_k = \hat{M}_2$, then

$$Z_k^*(t) = \begin{cases} \gamma(t) & \text{if } k = 1; \\ 1 - \gamma(t) & \text{if } k = 2; \\ 0 & \text{if } k = 3, \ldots, K, \end{cases} \qquad (7.55)$$

for all $t \ge 0$, where

$$\gamma(t) = \frac{\hat{W}^*(t) - a^*}{b^* - a^*} \text{ for all } t \ge 0. \qquad (7.56)$$

As in the single queue case, $(Z^*, U^*)$ is a pathwise solution to problem (7.45)–(7.49). The resulting sequencing policy (see [15] for an interpretation of the solution $(Z^*, U^*)$) is to rank each customer class $k = 1, \ldots, K$ by the index $\hat{M}_k$, and to award higher priority at station 1 (respectively, station 2) to the classes with smaller (respectively, larger) values of this index. Notice that, as in Section 7.2, this policy awards bottom priority at each station to the class that has a positive scaled queue length, thus maintaining consistency with existing heavy traffic limit theorems.

## 7.3.3   The $c = 0$ Case

Now let us analyze the other limiting case, where the objective is to minimize the sojourn time inequity. It is clear that the set of values $\hat{W}$ such that there exist $Z_1, \ldots, Z_k$ satisfying

$$\hat{W} = \sum_{k=1}^{K} \hat{M}_k Z_k, \tag{7.57}$$

$$\sum_{k=1}^{K} Z_k = 1, \tag{7.58}$$

$$Z_k \geq 0, \text{ for } k = 1, \ldots, K \text{ and} \tag{7.59}$$

$$\frac{\sum_{k \in \tau(i)} Z_k}{\bar{q}_i} - \frac{\sum_{k \in \tau(j)} Z_k}{\bar{q}_j} = 0 \text{ for } i \neq j, \tag{7.60}$$

is a closed interval on the real line that is a subset of the interval $[a^*, b^*]$. Let us denote this interval by $[a^0, b^0]$, where the superscript reminds us that we are analyzing the case $c = 0$. Therefore, any solution $(Z^0, U^0)$ that keeps $\hat{W}(t)$ within the interval $[a^0, b^0]$ will be a pathwise optimal solution to (7.45)–(7.49). There may be many pathwise solutions, and we propose to choose

$$U_1^0(t) = \frac{1}{\rho_2} \sup_{0 \leq s \leq t} [a^0 - \hat{B}(s) + \rho_1 U_2^0(s)]^+ \text{ and} \tag{7.61}$$

$$U_2^0(t) = \frac{1}{\rho_1} \sup_{0 \leq s \leq t} [\hat{B}(s) + \rho_2 U_1^0(s) - b^0]^+, \tag{7.62}$$

so that $\hat{W}(t)$ is a one-dimensional RBM on $[a^0, b^0]$. Among the pathwise solutions to (7.45)–(7.49), these control processes will maximize the mean throughput of the network (see Proposition 7.3.1 below), and hence will minimize the mean sojourn time.

In order to find an effective sequencing policy, we find solutions $Z^{a^0}$ and $Z^{b^0}$ that satisfy (7.57)–(7.60) under the two extreme points $\hat{W} = a^0$ and $\hat{W} = b^0$, respectively. All classes that have $Z_k^{a^0} = Z_k^{b^0} = 0$ will be in the higher priority bracket at their respective stations, and all other classes will be in the lower priority bracket. At each station, all classes within the higher priority bracket are given priority over all classes in the lower priority bracket. Within the higher priority bracket, classes are ranked in the same manner as when $c \to \infty$; this ranking maintains the spirit of minimizing mean sojourn time. A simple dynamic policy (that will be illustrated in the example in Section 7.5) is employed to attempt to maintain the actual queue lengths of the lower bracket classes in the same relative quantities as $Z^{a^0}$ and $Z^{b^0}$.

## 7.3.4   The Bi-Criteria Case

Now let us consider the general bi-criteria case where $0 < c < \infty$. Notice that our solution $(U_1, U_2)$ for both limiting cases (see (7.52)–(7.53) and (7.61)–(7.62)) are of a very special form (they are referred to as *control limit policies* in Harrison and Taksar [13]) and imply that $\hat{W}^*(t)$ in (7.54) is a RBM on some closed interval. We will restrict ourselves to this class of policies (this restriction will be justified shortly), so that a policy $(U_1, U_2)$ will be characterized by a particular closed interval $[a, b]$. It is clear that for $0 < c < \infty$, the optimal interval endpoints $a$ and $b$ will satisfy $a^* \leq a \leq a^0$ and $b^0 \leq b \leq b^*$, where $[a^*, b^*]$ characterizes the solution when $c \to \infty$, and $[a^0, b^0]$ characterizes the solution when $c = 0$.

For a control limit policy $(U_1, U_2)$ characterized by the interval $[a, b]$, the following two propositions are well-known results (see Chapter 5 of [11]).

**Proposition 7.3.1**

$$\lim_{T \to \infty} \frac{1}{T} E[U_1(T)] = \begin{cases} \frac{\mu}{\rho_2 (e^{\nu(b-a)} - 1)} & \text{if } \rho_1 \neq \rho_2; \\ \frac{\sigma^2}{2(b-a)} & \text{if } \rho_1 = \rho_2, \end{cases} \quad (7.63)$$

and

$$\lim_{T \to \infty} \frac{1}{T} E_x[U_2(T)] = \begin{cases} \frac{\mu}{\rho_1 (1 - e^{-\nu(b-a)})} & \text{if } \rho_1 \neq \rho_2; \\ \frac{\sigma^2}{2(b-a)} & \text{if } \rho_1 = \rho_2, \end{cases} \quad (7.64)$$

where $\nu = 2\mu/\sigma^2$.

**Proposition 7.3.2** If $\hat{W}(t)$ is a RBM on $[a, b]$, then $\hat{W}$ has a uniform steady-state distribution on $[a, b]$ if $\rho_1 = \rho_2$, and otherwise has a truncated exponential steady-state distribution with density function

$$p(x) = \frac{\nu e^{\nu(x-a)}}{e^{\nu(b-a)} - 1} \quad \text{for } a \leq x \leq b. \quad (7.65)$$

These results allow us to analyze (7.45)–(7.49) by considering the quadratic program

$$\min_{Z_k} \frac{1}{2} \sum_{i=1}^{J} \sum_{j=1}^{J} \left( \frac{\sum_{k \in \tau(i)} Z_k}{\bar{q}_i} - \frac{\sum_{k \in \tau(j)} Z_k}{\bar{q}_j} \right)^2 \quad (7.66)$$

$$\text{subject to } \sum_{k=1}^{K} \hat{M}_k Z_k = \hat{W}, \quad (7.67)$$

$$\sum_{K=1}^{K} Z_k = 1, \text{ and} \quad (7.68)$$

$$Z_k \geq 0, \text{ for } k = 1, \ldots, K, \quad (7.69)$$

as a function of the righthand side value $\hat{W}$. We will abbreviate the objective (7.66) by $\frac{1}{2}Z^T C Z$, where $C$ is a positive semidefinite matrix. The dual of this quadratic program (see [5]) is to choose $(Z_1, \ldots, Z_K, \pi_1, \pi_2)$ to

$$\max \quad -\frac{1}{2}Z^T C Z - \hat{W}\pi_1 - \pi_2 \tag{7.70}$$

$$\text{subject to } CZ - \hat{M}\pi_1 - e^T\pi_2 \geq 0, \tag{7.71}$$

where $\hat{M} = (\hat{M}_1, \ldots, \hat{M}_K)^T$ and $e = (1, \ldots, 1)^T$. Since the objective function in (7.66) is convex and the constraints (7.67)–(7.68) are linear, it follows that there is no duality gap. Furthermore, the dual objective function (7.70), which we denote by $h(\hat{W})$, is convex with respect to $\hat{W}$ on the interval $[a^*, b^*]$. Also, $h(\hat{W})$ achieves a minimum of zero on the interval $[a_0, b_0]$. By the convexity of $h(\hat{W})$, it follows from Taksar [40] that a control limit policy is indeed optimal for (7.45)–(7.49). Thus, under the policy characterized by the interval $[a, b]$, the value of the objective function (7.49), which we denote by $f(a, b)$, will be

$$f(a,b) = \begin{cases} \frac{c\mu}{\rho_2(e^{\nu(b-a)}-1)} + \int_a^b \frac{h(x)\nu e^{\nu(x-a)}}{(e^{\nu(b-a)}-1)}dx & \text{if } \rho_1 \neq \rho_2; \\ \frac{c\sigma^2}{2(b-a)} + \int_a^b \frac{h(x)}{(b-a)}dx & \text{if } \rho_1 = \rho_2. \end{cases} \tag{7.72}$$

Our solution can then be found by minimizing $f(a, b)$ subject to $a^* \leq a \leq a^0$ and $b^0 \leq b \leq b^*$. In order to develop a sequencing policy, we propose to proceed exactly as in the limiting case $c = 0$, except use the interval $[a, b]$ derived from the solution to (7.72) in place of the interval $[a^0, b^0]$ derived from (7.57)–(7.60).

## 7.4   A Network with Controllable Inputs

### 7.4.1   The Workload Formulation

The network considered in this section is identical to the closed network described in the previous section, except for the manner in which customers are released into the system. Here, customers are endogenously released according to the control process $\{N(t), t \geq 0\}$, where $N(t)$ is the number of customers released into the network up to time $t$. There is a constraint that the long run expected average number of customers departing the network per unit of time is at least $\bar{\lambda}$. The mix of customers released into the network is again exogenously generated according to the product mix $q = (q_k)$. As in Section 2, $v_i = \sum_{k=1}^K M_{ik}$ for $i = 1, 2$, but the traffic intensities are now defined by

$$\rho_i = v_i\bar{\lambda} \text{ for } i = 1, 2. \tag{7.73}$$

The balanced heavy loading conditions for the network assume the existence of a large integer $n$ such that $\sqrt{n}(1 - \rho_i)$ is positive and of moderate size for $i = 1, 2$.

Define the scaled *input process* $\{\theta(t), t \geq 0\}$ by

$$\theta(t) = \frac{\bar{\lambda}nt - N(nt)}{\sqrt{n}} \quad \text{for } t \geq 0, \tag{7.74}$$

and define the scaled queue length process $Z = (Z_k)$ and scaled idleness process $U = (U_1, U_2)$ as in Section 7.2. The workload formulation (see Section 3 of [43]) is to choose the RCLL processes $(U, Z, \theta)$ that are nonanticipating with respect to $B$ to minimize

$$\limsup_{T \to \infty} \frac{1}{T} E \left[ c \int_0^T \sum_{k=1}^K Z_k(t) \, dt + \right.$$
$$\left. \frac{1}{2} \int_0^T \sum_{i=1}^J \sum_{j=1}^J \left( \frac{\sum_{k \in \tau(i)} Z_k(t)}{\bar{q}_i} - \frac{\sum_{k \in \tau(j)} Z_k(t)}{\bar{q}_j} \right)^2 dt \right] \tag{7.75}$$

$$\text{subject to } \sum_{k=1}^K M_{ik} Z_k(t) = B_i(t) + U_i(t) - v_i \theta(t)$$
$$\text{for all } t \geq 0 \text{ and } i = 1, 2, \tag{7.76}$$

$$\limsup_{T \to \infty} \frac{1}{T} E[U_i(T)] \leq \gamma_i \text{ for } i = 1, 2, \tag{7.77}$$

$$Z_k(t) \geq 0 \text{ for } k = 1, \ldots, K \text{ and for all } t \geq 0, \text{ and} \tag{7.78}$$

$$U_1 \text{ and } U_2 \text{ are nondecreasing with } U_1(0) = U_2(0) = 0, \tag{7.79}$$

where $B$ is a two-dimensional Brownian motion and $\gamma_i = \sqrt{n}(1 - \rho_i)$, $i = 1, 2$.

## 7.4.2   Solution to the Workload Formulation

As in [42], this problem can be analyzed by first solving for the optimal control process $Z$ in terms of the control process $U$, and then deriving the optimal control process $U$. In particular, we can solve for $Z$ by solving, at each time $t$, the following quadratic program:

$$\min c \sum_{k=1}^K Z_k(t) + \frac{1}{2} \sum_{i=1}^J \sum_{j=1}^J \left( \frac{\sum_{k \in \tau(i)} Z_k(t)}{\bar{q}_i} - \frac{\sum_{k \in \tau(j)} Z_k(t)}{\bar{q}_j} \right)^2 \tag{7.80}$$

$$\text{subject to } \sum_{k=1}^K \hat{M}_k Z_k(t) = \hat{B}(t) + \rho_2 U_1(t) - \rho_1 U_2(t) \text{ for } t \geq 0, \tag{7.81}$$

$$Z_k(t) \geq 0, \text{ for } k = 1, \ldots, K, \tag{7.82}$$

where $\hat{M}_k$ is defined in (7.44), and $\hat{B}(t) = \rho_2 B_1(t) - \rho_1 B_2(t), t \geq 0$, is a one-dimensional Brownian motion with drift $\mu$ and variance $\sigma^2$. Notice that, by equation (7.73), the control process $\theta$ does not appear in equation (7.81). At each time $t$, this quadratic program has different values for the right side of (7.81), which is again denoted by $\hat{W}(t)$. The objective function will be abbreviated by $c^T Z(t) + \frac{1}{2} Z(t)^T C Z(t)$, where the matrix $C$ is positive semidefinite.

The dual of this quadratic program is to choose $Z(t)$ and $\pi(t)$ to

$$\max \quad -\frac{1}{2} Z^T C Z + \hat{W}\pi \qquad (7.83)$$

$$\text{subject to} \quad \hat{M}\pi - CZ \leq e^T c. \qquad (7.84)$$

Once again, there is no duality gap, and the optimal dual objective function $h(\hat{W})$ is convex with respect to $\hat{W}$ and achieves a minimum of zero at zero.

Given an optimal value of $Z^*(t)$, the following constrained singular control problem is then solved: choose nondecreasing, RCLL, nonanticipating (with respect to $\hat{B}$) processes $U_1$ and $U_2$ to

$$\min \quad \limsup_{T \to \infty} \frac{1}{T} E\left[ \int_0^T h(\hat{W}(t)) dt \right] \qquad (7.85)$$

$$\text{subject to} \quad \hat{W}(t) = \hat{B}(t) + \rho_2 U_1(t) - \rho_1 U_2(t) \text{ for } t \geq 0, \qquad (7.86)$$

$$\limsup_{T \to \infty} \frac{1}{T} E_x[U_1(T)] = \frac{(1 - \rho_1)\mu}{\rho_1 - \rho_2}, \qquad (7.87)$$

$$\limsup_{T \to \infty} \frac{1}{T} E_x[U_2(T)] = \frac{(1 - \rho_2)\mu}{\rho_1 - \rho_2}, \qquad (7.88)$$

if $\hat{B}$ has drift $\mu \neq 0$. If $\rho_1 = \rho_2$, then $\hat{B}$ is driftless, and the right sides of (7.87) and (7.88) are replaced by $\sqrt{n}\rho_1(1 - \rho_1)$.

Let us summarize the solution procedure to the workload formulation (7.75)–(7.79). The controller observes a two-dimensional Brownian motion $B$, from which can be observed the one-dimensional Brownian motion $\hat{B} = \rho_2 B_1 - \rho_1 B_2$. The solution $(Z^*, U^*, \theta^*)$ is given by the solution $Z^*$ to the quadratic program (7.80)–(7.82), which depends on the process $\hat{W}$, the solution $U^*$ to the Brownian control problem (7.85)–(7.88), and

$$\theta^*(t) = v_1^{-1}\left[B_1(t) + U_1^*(t) - \sum_{k=1}^{K} M_{1k} Z_k^*(t)\right] \text{ for all } t \geq 0. \qquad (7.89)$$

We now turn to solving the constrained control problem (7.85)–(7.88). This problem can be viewed as a variant of the *finite-fuel* problem for Brownian motion, in which there is a constraint on the total amount of controlling effort that can be exerted (or fuel that can be consumed). In the traditional finite-fuel problem, the amount of control exerted is constrained to be finite over some finite or infinite time interval; see Beneš, Shepp, and Witsenhausen [1], Chow, Menaldi, and Robin [4], and Karatzas [21] for variants of this problem. In contrast, the constraint in our problem is on the long-run expected average amount of control exerted.

Instead of analyzing the constrained control problem (7.85)–(7.88) directly, a Lagrangian approach will be used. In particular, let $r$ and $l$ be the Lagrange multipliers corresponding to constraints (7.87) and (7.88), respectively, and associate with a policy $(U_1, U_2)$ the *Lagrangian cost function*

$$k(x) = \limsup_{T \to \infty} \frac{1}{T} E_x \left[ \int_0^T h(\hat{W}(t))dt + rU_1(T) + lU_2(T) \right]. \qquad (7.90)$$

With the aid of the following proposition, which is given as Theorem 5.1 in [42], the constrained problem (7.85)–(7.88) can be solved by making an appropriate choice of multipliers and then minimizing the Lagrangian cost function. The problem of finding a policy $(U_1, U_2)$ that minimizes $k(x)$ will be referred to as the *Lagrangian problem*.

**Proposition 7.4.1** Suppose $r$ and $l$ are nonnegative real numbers and suppose $(U_1^*, U_2^*)$ is a solution to the Lagrangian problem. Furthermore, suppose

$$\limsup_{T \to \infty} \frac{1}{T} E_x[U_1^*(T)] = \frac{(1 - \rho_1)\mu}{\rho_1 - \rho_2} \qquad (7.91)$$

and

$$\limsup_{T \to \infty} \frac{1}{T} E_x[U_2^*(T)] = \frac{(1 - \rho_2)\mu}{\rho_1 - \rho_2}. \qquad (7.92)$$

Then $(U_1^*, U_2^*)$ is a solution to the constrained control problem (7.85)–(7.88).

Notice that, at this point, the Lagrange multipliers $r$ and $l$ are not known. In order to invoke Proposition 7.4.1, we need to find a pair of multipliers $(r, l)$ and a solution $(U_1^*, U_2^*)$ to the Lagrangian problem that simultaneously satisfy (7.91)–(7.92).

Given $r$ and $l$, the Lagrangian problem is a problem of *singular* (or *instantaneous*) control of Brownian motion. The name stems from the fact that the state of the controlled process can be instantaneously changed by the controller and, as a result, the optimal control processes $U_1$ and $U_2$ are continuous but singular (i.e., the set of time points at which $R$ and $L$ increase has measure zero). Such problems have been the subject of much study; see, for example, [13], Karatzas [20], Shreve, Lehoczky and Gaver [39], and [40]. In particular, [40] has solved the Lagrangian problem defined by (7.90) for a convex holding cost function $h$ that is finite everywhere or infinite on a finite interval. Since our holding cost function $h$ satisfies Taksar's requirement, his results can be used to derive sufficient conditions for optimality for the constrained problem (7.85)–(7.88). These conditions, which are stated as Theorem 6.2 of [42], are given below. Let the infinitesimal generator $\Gamma$ of $\hat{B}$ be given by

$$\frac{1}{2}\sigma^2 \frac{d^2}{dx^2} + \mu \frac{d}{dx}. \tag{7.93}$$

**Proposition 7.4.2** Suppose $(g, V(x), r, l, a, b)$ satisfy

$$\text{Min } \{\Gamma V(x) + h(x) - g, r + V'(x), l - V'(x)\} = 0, \tag{7.94}$$
$$V(0) = 0, \tag{7.95}$$
$$\Gamma V(x) + h(x) - g = 0 \text{ for } a \le x \le b, \tag{7.96}$$
$$V'(x) = -r \text{ for } x \le a, \tag{7.97}$$
$$V'(x) = l \text{ for } x \ge b, \tag{7.98}$$
$$\limsup_{T \to \infty} \frac{1}{T} E_x[U_1(T)] = \frac{(1 - \rho_1)\mu}{\rho_1 - \rho_2}, \text{ and} \tag{7.99}$$
$$\limsup_{T \to \infty} \frac{1}{T} E_x[U_2(T)] = \frac{(1 - \rho_2)\mu}{\rho_1 - \rho_2}, \tag{7.100}$$

where

$$U_1(t) = \frac{1}{\rho_2} \sup_{0 \le s \le t} [a - \hat{B}(s) + \rho_1 U_2(s)]^+, \text{ and} \tag{7.101}$$
$$U_2(t) = \frac{1}{\rho_1} \sup_{0 \le s \le t} [\hat{B}(s) + \rho_2 U_1^*(s) - b]^+. \tag{7.102}$$

Suppose $V \in \mathbf{C}^2$ and there exist constants $N_1$ and $N_2$ such that $V(x) \le N_1 + N_2 h(x)$. Then the optimal policy to the constrained problem (7.85)–(7.88) is (7.101)–(7.102).

Following Section 7 of [42], we use Propositions 7.3.1 and 7.3.2 in Section 7.3 to develop a candidate solution to (7.85)–(7.88), which is characterized by the interval endpoints $a^*$ and $b^*$. In particular, Proposition 7.3.1 is used to show that constraints (7.87)–(7.88), are satisfied with equality if and only if the interval width satisfies

$$b^* - a^* = \begin{cases} \nu^{-1} \ln\left(\frac{\rho_1(1-\rho_2)}{\rho_2(1-\rho_1)}\right) & \text{if } \rho_1 \neq \rho_2; \\ \frac{\sigma^2}{2\sqrt{n}\rho_1(1-\rho_1)} & \text{if } \rho_1 = \rho_2. \end{cases} \tag{7.103}$$

Proposition 7.3.2 is then used to show that the objective (7.85) is minimized by solving for $a^*$ to minimize $f(a)$, where

$$f(a) = \begin{cases} \int_a^{a+\nu^{-1}\ln\left(\frac{\rho_1(1-\rho_2)}{\rho_2(1-\rho_1)}\right)} \frac{h(x)\nu e^{\nu(x-a)}}{(e^{\nu(b-a)}-1)} dx & \text{if } \rho_1 \neq \rho_2; \\ \frac{2\sqrt{n}\rho_1(1-\rho_1)}{\sigma^2} \int_a^{a+\frac{\sigma^2}{2\sqrt{n}\rho_1(1-\rho_1)}} h(x) dx & \text{if } \rho_1 = \rho_2. \end{cases} \tag{7.104}$$

Given the candidate policy $(a^*, b^*)$, the obvious candidate for the gain $g^*$ that satisfies the optimality equations is the optimal long run expected average cost function of the Lagrangian, or

$$g^* = \begin{cases} f(a^*) + r\frac{(1-\rho_1)\mu}{\rho_1-\rho_2} + \frac{(1-\rho_2)\mu}{\rho_1-\rho_2} & \text{if } \rho_1 \neq \rho_2; \\ f(a^*) + (r+l)\sqrt{n}\rho_1(1-\rho_1) & \text{if } \rho_1 = \rho_2. \end{cases} \qquad (7.105)$$

The potential function $V^*(x)$ and the multipliers $r^*$ and $l^*$ that satisfy the optimality equations can then be found as in Section 8 of [42]. A closed form solution $(U_1^*, U_2^*)$ to the constrained problem (7.85)–(7.88) and a proof of optimality are given in [42] for the limiting case $c \to \infty$. The solution to (7.104) is more difficult in our general case where $0 \leq c < \infty$ (a numerical example is carried out in the next section), and the verification of optimality needs to be done on a case-by-case basis.

Now let us interpret the optimal solution to the workload formulation in terms of the original queueing system. The solution $(Z^*(t), \pi^*(t))$ to the dual quadratic program (7.83)–(7.84) yields the dynamic reduced costs

$$\bar{c}_k(t) = c + (CZ^*)_k(t) - \hat{M}_k\pi^*(t) \text{ for } k = 1, \ldots, K \text{ and } t \geq 0, \qquad (7.106)$$

where $(CZ^*)_k(t)$ denotes the $k$th element of $CZ^*(t)$. This value measures the increase in the objective function of problem (7.75)–(7.79) per unit of increase in the righthand side value of the nonnegativity constraint $Z_k(t) \geq 0$. Thus, the higher the value of $\bar{c}_k(t)$, the more costly it is to hold a class $k$ customer in queue at time $t$. As in [43], we propose the policy that awards higher priority at time $t$ to the classes with the higher dynamic reduced costs $\bar{c}_k(t)$. If more than one class at the same station has a dynamic reduced cost equal to zero, then we use the tie-breaking rule proposed in [51] and also described in Wein [45].

The proposed input policy is to release a customer into the network whenever the two-dimensional workload process enters a specific region in the nonnegative orthant of $R^2$. This region is derived from the interval endpoints $[a^*, b^*]$ and from the solution $Z^*$ of the quadratic program. The policy is most easily described with a concrete example, and so we defer its description until the next section.

## 7.5   An Example

We will illustrate the procedure described in Sections 7.3 and 7.4 with the simple example displayed in Figure 1, which was first studied in [15] and [43]. There are two customer types, $A$ and $B$, and type $A$ customers have two stages on their route, while type $B$ customers have four stages. Thus, there are six customer classes, and they will be designated (and ordered from $k = 1, \ldots, 6$) by $A1$, $A2$, $B1$, $B2$, $B3$, and $B4$. For concreteness, all processing times are assumed to be exponential, and the mean processing times for all six classes are displayed in Figure 1 . The specified product mix is $q = (1/2, 0, 1/2, 0, 0, 0)$, and customers are released into the network in the order $ABABAB\ldots$.

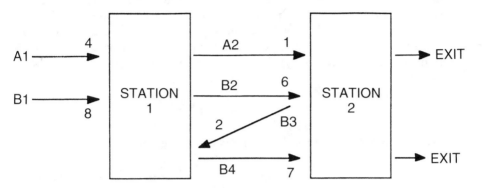

FIGURE 1. An example.

The workload profile matrix $M = (M_{ik})$ is given by

$$M = \begin{pmatrix} 4 & 0 & 10 & 2 & 2 & 0 \\ 1 & 1 & 13 & 13 & 7 & 7 \end{pmatrix}, \tag{7.107}$$

where $M_{ik}$ is the expected remaining processing time at station $i$ for a class $k$ customer until that customer exits. Also, the drift $\mu$ and variance $\sigma^2$ of the one-dimensional Brownian motion $\hat{B}$ was calculated in [43] to be zero and 10.93, respectively.

For the closed network problem of Section 7.3, we have $v_1 = v_2 = 7$ so that $\rho_1 = \rho_2 = 1$. Therefore, when $c \to \infty$, the proposed sequencing policy ranks each customer class by the index

$$\hat{M}_k = (3, \ -1, \ -3, \ -11, \ -5, \ -7) \quad \text{for } k = 1, \ldots, 6, \tag{7.108}$$

and gives priority (from highest to lowest) in the order (B3, B1, A1) at station 1 and (A2, B4, B2) at station 2.

Turning now to the limiting case $c = 0$, it can be calculated that the interval $[a^0, b^0]$ satisfying (7.57)–(7.60) is $[-6, 0]$, which is strictly contained in the interval $[a^*, b^*] = [-11, 3]$, which is calculated from (7.108). When $\hat{W} = -6$, the solution is $Z^{a^0} = (0, 1/2, 0, 1/2, 0, 0)$ and when $\hat{W} = 0$, the solution is $Z^{b^0} = (1/2, 0, 1/2, 0, 0, 0)$. Thus we give top priority to class $B3$ at station 1 and class $B4$ at station 2, since these classes are in the higher priority bracket.

In order to decide how to award priorities among the classes that are in the lower priority bracket at each station, a simple dynamic scheme is used that attempts to keep the number of customers in queue of each class in the relative proportions dictated by $Z^{a^0}$ and $Z^{b^0}$. For simplicity, we will describe this heuristic in the case where there are two classes, call them classes 1 and 2, in the lower priority bracket of a given station. Let $Z_1$ and $Z_2$ be the positive values of these classes from the solution $Z^{a^0}$ and $Z^{b^0}$. The idea behind the heuristic is to keep the proportion of class 1 customers in queue to be $Z_1/(Z_1 + Z_2)$. Suppose at time $t$, there are $Q_1(t) > 0$ class 1 customers and $Q_2(t) > 0$ class 2 customers in queue, and the server has just completed a service and is ready to begin serving a new customer. If the server serves a class 1 customer with probability $p(t)$ and a class 2 customer with probability $1 - p(t)$, then, after the choice is made, the expected proportion of total jobs in queue that are of class 1 is

$$\frac{p(t)(Q_1(t) - 1) + (1 - p(t))Q_1(t)}{Q_1(t) + Q_2(t) - 1}. \tag{7.109}$$

Setting this equal to the desired proportion $Z_1/(Z_1 + Z_2)$ and solving for $p(t)$ yields

$$p(t) = \frac{Z_1 + Z_2 Q_1(t) - Z_1 Q_2(t)}{Z_1 + Z_2}. \tag{7.110}$$

The dynamic heuristic is to serve class 1 customers at time $t$ if $p(t) > 1$, serve class 2 customers if $p(t) < 0$, and serve class 1 customer with probability $p(t)$ if $p(t) \in (0, 1)$.

In general, if there are $L$ classes in the lower priority bracket of a given station, then $L - 1$ linear equations need to be solved in order to determine $(p_1(t), \ldots, p_L(t))$, where $p_L(t) = 1 - \sum_{l=1}^{L-1} p_l(t)$. The dynamic heuristic is to serve class $l$ at time $t$ with probability $\max(0, p_l(t)/\sum_{\{j:p_j(t)>0\}} p_j(t))$.

Returning to our example, from the solution $Z^{a^0}$ (respectively, $Z^{b^0}$), it is desirable to keep the queue lengths of classes $A2$ and $B2$ (respectively, $A1$ and $B1$) at station 2 (respectively, station 1) as equal as possible, and thus our dynamic heuristic described in (7.110) takes on a particularly simple form. When no class $B3$ customers are available for processing at station 1, we serve class $A1$ customers when $Q_1(t) > Q_3(t)$ and serve class $B1$ customers when $Q_3(t) > Q_1(t)$, and alternate (or flip a fair coin) when there is a tie. Similarly, when there are no class $B4$ customers in queue at station 2, we serve class $A2$ customers when $Q_2(t) > Q_4(t)$ and serve $B2$ class customers when $Q_4(t) > Q_2(t)$.

For the general case where $0 < c < \infty$, the optimal dual objective function $h(\hat{W})$ in (7.70) is given by

$$h(\hat{W}) = \begin{cases} (\frac{6+\hat{W}}{5})^2 & \text{if } \hat{W} \in [-11, -6]; \\ 0 & \text{if } \hat{W} \in [-6, 0]; \\ \frac{\hat{W}^2}{9} & \text{if } \hat{W} \in [0, 3], \end{cases} \tag{7.111}$$

and thus $f(a, b)$ is given by

$$f(a, b) = \frac{1}{b - a}\left(\frac{c\sigma^2}{2} + \frac{b^3}{27} - \frac{a^3}{75} - \frac{18a^2}{75} - \frac{108a}{75} - \frac{216}{75}\right). \tag{7.112}$$

Therefore, our optimal interval endpoints can be found by minimizing $f(a, b)$ over $a \in [-11, -6]$ and $b \in [0, 3]$.

Now let us consider the numerical example in the context of a network with controllable inputs. If we choose a long run average throughput rate of .1286 customers per unit of time and choose the scaling parameter $n = 100$, then $\rho_1 = \rho_2 = 0.9$. The solution $(Z^*(t), \pi^*(t))$ to the dual quadratic program (7.83)–(7.84) is given in Table I, and the dynamic reduced costs (7.106) are given in Table II. In each of these tables, the solution and costs have been broken down into three regions (corresponding to the columns in the two tables), depending upon the value of the workload imbalance process $\hat{W}(t)$. The optimal dual objective function $h(\hat{W})$ in (7.83) is given by

$$h(\hat{W}) = \begin{cases} -\frac{25c^2}{144} - \frac{c\hat{W}}{6} & \text{if } \hat{W} \leq -55c/12; \\ -\frac{c\hat{W}}{11} + \frac{\hat{W}^2}{121} & \text{if } \hat{W} \in [-55c/12, 0]; \\ \frac{c\hat{W}}{3} + \frac{\hat{W}^2}{9} & \text{if } \hat{W} \geq 0. \end{cases} \tag{7.113}$$

By (7.103), it follows that $b^* - a^* = 6.072$, which we will denote by $k$. Solving (7.104) yields

$$a^* = \begin{cases} -\frac{9}{4}c - k + \sqrt{\frac{7}{2}c^2 + \frac{3}{2}ck} & \text{if } c \in [0, 6k/35]; \\ -\frac{11}{14}k & \text{if } c \geq 6k/35. \end{cases} \tag{7.114}$$

| VARIABLE | $\hat{W}(t) \leq -55c/12$ | $\hat{W}(t) \in [-55c/12, 0]$ | $\hat{W}(t) \geq 0$ |
|---|---|---|---|
| $Z_1^*(t)$ | $0$ | $0$ | $\frac{\hat{W}(t)}{3}$ |
| $Z_2^*(t)$ | $-\frac{\hat{W}(t)}{12} - \frac{55c}{144}$ | $0$ | $0$ |
| $Z_3^*(t)$ | $0$ | $0$ | $0$ |
| $Z_4^*(t)$ | $-\frac{\hat{W}(t)}{12} + \frac{5c}{144}$ | $-\frac{\hat{W}(t)}{11}$ | $0$ |
| $Z_5^*(t)$ | $0$ | $0$ | $0$ |
| $Z_6^*(t)$ | $0$ | $0$ | $0$ |
| $\pi^*(t)$ | $-\frac{c}{6}$ | $\frac{2\hat{W}(t)}{121} - \frac{c}{11}$ | $\frac{c}{3} + \frac{2\hat{W}(t)}{9}$ |

TABLE I. Solution to the Dual Quadratic Program (7.11)–(7.12).

In order to interpret the solution to the workload formulation given in Table I and (7.114), let us consider the limiting example $c \to \infty$ analyzed in [43]; readers may verify that the solution derived here in the limiting case is identical to the solution found in Section 7 of [43]. In this case, there are only two regions (i.e., two columns) to consider in Tables I and II, and it is easily seen that the sequencing policy based on the dynamic reduced costs in Table II ranks all classes by the index $\hat{M}_k$ in (7.108), and serves the class with the smallest (respectively, largest) value of the index when $\hat{W}(t) > 0$ (respectively, $\hat{W}(t) < 0$). From Table I, we see that only one component of $Z^*$ is positive at any time $t$ and only two components are ever positive. Thus the two-dimensional workload process defined by $W_i(t) = \sum_{k=1}^{6} M_{ik} Z_k(t)$ for $i = 1, 2$ and $t \geq 0$, stays on the boundary of a cone in the nonnegative orthant of $R^2$. Furthermore, the interval $[a^*, b^*]$, which equals $[-4.771, 1.301]$ by (7.114), determines cutoff points on the cone boundary beyond which the workload process may not enter (see Figure 2). As explained in [43], the control process $\theta(t)$, which can move either way along the 45 degree direction in Figure 2 (see (7.76)), is used to keep the workload process on the truncated cone boundary in Figure 2. Thus, when the workload process is in the region to the lower left of the truncated cone, then exerting $\theta$ corresponds to releasing more jobs into the system relative to the nominal input rate $\bar{\lambda}$.

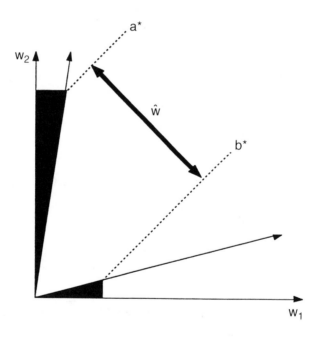

FIGURE 2. The release region when $c \to \infty$.

The resulting release policy is called a *workload regulating* release policy, and it releases a job into the network whenever the unscaled workload process $w(t)$, where $W(t) = w(nt)/\sqrt{n}$, enters a specific region. For our

| CLASS | $\hat{W}(t) \leq -55c/12$ | $\hat{W}(t) \in [-55c/12, 0]$ | $\hat{W}(t) \geq 0$ |
|---|---|---|---|
| $A1$ | $\frac{2c}{3}$ | $\frac{14c}{11} + \frac{16\hat{W}(t)}{121}$ | $0$ |
| $A2$ | $0$ | $\frac{10c}{11} + \frac{24\hat{W}(t)}{121}$ | $\frac{4c}{3} + \frac{8\hat{W}(t)}{9}$ |
| $B1$ | $\frac{4c}{3}$ | $\frac{8c}{11} - \frac{16\hat{W}(t)}{121}$ | $2c$ |
| $B2$ | $0$ | $0$ | $\frac{14c}{3} + \frac{16\hat{W}(t)}{9}$ |
| $B3$ | $c$ | $\frac{6c}{11} - \frac{12\hat{W}(t)}{121}$ | $\frac{8c}{3} + \frac{4\hat{W}(t)}{9}$ |
| $B4$ | $\frac{2c}{3}$ | $\frac{4c}{11} - \frac{8\hat{W}(t)}{121}$ | $\frac{10c}{3} + \frac{8\hat{W}(t)}{9}$ |

TABLE II. Dynamic Reduced Costs.

example, this region, which is shaded in Figure 2, is

$$w_1(t) \leq 19 \qquad \text{and} \tag{7.115}$$

$$w_2(t) - \frac{1}{4}w_1(t) \leq \frac{3}{4}\epsilon, \tag{7.116}$$

or

$$w_2(t) \leq 62 \qquad \text{and} \tag{7.117}$$

$$w_1(t) - \frac{2}{13}w_2(t) \leq \frac{11}{13}\epsilon, \tag{7.118}$$

where the parameter $\epsilon$, which shifts the cone vertex from the origin to the point $(\epsilon, \epsilon)$, is chosen so that the desired throughput rate is met. Choosing $\epsilon = 1$ achieved the target throughput rate in the simulation run that appears later in this section. A more detailed explanation that interprets the solution $(Z^*, U^*, \theta^*)$ of the workload formulation (7.75)–(7.79) in order to obtain the workload regulating release policy defined by (7.115)–(7.118) can be found in Section 6 of [43].

For the case when $0 \leq c < \infty$, the sequencing policy can easily be calculated from the dynamic reduced costs in Table II, but the determination of the release policy is more complicated. In the limiting case $c = 0$, equation (7.114) implies that $[a^*, b^*] = [-6.072, 0]$ and thus $\hat{W}(t)$ will always be in the leftmost region in Table I. From this table, it follows that $Z_2^*(t) = Z_4^*(t) = -\hat{W}(t)/12$, and so the workload process stays on a segment of the line $7W_1(t) = W_2(t)$. The release policy in this case (see [43] for an explanation) is to release a job whenever

$$w_2(t) \leq 71 \text{ and } 7w_1(t) - w_2(t) \leq 6\epsilon, \tag{7.119}$$

which is pictured in Figure 3. Once again, $\epsilon = 1$ achieved the desired throughput rate in the simulation experiment.

When $0 < c < \infty$, then the release region will be as pictured in Figure 4. The slope of the lower ray is $1/4$, just as it is in Figure 2. The upper shaded region in Figure 4 is formed by a line that has a slope of $13/2$ (the same as the upper ray in Figure 2) and another line that has a slope of 7 (which is parallel to the upper ray in Figure 3). The intersection of these two lines is at $\hat{W}(t) = -55c/12$, which is the cutoff point between two of the regions in Table I.

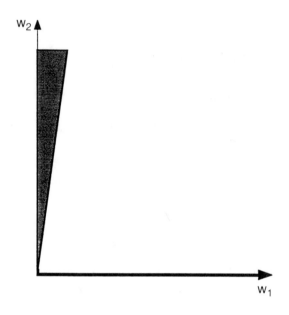

FIGURE 3. The release region when $c = 0$.

Before turning to the simulation results, there is one refinement that has been made to the scheduling policies described earlier. Notice in Table II that many of the scaled queue length processes are zero. Due to the rescaling, $Z$ measures how many *tens* of customers are in the actual network. This measurement is obviously too crude to account for the customers who are in service, and so we propose a slight refinement to the sojourn time inequality that essentially reinterprets $Z$ as only the scaled number of customers in queue, not including the customers in service. This refinement will hopefully cause a reduction in the sojourn time inequality, and it will be described in terms of the numerical example. For this numerical example, each server is to be utilized about 90% of the time, and we will denote this by $\rho = 0.9$. From Figure 1, the mean number of type $A$ customers in service is $5\rho/14$ and the mean number of type $B$ customers in service is

$23\rho/14$. The refinement changes the sojourn time inequality from

$$\left( \frac{Z_1(t) + Z_2(t)}{1/2} - \frac{Z_3(t) + Z_4(t) + Z_5(t) + Z_6(t)}{1/2} \right)^2 \tag{7.120}$$

in (7.66) and (7.80) to

$$\left( \frac{Z_1(t) + Z_2(t) + \frac{5\rho}{14N}}{1/2} - \frac{Z_3(t) + Z_4(t) + Z_5(t) + Z_6(t) + \frac{23\rho}{14N}}{1/2} \right)^2 \tag{7.121}$$

in (7.66) and

$$\left( \frac{Z_1(t) + Z_2(t) + \frac{5\rho}{14\sqrt{n}}}{1/2} - \frac{Z_3(t) + Z_4(t) + Z_5(t) + Z_6(t) + \frac{23\rho}{14\sqrt{n}}}{1/2} \right)^2 \tag{7.122}$$

in (7.80). In our simulation experiment, this refinement was only analyzed for the case $c = 0$ in the closed network. This is a particularly easy case to evaluate, since the only difference in the analysis is to change equation (7.60) from

$$Z_1 + Z_2 - Z_3 - Z_4 - Z_5 - Z_6 \;=\; 0 \tag{7.123}$$

to

$$Z_1 + Z_2 - Z_3 - Z_4 - Z_5 - Z_6 \;=\; \frac{18\rho}{14N}. \tag{7.124}$$

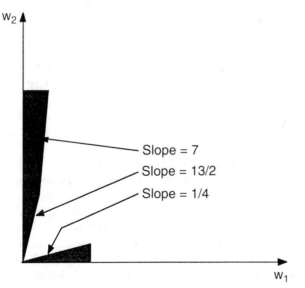

FIGURE 4. The release region when $0 < c < \infty$.

A simulation experiment was performed to assess the effectiveness of the analysis presented in Sections 7.3 and 7.4. Two conventional policies, which consist of a customer release policy and a priority sequencing policy, were tested. One policy was deterministic input (abbreviated by DET in Table III), where customers are released at constant intervals in the order $ABABAB\ldots$, paired with FCFS sequencing, and the second was closed loop input (CL), where the total population level was held constant, and FCFS. The closed release policy was also tested in conjunction with the sequencing policies derived in Section 7.3 under the two limiting cases, $c \to \infty$ and $c = 0$. The $c = 0$ policy used the refinement described in equation (7.124). The job release and priority sequencing policies derived in Section 7.4, which will be denoted by WR (for workload regulating), were also tested under the two limiting cases.

In order to allow for a comparison of the various cases, we have set the parameters $N$ and $\epsilon$ so that each policy achieves the same average throughput rate, which for convenience was chosen to be .127 customers per unit of time, which corresponds to a server utilization of 88.9%. Due to the discrete nature of the population parameter $N$, we were not always able to obtain this target rate exactly. In such cases, we have reported linear interpolations of the various performance measures so that the average throughput rate would be .127. For each policy tested, 20 independent runs were made, each consisting of 5000 customer completions and no initialization period. The mean sojourn time, the *actual* sojourn time standard deviation, and the mean sojourn time inequity, along with 95% confidence intervals, are recorded in Table III.

Referring to the results in Table III, it is seen that the (DET,FCFS) policy achieves a sojourn time standard deviation that is twice as high as most of the other policies, implying that job release has a large impact on the sojourn time variance. Of course, in many manufacturing systems, the amount of time a job spends waiting to gain entrance onto the shop floor is also of importance, and that time is ignored in this study; readers are referred to Wein and Chevalier [47] for a scheduling study where this time is taken into account.

The mean sojourn time inequity is dramatically reduced by the proposed scheduling policies under the two $c = 0$ cases. Although not reported here, the mean sojourn times of the two customer types are also much closer in value under these two cases than under the other four cases. For example, the mean sojourn times of type $A$ and $B$ customers, respectively, are 47.8 and 95.6 under (CL,FCFS), and 61.4 and 76.5 under (CL,$c = 0$). However, large reductions in sojourn time inequity lead to only modest reductions in sojourn time standard deviation, since the inequity reductions (from $c \to \infty$ to $c = 0$) are coupled with significant increases in mean sojourn time. The (CL,$c = 0$) case achieves the lowest sojourn time inequity and the lowest sojourn time variance, perhaps in part because of the refinement described in (7.124).

| Scheduling Policy | Mean Sojourn Time | Sojourn Time Std. Deviation | Mean Sojourn Time Inequity |
|---|---|---|---|
| DET,FCFS | 90.6 ($\pm$5.0) | 61.3 ($\pm$3.83) | 86.1 ($\pm$8.85) |
| CL,FCFS | 71.7 ($\pm$.45) | 31.6 ($\pm$.54) | 36.0 ($\pm$.01) |
| CL,$c \to \infty$ | 50.4 ($\pm$.31) | 27.9 ($\pm$.27) | 55.1 ($\pm$1.34) |
| CL,$c = 0$ | 68.9 ($\pm$.43) | 25.4 ($\pm$.26) | 15.3 ($\pm$1.12) |
| WR,$c \to \infty$ | 39.1 ($\pm$.52) | 33.0 ($\pm$.53) | 55.0 ($\pm$2.08) |
| WR,$c = 0$ | 53.3 ($\pm$1.45) | 29.5 ($\pm$.71) | 19.0 ($\pm$.45) |

TABLE III. Simulation Results for Example 1.

For this particular example, the difference in mean sojourn times between the $c = 0$ and $c \to \infty$ cases is much larger than the corresponding difference in sojourn time standard deviation. Thus, relative to the $c \to \infty$ case, the queueing system would have to incur a large increase in mean sojourn time in order to achieve a relatively small decrease in sojourn time standard deviation. Finally, it is also interesting to note that the (CL,$c \to \infty$) and the (CL,$c = 0$) policies both simultaneously reduced the mean sojourn time and sojourn time variance with respect to (CL,FCFS).

Now let us consider the same example, but with the mean processing times for the six classes altered from (4, 1, 8, 6, 2, 7) to (2, 6, 4, 1, 8, 7); we will denote the example using this new data set as example 2. For simplicity, we will only look at the closed network problem for example 2. When $c \to \infty$, the proposed sequencing ranks each customer class by the index

$$\hat{M}_k = (-4, -6, 4, 0, 1, -7) \qquad \text{for } k = 1, \ldots, 6, \qquad (7.125)$$

and gives priority in the order (A1, B3, B1) at station 1 and (B2, A2, B4) at station 2.

In the limiting case $c = 0$, the interval $[a^0, b^0]$ satisfying (7.57)–(7.60) is $[-6.5, 0]$, which is strictly contained in the interval $[a^*, b^*] = [-7, 4]$. When $\hat{W} = -6.5$, the solution is $Z^{a^0} = (0, 0, 0, 1/2, 0, 1/2)$ and when $\hat{W} = 0$, the solution is $Z^{b^0} = (1/2, 0, 0, 0, 1/2, 0)$. Thus we give top priority to class $B3$ at station 1 and class $B4$ at station 2.

The numerical results for example 2 are given in Table IV. Once again, the mean sojourn time inequity is drastically reduced under the $c = 0$ policy, and a corresponding reduction in sojourn time variance is also incurred. Also, as in the original example, example 2 offers a policy (in this case, the (CL,$c = 0$) policy) that simultaneously reduces the mean and variance of sojourn times relative to FCFS. However, these simulation results differ qualitatively from example 1 in several respects. The sojourn time inequity of the $c \to \infty$ policy is much larger than FCFS, and the sojourn time variance is larger than FCFS. Also, there is a large difference in sojourn time variance between the two extreme cases of $c \to \infty$ and $c = 0$. Thus, relative to the $c \to \infty$ case, a large decrease in sojourn time variance can be achieved while incurring a moderate increase in mean sojourn time.

| SCHEDULING POLICY | MEAN SOJOURN TIME | SOJOURN TIME STD. DEVIATION | MEAN SOJOURN TIME INEQUITY |
|---|---|---|---|
| CL,FCFS | 71.6 (±.36) | 31.6 (±.22) | 36.0 (±.02) |
| CL,$c \to \infty$ | 52.8 (±.21) | 37.9 (±.21) | 86.6 (±1.08) |
| CL,$c = 0$ | 63.8 (±.24) | 23.2 (±.20) | 14.3 (±.92) |

TABLE IV. Simulation Results for Example 2.

Thus, the nature of the tradeoff between mean sojourn time and sojourn time variance is problem dependent; in example 1, a small decrease in sojourn time variance is coupled with a large increase in mean sojourn time, and in example 2, a large decrease in sojourn time variance is coupled with a moderate increase in mean sojourn time. Fortunately, the rough nature of this tradeoff can be predicted from our Brownian analysis. In particular, the difference in the mean sojourn time and the sojourn time inequity between the (CL,$c = 0$) and (CL,$c \to \infty$) policies can be estimated from the network data. In order to analyze the difference in mean sojourn time inequity between the two policies, let us recall the following fact about priority queueing systems. When a queueing system is heavy loaded and static priorities are used, the bottom priority class at each server incurs much more delay in queue than the other classes; as mentioned earlier, this has been quantified in several heavy traffic limit theorems. Referring back to (7.108), we see that type $A$ gets bottom priority at station 1 and type $B$ gets bottom priority at station 2 under the (CL,$c \to \infty$) policy in example 1, and thus the sojourn time inequity for this policy was not that large. From (7.125), it can be seen that the (CL,$c \to \infty$) policy awards lowest priority to type $B$ customers at both stations, and thus the mean sojourn time inequity is very large for this policy. Thus, it is not surprising that (CL,$c \to \infty$) has a larger sojourn time variance in example 2 than in example 1, and that a larger reduction in sojourn time variance was achieved in example 2.

In order to determine the difference in mean sojourn time between the (CL,$c \to \infty$) and (CL,$c = 0$) policies, recall that in the Brownian model, the mean sojourn time is inversely proportional to the quantity $b^* - a^*$ for the (CL,$c \to \infty$) policy, and inversely proportional to $b^0 - a^0$ for the (CL,$c = 0$) policy. In example 1, $b^* - a^* = 14$ and $b^0 - a^0 = 6$, whereas $b^* - a^* = 11$ and $b^0 - a^0 = 6.5$ in example 2. Thus, one would predict that the difference in mean sojourn time between the two policies is larger in example 1 than example 2.

In summary, perhaps the most interesting result from this study is that FCFS is not particularly effective at minimizing sojourn time variance in complex queueing systems. This chapter offers some aid in developing release and sequencing policies to reduce the sojourn time inequity (and perhaps the sojourn time variance) in such systems, and in understanding the tradeoff between minimizing mean sojourn time and sojourn time variance.

## 7.6    A Review of Related Results

In this final section, we briefly review the existing literature on employing Brownian approximations to address queueing network scheduling problems.

### 7.6.1    Open Networks

Queueing networks with exogenous customer arrivals are referred to as *open* networks. Harrison [12] developed the workload formulation of the limiting control problem for a general multiclass open queueing network and derived the pathwise solution to minimize the mean sojourn time in a single server multiclass queue (see Section 7.2 of the present chapter). Harrison and Wein [14], and Wein and Ou [48] have derived pathwise solutions to particular two-station queueing networks, and Yang [51] has established sufficient conditions on the network data for the workload formulation to admit a pathwise solution. Not surprisingly, most interesting queueing network scheduling problems, including many two-station problems, have workload formulations that do not admit pathwise solutions. Although open queueing network scheduling problems without pathwise solutions have yet to be addressed, it is clear how one can proceed if the objective is to minimize the long run expected average sojourn time. In particular, a two-step procedure can be employed for a network with $I$ stations and $K$ customer classes: in step one, the following parametric linear program is solved at each point in time (that is, for all nonnegative values of the $I$-dimensional workload process $W(t)$):

$$\min_{Z(t)} \sum_{k=1}^{K} Z_k(t) \tag{7.126}$$

$$\text{subject to } \sum_{k=1}^{K} M_{ik} Z_k(t) = W_i(t) \text{ for } i = 1, \ldots, I \text{ and } t \geq 0, \tag{7.127}$$

$$Z_k(t) \geq 0 \text{ for } k = 1, \ldots, K, \tag{7.128}$$

where the $I \times K$ matrix $M = (M_{ik})$ is the workload profile matrix defined in Subsection 7.3.1. Let the optimal objective function value be denoted by $f(W(t))$, where $f$ is a convex function. Define the convex polyhedral cone $C$ by

$$C = \{(w_1, \ldots, w_I) : w_i = \sum_{k=1}^{K} z_k, z_k \geq 0, k = 1, \ldots, K\}, \qquad (7.129)$$

and let $B$ be an $I$-dimensional Brownian motion with known drift and covariance. In step two, the following multidimensional singular control problem needs to be solved:

$$\min_{U} \limsup_{T \to \infty} \frac{1}{T} E\left[\int_0^T f(W(t))dt\right] \qquad (7.130)$$

subject to $W_i(t) = B_i(t) + U_i(t)$ for $i = 1, \ldots, I$ and $t \geq 0$, (7.131)

$\qquad\qquad U$ is nondecreasing with $U(0) = 0$, $\qquad\qquad$ (7.132)

$\qquad\qquad U$ is nonanticipating with respect to $B$, $\qquad\qquad$ (7.133)

$\qquad\qquad W$ must reside in $C$. $\qquad\qquad$ (7.134)

The control problem (7.130)–(7.134) appears to be very difficult to solve in closed form when $I \geq 2$. However, numerical techniques developed by Kushner (see below) can be used to numerically calculate the solution, although the procedure becomes very computer intensive for three or more stations. I have calculated solutions to (7.130)–(7.134) for several two-station examples that do not possess pathwise solutions, and the resulting control boundaries (that is, the boundaries where the singular control is exerted) are nonlinear, further dimming the hope for a closed form solution. Notice that when a pathwise solution does exist, the control boundaries coincide with the boundaries of the cone $C$.

Since problems (7.126)–(7.129) and (7.130)–(7.134) are difficult to solve and since interpreting the solution would be a nontrivial task, the Brownian procedure may not be very useful for developing scheduling policies for open queueing networks with more than two stations.

## 7.6.2 Closed Networks

As described in Subsection 7.3.2, Harrison and Wein [15] analyzed the problem of maximizing the throughput rate of a two-station closed queueing network, and proposed a scheduling policy based on the index $\hat{M}_k$ defined in equation (7.44), which they refer to as the workload balancing sequencing policy. In Section 5 of that paper, they also develop an analytic performance comparison between the workload balancing policy and any other static policy, such as the shortest expected processing time rule (SEPT), where priority is given to the class with the shortest expected processing time for its upcoming operation, and the shortest expected remaining processing time rule (SERPT), where priority is given to the class with the least expected amount of work remaining before exiting the network.

For the general multistation problem, Chevalier and Wein [3] again reformulate the Brownian control problem in terms of workload imbalances, but a unique, closed form solution to the workload imbalance formulation is not obtained. However, the corresponding relationship between workload imbalance, server idleness, and the lowest priority classes is generalized to the multistation setting. In particular, when there are $I$ stations in the network, an $(I-1)$-dimensional workload imbalance process is defined that stays in a workload imbalance polytope in $R^{I-1}$. Also, server idleness is incurred only when the workload imbalance process is at the boundary of the workload imbalance polytope. Each extreme point of the polytope corresponds to a particular customer class, and these extremal classes are the only classes in the network that are ever given bottom priority at their respective stations. Unlike the two-station case, there will in general be more extremal classes than stations.

Chevalier and Wein exploit this intricate relationship to propose an effective static sequencing policy that is relatively easy to derive for large networks, and to approximately compare the performance of arbitrary static policies. Their numerical results show that the proposed policies perform surprisingly well in networks that are moderately loaded and moderately imbalanced.

### 7.6.3   Networks with Controllable Inputs

Section 7.4.2 reviews Wein's [42], [43] analysis of finding a release and sequencing policy to minimize the mean sojourn time in a two-station network subject to a throughput rate constraint. Wein [45] analyzed the general multistation problem where the resulting sequencing policy awards priority according to dynamic reduced costs derived from a linear program. A numercial solution to the imbedded multidimensional constrained singular control problem is found via a finite difference approximation method developed by Kushner [28]. This numerical procedure is rather difficult to implement for networks with four or more stations.

### 7.6.4   Networks with Discretionary Routing

Thus far, we have assumed that each customer class must be served at a particular station. However, Harrison's [12] original framework allows various types of discretionary routing. Motivated by communication networks, Laws and Louth [31] consider a particular four station open network where each of two customer types have two two different possible routes through the network. Using the five step procedure, they find a workload formulation that yields a pathwise solution. Motivated by flexible manufacturing systems, Wein [44] considers the case where each customer class can be served at each of several different stations, and provides a heuristic procedure to simultaneously address the problem of job release, sequencing and routing. The procedure is based on the observation that a set of servers who share flexible customers (that is, customers who can be served by any of the servers in the set) behave in heavy traffic as if they were a pooled set of servers, even if each server receives some dedicated side traffic. This observation was originally made by Foschini and Salz [8] and Foschini [7], which is probably the earliest work on heavy traffic analysis of scheduling problems.

### 7.6.5   Production/Inventory Systems

Many production facilities operate in a *make-to-stock* mode, meaning that they produce according to a forecast of customer demand, and completed jobs enter a finished goods inventory, which in turn services actual customer demand. Wein [46] considers a single server multiclass queue in a make-to-stock environment. The problem is to decide which class of customer, if any, to serve next, in order to minimize the long run expected average cost incurred per unit of time, which includes linear costs (which may differ by class) for backordering and holding finished goods inventory. The five step Brownian procedure is used to propose the following scheduling policy: the server stays busy as long as the weighted sum of the finished goods inventory (where the inventory of each class is weighted by its expected processing time) is not too large. When the server is working, the system gives priority to backordered classes that are expensive to backorder and have short expected processing times, and when the system has no backordered jobs, it gives priority to jobs that are inexpensive to hold in finished goods inventory and have long expected processing times.

Ou and Wein [34] generalize these results in several directions that are motivated by semiconductor manufacturing. In particular, they incorporate feedback to this single server facility, which allows them to model semiconductor wafer fabrication facilities, which often have only one bottleneck station to which the jobs make many visits (the photolithography workstation), and usually produce to stock, due to its long manufacturing cycle times. Also, the production facility can produce wafers according to a variety of different process types, and due to random yield, a wafer produced according to each process will yield, on average, a certain number of chips of each type.

### 7.6.6   Weak Convergence Results

Ideally, one would like to prove that the scheduling policies that arise from the five step procedure are, in some sense, asymptotically optimal in heavy traffic. None of the results described earlier in this section have included a rigorous justification of asymptotic optimality. In particular, the model development in [12] contains a persuasive verbal argument, but lacks a heavy traffic limit theorem claiming that a sequence of queueing network scheduling problems converges to the limiting Brownian control problem as the network approaches heavy traffic. Furthermore, the interpretation of the workload formulation solution is typically based on intuition gained from existing heavy traffic limit theorems, and no attempt is made to rigorously justify this interpretation with a weak convergence result. However, the scheduling policy and corresponding cost derived for some simple cases (the single server multiclass queue in [12] and the routing problem in [8]) are consistent with existing heavy traffic limit theorems (see [49] and [36], respectively). In lieu of weak convergence results, most of the papers include simulation studies (similar to the one undertaken in Section 7.5) that display the effectiveness of the proposed policies relative to scheduling policies from the job-shop scheduling literature. The studies in [14] and [31] go one step further by developing a pathwise lower bound (for the total number of customers in the system under any scheduling policy) and showing that the relative difference between the performance of the proposed policy and the pathwise lower bound becomes small as the load on the network is increased toward the heavy traffic limit.

Kushner and his co-workers have developed a complementary approach to the heavy traffic analysis of queueing network control problems, where the service rates, arrival rates and routing probabilities can be controlled. In a series of papers (Kushner and Ramachandran [30], Martins and Kushner [33], and Kushner and Martins [29]), they define (as opposed to derive) a particular control policy and prove the convergence of the controlled processes to a controlled reflected diffusion process, the convergence of the associated costs, and the convergence of the optimal value function of the queueing system to the optimal value function of the limit process.

*Acknowledgments:* This research was partially supported by a grant from the Leaders for Manufacturing Program at MIT and by National Science Foundation Grant Award No. DDM-9057297.

## 7.7  References

[1] Beneš, V. E., Shepp, L. A. and Witsenhausen, H. S. (1980). Some Solvable Stochastic Control Problems. *Stochastics* 4, 39–83.

[2] Billingsley, P. (1968). *Convergence of Probability Measures.* John Wiley and Sons, New York.

[3] Chevalier, P. B. and Wein, L. M. (1993). Scheduling Networks of

320    Lawrence M. Wein

Queues: Heavy Traffic Analysis of a Multistation Closed Network. *Operations Research*.

[4] Chow, P. L., Menaldi, J. L., and M. Robin (1985). Additive Control of Stochastic Linear Systems With Finite Horizon. *SIAM J. Control and Opt.* **23**, 858–899.

[5] Dorn, W. S. (1960). Duality in Quadratic Programming. *Q. Appl. Math.* **18**, 155–162.

[6] Federgruen, A. and Groenevelt, H. (1988). $M/G/c$ Queueing Systems with Multiple Customer Classes: Characterization and Control of Achievable Performance under Nonpreemptive Priority Rules. *Management Science* **9**, 1121–1138.

[7] Foschini, G. J. (1977). On Heavy Traffic Diffusion Analysis and Dynamic Routing in Packet Switched Networks. In Chandy, K. M. and Reiser, M., editors, *Computer Performance*, North Holland, Amsterdam.

[8] Foschini, G. J. and Salz, J. (1978). A Basic Dynamic Routing Problem and Diffusion Approximation. *IEEE Trans. Comm.* **COM-26**, 320–327.

[9] Groenevelt, H. (1990). The Variances of Waiting Times in Multi-Class Non-Preemptive $M/G/1$ Queues. Working Paper, Simon Graduate School of Business Administration, U. of Rochester, N.Y.

[10] Harrison, J. M. (1973). A Limit Theorem for Priority Queues in Heavy Traffic. *J. Appl. Prob.* **10**, 907–912.

[11] Harrison, J. M. (1985). *Brownian Motion and Stochastic Flow Systems*. John Wiley and Sons, New York.

[12] Harrison, J. M. (1988). Brownian Models of Queueing Networks with Heterogeneous Customer Populations. In W. Fleming and P. L. Lions (eds.), *Stochastic Differential Systems, Stochastic Control Theory and Applications*, IMA Volume **10**, Springer-Verlag, New York, 147–186.

[13] Harrison, J. M. and Taksar, M. I. (1983). Instantaneous Control of Brownian Motion. *Math. of Oper. Res.* **3**, 439–453.

[14] Harrison, J. M. and Wein, L. M. (1989). Scheduling Networks of Queues: Heavy Traffic Analysis of a Simple Open Network. *Queueing Systems* **5**, 265–180.

[15] Harrison, J. M. and Wein, L. M. (1990). Scheduling Networks of Queues: Heavy Traffic Analysis of a Two-Station Closed Network. *Operations Research* **38**, 1052–1064.

[16] Jackson, J. R. (1960). Some Problems in Queueing with Dynamic Priorities. *Naval Res. Log. Quart.* **7**, 235–249.

[17] Jackson, J. R. (1961). Queues with Dynamic Priorities. *Management Science* **1**, 18–34.

[18] Jackson, J. R. (1962). Waiting Time Distributions for Queues with Dynamic Priorities. *Naval Res. Log. Quart.* **9**, 31–36.

[19] Johnson, D. P. (1983). Diffusion Approximations for Optimal Filtering of Jump Processes and for Queueing Networks. Unpublished Ph.D. thesis, Dept. of Mathematics, Univ. of Wisconsin, Madison.

[20] Karatzas, I. (1983). A Class of Singular Stochastic Control Problems. *Adv. Appl. Prob.* **15**, 225–254.

[21] Karatzas, I. (1988). Stochastic Control Under Finite-fuel Constraints, in W. Fleming and P. L. Lions (eds.), *Stochastic Differential Systems, Stochastic Control Theory and Applications*, IMA Volume **10**, Springer-Verlag, New York, 225–240.

[22] Karatzas, I. and Shreve, S. E. (1988). *Brownian Motion and Stochastic Calculus*. Springer-Verlag, New York.

[23] Kelly, F. P. (1979). *Reversibility and Stochastic Networks*, John Wiley and Sons, New York.

[24] Kingman, J. F. C. (1962). The Effect of Queue Discipline on Waiting Time Variance. *Proc. Camb. Phil. Soc.* **58**, 163–164.

[25] Kleinrock, L. (1964). A Delay Dependent Queue Discipline. *Naval Res. Log. Quart.* **11**, 329–341.

[26] Kleinrock, L. (1976). *Queueing Systems Vol. II: Computer Applications.* John Wiley and Sons, New York.

[27] Klimov, G. P. (1974). Time Sharing Service Systems I. *Th. Prob. Appl.* **19**, 532–551.

[28] Kushner, H. J. (1977). *Probability Methods for Approximations in Stochastic Control and for Elliptic Equations.* Academic Press, New York.

[29] Kushner, H. J., and L. F. Martins, (1993). Limit Theorems for Pathwise Average Cost Per Unit Time Problems for Controlled Queues in Heavy Traffic. *Stochastics and Stochastic Reports* **42**, 25–51.

[30] Kushner, H. J., and Ramachandran, K. M. (1989). Optimal and Approximately Optimal Control Policies for Queues in Heavy Traffic. *SIAM J. Control and Optimization* **27**, 1293–1318.

[31] Laws, C. N. and Louth, G. M. (1990). Dynamic Scheduling of a Four Station Network. *Probability in the Engineering and Information Sciences* **4**, 131–156.

[32] Little, J. D. C. (1961). A Proof of the Queueing Formula $L = \lambda W$. *Operations Research* **9**, 383–387.

[33] Martins, L. F., and Kushner, H. J. (1989). Routing and Singular Control for Queueing Networks in Heavy Traffic. *SIAM J. Control and Optimization* **28**, 1209–1233.

[34] Ou, J. and Wein, L. M. (1991). Dynamic Scheduling of a Production/Inventory System with By-Products and Random Yield. To appear in *Management Science*.

[35] Peterson, W. P. (1991). A Heavy Traffic Limit Theorem for Networks of Queues with Multiple Customer Types. *Math. Operations Research* **16**, 90–118.

[36] Reiman, M. I. (1983). Some Diffusion Approximations with State Space Collapse. *Proc. Intl. Seminar on Modeling and Performance Evaluation Methodology*, Springer-Verlag, Berlin.

[37] Schonberger, R. J. (1982). *Japanese Manufacturing Techniques*. Free Press.

[38] Shanthikumar, J. G. (1982). On Reducing Time Spent in $M/G/1$ Systems. *European J. Operational Research* **9**, 286–294.

[39] Shreve, S. E., Lehoczky, J. P. and Gaver, D. P. (1984). Optimal Consumption for General Diffusions with Absorbing and Reflecting Barriers. *SIAM J. Control and Opt.* **22**, 55–75.

[40] Taksar, M. I. (1985). Average Optimal Singular Control and a Related Stopping Problem. *Math. Operations Research* **10**, 63–81.

[41] Walrand, J. (1988). *An Introduction to Queueing Networks*. Prentice-Hall, Englewood Cliffs, New Jersey.

[42] Wein, L. M. (1990a). Optimal Control of a Two-Station Brownian Network. *Math. of Operations Research* **15**, 215–242.

[43] Wein, L. M. (1990b). Scheduling Networks of Queues: Heavy Traffic Analysis of a Two-Station Network with Controllable Inputs. *Operations Research* **38**, 1065–1078.

[44] Wein, L. M. (1991). Brownian Networks with Discretionary Routing. *Operations Research* **39**, 322–340.

[45] Wein, L. M. (1992b). Scheduling Networks of Queues: Heavy Traffic Analysis of a Multistation Network with Controllable Inputs. *Operations Research* **40**, S312–S334.

[46] Wein, L. M. (1992b). Dynamic Scheduling of a Multiclass Make-to-Stock Queue. *Operations Research* **40**, 724–735.

[47] Wein, L. M. and Chevalier, P. B. (1992). A Broader View of the Job-Shop Scheduling Problem. *Management Science* **38**, 1018–1033.

[48] Wein, L. M. and Ou, J. (1991). The Impact of Processing Time Knowledge on Dynamic Job-Shop Scheduling. *Management Science* **37**, 1002–1014.

[49] Whitt, W. (1971). Weak Convergence Theorems for Priority Queues: Preemptive-Resume Discipline. *J. Appl. Prob.* **8**, 74–94.

[50] Wood, D. and Sargeant, R. (1984). The Synthesis of Multiclass Single Server Queueing Systems. Unpublished manuscript.

[51] P. Yang (1988). Pathwise Solutions for a Class of Linear Stochastic Systems. Unpublished Ph. D. Thesis, Dept. of Operations Research, Stanford University, Stanford, CA.

# 8

# Scheduling Manufacturing Systems of Re-Entrant Lines

## P. R. Kumar

ABSTRACT Re–entrant lines are manufacturing systems where parts may return more than once to the same machine, for repeated stages of processing. Examples of such systems are semiconductor manufacturing plants. We consider the problems of scheduling such systems to reduce manufacturing lead times, variations in the manufacturing lead times, or holding costs.

We assume a deterministic model, which allows for bursty arrivals. We show how one may design scheduling policies to help in meeting these objectives. To reduce the mean or variance of manufacturing lead time, we design a class of scheduling policies called Fluctuation Smoothing policies. To reduce the holding costs in systems with set–up times, we introduce the class of Clear–A–Fraction scheduling policies.

We study the stability and performance of these scheduling policies. We illustrate how scheduling policies can be unstable in that the levels of the buffers become unbounded. However, we show that all Least Slack policies, including the well known Earliest Due Date policy and all the Fluctuation Smoothing policies, are stable.

## 8.1 Introduction

Manufacturing systems consist of one or many machines, processing many parts. Arriving parts may require processing by specific machines, usually in a fixed order (a route). They may come with pre-determined processing times at each machine, or they could be random. The arrival of parts into the system may be either at our control, or exogenously determined. Machines may fail at random repair times, and be subject to random repair times. If a machine can cater to different types of parts, or the same part-type at different stages, it may incur a set-up or change-over time when switching between part-types.

While many of these contingencies are outside our control, there are several decisions that are at our disposal. We can decide which of several parts, waiting for processing at a machine, is processed next when the machine becomes available. This can be executed by a machine *scheduling policy*. In some cases we may even be allowed to regulate the release of new parts to the system, subject to certain constraints such as maintaining an average throughput. This can be governed by a part *release policy*.

The goal of scheduling is to choose such policies to provide good performance with respect to performance measures of interest. Such performance measures may be the cost of the total work-in-process, the mean manufacturing lead-time, or even the variance of the manufacturing lead time.

Depending on the particular issues being addressed, one should adopt a different model of the system that captures the relevant features. In turn, depending on the model adopted and the problem being addressed, one may adopt different strategies to design scheduling policies and analyze them. The choice of the model or framework adopted to address the relevant issues is usually a compromise between faithfulness to the situation, and tractability of subsequent design and analysis.

The model of a manufacturing system can be based on either discrete or fluid flows, and the various unpredictable events can be viewed as either deterministic but uncertain, or stochastic. The design procedure can range between pure intuition based, for example, on hypotheses about large scale system behavior, or derived from an optimal control formulation. In some cases, analysis can provide proofs of important properties of scheduling policies, or bounds on their performance, while in other cases recourse has to be made to carefully designed simulation experiments.

In this chapter, we shall study the design and analysis of scheduling policies for two models of systems. Together they illustrate some of the choices outlined above. Our goal here is to not only show new strategies for handling specific problems in manufacturing systems, but also to exhibit the flexibility available in modeling, design and analysis. By exploiting this richness of problems, solutions and analyses, a more comprehensive and applicable theory of manufacturing systems may emerge.

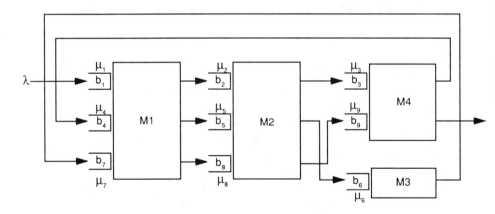

FIGURE 1. A Re-entrant line.

## 8.2    Re-Entrant Lines: The Models

Consider a manufacturing system as in Figure 1. It consists of four machines labelled M1 through M4. Parts arrive to the system at machine 1. It is convenient to suppose that while they are waiting for service at M1 on their first visit to it, they are stored in a (real or virtual) buffer called $b_1$. After processing is completed at M1 they visit machine M2 where they are stored in a buffer $b_2$, and so on. The last buffer visited is $b_9$ at machine M4, from which they then exit the system.

A very important feature of the system in Figure 1, is that parts return more than once to some of the machines, for repeated stages of processing. For example, machine M1 is visited thrice by parts during their route, at which time they are stored in buffers $b_1$, $b_4$ or $b_7$. We shall call such systems as *re-entrant lines*. A fundamental consequence is that when a machine, say M1, becomes idle, there may be parts waiting in all of the buffers $b_1$, $b_4$ and $b_7$. These are parts at different stages of their manufacturing lives, but all clamouring for attention from machine M1. The machine M1 then has to decide which part from which buffer it will process next. We therefore have the problem of resolving the competition for machines, by parts at different stages of production. We thus need to choose some machine *scheduling policy* to resolve which part to serve next at machine M1. Our choice of a scheduling policy will affect the performance of the overall system.

These systems of re-entrant lines can be contrasted with flow shops which produce automobiles. No machine or worker is ever revisited, and each worker simply serves the next car in line[1]. Thus, the issue of machine scheduling to resolve competition, as posed here, does not arise.

To complete the specification of the system, it is necessary to specify how new arrivals to the system are generated, and also the service requirements for parts in different buffers.

For example, a Poisson process may faithfully model the arrival process. Clearly, in that case, the arrivals are outside our control. Alternatively, the inter-arrival time between parts may be a constant. We shall label such periodic arrivals as *deterministic*. It may however be the case that arrivals are not so regular as to be periodic. The arrivals may simply be *bursty*. One may model such arrivals by requiring that

$$\text{Number of arrivals in } [t, T] \leq \lambda(T - t) + \delta \text{ for every } 0 \leq t \leq T. \qquad (8.1)$$

The constant $\delta$ above allows some burstiness, and $\lambda$ is an upper bound on the long term rate of arrivals. We shall simply call $\lambda$ as the *arrival rate*, and refer to such arrival processes as *bursty arrivals*.

---

[1]Strictly speaking, this is not true. To address problems associated with quality control, a car may on occasion return to the same worker. We are grateful to Semyon Meerkov for pointing this out.

If the arrivals, or more properly, releases of raw parts into the system, are fully at our disposal, then we have several possibilities for regulating them. For example, one could try to maintain the total number of parts in the system at a constant level $N$. Thus, whenever one part exits the system, another raw part is released into the system. Such a policy will be called a *closed-loop release policy*. It can be simply viewed as creating a direct link between the exit buffer $b_9$ and the entry buffer $b_1$, in Figure 1. One can simply envision the system as a closed queueing network which contains $N$ trapped parts that are constantly circulating round the network. Another possibility is to try to release new parts into the system whenever the number of parts, or work, destined for a certain machine in the system, drops below a threshold. Such a release policy is often used to alleviate starvation of certain critical bottleneck machines. It is called a *workload regulation* policy.

Finally, one needs to specify the service requirements for parts. At one extreme, service requirements, or processing times, may be deterministic. In that case, we simply suppose that parts in buffer $b_i$ require $\tau_i$ time units of processing, from the machine serving $b_i$. We call $\mu_i := \frac{1}{\tau_i}$ the processing rate. Alternatively, the service times may be random variables, with a probability distribution that is possibly different for each buffer, together with some independence assumptions.

Let us turn next to examining what performance measures may be of possible interest. The most common performance measure of interest is the *manufacturing lead time* (MLT). This is the time elapsed from the moment of entry of a raw part, to its exit as a finished product, i.e., the time spent by a part in the system. It is called the sojourn time in queueing networks, the delay in communication networks, and the *cycle-time* in semiconductor manufacturing parlance. Since the manufacturing lead times of different parts may be different, one may want to take as the objective to minimize, or reduce, the *mean* manufacturing lead time. It is worth noting that by Little's Law, under some stability assumptions,

Mean Number of Parts in System  =  (Mean Arrival Rate of Parts)

× (Mean Manufacturing Lead Time).

Thus, for a fixed mean arrival rate of parts, reducing the mean manufacturing lead time is equivalent to reducing the mean total number of parts in the system. The parts in the system are called the *work-in-process (WIP)*. Hence, minimizing the mean manufacturing lead time minimizes the cost associated with the WIP.

The manufacturing lead time of parts may vary dramatically, and in that case one may want to reduce the *variance* of the manufacturing lead time. A small variance ensures that the exit time of a part may be well predicted, important in make to order situations, since we can reliably predict when the product will be available. This allows better planning of releases into the system, as well as better coordination with respect to further operations (such as assembly) on the output of finished parts produced by the plant.

Another performance measure of interest is the *throughput* of the plant, i.e., the rate at which finished parts leave the plant. If the manufacturing system is *stably* operated, by which we mean that there is no accumulation of parts in the system, then the rate of departure of parts from the system is the same as the rate of arrivals. If arrivals are outside our control, then this is not a performance measure that we can alter. On the other hand, for some release policies, such as the closed-loop release policy, the number of parts in the system is maintained at $N$. However the rate of circulation of parts, i.e., the throughput, may depend on the scheduling policy. Therefore, maximizing throughput is usually the objective of interest in such situations.

## 8.3   Fluctuation Smoothing Scheduling Policies to Reduce Variance of Lateness, Variance of Cycle–Time, and Mean Cycle–Time

In this section we will consider the problem of designing good scheduling policies for re-entrant lines. Our goal is to reduce both the mean and variance of manufacturing lead time. Of course, it is unlikely that two performance measures can be simultaneously optimized. However, in what follows, we will design policies that do well with respect to both criteria, compared to many other policies. First, we need to be a bit more specific about the model.

Let us suppose initially that the arrivals are exogenously determined, say deterministic or Poisson. We shall suppose that all processing times are independent, and that the processing times for parts in buffer $b_i$ are random variables with a certain probability distribution, say $F_i$.

Our design will be based on intuitive considerations, using some intuition gleaned from queueing theory. It is convenient to start by supposing that each part arriving to the system has a *due-date*, and that the goal is to minimize the variance of *lateness*. By lateness, we mean the difference between the *exit time* and the due date. If $\pi$ denotes a part, let $\alpha(\pi)$, $\delta(\pi)$ and $e(\pi)$ denote, respectively, its arrival time, due-date, and exit time.

Suppose that $\zeta_i$ is the mean, or an estimate of the mean, of the time required by parts to move from $b_i$ to the exit. Consider a time $t$ at which a part $\pi$ is in buffer $b_i$. Then $(\delta(\pi)-t)$ is the time remaining till the due-date, while $\zeta_i$ is an estimate of the remaining sojourn time in the system. Thus, $(\delta(\pi) - t - \zeta_i)$ is an estimate of the lateness of the part $\pi$. Let us call

$$s(\pi) \quad := \quad \delta(\pi) - t - \zeta_i$$

the *slack* of part $\pi$. Since the current time $t$ is the same for all parts, we could simply redefine $s(\pi)$ as,

$$s(\pi) \quad := \quad \delta(\pi) - \zeta_i.$$

It seems "fair" that a machine should process that part $\pi$, waiting in one of its buffers, that has the *least* slack. We shall say that this is a *Least Slack* (LS) policy. (Note that if there are waiting parts, the machine is not allowed to stay idle, but must choose between them based on their slacks). Now let us ponder over what such "fairness" amounts to. First, such a policy will tend to make all parts equally late or equally early. Thus it tends to reduce the *variance of lateness.*

Now let us turn to the issue of reducing the *variance of manufacturing lead-time.* Suppose that the *mean* manufacturing lead time is $M$. If we now set the due-date as $\delta(\pi) := \alpha(\pi) + M$, then the lateness is $e(\pi) - \delta(\pi) = e(\pi) - \alpha(\pi) - M$. Since $M$ is a constant, the variance of the lateness is also the variance of the manufacturing lead time $e(\pi) - \alpha(\pi)$. Thus, the policy which chooses the part with least slack,

$$s(\pi) \quad := \quad \alpha(\pi) + M - \zeta_i,$$

tends to reduce the variance of manufacturing lead time. One should note that since $M$ does not depend on $\pi$, it does not play any role in selecting the part $\pi$ with the least slack. One can therefore simply redefine the slack as $s(\pi) := \alpha(\pi) - \zeta_i$. This is also a Least Slack policy, though with a different

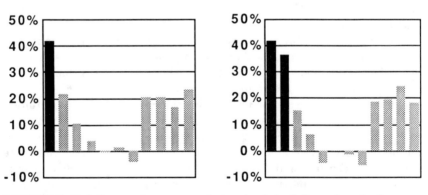

FIGURE 2. Relative performance of standard deviation of cycle-times under deterministic (left) and **Poisson** (right) releases. Shown are the percentage improvements in the standard deviation of cycle-time, over the baseline FIFO policy. The new FSMCT and FSVCT policies are highlighted in black. For deterministic releases, the policies FSMCT and FSVCT are the same. In all figures, the policies shown from left to right are: FSMCT, FSVCT, CYCLIC, LTNV, FIFO+, FIFO, LWNQ, FGCA, SRPT++, SRPT+, SRPT, and EDD.

definition for slack. We shall identify it as the *Fluctuation Smoothing Policy for Variance of Cycle-Time* (FSVCT).

One should note that the above policies are parametrized by the estimates of the mean remaining time, the $\zeta_i$'s. However, these estimates are themselves determined by the scheduling policy employed. Thus we have a mutual dependence. To resolve this we use a fixed point iteration scheme. First, we set all the estimates $\zeta_i$ to zero, and simulate the resulting policy. Next, we use the results of the simulation to refine the estimates. Then we conduct a new simulation using the same seeds (to fix the behavior of extraneous events) but employing the refined estimates. This process is repeated, and typically converges in just a few iterations, less than ten. We can also average over the results of several such simulations using different seeds.

A simulation study of a model of a semiconductor plant, which is a large re-entrant line that is also subject to machine failures and repairs, shows that the FSVCT policy is effective. The result is shown in Figure 2, which compares several policies. The strategy appears to lead to a sizable reduction in the variance of the manufacturing lead time.

Now let us address the problem of minimizing the *mean* manufacturing lead time. It is convenient to start with the simplest case, where arrivals are deterministic, i.e., periodic.

We shall take our cue from queueing theory for single-server queues. Consider first an M/G/1 queue. It is known from the Pollaczek-Khintchine formula that the mean delay is given by $\frac{2\rho-\rho^2+\lambda^2\sigma_s^2}{2\lambda(1-\rho)}$, where $\lambda$ is the arrival rate, $\rho$ is the mean server utilization, and $\sigma_s^2$ is the variance of the service times. We see that when $\sigma_s^2$ is reduced, the mean delay is also reduced. One can paraphrase this by saying that the smaller the *burstiness* in service times, the smaller the delay. More generally, consider a GI/GI/1 queue, where the mean interarrival time is $\frac{1}{\lambda}$, and the variance of the interarrival times is $\sigma_a^2$, while $\rho$ and $\sigma_s^2$ are as above. Kingman has shown that a bound on the mean delay is $\frac{2\rho-2\rho^2+\lambda^2\sigma_a^2+\lambda^2\sigma_s^2}{2\lambda[1-\rho]}$. Again, we see that large values of $\sigma_s^2$ produce large bounds. Additionally, we see that large values of $\sigma_a^2$ also produce large bounds. We thus see that the larger the burstiness in interarrival times, the larger is the upper bound on mean delay. This is in fact a general maxim in queueing theory. Burstiness increases delay.

We will now attempt to reduce delays *throughout* the manufacturing system by *simultaneously* attempting to reduce the burstiness of arrivals to all nodes. Since the arrivals to the system, i.e., arrivals to $b_1$, have been assumed to be deterministic, they have no burstiness at all.

Hence, to reduce the burstiness of arrivals to a certain buffer $b_k$, it is reasonable to attempt to reduce the variance of the delay incurred by parts in going from $b_1$ to $b_k$. But this is the same as the problem of reducing the variance of the manufacturing lead time, except that one truncates and excises the system after $b_{k-1}$. Thus, one would form estimates of mean time to go from every $b_i$, with $i < k$, to $b_k$; call it $\zeta_i^k$, and define the slack as $s(\pi) = \alpha(\pi) - \zeta_i^k$, for a part in buffer $b_i$. (We will not fully ignore all buffers $b_i$ for $i \geq k$, since that would be unrealistic.)

So far we have argued that this policy reduces the burstiness of arrivals to a particular buffer, namely $b_k$. Now note that $\zeta_i = \zeta_i^k + \zeta_k$, and since $k$ was fixed in our argument above, we could redefine the slack as $s(\pi) := \alpha(\pi) - \zeta_i$, for a part in $b_i$. However, now we have a policy which is *uniform* in $k$. Thus, the Least Slack policy with slack defined as $s(\pi) := \alpha(\pi) - \zeta_i$, for a part in $b_i$, should be a reasonable policy to reduce the burstiness of *all* flows in the network simultaneously, i.e., to all buffers, when the arrivals of raw parts to the system are periodic. It should therefore (one hopes) lead to a small mean manufacturing lead time.

Above, we have only considered deterministic, i.e., periodic, arrivals. Now let us consider more general arrivals. First note that to reduce the burstiness of exits from the system, one can simply set periodic due dates, and then reduce the variance of lateness. Define $\delta(\pi) = n/\lambda$, if $\pi$ is the $n$-th release into the system, and $\frac{1}{\lambda}$ is the mean interarrival (equivalently, interdeparture) time. This gives rise to the Least Slack policy with slack $s(\pi)$ defined as

$$ s(\pi) \quad := \quad \frac{n}{\lambda} - \zeta_i, $$

if $\pi$ is the $n$-th part released into the system, and it is located in buffer $b_i$. By the same argument as above, this scheduling policy can be used to reduce burstiness of flows *throughout* the network.

Thus, we arrive at the Least Slack policy with $s(\pi)$ defined as $s(\pi) = \frac{n}{\lambda} - \zeta_i$ for reducing the mean manufacturing lead time. Let us call this the *Fluctuation Smoothing policy for Mean Cycle-Time* (FSMCT).

One may note that it agrees with the policy derived earlier for deterministic, i.e., periodic releases, since there $\alpha(\pi) = \frac{n}{\lambda}$. In fact, for such arrivals, FSMCT = FSVCT, and so the *same* policy reduces both mean and variance of cycle-time.

There is a very appealing interpretation of the FSMCT policy as trying to equalize and reduce the total *downstream* shortfall from each buffer. To see this, let $x_i(t)$ be the number of parts in buffer $b_i$ at time $t$, and let $\bar{x}_i$ be its mean value in steady state. Consider the quantity ($\lambda s(\pi)$ - Total Number of Exits from the System). This is a monotone increasing function of $s(\pi)$, and so the FSMCT policy simply chooses that part $\pi$ for which this quantity is smallest. However, this quantity has a nice interpretation, which can be seen as follows:

$\lambda s(\pi)$   &minus;   Total Number of Exits from the System

$\quad = \quad \lambda(n/\lambda - \zeta_i) -$ Total Number of Exits from the System

$$\begin{aligned}
&= \ (n - \text{ Total Number of Exits from the System}) \ - \lambda\zeta_i \\
&= \ \text{Number of Parts Downstream from } b_i \text{ in the System} \\
&\quad - \text{ Mean Number of Parts Downstream from } b_i \text{ in Steady State} \\
&= \ \sum_{j=i}^{L} x_j(t) - \sum_{j=i}^{L} \bar{x}_j.
\end{aligned}$$

Above, the second to last equality is true because the number of parts currently downstream from $b_i$ is ($n$ - Total Number of Exits from the System), since the $n$-th release is at the head of buffer $b_i$, and parts leave the system in the order that they arrive. (We are implicitly assuming here that the system is started empty). Also, by Little's Theorem, $\lambda\zeta_i =$ Mean Number of Parts Downstream from $b_i$. Thus we see that the FSMCT policy has the very appealing property of trying to equalize and reduce the *total downstream shortfall* from every buffer.

The above equivalent representation also shows that FSMCT is a *stationary* policy, in the sense of Markov Decision Processes. By this, we mean that its actions are based only on the numbers of parts in each buffer.

Figure 3 shows a comparison of several policies for a model of a semiconductor manufacturing plant. We see that our FSMCT strategy seems very effective.

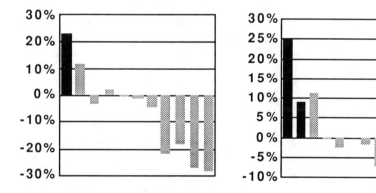

FIGURE 3. Relative performance of mean queueing times under determisnistic (left) and **Poisson** (right) releases. Shown are the percentage improvements in the mean queueing time, over the baseline FIFO policy. The new FSMCT and FSVCT policies are highlighted in black. For deterministic releases, the policies FSMCT and FSVCT are the same. In all figures, the policies shown from left to right are: FSMCT, FSVCT,CYCLIC, LTNV, FIFO+, FIFO, LWNQ, FGCA, SRPT++, SRPT+, SRPT, and EDD.

## 8.4  Stability of LBFS, SRPTS, EA, EDD and All Least Slack Scheduling Policies

In Section 3, we have motivated the use of various Least Slack policies. All of them define the slack of a part $\pi$ in buffer $b_i$ as $s(\pi) := \gamma(\pi) - \zeta_i$. Here $\gamma(\pi)$ is an attribute of the part, while $\zeta_i$ is an attribute of the buffer $b_i$ in which the part $\pi$ is located. The choices $\gamma(\pi) = \delta(\pi)$, the due-date, $\gamma(\pi) = \alpha(\pi)$, the arrival time, and $\gamma(\pi) = \frac{n}{\lambda}$, were all shown to be useful.

Also, $\zeta_i$ was a number, chosen for each buffer $b_i$. While $\zeta_i$ was in all cases taken to be an "estimate of remaining delay from $b_i$," let us allow $\zeta_i$ here to be any real number. We can then regard $(\zeta_1, \ldots, \zeta_L)$ as a vector which *parametrizes* the least slack policies.

We now wish to analyze the behavior of such Least Slack policies. To do so for general stochastic models is currently infeasible. Let us simplify the situation, and assume a bursty model for arrivals, and a deterministic model for service times. The latter could be relaxed somewhat.

Let us suppose that arrivals to the system satisfy (8.1). Also, suppose that every part in buffer $b_i$ requires $\tau_i$ time units of processing from the machine serving $b_i$. Regarding the

definition of slacks, we will only assume that for every part $\pi$, the part attribute $\gamma(\pi)$ satisfies,

$$|\gamma(\pi) - \alpha(\pi)| \leq M \text{ for all } \pi, \tag{8.2}$$

for some $M < +\infty$. It clearly covers the situation $\gamma(\pi) = \alpha(\pi)$. It covers $\gamma(\pi) = \frac{n}{\lambda}$, if $\pi$ is the $n$-th part released into the system too, by virtue of (8.1). Finally, it will cover $\gamma(\pi) = \delta(\pi)$, if one assumes that

$$|\delta(\pi) - \alpha(\pi)| \leq M' \text{ for all } \pi, \tag{8.3}$$

for some $M' < +\infty$, i.e., if the due-date is set to within some bounded time of the arrival time – a reasonable assumption.

One would like to quantify the performance of such Least Slack policies. However, an even more fundamental issue needs to be resolved first. Can the performance be so bad that the delay of parts is unbounded? This is the problem of *stability* of a scheduling policy. Let $e(\pi)$ denote the time that part $\pi$ exits from the system. We shall say that a scheduling policy is *stable* if

$$e(\pi) - \alpha(\pi) \leq M'' \text{ for all } \pi,$$

for some $M'' < +\infty$, i.e., the manufacturing lead time is bounded. Note that when the due-date setting satisfies (8.3), stability is equivalent to

$$|\delta(\pi) - e(\pi)| \leq M''' \text{ for all } \pi,$$

for some $M''' < +\infty$, i.e., boundedness of lateness of parts.

Clearly, for *any* scheduling policy, a necessary condition for its stability is that

$$\sum_{\{i:b_i \text{ is served by } \sigma\}} \lambda \tau_i \; < \; 1 \text{ for all machines } \sigma. \qquad (8.4)$$

This is simply the requirement that each machine be fast enough to serve the needs of arriving parts, if they arrive at rate $\lambda$. Let us call this the *capacity condition*.

Is it true that all scheduling policies are stable whenever the arrival rate is within the capacity of the system? Clearly not, since a scheduling policy that insists on keeping all machines always idle, is unstable.

Let us say that a scheduling policy is *non-idling* if no machine is ever allowed to stay idle whenever any of its buffers is non-empty. It is clear that some policies which are *not* non-idling are unstable; an extreme example is the always idling policy above. However, a policy which is not non-idling need not necessarily be unstable, or even unreasonable, for that matter.

Let us restrict our attention to non-idling policies. There are several examples of such scheduling policies. One example is the well known First Come First Serve (FCFS) policy, where a machine provides service to the part which arrived first to that machine. (We should note here that by the arrival time of a part to the machine we mean the arrival time for the current visit to the machine, since a part may revisit a machine more than once.) Also, the class of Least Slack policies is non-idling, as noted earlier.

Another class of non–idling policies is the class of *buffer priority* policies. These are policies where a priority order is chosen for the buffers at each machine, and the machine then provides service according to the ordering. For choosing parts from within a buffer, the service priority could, for example, choose from the head of the buffer.

As an example, consider ordering buffers in a re-entrant line according to the order visited, i.e., $\{b_1, \ldots, b_L\}$. We shall call this the *First Buffer First Serve* policy (FBFS). Thus, if $b_i$ and $b_j$, with $i < j$, are in contention for the same machine, then $b_i$ has higher priority. A part in $b_j$ gets taken up for processing only when all buffers $b_k$ with $k < j$, which are located at the same machine as $b_j$, are empty.

In all cases, we could let the service priority be pre-emptive resume or non-preemptive. Under a *pre-emptive resume* priority, a part arriving to a higher priority buffer pre-empts the part currently undergoing processing, which then has to wait till the next time that there are no other higher priority parts at the machine, for the resumption of its remaining processing. Under a *non-preemptive* priority policy, a new part is taken up for processing only when the part currently undergoing processing completes its service. For many manufacturing operations, a non-preemptive priority is more realistic[2].

Diametrically opposed to the FBFS policy is the *Last Buffer First Serve* policy (LBFS), where the priority ordering of the buffers is $\{b_L, b_{L-1}, \ldots, b_1\}$. Thus, buffers visited later in the route are given higher priority.

The LBFS policy can also be regarded as a *Shortest Remaining Processing Time in System* (SRPTS) policy. Assuming deterministic processing times, a part closer to exit has a lesser total of remaining processing times left, and an SRPTS policy gives priority to such parts – just as the LBFS policy does.

A little thought should convince the reader that the LBFS policy is the *system-wide* analog of the FCFS policy, where the arrival time *to the system* dictates the priority. Clearly, if every machine gives priority to parts which arrived first to the system, then parts which arrived first would be located in buffers nearer the exiting end of the system. Thus the LBFS policy which gives priority to buffers nearer the exiting end of the system also gives priority to the parts which arrived first to the system. Therefore, it could also be called an *Earliest Arrival* (EA) policy.

In turn, the EA policy, and thus the LBFS policy too, is a special case of a Least Slack policy, which is obtained by defining the slack as $s(\pi) = \alpha(\pi)$, the arrival time to the system, and setting all $\zeta_i \equiv 0$.

Finally, the EA policy, is the same as the well known *Earliest Due Date* (EDD) policy, provided the due-dates assigned to parts are monotone increasing in the arrival times of the parts to the system, i.e., if $\alpha(\pi) < \alpha(\pi') \Rightarrow \delta(\pi) < \delta(\pi')$. Another way to state this is to say that parts arrive in the order of their due dates.

One therefore notes that the LBFS policy coincides with EA, SRPTS, and EDD policies. For these reasons, the LBFS policy is a useful policy to analyze. Another perhaps more important reason is that since it is a special case of the family of Least Slack policies, one may hope to learn something about this more general class of policies. We have already seen in Section 3 that such Least Slack policies can yield useful results.

To show that stability of non-idling scheduling policies cannot be taken for granted, we now give an example of an unstable buffer priority policy.

*Example: An Unstable Buffer Priority Policy.*

Consider the re-entrant line of Figure 4. Parts arrive periodically to buffer $b_1$, one every hour. Each part requires 0 hrs, 2/3 hrs, 0 hrs and

---

[2]However, in the operation of computer systems, a pre-emptive resume priority is often used.

$2/3$ hrs of processing, at buffers $b_1$, $b_2$, $b_3$ and $b_4$, respectively. The requirement of 0 hrs means that the processing time is very small; however a part
may still have to wait for processing due to the nature of the scheduling
policy. Clearly, the capacity condition (8.4) is satisfied at each machine,
since each part requires $2/3$ hrs of total processing at each machine, and
parts only arrive 1 per hour.

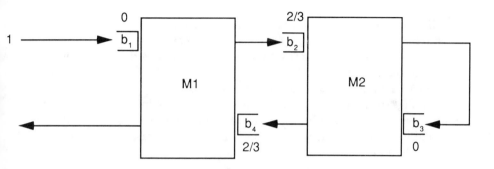

FIGURE 4. An unstable system under the buffer priority ordering $(b_4, b_2, b_3, b_1)$.

Consider now the buffer priority ordering $\{b_4, b_2, b_3, b_1\}$. This is slightly
different from LBFS. It gives priority to $b_4$ over $b_1$ at machine M1, and
priority to $b_2$ over $b_3$ at machine M2. Consider now the initial condition
$(x, 0, 0, 0)$ at time $t = 0$, which denotes that buffer $b_1$ has $x$ parts in it, and
all other buffers are empty.

Let us now trace the evolution of the system forward from time $t = 0$.
Since $b_4$ is empty, machine M1 works on $b_1$, and immediately transfers all
$x$ parts to $b_2$. Machine M2, which gives priority to $b_2$ over $b_3$, then goes
into a busy period working on buffer $b_2$. While it is working on buffer $b_2$,
new parts are arriving to buffer $b_1$, one every hour. Since $b_4$ is still empty,
machine M1 can work on these new arrivals, and so they are promptly
transferred to $b_2$. The buffer $b_2$ finally empties for the first time at $t = 2x$.
To see this, note that at $t = 2x$, the $x$ original parts, plus the $2x$ new parts
which arrived to $b_1$, a total of $3x$ parts, have been sent to $b_2$. These $3x$
parts take up $2x$ hours of processing time ($2/3$ hours per part). Thus, at
$t = 2x$, buffers $b_1$, $b_2$ and $b_4$ are empty, while $b_3$ has $3x$ parts. Machine M2
can then work on $b_3$ since $b_2$ is empty, and so it promptly dispatches all $3x$
parts to $b_4$. At M1, $b_4$ has higher priority than $b_1$, and so M2 goes into a

busy period while processing the $3x$ parts in $b_4$. During this busy period, new parts arriving to $b_1$ are held up, and thus machine M2 undergoes an enforced *starvation*. The busy period to process $3x$ parts at $b_4$ lasts $2x$ hours. During this busy period, $2x$ new parts have arrived to $b_1$.

Thus, we see that at the end of this busy period, the new state of the system is $(2x, 0, 0, 0)$.

Hence the number of parts in the system has doubled. This process continues indefinitely, and so the buffer levels are all unbounded.    □

The key feature to notice in the above example is that when working on parts in one buffer, the scheduling policy may cause starvation of some machine. Due to the re–entrant nature of the line, and the consequent flow of material in both directions between machines, the build-up of parts in buffers can undergo back and forth amplification, which leads to instability.

In fact, such instability can be latent in any scheduling policy, and it is of interest to see which scheduling policies are unstable. In particular, we would like to determine whether the class of Least Slack policies developed in Section 3 is stable.

We shall show below that the entire class of Least Slack policies, i.e., for all choices of parameters $\{\zeta_i\}$, is stable for all re-entrant lines with arrival rate within the capacity of the system.

It is convenient to begin however with the LBFS policy. The key result in establishing the stability of LBFS is a bound on the delay experienced by a new part, as a function of the number of parts already in the system when it arrives.

**Theorem: Bound on Delay of a New Part.** Consider a re-entrant line with service times $\tau_i$ at buffer $b_i$, operating under the pre-emptive resume LBFS policy. For every $\epsilon > 0$, there exists a constant $c(\epsilon)$ with the following property. If a new part $\pi$ arrives to the system to find $x$ parts already in the system, then

Manufacturing Lead Time of $\pi \leq (\bar{w} + \epsilon)x + c(\epsilon)$ for every $\epsilon > 0$, and all $x$.

Above, $\bar{w}$ is the maximum work brought to a machine by an incoming part, i.e.,

$$\bar{w} := \max_{\{\sigma:\sigma \ is \ a \ machine \ \}} \sum_{\{i:b_i \ is \ served \ by \ \sigma\}} \tau_i.$$

Ignoring the $\epsilon$, the above result says that the delay to clear $x$ parts from the system is essentially only the delay experienced by the $x$ parts in traversing the *bottleneck* machine. Thus, it rules out excessive enforced starvation.

**Proof of Theorem.**

Let us define by $B_i := \{b_i, b_{i+1}, \ldots, b_L\}$ the *head section* of the manufacturing system. Thus $B_1$ is the entire system.

Let

$$\bar{w}_i := \max_{\{\sigma : \sigma \text{ is a machine}\}} \sum_{\{j : b_j \text{ is served by } \sigma \text{ and } j \geq i\}} \tau_j$$

be the maximum work contributed to a machine by a part in the head section $B_i$. Note that $\bar{w} = \bar{w}_1 \geq \bar{w}_2 \geq \cdots \geq \bar{w}_L = \tau_L$.

Consider a part $\pi$ which arrives to the head section $B_L$, i.e., to $b_L$, to find $x$ parts in $B_L$. Clearly, since the highest priority under pre-emptive LBFS is given to parts in $b_L$, the delay suffered by $\pi$ is

$$\text{Delay} \leq x\tau_L + \tau_L.$$

Noting that $\tau_L = \bar{w}_L$, we have proved,

$$\begin{pmatrix} \text{Delay experienced by a part } \pi \text{ arriving to} \\ B_L \text{ to find } x \text{ parts in } B_L \end{pmatrix} \leq (\bar{w}_L + \epsilon)x + c_L(\epsilon)$$

where $c_L(\epsilon) := \tau_L$ for all $\epsilon > 0$.

Our proof is by induction on $i$, starting with $i = L$, that there is a constant $c_i(\epsilon)$, for every $\epsilon > 0$, so that

$$\begin{pmatrix} \text{Delay experienced by a part } \pi \text{ arriving to} \\ B_i \text{ to find } x \text{ parts in } B_i \end{pmatrix}$$
$$\leq (\bar{w}_i + \epsilon)x + c_i(\epsilon) \text{ for every } \epsilon > 0.$$

Now suppose that the induction hypothesis is true for $i + 1$, $i + 2, \ldots, L$. Consider a part $\pi$ arriving to $B_i$, to find $x$ parts already in $B_i$.

When part $\pi$ arrives to $B_i$, i.e., to $b_i$, say at time 0, it may find some number $n$ of parts already in $b_i$. The value of $n$ may range between 0 and $x$.

Consider $n = 0$. Let us denote by $\pi'$ the part that arrived just prior to $\pi$. Alternatively, $\pi'$ is the part which has second lowest priority in $B_i$; its priority being higher only than that of $\pi$. Since $n = 0$, $\pi'$ has to be in $B_{i+1}$. Moreover, $\pi'$ has $(x - 1)$ parts ahead of it in $B_{i+1}$. Hence, using the validity of our induction hypothesis for the head section $B_{i+1}$, we have

$$\begin{aligned} \text{Exit time of } \pi' &\leq (\bar{w}_{i+1} + \epsilon)(x - 1) + c_{i+1}(\epsilon) \\ &= (\bar{w}_{i+1} + \epsilon)x + (c_{i+1}(\epsilon) - \bar{w}_{i+1} - \epsilon) \\ &\leq (\bar{w}_i + \epsilon)x + (c_{i+1}(\epsilon) - \bar{w}_{i+1} - \epsilon), \text{ for every } \epsilon > 0. \end{aligned}$$

Above, we have used the fact that $\bar{w}_{i+1} \leq \bar{w}_i$. Note now that after $\pi'$ has exited the system, the part $\pi$ has a clear run through the empty buffers ahead of it. Hence, it exits no more than $\sum_{j=i}^{L} \tau_j$ time units after $\pi'$. Thus,

$$\text{Delay of } \pi \quad \leq \quad (\bar{w}_i + \epsilon)x + \left(c_{i+1}(\epsilon) - \bar{w}_{i+1} - \epsilon + \sum_{j=i}^{L} \tau_j\right).$$

Now we perform a second layer of induction on $n$ starting with $n = 0$. We will show that there exist constants $c_i^{(n)}(\epsilon)$ for every $\epsilon > 0$, so that

$$\begin{pmatrix} \text{Delay experienced by a part } \pi \text{ which ar-} \\ \text{rives to find } n \text{ parts in } b_i \text{ and } x \text{ parts in} \\ B_i \end{pmatrix} \leq (\bar{w}_i + \epsilon)x + c_i^{(n)}(\epsilon)$$

for every $\epsilon > 0$ and all $x$.

Note that this induction hypothesis has been shown above to be true for $n = 0$ if we choose

$$c_i^{(0)}(\epsilon) \quad \geq \quad c_{i+1}(\epsilon) - \bar{w}_{i+1} - \epsilon + \sum_{j=i}^{L} \tau_j.$$

Now suppose the induction hypothesis has been established for $0, 1, 2, \ldots, n-1$. Consider a part $\pi$ arriving to $B_i$, at time 0, to find $n$ parts in $b_i$, and $(x - n)$ parts in $B_{i+1}$ – making for a total of $x$ parts in $B_i$.

We need to introduce a bit of notation. Let $T$ denote the time at which $\pi$ moves from $b_i$ to $b_{i+1}$. (It is easy to see that $T < +\infty$; in fact every part entering the system eventually leaves it). Also, let $y$ be the number of parts in $B_{i+1}$ when $\pi$ enters $b_{i+1}$.

We will fix $\epsilon > 0$, and consider three cases.

*Case 1:*

Suppose $y \leq \Gamma(\epsilon)$, where $\Gamma(\epsilon) := \frac{2c_{i+1}\left(\frac{\epsilon}{2}\right)}{\epsilon}$.

Note that $\pi$ can wait no more than $\bar{w}_i x$ time units in $b_i$, before its processing starts. This is the worst case even if all $x$ parts require attention from the machine serving $b_i$. Hence

$$T \quad \leq \quad \bar{w}_i x + \tau_i.$$

After entering $b_{i+1}$, $\pi$ finds $y \leq \Gamma(\epsilon)$ parts ahead of it, and its further delay is therefore no more than $(\bar{w}_{i+1} + \epsilon)\Gamma(\epsilon) + c_{i+1}(\epsilon)$. Hence, the total delay incurred by $\pi$ is no more than $\bar{w}_i x + \tau_i + (\bar{w}_{i+1} + \epsilon)\Gamma(\epsilon) + c_{i+1}(\epsilon)$. Therefore, the choice of $c_i^{(n)}(\epsilon) \geq (\bar{w}_{i+1} + \epsilon)\Gamma(\epsilon) + c_{i+1}(\epsilon) + \tau_i$ will suffice for this case.

*Case 2:*

Suppose $\Gamma(\epsilon) < y \leq n$.

Note that when $\pi$ enters $b_i$, there are $n$ parts already in $b_i$. When it enters $b_{i+1}$, the assumption in this case is that the number of parts in $B_{i+1}$

is $y \leq n$. Together, these imply that the part with highest priority in $B_{i+1}$, at the time that $\pi$ enters $B_{i+1}$, was originally in buffer $b_i$ with $(n-y)$ parts ahead of it in $b_i$, at time 0. Call this part $\pi''$.

Hence, at time 0, the part $\pi''$ has $(x-y)$ parts ahead of it in $B_i$, and $(n-y)$ parts ahead of it in $b_i$. Thus, its delay is no more than $(\bar{w}_i + \epsilon)(x - y) + c_i^{(n-y)}(\epsilon)$, since the induction hypothesis is true for $(n-y)$. Since at time $T$, $\pi''$ still has not exited the system, we see that

$$T \leq (\bar{w}_i + \epsilon)(x - y) + c_i^{(n-y)}(\epsilon).$$

After $\pi$ enters $B_{i+1}$, it sees $y$ parts ahead of it. Hence the further delay experienced by $\pi$ is no more than $\left(\bar{w}_{i+1} + \frac{\epsilon}{2}\right) y + c_{i+1}\left(\frac{\epsilon}{2}\right)$. Here we have used the crucial fact that the induction hypothesis is true for all $\epsilon > 0$, and in fact true for $\frac{\epsilon}{2}$.

Taking the sum of the delay to enter $b_{i+1}$, and the delay to thereafter exit $B_{i+1}$, we see that

$$
\begin{aligned}
\text{Delay of } \pi \;\leq\;& (\bar{w}_i + \epsilon)(x - y) + c_i^{(n-y)}(\epsilon) + \left(\bar{w}_{i+1} + \frac{\epsilon}{2}\right) y + c_{i+1}\left(\frac{\epsilon}{2}\right) \\
=\;& (\bar{w}_i + \epsilon)x + \left(\bar{w}_{i+1} - \bar{w}_i - \frac{\epsilon}{2}\right) y + c_{i+1}\left(\frac{\epsilon}{2}\right) + c_i^{(n-y)}(\epsilon) \\
\leq\;& (\bar{w}_i + \epsilon)x - \frac{\epsilon}{2}y + c_{i+1}\left(\frac{\epsilon}{2}\right) + c_i^{(n-y)}(\epsilon) \quad \text{(using } \bar{w}_{i+1} \leq \bar{w}_i) \\
\leq\;& (\bar{w}_i + \epsilon)x + c_i^{(n-y)}(\epsilon) \quad \left(\text{using } y > \Gamma(\epsilon) = \frac{2c_{i+1}\left(\frac{\epsilon}{2}\right)}{\epsilon}\right).
\end{aligned}
$$

Thus the induction hypothesis is true for this case if we choose $c_i^{(n)}(\epsilon) \geq c_i^{(j)}(\epsilon)$ for all $0 \leq j \leq n-1$.

*Case 3:*

Suppose $y > \max\{n, \Gamma(\epsilon)\}$.

Again, consider the part $\pi''$ which has highest priority in $B_{i+1}$, at the time $T$ that $\pi$ enters $b_{i+1}$. Note that at time 0, $\pi$ had $n$ parts ahead of it in $b_i$, while at time $T$ it has $y$ parts ahead of it in $B_{i+1}$. Since $y > n$, it follows that the part $\pi''$ was originally already in $B_{i+1}$ at time 0. Hence the exit time of $\pi''$ from $B_{i+1}$ is no more than $(\bar{w}_{i+1} + \epsilon)(x - y) + c_{i+1}(\epsilon)$. Since such exit has not yet occurred at time $T$, it follows that

$$T \leq (\bar{w}_{i+1} + \epsilon)(x - y) + c_{i+1}(\epsilon).$$

At time $T$, part $\pi$ enters $B_{i+1}$ to find $y$ parts ahead of it. Hence its further delay is no more than $(\bar{w}_{i+1} + \epsilon)y + c_{i+1}(\epsilon)$.

Summing the delay incurred by $\pi$ to enter $B_{i+1}$, and its further delay to exit the system, we see that

$$
\begin{aligned}
\text{Delay of } \pi \;\leq\;& (\bar{w}_{i+1} + \epsilon)(x - y) + c_{i+1}(\epsilon) + (\bar{w}_{i+1} + \epsilon)y + c_{i+1}(\epsilon) \\
=\;& (\bar{w}_{i+1} + \epsilon)x + 2c_{i+1}(\epsilon).
\end{aligned}
$$

Thus, the induction hypothesis is satisfied for this case if we take $c_i^{(n)}(\epsilon) \geq 2c_{i+1}(\epsilon)$.

Combining all three cases together, we see that the requirements on the constants $c_i^{(n)}(\epsilon)$ are

$$c_i^{(0)} \geq c_{i+1}(\epsilon) - \bar{w}_{i+1} - \epsilon + \sum_{j=1}^{L} \tau_j$$

and

$$c_i^{(n)} \geq \max\{(\bar{w}_{i+1} + \epsilon)\Gamma(\epsilon) + c_{i+1}(\epsilon) + \tau_i, c_i^{(0)}(\epsilon), c_i^{(1)}(\epsilon), \ldots, c_i^{(n-1)}(\epsilon), 2c_{i+1}(\epsilon)\}.$$

They are met by simply choosing,

$$c_i^{(n)}(\epsilon) := \max\{0, c_{i+1}(\epsilon) - \bar{w}_{i+1} - \epsilon + \sum_{j=i}^{L} \tau_j, \frac{2(\bar{w}_{i+1} + \epsilon)c_{i+1}\left(\frac{\epsilon}{2}\right)}{\epsilon}$$
$$+ c_{i+1}(\epsilon) + \tau_i, 2c_{i+1}(\epsilon)\}.$$

Thus the induction on $n$ is complete, and that also completes the induction on $i$.   $\square$

From the proof of the preceding Theorem, by taking the explicit values of the constants into account, we have the following more explicit result.

$$\begin{pmatrix} \text{Delay experienced by a part } \pi \text{ that ar-} \\ \text{rives to } b_i \text{ to find } x \text{ parts already in} \\ \{b_i, b_{i+1}, \ldots, b_L\} \end{pmatrix}$$
$$\leq (\bar{w}_i + \epsilon)x + c_i(\epsilon) \text{ for every } \epsilon > 0,$$

where

$$\bar{w}_i := \max_{\{\sigma : \sigma \text{ is a machine}\}} \sum_{\{j : b_j \text{ is served by } \sigma \text{ and } j \geq i\}} \tau_j$$

$$c_L(\epsilon) := \tau_L$$

$$c_i(\epsilon) := 2c_{i+1}(\epsilon) + \frac{2(\bar{w}_{i+1} + \epsilon)c_{i+1}\left(\frac{\epsilon}{2}\right)}{\epsilon} + \sum_{j=i}^{L} \tau_j.$$

Keeping track of the powers of $\epsilon$ so generated shows that,

$$c_i(\epsilon) = \sum_{j=0}^{L-i} \frac{a_j}{\epsilon^j}, \text{ for some system dependent constants } a_j, \ldots, a_{L-1}.$$

A particular corollary is the following result, which shows that even re-entrant lines, possessing cycles, satisfy a "pipeline" property, when operated under an LBFS policy.

**Corollary: The Pipeline Property of LBFS.**

$$\begin{pmatrix} \text{Delay of part } \pi \text{ which arrives to} \\ \text{find } x \text{ parts ahead of it in system} \end{pmatrix} \leq \bar{w}x + o(x).$$

**Proof.**

Note that,

$$\frac{\text{Delay of } \pi - \bar{w}x}{x} \leq \epsilon + \frac{c(\epsilon)}{x} \text{ for every } \epsilon > 0.$$

Hence

$$\limsup_{x \to +\infty} \frac{\text{Delay of } \pi - \bar{w}x}{x} \leq \epsilon \text{ for every } \epsilon > 0.$$

Thus,

$$\limsup_{x \to +\infty} \frac{\text{Delay of } \pi - \bar{w}x}{x} \leq 0.$$

$\square$

Using the above result on the delay experienced by an incoming part, one can prove the stability of the LBFS policy for *all* arrival rates within the capacity of the system.

**Theorem: Stability of the LBFS Policy.** Consider any bursty arrival process satisfying (8.1), with arrival rate $\lambda$. Suppose that the arrival rate is within the capacity of the system, i.e., (8.4) is satisfied. Assume that the system is operating under the LBFS policy. Then the system is stable, i.e., the number of parts in the system is bounded. If $x(t)$ denotes the number of parts in the system at time $t$, then the asymptotic number of parts in the system is bounded by,

$$\limsup_{t \to +\infty} x(t) \leq \frac{\lambda c(\epsilon) + \delta}{1 - \rho - \lambda \epsilon},$$

where $\rho := \lambda \bar{w}$ is the utilization ratio of the bottleneck machine, and $\epsilon > 0$ is any number with $\rho + \lambda \epsilon < 1$.

**Proof.**

Let $t_0 := 0$ and denote by $\pi^{(0)}$ the part which has the lowest priority among the $x(0)$ parts in the system at $t_0$, i.e., it is in the tail of some buffer $b_j$ with buffers $b_1, \ldots, b_{j-1}$ behind it being empty. Recursively define for $n = 1, 2, \ldots$

$$t_n := \text{time at which } \pi^{(n-1)} \text{ exits the system,}$$

where,

$$\pi^{(n)} := \text{part with lowest priority in system at time } t_n.$$

We will analyze the system in the time intervals $[t_{n-1}, t_n]$ for $n \geq 1$. Note that

$$t_n - t_{n-1} = \text{remaining manufacturing lead time, after } t_{n-1}, \text{ of } \pi^{(n-1)}.$$

However, at time $t_{n-1}$, the part $\pi^{(n-1)}$ has $x(t_{n-1}) - 1$ parts ahead of it in the system. Hence

$$t_n - t_{n-1} \leq (\bar{w} + \epsilon)x(t_{n-1}) + c(\epsilon) \text{ for every } \epsilon > 0.$$

Now note that at time $t_{n-1}$, there are no parts *behind* $\pi^{(n-1)}$. Hence, when it exits at time $t_n$, it leaves behind it in the system only those parts which arrived in the time interval $[t_{n-1}, t_n]$. Therefore, by the assumption (8.1) on the arrival process,

$$x(t_n) \leq \lambda(t_n - t_{n-1}) + \delta.$$

Combining the two inequalities above, we see that

$$
\begin{aligned}
x(t_n) &\leq \lambda(\bar{w} + \epsilon)x(t_{n-1}) + \lambda c(\epsilon) + \delta \qquad (8.5)\\
&= (\rho + \lambda\epsilon)x(t_{n-1}) + \lambda c(\epsilon) + \delta \text{ for every } \epsilon > 0.
\end{aligned}
$$

Since the arrival rate is within capacity, $\rho < 1$. Hence, one can choose $\epsilon > 0$ so small that $\rho + \lambda\epsilon < 1$. Consider any such $\epsilon$. Then, the above difference equation is stable, and one obtains,

$$\limsup_{n \to \infty} x(t_n) \leq \frac{\lambda c(\epsilon) + \delta}{1 - \rho - \lambda\epsilon}.$$

This proves that the number of parts in the system is bounded. It also shows that the bound on the asymptotic number of parts in the system is valid if we sample the system at the times $\{t_n\}$. The demonstration that it is valid for all large $t$ involves a slight extension of the above argument, and is omitted. $\qquad \square$

So far, we have analyzed only the pre-emptive resume version of the LBFS policy. However, the arguments above are easily extended to the non-preemptive case, and in fact to the class of all Least Slack policies.

Let us directly turn to non-preemptive Least Slack policies, and see how one may prove a bound on the manufacturing lead time of a part which arrives to find $x$ parts in the system. The heart of the matter is as follows. Consider a part $\pi$ at a buffer $b_i$. If the system is operated under a pre-emptive resume LBFS policy, then the part $\pi$ is delayed only by parts ahead of it. Now turn to a non–pre-emptive Least Slack policy. The part $\pi$ may have to wait $\tau_i$ time units for a part to complete processing, because we are now operating in a non-preemptive mode. After this, it has to defer, at most, to those parts $\pi'$ which satisfy

$$\gamma(\pi') - \zeta_k \quad < \quad \gamma(\pi) - \zeta_i,$$

where $b_i$ and $b_k$ share the same machine. Such a part $\pi'$ must satisfy

$$\gamma(\pi') \quad < \quad \gamma(\pi) - \zeta_i + \zeta_k.$$

Recall now our assumption that the attribute $\gamma(\pi')$ for Least Slack policies satisfies (8.2). Thus, we see that a necessary condition for a part $\pi'$ to delay $\pi$ at $b_i$ is that the arrival time $\alpha(\pi')$ of the part $\pi'$ must satisfy,

$$\alpha(\pi') < \quad \alpha(\pi) - \zeta_i + \zeta_k + 2M \leq \quad \alpha(\pi) + 2M + 2\bar{\zeta},$$

where $\bar{\zeta} := \max_j |\zeta_j|$.

Under LBFS, a part $\pi$ can be delayed at a buffer $b_i$ only by parts that arrived in $(-\infty, \alpha(\pi)]$, i.e., by the parts that arrived before it. In comparison, under LS, a part may also be delayed by parts that arrived in $(\alpha(\pi), \alpha(\pi) + 2M + 2\bar{\zeta}]$. The number of such additional parts is at most $\lambda(2M + 2\bar{\zeta}) + \delta$. Together, these parts can delay $\pi$ by at most $[\lambda(2M + 2\bar{\zeta}) + \delta] (\max_j \tau_j)$. Adding up the non-preemptive delay, and the delay that can possibly be caused by parts arriving after $\pi$, we see that their effect is bounded.

Such a bound can be propagated through the arguments of the stability Theorem above. We can thus prove the stability of all Least Slack policies.

**Theorem: Stability of all Least Slack policies.** Consider a re-entrant line with processing times $\tau_i$ at $b_i$, with arrivals satisfying the burstiness constraint (8.1), and the capacity condition (8.4). Consider any Least Slack policy, where the part attributes $\gamma(\pi)$ satisfy (8.2), and $\{\zeta_i, \zeta_2, \ldots, \zeta_L\}$ are any real numbers associated with the buffers $\{b_1, b_2, \ldots, b_L\}$, respectively. Then the system is stable, i.e., the number of parts in the system is bounded.

# 8.5   Dynamic Scheduling of a Single Machine with Set-Up Times: A Push Model

In this section we will address the problem of scheduling a machine producing several types of parts. The critical new issue we examine is how to schedule the machine if it incurs set-up times whenever it changes the part-type it is processing. For notational convenience, it is useful to adopt a *fluid* model.

Consider the single machine system shown in Figure 5. There are $P$ types of parts, labeled $1, 2, \ldots, P$ which arrive to the machine at the rates $\lambda_1$ parts/hr, $\lambda_2$ parts/hr $,\ldots,$ and $\lambda_P$ parts/hr, respectively.

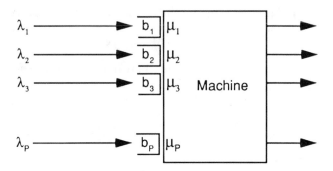

FIGURE 5. Machine with set-up times.

Parts of type $i$ take $\tau_i$ units of processing time; equivalently the processing *rate* for parts of type $i$ is $\frac{1}{\tau_i}$. Moreover, the machine incurs $\delta$ hours of *set-up time* whenever it switches between part-types.

Let us suppose that parts of type $i$ are held in buffer $b_i$, while awaiting processing. We denote by $x_i(t)$ the number of such parts in buffer $b_i$ at time $t$, and suppose that there is a holding cost of $c_i$ units per part of type $i$, per unit time. Thus, over a time interval $[0, T]$, the total cost incurred is

$$\int_0^T \sum_{i=1}^P c_i x_i(t) dt.$$

Let us suppose that our goal is to choose a scheduling policy which reduces the long-term average cost per unit time,

$$\limsup_{T \to \infty} \frac{1}{T} \int_0^T \sum_{i=1}^P c_i x_i(t) dt. \qquad (8.6)$$

As in the previous section, we shall say that a scheduling policy is *stable* if $x_i(t)$ is bounded over $t \geq 0$ for $i = 1, 2, \ldots P$. In addition to stability, we will also examine how to attain good *performance*, i.e., a small value of the cost (8.6).

## 8.6   Clear-A-Fraction Policies

Let us first examine the issue of stability. Clearly, it is necessary that the arrival rate vector $(\lambda_1, \lambda_2, \ldots, \lambda_L)$ be within the *capacity* of the machine to handle. This translates to the requirement that

$$\rho := \sum_{i=1}^{P} \lambda_i \tau_i < 1. \tag{8.7}$$

Note that $\rho$ is the average fraction of time that the machine needs to be busy processing parts, if it is to keep up with the incoming flow of parts. Thus, it can only afford to spend a fraction $(1 - \rho)$ of its time, at most, not processing any parts. This includes the time lost to set-up changes. Since each set-up incurs $\delta$ hours, the average time between set-ups can be no less than $\frac{\delta}{1-\rho}$.

This argument shows the danger of making too frequent set-up changes. In fact, a policy which changes set-ups too frequently will be unstable. As an example, a policy which produces that part-type $i$ for which $x_i(t)$ is largest, may be unstable.

Thus, once a part-type is taken up for production, it should be continued for a sufficient length of time, before the set-up is changed. However, there is also a disadvantage to having production runs which are too long; the buffer levels can reach unacceptably high levels resulting in too large a value of the cost (8.6). This gives rise to a need to maintain long, but not excessively long, production runs.

We will now study the dynamics of scheduling policies which attempt to regulate the lengths of production runs.

First, let us call a scheduling policy *clearing* if it always continues to work on a part-type until its buffer level hit zero. We shall say that a policy is *non-idling*, if no fraction of its capacity is unutilized whenever it is not changing a set-up. Thus, we exclude here policies which work on a part-type $i$ at rate $\lambda_i$, rather than at the maximum possible rate $\frac{1}{\tau_i}$. Hence, as soon as a buffer level hits zero, a non-idling policy necessarily forces a change in set-up.

We shall say that a policy has the "clear-a-fraction" property if it is clearing, non-idling, and if there is an $\epsilon > 0$ such that whenever it begins a set up to a new part type $p$ at time $\tau$, then that part type's buffer level $x_p(\tau)$ is at least a fraction $\epsilon$ of the total of the buffer levels of all part-types, i.e.,

$$x_p(\tau) \geq \epsilon \sum_{i=1}^{P} x_i(\tau). \qquad (8.8)$$

The first fundamental fact about such *Clear-A-Fraction* (CAF) policies is that they are always stable.

**Theorem: Stability of Clear-A-Fraction Policies.** Consider a single machine system as in Figure 5, satisfying the capacity condition (8.7). If a CAF policy is used, then the system is stable. Moreover,

$$\limsup_{t\to\infty} \sum_{i=1}^{P} x_i(t) \leq \frac{\delta\rho}{\underline{\tau}} + \frac{\delta\overline{\tau}}{\epsilon\underline{\tau}(1-\rho)} \max_i(\frac{\rho-\rho_i}{\tau_i}).$$

Above,

$$\underline{\tau} := \min_i \tau_i$$
$$\overline{\tau} := \max_i \tau_i$$
$$\rho_i := \lambda\tau_i, \text{ and } \rho = \sum_{i=1}^{P} \rho_i.$$

*Proof.*

Let $w(t) := \sum_{i=1}^{P} \tau_i x_i(t)$ denote the *work* in the system. Let $\{\tau_n\}$ denote the sequence of times at which set-ups are commenced, with $\tau_0 := 0$, and let $p_n$ be the corresponding sequence of part-types chosen for the set-ups. Note that

$$t_{n+1} - t_n = \frac{x_{p_n}(t_n) + \delta\lambda_{p_n}}{\frac{1}{\tau_{p_n}} - \lambda_{p_n}} + \delta.$$

The reasoning here is that the machine is actively working at rate $\frac{1}{\tau_{p_n}}$ on part-type $p_n$ during the entire time interval $[t_n+\delta, t_{n+1}]$. During this period it produces exactly as many parts as needed to clear both the $x_p(t_n)+\delta\lambda_{p_n}$ parts originally there at time $(t_n+\delta)$, plus the $\lambda_{p_n}(t_{n+1}-t_n-\delta)$ new parts that have arrived.

Hence, the net work in the system satisfies,

$$\begin{aligned} w(t_{n+1}) &= w(t_n) + \rho(t_{n+1} - t_n) - (t_{n+1} - t_n - \delta) \\ &= w(t_n) - (1-\rho)(t_{n+1} - t_n) + \delta. \end{aligned}$$

Clearly, if we can guarantee that there is an $\epsilon'$ such that $(t_{n+1} - t_n) \geq \epsilon' w(t_n)$, then the above equation will be stable, guaranteeing bounded buffer levels $\{w(t_n)\}$. Moreover, using the at most linear growth between $t_n$ and $t_{n+1}$, one also obtains that $w(t)$ is bounded.

The rest of the proof simply consists of noting that the CAF condition (8.8) guarantees the existence of such an $\epsilon'$.                                    □

We have seen earlier that the class of Least Slack policies is a large class containing some useful policies for scheduling re-entrant lines. So also, for single machine systems, the class of CAF policies is a large class, which also contains policies which yield good performance.

## 8.7   A Lower Bound on Optimal Cost

In this section, we obtain a lower bound on the long-term average cost of any non-idling stable policy.

Consider any stable policy, i.e., one which ensures that $\sup_t x_i(t) \leq c$ for all $i$. Let $T$ be a large time. We shall consider the trajectories of the system over the time interval $[0, T]$. Let $n_i$ be the total number of production runs of part-type $i$ in $[0, T]$, and let $T_i$ be the total time of all the production runs for part-type $i$. Clearly, $x_i(T) = x_i(0) + \lambda_i T - \frac{1}{\tau_i} T_i$. Since $\sup_t x_i(t) \leq c$, we obtain $\sum_{i=1}^{P} T_i \geq \rho T - \hat{c}$ for

$$\hat{c} := c \sum_{i=1}^{P} \tau_i. \tag{8.9}$$

Note that $\hat{c}$ is bounded independently of the value of $T$.

Moreover, $\sum_{i=1}^{P} T_i + \delta \left( \sum_{i=1}^{P} n_i - 1 \right) \leq T$, since each set-up consumes $\delta$ time units. Hence

$$\delta \sum_{i=1}^{P} n_i \leq (1 - \rho)T + \delta + \hat{c}. \tag{8.10}$$

Now we shall consider a single part-type "relaxation." We shall determine the smallest (there is a minimizer) possible value of

$$\frac{1}{T} \int_0^T c_i y_i(t) dt, \tag{8.11}$$

subject to just four requirements:

i) $y_i(t)$ is piecewise linear, and has a slope of either $\left( \lambda_i - \frac{1}{\tau_i} \right) < 0$ or $\lambda_i > 0$,

ii) there are at most $n_i$ segments of slope $\left( \lambda_i - \frac{1}{\tau_i} \right)$,

iii) the total length of all segments with slope $\left(\lambda_i - \frac{1}{\tau_i}\right)$ is no more than $T_i$, and

iv) $0 \le y_i(t) \le c$ for all $t$.

Clearly, the actual trajectory $x_i(t)$ of part-type $i$ satisfies these requirements. It however also satisfies the additional constraints induced by the fact that the machine cannot work on more than one part-type at a given time. This implies that two part types $i$ and $j$ cannot both have decreasing slopes at the same time. However, this last constraint is *relaxed* for $y_i(t)$.

It can be shown by a series of swapping arguments that the trajectory with smallest value of (8.11) has the form shown in Figure 6. Except for an initial and a final segment, the optimal trajectory consists of number $m_i$ of alternating non-production and production runs, with all production runs being of equal lengths, and all non-production runs also being of equal length.

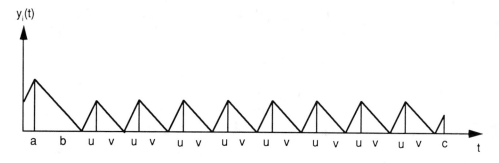

FIGURE 6. A relaxation of a trajectory for a part-type providing a lower bound.

Let $a, b, u, v, u, v, \ldots, u, v, c$ be the corresponding lengths of the line segments, as in Figure 6. Then

$$\lambda_i(u + v) = \frac{1}{\tau_i}v$$

and

$$m_i(u + v) = T - (a + b + c).$$

Together these yield $u + v = \frac{v}{\rho_i} = \frac{(T-\bar{c})}{m_i-1}$, where $\bar{c} := a + b + c$. Earlier, in (8.9), we saw that $\hat{c}$ was bounded independently of the value of $T$. Similarly, due to the boundedness constraint $\sup_t x_i(t) \leq c$, the constant $\bar{c}$ is also bounded independently of the value of $T$.

Utilizing the values for $u$ and $v$, the sum of the areas of the $m_i$ triangles in Figure 6 is $\frac{1}{2} \frac{(T-\bar{c})^2 \lambda_i(1-\rho_i)}{m_i}$. Thus, we obtain

$$\int_0^T x_i(t)dt \geq \int_0^T y_i(t)dt \geq \frac{1}{2} \frac{(T-\bar{c})^2 \lambda_i(1-\rho_i)}{(m_i-1)}.$$

Hence we see that a lower bound on the cost $\frac{1}{T} \int_0^T \sum_{i=1}^P c_i x_i(t)dt$ is,

$$\min \sum_{i=1}^P \frac{1}{2} \frac{c_i(T-\bar{c})^2 \lambda_i(1-\rho_i)}{T m_i}$$

subject to the constraints

$$\delta \sum_{i=1}^P m_i \leq (1-\rho)T + \delta + \hat{c}$$

$$m_i \geq 0.$$

Above, we have used the constraint (8.10). We have also relaxed the constraint that $m_i$ be an integer.

This convex program can be explicitly solved, to yield

$$m_i = k\sqrt{c_i \lambda_i(1-\rho_i)}$$

where the constant $k$ satisfies

$$k = \frac{(1-\rho)T + \delta + \hat{c}}{\delta \sum_{i=1}^P \sqrt{c_i \lambda_i(1-\rho_i)}}.$$

Hence

$$\frac{1}{T} \int_0^T \sum_{i=1}^P c_i x_i(t)dt \geq \frac{(T-\bar{c})^2 \delta \left[\sum_{i=1}^P \sqrt{c_i \lambda_i(1-\rho_i)}\right]^2}{2T\left[(1-\rho)T + \delta + \hat{c}\right]}.$$

The constants $\hat{c}$ and $\bar{c}$ are bounded as $T \to \infty$. Taking the limit, we obtain the following lower bound on long-term average cost.

**Theorem: Lower Bound on Long-Term Average Cost of Any Non-Idling Stable Policy.** Consider a single machine system, satisfying the capacity condition (8.7). The long term average cost of any stable, non-idling scheduling policy is lower bounded as follows:

$$\liminf_{T \to +\infty} \frac{1}{T} \int_0^T \sum_{i=1}^P c_i x_i(t) dt \;\geq\; \frac{\delta \left[ \sum_{i=1}^P \sqrt{c_i \lambda_i (1 - \rho_i)} \right]^2}{2(1 - \rho)}$$

## 8.8   A Good CAF Policy

In our definition of CAF policies, let us loosen the requirement (8.8), to

$$x_{p_n}(\tau_n) \;\geq\; \epsilon \sum_{i=1}^P x_i(\tau_n) - c \tag{8.12}$$

where $c \geq 0$ is any constant. Earlier, we took $c = 0$. Let us continue to call policies which satisfy (8.12) as CAF policies. Even with this extension, the CAF policies are stable. Moreover, as earlier, an upper bound on buffer levels can be obtained.

Within the class of CAF policies, one can design good scheduling policies. For our intuition, we turn to the proof of the lower bound on the optimal cost. There, we saw that the peak value of the triangles for part-type $i$ in Figure 6 is $v \left( \frac{1}{\tau_i} - \lambda_i \right)$, where $v = \frac{\rho_i(T - \bar{c})}{m_i - 1}$. Moreover, $m_i = k\sqrt{c_i \lambda_i (1 - \rho_i)}$. These relations suggest that the peak value of $x_i(t)$ is roughly proportional to $\frac{\rho_i \left( \frac{1}{\tau_i} - \lambda_i \right)}{\sqrt{c_i \lambda_i (1 - \rho_i)}} = \sqrt{\frac{\lambda_i (1 - \rho_i)}{c_i}}$. This shows that the "superoptimal" policy, shown in Figure 6, that attains the lower bound, attempts to equalize peak values of $\frac{x_i \sqrt{c_i}}{\sqrt{\lambda_i (1 - \rho_i)}}$ for all $i$. Thus, it demonstrates what are desirable "scalings" for the buffers.

Since the peak value of a buffer is obtained just after a set-up to it, the following CAF policy suggests itself. At the end of a clearing run, choose a part-type $i$, for which $(x_i + \lambda_i \delta) \frac{\sqrt{c_i}}{\sqrt{\lambda_i (1 - \rho_i)}}$ is maximal. Since the above expression can be written as $\sqrt{\frac{c_i}{\lambda_i (1 - \rho_i)}} x_i(\tau_n) + \frac{\delta \sqrt{c_i \lambda_i}}{\sqrt{(1 - \rho_i)}}$, we see that it is a CAF policy.

One may simulate this CAF policy, and compare its performance with respect to the lower bound.

*Example:*

Consider a system producing 10 part types with $\lambda_1 = 0.24$, $\lambda_2 = 0.16$, $\lambda_3 = 0.12$, $\lambda_4 = 0.09$, $\lambda_5 = 0.08$, $\lambda_6 = 0.06$, $\lambda_7 = 0.04$, $\lambda_8 = 0.03$,

$\lambda_9 = 0.02$, $\lambda_{10} = 0.01$, and $\tau_1 \equiv 1$ for all $i$. Let $c_i \equiv 1$ for all $i$, and $\delta = 1$. Then

$$\frac{\text{Average cost in simulation of } 10,000 \text{ production runs}}{\text{Lower bound on average cost}} = 1.0225$$

was observed. Thus, the CAF policy designed by us yielded a cost no more than 2.25% away from the optimal.

## 8.9  Non-Acyclic Manufacturing Systems with Set-Up Times

Let us now turn to the fairly general model of a manufacturing system shown in Figure 7. There are $M$ machines labeled $1, 2, \ldots, M$ in the system which produces $P$ types of parts labeled $1, 2, \ldots, P$. Parts of type $i$ arrive at rate $\lambda_i$. They visit the machines $\mu_{i,1}, \mu_{i,2}, \ldots, \mu_{i,n_i}$ in order, where $1 \leq \mu_{i,j} \leq M$ for each $j$. They exit from $\mu_{i,n_i}$ as a finished product. We suppose that at machine $\mu_{i,j}$, parts of type $i$ require $\tau_{i,j}$ units of processing time, and that they await processing in a buffer labeled $b_{i,j}$. Since the directed graph obtained from the union of the routes of all the part–types may contain cycles, we say that such a manufacturing system is *non–acyclic*.

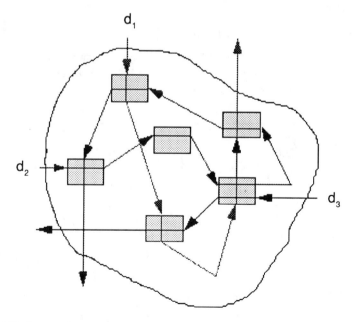

FIGURE 7. General multi-part-type multi-machine system with set-up times.

We will allow two features. First, we suppose that a machine incurs a set-up time $\delta_{b,b'}$ when it switches from processing parts in buffer $b$ to parts in buffer $b'$.

We will also allow a transportation delay when parts move between buffers. We will simply assume that the transportation delay is bounded by some $\tau$.

Our goal now is to schedule this entire system in such a way that all buffer levels are bounded. Such a scheduling policy will be called *stable*. Clearly, the vector of arrival rates $(\lambda_1, \ldots \lambda_P)$ should be within the capacity of every machine to handle, if such a goal is to be attained. Hence we suppose that the *capacity* condition,

$$\rho_m := \sum_{\{(i,j):b_{i,j} \; is \; served \; by \; m\}} \lambda_i \tau_{i,j} < 1 \text{ for every machine } m \quad (8.13)$$

There are some further attributes that we may desire of the scheduling policy. First, it should not be stymied by the computational complexity, even for large systems. Second, we may also wish it to be robust; for example tolerant to the bound on the transportation delay.

Below we will provide examples of such policies, which still yield bounded buffer levels. Our scheduling policies will be "distributed." They will neither require any information exchange between machines, nor any coordination of action across machines.

First we show the intricacies involved in establishing stability of non–acyclic systems.

*Example: A System Where All Clearing Policies are Unstable.*

Consider the system shown in Figure 8. There are two machines, labeled M1 and M2. There is only type of part, which arrives at rate 1. The parts

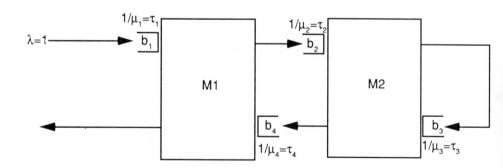

FIGURE 8. An unstable system under any clearing policy.

visit the four buffers $b_1$, $b_2$, $b_3$ and $b_4$ in that order, located at machines M1, M2, M2 and M1. Parts in buffer $b_i$ take $\tau_i$ units of processing time. For simplicity we will assume that set-up times are zero. We assume that $\tau_1 + \tau_4 < 1$ and $\tau_2 + \tau_3 < 1$, which imply that the capacity condition (8.13) is satisfied. However, we suppose that $\tau_2 + \tau_4 > 1$.

Let us consider perhaps the simplest class of distributed scheduling policies. Suppose that each machine simply adopts a clearing policy, which continues to work on a buffer until it is empty, and another buffer is non-empty. (In this case, there can only be one other non-empty buffer).

We will now show that such a policy is unstable. Consider the initial state $x(t) = (x, 0, 0, 0)$, where $x_i(t)$ is the number of parts in buffer $i$. At time $t_1 := \frac{x\tau_1}{1-\tau_1}$, buffer $b_1$ clears, and $x(t_1) = \left(0, x - \left(\frac{1}{\tau_2} - 1\right) t_1, \frac{t_1}{\tau_2}, 0\right)$. After $t_1$, $b_4$ is empty and so M1 continues to work on $b_1$, but at the reduced rate of 1, since it is *starved* of parts. At time $t_2 := t_1 + \frac{x_2(t_1)\tau_2}{1-\tau_2}$, buffer $b_2$ is cleared, and $x(t_2) = (0, 0, x + t_2, 0)$. At time $t_3 := t_2 + \tau_3 x_3(t_2)$, buffer $b_3$ clears, and $x(t_3) = \left(t_3 - t_2, 0, 0, \left(\frac{1}{\tau_3} - \frac{1}{\tau_4}\right)(t_3 - t_2)\right)$. Finally (for our analysis), at time $t_4 := t_3 + \tau_4 x_4(t_3)$, buffer $b_4$ also clears, and the state is $x(t_4) = \left(\frac{\tau_4}{1-\tau_2}x, 0, 0, 0\right)$.

Thus, after some time the system has returned to an amplified version of its original state; it is an amplification since $\frac{\tau_4}{1-\tau_2} > 1$. This process continues, and so we see that the buffer levels are unbounded.    □

The cause of instability is the enforced starvation of M2 during intervals such as $[t_1, t_2]$. Thus, the scheduling policy will have to somehow prevent excessive starvation.

There are many strategies for doing so. We will now describe a class of scheduling policies, that we call *Universally Stabilizing Supervisors* (USS), which guarantee stability.

The key idea is to enforce some sort of high level mechanism which provides some "discipline." We will assume that there is some "lower level" scheduling policy, which is in operation. However, at certain times, a supervisor steps in to intervene. What we show is that by implementing a few simple rules the supervisor can guarantee stability, irrespective of the details of the "lower level" scheduling policy. Moreover, the supervisor is really a set of *distributed* supervisors, one for each machine.

For each machine $m$, let $\gamma_m$ be a number which is large enough to satisfy

$$\gamma_m(1 - \rho_m) > \sum_{\{b: b \text{ is served by } m\}} \max_{\{b': b' \text{ is a buffer served by } m\}} \delta_{b'b}.$$

Also, for each buffer $b_{ij}$, we choose an arbitrary nonnegative number $z_{ij}$.

The operation of the supervisor is governed by the following five rules.

*The Truncation Rule:*

The processing time for buffer $b_{ij}$ is truncated at machine $m$ after $\gamma_m \lambda_i \tau_{ij}$ time units.

*Rule for entering an FCFS Queue:*

Each machine $m$ maintains an FCFS queue $Q_m$ of *buffers* that it is serving. A buffer $b_{ij}$ located at machine $m$ enters $Q_m$ when i) its buffer level exceeds $z_{ij}$ *and* ii) it is not being processed or set-up.

*Serving the FCFS Queue of Buffers:*

If the queue $Q_m$ of buffers is non-empty, then it is served in the FCFS order, i.e., the order in which buffers enter it.

*Rule for leaving the FCFS queue*

A buffer leaves the queue $Q_m$ when it is taken up for processing.

*The Processing Time for buffers in $Q_m$*

When a buffer $b_{ij}$ in $Q_m$ is taken up for processing, it is given exactly $\gamma_m \lambda_i \tau_{ij}$ time units of processing, unless it is cleared even before this.

One may note the following features. As long as $Q_m$ is empty, the lower level scheduling policy is free to proceed as it pleases. The supervisor only intervenes when $Q_m$ is non-empty. The numbers $z_{ij}$ determine the frequency with which the supervisor intervenes. If the $z_{ij}$'s are small, the supervisor intervenes frequently. In the extreme case, if the $z_{ij}$'s and $\gamma_m$'s are chosen large, and the lower level scheduling policy already stabilizes the system, then the supervisor never intervenes.

Irrespective of the lower level policy, the USS guarantees stability. What is not known, however, is how to obtain good performance, i.e., small values of buffer levels.

## 8.10   Concluding Remarks

We have shown how one may design dynamic scheduling policies through a combination of intuition and analysis. We have also analyzed their properties. In all cases, our scheduling policies are easy to implement. We believe that more work is clearly necessary to further develop our understanding about the dynamics of manufacturing systems, and also to provide a more definitive analysis, especially concerning the performance of scheduling policies. Instead of adopting the traditional deductive mode, where one attempts to deduce the optimal policy from, say, the theory of optimal control – which usually is intractable – more attention should be paid to what are usually called "heuristics." However, that term has come to acquire a pejorative meaning because it is frequently not backed up either by any analysis or a careful comparative evaluation. Such heuristics need more careful justification and analysis than has been traditional in manufacturing systems. Finally, careful comparative analysis of heuristics is necessary.

## 8.11   Notes

We have avoided all references to the literature in this Chapter. We make no attempt to properly attribute results, and apologize to authors in advance. A few pertinent references, which could be used to begin delving into the literature, are provided below:

1. An excellent comparative analysis of various scheduling policies, and a model of a semiconductor manufacturing plant is provided in Wein [1]. The Fluctuation Smoothing policies of Section 3, and the simulation results are from Lu, Ramaswamy and Kumar [2]. A statistical analysis can also be found there. The argument that reducing the variations in the interarrival times leads to smaller delays can be made precise by considering the convexity properties of Lindley's equation; see Ross [3]. The appealing interpretation of FSMCT, as attempting to equalize and reduce the total downstream shortfall from each buffer, is from Lu and Kumar [4]. This is different from an alternative policy of making each buffer's value tend to its own mean value, proposed by Li [5, 6].

2. The stability analysis of Least Slack scheduling policies in Section 4 is from Lu and Kumar [7]. There, the FBFS policy is also shown to be stable. Also some stable buffer priority policies are provided for systems consisting of multiple re-entrant lines. A broader account of re-entrant lines can be found in Kumar [8]. Recently, Kumar and Meyn [9] have developed linear programming tests to establish the stability of queueing networks and scheduling policies. These tests have been extended more recently in Kumar and Meyn [10]. Also, Rybko and Stolyar [11], Dai [12], and Chen [13], have shown that one may establish the stability of systems by establishing the stability of associated fluid models. The stability of such fluid models, and their connection to the linear program tests, is also examined in Kumar and Meyn [10].

3. Recently Bertsimas, Paschalidis and Tsitsiklis [14, 15] and Kumar and Kumar [16] have shown how one may obtain performance bounds for queueing networks and scheduling policies. There, bounds can be found for the performance of any policy, as well as buffer priority

policies. More recently, Kumar and Meyn [10] show that the stability and performance problems are related by duality.

4. The treatment of set-up times in Sections 5 and 6 is from Perkins and Kumar [17] and Kumar and Seidman [18]. Chase and Ramadge [19] have shown that sometimes one can obtain a lower cost by selectively idling, and obtain a performance bound, as well as a good policy. In Perkins and Kumar [17] and Kumar and Seidman [18], other stable distributed scheduling policies are also developed. Also, sufficient conditions for the stability of distributed CAF policies are presented in [18]. Further recent results on stability and performance can be found in Perkins, Humes and Kumar [20].

*Acknowledgments:* The research reported here has been supported by the National Science Foundation under Grant No. NSF-ECS-90-25007, and the Joint Services Electronics Program under Contract No. N00014–90–J1270.

## 8.12   References

[1] L. M. Wein. Scheduling semiconductor wafer fabrication. *IEEE Transactions on Semiconductor Manufacturing*, 1(3):115–130, August 1988.

[2] Steve C. H. Lu, Deepa Ramaswamy, and P. R. Kumar. Efficient scheduling policies to reduce mean and variance of cycle–time in semiconductor manufacturing plants. Technical report, University of Illinois, Urbana, IL, 1992.

[3] Sheldon M. Ross. *Stochastic Processes*. John Wiley, New York, 1982.

[4] Steve H. Lu and P. R. Kumar. Fluctuation smoothing scheduling policies for queueing systems. To appear in *Proceedings of the Silver Jubilee Workshop on Computing and Intelligent Systems*, Bangalore, India, December 1993.

[5] S. Li. Private Communication. 1992.

[6] S. Li. An introduction to basic principles of production. In *Semiconductor Manufacturing Technology Workshop*, pages 3–20, Hsinchu, Taiwan, R.O.C., March 1993.

[7] S. H. Lu and P. R. Kumar. Distributed scheduling based on due dates and buffer priorities. *IEEE Transactions on Automatic Control*, 36(12):1406–1416, December 1991.

[8] P. R. Kumar. Re–entrant lines. *Queueing Systems: Theory and Applications: Special Issue on Queueing Networks*, 13(1–3):87–110, May 1993.

[9] P. R. Kumar and Sean Meyn. Stability of queueing networks and scheduling policies. Technical report, C. S. L., University of Illinois, 1993.

[10] P. R. Kumar and Sean Meyn. Duality and linear programs for stability and performance analysis of queueing networks and scheduling policies. Technical report, C. S. L., University of Illinois, 1993.

[11] A. N. Rybko and A. L. Stolyar. On the ergodicity of stochastic processes describing open queueing networks. *Problemy Peredachi Informatsii*, 28:2–26, 1991.

[12] J. G. Dai. On the positive Harris recurrence for multiclass queueing networks: A unified approach via fluid models. Technical report, Georgia Institute of Technology, 1993.

[13] Hong Chen. Fluid approximations and stability of multiclass queueing networks I: Work conserving disciplines. Technical report, University of British Columbia, 1993.

[14] D. Bertsimas, I. Ch. Paschalidis and J. N. Tsitsiklis. Scheduling of multiclass queueing networks: Bounds on achievable performance. In *Workshop on Hierarchical Control for Real–Time Scheduling of Manufacturing Systems*, Lincoln, New Hampshire, October 16–18, 1992.

[15] D. Bertsimas, I. Ch. Paschalidis and J. N. Tsitsiklis. Optimization of multiclass queueing networks: Polyhedral and nonlinear characterizations of achievable performance. Laboratory for Information and Decision Systems and Operations Research Center, M. I. T., December 1992.

[16] S. Kumar and P. R. Kumar. Performance bounds for queueing networks and scheduling policies. Technical report, Coordinated Science Laboratory, University of Illinois, Urbana, IL, 1992. To appear in *IEEE Transactions on Automatic Control*, August 1994.

[17] J. R. Perkins and P. R. Kumar. Stable distributed real-time scheduling of flexible manufacturing/assembly/disassembly systems. *IEEE Trans. Automat. Control*, AC-34(2):139–148, February 1989.

[18] P. R. Kumar and T. I. Seidman. Dynamic instabilities and stabilization methods in distributed real-time scheduling of manufacturing systems. *IEEE Trans. Automat. Control*, AC-35(3):289–298, March 1990.

[19] C. J. Chase and P. J. Ramadge. On the real time control of flexible manufacturing systems. In *Proc. IEEE 28th Conf. on Decision and Control*, pages 2026–2027, Tampa, FL, 1989.

[20] J. R. Perkins, C. Humes, Jr., and P. R. Kumar. Distributed control of flexible manufacturing systems: Stability and performance. Technical report, University of Illinois, Urbana, IL, 1993. To appear in *IEEE Transactions on Robotics and Automation*, 1994.